Applied Computing

Springer

London
Berlin
Heidelberg
New York
Barcelona
Hong Kong
Milan
Paris
Santa Clara
Singapore
Tokyo

Applied Computing

Series Editors
Professor Ray Paul and Professor Peter Thomas

The Springer-Verlag Series on Applied Computing is an advanced series of innovative textbooks that span the full range of topics in applied computing technology.

Books in the series provide a grounding in theoretical concepts in computer science alongside real-world examples of how those concepts can be applied in the development of effective computer systems.

The series should be essential reading for advanced undergraduate and postgraduate students in computing and information systems.

Books in the series are contributed by international specialist researchers and educators in applied computing who will draw together the full range of issues in their specialist area into one concise authoritative textbook.

Titles already available

Linda Macauley
Requirements Engineering

Derrick Morris, Gareth Evans, Peter Green, Colin Theaker
Object Oriented Computer Systems Engineering

Deryn Graham and Tony Barrett
Knowledge Based Image Processing

John Hunt
Java and Object Orientation: An Introduction

Sarah Douglas and Anant Mithal
The Ergonomics of Computer Pointing Devices

David Gray

Introduction to the Formal Design of Real-Time Systems

 Springer

David Gray, BSc, MSc, PhD, CEng

Series Editors

Professor Peter J. Thomas, BA (Hons), PhD, AIMgt, FRSA, FVRS
Centre for Personal Information Management, University of the West of England, Coldharbour Lane, Bristol, BS16 1QY, UK

Professor Ray J. Paul, BSc, MSc, PhD
Department of Information Systems and Computing, Brunel University, Uxbridge UB8 3PH, UK

ISBN 3-540-76140-3 Springer-Verlag Berlin Heidelberg New York

British Library Cataloguing in Publication Data
Gray, David
        Introduction the Formal Design of Real-Time Systems - (Applied computing)
        1.Real-time data processing 2.System design
        I.Title
        004.3'38'1
        ISBN 3540761403

Library of Congress Cataloging-in-Publication Data
Gray, David, 1946-
        Introduction the formal design of real-time systems / David Gray
            p.   cm. -- (Applied computing)
        Includes bibliographical references and index.
        ISBN 3-540-76140-3 (pbk. : alk. paper)
        1. Real-time data processing   2. System design   I. Title   II. Series
        QA76.54.G73   1997
        005.2'.73--dc21   97-29239

Illustrations by the author
Typesetting by Editburo, Lewes, East Sussex
Printed and bound at the Athenæum Press Ltd., Gateshead, Tyne and Wear
34/3830-543210 Printed on acid-free paper

Preface

This book is about applying an easily understood formal method, the process algebra SCCS, to the design of concurrent and real time systems. It charts the progress of a non-mathematician through the process of learning a formal method from the creation of designs to their validation using automated tools.

But why formal methods? As a young electrical engineer I was taught by people who believed that engineers, by employing rigorous mathematical theories, correctly predict how designs will behave before they are built; if they couldn't they weren't engineers. It came as something as a shock on first entering the world of software programming to find that such techniques were thought foolish and unnecessary. It was with some relief that I eventually stumbled upon several groups of people applying the rigour of mathematics to the design of correct software systems – perhaps they were taught by the same sort of lecturers as I was?

Based on formal methods, the book's main premise is that, in order to design something correctly, one has to understand it fully. One does not understand something if one's theories about it are incorrect, contradictory or incomplete, and only by expressing our theories in a formal way can they be checked with sufficient rigour. As Martin Thomas of Praxis put it cogently in 1989, 'If you cannot write down a mathematical behaviour of the system you're designing, you don't understand it'. This is not to say that formal methods are a philosopher's stone; rather than replace traditional methods, they complement them. The ideas that drive a design may still come from many sources – your experience, the experience of others, educated guesses, inspiration, hunches, tarot cards, runes, or whatever – but, to check if your ideas hold water, what better than formal tools to animate and apply some rigour to the design process?

The formal method used here is the process algebra SCCS. No previous knowledge of SCCS is presumed: it's both introduced and applied here. SCCS was selected for the task because not only does it capture the behaviour of real-time systems, it does so in a simple and elegant way based on the natural concept of observation – things are considered equivalent if an observer cannot tell them apart. Equally as important, SCCS is a member of an extended family of algebras for which automated tools are available.

Intended Audience

The material that forms the book's content was developed as part of a set of modules given to a variety of students at Brunel and Surrey Universities. The students included undergraduates majoring in electronic and electrical engineering, information technology, mathematics and computer science, as well as graduate students studying telematics, microelectronics and computer engineering. To cater for such disparate backgrounds the material is, as far as possible, self-contained; it is aimed at people who already have some experience with computer systems – about as much as might be achieved by a couple of years of a full-time academic course, or the equivalent in practical experience. Readers should be able to follow the programming examples, and ideally have some understanding of, or may even have met, the problems addressed here. At first I thought a reasonable knowledge of discrete mathematics would be mandatory, but all of the students who followed the original modules took to the formalism like ducks to water, finding the concepts and theories intuitive, process algebras common sense, and only the act of linking the concepts to the notations problematic.

Layout

The book has four main parts:

- The first introduces and defines the problems associated with the correct design of concurrent and real-time systems, and stimulates awareness of the pitfalls of concurrent systems design in addressing some examples by adding special extensions to sequential programming languages.
- The second section introduces the process algebra SCCS in a multi-pass fashion. An informal overview of the complete calculus is followed by a formal introduction to the basic algebra. Examples are given which extend the basic algebra to directly address particular classes of problems, which are then used to devise further extensions.
- The third section dwells on the role of equality. It is one thing to say that our objective is to prove a design equivalent to a specification,

but when we state that A 'equals' B , as well having to know what we mean by A and B we also have know what we mean by 'equals'. This section explores the role of observers; how different types of observer see different things as being equal, and how we can produce algorithms to decide on such equalities. It also explores how we go about writing specifications to which we may compare our SCCS designs.

- The final section is the one which the students like best. Once enough of SCCS is grasped to decide upon the component parts of a design, the 'turning the handle' steps of composition and checking that the design meets its specification are both error-prone and tedious. This section introduces the concurrency work bench, which shoulders most of the burden.

How you use the book is up to you; I'm not even going to suggest pathways. Individual readers know what knowledge they seek, and course leaders know which concepts they are trying to impart and in what order.

Acknowledgements

The list of people I wish to thank includes my parents and teachers; responsible for most of my training, I only hope they're not too dissatisfied with the outcome. I'd also like to thank the following. The students at both Brunel and Surrey Universities, for their forbearance and active feedback while the material was being developed; it was their input that resulted in the multi-pass nature of the book. In particular, one of my PhD students, Jason Cozens, whose work on higher order SCCS gave rise to impassioned discussions which made me rethink certain concepts expressed here. Bernie Cohen, for encouraging my first formal steps. Steve Schumann and Mike Shields, with whom I gave courses and from whom I 'borrowed' the odd example. Stephan Zuldt, an experienced engineer with an interest but no formal training in this area, who gave an outsider's view of the text. Perdita Stephens, who answered my questions about the Concurrency Workbench. My wife, who walked the dogs when it was my turn. But mainly the authors of books and papers and the givers of presentations and seminars, who began and then nurtured my interest in formal methods, foremost amongst whom are Professor Milner, the originator of SCCS, whose book [Mil89] I still return to for insights missed in previous readings, and Professor Stirling, whose clarity of writing does much to demystify modal logic. I also have to thank Professors Milner and Joseph for introducing me to Tomasz Janowski, and Professor Stirling for introducing me to Sibylle Froschle, both of whose reviews changed the eventual content and presentation of the material.

Finally I wish to dedicate this book to Rachel Rochester Warlow.

Contents

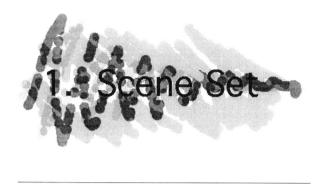 

1. Scene Set

Introduction

One of the most endearing preoccupations of human beings is the way they attempt to understand the world around them and then try to improve it, with varying degrees of success. Over the years it's been man's insatiable curiosity – '…but what happens next?' – that has driven advances in both science and engineering. As engineers we make our living out of this desire; we don't just design things, we know how objects, yet to be built, will behave, and we can predict whether they will answer to our customers' requirements (and even if we don't, we should). In more formal terms, engineers not only design systems but prove these designs satisfy their specifications.

But how do we build things that behave correctly? The artisan approach is just to go ahead and start building, beginning with something with a behaviour near to what is required and then repeatedly testing and modifying it until we get what we want. One problem with this method is its lack of scalability – we can use it to build simple systems but the method doesn't scale up to complex ones. Proving a system meets its specification also has scalability problems. To prove a system correct we need to test it exhaustively. While smaller systems may need few tests (for example, to test a lamp and switch to exhaustion we only need to show that pressing the switch turns the light on and releasing it turns the light off), to test to exhaustion even medium-sized systems, for example a single computer chip, can take man years. During that time the customer may get impatient and think of the wait to get paid.

Unfortunately, many of the objects we might wish to create are just too complex to build, test and modify as a prototype, or even as an accurate physical model. We need a more abstract modelling system, preferably one with a mathematical framework, so that we can design with pencil on paper, test by computer simulation, and use automated provers to check for correctness. Such an abstract modelling method must faithfully capture the behaviours of objects, enable us to manipulate those behaviours in a predictable way, predict the behaviours of objects composed of other objects, and finally compare behaviours so that we can check whether the object meets its specification. What we need is a modelling method which has operations, and laws over those operations, that replicate objects' behaviours. We need an algebra of objects.

How would such an algebra-based modelling method revise our design approach?

We commence any design with a set of requirements which state how we wish the final object to behave. We then propose, in the abstract world of models, a design that may satisfy those requirements

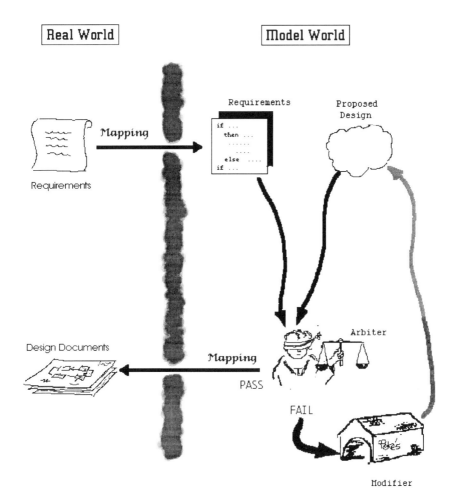

Using our algebra upon models we can predict how the design will behave; then, using an arbiter, we can test if this behaviour satisfies the requirements. If the arbiter decides the design is satisfactory we can proceed to build the real-world

object. If not, we revise the design, before submitting it again to the arbiter. There's a small problem with this scenario. When making comparisons, an arbiter can only compare like with like. To compare an expression in our algebra of models with a specification, both must be defined in the same terms. The specification must either be expressed in terms of the algebra of models or isomorphic to them.

While this process is similar to the artisan method, the design is no longer carried out in the physical world but in the more tractable world of abstract models. When we avail ourselves of strong mathematical underpinnings, the construction, testing, and modification of a design can be carried out more simply, reliably and quickly.

For our design method to be successful, we require that our models behave like the real thing – but only in those aspects in which we are interested. A model aircraft might fly, but it need not contain all the detail of a real one. By reducing complexity we reduce the possibility of error. But how do we know what behaviour is essential? What not? And how do we represent such behaviour in a model?

1.1 Making Models

When modelling the behaviour of a thing

we have conflicting goals. We want the model to be simple – the simpler the better – but it must also completely capture the important behaviour of the thing. As we define the behaviour of a real-world object in terms of the actions in which it is seen to engage we will have created an adequate model if an observer cannot distinguish between the actions of our creation and those of the real thing.

As actions are to be the basis of all our models, we need to know more about them. In the simplest terms, an action is something which moves an object between discernible states.

We can label actions with abstract names. Here, instead of an_action, we substitute the label 'a',

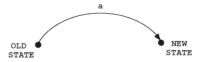

and the states of a system are defined purely in terms of these observed and labelled actions.

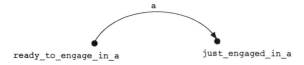

Here, action a moves the system from state ready_to_engage_in_a to state just_engaged_in_a. The states are only significant with respect to actions. If a was the last observed action, we can only be in state just_engaged_in_a. If we've not observed any action, we must be in the initial state ready_to_engage_in_a.

We can, if we wish, label the states and actions with names relevant to the states and actions in the system being modelled. For example, in

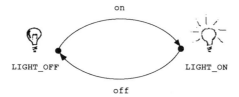

the state of the light is switched between LIGHT_ON and LIGHT_OFF by the on and off actions.

The same model can be interpreted using different objects in different environments. The light model behaves the same as these flag and clock models.

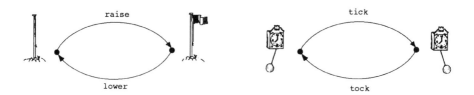

All have two actions moving the systems between two states. We could abstract this to a system in which a and b actions move the system between states P and Q.

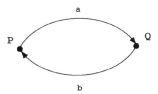

Devising laws over behaviours for such generalised models allows us to make subsequent interpretations as to how a particular instantiation will behave. Renaming the general (a, b) in terms of the particular gives us the light system (on, off), the flag system (raise, lower), and the clock system (tick, tock). The benefit of taking abstract views is that one system containing certain action sequences is the same as any other with the same sequences; only the action and state names are changed to better reflect the system modelled.

Instead of the pretty, but difficult to manipulate, pictures, we can represent a model's actions and subsequent state changes in terms of formulae. 'A system in state P can engage in action a and in so doing move to state Q.' The states P and Q represent agents – they portray, in mathematical terms, the behaviour of an associated real-world system. Agent P is defined by expression a→Q.

$$P \stackrel{\text{def}}{=} a \rightarrow Q$$

In other words, 'Agent P can engage in action a and in so doing become agent Q.' Similarly 'Agent Q can engage in action b and in so doing become agent P.'

$$Q \stackrel{\text{def}}{=} b \rightarrow P$$

Finally, the complete system can be expressed as a recursive equation. 'Agent P can engage in actions a then b and so become agent P again.'

$$P \stackrel{\text{def}}{=} a \rightarrow b \rightarrow P$$

These general action and agent names can be instantiated to particular systems.

$$\text{LIGHT} \stackrel{\text{def}}{=} \text{off} \rightarrow \text{on} \rightarrow \text{LIGHT}$$
$$\text{FLAG} \stackrel{\text{def}}{=} \text{lower} \rightarrow \text{raise} \rightarrow \text{FLAG}$$
$$\text{CLOCK} \stackrel{\text{def}}{=} \text{tick} \rightarrow \text{tock} \rightarrow \text{CLOCK}$$

And so on.

Such state- and action-based mathematical models are not new. In the world of electronics, Meally–More diagrams, a type of labelled transition system, are used to design and check the correct operation of digital circuitry. In the field of computer systems vector diagrams, showing how processors change state when they engage in software instructions, have long been used to check if a program performs correctly.

The ability to model single objects is only part of the picture. Objects do not exist in isolation. Something must raise the flag, switch on the light, hear the clock tick, etc.. Objects exist in environments with which they interact. For example, when we observe and record an object's actions, the observer is part of that object's environment. The existence of environments means that an object must engage in not one but two types of actions: private, internal actions, to progress towards a personal goal which cannot interact with, nor be influenced by, the object's environment;

internal actions

and external actions to communicate with that environment.

external actions

Our basic model of a system is thus something which can engage both in internal actions which progress its private task, and external actions by which those private tasks can modify or be modified by an environment. For example, the following computer function has an external action that inputs data, an internal action that acts upon the data, and finally another external action which outputs the result of the internal action.

```
double (x)
    y := x + x
return (y)
```

Any caller of the function takes the role of the function's environment.

We now have two objects to model: the thing itself, and its environment. We can assimilate such a view by simply making a thing's environment another thing. By doing this we can now use our modelling method to build systems of increasing complexity. Objects placed in environments and interacting with them are just more complex objects.

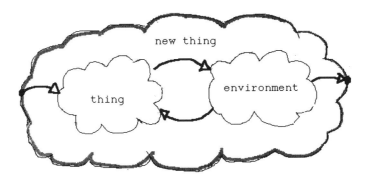

The new thing thus created can, in turn, be placed in further environments to become newer things, and so on.

In this way we can model systems of any complexity as multiple objects, each viewing the rest as an environment with which to interact. Individual objects engage in internal actions to progress a local task, and in external actions to communicate with other objects to forward a global task.

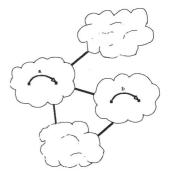

If we can construct theories of how combinations of individual models behave, we will be able to predict the behaviour of a complete system from a knowledge of the behaviours of the system's constituent parts.

This has a direct influence on our design process. After mapping the requirements into a set of models, we can initially propose not a complete design but a collection of simpler subdesigns which, together, form our proposed solution. Each design fragment defines the behaviour of an identifiable part of the overall design in terms of both its own actions and its interactions with other fragments. This 'divide and conquer' technique should greatly simplify the design process.

Now, using the mathematical underpinning of our modelling system, we provide a mathematical machine which can determine the behaviour of a system composed of design fragments. By passing the composition to an arbiter, we can test if the complete design satisfies the requirements. If the arbiter approves the design, we can then proceed to build the real-world object. If the arbiter rejects the design, we will need to revise certain fragments before once again turning the handle on the mathematical machine, establishing a revised composite behaviour, and submitting this new solution to the arbiter.

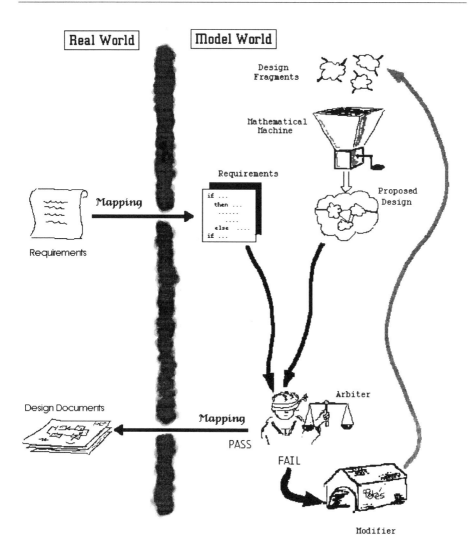

If we had an algebra which could capture a desired behaviour in models in terms of the internal and external actions of their fragments, predict the behaviour of systems composed of one or more fragments, and finally prove that the solution behaves as required, we would be able correctly to design fairly complex objects. If only we had such an algebra. However, not only do we not have such an algebra, we have yet fully to establish how to create the models it would operate on. So far we have only established that models are created by making them duplicate the actions of real-world systems. We've neglected to define which actions we record and what limitations models so created have. We put that right in the next section.

1.2 Lies, Damn Lies and Models

To record all the actions of a system and then incorporate them in a model would be insane. Why bother making a model which behaves identically to the real object in all respects? It would be as complex as the real thing, and just as difficult to work with. No. We want a model that is simpler than the real thing, capturing only the behaviours of current interest. We record what is considered to be important about an object, ignoring the unimportant. To do this, the designer nominates which actions are of significance to a particular design and places them in a list; then, when observing an object, only the occurrences of actions in this list are considered. For example, our model of a light considered only the on and off actions to be significant. How the electric circuit was made and broken, and the passage of individual electrons along the wire, were considered unimportant. This restriction of observed actions to those considered relevant has obvious practical importance. The smaller the number of actions, the simpler the model and the simpler the theories associated with that model will be. The falling of an apple can, in all reasonable circumstances, be described by Newton's laws, and it is unnecessary to take into account the effects of windage or of dehydration of the apple on the way down. These effects are there, but their influence upon the behaviour in which we are interested is insignificant.

Limiting the scope of models and the theories over them has an honourable history in science, many advances have been made by suggesting partial theories to a limited range of happenings, ignoring other effects or approximating them to some constant. Physicists predict change in gas pressure under volume change without resource to the laws of molecular interaction; chemists predict the results of adding another element to a compound without delving into the atomic interactions taking place; and so on. By ignoring unimportant detail we can contain the complexity of system models. But what if we get it wrong? If we include in our model irrelevant actions, apart from adding unnecessary complexity, no harm is done. If, however, we fail to include significant actions, our model will be of little use - its predictive powers will be constrained by what the model should, but doesn't, know.

So, to imitate faithfully those behaviours of real objects relevant to our designs, we consider only those actions related to these behaviours as being of sufficient importance to include in our models. To decide which actions we select for inclusion in a model is a problem that we'll sidle up to, by first addressing the more basic question of what exactly does an action consist.

Most actions can be broken down into sequences of smaller, lower-level actions. For example, eating lunch at a restaurant could, at one level, be defined by a selection of dishes from the menu.

Table D'Hote Menu

TO START

Fan of Melon with Citrus Sauce
Avacado & Peppers with Walnut Vinigrette

MAIN COURSE

Steaks of the Sea – Pan fried salmon, shark & swordfish
in garlic butter, served with cream sauce

Lemon Chicken with Coriander – Supreme of chicken
marinaded in special sauce served with rice

Roast Leg of Lamb – Welsh leg of lamb cooked in rosemary,
served with redcurrent stuffing

Sirloin Steak – 6oz prime steak cooked to order
traditional – charcoal brazed rare, medium or well done
balmoral – pate filled and flamed in malt whisky
boursin – flamed in brandy, poached in borsin and cream

SWEETS

Selection from trolley

Coffees, Teas, Beers and Wines available from Waiters

In order to create each dish, a sequence of actions – the recipe – is followed in the kitchen. For example, a fragment from the recipe for roast lamb could contain

```
..........
Brush the lamb with melted fat or butter and oil.
Place it on a rack in a roasting tin and place in the
upper part of a preheated oven (300°F., Mark 3).
Turn and baste it every 4 to 5 minutes, or until it has
browned lightly on all sides. This sears the outside
of the meat and prevents its juices form bursting
out.

Reset oven for 350°F., Mark 4. Insert a meat
thermometer into the fleshiest part of the lamb.
Strew vegetables in the bottom of the tin. Place
lamb in middle of oven and ........
```

To create the cream sauce for the 'Steaks of the Sea', several items are combined, and so on. Different levels in this hierarchy of actions are important at different levels of abstraction of the same event.

This process is not only regressive. At a higher level the whole visit to the restaurant can be recorded as an action in a diary.

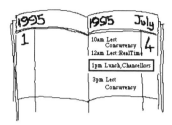

Here it has equal importance with other appointments but not to the depth of detail required by the menu and recipe levels. Each set of actions is relevant to the context it is used in. If I'm asked what I'm doing at 1300hrs on the 4th of July 1995, I reply, 'Eating at Chancellors'. I don't delve into the recipe for 'Steaks of the Sea'. This is a detail which the waiter, to take my order, and the sous chef, to prepare it, need to know; and while neither of these two need be aware of the quayside price of the salmon, both the owner and his accountant do. We all have our areas of concern and objectives to meet, and only when everyone pulls together will the restaurant be successful.

The choice of an abstract level at which to base a design is as important for us in our domain of interest as it is to restaurateurs and diarists in theirs. In the world of electronics, when designing a system one deals with the actions of data-processing blocks such as adders, memory elements, processors, etc. The behaviour of these devices is dictated by the activities of the components, transistors, resistors, etc., from which they are made. The actions of these components depend upon the behaviour of electrons flowing through them, down to the limit, for example, of individual bosons. In the world of software, when we write programs in C, Pascal, Miranda, SML and so on, we visualise their behaviour in terms of a sequence of lines of code following an underlying algorithm. We do this despite the knowledge that individual lines are translated into machine code for execution by a processor, and machine code statements are translated to equivalent microcode fragments for execution within the processor where the aforementioned electronic hardware hierarchy takes over.

We have already proposed that we can simplify our models to the benefit of the design process by considering only actions relevant to the current concern, implying that when we design a system at a higher level we can ignore what is happening at lower levels. By choosing one level in the hierarchy of actions as relevant to our problem, its actions represent, for all meaningful purposes, the hierarchy of actions underpinning them. After all, we do not want to consider what's happening down to the boson level every time we design an electronic circuit or write a computer program.

The actions we chose are modelled as something which moves a system between two states.

By nominating a as an action relevant to the level of abstraction at which we wish to work, we imply that states P and Q are also relevant to our model and at the correct level of abstraction. With only two states, the system must either be in state P, awaiting action a, or state Q, just completed action a. As there are no intermediate states, action a must be indivisible, i.e. atomic, and execute in zero time.

There is an apparent agreement, which is a good thing, between the behaviour of our models and their real-world counterparts. In both we only pay heed to actions of current interest, and those actions we do select are considered representative of lower internal actions. In both, internal actions are explicitly hidden by making the selected actions atomic.

Unfortunately we cannot leave it there. There still remains the question: 'In the hierarchy of actions, which level do we choose as representative, and who says the actions are atomic?'. This is important for, if actions in the model are assumed to be atomic but their counterparts in the real word are not, the model would be about as useful as a sandcastle facing the incoming tide. A model which behaves differently from its real-world counterpart could not reliably predict anything about the system it was modelling.

Consider the following example. We wish to model the actions of a computer system which reads and writes values into memory. If a write is completed before a

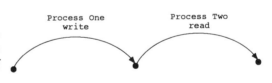

read, the data reader would obtain the correct value. By making the read and write actions atomic, we make them indivisible and ensure that a read action cannot interrupt a write action. This is easily done in a model, but in the real world things are more complex. Computer hardware operations take time. When writing an n -bit number, not all the bits are modified simultaneously, and if there are intermediate states in a write we could get

A read performed during the write process would return not the previous value or the one intended by the data writer but some random intermediate. In the real

world, lower-level actions, ignored in our model, have effected the outcome. Actions we've assumed to be atomic in the model are not atomic in the real world. The model and the real-world system have different behaviours and the model fails.

Why all this emphasis on atomic actions? Well, atomic actions have useful attributes for both engineer and scientist: they make things easier. Indivisible atomic actions cannot be dissected into smaller parts, and thus their constituent parts cannot be observed nor experimented with. By definition, what goes on inside an atomic action is hidden from all environments and cannot be influenced by them. The level of action atomicity thus determines the level of abstraction of the system being modelled forming a base level below which everything is hidden. As such, atomicity of actions, rather than being a limitation, is a powerful aid without which we would be overwhelmed with detail. Models of interesting systems would be too complex to be comprehensible, and we would never be sure if they were error-free.

Atomic action-based state modelling has widespread application as a design method. In electronics, the designer of a digital circuit predicts whether an implementation will meet its specification using methods (Boolean Algebra, Meally–More state diagrams, etc.) which only concern themselves with the idealised behaviours of hardware elements, gates, flip-flops and so on, ignoring the behaviour of their constituent transistors, resistors, etc. By ignoring these unimportant details a designer can concentrate in the abstract on those attributes of the system pertinent to the problem at hand.

Our models are not true models, in that they record only certain behaviours of an object, making the assumption that these recorded actions are atomic. They lie. Or rather, by representing only certain aspects of systems, they are economic with the truth.

So we construct models as simplification of real objects. This simplification makes it viable to construct an algebra over model actions; the algebra in turn enables us to make predictions about the composite behaviour of models; supports the design of fairly complex systems, and assists in proving that their behaviour meets given specifications. For this impressive edifice to work, we have to assume that the actions of our models are atomic and that they map to equivalent actions in the real world – which brings us to the questions of how, when carrying out a design, do we decide the level of abstraction at which to base the actions of our algebra, and who decides that these action are atomic?

1.3 Abstraction, Atomicity and Algebras

Sometimes we have a correspondence, natural or contrived, between the atomic actions of a model and the real world. The electronic and computer systems that are of concern to us did not spring, fully-formed, into this world without anxious designers acting as midwives. These early designers had the same requirement to contain complexity. They, too, needed the simplicity of atomic actions guaranteed to execute without interference. In conventional processors, to contain the complexity of environmental interrupts and so on, designers made sure that machine-code instructions were executed atomically, making any software modelled by atomic actions at this level a true representation of the real world of the processor. Electronic circuit designers use Boolean algebra to describe the behaviour of digital circuits. The inputs and outputs of all digital devices are considered to be made at 0, a low voltage, or 1, a high voltage. In the real world things are not so convenient: digital signals do not instantaneously move between low and high, and, when they get there, they have a tendency to wobble about a bit. The designers countered these real-world problems by setting voltage bands which map to 0 and 1.

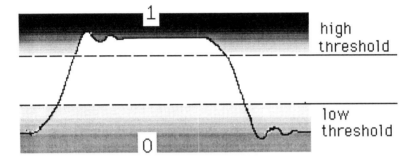

The threshold levels are built into the hardware so that, to switch from a 1 to a 0 the voltage has to fall past a low threshold, and to switch from a 0 to 1 the voltage has to rise past a high threshold. For operational integrity, the thresholds are set a safe distance from each other – the noise margin – as well as from the nominal voltages representing 0 and 1. This built-in hysteresis means that, for all practical purposes, changes at the Boolean level in digital circuits can be considered atomic. Once the hardware itself ensures that it models the same level of abstraction as Boolean algebra, the latter can be used with confidence. If it weren't so, we would not have the computer systems we do today – definitely a bad thing. And I wouldn't be writing this on my Apple Macintosh – probably a bad thing.

If we can ensure that the atomic actions of our models represent equivalent real-world atomic action, designs based on that modelling system will be correct in this regard. In the examples above, this was ensured by building an atomic level into the real-world implementation. We could extend this concept to computer languages: if statements in C, Pascal, Miranda, etc., were mapped to implementable atomic actions, we would then be safe to use the language statements as actions in a design model.

While the internals of some real-world objects – for example, the escapement mechanism of a clock – are atomic, not all such systems are so obliging, and, as these internals tend to be beyond our control, the best we can do is to confer atomicity at what we consider an appropriate level of abstraction for the design in hand.

When modelling the purchase of a stamp from a machine, the behaviour of interest is the repeated payment for, and subsequent delivery of, a stamp. This can be expressed as

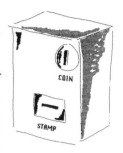

$$\text{MACHINE} \stackrel{\text{def}}{=} \texttt{coin} \rightarrow \texttt{stamp} \rightarrow \text{MACHINE}$$

Actions such as refilling the machine, emptying it of cash, maintaining its internals, etc., are not of current concern, and are thus ignored. All well and good. The only remaining proviso, discussed earlier, is that as all actions of our models are atomic, the model will only properly represent the machine if the actions map to atomic actions in the machine itself. But machine actions like `coin` will consist of lower-level activities which check for the validity of coins, reject incorrect ones, store correct coins, trigger stamp release, etc.. By assuming an action to be atomic we must be able to assume that, for all practical purposes, all its lower-level actions are subsumed within it. If this is true the design will viable. If not, predictions from the design will be uncertain to some extent. Such limitations of a model must not be concealed but declared. It is the obligation of every designer to state the assumptions made in the design and to indicate any consequences before the design is acted upon.

We've now sketched out the components of a design system. To meet stated requirements, we propose an abstract model, or a set of abstract models, as a solution. To make models as simple as possible we limit them to actions considered relevant to the design. These can either be internal actions furthering individual goals, or external actions forwarding a joint goal. At the lowest level, actions of models are atomic and map one-to-one to equivalent atomic actions in an implementation of the model. To check whether or not the proposed design meets its requirements we express both in terms of an algebra over actions. If an arbiter is satisfied that the model meets the requirements, the design can be refined into an implementation. If the arbiter finds the design deficient, (and hopefully indicates why it has failed), the design is modified and resubmitted to the arbiter.

All we have to do is convince ourselves that an algebra over actions can be built to capture the behaviour of such models, and to answer questions such as: 'How can we compare models and specifications?'; and 'If we have systems A and B with known behaviours, how does a combination of A and B behave?'

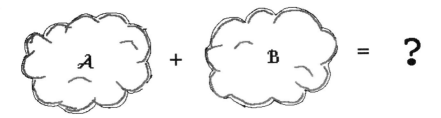

But before we approach such questions, we have first to satisfy ourselves on the following points: what are algebras and specifications?; why do we need them?; what relationship do they have with each other?

1.3.1 Algebras, Specifications and Other Related Things

When we were at school, most of us probably had a slot in our timetable labelled 'algebra'. But what precisely is an algebra? Simple algebras consist of a set of values and a number of operations acting on those values. One of the first algebras we're taught is that over integers, which has a set of values '$1, 2, 3, 4, \ldots$,', a number of binary operators '$=, +, -, \times, \ldots$', and a consistent set of laws in which valid expressions built of values and operators can be equated. The laws form the basis of provable formulas. The formula $2 \times 3 = 6$ states that the expression 2×3 is identical to the value 6, thus everywhere 2×3 appears it can be replaced by 6. So, for example, $4 + (2 \times 3) - 3 = 7$ can be replaced by $4 + 6 - 3 = 7$; the formula $5 + 2 = 2 + 5$ means $5 + 2$ is the same as $2 + 5$; and so on.

In a wider context, an algebra is an abstract, internally consistent mathematical entity which exists in its own right. Its usefulness in modelling things in our world is purely serendipitous – but once this relation is found, the algebra can be used to predict the behaviour of real-world systems. The integer algebra is considered applicable where a count of different objects is needed in a design. Consider the integer identifier AppleCount, which represents only a count of apples, nothing else, and the operators '$+, -, \times$, etc.', which precisely capture the real world operations we intend subjecting these apples to.

If a box of BoxCapacity holds an AppleCount of 20 apples, we can predict that, to hold 80 apples, we need 4 boxes using AppleCount/BoxCapacity = 80/20 = 4. However, if we want to transport 81 apples, the algebra breaks down, as 81/20 is not an integer and the algebra knows nothing about real numbers.

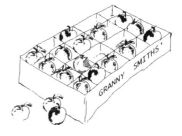

We need to upgrade our algebra to treat this new case, or reject the algebra in favour of a new one. In this case a simple upgrade suffices. If we add to our existing operators an infix binary operator mod which, applied to a pair of integers, delivers the integer part of the result of dividing its leftmost parameter by its rightmost, as in 7mod2 = 3, we restore the consistency and predictive powers of our algebra, correctly predicting that 5 boxes are needed to hold 81 apples from (AppleCount + BoxCapacity -1) mod BoxCapacity.

We can not only write formulas in an algebra, we can also ask questions about these formulas. For example, in the algebra of integer numbers we can ask if 3×3 is the same as 9, or what formula we should apply to the value 3 to give the value 9; not all that useful, perhaps, but by rewriting such questions as predicates, expressions which evaluate to true or false, we can rephrase them as specifications to test possible solutions. For example, we could ask the question: 'Does x=3 in the expression y=x×x satisfy the specification y=square(x)?'.

An expression Expr satisfies the specification Spec if the logical statement Expr **sat** Spec is true, where **sat** is a logical connective of comparison. For this to be true, Expr must satisfy Spec for all values of variables common to both. More formally, Expr **sat** Spec is true only if

$$\forall x. \; Expr(x) \; \textbf{sat} \; Spec(x)$$

But what logical connective do we use for such comparisons? What is **sat**? The obvious logical connective to use for comparison in the algebra of integers is equality, =, as defined in

Expr	Spec	Expr = Spec
true	true	true
true	false	false
false	true	false
false	false	true

Now, to prove that Expr satisfies Spec, we need only to prove that (Spec=Expr) is true. Or rather, for all relevant values x, with both specification and solution parametrised by x, that Expr(x)=Spec(x) is true.

In asking: Does f(x)=x×x satisfy the specification f(x)=square(x) for particular value x=3? we only have to prove that

$$\text{For } x=3, \; ((y=(x\times x))=(y=square(x))) = true$$

applying x=3

$$((y=(3\times 3))=(y=square(3))) = true$$
$$((y=9)=(y=square(3))) = true$$

```
(9=square(3)) = true
      true = true
        true
```

So the formula meets its specification for `x=3`.

To prove something incorrect is a similar exercise. If we'd proposed function `y=x+x` as a solution to the specification `y=square(x)`. Again we need to establish that

       For `x=3`, `((y=(x+x))=(y=square(x)))` = true

applying `x=3`

```
((y=(3+3))=(y=square(3))) = true
  ((y=6)=(y=square(3))) = true
     (6=square(3)) = true
          false = true
            false
```

The formula has failed to meet its specification.

If we wanted to establish if `((y=xxx)` satisfies `(y=square(x))` not just for `x=3` but for all integers, we would have to prove that `(y=xxx)` satisfies `(y=square(x))` for all x, written as $\forall$ x, which are members of the set of non-negative integers, $\mathbb{N}$, written as $x \in \mathbb{N}$

       For $\forall$ x and $x \in \mathbb{N}$, `((y=(xxx))=(y=square(x)))` = true

But the set of integers is infinite and to test the proposed solution to exhaustion will need an infinite number of tests and a commensurately infinite amount of time. In the above case we can resort to iteration to prove the solution correct in a reasonable time, and we'll touch on that later in the book. To prove a system incorrect is, on the face of it, easier. After all, we only need one counter-example to reject a solution. But it's not always that easy – that sole counter-example could be the last of an infinite number left to be tested.

In the natural world, not all objects can be described by integers. We'll need other algebras for other systems. Such algebras are useful only if they can simplify the process of accurate prediction of system behaviours. Consider the problem of inserting identical things, quanta, into a finite receptacle, the energy required to add each quanta increasing with the number of quanta already inserted. As an example, think of blowing up a balloon. The laws predicting the energy needed to add extra quanta all involve the *natural number* e≈2.71828. Engineers use these laws to predict changes in the energy stored in devices like capacitors, inductors, etc. The storage capabilities of these devices provide the engines to drive the sinusoidal changes of currents and voltages in electrical circuits. To analyse such circuits can require complicated expressions peppered with integrals and differentiations over time. However, as the small signal behaviour of analogue circuits is rooted in the exponential, Laplace transforms, which map expressions involving calculus over time into equivalent expressions in the Laplace domain, can be used map complex small signal behaviours into terms in a simple and straightforward algebra which can accurately predict behaviours with a few lines scribbled on the back of an envelope. Boolean algebra, initially conceived as a logic over object properties (e.g. Rome is the capital of France – `false`; New York is north of Rio de Janero – `true`), nowadays is used to design fairly complex digital electronic products – not what Boole had in mind at all.

Examples of calculi in the design of computer software are more rare – perhaps supporting the premise that most practising software writers are more craftsmen than they are engineers. One can think of niche market exceptions. Examples would include: the the use of probabilities to predict search and build times for tables; hit rates in cache memory and databases; response times in interactive systems, etc.; but these are rare. It is only relatively recently that tools and methods founded in discrete mathematics (e.g. Petri nets, Temporal Logic, VDM, Z, Hoare pre-post, weakest precondition, etc.), proving the correctness of sequential programs, have been finding adherents among practising programmers.

But not any old algebra can be pressed into service as a design tool. To be considered for adoption, an algebra has to be correct. In more formal terms it has to be consistent – one should not be able to prove an assertion and the contrary of that assertion (proving both A and ¬A correct would be rather embarrassing); and it has to be complete – one should be able to settle a meaningful assertion one way or the other (that either A and ¬A holds should be provable using the algebra alone). As well as being correct, the algebra must also be appropriate – it must faithfully capture the behaviours of the systems of interest and reliably predict the outcome of valid operations upon them (the adoption of Boolean algebra for digital systems and Laplace transforms for analogue systems are cases in point). It is also essential that the algebra selected must help prove a proposed design correct – it must support the comparison between a proposed design and a specification. It would also be convenient if the algebra were simple, easy to learn, and contained representations which would aid the user's understanding without requiring too much exposure to the underlying mathematics. It is all quite a bill to fill.

Just as they have different values and operators, different algebras have different ways of expressing specifications and different ways of establishing if an expression meets a specification. In the algebra over integers, the logical operator '=' was used to equate expression and specifications, and, as logical operators only compare like with like, the specification had to be written in the same algebra as the expression.

We've looked at what our algebras have in common, namely that for sequential, concurrent and real-time systems they describe systems in terms of state changes driven by atomic actions, in other words labelled transition systems. While this general approach holds for most algebras, the details may be different. But before we go on to look at differences, and to develop an algebra over labelled transition systems, we should first properly define what labelled transitions are.

1.4 Labelled Transition Systems

A labelled transition system describes the behaviour of a system in terms of states and the actions which move the system between its states. In more mathematical terms, a transition system, T, is a triple, $(S, A, \rightarrow)$ where:

S	is the set of states of the system
A	is the set of actions it can engage in
$\rightarrow$	is a relation, the state transition relation.

It is conventional, i.e. saves a lot of problems, to consider that all transition systems are finite by insisting that the number of states S is finite.

States and actions we know about, but what is $\rightarrow$? The state transition relation $\rightarrow$ is a set of transitions which, for given initial states in S, can, via an action from set A, move to another state in S. More formally, $\rightarrow$ is some subset of $(S \times A \times S)$

$$\rightarrow \subseteq (S \times A \times S).$$

A typical member of set $\rightarrow$ is a triple (s, α, s') where $s, s' \in S$ and $\alpha \in A$. This can be interpreted as that transition system T in state s can engage in action α and by doing so move to state s'. The state transition triple can be expressed as $s \xrightarrow{\alpha} s'$, or pictured as

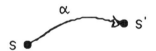

To enable us to define and analyse a system's properties its associated labelled transition system must be capable of describing: what it's next action will be; what happens if it has a choice of actions; and so on. In other words, we need an algebra over transition systems.

1.4.1 An Algebra of Transition Systems

A labelled transition system T_{Act} is an abstract representation of a real-world system. It consists of a set of atomic actions Act which contains individual actions, labelled by lower case letters from the Greek alphabet α, β, χ, ... , which model transitions between states named P, Q, R, ... Given a set of actions Act we can define $Expr(Act)$ as a set of those expressions containing actions from Act. As expressions are formed from operators ranging over actions they define system behaviour in particular states, and as such they label those same states. Now, given that expressions $\mathit{Expr}(\mathit{Act})$ are state-like, we can redefine a transition system over the set of actions Act, $\mathcal{T}_{\mathit{Act}}$, by a triple based only on two ingredients

$$\mathcal{T}_{\mathit{Act}} = (\mathit{Expr}(\mathit{Act}), \; \mathit{Act}, \; \rightarrow_{\mathit{Act}})$$

Knowing what Act and $\mathit{Expr}(\mathit{Act})$ are, we only have to establish what the mechanism which effects a change of state, $\rightarrow_{\mathit{Act}}$, is. We can define $\rightarrow_{\mathit{Act}}$ recursively on the structure of expressions reinforced by several significant cases (where the transition system in use is fairly obvious, we will write $\rightarrow$ in place of $\rightarrow_{\mathit{Act}}$ and $\mathcal{T}$ for $\mathcal{T}_{\mathit{Act}}$).

First, we define inaction, a process which as it cannot perform any action in Act is only one state

Inaction

Nil is a single-state system which has no actions and no future transitions, as in

The agent can be defined in terms of transition systems as $(\{Q\}, \{\}, \{\})$ for some Q.

Sequentiality can be modelled by prefixing a transition system with an action

Prefix

Intuitively, as a prefix must be performed before a system behaves as a particular agent, it is equivalent to inserting an arc labelled α pointing to an initial state of a transition systems defining that agent, as in

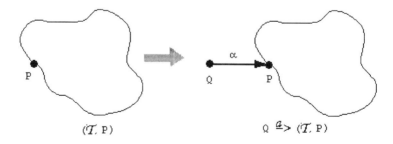

$(\mathcal{T}, P)$ $Q \xrightarrow{a} (\mathcal{T}, P)$

In label transition terms:
Where $(\mathcal{T}, P)$ represents the transition system $\mathcal{T}$ in state P then
if $\mathcal{T} = (S, \mathcal{A}, \rightarrow)$ and $Q \in S$ then $Q \xrightarrow{\alpha} (\mathcal{T}, P) = (\mathcal{T}', Q)$

$$\text{where } T' = (S', \mathcal{A}', \rightarrow');$$
$$S' = S \cup \{Q\};$$
$$\mathcal{A}' = \mathcal{A} \cup \{\alpha\};$$
$$\rightarrow' = \rightarrow \cup \{(P, \alpha, Q)\}$$

Choice between two behaviours is the same as adding two transition systems.

Summation

Intuitively, joining two initial nodes of two transition systems together forms a transition system which can perform as either one or the other of the original transition systems.

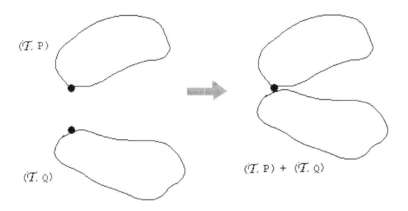

if $T = (S, \mathcal{A}, \rightarrow)$, $T' = (S', \mathcal{A}', \rightarrow')$ then $(T, P) + (T', Q) = (T'', R)$
where $T'' = (S'', \mathcal{A}'', \rightarrow'')$ and
$$S'' = S \cup S';$$
$$\mathcal{A}'' = \mathcal{A} \cup \mathcal{A}';$$
$$\rightarrow'' = \rightarrow \cup \rightarrow';$$

We can remove certain behaviours by hiding, or perhaps more accurately pruning, the actions leading to them.

Hiding

Intuitively, $(T, P) \setminus \alpha$ is obtained from (T, P) by deleting all edges labelled α.

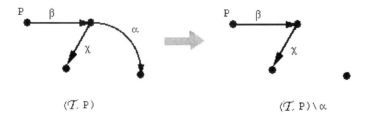

if $\mathcal{T} = (S, \mathcal{A}, \rightarrow)$ then $(\mathcal{T}, P) \setminus \alpha = (\mathcal{T}', P)$ where $\mathcal{T}' = (S', \mathcal{A}', \rightarrow')$
    given
$$S' = S$$
$$\mathcal{A}' = \mathcal{A} - \{\alpha\};$$
$$\rightarrow' = \rightarrow - S \times \{\alpha\} \times S;$$

The state previously reached in transition system $\mathcal{T}$ remains in the new transition system $\mathcal{T}'$, post pruning, but can no longer be reached by any action of $\mathcal{T}'$.

A benefit of taking an abstract view is that, to the modelling system, something engaging in a particular action sequence is the same as all other somethings with the same action sequences, e.g.: agents LIGHT $\stackrel{\text{def}}{=}$ off→on→LIGHT, FLAG $\stackrel{\text{def}}{=}$ lower→raise→FLAG, and CLOCK $\stackrel{\text{def}}{=}$ tick→tock→CLOCK, are all seen as systems continually engaging in two distinct actions turn and turn about, and conclusions draw from one model apply equally well to the others. We can thus create models with the same behaviour as existing models by changing action names, but we cannot do this as we please and we need the formal framework provided by renaming to ensure we do not unknowingly introduce errors.

Renaming

Intuitively, $(\mathcal{T}, Q) [\beta/\alpha]$ is obtained from $(\mathcal{T}, Q)$ by replacing each arc labelled α by an arc β, where β does not already label any arc in $(\mathcal{T}, Q)$.

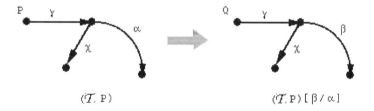

                $(\mathcal{T}, P)$ $(\mathcal{T}, P) [\beta/\alpha]$

if $\mathcal{T} = (S, \mathcal{A}, \rightarrow)$ then $(\mathcal{T}, P) [\beta/\alpha] = (\mathcal{T}', Q)$ where $\mathcal{T}' = (S', \mathcal{A}', \rightarrow')$
    and
$$S' = S$$
$$\mathcal{A}' = (\mathcal{A} - \{\alpha\}) \cup \{\beta\};$$
$$\rightarrow' = (\rightarrow - S \times \{\alpha\} \times S) \cup S \times \{\beta\} \times S;$$

When defining renaming it was necessary to establish whether action, β, was a possible action of expression, $\mathcal{E}xpr$, and it would help if we had a formal framework to decide such issues. We define *Sort* as the set of actions present in an expression.

Sort

The *sort* of expression *Expr* is the set of actions that *Expr* can engage in and is denoted by $\mathcal{L}(\mathit{Expr})$.

Using this definition we can define the sorts of the recently introduced operators over expressions:

$$\mathcal{L}(\text{NIL}) = \{\}$$

and the sorts of expression operators can be defined recursively as:

$$\mathcal{L}(\alpha \, . \, \mathit{Expr}) = \{\alpha\} \cup \mathcal{L}(\mathit{Expr})$$
$$\mathcal{L}(\mathit{Expr}_1 + \mathit{Expr}_2) = \mathcal{L}(\mathit{Expr}_1) \cup \mathcal{L}(\mathit{Expr}_2)$$
$$\mathcal{L}(\mathit{Expr} \backslash \alpha) = \mathcal{L}(\mathit{Expr}) - \{\alpha\}$$
$$\mathcal{L}(\mathit{Expr}[\beta / \alpha]) = (\mathcal{L}(\mathit{Expr}) - \{\alpha\}) \cup \{\beta\}$$

To compare systems, we need to observe their actions, record and compare what we've observed. Expressing a system's behaviour in terms of sequences of observed actions, *traces*, would seem the next logical step.

Traces

Traces are lists of actions seen by an observer as an agent moves from state to state. OLD_CLOCK would be observed to repeat the sequence tick, tock forever.

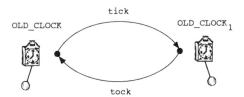

We define traces in the following way:

The trace of an agent is a finite sequence recording the actions of an agent from a particular state. Individual traces are written as lists of actions enclosed in <brackets>. For example:

<α, β>	a two-action trace, α followed by β;
<α>	a one-action trace;
<>	an empty trace, recording no actions.

The empty trace describes the behaviour of an agent before it engages in its first action.

The future behaviour of any agent is described by a set of traces. The future traces of P are <>, before it engages in any actions, <α>, after it engages in its first action, <α, α>, after it engages in its second action, and so on up to <α>^{n}, for some integer n, giving the set of traces

$$\{<>, <\alpha>, <\alpha, \alpha>, \quad ... \quad ., <\alpha>^n\}$$

It is convenient to define $A*$ as the set of all finite traces, including $<>$, which can be formed from symbols in the set A, $A*$ describes all possible behaviours of an agent with alphabet A.

In our example $A = \{\alpha\}$ so $A* = \{<>, <\alpha>, <\alpha, \alpha>, \ \ldots \ ., <\alpha>^n\}$

To predict the behaviour of agent P, where the agent's name is associated with a state in a derivation tree, we use the function $\texttt{Traces(P)}$. The above example agent has $\texttt{Traces(P)} = \{\alpha\}*$.

Some more examples:

Agent $\texttt{OLD\_CLOCK}$ represents a clock which ticks before it tocks.

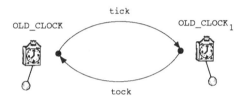

$$\texttt{OLD\_CLOCK} \ \overset{\text{def}}{=} \ \texttt{tick:OLD\_CLOCK}_1$$
$$\texttt{OLD\_CLOCK}_1 \ \overset{\text{def}}{=} \ \texttt{tock:OLD\_CLOCK}$$
and
$$\texttt{Traces(OLD\_CLOCK)} =$$
$$\{<>, <\texttt{tick}>, <\texttt{tick}, \texttt{tock}>, <\texttt{tick}, \texttt{tock}, \texttt{tick}>, \ \ldots \ \text{etc.}\}$$

$$\texttt{Traces(OLD\_CLOCK}_1) =$$
$$\{<>, <\texttt{tock}>, <\texttt{tock}, \texttt{tick}>, <\texttt{tock}, \texttt{tick}, \texttt{tock}>, \ \ldots \ \text{etc.}\}$$

Agent $\texttt{STAMP\_MACHINE}$ represents a system which usually accepts a coin and delivers a stamp in a pull-out drawer:

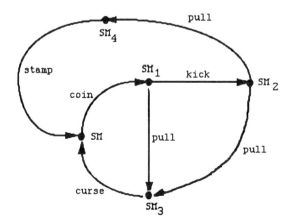

Occasionally the machine needs a kick before the drawer can be opened, and even then it sometimes fails to deliver a stamp, evoking a curse from the customer.

```
STAMP_MACHINE = SM
        SM def coin:(kick:(pull:stamp:SM + pull:curse:SM)
                          + (pull:curse:SM)
```

and

```
        Traces(SM) = {<>,<coin>,<coin,kick>,<coin,pull>,
                          <coin,pull,curse>,...etc.}
        Traces(SM₁) ={<>,<kick>,<pull>,<kick,pull>,
                          <pull,curse>,...etc.}
```

The complete behaviour of any system P is described by `Traces(P)` the set of all possible sequences of actions of P from its initial state. For example `Traces(SM)` generates all the traces of `STAMP_MACHINE` from its initial state and fully describes `STAMP_MACHINE` just as `Traces(P) = {α}*` fully describes $P \overset{def}{=} \alpha : P$.

We may wish to ask other pertinent questions of an agent. For example: What are the initial actions of a given system?; Does a given system always return to its initial state?; Are all states reachable?; Does there exist a sub-set of states where the system can cycle indefinitely?; Can the system reach a state from which no further action is possible? We can define a basic set of questions in the form of functions.

Next Actions
Set of next actions of an agent
```
        NextActions(agent_name) = SetOfActions
```
For example
```
        NextActions(SM₁) = {kick,pull}
```
and the special case of initial actions
```
        NextActions(SM) = {coin}
```

Final states
States reached from the initial state of an agent, P, by a sequence of actions, `seq`, are elements of the set `Final(P,seq)`.
```
        Final(agent_name,trace) = SetOfStates
```
For example
```
        Final(SM, <>) = {SM}
        Final(SM, <coin>) = {SM₁}
        Final(SM, <coin,kick,pull>) = {SM₃, SM₄}
```

We now use these basic functions to ask fairly complex questions of an agent.

Does a given agent ever stop? Is it incomplete? Does it exhibit livelock? Or deadlock? And so on. For example, P will deadlock if the following predicate evaluates to true:

$$\exists \alpha \in \texttt{Traces(P)} \; \exists P' \in \texttt{Final(P,}\alpha\texttt{)} \; : \; \texttt{Traces(P')} = <>$$

By expressing a required system behaviour in terms of such questions, we can build a specification which a proposed design will have to satisfy.

Having gone over the common basis for sequential, concurrent and real-time algebras, we can now look at their differences.

1.5 One at Once, All Together and In Time

We describe systems in terms of their observed actions. If an observer cannot distinguish between systems by observation alone, the systems are considered equal; i.e., systems are considered equal if they cannot be told apart without taking them apart. For example, a system which accepts an integer x and outputs its square x^2 can be constructed from several types of hardware, or from a mixture of hardware and software. It could even be a student with a calculator. Providing they behave identically, to all intents and purposes they are identical, and any of these squaring systems which formed part of a larger system could be replaced by any other without affecting the performance of that larger system. What they do internally to achieve this equality is not our concern.

By their actions we can place systems in one of three categories. These are:

- **Sequential** systems, where actions cannot overlap in time;
- **Concurrent** systems, where they can; and
- **Real-time** systems, where actions can not only overlap but have to occur within certain time limits.

Sequential systems are the simplest of our three categories. They engage in one action at a time, each action causing one change of state. Concurrent systems are more complex. They are composed of one or more subsystems, and the ordering of which actions overlap when they can change each time the systems runs. To model such systems, we need to describe their behaviours for all possible interleavings of the actions of their subsystems. Real-time systems are the most complex of all. Like concurrent systems, they can be composed of several subsystems, with as many different behaviours as the number of interleavings of their subcomponents, with the additional proviso that their actions are constrained by when they can be executed.

The level of difficulty in designing systems is directly related to their complexity. The more complex a system, the higher the probability of getting things wrong.

But one thing sequential, concurrent or real-time systems have in common is that algebras are needed to help us design, and subsequently to check these designs against their specifications. But we may need different algebras for each type of system.

1.5.1 A Process Algebra for Sequential Systems

Sequential systems follow one thread of control and engage in a single sequence of actions, each action being completed before the next one commences. Any sequential computer program which defines a sequence of actions to be executed is a sequential system. While programming language statements can be grouped into fairly complex structures, such as: *if…else, case…esac* predicated clauses; *do…until, while…do* loops; *call…return* procedure calls, and so on, they are all sequential systems with one thread of control.

Sequential systems need not be monolithic, but can be composed of smaller components, with the proviso that only one action of one component can be live at a time. An example of such a composite system is time-slice multiprocessing, where an inherently sequential processor, capable of executing one programming instruction at a time, can be shared between many processes. Apparent multiprocessing is orchestrated by a scheduler which selects one of the waiting set of programs for the sequential processor to execute in each time slice.

To design a sequential system we need to model: sequentiality where we have sequences of actions which define a system's behaviour; choice in which alternative system behaviours can be chosen; morphism, in which actions and hence behaviours can be renamed; and hiding, in which actions can be removed. And these features happen to be the very things we developed in our algebra of transition systems; what remains is to present them as operators in an algebra over sequential systems.

Prefix

Sequentiality is modelled by the simplest operator, prefix →. Prefixing actions to existing agents creates new agents.

Expression P $\stackrel{\text{def}}{=}$ a→Q defines agent P which engages in action a before behaving as a previously defined agent Q. By stringing actions together with the prefix operator we can model sequential behaviours. A system in state P engages in action a and by so doing performs a transition to state Q. Subsequent engagement in action b moves the system from state Q to state R. The transition from state P to S is unla-

P   Q   R   S

belled and the system can move between these states at any time with no discernible cause. The pictured system can thus move from state P to state S by engaging in action sequence a,b.

A recursive system, by engaging in a sequence of actions, can forever return to its original state, ready to engage in the same sequence again, as for example a system which returns to state P after sequentially engaging in action a followed by b.

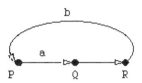

For example, a stamp machine MACHINE which, for each coin inserted, delivers a stamp, then stands ready to repeat the process, can be described by the expression

$$\text{MACHINE} \stackrel{\text{def}}{=} \text{coin}{\rightarrow}\text{stamp}{\rightarrow}\text{MACHINE}$$

Choice

Alternative behaviours are modelled by the choice operator, |. Choice forms a new agent by offering a choice over existing agents.

Expression P $\stackrel{\text{def}}{=}$ (a→Q) | (b→R) defines agent P which can engage in action a and behave as Q, or, by engaging in b, behave as R.

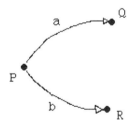

We could, for example, create a new stamp machine 10/20MACHINE, offering to deliver 10p or 20p stamps, from two older machines 10MACHINE and 20MACHINE, with

    10MACHINE $\stackrel{\text{def}}{=}$ (10pcoin→10pstamp→10MACHINE)
    20MACHINE $\stackrel{\text{def}}{=}$ (20pcoin→20pstamp→20MACHINE)
then

```
10/20MACHINE def 10MACHINE | 20MACHINE
            = (10pcoin→10pstamp→10/20MACHINE)
            | (20pcoin→20pstamp→10/20MACHINE)
```

Morphism

To change action names, instead of direct relabelling we use a more general morphism operator [φ]. With morphism we can create new agents with the same behaviour as existing ones. For example, with morphism function [φ]:a→b, we can create P[φ] = (b→Q[φ]) from P def (a→Q).

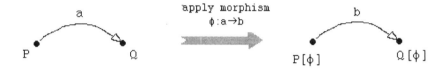

Using morphism we can create a new stamp machine USA_MACHINE which behaves like the previous one but, adjusted for the USA, offers to deliver 10¢ or 20¢ stamps.

```
USA_MACHINE = (10¢coin→10¢stamp→USA_MACHINE)
            | (20¢coin→20¢stamp→USA_MACHINE)
```

Hiding

Finally, by removing certain actions from our observations, we can change the observed behaviour of a process. For this we use the hiding operator \ in collaboration with a hiding set A. We express the removal of actions in set A from process P as P\A.

With A = {a}, we can take P def a→b→Q | c→d→Q and create P\A = c→d→Q\A.

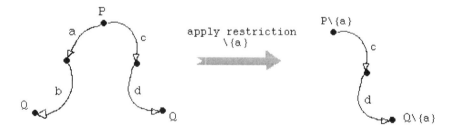

By hiding the 10¢coin actions of USA_MACHINE we can create a stamp machine which only deals in 20¢ stamps:
```
USA_MACHINE\10¢coin
    = (20¢coin→20¢stamp→USA_MACHINE\10¢coin)
```

We can now define our algebra over actions. We do this using the Backus–Naur Form (BNF), a conventional, and concise, way to define an algebra by defining the expressions, Expr, to the left of a ': :=' that can be replaced by what forms to its right. Where the expression separator '|' is read as an *or*. Using BNF we can now define an algebra over actions in terms of expressions and operators over them. Given a set $\mathcal{A}$ of actions, a, b∈ $\mathcal{A}$, and STOP is a process which engages in no actions, expressions over $\mathcal{A}$ are the sequences generated by the following BNF grammar:

$$\text{Expr} ::= \text{STOP} \| (\text{a} \rightarrow \text{Expr}) \| (\text{Expr} \mid \text{Expr})$$
$$\| (\text{Expr}) \backslash \text{a} \| (\text{Expr}) [\phi : \text{a} \rightarrow \text{b}]$$

From the BNF definition, valid expressions in the algebra include:

$$\text{Expr} ::= \text{STOP}$$
$$\text{Expr} ::= (\text{a} \rightarrow \text{Expr})$$

and so on.

The BNF form is recursive. Expressions to the left of the 'can be replaced by' can be reinserted on its right, giving as valid expressions:

$$\text{a} \rightarrow (\text{Expr} \mid \text{Expr})$$
$$\text{a} \rightarrow (\text{STOP} \mid (\text{Expr}) \backslash \text{a})$$

and so on.

Now that we have a process algebra over sequential systems, we can make good our promise to explore the production and use of specifications as each process algebra was introduced.

If we can express a specification as a predicate over the actions of the system to be built, we can check if a proposed solution satisfies this specification by showing it never acts outside the specification. To do this, we check all possible sequences of actions of our solution against a specification to determine if the statement Expr **sat** Spec is always true.

But the first thing we have to do is establish how we compare a design with a specification. What is the **sat** in Expr **sat** Spec? When we discussed proofs earlier in this chapter it was noted that, while '=' was used for **sat** in the algebra over integers, this did not have to be so for all algebras. For each algebra we must establish which logical connective is the most appropriate.

Candidates as possible connectives for our process algebra of sequential systems are and ^; equality =; and implication ⇒, as defined in

Expr	Spec	Expr^Spec	Expr=Spec	Expr⇒Spec
true	true	true	true	true
true	false	false	false	false
false	true	false	false	true
false	false	false	true	true

Expr^Spec is true only when both Expr and Spec are true. Expr=Spec, in addition to the conditions for ^, is also true when both Expr and Spec are false. Expr⇒Spec, in addition to the conditions for =, is also true when Expr is false and Spec is true.

The greater the number of solutions satisfying a specification, the weaker that specification is said to be. The fewer, the stronger. In the above table, the number of trues in the columns associated with each operator speaks of the comparative strength of the statement Expr **sat** Spec. The ^ operator embodies the strongest comparison. Expressions proved to meet their specifications with ^ automatically meet their specifications under the other two, weaker, operators. The = operator is the next strongest. Expressions proved to meet their specifications under = also meet their specifications under ⇒ but not the stronger ^. The weakest operator is ⇒. Expressions proved to meet their specifications under ⇒ do not automatically meet their specifications under the other, and hence stronger, operators.

So what? Well, as we've already said, the easier it is to meet a specification the more possible solutions there are. And the more solutions there are the easier it will be to find one of them, and if we have several solutions we can choose to implement the simplest one. In other words we do not want to over-specify our problem as this will unnecessarily complicate both design and implementation.

Given this argument, we'd obviously prefer it if the ⇒ operator could be used as the **sat** in Expr **sat** Spec. But whilst it's fairly obvious that if Expr^Spec and Expr=Spec are true then so is Expr **sat** Spec, this is less obvious with ⇒.

But look again at the truth table.

Expr	Spec	Expr⇒Spec
true	true	true
true	false	false
false	true	true
false	false	true

The first two rows are fairly obvious. It is only in the last two that things get a bit obscure. To make things clearer, remember that an implication, p⇒q, links two, perhaps unrelated, statements, p and q, into a causal 'if p then q' statement which we can think of as a contract to be met. As an example, consider a father who, feeling his age, is finding it increasingly difficult to beat his son in their weekly tennis game. To keep on winning he knows he must get fitter, and consequently he makes the following contract with himself: 'If my son wins next week then I will take up jogging.' We can check if the contract is met, (p⇒q) = true, for all possible cases, by applying the truth table row by row. Let's start with the easier pair of:

- true⇒true: The following week the son beats the father. The father takes down his running shoes and starts jogging. The contract is satisfied, (true⇒true) = true.
- true⇒false: The following week the son beats the father, not by much, but by enough. The father, whilst feeling his age, makes no attempt to start jogging. The father has broken the contract, (true⇒false) = false.

Now the less intuitive cases:

- false⇒false: The following week the father beats the son. The father breathes a sigh of relief and postpones any thought of jogging for at least another week. The contract, by not being violated, is satisfied, (false⇒false) = true.
- false⇒true: The last case finds the father still beating the son but also starting to jog. Perhaps he's decided to get fitter anyway. Or he doesn't want to waste the money he's already spent on a new pair of jogging shoes. The reason doesn't matter, he has not violated the contract, (false⇒true) = true.

Now, thinking of Expr⇒Spec as a contract to prove Expr satisfies Spec, we need only to prove Expr⇒Spec holds. Or rather, for all relevant actions act, Expr(act)⇒Spec(act) is true. Consider the expression

$$\text{MACHINE} \stackrel{\text{def}}{=} \text{coin}\rightarrow\text{stamp}\rightarrow\text{MACHINE}$$

which models the purchase of a stamp from a machine in terms of the observed actions coin and stamp. The specification is written as a predicate in terms of these same actions. For example, the manufacturer of the machine would like the machine to dispense a stamp for every coin received, but would be quite happy if the machine accepted the occasional coin without giving out a stamp. As a specification, for every stamp dispensed a coin must have been inserted. The running total of stamps dispensed #stamp must never exceed that of coins received #coin

$$\text{MACHINE\_SPEC} = (\#\text{stamp} \le \#\text{coin})$$

and this must hold for all states of the machine. To prove that our machine satisfies this expression we have to prove that

$$(\text{MACHINE} \stackrel{\text{def}}{=} \text{coin}\rightarrow\text{stamp}\rightarrow\text{MACHINE}) \Rightarrow (\#\text{stamp} \le \#\text{coin})$$

holds in the states before the first coin action, before the first stamp action and before all subsequent coin and stamp actions. This we will do, but later on in the text.

There is, of course, more to sequential systems design than we've covered here. Nevertheless, we've done sufficient to move on and consider algebras for concurrent and real-time systems design.

1.5.2 A Process Algebra for Concurrent Systems

Concurrent systems, whose individual actions can overlap in time, may have several threads of control and are intrinsically more difficult to theorise about than sequential systems. As the possibility of error increases with the complexity of a system, it is going to be more difficult to correctly design a concurrent system than it is a sequential one. But that's not all. Concurrent system are also more arduous to prove correct.

To prove a system correct, we need to show that whatever state it reaches, none of its subsequent actions run counter to the specification.

Consider a sequential system with five states, represented by the fingers of one hand; four actions move the system from state ❶ to state ❺.

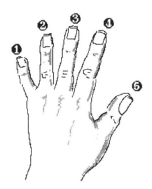

To prove the system meets its specification, we only have to test the system in its five states and prove that, in each state, the system cannot engage in any action which would violate the specification. Two such sequential systems in series would require the testing of ten states.

Now, consider these same two sequential systems combined as a concurrent system. As actions can overlap in time, sometimes the system will run with all the actions of one hand preceding those of the other, sometimes vice versa, and sometimes in any combination (interleaving) between the two. To ensure the system meets its specification, we have to prove the system correct for all these possible interleavings. With ten states per interleaving, and ten possible interleavings, we have one hundred system states to check for specification violations. And this is a very simple system. Consider trying to prove systems correct that have many complex concurrent parts with hundreds of states each.

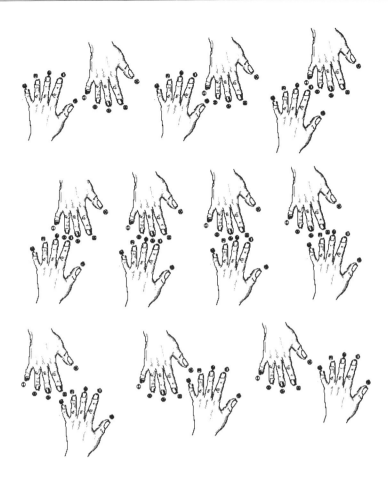

Things will, of course, be easier if we have the help of an algebra over concurrent systems. But such an algebra will only really help if it simplifies concurrent system design and doesn't add to its complexity. The easiest path would be to upgrade an existing algebra. The only candidate at our disposal is our algebra for sequential systems. If we can upgrade this to cover concurrent systems, not only will we be able to capitalise on our knowledge of sequential systems, but the resultant algebra (and associated tools) will, by definition, be capable of addressing both concurrent and sequential systems design.

We establish the link between sequential and concurrent systems by making the observation that any concurrent system can be considered as a collection of cooperating sequential systems. This makes sequential systems a special case of concurrent systems – a sequential system is a concurrent system with only one component. This hierarchy is strongly founded in our current sequential systems model, in which objects can engage in internal actions which are the concern of the object itself, and in external actions by which an object interacts with its environment. All environments are composed of sequential systems and it takes external actions, the agency of communication, to turn them into a concurrent system.

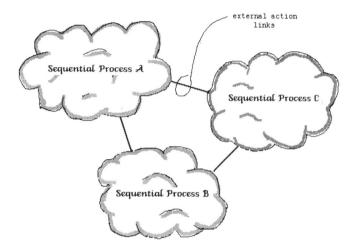

Defining concurrent systems as cooperating sequential systems does not preclude the construction of concurrent systems out of cooperating concurrent systems, or out of a mixture of both. It only requires that each component of a concurrent system can be decomposed into one or more sequential systems. Having established the link, we are now justified in extending the existing sequential process algebra with its prefix, choice, morphism and hiding operators to an algebra over concurrent systems. All we are missing are an operator and laws to predict what happens when two sequential systems P and Q operate concurrently as P∥Q.

How a concurrent system behaves is dependent upon when its individual components engage in their own actions. But we have a problem if the timing of actions is significant. The sequential algebra, on which we hope to base our new algebra, is asynchronous – it ignores time, and only records the order of actions. For example, the sequential system P $\stackrel{\text{def}}{=}$ a→b→P says action a is followed by action b, but at what time they occur is not given. We read P $\stackrel{\text{def}}{=}$ a→b→P as 'sometime in the future, P can engage in action a followed sometime later by action b which returns the systems to its initial state'.

But how relevant is time to the modelling of concurrent systems? For two systems to communicate successfully they must simultaneously engage in the same external actions. For example, systems a→P and a→Q can communicate by simultaneously engaging in action a. But systems progress asynchronously, and it would only be by the blindest chance that two system which want to communicate would be ready to do so at the same time. Normally the first one ready would simply have to wait for the other, and only when both are ready would communication

proceed. As a law,
$$(a{\to}P)\,\|\,(a{\to}Q)\ =\ a{\to}P\|Q$$
So by insisting that all process communication between sequential components is done using a 'stop and wait' protocol, our asynchronous model of sequential systems can be upgraded to cover process interaction.

Take an example. Consider someone who needs to buy a stamp to post a letter. The process WRITER can be modelled by the sequential process
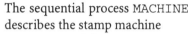
WRITER $\stackrel{\text{def}}{=}$ write${\to}$coin${\to}$ stamp${\to}$post${\to}$WRITER$'$
After completing the letter the writer goes to a stamp machine, inserts a coin, takes the offered stamp, uses it to post the letter, then gets on with the rest of her life.

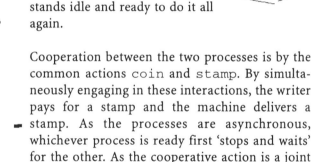

The sequential process MACHINE describes the stamp machine
    MACHINE $\stackrel{\text{def}}{=}$
    coin${\to}$stamp${\to}$MACHINE

For each coin inserted, the machine delivers a stamp, then stands idle and ready to do it all again.

Cooperation between the two processes is by the common actions coin and stamp. By simultaneously engaging in these interactions, the writer pays for a stamp and the machine delivers a stamp. As the processes are asynchronous, whichever process is ready first 'stops and waits' for the other. As the cooperative action is a joint action, engaged in simultaneously by the interacting parties, it has the effect of temporarily synchronising the participating asynchronous processes.

For potential cooperating process to succeed, they must somehow be aware of offers of interaction by other processes. As the only actions an environment can engage in are the external actions of a process, it must be these same actions by which they communicate. This leads us to define external actions, requiring cooperation of an environment, as the shared actions of a system; for example, the coin and stamp actions in the stamp transaction. Similarly, we define internal actions, which cannot be influenced by an environment, as actions unique to each process in a system, as the write and post actions in the stamp transaction.

We've described what role external actions play in concurrently composed sequential processes, but what happens to internal actions? For example, given a→P and b→Q where both a and b are internal actions, as a and b are independent of each other they can happen at any time. We have three possible behaviours: a happens before b; b happens before a ; or they occur simultaneously. We need an answer for each case.

Combine the first two cases. As actions are atomic, indivisible and instantaneous, a can occur before b, giving
$$(a{\rightarrow}P)\,||\,(b{\rightarrow}Q) = a{\rightarrow}(P||(b{\rightarrow}Q))$$
and internal action b has yet to happen.

Or, if b occurs before a, giving
$$(a{\rightarrow}P)\,||\,(b{\rightarrow}Q) = b{\rightarrow}(P||(a{\rightarrow}Q))$$
and internal action a has yet to happen.

If we combine them, using | as the or operator, we get the law
$$(a{\rightarrow}P)\,||\,(b{\rightarrow}Q) = (a{\rightarrow}(P||(b{\rightarrow}Q)))\ |\ (b{\rightarrow}(P||(a{\rightarrow}Q)))$$
The parallel composition of two processes reduces to a choice between two interleaved sequential behaviours, and, as which choice will be made cannot be determined, the choice between these behaviours is non-deterministic.

But what happens if these independent actions occur simultaneously? Surprising enough the results are the same, because, in our model, such actions just cannot happen simultaneously. In an asynchronous algebra, time is continuous, It can be divided and subdivided without limit. Thus, if two action appear to happen simultaneously, we can always use a finer scale of time until we can distinguish an order between them. As actions are atomic and instantaneous, the first action completes before the other starts. So actions which appear simultaneous can be resolved into our existing law.

Any surprise one might have at this result may well be a consequence of our not being sufficiently clear about how the algebra views atomic actions. Our thoughts about actions may be captured in the following diagram, where **a** and **b** are actions of two components of a concurrent system.

In this model, the actions have width, they take time to execute, and the model agrees with our original definition of concurrent systems as ones whose actions can overlap in time. Our interleaving model/algebra takes a simpler view; no actions are allowed to overlap. Only the first and last examples of interleaving are valid.

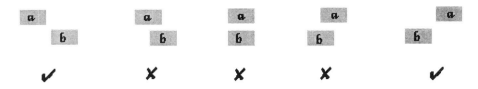

If we allowed actions to overlap we would, by definition, create non-atomic actions. As we don't want to make things complex for the sake of it, if interleaving/atomic actions model concurrent systems sufficiently well we would be foolish to reject our algebra in favour of a more complex one over non-atomic actions.

The actions of an algebra over atomic actions can be more faithfully represented as

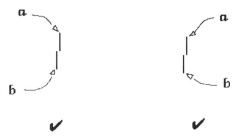

where, because actions are instantaneous, only interleaving is required. The only time two agents act simultaneously is when they synchronise by engaging in the same external action. The resultant shared actions are themselves atomic and can be interleaved with other actions. For example,

WRITER $\stackrel{\text{def}}{=}$ write→coin→stamp→post→MACHINE

MACHINE $\stackrel{\text{def}}{=}$ coin→stamp→MACHINE

synchronise using the common actions coin and stamp

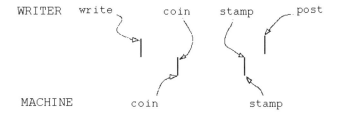

giving their composite

WRITER‖MACHINE $\stackrel{\text{def}}{=}$ write→coin→stamp→post→WRITER‖MACHINE

Smart, or what?

The complete algebra can now be defined as

Expr ::= STOP ‖ (a→Expr) ‖ (Expr | Expr) ‖ (Expr‖Expr) ‖
(Expr)\a ‖ (Expr) [ϕ:a→b]

We've only added one new operator to our process algebra for sequential system to form this new algebra. But it's a powerful one. It enables us to predict the behaviour of a concurrent system from a knowledge of the behaviour of its sequential parts. For example, we can now formally determine the emergent behaviour of a WRITER composed with a MACHINE that we pictured above

$$\text{WRITER} \| \text{MACHINE} \overset{\text{def}}{=} (\text{write} \to \text{coin} \to \text{stamp} \to \text{post} \to \text{WRITER}')$$
$$\| (\text{coin} \to \text{stamp} \to \text{MACHINE})$$

The write action is a private internal action of WRITER. It does not interact with an environment and can go ahead at any time. The coin action is a joint action of MACHINE and WRITER and, as such, is an external action of both. It can only proceed if both are ready. As they are not, the system's only option is to engage in write.

$$\overset{\text{def}}{=} \text{write} \to ((\text{coin} \to \text{stamp} \to \text{post} \to \text{WRITER}')$$
$$\| (\text{coin} \to \text{stamp} \to \text{MACHINE}))$$

The coin action is an external action of both MACHINE and WRITER and can proceed if both are ready. Hence MACHINE and WRITER interact by engaging in coin.

$$\overset{\text{def}}{=} \text{write} \to \text{coin} \to ((\text{stamp} \to \text{post} \to \text{WRITER}')$$
$$\| (\text{stamp} \to \text{MACHINE}))$$

Now MACHINE and WRITER interact, using the stamp action.

$$\overset{\text{def}}{=} \text{write} \to \text{coin} \to \text{stamp} \to ((\text{post} \to \text{WRITER}')$$
$$\| (\text{MACHINE}))$$

The post action is a private internal action of WRITER and can be executed at any time. As the MACHINE is waiting to engage in the joint coin action, only the private post action can proceed, giving

$$\text{WRITER} \| \text{MACHINE} \overset{\text{def}}{=} \text{write} \to \text{coin} \to \text{stamp} \to \text{post}$$
$$\to (\text{WRITER}' \| \text{MACHINE})$$

The writer and machine correctly negotiate the buying of a stamp.

'All' that remains for us to do is to prove that proposed solutions Expr meet their specifications Spec in this concurrent world. As the algebra is essentially the same, we prove concurrent systems correct just as we did sequential ones, by showing that the actions of the proposed solution do not violate a specification written as a predicate over those same actions. The arguments for using Expr⇒Spec for Expr **sat** Spec also hold, and to prove that a proposed solution is correct we need only prove (Spec⇒Expr) is true. Or rather, for all relevant actions act, that Expr(act)⇒Spec(act) is true.

Back to the stamp machine and the writer, where we consider only the joint stamp and coin actions involved in the transaction. We already have a specification for MACHINE:

MACHINE_SPEC = (#stamp ≤ #coin)

But the writer may cavil at paying for stamps she doesn't receive and would rather receive a stamp for every coin inserted – but would be content to receive the occasional stamp for free. Consumers require that the machine never accepts a request for another stamp until it has satisfied previous requests, allowing at most one request to be outstanding. Where the observed number of coins inserted is #coin and the observed number of stamps dispensed is #stamp,

WRITER_SPEC = (#coin ≤ #stamp +1)

The actual machine must satisfy both specifications

STAMP_SPEC = (#stamp ≤ #coin) ^ (#coin ≤ #stamp +1)

and this must hold for all states of the machine. To prove our machine satisfies this expression, we have to prove that

(MACHINE‖WRITER) ⇒ (#stamp ≤ #coin) ^ (#coin ≤ #stamp +1)

holds in the states before the first coin action, before the first stamp action and before all subsequent coin and stamp actions.

The specification is actually rather loose, and could be satisfied by a system which accepts a coin then stops. We'll tighten up such specifications later on. At this point, real-time systems call.

1.6 Real-Time Systems

Unlike in the preceding sections, we're not going to develop a real-time algebra here – we have the rest of the book in which to do that – but, rather, we will concentrate on why we need a different algebra for real-time work and outline the sort of algebra required.

First of all we should define what we mean by a real-time system. A real-time system is one in which the time at which inputs are accepted and outputs produced is significant. This is usually because the inputs and outputs correspond to some activity in its environment and the time delay between inputs and related outputs must be acceptable to that environment. Usually the environment is the real world, and the real-time system must react so that the system to which it is connected is not compromised – it's better if an aircraft's autopilot lowers the plane's wheels before, rather than after, landing.

Real-time systems can be subdivided into two categories: 'hard' real time, where it is imperative that responses occur within specified tolerances; and 'soft' real time, where response times are important but the system will function correctly if deadlines are occasionally missed. Hard real-time systems include safety-critical applications where, if things go, wrong life and limb can be endangered, or large lawsuits could ensue. Soft systems are where certain failures are of little consequence: for example, a washing machine which exceeds its specified cycle time. In both cases the design strategies have to be appropriate to the end objective. Spending \$5,000 so that every washing machine works within tight time tolerances, when each machine only costs \$500 to build, may not be a smart move, whereas spending \$10,000 to design a widget costing \$100 whose failure would result in irradiating the population of a large city would be quite rational.

But how do we design real-time systems correctly? Asynchronous algebras, while useful in the design of concurrent systems, have one major failing as tools for designing real-time systems. They do not model real-time. Knowing that action b follows sometime after action a in $P \stackrel{def}{=} a{\to}b{\to}P$ isn't very useful when the specification requires that action b must follow action a by one second, plus or minus ten milliseconds. To design such systems we need an algebra in which time is an implicit parameter.

It is tempting to follow our previous route of upgrading, by adding time to our asynchronous algebra. The benefits would be huge. Unfortunately, there's a problem. Time has a more insidious influence than appears at first glance. If actions a and b happen at the same time, our algebra must model these actions as simultaneous – it must model overlapping actions, the very thing ruled out by the interleaving model. To check if overlapping actions are necessary we'll take a look at what are termed 'truly' concurrent systems in which overlapping actions are allowed, and in particular at the so called 'glitch' problem. Consider the behaviour of a binary exclusive-or, EXOR, gate $f = x{\oplus}y$ defined in the following truth table

x	y	f
0	0	0
0	1	1
1	0	1
1	1	0

If the input signals differ, the output is a 1. If the inputs are the same the output is a 0. Consider how the gate behaves when its x and y inputs change as follows:

The x signal changes from a 1 to a 0 before the y signal changes from a 0 to a 1. This gives a 0 'blip' in the f output for the period when the two input signals are the same. This is the infamous 'glitch'.

x

y

f=x⊕y

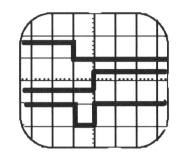

Similarly, if the x signal changes from a 1 to a 0 after the y signal changes from a 0 to a 1, we also get a 0 'blip' in the f output while the two inputs are the same.

x

y

f=x⊕y

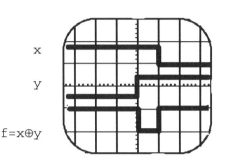

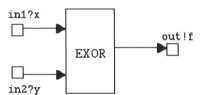

Describing a typical EXOR gate with our interleaving algebra we get the model

EXOR $\overset{\text{def}}{=}$ in1?x→in2?y→out!(x⊕y)
| in2?y→in1?x→out!(x⊕y)

By assuming that inputs interleave, either input can precede the other, the model captures both of the above behaviours. But before we think all is well with the world, let us look in more detail at what is actually going on, by conducting a state analysis on the gate.

The gate's inputs, x and y, and its output, f, can as (x,y/f) be used to label its states. The transitions which are of interest to us are between states (0,0/0), (0,1/1),(1,0/1) and (1,1/0). In particular, the input changing from (1,0) to (0,1) is pictured as

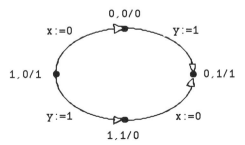

Whichever way we get from the leftmost state to the rightmost state, the output goes from a 1, through a 0, and back to a 1. In more formal terms the output trace, the list of observed output actions as the transition system moves from $(1,0/1)$ to $(0,1/1)$, its x and y inputs changing in any order, is $<1,0,1>$.

Reasonable? Well, yes, but an interleaving model cannot capture the case of things happening truly concurrently. What happens if both input signals change simultaneously? They can, as in

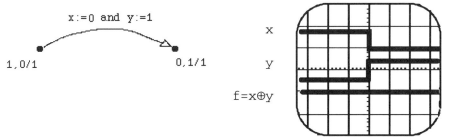

An observer would see both inputs change
but the output remain the same – no glitch.

The interleaving model defines an EXOR as a gate whose inputs change in sequence. However, in the real world an EXOR gate has no control over its inputs and these can change simultaneously. And, as long as these changes occur within a certain time window, the behaviour of a real EXOR gate may differ from that predicted by the interleaving model. In the real world, the output does not change – no glitch – if the inputs change simultaneously; but it does change – with a glitch – if the inputs change sequentially.

So it's true. For certain real-world systems, the so-called truly concurrent ones, the interleaving model with atomic actions fails to capture all behaviours. Why is this? Well, it all stems from the assumption on the part of our interleaving algebra that actions are atomic, instantaneous and cannot overlap in time. By mapping simultaneous actions to interleaving actions, such an algebra maps concurrent actions to a non-determinstic choice between those same actions in series. By making such a mapping, the algebra will be unable to distinguish between systems whose behaviours differ for overlapping and non-overlapping actions.

Remember that, while in the last section we defined concurrent systems as those whose actions can overlap in time, an interleaving algebra models systems by assuming that actions never overlap and their combinations remain atomic.

For example, where actions a and b are from different components of a concurrent system, an interleaving model would see either action a occurring before action b, or vice versa. The actions never overlap. Concurrent actions of component systems map to serial, and still atomic, actions in a composite system.

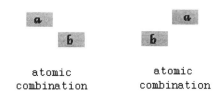

atomic   atomic
combination   combination

non-atomic   non-atomic   non-atomic
combination   combination   combination

An interleaving algebra which only recognises atomic actions will not be able to accommodate overlapping actions which combine into non-atomic actions.

Unfortunately, life is not sufficiently accommodating to make the actions of all real-world objects atomic and instantaneous so as to allow us to fit simultaneous actions into an interleaving model. Some objects have an implicit inertia and behave as if they have a minimum grain size to their behaviours. Such behaviours are better modelled by an algebra which accommodates simultaneous, overlapping, non-atomic actions. In our EXOR example, the glitch-free state change from $1,0/1$ to $0,1/1$ is the result of a non-atomic action composed of x changing from 1 to 0 simultaneously with y changing from 0 to 1.

In the real world, surely we can reconcile such differences in behaviour by waiting until all intermediate fluctuations have settled, only acting when the final stable state of the system is reached? Unfortunately, this is not the case. Intermediate states cannot always be ignored, as they may be instrumental in generating an alternative behaviour no matter how long we wait. Consider the EXOR gate feeding an edge-triggered flipflop. Errors caused by ignoring possible behaviours are not restricted to hardware but also occur in other real-world situations. A system which energises if two buttons are pressed at the same time should remain inactive if one button is pressed as the other is released, but an interleaving algebra would predict that the system would energise, which may be a problem if the buttons form an interlock for a safety-critical system.

Algebras are only as useful as long as their basic assumptions hold true. If a system's actions are atomic and can never overlap in time, the interleaving model holds good; but if a system can engage in overlapping, and hence non-atomic, actions, an interleaving model will ignore possible behaviours. Interleaving algebras, by imposing a strict sequentiality on the actions of concurrent systems, distort reality. But while interleaving algebras have problems with true concurrency, it is only a minor imperfection, and for designing the vast majority of concurrent systems an interleaving approach is perfectly sound. Only for the likes of real-time systems do we need an algebra that also models time. For this, we could seek to extend an interleaving algebra by, for example, time-stamping actions, but if we attempt to retrofit time to an existing asynchronous algebra, the same algebra has to accommodate two views of the world, with discrete actions and continuous time, and things would be simpler if we considered discrete time and discrete actions.

We can introduce discrete time into an algebra using the concept of synchronous systems from the world of electronics. Here, systems are not continually observed but rather viewed at the dictates of a global clock, at fixed and periodic times, tied to system activities, and hence our observations implicitly incorporate time as a parameter.

When modelling systems which are themselves synchronous, it is usual to synchronise observations with the actions in the system under observation. For example, we observe the behaviour of a clock that ticks every second as

$$\text{CLOCK} \stackrel{\text{def}}{=} \texttt{tick:CLOCK}$$

where the : denotes the passage of one time increment, in this case a second, giving a truer representation of the clock than that of the asynchronous algebra form of $\text{CLOCK} \stackrel{\text{def}}{=} \texttt{tick} \rightarrow \text{CLOCK}$, which doesn't define the time between its ticks (it can be anything from zero to infinity – not the best basis for designing a clock).

This viewing of systems at specific times has the following consequence. As all actions active at observation time must be recorded, if a system is engaging in multiple actions they all must be recorded. In other words, a synchronous algebra models overlapping, and hence the non-atomic, actions of truly concurrent systems. In other words, adding discrete time adds true concurrency.

The adoption of synchronous algebras as a possible modelling system for real-time systems, since they implicitly incorporate time-based and non-atomic actions, has promise, particularly if, by relaxing the time constraint, they could model concurrent and sequential systems. The rest of this book, after a more formal introduction to the problems of designing concurrent and real-time systems, introduces SCCS, the Synchronous Calculus of Communicating Systems, an algebra first proposed by Professor Milner of Edinburgh University in [Mil82a, Mil83] as a self-contained, complete and consistent mathematical theory of real-time systems.

2. Concurrency and Communication

Overview

Concurrency is the instinctive model we use to describe the behaviour of most real-world systems. A concurrent system is something composed of simultaneously active subsystems, all cooperating to achieve some global aim which we can define as 'a system composed of cooperating subsystems whose separate internal actions can overlap in time'.

Concurrent systems include things like human beings – composed of subsystems including heart, liver, lungs, brain, etc. A human wouldn't perform particularly well if the heart worked for a bit, then the lungs took over, followed by the brain, and so on. And it's no use these systems just co-existing, pursuing their own life cycles; for the good of the complete entity, they must cooperate. But things don't stop there. Even the concurrently operating heart, liver, etc., are composed of smaller cooperating systems which in turn are composed of smaller systems, and so on.

The strength of a concurrent system, that many things can be happening at once, is also, from a designers point of view, its weakness. Sequential systems on their own do not get into too much trouble, but as soon as they congregate they begin to get in each others way.

A customer at a restaurant can be seen as a single sequential system; he orders his meal, and eats his way through first, second and third courses, coffee and brandy, before paying the bill. But the customer doesn't exist in isolation. For him to be served we need a waiter, who acts as a conduit between customer and kitchen, taking and passing on the customers orders, to return some time later with the dishes created by the experts in the kitchen. While customer, waiter and kitchen staff operate as concurrent agents to get the customer his meal, they have to cooperate. Although they have their separate activities, they all reach states from which they cannot proceed until other agents reach certain other states. The waiter can only dispatch the customer's order after the customer has decided what he wants; the chef can only proceed when she knows what's been ordered; and so on. For the whole system to work, these agents must communicate with other agents, and to communicate they must be *ready* to do so – they must *synchronise* their activities. When not engaged in these external actions of communication, the agents pursue private goals by engaging in internal actions which, for the health of the overall system, are not the concern of other agents: the chef fries a better egg without the interference of customer or waiter. Such a concurrent system works as each participating agent assumes the other agents perform the tasks allotted to them; each agent is capable of acting as a server to the others.

No restaurant would be profitable catering for one customer – it needs as many concurrently active patrons as it can get. Similarly, in the kitchen the cooks don't all concentrate on one dish; they, too, operate concurrently, working simultaneously on many dishes. But the very act of operating concurrently introduces problems not present if the same agents were to operate sequentially; customers who can successfully negotiate a restaurant on their own can trip over each each when operating concurrently.

One cause of such fallings out is resource sharing: two customers cannot eat at the same time with the same fork, two waiters cannot use the same pencil at the same time, and so on. All such unshareable resources can only be used by one agent at a time; such resources must be used with *mutual exclusion*. The very act of attempting to use such unshareable resources can lead to problems: if each customer needs two forks to eat spaghetti and, of the two forks available, one customer has one, which he refuses to give up, and the other has the other, which she refuses to give up, then both will sit, fork in hand, and starve. The two customers are *deadlocked*. If, on the other hand, both insist on the other having the forks; they will be so busy giving forks to each other that neither will actually get to the eating stage. The customers are *livelocked*.

While in both cases the system fails, the causes are different: with deadlock, neither customer gets to eat as both are inactive, waiting for something that will never happen; with livelock, both customers are active but these activities do not advance them to the eating stage. The only way we can be sure that resource sharing does not violate mutual exclusion, lead to deadlock or livelock, is formally to prove that in each design such conditions never arise.

Competition for resources also leads to other considerations. Systems will only behave *fairly* to their clients if each client gets a fair share of common resources. If the restaurant becomes successful it may instigate a priority scheme for tables, running from food critics at the top, through the owner's friends and those customers who have booked, down to those who just turn up. If the higher-priority customers come regularly enough, so there's always at least one waiting, those in the last category will always be passed over and never served – for this group the system isn't fair. If enough food critics arrive, or even if once they've eaten they are ready to eat again, other classes of customer will be continually passed over and never get a table.

We can set other criteria to measure the success of a design by specifying that certain properties must hold; in a restaurant, these criteria could be that customers always get what they've ordered, no dish is served badly cooked, no one is overcharged, and so on. As we can express such properties in terms of things that must always be true, these invariants can act as a specification against which to check the correctness of a design. If a design meets such a specification it's said to be *safe*. But being safe doesn't mean being correct; a deadlocked system is safe, as, by doing nothing, it does nothing wrong. Before accepting a design we have not only to show that it is safe but that it is fair, and free from deadlock and livelock. For concurrent systems to perform correctly, not only must each subsystem operate correctly, they must interact correctly, too. We need solutions to the problems introduced by concurrency, but first we need to define these same problems more formally. This we do in the next section.

2.1 Concurrency – Defining the Problems

Our basic design strategy remains to consider a system, dedicated to some global task, as a set of subsystems which perform identifiable sub-tasks. These sub-task processes operate concurrently, and cooperate to forward the global task. This simplification is repeated until all sub-tasks are described by sequential processes. This approach makes things easier. Thus, all concurrent systems design decomposes to sequential system design, including labelled transition systems, supplemented with bits peculiar to the problems of concurrency. As the last part is the tricky bit. We need to spend some time defining the problems that concurrency introduces into systems design before we can go on to use these definitions to propose some general solutions.

To support such a strategy we need to be able to divide, or partition, a system into separate processes. This can be done formally by cluster analysis of the labelled transition systems to minimise the cluster relations between sub-processes, looking for synonyms and so on, or it can be done informally by identifying process interfaces and the mechanisms by which they cooperate. Whichever way we partition the system, it has to be done with care; if we partition too grossly, the resultant processes will be difficult to understand, design and implement; if we partition too finely, interprocess communication overheads will make the system operationally inefficient. Desirable properties of systems after partitioning include the following:

- each constituent process should be logically simple and closely related to the function it performs;
- each processes contributes to the logical simplicity of the overall system;
- run-time interprocess communication is minimised;
- possible system concurrency is maximised.

These requirements suggest that the processes created by partitioning have to cooperate to work properly, for example to negotiate the use of shared resources, while being as independent as possible to simplify the design. Obviously we cannot fully satisfy both criteria, but how close we get will be a measure of the success of the partitioning. First, some definitions of terms.

Process Dependence
Independent
Completely independent processes do not cooperate. As no inter-process communication is supported, the design and implementation will be relatively simple. However, as non-interacting process do not contribute to an overall task, by definition they cannot be part of a concurrent system.

Dependent
By definition, processes cooperate to progress a global task. They interact to pass information, so they can safely compete for resources.

Two cats eating their dinner from separate bowls and ignoring each other represent few problems. It's not until the component parts begin to interact – if one cat covets his neighbour's bowl – that the fur begins to fly. Many of the problems in concurrent systems come from interactions necessitated by the management of resources like cat bowls.

Resource Use
The behaviour of resources can be categorised by what they are…
- Static resources have one state which doesn't change.
- Dynamic resources have several states which they change between.
For example, a data constant is a static resource and a data variable is a dynamic resource.

…and who can use them…

- Dedicated resources are private to and used by one process.
- Shared resources can be used by more than one process.

Systems whose processes using different categories of resource have different properties:
- Processes with dedicated resources which are either static or dynamic. The resource goes with the process that needs it. No competition, no problems.
- Processes with shared but static resources. Copies of the invariable resource go with the processes that require it. Again, no competition and no problems.
- Processes with shared but dynamic resources. The state of a shared and dynamic resource depends upon the interleaving of actions from processes competing to use the resource. The interleaving of actions, and hence states, depends upon which process is successful, and when. To check a design, we must find out if our system behaves correctly for all possible interleaving of all resource-related actions.

So in actual fact only certain combinations of resources and processes in concurrent systems give rise to problems which are not already covered by sequential systems design. We have a general model of concurrent system composed of cooperating sequential subsystems, and we can design the sequential bits, here called processes, using labelled transition systems. No horrors there. The problems only really surface when we consider the interactions between the component parts of concurrent systems. These we place in four categories: synchronisation, mutual exclusion, deadlock, and correctness:
- synchronisation: necessary for processes to cooperate;
- mutual exclusion: to be enforced when unshareable resources are used;
- deadlock: a system with deadlock irretrievably stops;
- correctness: a system behaves as required at all times.

We can divide correctness into more useful subcategories:
- liveness: a system component with liveness advances towards its goal;
- fairness: a systems resources are shared fairly amongst its subsystems;
- safeness: a system is safe if certain of its properties are always true;
- satisfaction: a system is shown always to meet defined requirements.

Synchronisation

The state of a concurrent system depends, among other things, upon the previous availability of resources. For example: upon how many times it has been blocked and waiting for resources; how long it waited for them; how long it held them; and so on. The speed of a process relative to others is thus unpredictable: processes run in their own time frames with their own clocks; but to cooperate, these same processes must pass information to each other for which they first must be put into step, be synchronised.

example

One process produces items and a second oversees their display on a terminal. For the system to work, the processes must synchronise at some point. The second cannot proceed, must wait, until the first has produced something to display.

▨

Synchronisation isn't a problem with sequential systems. As there's never more than one process active at a time, and one process can leave information for another in a known place to be picked up when that process becomes active. By definition, synchronisation is a problem specific to concurrent systems.

As a general rule, no process in a concurrent system can dictate the states of others – all processes run as peers – nor can they know the state of another without the others cooperation. For a concurrent system successfully to reach its goal, its constituent processes must cooperate, and, to cooperate, processes must first synchronise.

Some types of cooperation – for example, managing the safe access of unshareable resources – are more fraught than others.

Mutual Exclusion

Resources can be classified as either *shareable*, usable by several process simultaneously, or *unshareable*, usable by only one process at a time. How shareable resources are may depend upon their physical attributes: for example, printers are unshareable, as interleaving words or characters from several sources isn't recommended.

example

The classical 'last seat' problem. An agent for an international airline uses a centralised database to hold the times, destinations and number of seats remaining on all the airline's flights. When a prospective passenger requests a flight, the agent checks the database, consults the client for confirmation, and reserves the seat. The booking is error-free.

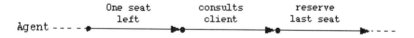

But if two clients walk off the street into different agencies to book a seat on the same flight, and only one unreserved seat remains, what then? With agents performing the same procedures,

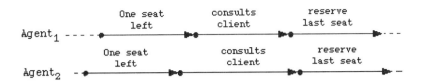

As both agents book after consulting their clients, both clients go away unaware of the false booking and the trouble in store.

We can prevent shared resources being left in an unsafe state by restricting access to one client at a time – by effectively treating such resources as unshareable. Such unshareable resources are said to be accessed under mutual exclusion.

Our model of concurrent systems and any subsequent implementation must support the concept of mutual exclusion and guarantee sole use of an unshareable resource when required.

Deadlock

When several processes compete for an unshareable resource, a state can arise in which no process can proceed, as the resource it needs is held by another. Processes in this state are said to be deadlocked.

There is no problem about sequential systems using unshareable resources, since a process acquires, uses, then releases resources as it needs them.

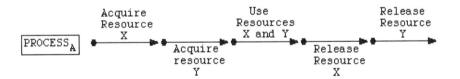

Only with concurrency does the problem arise. Consider two concurrent processes needing the same two resources, but in a different order. One possible action interleaving puts the processes in the states highlighted with square halos below.

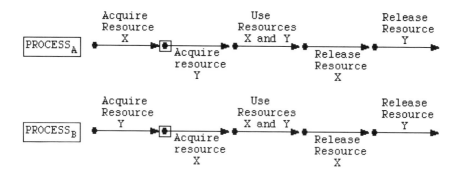

Each process now tries to acquire the other resource. In both cases this resource isn't free, neither can continue, and we have deadlock, independent of whether we consider simultaneous or interleaved actions. For concurrent systems to be shown to be deadlock-free they must be shown such for all possible action interleavings.

Even if the number of unshareable resources of one type is increased to some large amount, the problem persists. Infinite resources are an impossibility and, for any number smaller than infinity, there will always come a time when there is only one resource left at which point we can get a replication of the above scenario.[†]

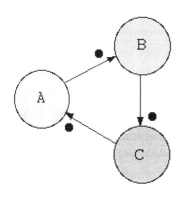

Deadlock doesn't just occur with two processes, it can happen with any number. Consider three sequential systems A, B and C which act as nodes in a network. Each node operates sequentially and can either receive or transmit a packet. Using a notation adapted for Petri Nets where a token '●' is used to indicate the next action of each node, we can get the state where all the sequential components of the concurrent system are waiting to receive and they need the unavailable transmitter resource of their upstream companion to continue. The individual processes in the system work perfectly correctly apart, but when composed as a system they can deadlock.

Deadlock is a possibility in any system which can form such closed dependency loops.

Correctness

The problem areas we have identified so far are facets of the larger concern of *correctness*, for which we need to show that a system does what we want, and only

---

† This supports the old computer science maxim that 'one only needs to check what happens with 0, 1 or an infinite number of things'.

what we want, at all times and has no predictable suicidal tendencies. How correct a system is can be determined by looking at two subsidiary properties: *liveness* – whether a system progresses in its allotted task; and *safeness* – whether the system always stays within certain acceptable boundaries.

Liveness

A component process of a system is live if desired properties are eventually attained, where *now* is included in *eventually*. For example, if a component requests a resource from its environment and eventually gets it, the component is live with respect to that resource. If a system is not live it is said to be livelocked. By this definition, a process can be livelocked if it deadlocks before the desired property is made true. However, a deadlock-free system is not necessarily live. A system that gets into an idle loop before it can make a desired property true is livelocked rather than deadlocked.

The difference between a deadlocked system and a livelocked one is that the former does nothing, while the latter does something but what it does does not progress its overall task. In terms of agents, a livelocked system can engage only in internal actions while a deadlocked system engages in no actions at all. As agents use external actions to interact with their environment, this gives rise to an alternative, and probably more useful, definition of a livelocked system as one which does not interact with its environment; and to the corollary that a live system is one which will eventually interact with its environment.

A corollary of liveness is *fairness*. A process may not be live because it is waiting for resources allocated (unfairly?) to others. A primary cause of lack of fairness is the overtaking of resource requests. For example, in a priority-based system, the highest-priority process requesting a resource will be granted that resource in preference to others of lower priority which may have been waiting longer – they are overtaken, and if higher-priority processes keep arriving, the lower-priority processes will never get the resource – and starved processes are no longer live.

examples

a) Process A has a higher priority than process B. When both processes are waiting to use the processor, a priority-based scheduler always selects A in preference to B irrespective of which has been waiting the longer. If upon completion process A immediately requests to run again, A will repeatedly overtake B which, never getting the processor, will never execute and thus will not be live.

b) A receiver accepts messages from three separate transmitters over three communication channels. The channels are accessed in sequence, and only when no messages are outstanding does the receiver move on to service the next channel. If one channel sends as quickly as the receiver can consume, it will 'hog' the receiver and its messages will overtake those messages sent by other transmitters. The originators of the overtaken messages will be livelocked, waiting for responses that never arrive.

■

Any system in which overtaking can occur is prone to lack of liveness. To ensure fairness, we prevent overtaking by enforcing some ordering on requests. This can be achieved, for example, by:
- linear waiting – if a process makes a request, the request will be granted before any other process is granted the same request more than once; or by
- first-in-first-out (FIFO) waiting – if a process makes a request, the request will be granted before that of any other process making the same request later.

Safeness
A system is safe if it always has certain desired properties. For example: in any design we would want it to be always true, invariant, that all unshareable resources are never used by more than one process at a time – that they are accessed under mutual exclusion; or, in a particular design, that the value of out in process out = square(in) is never negative; or again, that the number of items stored in a buffer of size N is never less than zero or never greater than N; and so on.

A collection of these desired properties can fully define the behaviour required of a system, and if we define these properties as a set of invariants, each stating some property that must remain true throughout the life of the system, we will have produced a specification against which to check proposed designs. A safe design is one which satisfies its specification.

Satisfaction
A specification defines a set of safety properties for a particular system by specifying what parameters a proposed design must stay within at all times, i.e. in all system states. In more formal terms, specification Spec is an invariant, or collection of invariants, to be satisfied by system Sys, written as Sys **sat** Spec. The implication is that every possible observation of system Sys is described by specification Spec. As system states and action sequences can be used interchangeably, we can express this requirement as a theory – namely that system SYS1 must satisfy its specification SPEC1 for every state x from the set of all its possible states D

$$\forall x \in D . (SYS1(x) \text{ sat } SPEC1)$$
if (SYS1(x) **sat** SPEC1) for all x∈D then SYS1 **sat** SPEC1.
Which means that if SYS1(x) fails to satisfy its SPEC1 in any one state
SYS1 **sat** SPEC1 is false.

In practical terms, the greater the number of distinct states, the larger the set D, the greater the complexity and the more laboured proving the system correct will be. If the set D is sufficiently small, we can test all its possible states, by *exhaustive testing*, to prove correctness. Conversely we only need to find one example where the specification fails, a *counter example*, to prove that the complete system fails to meet its specification.

More formally, if there exists a state x from the possible set of states D in which the system fails to satisfy its specification, then

$$\exists x \in D \,.\, (\text{SYS1}(x) \ \textbf{does not sat} \ \text{SPEC1})$$

This means we could test D-1 states and find that the system meets its specification, only to find that in the last state it fails. Hence the need for 'exhaustive testing', as it may be necessary to test all states of a system to prove a specification holds. But even if we test a design in all its states, when can we say a design is correct? As a system is safe if it meets its specification, surely that is sufficient? But a deadlocked system, by doing nothing at all, is by definition safe, as it never does anything wrong. A deadlocked system will meet all its specifications, which isn't quite what we had in mind. The fact that a system satisfies its specification is insufficient to accept it as a valid solution – after all, a specification simply states the rules by which a system is deemed to behave correctly.

When we compose a system, the act of putting together subsystems can cause them to 'trip over each other', resulting in incorrect performance of the complete system due to deadlock, lack of liveness, synchronisation, problems with mutual exclusion, and so on. It is thus essential that we prove not only that processes meet their specifications but also that they are free from these interaction problems.

Conclusions

We must ensure in a design, and also in any subsequent implementation, that: resources are allocated with *fairness*; individual processes *synchronise* so they can cooperate in progressing the overall task; unshareable resources are accessed with *mutual exclusion*; processes never get into states of *livelock,* where parts of the system cannot interact; or of *deadlock,* where the complete system cannot proceed. In fact we must solve all the problems introduced by concurrently operating sequential systems, and then prove that the design meets a given specification. But how do we achieve this?

One obvious way of tackling concurrent systems design is to modify existing sequential programming languages to address the concurrency-specific problems we have identified here, using the resulting languages both to design and to implement our concurrent systems. We commence this exploration by seeing if we can ensure mutual exclusion in such programming domains.

2.2 Programming Domain Solutions

2.2.1 Mutual Exclusion

Mutual exclusion needs enforcing when processes access unshareable resources. A resource under mutual exclusion can only be accessed by one process at a time. As designers, we don't need to intervene to protect all unshareable resources; some are implicitly safe – for example, by definition resources accessed by atomic transactions always operate under mutual exclusion and never get into unsafe states. The resources we have problems with are those with transactions that require the performance of several actions in order to work – it is only when accessing these latter resources that client actions can interleave and get the resource into an unsafe state. We can prevent such unsafe states by fooling a client action into thinking it is accessing an atomic resource. One way to do this is by serialising all transactions on that resource, locking out all other process actions during a transaction, to make that transaction appear atomic.

Intelligent resources serving perhaps several clients, data bases for example, are independent entities whose internal structure and actions are under their own control, and clients of such resources rely upon the resources themselves to ensure mutual exclusion. For less intelligent resources, for example data structures, it is up to the clients to guarantee mutual exclusion amongst themselves, which they can only do by controlling access to the resource. With resource access under program control, we can ensure mutual exclusion by ensuring that only one client executes this access code – known as *critical sections*.

For mutual exclusion purposes, client processes have two parts: critical sections, when processes access a resource; and non-critical sections, when they do not. We can now define in process terms what objectives systems with mutual exclusion must satisfy:

- When one process is in its critical section, all other processes which can possibly access the data/resource must be excluded from their critical sections which access the same resource.
- All processes must be allowed to proceed while not in a critical section, in order to maximise possible concurrency.
- When one process leaves a critical section associated with a resource, another must be allowed to enter its critical section for the same resource.
- One, and only one, process can be in a critical section and accessing a particular resource at any one time.
- The solution should not, of itself, introduce other problems into the system.

Solving mutual exclusion

Enforcing mutual exclusion is one of the key problems in concurrent systems. Many solutions have been tendered, some of them hardware solutions, some software, and at both low and high levels of abstraction.

The constraints that any solution must obey include :

- no assumptions is made about the relative speeds of the processes – they are considered asynchronous;
- processes in their critical sections cannot of themselves prevent other processes entering theirs – as processes run as peers, there is no dictator process;
- processes must not be indefinitely held from entering critical sections – access must be fair;
- processes must remain live, and deadlock-free, with respect to accessing resources;
- there must exist a level of execution for which process actions can be considered atomic, so that, once started, it completes without interruption;
- mutual exclusion must be preserved in all interleavings of constituent processes actions.

In the most trivial case, mutual exclusion is guaranteed if resource access is naturally atomic or the critical sections are guaranteed indivisible. But guaranteeing mutual exclusion does not eliminate all problems related to resource access. We saw earlier that, when reading and writing the variable x under mutual exclusion, only the last writer was guaranteed success when reading.

Further, even if a design is proved error-free, it is still the designer's responsibility to ensure that subsequent implementations are also correct.

To highlight some of the problems implicit in using critical sections to provide mutual exclusion, we will examine the simple case of two processes procone and proctwo executing concurrently, and both needing access to an unshared resource. Using this example we can demonstrate the difficulty of proving any solutions meets our objective of ensuring mutual exclusion.

2.2.2 Critical Sections

By ensuring the mutual exclusion of critical sections accessing a resource, we provide mutual exclusion to the resource itself. If the critical sections are naturally atomic, then, by definition, they execute under mutual exclusion – if not, we must make them appear atomic by bracketing each with guards.

An *entry guard* monitors entry into a critical section and an *exit guard* monitors departure from it. The guards use information held in a *resource access control* data structure which echoes relevant parts of the resources state, to ensure mutual exclusion. In its simplest form the resource access control maintains the count of available resources in a class. A client wanting to enter its critical section and access a particular resource calls its entry guard, which checks with resource access control that no other client is in a critical section associated with this resource; if the resource is free, the input guard tells the client it can enter its critical section, and updates the resource access control; if the resource is in use – another client is in its critical section – the client process waits until the resource is freed. Clients exiting a critical section use their exit guards to update resource access control to reflect the new state, thus allowing a previously blocked client entry.

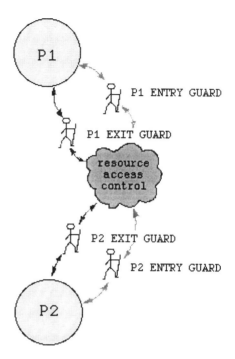

In the following example, we've added to our serial programming language the parbegin and parend statements, which ensure that the instructions they bracket execute concurrently. The two procedures processone and processtwo thus become concurrent processes which repeatedly attempt to access a resource via their critical sections, using their entry and exit guards to oversee resource access.

```
program mutual;
  declare resource access control;

        procedure processone;
          begin
            while TRUE do
                non-critical section;
                enter ME;   (* P1 entry guard *)
                critical section;
                exit ME;    (* P1 exit guard *)
                non-critical section;
            endwhile
          end (*processone*)
```

```
          procedure processtwo;
            begin
              while TRUE do
                non-critical section;
                enter ME;   (* P2 entry guard *)
                critical section;
                exit ME;    (* P2 exit guard *)
                non-critical section;
              endwhile
            end (*processtwo*)

    begin
          initialise resource access control;
          parbegin
                processone;
                processtwo;
          parend
    end (*mutual*)
```

But how does a client actually enter and exit mutual exclusion?

Clients wishing to use an unshareable resource request entry into their critical sections from their associated entry guards. The guard checks with resource access control that no other client is in a critical section associated with this resource; if the resource is free the input guard tells the client it can enter its critical section and updates resource access control; if the resource is in use, the guard, by not returning until the resource is free, forces the client to wait. Clients exiting a critical section use the section's exit guard to update resource access control, reflecting the new state and allowing a blocked client entry. In essence, the guards act in concert to ensure that one, and only one, process is in its critical section at any one time.

But how does the programmer know that mutual exclusion has been achieved?

To prove the system correct, we must prove that it meets its specification. In this case it is safe with mutual exclusion as an invariant; it is never the case that both critical sections are active simultaneously. We must also establish that the system is live and never deadlocks. This correctness must be demonstrated for all possible states of the system.

We currently know of two methods of proof of correctness. If system Sys1 satisfies its specification Spec1 for every state x from its set of possible states D

$$\forall x \in D. (Sys1(x) \textbf{ sat } Spec1)$$

then the system satisfies its specification, Sys **sat** Spec. However, if the the system does not satisfy its specification in even one of its states the theory is false, the system has failed to satisfy its specification, Sys **sat** Spec is false.

It is not unusual to 'test' proposed programming solutions informally by manually checking that the program has all the desirable characteristics and none of the undesirable ones. This is done by 'walking through' the program as if it were executing on a real machine and confirming if the requirements are met after each instruction. To check a program is correct by this *operational proof* method requires us to visit every possible state. It only needs one state where the requirements are not met to prove the complete solution invalid. This operational proof method is beloved of programmers as it is straightforward, can be driven by experience and is not tainted by any mathematics or formal methods.

We'll try using this operational proof method to sieve out incorrect solutions to our mutual exclusion problem. The following examples and their treatment are sourced from [Ben82], and adaptations of them can be found in [Dei84] and [Ben90]. They nicely illuminate the problems of proving things correct by operational proofs and it seems perverse to tamper with them too much.

We base our analysis on the assumption that individual statements in our programming languages are implemented atomically and so can be represented by transitions in related labelled transition diagrams.

Solution (1)

For the simple case where the processes share an SISD processor we extend our programming language by adding two utilities, **lock()** and **unlock()**, to act as critical section guards. When executing in a multiprocess environment a user process executes a lock() procedure to raise the calling processes' priority above the maximum normally allowed to user processes, disables all interrupts, and gets sole use of the processor. An unlock() returns the process to its previous priority. Instructions bracketed by the utilities are ensured sole use of the processor and, as they executed atomically, this should give the desired mutual exclusion.

In this example, no resource access control data is necessary, just the entry and exit guards.

```
program mutual V1;

procedure processone;
    begin
        while TRUE do
            first part of processone;
            lock();         (* P1 entry guard *)
            critical section one;
            unlock();       (* P1 exit guard *)
            rest of processone;
```

```
            endwhile
    end (*processone*)


procedure processtwo;
    begin
        while TRUE do
            first part of processtwo;
            lock();          (* P2 entry guard *)
            critical section two;
            unlock();        (* P2 exit guard *)
            rest of processtwo;
        endwhile
    end (*processtwo*)


begin
    parbegin
        processone;
        processtwo;
    parend
end (*mutual V1*)
```

We can represent the processes in labelled transition form as:

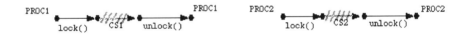

There seems to be no obvious failure of mutual exclusion if the clients run one after the other, and we will move smartly on to look at a more probable failure mode – clients operating in parallel.

If lock() is an atomic action it either doesn't start, or, once it has started it executes to completion. On a shared processor, one, and only one, process can execute a lock() – even if more than one attempt to do so simultaneously. A process, by executing a lock(), grabs the processor, thus locking out all other processes. The processor is freed for use by other processes only when the successful process executes an unlock().

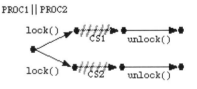

The correct use of lock() and unlock() change the concurrent activity of the processes to a non-deterministic choice between sequential processes. The first process to execute a lock() gets sole use of the processor; other processes, denied the processor, are forced to wait. Critical sections are thus indivisible, atomic, and mutual exclusion is ensured – provided of course that `lock()` and `unlock()` are implemented atomically.

We seem to have an algorithm that works: game over. But is it safe in all circumstances?

Each `lock()` will delay action on interrupts that inform the system of environment changes, which can delay responses in interactive systems, ignore a disaster in a safety critical system until it's too late, and so on. For the algorithm to work we have to give programmers access to the `lock()` and `unlock()` utilities and, by so doing, we give programmers total power over the processor. Such power can be abused; programmers can selfishly `lock()` a program into the processor, denying access to others; they can write critical sections and forget to add the `unlock()`, and so on. These reasons explain why, even though `lock()` and `unlock()` are normally found in operating systems, in most, as in Unix, they are sensibly kept well hidden from programmers. Our solution has also assumed that the processes execute on a single SISD processor, but what happens if, after a cash windfall, we buy a multiprocessor to speed up the execution of the system? If processes `procone` and `proctwo` run on separate processors, one of the assumptions the solution relies upon – that one process can lock out all others – is false; processes can now `lock()` and `unlock()` to their hearts' content without in any way affecting the running of the others. But, more importantly, as we've assumed in the design that `lock()` and `unlock()` are atomic, for the solution to work at all `lock()` and `unlock()` must be guaranteed to be atomic in the implementation – we've simply moved the problem from one area to another.

So the solution is nasty, error prone, lacking in generality and reliant upon the implementation used; but, because its looks simple, and seems to work then, you've guessed it, if programmers had a top ten it would be number one. But as it fails to meet our requirement – that a solution should not introduce more problems – we will continue our search for something less open to abuse.

Solution (2)

In this proposal, critical sections are scheduled turn and turn about. The content of variable `proc` held as resource access control data is used to determine process access, and a process is only allowed into its critical section if its process number is the same as variable `proc`. On completion of a critical section the exit guard sets `proc` to another process's number.

The shared global variable `proc` is arbitrarily initialised to one of the two processes in:

```
program mutual V2;
var proc : integer;   (* resource access control *)

        procedure processone;
          begin
            while TRUE do
                first part of processone;
                while proc = 2 do
                   nothing;                (* P1 entry guard *)
                endwhile
                critical section one;
                proc := 2;                 (* P1 exit guard *)
                rest of processone;
            endwhile
          end (*processone*)


        procedure processtwo;
          begin
            while TRUE do
                first part of processtwo;
                while proc = 1 do
                   nothing;                (* P2 entry guard *)
                endwhile
                critical section two;
                proc := 1;                 (* P2 exit guard *)
                rest of processtwo;
            endwhile
          end (*processtwo*)

  begin
        proc := 1; (* resource access control initialisation *)
        parbegin
          processone;
          processtwo;
        parend
  end (*mutual V2*)
```

Mutual exclusion is probably guaranteed as there's no obvious counter example. The process appears correct and fair as access to the resource is turn and turn about. But is the solution a satisfactory one?

We can define the relevant parts of the two processes as

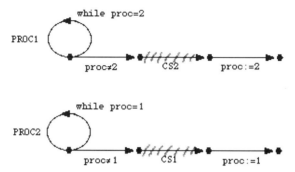

Again, looking at the most probable failure case – when both processes simultaneously request entry to their critical sections, system behaviour is serialised to:

PROC1 || PROC2

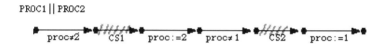

As dictated by the global `proc` variable, PROC1 is the only process initially allowed to enter its critical section, then processes enter their critical regions turn and turn about. Mutual exclusion is preserved. But at what cost?

With this algorithm, one process is nominated to access the resource whether it has requested to or not; other processes needing to enter their critical regions will have to wait until after the nominated process indicates it has used the resource. As a result, all processes are constrained to operate at the speed of the slowest; and, worse, processes can be made to wait for a resource as, even though it is free if it has been promised to another process. The requirement to maximise concurrency has been violated.

The algorithm, by deciding the order in which processes gain access to the resource, has pre-empted the role of the system scheduler and doesn't do it as well. If the first nominated process never actually needs the resource, others which do will never get it, demonstrating a gross lack of liveness and a direct failure to meet our requirements. We reject this solution and try yet again.

Solution (3)
The problem with Solution(2) seems to be the shared variable `proc` enforcing an intrinsically unfair 'hidden scheduler'. Perhaps we can circumvent the problem

by replacing `proc` within the resource access control with variables echoing actual process state, as in:

inprocone = TRUE when `procone` is in its critical region,
            FALSE otherwise
inproctwo = TRUE when `proctwo` is in its critical region,
            FALSE otherwise

Processes can now use this information to 'get to know' the state of the other, and with this information, entry guards can block further requests if any process is in its critical section.

```
program mutual V3;
var inprocone, inproctwo : integer;     (* resource *)
                                        (* access control *)


        procedure processone;
           begin
              while TRUE do
                 first part of processone;
                 while inproctwo do
                    nothing;              (* P1 entry guard *)
                 endwhile
                 inprocone := TRUE;
                 critical section one;
                 inprocone := FALSE; (* P1 exit guard *)
                 rest of processone;
              endwhile
           end (*processone*)


        procedure processtwo;
           begin
              while TRUE do
                 first part of processtwo;
                 while inprocone do
                    nothing;              (* P2 entry guard *)
                 endwhile
                 inproctwo := TRUE;
                 critical section two;
                 inproctwo := FALSE; (* P2 exit guard *)
                 rest of processtwo;
              endwhile
           end (*processtwo*)
```

```
begin
        inprocone := FALSE;     (* resource access *)
        inproctwo := FALSE;     (* control initialisation *)
    parbegin
        processone;
        processtwo;
    parend
end  (*mutual V3*)
```

The relevant behaviours of the two processes are:

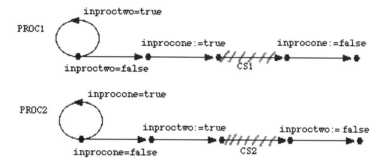

Now consider the following scenario. During initialisation `inprocone` and `inproctwo` are both set to `false`

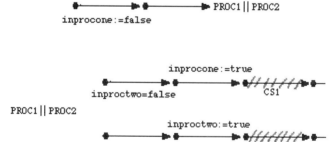

then

As the processes operate concurrently, both `procone` and `proctwo` could simultaneously attempt to enter their critical regions, their entry guards simultaneously test their `inproc` flags, find them FALSE, set their `inproc` flags to TRUE and simultaneously enter their critical regions – just like the customers in the 'last airplane seat' example.

The algorithm does not guarantee mutual exclusion. Another failure, and the search continues.

Solution (4)

The problem with Solution(3) was that, during the time a process was testing the others' inproc flags to see if it was opportune to enter its critical region, and setting its inproc flag to claim the resource, the other process could have been doing the same.

Perhaps we can amend the solution so that each process informs others when it is about to try and enter its critical region by setting a want flag to TRUE, which tells the others to wait. This should allow a process to check if another process also wants the resource, defer to it, and only access the resource after the other has been serviced. Adding such variables to resource access control gives:

```
program mutual V4;
var     p1wants, p2wants : boolean;      (* resource *)
                                         (* access control *)

        procedure processone;
          begin
            while TRUE do
              first part of processone;
              p1wants := TRUE;
              while p2wants do           (* P1 entry guard *)
                nothing;
              endwhile;
              critical section one;
              p1wants := FALSE;          (* P1 exit guard *)
              rest of processone;
            endwhile
          end (*processone*)

        procedure processtwo;
          begin
            while TRUE do
              first part of processtwo;
              p2wants := TRUE
              while p1wants do           (* P2 entry guard *)
                nothing;
              endwhile;
              critical section two;
              p2wants := FALSE;          (* P2 exit guard *)
              rest of processtwo;
            endwhile
          end (*processtwo*)
```

```
begin
        p1wants := FALSE;      (* resource access *)
                               (* control initialisation *)
        p2wants := FALSE;      (* neither process *)
                               (* in its critical section *)
    parbegin
        processone;
        processtwo;
    parend
end  (*mutual V4*)
```

The relevant parts of the processes are:

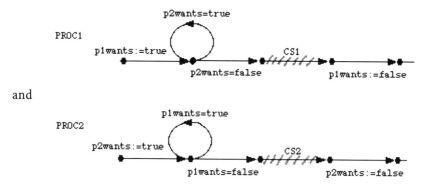

and

As we cannot find an obvious counter-example, perhaps we have restored the desired mutual exclusion? But if each process simultaneously sets its wants flag to TRUE,

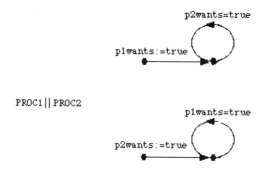

each process loops forever round its inner while ... do statements as p1wants and p2wants always remain TRUE. We have re-established mutual exclusion at the expense of liveness.

The solution has once more failed to meet our requirements. We try yet again.

Solution (5)

The problem with Solution (4) was the possibility of both process getting locked in a while loop waiting for something that would never happen. Adding a method of breaking out of these loops should help resolve the problem.

To do this we will modify the algorithm so that, if both the processes find themselves wanting the resource, they both lie by setting their want flags to FALSE, for a random time interval. The first process returning from its random sojourn reasserts its need for the resource by setting its want flag to TRUE, and will get it. When the losing process returns, it also reasserts its desire by setting its want flag to TRUE, and will eventually be granted access. This serialisation of the contention should resolve the problem of Solution (4).

```
program mutual V5;
var p1wants, p2wants : boolean;    (* resource access control *)


      procedure processone;
        begin
          while TRUE do
            first part of processone;
            p1wants := TRUE;
            while p2wants do
                p1wants := FALSE;              (* P1 entry guard *)
                delay(random);
                p1wants := TRUE;
            endwhile
            critical section one;
            p1wants := FALSE;                  (* P1 exit guard *)
            rest of processone;
          endwhile
        end (*processone*)


      procedure processtwo;
        begin
          while TRUE do
            first part of processtwo;
            p2wants := TRUE;
            while p1wants do
                p2wants := FALSE;              (* P2 entry guard *)
                delay(random);
                p2wants := TRUE;
            endwhile
            critical section two;
            p2wants := FALSE;                  (* P2 exit guard *)
```

```
                    rest of processtwo;
                endwhile
            end (*processtwo*)

    begin
            p1wants := FALSE;        (* resource access *)
                                     (* control initialisation *)
            p2wants := FALSE;        (* neither process in *)
                                     (* its critical section *)
            parbegin
                processone;
                processtwo;
            parend
    end (*mutual V5*)
```

When both processes wish to access the resource, they both temporarily lie, by setting their want flags to FALSE and embark on a random delay. The first one to return from its delay reasserts its desire for the resource and, finding the other apparently not wishing to enter its critical section, enters its own. The choice between simultaneous request is thus made at random, no preference being given to any process. The victorious process reasserts its resource request and enters its critical section before the other process has returned from its random sojourn. It appears that mutual exclusion is guaranteed without the deadlock of the previous solution.

The sequence of action processone must pass through to enter its critical section are:

PROC1

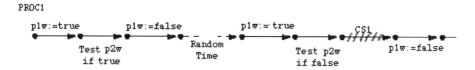

Simplifying the diagram by leaving out operations on the want flags and only reporting the resultant state changes, we get:

When the two processes operate in parallel, both requesting to enter their critical sections simultaneously, both set their want flags to TRUE and, on finding the other's want flag set, in an attempt to resolve the conflict both set their want flags to FALSE and evoke random delays:

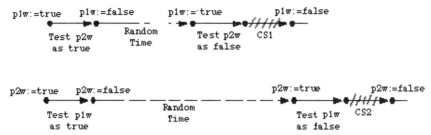

Access to the critical sections has been serialised and mutual exclusion obtained.

But what happens if processes are quick and resources slow? As soon as a successful process uses a resource it may immediately make another request and the process that was victorious last time can be so again, and again – and so on. The very randomisation we've added to resolve conflicts can lead to overtaking, which introduces a possible lack of fairness leading, in turn, to a lack of system liveness.

Even more seriously, as process proceed asynchronously, a case exists whereby they can set their want flags to TRUE; enter the body of their while loops, set their want flags to FALSE then TRUE in the same sequence, and do so for an indeterminate time. For this to happen, the time of their random delays needs only to be sufficiently similar.

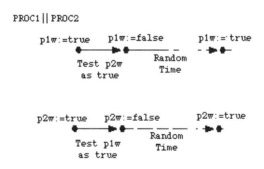

The last states of both processes are the same as their initial ones, and if this can happen once it can happen any number of times, even indefinitely. The solution is livelock-prone.

So, while this algorithm gives mutual exclusion, it also introduces possible livelock and lack of fairness and so fails to meet our requirements. We are almost there, but we can do better.

Solution (6)

Dekker's algorithm resolves the livelock problem when resolving conflicts between simultaneous requests by replacing the random delay of the previous solution with a more deterministic solution based on a `favouredproc` variable. Notice how many more lines of code this 'better' solution takes – the closer we get to an acceptable solution, the more complex they seem to be. But this is the first solution bearing its authors name – a good portent?

```
program DEKKER;
var favouredproc : (first,second);  (* resource access *)
                                     (* control *)
    p1wants, p2wants : boolean;

    procedure processone;
      begin
        while TRUE do
          first part of processone;
          p1wants := TRUE;
          while p2wants do
            if favouredproc = second then
              p1wants := FALSE;
              while
                favouredproc = second do        (* P1 entry *)
                  nothing                        (* guard *)
              endwhile
              p1wants := TRUE;
            endif
          endwhile
          critical section one;
          favouredproc := second;                (* P1 exit *)
          p1wants := FALSE;                       (* guard *)
          rest of processone;
        endwhile
      end (*processone*)

    procedure processtwo;
      begin
        while TRUE do
          first part of processtwo;
          p2wants := TRUE;
          while p1wants do
            if favouredproc = first then
              p2wants := FALSE;
```

```
                    while favouredproc = first do    (* P2 entry *)
                        nothing                       (* guard *)
                    endwhile
                    p2wants := TRUE;
                  endif
                endwhile
                critical section two;
                favouredproc := first;               (* P2 exit *)
                p2wants := FALSE;                     (* guard *)
                rest of processtwo;
              endwhile
          end (*processtwo*)


      begin
          p1wants := FALSE;        (* resource access *)
                                   (* control initialisation *)
          p2wants := FALSE;        (* neither process *)
                                   (* in its critical section *)
          favouredproc := first;   (* P1 to be favoured in *)
                                   (* first contention *)
      parbegin
          processone;
          processtwo;
      parend
      end (*Dekker*)
```

Like the previous algorithms, to check this one we will 'walk through' a possible scenario. Initially, both want flags are set to FALSE and, while the processes have no interest in the resource; they remain at FALSE. Only when a process desires entry to its critical section does it set its want flag to TRUE and, if no other want flag is set to TRUE, enters its critical section. When there's contention, both p1wants and p2wants set, the processes enter arbitration mode.

● When procone, p1wants flag flying, finds that proctwo's p2wants flag is set, and vice versa, both circle round their entry guard's outer **while** loops.

The only process that can exit its loop is the one named in favouredproc, initialised to procone in our case. The non-favoured process tells the world it has lost, by setting it's want flag to FALSE, and waits, circling its entry guard's inner **while** loop. The favoured process, still with want flag flying, is allowed out of its outer **while** loop and given entry to its critical section when its competitor's want flag is set to FALSE.

● In our case, the entry guard of the non-favoured process, proctwo, sets its want flag to FALSE, then waits in its inner **while** loop. The entry guard of the favoured process, procone, waits in its outer **while** loop until proctwo concedes, indicated by setting its want flag to FALSE, which allows procone to enter its critical section.

After the favoured process has finished with the resource, it releases mutual exclusion, its exit guard informing the world by setting its want flag to FALSE, and nominates the other process as favouredproc – all of which allows the waiting, previously non-favoured process, to exit its inner and outer **while** loops, reassert its want flag and enter its critical section – so maintaining fairness of resource allocation.

- Upon exit from its critical section procone's exit guard nominates proctwo as favouredproc, allowing proctwo to complete its inner **while** loop, and reasserts its resource request by setting its p2wants flag to TRUE; Procone then sets its p1wants flag to FALSE, allowing proctwo to complete its outer **while** loop and enter its critical section.

It looks like mutual exclusion has been achieved with fairness, for, even if procone quickly tries to re-enter its critical section, it will be forced to wait in its inner **while** loop as p2wants=TRUE and favouredproc=second (as nominated by procone). Proctwo is dominant until it gains access to its critical section, and so on.

Dekker's algorithm seems to meet our stated requirements. Processes proceed concurrently when not in their critical sections; conflicts are resolved alternately, with fairness, by the input guards acting as FIFO schedulers; and the longest waiting process in a conflict is always nominated as the next favoured process, ensuring it will win the next conflict.

While we have not disproved Dekker's algorithm, neither have we proved it. All we've really done is look at it informally, and, to actually prove it meets our requirements, we have to prove that mutual exclusion is preserved in all possible states – a rather daunting task which we will defer until we have some better tools. But even given that Dekker's solution is correct, it only applies to two processes, and what we really want is something that will arbitrate for mutual exclusion over an arbitrary number of processes. An obvious way forward is to to incorporate a full n-process FIFO scheduler in the guards. Knuth [Knu66] produced such an algorithm, which also removed a possible liveness flaw in a previous algorithm by Dijkstra [Dijk65]. However, nothing comes for free, and, as this solution adds further complication, it only magnifies the difficulty of proving correctness.

The FIFO queue idea suggests an ordered queue of waiting clients, which is ordered by the clients themselves, by arrival time. Such FIFO queues are fine for centralised systems where queues can be kept consistent, but in the more abstract domain of distributed systems a better model would not rely upon the clients to control the queue but on the server which provides the resource. Such systems are organised like the service in a bakery, where customers coming into the shop take consecutively numbered tickets that denote their queue position and determine the order, first come first served, in which they will receive their bread. Such is the basis for Lamport's [Lam74] solution to the n-process distributed mutual exclusion algorithm, better known as *Lamport's Bakery Algorithm.*

Two More Algorithms

Now's your chance. Here are two algorithms proposed as simplifications of Dekker's algorithm, one by Hyman [Hym66] and one by Peterson [Pet85]. Using operational proof methods, can you prove whether they preserve mutual exclusion?

```
program HYMAN;
var    favouredproc : (first,second);
       p1wants, p2wants : boolean;


       procedure processone;
          begin
             while TRUE do
                 first part of processone;
                 p1wants := TRUE;
                 while favouredproc = second do
                    while p2wants do
                       nothing
                    endwhile
                    favouredproc := first;
                 endwhile
                 critical section one;
                 p1wants := FALSE;
                 rest of processone;
             endwhile
          end (*processone*)


       procedure processtwo;
          begin
             while TRUE do
                 first part of processtwo;
                 p2wants := TRUE
                 while favouredproc = first do
                    while p1wants do
                       nothing
                    endwhile
                    favouredproc = second;
                 endwhile
```

```
        critical section two;
        p2wants := FALSE;
        rest of processtwo;
      endwhile
    end (*processtwo*)


begin
      p1wants := FALSE;
      p2wants := FALSE;
      favouredproc := second;
      parbegin
        processone;
        processtwo;
      parend
end (*Hyman*)
```

And

```
program PETERSON;
var     favouredproc : (first,second);
        p1wants, p2wants : boolean;

      procedure processone;
        begin
          while TRUE do
            first part of processone;
            p1wants := TRUE;
            favouredproc := second;
            while (p1wants = TRUE and favouredproc = second) do
                nothing
            endwhile
            critical section one;
            p1wants := FALSE;
            rest of processone;
          endwhile
        end (*processone*)

      procedure processtwo;
        begin
          while TRUE do
            first part of processtwo;
            p2wants := TRUE
            favouredproc := first
            while (p2wants = TRUE and favouredproc = first) do
              nothing
```

```
            endwhile
            critical section two;
            p2wants := FALSE;
            rest of processtwo;
         endwhile
      end (*processtwo*)

begin
         p1wants := FALSE;
         p2wants := FALSE;
      parbegin
         processone;
         processtwo;
      parend
end (*Peterson*)
```

Not that easy, is it?

We've explored critical sections as a method of thinking about, designing and implementing mutual exclusion, and, while it's been fairly easy to propose algorithms that seem to work, it is more difficult to explain to others how they work – and even more difficult to prove they do work. Only for the Dekker algorithm have we been unable to find a counter-example, and failure to find a counter-example doesn't mean the algorithm is successful.

Overview

Our first foray into solving what seemed the simplest of the concurrency problems has been singularly unsuccessful. We haven't proved that any of our proposed solutions solve the mutual exclusion problem; our leading candidate, Dekker's algorithm, only applies to two competing processes, and is not the general solution we seek.

If all processes could access all resources with one atomic action, mutual exclusion over those resources would be ensured and the problem of unshareable resources access would conveniently disappear. Unfortunately, the resources we normally deal with are unlikely to be naturally atomic, and we introduce things like critical sections in an attempt to make them appear so. But in subscribing to critical sections as possible solutions, haven't we been 'chasing our tails'?

For critical sections to work, they have to operate atomically, be mutually exclusive. To make them so we use guards. And, for guards to work, they must access their shared data atomically, under mutual exclusion. Are we addressing the same problem, only in different guises? The advantage of all this is that we've collected the mutual exclusion code into one place, the guards, and it should be easier to perform an operational proof on the resultant code. By collecting code distributed through out the system into one place, like `lock()`/`unlock()`, means we can ensure these 'hot spots' are designed correctly, so at least one part of the design error free. But how do we prove things error free? Can we use labelled transition systems?

For labelled transition systems to work, the design language must have some semantic underpinning, so that each statement means one thing unambiguously. Even if we did our design using a computer language which has such a semantics, the compiler, run-time system and processor used in an implementation would need to be validated to ensure that the behaviours captured in the design were correctly translated to the implementation. In the real world, no such integrated set of languages, compilers, run-time systems and hardware platforms exists, and to use such a programming language both to design and to implement a system is implicitly flawed, for, with no associated semantics, one cannot be sure what that the behaviour of any design will be – not a strong basis upon which to state a design satisfies its specification.

But the exercise has been useful, since it has shown the dangers in using pro-gramming languages as design notations and drawing conclusions from informal 'proof' methods which, despite their disarming simplicity, are neither easy nor secure, but only giving a false impression that we've proved things correct. To really decide issues of correctness we need a more formal design method.

In all, this exercise has resulted in rather a trouncing. But, ever the optimists, per-haps we'll have better success when we look at another concurrency problem: that of synchronisation.

2.2.3 Synchronisation

We visualise a concurrent systems as separate sequential processes which, by passing information, cooperate to progress a global task.

In its simplest form, two processes communicate by one process, A, sending a message to another process, B.

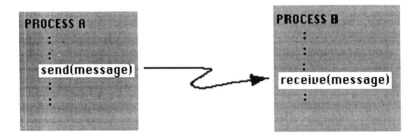

In order to pass information, both sides must in the state of readiness to communicate, *be synchronised,* but to work efficiently the component parts of a concurrent system must work in their own time frames, operate *asynchronously,* individual processes progressing as and when resources allow, with no central authority dictating their progress.

We need a method by which a SENDER and a RECEIVER, when not communicating, progress asynchronously, synchronise to communicate, and return to an asynchronous mode after each communication.

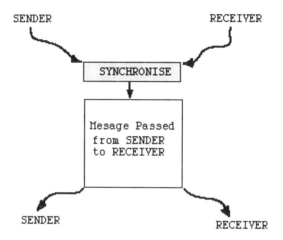

In its simplest form, two processes synchronise if one, process A, cannot proceed beyond a certain point X until another, process B, has reached a certain point Y, and vice versa.

The first process to reach its synchronisation point waits for the other to reach *its* synchronisation point, they synchronise and pass information, before they continue on their asynchronous ways.

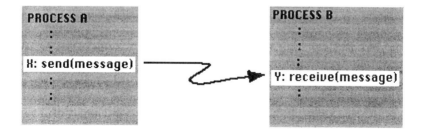

Would having one process wait, by going to sleep, until another process reaches a certain state and issues the associated wake-up call, solve the problem?

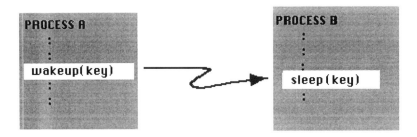

First we define the utilities, 'sleep' and 'wakeup', that we are going to add to our language. Sleep(key) halts its calling process where key is an identifier uniquely associated with the reason for the process being halted. When that reason no longer holds, the calling of utility wkup(key) will restore the process environment and restart the sleeping process.

Process A passes data to process B. For simplicity we'll use integer numbers as the data items, rename process A as PRODUCER, the producer of integers, and process B as CONSUMER, the consumer of integers. We will also generalise things a little by allowing not one, but several, data messages to be outstanding between PRODUCER and CONSUMER.

The PRODUCER passes data to the CONSUMER in individual buffers. Empty buffers are held as a list in freelist, and an associated freelist_count variable contains the number of buffers in the list. Filled buffers are held as a list in queue with an associated variable queue_count containing the list's size. There is a fixed number of buffers N, where N is a system invariant N = freelist_count + queue_count.

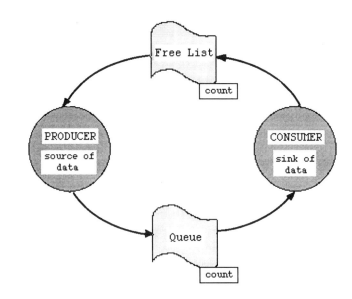

The algorithms for PRODUCER and CONSUMER are outlined thus:

PRODUCER produces integers, one at a time. When it has an integer to transmit, it obtains a buffer from freelist, decrements freelist_count, places the integer in the buffer, adds the buffer to queue and increments the queue_count, then goes back to the task of producing integers.

CONSUMER takes buffers from queue, decrements queue_count, removes the integer contained in the buffer, returns the buffer to freelist, increments freelist_count, uses the integer, and then waits for more.

As the system has two symmetrical parts, we can simplify things by investigating the behaviour of one half, here the management of the PRODUCER to CONSUMER queue. The relevant parts of the PRODUCER and CONSUMER algorithms could be:

If PRODUCER discovers the buffer queue full it halts, to be restarted by CONSUMER when it removes an item from the full queue. Similarly, when CONSUMER finds the queue empty it halts, to be restarted when PRODUCER adds a buffer to the empty queue.

The objective of introducing buffering is to maximise concurrency; the producer and the consumer do not have to wait to synchronise every time they wish to pass data, they simply add and remove buffers from the relevant lists. Direct inter-process communication is only required to restart processes waiting on full or empty lists.

We could postulate a possible design for the queue-handling parts of PRODUCER and CONSUMER using sleep and wake-up:

```
PRODUCER produces until the queue is full
        if (queue_count = maximum) then go to sleep
        if (0 < queue_count < maximum) then
          add buffer to queue, increment queue_count
        if (queue_count = 0) then
          add buffer to queue, increment queue_count
          and send wakeup to CONSUMER.
CONSUMER consumes until the queue is empty
        if(queue_count = 0) then go to sleep
        if(0 < queue_count < maximum) then
          remove item from queue, decrement
          queue_count
        if(queue_count = maximum) then
          remove item from queue, decrement
          queue_count and send wakeup to PRODUCER
```

Seems reasonable?

We can refine the above algorithms into more familiar programming terms as:

```
PRODUCER                              CONSUMER
repeat forever                        repeat forever
 /* wait for item */                   /* read queue_count */
 /* read queue_count and test it */    /* test it */
 if queue full                         if queue empty
   sleep (full);                         sleep (empty);
 else if queue empty                   else if queue full
   wakeup(empty);                        wakeup (full);
 /* add buffer to queue */             /* remove buffer from queue */
 /* increment queue_count */           /* decrement queue_count */
end.                                  end.
```

We must now test the system to see if it performs as we require. We test operationally, 'walking through' the algorithms until we've either considered all possible states or discovered a case where the system fails to meet our requirements.

To test the system operationally we must consider the algorithms running on some implementation which has its own characteristics. We'll start with the simplest implementation, where PRODUCER and CONSUMER are processes on a multi-processing SISD machine. The scheduler of the machine is priority-based, and we will assume that PRODUCER has a higher priority than CONSUMER and processes negotiating with the queue have higher priority than those which are not. During the life of the processes, priority, and hence which process executes when, will 'ping-pong', depending upon their queue accesses.

Consider the following scenario. The state has been reached in which only one buffer remains, i.e. queue_count=1. PRODUCER is busy doing things not related to data transfer when CONSUMER is ready to remove data from the queue, and, as data transfers have a higher priority, it is scheduled and starts to remove an item. During this time, PRODUCER becomes ready to add data items to the queue as its priority is greater than that of CONSUMER the PRODUCER runs...

```
PRODUCER                        CONSUMER
do things to produce                 :
the next integer to send             :
           :                    read queue_count
           :                    as queue_count > 0
           :                         remove last item
           :                         decrement
           :                         queue_count to 0
           :                    read queue_count
have data item to transmit           :
```

```
read queue_count                            :
as queue_count= 0                           :
    wakeup CONSUMER                         :
    add buffer to queue                     :
    increment queue_count                   :
    to 1                                    :
```
do things to produce   :
the next integer to send   :
```
    :                                       :
    :                           as queue_count = 0
    :                               go to sleep
    :                                       :
```
have data item to transmit   :
```
read queue_count                            :
as queue_count= 1                           :
    add buffer to queue                     :
    increment queue_count                   :
    to 2                                    :
    etc.                                    :
```
until eventually   :
have data item to transmit   :
```
read queue_count                            :
as queue_count= maximum - 1                 :
    add buffer to queue                     :
    increment queue_count                   :
    to maximum                              :
    :                                       :
```
have data item to transmit   :
```
read queue_count                            :
as queue_count= maximum                     :
        go to sleep                         :
```

The system has failed: there is a situation where both processes go to sleep and remain asleep.

In detail, if there remains 1 item in the queue and CONSUMER starts to fetch, it reads queue_count as 1, applies its test to the queue_count and as the count is greater than zero, CONSUMER removes a buffer from the queue and decrements queue_count to 0. CONSUMER uses the data in the buffer and returns for the next one.

CONSUMER reads queue_count, which is 0, but, before it can apply its test, the higher-priority PRODUCER is ready to transmit data and is scheduled in preference to CONSUMER. When PRODUCER tests queue_count it is 0 and its algorithm incorrectly assumes that CONSUMER is blocked, asleep, and sends it a wakeup, which is ignored. PRODUCER continues by adding an item to the queue, increments queue_count to 1, and continues producing.

When CONSUMER recommences, it applies its test to the count it read earlier, it finds that queue_count is 0, so it sleeps. PRODUCER can continue producing until the queue is full, when it, too, will sleep.

Both PRODUCER and CONSUMER are now halted, sleeping, and will remain so forever.

The difficulty has arisen because of the shared variable queue_count. Between the time CONSUMER fetches the queue_count and the time it tests it, PRODUCER sneaks in, reads queue_count as 0, wrongly assumes CONSUMER is asleep, and the wake-up signal it sends is lost. It is a *race condition*. System behaviour, success or failure, depends upon when PRODUCER and CONSUMER access queue_count.

We can also describe the 'failure zone' of this example in terms of labelled transition systems. PRODUCER contains the actions:

and CONSUMER contains:

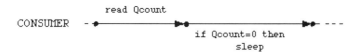

giving a possible interleaving, where C:x is consumer action x and P:x producer action x, of:

C:read Qcount:=0; P:read Qcount:=0; P:wkup CONSUMER;
              P:Qcount=1; C:sleep; ...

The use of sleep and wake-up primitives to support interprocess communication in a fairly straight algorithm has failed. Can we alter the implementation's environment to get us back on track?

One cause of the race condition is PRODUCER having a higher priority than CONSUMER. This allows PRODUCER to 'sneak in' and alter the count value without CONSUMER's knowledge. Would the problem disappear if we gave CONSUMER higher priority than PRODUCER? Unfortunately not; the problem is simply relocated from queue to freelist. What if PRODUCER and CONSUMER had the same priorities: would that solve things? Once more, no; as processes with the same priorities can execute with any interleaving of their statements, their behaviour will also include the race condition. What if we had true concurrency and the PRODUCER and CONSUMER processes executed on separate processors? Good try, but, again, as such processes can execute with any interleaving of their actions, they will eventually replicate the race condition.

Can we approach the problem from another direction? The cause of the race problem is that the wake-up sent by PRODUCER is lost, as CONSUMER was not yet asleep. We could have a *wakeup waiting bit*, wwb, which is set when a wake-up is received by a non-sleeping process. The next time the process is about to go to sleep the wwb is checked, and if it is non-zero the process decrements the wwb by one and continues. Only when the wwb is zero is a process actually allowed to sleep. The wwb effectively stores a superfluous wake-up signal for future use. This would appear to solve our problem, but to be certain, further analysis is necessary to check that it works in all cases and does not introduce further problems in its own right. The wwb looks like a reasonable solution, but as we saw in the section on mutual exclusion, things that look reasonable are not necessarily correct.

We will not carry out this further analysis, since we are about to reject the wake-up waking bit on other grounds. The simpler and more general a solution, the more likely it is to be understood and be correct. The addition of wwb for two processes to any system adds undesirable complexity, as each wwb needs to be stored somewhere and needs housekeeping support, etc. This complexity will escalate as more and more processes are involved. As complexity leads to error, if we can devise a simpler, more general solution to our problem, the wwb should be shown the door.

We could remove any race condition involving variable queue_count by making the parts of the code which access it indivisible, making access mutually exclusive. This could be done by bracketing these access code segments with lock() and unlock() primitives. But didn't we previously reject a similar solution when last trying to provide mutual exclusion? For the same reasons we reject its use here and continue the search for a better solution.

Looking at the problem more objectively, the system we're investigating can be considered from two perspectives:

- The system can be seen as two processes attempt to synchronise using the message-passing inherent in a sleep–wake-up pairing. Really this was never going to work for sleep–wake-up acting on queue_count does not satisfy the synchronisation requirements stated at the beginning of the section ('the first process ready to data transfer waits for the other, they synchronise, pass the data and finally continue on their asynchronous ways'), as, while a process executing a sleep will wait for one executing a wakeup, it doesn't work the other way round, and only if the primitives were balanced, both waiting for each other, would PRODUCER and CONSUMER synchronise correctly.

- The system can be seen as two processes accessing a shared variable, in this case queue_count, and the sharing causes our synchronisation problem: both processes take a snapshot of queue_count, record it, and later on use this stored value to decide their future behaviours – in this case, whether to sleep or not. As the processes act on some past value of queue_count, the outcome is unpredictable.

The first argument leads us to a solution based on message-passing, a view of such importance that we are about to devote a complete section to it. The second point indicates that our solution to the problem of synchronisation has devolved to a problem of mutual exclusion. For our synchronisation solution to work, reading and acting upon values of the shared variable queue_count must be done atomically under mutual exclusion. But isn't this just what we failed to do in the previous section? We have no need to increase our embarrassment by repeating such attempts here.

What we need is a new look at mutual exclusion, producing a simple and general solution and going on to use this solution to solve the problem of synchronisation.

2.2.4 Semaphores

Our previous attempts to 'solve' the problems of mutual exclusion and synchronisation have met with little success. We were unable to prove mutual exclusion for systems of two processes, never mind those of more. The only reliable way we've found to provide mutual exclusion is to ensure that transactions on an unshareable resource are done indivisibly, atomically. Critical sections, by simply relocating the problem from resource to guards, have been unable to guarantee such atomicity.

When using guarded critical sections, we always seemed to stumble across the problem of providing mutual exclusion over shared variables, for example the sharing of procno in Solution (2), sharing p1wants, p2wants in Solution(3), and so on. When addressing synchronisation we also met the same obstacle – this time with the shared count variables of the buffer queues. To address mutual exclusion and synchronisation we need either to dispense with these error-prone shared variables or to ensure that transactions over them are safe. We could make them safe by making all transactions on them mutually exclusive. Our best hope for solving the problem of mutual exclusion, and hence synchronisation, would appear to be the provision of pseudo-atomic guarded critical sections that actively minimise programmer error, which is best achieved by abstracting guards and their environments to their simplest form. After all, all we need to know about resources is how many are available to clients, and this count, never less than zero, can be held in a variable associated with each resource. Now, if transactions on this variable are done under mutual exclusion, by making the access code atomic, we may have circumvented the problem of safe resource allocation in a concurrent environment. Such is the impetus behind the concept of Dijkstra semaphores.

Dijkstra Semaphores

Dijkstra pared the notions of mutual exclusion to the bone by suggesting that all that is required in a solution is the presence of two pseudo-atomic guards acting on a protected shareable resource count. In [Dijk68], this was implemented as two indivisible procedures acting on a protected non-negative counter termed a *semaphore*. The semaphore is a virtual abstract data type; after initialisation it should only be accessed via its two associated procedures. It is virtual as it relies upon the programmer to ensure it is accessed correctly; it's not enforced by the construct itself.

We add to our programming language the semaphore s and its associated procedures:[†]

signal(s)	adds 1 to a semaphore
wait(s)	subtracts 1 from a semaphore

> If a **wait(s)** is performed on a semaphore whose value $s>0$ the semaphore is decremented by one and the wait procedure returns, otherwise the calling process is suspended, sent to sleep, on the semaphore until a corresponding signal(s) is performed.

> If a **signal(s)** is performed and there are processes suspended on semaphore s, wake one of them, otherwise increment the semaphore s by one and return.[††]

An essential property of the signal(s) and wait(s) procedures is their indivisibility – once they are initiated, no other process may access semaphores until the wait or signal completes, or the process accessing it is suspended. Semaphore procedures thus behave as primitive instructions, making designs of which they

---

[†] A semaphore which can take any non-negative integer value is termed a *general semaphore*, and one restricted to values of 0 or 1 is called a *binary semaphore*.

[††] A signal(s) command wakes only one process suspended on s, and the way this process is selected from the set of waiting processes – randomly chosen, woken in the order of suspension, etc. – will give the programs using such semaphores different properties.

are part easier to comprehend and more difficult to get wrong.

We will now see if this new tool can help solve our synchronisation, mutual exclusion and deadlock problems. If they do, how do we add them to our implementation language, and so on? First let's see if it works.

Semaphores and Mutual Exclusion

We obtain mutual exclusion of unshareable resources by withholding access to a resource by more than one process at a time and this we do by preventing concurrent execution of critical sections of code associated with that resource. To provide mutual exclusion, the semaphore procedures act as guards, their indivisibility ensured by the implementation. The non-negative semaphore, holding the number of available resources, is initialised to the maximum number of resources available.

Keeping the critical section conventions used in the previous mutual exclusion section, we enclose critical sections by an entry guard, wait(muex), and an exit guard, signal(muex), operating on a single binary semaphore muex with initial value 1.

```
program mutualsem
var     muex: boolean; (* semaphore declaration *)

        process procone
        begin
            while true do
                first part process one
                wait(muex);        (* P1 entry guard *)
                critical section one
                signal(muex);      (* P1 exit guard *)
                second part process one
            end while
        end (* procone *).

        process proctwo
        begin
            while true do
                first part process two
                wait(muex);        (* P2 entry guard *)
                critical section two
                signal(muex);      (* P2 exit guard *)
                second part process two
            end while
        end (* proctwo *).
```

```
begin
        muex := 1;  (* semaphore initialisation *)
        parbegin
            procone;
            proctwo;
end (*mutualsem*)
```

By inspection, as semaphore procedures are atomic, only one of the processes will gain access to a critical section, thus allowing access to the resource, at a time. We have the mutual exclusion we desire.

Semaphores and Synchronisation

We will approach this topic via a re-examination of the synchronisation problem introduced earlier. The obvious solution is to use two semaphores: one to control the allocation buffers in the queue from PRODUCER to CONSUMER, and the other to manage those in the free list from CONSUMER to PRODUCER.

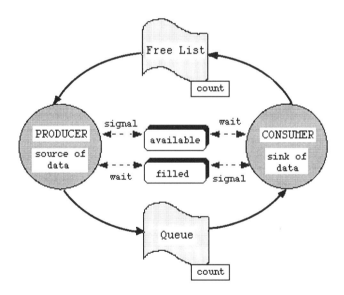

Let's assume that initially we have 100 buffers in the free list and 0 buffers in the queue. The two associated semaphores have cardinal values available (=100) and filled (=0).

An initial stab at the design of a producer/consumer system using semaphores could be:

Producer

```
repeat forever
   /* produce an item */
   wait(available);          /* see if a buffer is */
                             /* available in freelist */
   /* get a buffer */
   /* put item in buffer */
   /* add buffer to queue */
   signal(filled);          /* signal that queue has */
                            /* an extra buffer */
end
```

Consumer

```
repeat forever
   wait(filled);            /* see if a buffer is */
                            /* available in queue */
   /* get a buffer */
   /* get item from buffer */
   /* return buffer to freelist */
   signal(available);       /* signal buffer added */
                            /* to freelist */
   /* use item */
end
```

This is fairly straightforward, simple and understandable. Now, applying our operational proof technique, we can 'walk through' the design to establish if it is successful.

> If CONSUMER runs first, and filled=0, it will be suspended and sent to sleep on semaphore filled. If PRODUCER runs first, it produces an item and calls wait(available) to obtain an empty buffer from the free list, decrementing available=99, then returning. PRODUCER places its item in the just-acquired buffer, places filled buffer in queue, and calls signal(filled), which increments filled=1 before waking CONSUMER; signal(filled) returns and PRODUCER continues. CONSUMER is woken and, as filled=1, wait(filled) completes. Both processes are now active.

Both processes will remain active until either the free list or the queue become empty, in which case the system will restart as outlined above.

This seems OK. But will the semaphore-based solution successfully handle the case where the previous sleep/wake-up solution failed? The previous solution failed when CONSUMER was attempting to get a buffer from the empty queue, PRODUCER snuck in, and...

Reconstructing previous failure mode

CONSUMER has serviced the last item in queue. At this point the semaphores would read filled=0 and available=100. CONSUMER returns for the next item, executing a wait(filled) which, as the queue is empty, sends CONSUMER to sleep on the filled semaphore.

As the wait is indivisible (atomic), PRODUCER is inhibited from running until CONSUMER is suspended, which removes the race hazard – it's as simple as that. PRODUCER can now run, adding an item to the queue and, by sending a wake-up to CONSUMER via signal(filled), waking CONSUMER which takes this item from the queue. Both PRODUCER and CONSUMER are still active, and the previous problem is resolved.

Having shown that semaphores can address synchronisation and mutual exclusion, is this the solution we require: for example, can it address deadlock?

Semaphores and Deadlock

Deadlock can occur when suspended processes form a cycle, and each waits for the next in the chain to complete.

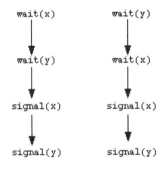

Consider two processes with semaphores x and y controlling access to two distinct unshareable resources.

As the resources are unshareable their associated semaphores will be initialised to x=y=1. Now, if each of the processes has completed its first wait, it will not be able to complete the second: deadlock. Use of semaphores in a design does not of itself prevent deadlock.

We need another way to circumvent deadlock. First we need to understand under what conditions deadlock arises. Some obviously reasons are:

1. The resources involved are unshareable.
2. Processes hold resources they have been allocated while waiting for others.
3. Resources cannot be taken from processes by others.
4. A circular chain of processes exists such that each process holds a resource necessary to the next process in the chain.

Deadlocks can be removed or circumvented if we can ensure that, at all times, at least one of the above conditions does not hold. Removal of the reasons will prevent deadlock, as shown in the following examples.

Reason 1.   This is simple in some circumstances, e.g. sharing a disk drive, by spooling to a shareable manager process which then negotiates with the unshareable resource.

Reason 2.   Processes are given all resources necessary to complete before they commence. This is implicitly unfair. Processes ready to proceed may be prevented from doing so, as a necessary resource has been allocated to, but not used by, another.

Reason 3.   Refused processes are made to release all held resources. This is inherently complex. Housekeeping duties, such as check pointing and rolling back, will be required.

Reason 4.   Processes may be rewritten so that a process holding resource R can only request further resources of type R.

The alternative, as we'll see later, is to design a system which is provably free of deadlocks.

Semaphores Overview

For concurrent systems of fairly low complexity Dijkstra semaphores are simple to comprehend and easy to use – a sort of guarded critical section with clothes on. However, being low-level unstructured constructs, at the assembly code level of concurrency, they do little to assist the understanding of complex systems. Such a lack of understanding inevitably leads to programmer error.

While semaphores are a neat solution to the problem of resource allocation, they only work correctly if the signal and wait calls are correctly paired, in the correct order and correctly initialised to the number of resources available. Further, as Dijkstra semaphores are not abstract data types, the semaphore is left 'dangling' in the programmer domain and any user can access, and change, the shared semaphore at will. It is thus untenable to claim that using semaphores ensures mutual exclusion. Worse, as programming language constructs, semaphores have no associated semantics, so we cannot use them to predict unambiguously the behaviour of any system they describe and we cannot easily prove that our semaphore 'solutions' to the problem of mutual exclusion actually work. As was the case with critical sections, a correct design would need to be validated to ensure that behaviours in the design were correctly translated to the implementation. Such systems are as rare as hen's teeth.

So, though semaphores are a definite improvement over guarded critical sections, they are not the universal solution we need. The search continues.

The obvious next step, which has the effect of removing programmer errors, would be to encapsulate semaphores and associated resource access into one structure, hiding all the internals – which is just what monitors do.

2.2.5 Monitors

For concurrent systems with straightforward synchronisation and mutual exclusion requirements, Dijkstra semaphores are simple to comprehend and easy to use. However, as a general model to use in the design of concurrent systems, they have major weaknesses.

- As low-level constructs it is difficult to use semaphores to address complex concurrent problems.
- Their presence does little to help prove systems correct.
- They are open to user abuse.
- They cannot be directly used to model higher levels of abstraction.
- They are only effective when a single serial processor is used as the implementation vehicle.

Hence the search for design models that better support the human-level concept of client server and are mathematically tractable, so that we can get meaningful answers to questions about system behaviour; this implicitly simplifies our problems and, by doing so, reduces programmer error. We want a mechanism which:

- facilitates capturing the behaviour of complex concurrency problems;
- facilitates proving systems correct;
- is difficult, if not impossible, for the programmer to misuse;
- supports implicitly comprehensible models – the clarity of understanding conferred reduces design errors and implementation errors, and aids proving designs correct.

Not wanting to throw out the baby with the bath water, before dispensing with the accumulated knowledge of previous models we'll sift them carefully and retain any useful concepts in the new one.

When using guarded critical sections to provide mutual exclusion it was found that the guards and associated dynamic shared data, together representing resource access control, had themselves to be used under mutual exclusion. This train of thought led us to the atomic procedures `signal(s)` and `wait(s)`, operating on a shared semaphore. The semaphore representing the number of available resources. Whatever solution we now propose must preserve this concept of treating dynamic shared data as unshareable resources.

Dekker's algorithm, by serialising and making indivisible interleavings which would otherwise be unsafe, was presented as a successful critical section algorithm. At the heart of the algorithm is a scheduler which only intervenes when several clients simultaneously attempt to use an unshareable resource, the scheduler deciding which client gets which resource, when, and ensuring that initially refused clients eventually acquire the resource. If a scheduler can provide mutual exclusion in this specialised algorithm, why can it not be used as a basis of more general client-server systems? This argument isn't original. Monitors conceived in the 1970s took the form of servers with internal schedulers. Individual monitors oversee sets of related resources and clients access resources only through such monitors. If a service is simultaneously requested by several clients the controlling monitor ensures that clients are individually served under mutual exclusion. The use of monitors to control access to general resources is ably presented in [Hoa74] and [Bri77]. Their use in the programming languages Pascal and Modula can be found in [Bri75] and [Wir77].

Monitors as Resource Schedulers

Monitors contain the only sequences of instructions that access a resource. The concentration of responsibility for resource access in one place makes our obligation to prove designs correct somewhat easier.

A most important concept to get clear is that monitors are not processes. A monitor only becomes active when called by a process. A monitor's a static structure consists of local administrative *data* and *procedures* which are used by a client to determine if it can have access to which resource, when. Sounds familiar? These procedures mirror critical section entry and exit guards and the local data resource access control. A monitor is in effect a critical section 'package', its local data only accessible via its own procedures. So packaged monitors are simple to understand and use. The packetisation also removes the possibility of errors when programmers have access to the separate bits of the package as with semaphores.

From our previous experiences we know that, if several clients were simultaneously to enter a monitor, its local data, keeping track of resources use, would behave as a shared variable, and chaos probably be the result. It is thus necessary to enforce mutual exclusion; only one client can be 'inside' a monitor at a time, and we rely upon the implementation to provide this mutual exclusion.

Clients can only access a service from within the monitor, but as a server may provide more than one service, clients have to specify what service they require. If the monitor is provided with several entry points, each associated with one type of service on offer, whichever one a particular client wants is communicated to the monitor by which entry point the client selects. A client requests entry by executing the monitor entry procedure associated with that service, and, once inside, a client negotiates access to the resource it wants.

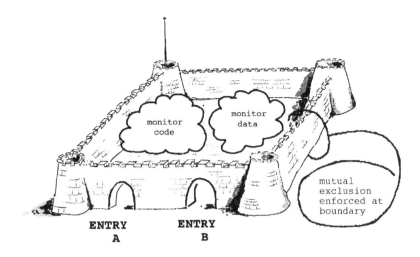

In particular, the above monitor controls access to a resource by ensuring that one, and only one, process can be 'inside' the monitor, using monitor procedures which access that resource. Entry to the monitor is via entry points A or B, which are mapped to monitor procedures.

As only one client can be inside a monitor, if several clients simultaneously want to enter an available monitor only one will succeed. Refused clients have to wait, and, to preserve fairness, the monitor organises waiting clients in FIFO queues outside the monitor, each queue associated with the client's intended entry point. There is no analogue for clients leaving a monitor; processes leaving simply release the monitor's mutual exclusion, thus allowing another process to enter.

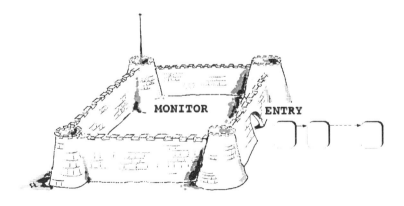

A client process allowed inside the monitor has, by definition, been granted permission to negotiate with a resource – but no more than that. If the client finds that the resource it wants is not available, what does it do? it can only wait for the resource to become available, but where does it wait? Waiting processes cannot wait 'inside' a monitor; as monitors operate under mutual exclusion, they would prevent processes entering and releasing the very resource they were waiting for. Instead, waiting processes are made to execute a monitor `wait` procedure, causing them to vacate the monitor to wait until the requested resource becomes available. Waiting clients are held in `FIFO` queues outside the monitor, each queue related to a reason for waiting: for example, waiting for the condition 'resource in use' to become `false`. Thus, clients wishing to access a resource may have to wait to enter the monitor handling access to that resource, and wait again for the resource to be free, but, as clients in condition queues wait for a different reason to those in entry queues, the queues are kept distinct.

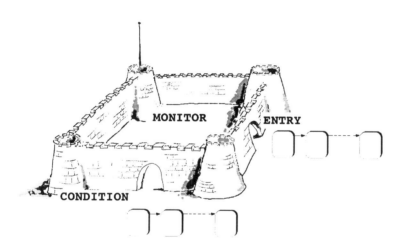

A client returning a resource executes a monitor `signal` procedure which allows the client at the head of the associated condition queue to re-enter the monitor.

Implementation of Monitors
All this client-server negotiation must be handled in a way which is transparent to clients. A client must simply ask for the resource and eventually be given it; the 'sleight of hand' is performed by the code used to implement each monitor. Further, the preservation of a monitor's mutual exclusion, and hence the atomicity of its

actions, are not the concern of the user but are ensured by the compiler and run-time system associated with the computer language(s) of which they are part.

To relieve the user of further burdens, the implementation language also includes support for the condition queues by providing two special 'monitor-associated' procedures usually named `signal` and `wait`. The user is only required to known what these procedures do and how to use them. As only one client can be inside a monitor, there is need for only one pair of monitor `wait` and `signal` procedures, parametrised by the condition associated with each waiting queue, akin to a key in sleep and wake-up procedures. These procedures can be described as follows:

> **wait(ConditionVariableName)** This places the calling process at the tail of a `FIFO` queue associated with condition `ConditionVariableName`. Monitor mutual exclusion is released.
> **signal(ConditionVariableName)** If the queue associated with condition `ConditionVariableName` is empty, no action is taken. Otherwise, the process at the head of the queue is revived.

While monitors can be considered generalisations of semaphores, one should not confuse their wait and signal procedures. Both oversee resource access, but the monitor procedures also manage the associated queues of waiting clients.

But how easily do monitors address the problems of concurrency? We'll start to answer this by considering monitors not acting as resource servers, which we'll leave until later, but being used as critical section guards for processes accessing an unshareable resource.

Mutual Exclusive Access to an Unshareable Resource
Monitors totally control resource access by containing the only copies of the the critical sections of code which negotiate with resources. Critical sections are viewed as resources in their own right, and, by controlling access to them, we control access to the resource. As monitors have implicit mutual exclusion, conferring this property on the resources they control should be fairly straightforward.

Monitors can be used in two main roles: as critical sections and guards; or just as guards. The latter view fits better when comparing monitors with semaphores, and we will follow this view first.

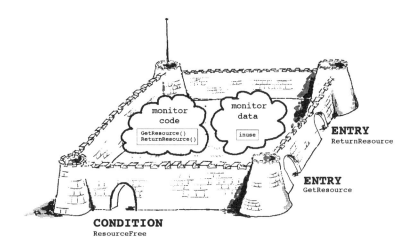

As an overview, client processes contain procedure calls GetResource() and ReturnResource(), which have access to variable inuse, are used to acquire and return access permission to the unshareable resource. Both are held within the monitor. Clients wishing to access the resource do so by executing GetResource. Seen by the user, this can loosely be defined in pseudo code as:

```
procedure GetResource()
        if resource in use, inuse = true then
            calling process executes
            wait(ResourceFree),
            is sent to sleep by monitor queued
            on condition free.
        else
            client sets inuse := true
            and accesses the resource.
        endif
end (*GetResource*)
```

Only one user procedure contained in a monitor can be executed at a time; this is guaranteed if only one process, executing such procedures, is allowed 'inside' the monitor at a time. This in turn is ensured if we can guarantee that monitors are accessed with mutual exclusion. Here is where monitors show their subtlety. Access to a monitor is controlled by that monitor, it ensures that one, and only one, user can be using its facilities at one time. Mutual exclusion is provided by the compiler bracketing all monitor-resident procedures with code which, though the procedure-calling mechanism is unaltered, enables the run-time system to ensure that only one process can be in a monitor at a time, holding refused processess in queues at their intended entry points. This code, added by the language compiler, acts as a scheduler, allocating the monitor between users as a unshareable resource.

```
procedure GetResource()
    if monitor unoccupied then
        client process allowed entry into the monitor
        if resource in use, inuse = true then
            calling process executes
            wait(ResourceFree),
            is sent to sleep by monitor
            queued on condition free.
        else
            client sets inuse := true
            and returns allowing caller to
            accesses the resource.
        endif
    else
        client process made to wait in queue at entry
        point
    endif
end (*GetResource*)
```

added by compiler,
executed by
run-time system

The client first attempts to gain access to the monitor. If the monitor is already occupied, the client is forced to wait in a FIFO queue at the entry point. If the monitor is free, the client is allowed entry and tests the state of the resource using monitor-local data variable inuse. If the resource is in use, inuse=true, the client blocks with a call to the general built-in monitor routine wait(ConditionVariableName). In this case, ConditionVariableName=ResourceFree places the client at the tail of the queue associated with condition ResourceFree. If the resource is available, inuse=false, the client exits from the monitor with permission to use the resource under mutual exclusion, guaranteed by the monitor.

Similarly, `ReturnResource` can be loosely defined in pseudo code as:

```
procedure ReturnResource()
    if monitor unoccupied then
        client process allowed entry into the monitor

            sets inuse := false and calls
            signal(ResourceFree), the
            monitor thus wakes a process        added by compiler,
            queued on condition ResourceFree       executed by
            allowing it entry into the            run-time system
            monitor after the current
            process vacates it.

    else
        client process made to wait in queue at entry
        point
    endif
end (*GetResource*)
```

The client first attempts to gain access to the monitor. If the monitor is already occupied, the client is forced to wait in a `FIFO` queue at the entry point. If the monitor is free, the client is allowed entry and informs the world that the resource is free by setting monitor-local data variable `inuse` to `false` and unblocks a client with a call to general built-in monitor routine `signal(ConditionVariableName)`. In this case, with `ConditionVariableName=ResourceFree` the client at the head of the queue associated with condition `ResourceFree` is allowed to enter the monitor.

We can now code a suitable client-server system based on these monitor procedures. A typical client would contain fragments of code, as:

```
process Client
        begin
            { not using Resource}
            GetResource;        (* entry guard *)
            { critical section accessing the resource }
            ReturnResource;    (* exit guard *)
            { not using resource }
        end (* Client *)
```

The actual guard procedures `GetResource()` and `ReturnResource()` are called by clients but implemented in the monitor. These procedures access monitor-local data, in this case variable `inuse`, and call other monitor routines, in this case the `wait(ResourceFree)` and `signal(ResourceFree)` procedures, with mutual exclusion guaranteed.

```
monitor ResourceSupervisor
        var inuse: boolean;            (* declare local variables *)
          ResourceFree: condition;     (* and conditions to *)
                                       (* control resource access *)

        procedure GetResource          (* request permission *)
                                       (* to use resource *)
          begin
            if inuse then
                wait(ResourceFree);
            endif
            inuse := true;
          end (*GetResource*)

        procedure ReturnResource       (* return permission *)
                                       (* to use resource *)
          begin
            inuse := false;
            signal(ResourceFree);
          end (*ReturnResource*)

        begin
          inuse := false;              (* initialise monitor *)
                                       (* local variables *)
        end (*ResourceSupervisor*)
```

Clients cannot access the resource environment `inuse`, as this variable is held within the monitor as local data. Thus, as only one process can be inside a monitor at any time, all problems introduced by having resource environments as shared variables, accessible at all times by all clients, are neatly removed.

Showing that a monitor can provide mutual exclusion of one unshareable resource is hardly exciting. We achieved the same result using semaphores. But monitors are higher-level abstractions which can directly address fairly complex concurrent systems. Building monitors to be servers offering several different types of resource is no more difficult than the previous example; all we need is monitor entries to obtain and return each type of service offered and, as there may be several reasons why a client has to wait for access to a particular resource, the monitor must associate a condition plus waiting and signalling actions with each reason for waiting, a signal on a particular resource resuscitating clients waiting for that resource only. The next example looks at such a general case.

A Floppy Disk Controller

The associated monitor has three entry points representing read a file, write a file and seek a file on a floppy disk, and two conditions for disk inaccessibility namely read_only and disk_not_inserted.

We'll consider the monitor in a state where user process P_5 is inside the monitor performing a read after entry via the read entry point, processes P_1 and P_2 are blocked at entry point read, and P_4 is blocked at entry point seek, processes P_3 and P_6 are waiting on condition read_only, having previously entered the monitor via entry write.

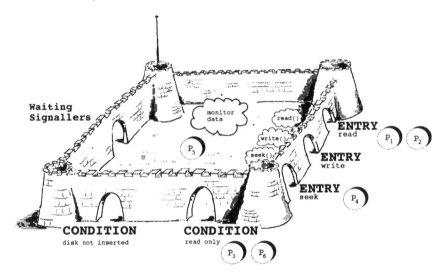

When a client completes a resource access, it leaves the monitor, mutual exclusion is released, and the client at the head of one of the entry or waiting signaller's queues can enter.

- When P_5 has completed its read action it leaves the monitor, and either P_2, the head of the read queue, or P_4, the head of the seek queue, enters.

As only a client in the monitor can access resources and detect any state changes, the determination that conditions requested by a waiting client hold can only be signalled by a client inside the monitor. If a client checks and finds such conditions are now true, its signals should wake the waiting client and, for safety reasons,[†] a woken client takes precedence over the signaller and enters the monitor to continue its execution. However, to preserve mutual exclusion,

---

†   Consider the case of a client which generates several different signals.

the signaller must exit the monitor. Such signalling clients are not waiting on a resource condition but simply waiting to re-enter the monitor; they are not in their original entry state, and a separate time ordered FIFO queue of waiting signallers is provided.

- If P_5 executes a signal on condition read_only, P_3, as head of the queue waiting on this condition, will be allowed to enter. P_5 must evacuate the monitor to preserve its mutual exclusion, but, as it needs to re-enter at a later date, P_5 is queued as a waiting signaller. Waiting signallers have the same priority as clients at other entry points.

We will conclude our examples of monitors by re-addressing the synchronisation problem of the producer–consumer system, and here we'll use monitors in their other guise – not just that of granting access to a resource but overseeing all transactions on that resource.

We can outline the algorithms for PRODUCER and CONSUMER as follows:

> PRODUCER produces integers, one at a time. When it has an integer to transmit, it obtains an empty buffer from a finite list of free buffers, decrements the free list count, places the integer in the buffer, adds the now filled buffer to a finite queue, increments the queue count, and goes back to the task that produces integers.
>
> CONSUMER takes filled buffers from the queue, decrements the queue count, removes the integer contained in the buffer, returns the now empty buffer to the free list, increments the free list count, and then gets on with the task that consumes integers.

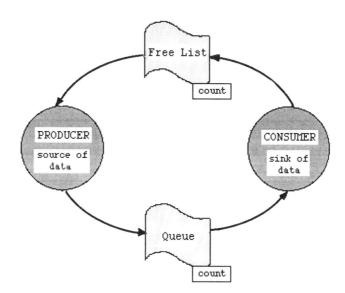

First of all we will attempt to outline a monitor to control the queue of filled buffers from PRODUCER to CONSUMER. Internal queue management is irrelevant to our protocol and will be ignored. The protocol between the queue and its users operates as follows:

> PRODUCER halts if it discovers the buffer queue, queue, full, to be restarted by CONSUMER when it removes an item from the full queue. Similarly, when CONSUMER finds the queue empty, it halts, to be restarted when PRODUCER adds a buffer to the empty queue.

At start-up all buffers, MAX of them, are in the free list and none in the queue.

```
monitor QueueManager
        var    Qcount: integer;
               QNotFull, QNotEmpty: condition;

        procedure PutQueueItem(FilledBuffer: in buffertype)
           begin
              if Qcount = MAX then
                 wait(QNotFull);
              endif
              (* append filled buffer to Queue *)
              Qcount := Qcount +1;
              signal(QNotEmpty);
           end (*PutQueueItem*)

        procedure GetQueueItem(FilledBuffer: out buffertype)
           begin
              if Qcount = 0 then
                 wait(QNotEmpty);
              endif
              (* get a buffer from the Queue *)
              Qcount := Qcount -1;
              signal(QNotFull);
           end (*GetQueueItem*)

        begin
           Qcount := 0;
        end (*QueueManager*)
```

As the free list has a similar behaviour to the queue we can use the same algorithm, with appropriate changes to procedure and variable names, as a description of the freelist monitor – and rather than spell it out we'll conclude this section of monitor applications with a monitor defining the user interfaces of the complete buffer system.[†]

```
monitor BufferManager
        var   Qcount, FreeCount: integer;
              QNotFull, QNotEmpty: condition;
              FreeNotFull, FreeNotEmpty: condition;

        procedure PutQueueBuffer(FilledBuffer: in buffertype)
           begin
              if Qcount = MAX then
                 wait(QNotFull);
              endif
              (* append filled buffer to Queue *)
              Qcount := Qcount +1;
              signal(QNotEmpty);
           end (*PutQueueBuffer*)

        procedure GetQueueBuffer(FilledBuffer: out buffertype)
           begin
              if Qcount = 0 then
                 wait(QNotEmpty);
              endif
              (* get a filled buffer from the Queue *)
              Qcount := Qcount -1;
              signal(QNotFull);
           end (*GetQueueBuffer*)

        procedure PutFreelistBuffer(EmptyBuffer: in buffertype)
           begin
              if FreeCount = MAX then
                 wait(FreeNotFull);
              endif
              (* append empty buffer to Freelist *)
              FreeCount := FreeCount +1;
              signal(FreeNotEmpty);
           end (*PutFreelistBuffer*)

        procedure GetFreelistBuffer(EmptyBuffer: out buffertype)
           begin
              if FreeCount = 0 then
```

[†] While system throughput would be improved if we divided this monitor into two – one monitor controlling the full buffer queue and one the free list – this is not explored here.

```
            wait(FreeNotEmpty);
        endif
        (* get empty buffer from the Freelist *)
        FreeCount := FreeCount -1;
        signal(FreeNotFull);
    end (*GetFreelistBuffer*)


begin
    Qcount := 0;
    FreeCount := MAX;
end (*BufferManager*)
```

The associated producer and consumer processes are simplicity itself. All buffer management is handled by the monitor.

```
process Producer
    begin
        while TRUE do
            (* produce next Prime *)
            GetFreelistBuffer(buffer);
            (* copy Prime into empty buffer *)
            PutQueueBuffer(buffer);
        endwhile
    end (*Producer*)


process Consumer
    begin
        while TRUE do
            GetQueueBuffer(buffer);
            (* copy Prime from buffer *)
            PutFreelistBuffer(buffer);
            (* consume Prime *)
        endwhile
    end (*Consumer*)
```

Semaphore Emulation

If we can emulate general semaphores by a monitor, this will support our claim that monitors are at a higher level of abstraction, or at least the equal of semaphores.[†]

---

† Using monitors to emulate semaphores is not the end of their interdependence. To be effective, each monitor must be used under mutual exclusion, and what could be simpler than to use semaphores to provide this mutual exclusion? Each monitor is given an operating-system-level binary semaphore, to track if it is in use or not, plus a set of signal and wait primitives to control client access.

```
monitor SemaphoreEmulator
        var    s:integer;
               NotZero: condition;

        procedure SemaphoreWait
          begin
            if s=0 then
               wait(NotZero);
            endif
            s := s -1;
          end (*SemaphoreWait*)

        procedure SemaphoreSignal
          begin
            s := s +1;
            signal(NonZero);
          end (*SemaphoreSignal*)

        begin
          s := sInitial;
        end (*SemaphoreEmulator*)
```

where sInitial is the initial value assigned to the semaphore.

Showing that monitors can emulate semaphores means that monitors will inherit all the attributes of semaphores, and any system designed and proved correct using semaphores can be rewritten using monitors without a change of properties.

The Problems with Monitors

For each service there is one copy of a monitor shared by all processes that access it. Any client executing any part of a monitor has access to this single copy, and there must exist an arbiter to ensure that only one client is 'inside' a monitor at any time. Mutual exclusion between the clients accessing the monitor must be enforced, which is fine in systems where monitors can be placed in shared memory, accessible to all involved processes; but what about truly distributed systems, and systems where messages may 'pass' each other in transit? For, as we know, overtaking can lead to liveness problems.

Monitors as described here are rather complex to nest. Consider a client accessing a resource under the control of one monitor having to use another monitor to access a sub-resource – for example, a client given permission to write to a file-server by one monitor having to pass through another monitor which allocates disk drives. In such nested monitors, what happens when the client is blocked in a monitor low down in the hierarchy? But that is the sort of thing we want to model in the real world; the concept is beginning to run out of steam.

However, these problems are incidental to proving that systems incorporating monitors meet their specifications. Do we achieve this using operational proofs? The behaviour of monitors, like semaphores, is implementation-dependent. One cannot predict their behaviour as they have no intrinsic semantics from which to derive formal proof rules. One can apply general mathematical semantics to them [Ben90] by assuming that the instructions of the implementation language statements are unambiguous and atomic. While not isomorphic, to a real implementation use of these methods does promote better understanding of concurrent systems.

Nor are monitors the general solution we seek, for, as devices to allocate resources, their primary use is to provide mutually exclusive access to unsharable resources. True, they can be used to pass messages, but they do not support process synchronisation, nor do they help in proving systems live and deadlock free.

2.3 Review and Rethink

This concludes the section which addresses the inherent problems of concurrent systems by proposing 'programming' solutions, adding extensions to sequential programming languages and using the resultant language as both design and implementation media. Such methods have ranged from simple critical section guards, with shared variables, through to monitors as fully abstract data types. Such a progression provides the designer/programmer with a spectrum of solutions, some easier to use than others, but all have failed to provide proof systems to determine whether the resultant design meets the user's requirements or not.

In systems where the occasional malfunction does no irreparable harm, the odd undiscovered error in the design is not serious, and these programming methods are adequate – if a washing machine fails, the cost to the supplier would at worst be a new machine and some compensation, and it's a lot cheaper than ensuring that no machine never fails. It is different in safety-critical systems where failure puts human life (or the company's finances) at risk. When the telemetry and control systems of chemical plants, motor cars and aircraft fail, they can kill and/or generate large law suits. Here, it is essential to minimise system failure, and proving designs correct may be cheaper, as well as more humanitarian, than accepting the consequences of system failure. The time is not far away when software engineers will be held legally responsible for the consequences of errors in design, as medical practitioners are for their failures today. The designers, programmers and implementers of any system have an obligation, a 'proof obligation'. Not only should they fully understand what they are doing, they must prove, and convince others, that a proposed solution works. The more complex the task, the more likely it is to fail, and, unfortunately, the more difficult and costly it is to satisfy this obligation. In general we satisfy this obligation only where necessary, expressed in a 'fitness for use' caveat as 'the amount of effort expended on proving a particular system correct should be commensurate with its eventual use'.

If we need to prove designs correct, the programming approaches presented in this section are simply inadequate, as no programming language in common use has a defined semantics. It is usually left to a compiler to associate meaning to language statements. If the compiler authors all get together and formally define the language syntax, and agree to write complilers which map this syntax into one uniquely defined behaviour, and the compilers are validated to show that their output does not distort the semantics captured in the programmes, will we then have sidestepped the problem? Unfortunately not, the run-time support system, the lower-level translators and, ultimately, the hardware itself have a hand in determining the operational semantics of any program. As it's not practical to validate all program/machine couplings, the actions associated with language statements are ambiguous: different states can result from identical instructions operating on systems in the same initial state.

Even if we restricted programs to one fully validated system, we would still have the problem that our design method was founded on the concept that individual language statements are atomic and can map to the actions of our labelled transition systems. This is not generally true. These so-called 'programming' solutions, by not having a defined semantics, fail to address our concurrency problems adequately, and their non-deterministic behaviours have no place in a design method which trys to predict behaviours.

It took computer scientists several years to get to this point and realise that these programming solutions, while of use as methods by which to navigate, are of marginal use to designers attempting to satisfy a proof obligation. We need a total rethink about the way forward.

3. Message Passing

Introduction

Our attempt to provide a design framework for concurrent systems by extending familiar sequential programming languages was something of a failure. In their favour, extensions are understandable, and no more than common sense is required to use them; they simplify the design of modest concurrent systems to such a degree that even the inexperienced can get things right most of the time without the involvement of nasty things like discrete mathematics.

On the down side, these methods only really address the problem of mutual exclusion. The simpler extensions provide users with the tools to serialise access to unsafe areas, while higher-level semaphores and monitors actively prevent unsafe access. As such, the successes of extensions ultimately rely upon programmers getting things right, as just using them doesn't guarantee valid concurrent systems. The only way we could prove such designs to be correct is to test them; unfortunately the statements of programming languages plus extensions can have more than one interpretation, and we cannot test a design described in ambiguous terms. For simple, non-critical systems, programming languages plus extensions are better than nothing, but to use them for complex and/or safety critical systems would be unprofessional.

What we want is a formal design method, based on a generally applicable model, which can be used to design concurrent systems and then prove them correct. Our mental model of concurrent systems – a set of simultaneously active sequential subsystems that interact by passing messages to progress some global task(s) – is a useful starting point. With formal models for the sequential bits we need only add a model of message passing to create the design method we seek.

3.1 Choosing the Best

The better we understand a problem, the easier it becomes to design a solution, the simpler it is to implement and the less likelihood there is of introducing errors along the way. We better understand problems by describing their behaviour using simple models. Our problem is how correctly to design concurrent systems. Our simple model is a set of objects engaged in local tasks that communicate to forward global tasks.

If, at some level, the objects forming concurrent systems are familiar sequential processes, the only unknown is how to model interprocess communication. As before, the simpler our model, the easier it will be to write clear specifications, understandable designs, realisable implementations, and the less will be the likelihood of error; and the closer the model to the problem domain, the easier it will be to validate designs. In short, our communications model must not only capture message passing; it must also support the formalisation of the design process by complementing an algebra for concurrent systems.

As well as supporting the formal aspects of design, the communications model we select must be a general one, capable of modelling the other types of communication we're likely to employ in a design. The best model will be the one that, together with the chosen design framework, can describe these other communication systems.

It would also be an advantage if the model chosen did not, of itself, reduce the available concurrency in a system – the communication system shouldn't cause otherwise active processes to idle. To compare the effectiveness of communication models in maintaining concurrency we use something called a decoupling factor, d, representing the maximum number of outstanding messages a model can maintain between sender and receiver. In a system with N buffers, holding one message each, the sender and receiver can proceed asynchronously until either zero messages are outstanding, when the receiver has to wait, or N messages are outstanding, when the sender has to wait. Such a system has a decoupling of $d=N$. In general, the larger d is, the less a model limits its users' concurrency.

Finally, we want the communications model to be safe and secure. We don't want a model which, by design, can lose and/or duplicate messages.

Briefly we want a communications model which is:
- tractable – forms a component of an algebra in which concurrent systems can be designed and designs verified;
- general – capable of describing a maximum number of other communication methods;

- simple – captures interprocess communication in an easy and understandable way;
- appropriate – close to the problem domain of concurrent systems, and can capture as many of the problems implicit in concurrent systems as possible without, of course, introducing any of its own;
- realisable – close to physical implementation;
- unconstraining – does not limit user concurrency
- safe – does not duplicate or lose messages.

The act of communication can be generalised as a server passing message between users.

We'll now consider several communications models of this type to choose the best for our purposes.

3.1.1 The Contenders

Based on an idea I first saw used by Professor Milner in a concurrency workshop he led at Strathclyde University in the 1970s, here we meet some contenders for the crown of Most Suitable Communication System, with comments on their effectiveness. To keep things simple, we'll initially consider a system with one sender and one receiver.

An Ether
We define an ether as an infinite, unorganised, holder of messages. Messages can always be put into the ether and messages can be removed in any order.

An ether has the following attributes:
- sender never waits;
- receiver waits if no message pending;
- receive order may differ from send order.

The decoupling of this model is infinite, $d=\infty$. The system doesn't affect the concurrency of its users. However, as messages can be removed in any order, they can overtake – the receive order may not be the same as the send order, and, in the extreme, if a message can be overtaken once it can be overtaken an infinite number of times: messages sent may never be received. The model is inherently unfair, and systems using this model may not be live. We can resolve the liveness issue by moving to a serial unbounded buffer.

Serial Unbounded Buffer

This consists of an infinite set of buffers, each capable of holding one message, connected as an ordered, first-in-first-out pipeline. As the capacity of the pipe is infinite, it can always accept incoming messages. Messages are delivered in the order accepted.

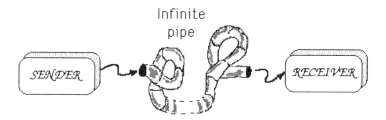

A serial unbounded buffer has the following attributes:
- sender never waits;
- receiver waits if no message pending;
- receive order is the same as send order.

The decoupling of this model if infinite, $d=\infty$. The system has no effect on the inherent concurrency of its users. With the removal of possible message overtaking, the model is fair; but, as with the ether before it, it is not implementable. So, we limit the number of buffers.

Serial Bounded Buffer

The pipe now has some finite number, N, of message buffers. The pipe can only accept messages while not full, and deliver them while not empty. Messages are delivered in the order received.

A serial bounded buffer has the following attributes:
- sender waits if buffer full;
- receiver waits if no message pending;
- receive order is the same as send order.

The decoupling factor of this model is the size of the pipeline, $d=N$, the number of buffers placing a limit on the concurrency of its users. As messages cannot overtake, the model is fair. With a finite number of buffers, the model is implementable.

There is no need to limit ourselves to serial systems. By changing the buffer topology from long and thin to short and fat, we can also have parallel models.

Parallel Buffers

By giving user processes equal access to a set of shared buffers, a serial system becomes a parallel one. However, this equality of access reintroduces message overtaking.

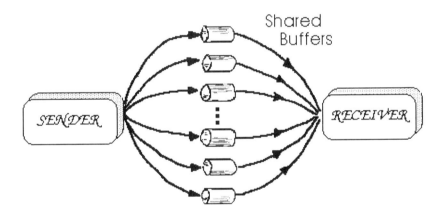

Rather than copy the serial buffer model, where a filled buffer must be read before being written to again, for parallel buffers we will consider an interesting variant in which a sender can write and overwrite any buffer and a receiver can read and reread any buffer – like memory elements in a computer system. In this system:
- neither sender nor receiver ever waits;
- receive order may differ from send order;
- messages can be lost;
- messages can be duplicated.

If the sender could never overwrite a buffer and the receiver could never reread the same message, the decoupling would be the number of shared buffers, N. But, if messages can be overwritten and read more than once, and as individual messages can be lost and duplicated, the effective decoupling is infinity, $d=\infty$. In this case the shared buffer model emulates interprocess communication using shared variables and provides a design platform for the analysis of the (many) problems associated with such algorithms.

3.1.2 The Choosing

Which of these models do we choose as best for our purposes? We'll use our stated requirements to sift out the inadequate ones.

While all the models pass the test for *simplicity*, in that they capture interprocess communication in an easy and understandable way, not all are safe as, by design, parallel bounded buffers can both duplicate and lose messages. Nor are all the models realisable for, as there is no such thing in the real world as an infinite number of anything, certainly not an infinite number of buffers in a computer system, we can implement neither the *ether* nor the *serial unbounded buffer*. Worse is to come.

None of the models ensure that processes synchronise correctly, are live, or use resources with fairness and mutual exclusion. In particular, by allowing message overtaking, the *ether* and *parallel bounded buffer* models can introduce unfairness into previously fair systems.

Of the original models, the only survivor of the sieve is the *serial bounded buffer*, which has yet to be shown to be tractable, general, unconstraining or fully appropriate. To do this we need a more searching look, but rather than limit the discussion to a particular serial buffer system, we will consider a more general form called (for reasons which will become clear) the *asynchronous FIFO message passing* model – a first-in-first-out (FIFO) pipeline with a finite decoupling of $d>0$.

Generalised Asynchronous FIFO Message Passing
A FIFO message server with finite d, $d>0$:

has the following attributes:
- messages are delivered in the order received;
- receiver waits if no message is pending;
- sender only waits if N messages are outstanding, $d=N$.

As the sender can continue processing after a send, we must store outstanding messages somewhere. Such messages are stored in buffers, also referred to as mailboxes, connected as a pipeline whose length defines the decoupling between sender and receiver.

The sender process can, in its own time, give a message to the mail server for subsequent removal by the receiver, again in its own time. While the message pipeline is neither empty nor full, both the sender and the receiver can remain active, doing their own things, operating asynchronously with respect to each other. Although we can't do anything about keeping the receiver active when the sender has nothing to send, we can influence message saturation by our choice of d. With a d=∞, the message passing system places no extra constraint on the concurrency of its users, a d=n allows n messages to be outstanding before concurrency is proscribed, and with a d=1, one outstanding message can put a damper on concurrency.

To achieve a d>0 we'll need mailboxes, but if we have mailboxes we will need to know:
* What size should they be? If they are of fixed size, how do we store messages that are too big? If of variable size, who does the housekeeping of the fragments, the garbage collection, etc.?
* Where are mailboxes kept in a distributed system; and who 'owns' them?
* To maximise decoupling we need as many mailboxes as possible, but, as we cannot have an infinite number, what is the 'best' number?

There are answers to these questions, but it would be a relief if the questions disappeared and, with them, the necessity of finding answers. If the only reason we have mailboxes and d>0 is to maximise concurrency, the question we should be asking ourselves is 'do they?' If not, we can cheerfully dispense with mailboxes and their associated complications. Perhaps their disadvantages outweigh their advantages? A rethink is indicated.

Let's make things simpler (always a good move) and consider a system with no mailboxes. If such a system satisfies more of our requirements than one with mailboxes, we'll take the former. Such d=0 systems are better known as *zero-slot mailbox, synchronising message passing, handshake,* or *blocking send.* This plethora of names, bequeathed by various researchers, indicates that this communications model will reward closer scrutiny.

3.2 Blocking Send

In *blocking send*, the sender and receiver are directly coupled. The first one ready to communicate waits for the other; only when both are ready is a message transmitted. The sending and receiving of a message is simultaneous, performed by a joint action distinct from the independent actions of sender and receiver. These joint communication actions link the two processes in time and, by doing so, they synchronise sender and receiver – hence the alternative name of *synchronising message passing*.

Blocking send has the following attributes:
- sender and receiver wait until the other is ready to participate;
- sender and receiver communicate by a single indivisible (atomic) action – a handshake.

With a direct, memory-less link, the model's behaviour is simplicity itself. When ready to communicate, the sending process is delayed (blocked) until a corresponding receive is performed – the *blocking send* – and the receiver is blocked until the message is sent. In this way, only one message is ever outstanding, and the need for mailboxes disappears – the *zero-slot mailbox*. The message is part of the sender until the message is sent, when it becomes part of the receiver.

The *synchronising message passing* discipline is supported by an underlying *handshake* between sender and receiver. Processes wanting to communicate enter a synchronisation phase in which they wait until the other is ready. Once synchronised, the participants pass their message. A final disengagement phase 'signs off' the communication, returning sender and receiver to concurrent operation. During communication, the users have the same concept of time; they are synchronised. An example of such a handshake, here sender-initiated, is:

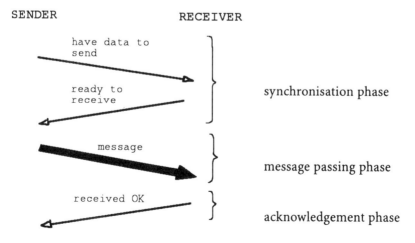

We can describe this handshake as a schematic:

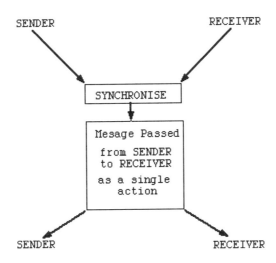

Two concurrent systems synchronise, then pass a message, before resuming independent concurrent operation. Unlike the asynchronous models, here the act of message passing tells each user the state of the other; the model supports a two-way flow of state information as well as a one-way flow of data. By sacrificing the requirement that message passing must be done with minimal effect upon the concurrency of its users, we have defined a simple model which directly represents synchronisation between processes.

The closer an algebra is to a class of systems, the the more appropriate it will be as a tool for capturing their behaviours, asking questions about them, and understanding the answers. The more an algebra's basic elements directly model behaviours of a class of systems, the more appropriate the algebra is to that problem area; having the or and and operators in Boolean algebra makes it an appropriate logic model. Similarly, *blocking send*, by directly modelling synchronisation, suggests that an algebra which includes it will be useful when predicting the composite behaviour of communicating systems.

We've considered the concept of blocking send in the abstract. To see if it's the best model for our purposes, we will build a set of communication commands to help us determine if it is tractable and appropriate, before going on to test its generality.

Is Blocking Send Tractable?
An implementation of *blocking send* as statements in an algebra could include the sending action, coded as:

```
send message
```

and the action of waiting for a message as:

        `wait` *message*

To operate correctly these commands need to spell out who to send a particular message to and who to accept a particular message from; we need to add process identifiers to the `send` and `wait`. For example:

        `send` *message* `to` *process_name*

and symmetrically:

        `wait` *message* `from` *process_name*

The sender has to wait – is blocked – until it sends a message to a particular receiver, and the receiver process is blocked until a message comes from a particular sender. The communication is *deterministic*: i.e. we know beforehand which sender will communicate with which receiver. In certain cases we want to get away from such determinism. We may, for example, want a server to accept a request from any one of a defined set of potential clients, so we modify the general commands to:

        `send` *message* `to` *process_name*

for a sender; and asymmetrically for a receiver:

        `choice`

                `{wait` *message* `from` *process_names*`}`

The server can receive a message request from any client in the set of `process_names`. The server serves whichever client is ready first; the outcome is determined by the clients. If several clients are ready simultaneously, the successful one is chosen at random; the choice is *non-deterministic*, as no one knows beforehand which client is going to be successful.

A receiver may be interested only in the message and not where it comes from – when we hear someone shout 'FIRE' it's the message that concerns us, not who is shouting. In our context, the receiver could be a server whose clients require no response: for example, a print server accepts a file from a client without reporting back when it has printed. We can accommodate such cases by modifying the general commands to:

        `send` *message* `to` *process_name*
        `wait` *message*

As *blocking send* contains an implicit synchronisation, the message part is redundant. If we simply want to synchronise two processes we can use:

        `send` *any_message* `to` *process_name*
        `wait` *any_message* `from` *process_name*

as the message is ignored by both parties; we need send no message at all:

        `send to` *process_name*
        `wait from` *process_name*

And if it doesn't matter which of a set of senders a receiver synchronises with, we can use:

```
send any_message to process_name
choice
          {wait any_message from process_names}
```

The server waits at the choice statement, ready to accept a message from any one of the named set of clients; the first client successfully to synchronise with the server gets the service, while the clients which request an allocated server will have to wait until it becomes free again. If client requests are made simultaneously, one is chosen at random while the others are forced to wait.

To be successful, the process issuing all these commands has to identify its companion by a name, or a set of names. In real life, such knowledge is not always available, as companions may be part of an as yet undefined part of the system.

It would be simpler if we could design processes in isolation, designing the internals of each process, up to its interface with its environment, and then connecting them together.

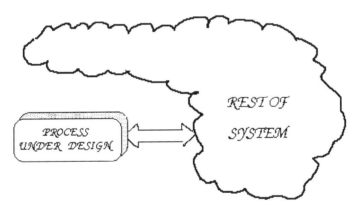

By making processes communicate over unidirectional channels and giving each channel a unique `channel_name`, we can use these channel names as aliases for process identifiers. Each process now only need be aware of these local channel names that define the process's interface to its environment, and not process identifiers.

A channel is a unique, point-to-point, unidirectional communication medium which faithfully delivers all messages in the order given.

For channel commands we simply replace the process names in our algebra with channel names. For example, the deterministic commands become:

> send *message* to *channel_name*

and

> wait *message* from *channel_name*

Once we have designed individual processes, how we connect them will define the behaviour of any resulting systems, and to connect processes we now only need to name and rename channels. This concept of channels connecting sequential systems forms the basis of CSP, the Communicating Sequential Processes algebra of Professor Tony Hoare [Hoa85], which can be used formally to determine the behaviour of a composite from a knowledge of its parts and their connection topology.

An alternative to naming channels is to give names to the ports at each end of a channel. Ports come in two flavours, those offering to send, denoted port_name!, and those offering to receive, denoted port_name?. Ports with the same name and different directionals are considered connected, as in:

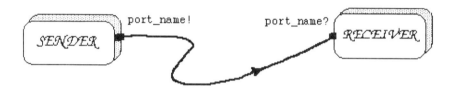

Again we can use port naming to define a connection topology, and hence the behaviour of any composite system. Ports are used by Professor Robin Milner as the basis of his Calculus of Communicating Systems (CCS) [Mil89], and his Synchronous Calculus of Communicating Systems (SCCS) [Mil82a] which we will meet later in this book. As a communications model, port naming delivers the same benefits as the channel model, plus a few added advantages which will be explored later.

We now return to the mainstream question: 'Is *blocking send* the best choice of communications model?'. We will have advanced our cause if we can establish that *blocking send* is *appropriate* – i.e. close to the problem domain of concurrent systems, so that it can as simply as possible capture as many of the problems implicit in concurrency without introducing any of its own.

Is Blocking Send Appropriate?

Formal proofs will have to wait. In the meantime we appeal to the reader's reason by considering blocking send in the contexts of mutual exclusion, synchronisation, deadlock, liveness and fairness.

Mutual Exclusion

For this illustration we'll use a server process, acting as resource manager of an unshareable resource, allocating the resource to one client at a time and reassigning the resource only after it is released by the previous user.

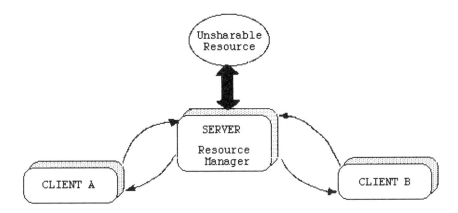

Clients include code, which emulate critical section entry and exit guards, to get and release the resource:

```
send get to MANAGER          /* input guard */
          :
          :
     {use the resource}      /* critical section */
          :
          :
send release to MANAGER      /* output guard */
```

The resource server includes code to manage the resource:

```
choice
    wait get from clientA
        wait release from clientA
    wait get from clientB
        wait release from clientB
```

When the server is ready to allocate the resource, it waits for client get requests at the choice statement. The first client to invoke a get synchronises with the server, and that client send and the server's wait instructions execute simultaneously. The client then moves on to use the resource and the server waits for that client's release message. When the client has finished with the resource, it sends a release to synchronise with the wait of the server and the resource is freed to serve other clients. The client continues with client-specific things and the server returns to wait at its choice statement for further clients.

More than one client simultaneously requesting the resource results in several `send` statements trying to synchronise with the server. As only one of the statements that `choice` ranges over can be executed in each pass, one (randomly chosen) synchronisation succeeds. Rejected clients are made to wait, as are clients who request an already allocated resource. By giving the resource to only one client at a time the server preserves mutual exclusion.

Synchronisation

Blocking send is synchronisation. Its first act is to synchronise sender and receiver. To synchronise processes, all we need is a blocking send with no message part. One process issues a

> `send to process_name`

the other a

> `wait from process_name`

Deadlock, Livelock and Fairness

As the emergent properties of a concurrent system depend upon the actions of its subcomponents, no communication method can, by itself, prevent the occurrence of deadlock or livelock, or ensure fairness. However, the blocking send model is powerful enough, and simple enough, to be incorporated into formal algebras which can determine if systems have these properties. We will see in a later chapter how one such algebra, SCCS, can be used to check if designs are free of deadlock and livelock. Proving they are fair is an order of difficulty greater, and here our algebras are more circumspect.

So we've now shown that blocking send is more appropriate for our task than the other models. We've also promised that its simplicity makes it tractable, which later on we will prove. What we haven't shown is that blocking send is general and unconstraining – if a design calls for messages to overtake, be overwritten, not read and so on, can we model them? Such doubts would be removed it we could show that blocking send is a primitive which can be used to model any other communications system of interest, including those that do not constrain the concurrency of their users.

Is Blocking Send General?

The act of communication can be generalised to a server which passes message between processes.

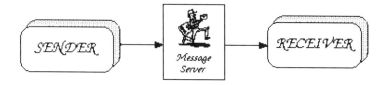

For blocking send, this server is a simple piece of wire. For other models we can think of it as a process which oversees the reception, transmission and storage of messages. A sender never talks directly to a receiver but always via the message server, users communicating with the server by blocking send.

Sender and receiver operate asynchronously, only synchronising with the server when they need to pass messages. The sender, by executing a `send`, synchronises with and outputs a message to the server; the receiver, by executing a `receive`, synchronises with and gets a message from the sever. The server stores any outstanding messages.

To accept the blocking send model as general, we must be able to use it, together with the chosen design framework, to describe all message servers of interest. We can square this circle if, by making its buffers intelligent, we promote message servers to concurrent systems in their own right. We do this by associating with each buffer a processes which oversees the reading, writing and storage of messages. By this means the design of all concurrent systems, including their internal communications, can be addressed within the same framework.

To convince ourselves that the blocking send model can model all communication systems of interest, we show that blocking send is a primitive which can model the realisable subset of the original contenders for the title of Best Communications Model. In later sections we'll prove this more formally, but here we'll appeal to the reader's reason using pictures alone.

examples
Particular examples include:
    a. Single buffer communication between sender and receiver.

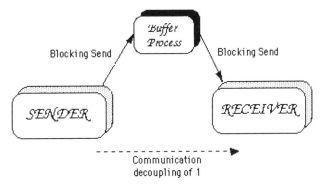

Two blocking sends and an intermediary one-message buffer models a communications system with $d=1$. The order of packets received is the same as that sent:

```
receive_order = send_order.
```

b. Piped communication.

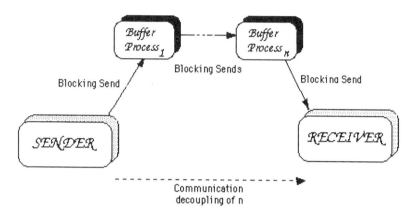

Decoupling factor $d=n$. Ordering is preserved:

```
receive_order = send_order.
```

c. Model (b) can be expanded into a multi-pipe model with a decoupling factor $d=n \times m$. Packets are not necessarily received in the order sent:

```
receive_order≠send_order.
```

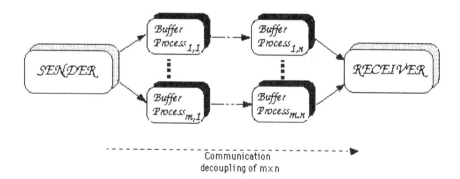

d. Communication between sender and receiver using shared variables to hold messages. Messages can be overwritten and read more than once. Ordering is not preserved.

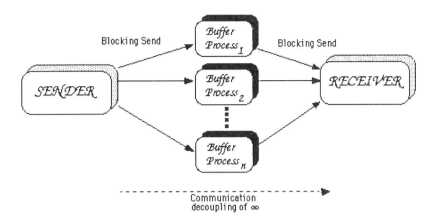

Blocking send is the most primitive of our models – it can model the others, but not vice versa.

Do We Have a Reasonable Model?

Our sacrifice of the requirement for the best message passing model to be one which initially doesn't constrain its users' concurrency has enabled us to define a simple blocking send model which was more appropriate, represented process synchronisation and tackled mutual exclusion. Being a simple model, blocking send was realisable and safe. And, while the basic blocking send model did constrain concurrency, it was also capable of describing higher-order models which do not; thus, in a circuitous way, blocking send also satisfied the general and unconstraining requirements.

While we tried to convince ourselves that blocking send would prove tractable, our arguments were hardly formal. This was unfortunate, as blocking send forms the basis of many process algebras, most noteworthy of which are CSP and CCS. Professor Hoare [Hoa85] introduced CSP, the calculus of communicating processes, later animated as the programming language OCCAM-1 [Inm84]; for a text relating the first version of OCCAM to concurrency, see [Dow88], and for later versions try [Bur88] or [Gal90]. But, as the main part of this book concerns Professor Milner's SCCS, we'll use his associated Calculus of Communicating Systems to illustrate the link between blocking send and an asynchronous algebra. With a few extensions, such as actions which have directionality, CCS turns out to be astonishingly similar to the algebra we developed in the 'Scene Set' chapter, Chapter 1.

3.3 CCS (Calculus of Communicating Systems)

This is not intended to be a full, nor a formal, treatment of the Calculus of Communicating Systems, CCS, introduced by Professor Milner [Mil89], but rather an illustration of algebras based on message passing as applied to concurrent systems.

Actions

There are three kinds of action in CCS, two types of external actions,[†] observable by other agents, used to interact with other agents, namely:
- `input actions`, written a?
- `output actions`, written a!

and internal actions, hidden from other agents, namely:
- `silent (unobservable) actions`, written τ.

Sequential execution of processes

This is modelled using action prefixing:

$$P \overset{\text{def}}{=} a?.b!.P$$

Agent P engages in action a?, then b!, before behaving as agent P again. P is both sequential and recursive. Action a? prefixes agent b!.P and action b! prefixes agent P.

An action which must be executed before an agent can become another agent is called a *guard* of that second agent: for example, action a is the guard of agent Q in a.Q; and any agent with a guard is said to be guarded: for example Q is guarded by a in a.Q.

Concurrent execution of processes

P and Q operating concurrently is represented as:

$$P \mid Q$$

Choice between processes

An agent which offers choice between two agents P and Q is:

$$P + Q$$

This agent will behave either like P or like Q, but not both. The choice of which is selected *may* be influenced by communication with an environment:
- If the environment attempts to exercise control through a communication which is a guard of Q but not of P, then Q will be chosen deterministically. For example, a?.P + b?.Q in the environment b!.R.
- If the environment communicates via an action which is a guard of P but not of Q, then P is chosen deterministically. For example, a?.P + b?.Q in the environment a!.R.
- If the guards of P and Q are the same and the environment communicates by

---

† Conventionally in CCS, action names associated with output are over-barred, for example ā, and input actions are not, for example a. For improved clarity, I use here what is becoming the *de facto* notation (borrowed from Hoare's CSP [Hoa85]) of a postfix ? for input and a postfix ! for output, as this reinforces the point that all visible actions in CCS are offers of communication.

this action, then the choice is non-deterministic; the choice between P and Q is made at random. For example, a?.P + a?.Q in the environment a!.R.

To denote the application of the binary choice operator + to more than two agents we use the operator with subscripting. For example:

$$\sum_{0 \leq i \leq 2} P_i \text{ means the same as } P_0 + P_1 + P_2$$

Communication

Taking existing agents and, by making them communicate, creating other agents, is the basis of CCS. Individual agents proceed independently and asynchronously when not communicating. To cooperate, they communicate over named ports using the blocking send protocol where ports support a point-to-point and unidirectional communication, one port supporting one communication at a time. While the behaviour of blocking send hasn't changed, CCS has its own syntax for it.

- By executing port!message, the sending agent A sends message over output port chan. The sending agent is blocked until message is received.
- By executing port?v, the receiving agent B receives message over input port chan, binding it to local variable v. The receiving agent is blocked until message is sent.

The first participant to arrive for a communication waits for the other. The sending agent is delayed (blocked) until the message is received, and the receiver is blocked until the message is sent.

Example of Message Passing

Consider a sequential agent BUFFER which can accept an integer over port in, bind it to variable x, and subsequently output it to port out.

In CCS, this is written:

$$\text{BUFFER} \stackrel{\text{def}}{=} \text{in?x.out!x.BUFFER}$$

We can build a larger system, 2BUFFER, which acts as a double buffer by taking two copies of agent BUFFER, and, by a renaming of ports, connect them together.

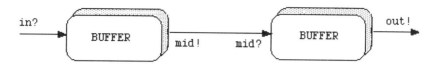

This is written as:

$$2\text{BUFFER} \overset{\text{def}}{=} (\text{in?x.mid!x.BUFFER})$$
$$|\ (\text{mid?y.out!y.BUFFER})$$

where | represents concurrent composition.

2BUFFER, formed from two BUFFER agents operating concurrently, acts as a pipeline and can input new data at the same time as it outputs data previously input.

■

But how can we use message passing and CCS to address the problems of concurrency? We'll start with the simplest problem, that of synchronisation. Message passing in CCS is synchronisation – agents passing messages always first synchronise. Agents that want only to synchronise have no need to include a message in the communication; instead of synchronisation and message passing, a?x and a?v, we only need the synchronisation bits a? and a!.

Example of Synchronisation

Consider a client agent, CLIENT, using a binary SEMAPHORE to ensure the correct use of some unshareable resource or other. The semaphore acts as the input and exit guards, by the usual wait and signal calls, for the critical time the client uses the resource. For the system to work, CLIENT and SEMAPHORE have to interact, and to interact they have to synchronise. For a binary semaphore, client/semaphore synchronisation is the only interaction required.

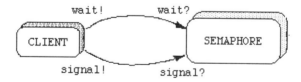

A client is:

$$\text{CLIENT} \overset{\text{def}}{=} noncritical.\text{wait!}.critical$$
$$.\text{signal!}.noncritical.\text{CLIENT}$$

in which semaphore commands bracket the critical section from the noncritical ones. The binary semaphore, where the state is S_n, is the semaphore with value n.

$$\text{SEMAPHORE} = S_1$$

$$S_1 \overset{\text{def}}{=} \texttt{wait?.}S_0$$
$$S_0 \overset{\text{def}}{=} \texttt{signal?.}S_1$$

(Note: a general semaphore would be something like:

$$\text{SEMAPHORE} = S_{max}$$
$$S_{max} \overset{\text{def}}{=} \texttt{wait?.}S_{max-1}$$
$$S_n \overset{\text{def}}{=} (\texttt{wait?.}S_{n-1}) + (\texttt{signal?.}S_{n+1}); \text{ for } 0<n<max$$
$$S_0 \overset{\text{def}}{=} \texttt{signal?.}S_1)$$

In this example, not only do we model synchronisation between agents, but, by showing that message passing can emulate semaphores, we've also shown that message passing can inherit all semaphore-based solutions to concurrency problems.

Examples of Mutual Exclusion

a) Consider the case of two clients competing to use an unshareable resource handled by a server.

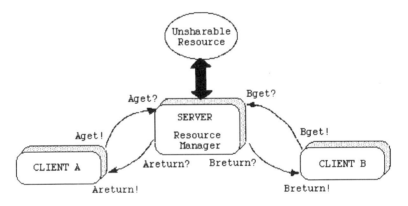

The clients use their `get` and `return` ports to negotiate with the server to acquire and release the resource.

$$\texttt{CLIENT}_A \overset{\text{def}}{=} \textit{doAthings}.\texttt{Aget!}.\textit{AUseResource}$$
$$.\texttt{Areturn!}.\texttt{CLIENT}_A$$
$$\texttt{CLIENT}_B \overset{\text{def}}{=} \textit{doBthings}.\texttt{Bget!}.\textit{BUseResource}$$
$$.\texttt{Breturn!}.\texttt{CLIENT}_B$$

The critical sections, clients using the resource, are the UseResource bits, the entry and exit guards, and the synchronisation actions `get!ANY` and `return!ANY`. The server's behaviour is captured in:

$$\texttt{SERVER} \overset{\text{def}}{=} (\texttt{Aget?.Areturn?.SERVER})$$
$$+ (\texttt{Bget?.Breturn?.SERVER})$$

Initially SERVER is ready to accept a request from either client. After one client successfully synchronises with the server, it waits for that client to release the resource before it can once again behave as a server.

b)   Mutual exclusion generalised to n clients competing for one unshareable resource handled by a server.

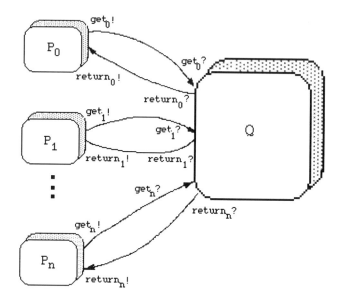

This is written as:

$$P_i \overset{\text{def}}{=} doP_i things.\texttt{get}_i!.P_iUseResource.\texttt{return}_i!.P_i$$

Client P_i, after doing private things, synchronises with server Q over port $\texttt{get}_i$; a successful synchronisation tells the client it has acquired control of the resource. After using the resource the client returns control of the resource using port $\texttt{return}_i$ before behaving as P_i again.

Agent Q synchronises with one client P_i over port $\texttt{get}_i$, assigns control of the resource to this successful client, then waits for the client to return control using port $\texttt{return}_i$. The server then behaves as Q again, ready to serve more clients:

$$Q \overset{\text{def}}{=} \sum_{0 \leq i \leq n}(\texttt{get}_i?.\texttt{return}_i!.Q)$$

where $\sum_{0 \leq i \leq n}$ represents Q ready to accept one communication over the set of $\texttt{in}_i$, $0 \leq i \leq n$, ports.

As regards the other problems intrinsic to concurrent systems, no communication method can prevent the occurrence of deadlock or livelock, or ensure fairness. It's too low a level to do that. But with process algebras we can determine if systems have these properties or not. We'll return to this later.

So message passing is simple, easy to comprehend and fits nicely with the human domain client–server model of concurrent and distributed systems. It can address mutual exclusion and synchronisation, and it forms the basis of a formal design method (CCS) in which properties such as deadlock and liveness can be identified. What more could one ask? Well, one thing that would be useful would be a higher-level construct, closer to the human domain, as the closer it is the easier and less error-prone will be any design. To represent things like client–server interactions we need a higher-level construct to model two-way transactions between client and server than we do for the one-way flow provided by blocking send. While we want formal tools to design such client–server systems, we want them to be extensions of, and firmly founded in, existing concepts. This is the concern of the next section.

3.4 Rendezvous

A concurrent system can be viewed as a set of processes running on a number of interconnected implementation vehicles. An example would be networked processors in which server processes, which manage resources, are used by client processes; servers can be clients of other servers, and so on. In such client–server systems we may require a two-way flow of data; the client tells a particular server which service it requires, the server carries out the specified task and informs the client when it's done.

To simplify the design of a sequential system we split a program into smaller, reusable bits called procedures; each procedure performs some specific task modified by data passed by its caller. Communication between system and individual procedure is by a two-way flow of data, input and output, all handled by a procedure-calling mechanism. The success of this simple concept encourages us to seek a similar model, a *remote procedure call*, for two-way data flow in concurrent systems. This is like the procedure call for sequential systems, except the procedure is called by one process and executed by another, a client process passing a procedure name and parameters specifying the service required to a server process, the server executing the named procedure and parameters to perform the service, before finally returning a result to the client.

But where should we start? Well, in blocking send we have a communications mechanism which supports a one-way flow of data between processes. Perhaps if we use it 'back-to back' it could provide a two-way flow which, with encouragement, could be extended to a full remote procedure-calling mechanism?

Take two CCS agents P and Q

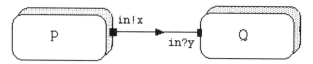

$$P \overset{\mathrm{def}}{=} \mathtt{in!x.P'}$$
$$Q \overset{\mathrm{def}}{=} \mathtt{in?y.Q'(y)}$$

wanting to communicate. P outputs data as message x over port in, then behaves as agent P'. Q inputs a message over port in, binds the data in the message to local variable y, then behaves as Q'(y). Operating P and Q concurrently,

$$P\,|\,Q = (\mathtt{in!x.P'})\,|\,(\mathtt{in?y.Q'(y)})$$

The communication between processes results in data from one being assigned to a variable in another. Here the x of P is assigned to the y of Q, resulting in y := x.

We have a *remote assignment* between processes.

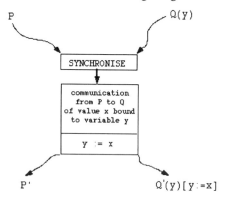

By combining two unidirectional remote assignments we can create one bidirectional remote procedure call, as in: A client synchronises with a server and uses remote assignments to specify which procedure, with which parameters, it wants the server to perform; the server executes the named procedure with the given parameters, and returns any results by another remote assignment.

The input, request, and output, accept, engage in a two-way communication, termed a *rendezvous* where rendezvous are:

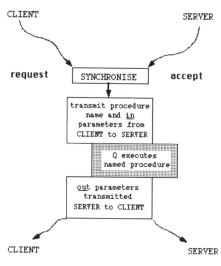

- symmetrical: whichever arrives first (client or server) waits for the other;

- singular: only one transaction is performed in each rendezvous;
- mutual: after a synchronisation between participants there can be a two-way exchange of data;
- safe: the complete rendezvous is indivisible, performed under mutual exclusion.

A rendezvous is an indivisible act involving synchronisation between two processes and a two-way exchange of information, request to server and reply to client, in comparison with a blocking send which is an indivisible act involving the synchronisation of two processes and a one-way exchange of information. To be safe, each rendezvous has to be indivisible. Once a client process is participating in a rendezvous, it is forced to wait until the rendezvous completes. Any system supporting rendezvous has to operate as advertised; the run-time systems of languages incorporating rendezvous must ensure the complete atomicity of the transaction.

To build a rendezvous using blocking sends we simply add `out` ports to our previous example, P taking the role of client and Q that of server:

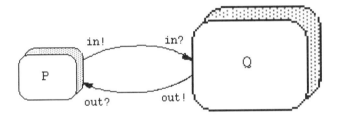

And by defining the two agents as

P $\stackrel{\text{def}}{=}$ *doPthings*.in!proc_name.in!parameters.out?result.P
Q $\stackrel{\text{def}}{=}$ in?proc.in?x.y:=proc(x).out!y:Q

Client P, after doing some private things, synchronises with server Q and passes a procedure name and parameters over `in` and then waits for a response from Q. Server Q accepts both procedure name and parameters over `in`, assigns the procedure name to variable `proc` and the parameters to x. It then executes the procedure and returns the results to the client over `out`, before being ready to act as a server again. The waiting client P receives the result and proceeds on its way.

We've now got our two way flow of information and data, but beware, all is not as it seems. For a rendezvous to be indivisible, the accept and reply statements in our CCS model must also be atomic.

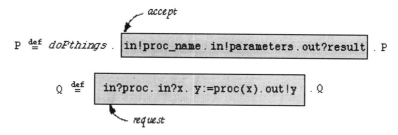

Unfortunately, only individual action are atomic in CCS; extending atomicity over a sequence of actions has to be ensured by other means.

OCCAM incorporates blocking send, while Ada incorporates rendezvous. However, this is a text on formal design and not on Ada. Ada, which started life as a formally defined language, as an innocent child was patted on its head, given a packed lunch and sent out into the world. But, once in the hands of programmers, it was led astray and away from the formal path. If you want to read more on rendezvous, Ada and the like, see [BuWe90, GeGe88].

3.5 Conclusion

Thinking of concurrent systems as communicating sequential processes has allowed us to outline a simple design framework which, for the first time, promises formal proofs that a design satisfies its specification. Central to the success of this framework was deciding how the sequential bits should communicate. Directly coupling processes and orchestrating communications with blocking sends was shown to be a simple and practical solution. Their very simplicity helped show that blocking send contributed to the tractability of the design framework and, as a component of that framework, could be used to model the types of communication needed for our designs.

The proud boast that communicating sequential processes was the basis of a formal design framework was supported by the use of the process algebra CCS to investigate problems implicit in the design of concurrent systems. The next chapter, devoted to SCCS, will deliver on that boast and show methods which are both usable and rigorous.

4. Synchronous Calculus of Communicating Systems

Introduction

Asynchronous algebras such as CCS can help us to understand and correctly design concurrent systems by viewing them as collections of concurrently operating sequential subsystems; the behaviour of each subsystem is defined in terms of sequences of atomic actions, internal ones to progress a subsystem's local task and external ones for subsystem interaction. By formalising such a view, the calculus predicts the behaviour of a composition from knowledge of the behaviours of its individual parts. But, being an asynchronous algebra, it is constrained to express system behaviours in terms of sequences of actions, independent of time, and cannot directly address real-time systems. On the other hand, synchronous algebras (which, by definition, contain a concept of global time – events only happen when some omnipresent clock ticks) define not only the order of actions but also when they occur.

Requirements of a Real-Time Calculus

We model real-time systems as concurrent systems plus time. They are concurrent as, by definition, even the simplest real-time system interacts with an environment, and the requirements for such a calculus are an extension of those for concurrency. Such a real-time calculus must:

- include a notation describing the behavioural properties of timed concurrent systems and how subsystems can be composed into larger systems;
- contain a calculus over that notation by which properties of a system can be deduced from those of its parts and their compositional structure;
- contain a concept of equivalence, enabling the behaviour of two designs to be equated or a design to be shown to meet a specification;
- address the effect of time naturally, and as easily as possible, without having to 'step outside' the calculus;
- support the derivation of new operators and notations tailored to particular problem domains;

- support abstraction, where the designer decides which details of the artifact modelled are sufficiently important to keep and which can be ignored;
- support encapsulation, where details relevant to a particular phase of the design can be kept local to that phase and hidden when the design moves on;
- reflect and predict the behaviours of real-time systems, for which the algebra must have a valid interpretation from, and eventually back to, real-world objects;
- be easy to implement. We use the calculus primarily as a design tool, but eventually our designs must be realised as objects in the real world – designs will be easier to implement if the components of the calculus are themselves easy to implement.

Quite a list, to which we can add that it would also be convenient if the calculus were simple, easy to learn and contained representations to aid in its understanding so that a designer could use the calculus without having fully to understanding the underlying mathematics.

SCCS Review

SCCS, the Synchronous Calculus of Communicating Systems, is the work of professor Robin Milner. It was first introduced in [Mil82a], with a revised version published in [Mil83]. The majority of this chapter, an adaptation of Milner's work, gives an SCCS view of the world. In brief:

- In SCCS, a system consists of a set of independent *agents* which perform *atomic actions* and engage in *synchronous communication* with other agents.
- Issues of synchrony and timing are addressed from within the calculus – time is assumed to proceed monotonically in fixed, discrete (but unspecified) units.
- SCCS describes systems in terms of their observable actions – the behaviour seen by an external observer.
- SCCS defines observational equivalence and its properties – two systems are considered identical if an observer cannot tell them apart by experimentation and observation alone.
- The algebra includes several different system models:
  - a spatial layout showing how agents can communicate;
  - a descriptive algebra to represent agent behaviours with respect to time;
  - a notation capturing the history of agent actions.

We have already met an asynchronous algebra, CCS, which supports an interpretation to and from most of the above constructs and which can be used to predict the behaviour of concurrent systems, that is, with the exception of real-time modelling – a property which most real-world systems exhibit. A real-time algebra must be as expressive as any other process algebra when dealing with sequential and concurrent systems, but it must also capture issues of synchrony and timing. And, we don't want this extra facility 'bolted on at the end'; it must be an integral part of the algebra. As such, a real-time algebra must contain a notion of time at the most primitive levels of actions and interactions – events happening not only in certain orders but at a specific times. We will approach this sideways by considering how time can be introduced into agent interactions, and to do this we re-evaluate the blocking send model which underpins so many asynchronous algebras.

Synchronisation Model

Any algebra attempting to model the real world must model cooperation between agents, which requires that it first models agent synchronisation. In most asynchronous algebras, this is modelled by blocking send.

Blocking Send

Discipline:
- Sending and receiving together constitute a single indivisible (atomic) action.
- Either sender or receiver waits if the other is not ready to communicate.

A slight change, actually to a simpler model, gives us the temporal behaviour required in a real time calculus:

The SCCS Model

Discipline:
- Sending and receiving together constitute a single indivisible (atomic) action.
- Neither sender nor receiver ever waits for the other.

In this model, the sender and receiver agents synchronise if they are ready *at the same time*. If they're not both ready at the same time, synchronisation fails.

As with trapeze artists, it's all down to cooperation and timing. If the catcher's not at the correct place at the correct time, the whole system fails.

The SCCS synchronisation model passes no data but exchanges information about the states of the participants – both agents are ready for this interaction. One can imagine a sender trying to synchronise by pulsing a connecting wire, and only if the receiver is ready to receive such a pulse at that same moment will synchronisation succeed.

In CSP, blocking send is extended to model the world as sequential processes, agents, communicating via channels – unidirectional, uniquely named, one-to-one communications media, the assignment of names to channels defining the connection topology of agents. SCCS renounces channels and opts for the more primitive ports which support one-to-one synchronisation between agents; this time the naming of ports establishes the connection topology of agents in a system. Ports come in two flavours: those supporting an output; and those supporting an input. In [Mil83] the port names associated with the former are over-barred: for example $\bar{a}$ represents an output port and a an input port. For improved clarity we borrow the CSP notation of a postfix ? for input and a ! for output, which reinforces the notion that all visible actions in SCCS are offers of synchronisation.

The SCCS model of a one-to-one synchronisation between agents SENDER and RECEIVER over ports a? and a! is

While channels must be uniquely named, ports need not be so, and we can represent agent SENDER simultaneously synchronising with agents RECEIVER$_1$ and RECEIVER$_2$ by multiple naming of ports.

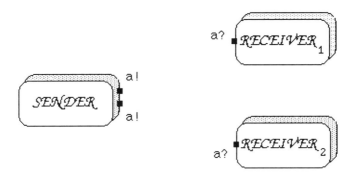

Based on the concept that one port can only support one synchronisation at any time, the connection topologies can be:

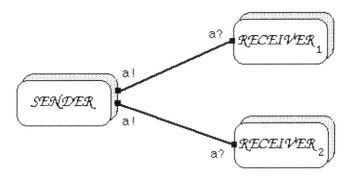

or, equally:

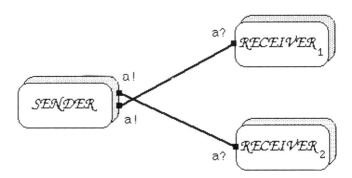

Whichever one we employ is irrelevant; in both cases SENDER simultaneously synchronises with RECEIVER$_1$ and RECEIVER$_2$, and both cases can be captured by combining the two active output ports a! and a! as a!×a!

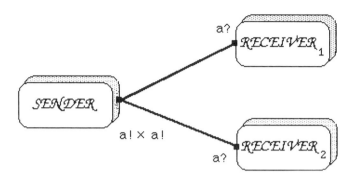

Ports and channels have advantages in common – individual agents do not have to identify (name) the companion agent they wish to communicate with; they need only name the port (channel) by which communication is to be made, the resultant static interconnection topology ensuring the rest. However, the more primitive method of naming the ends of the communications medium, rather than the medium itself, has added advantages. An example: the non-uniqueness of port names means it's legal to have the following:

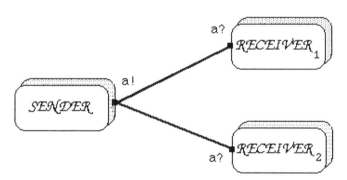

Interactions in SCCS are unidirectional and one-to-one; a port can support only one communication at once, and in the above diagram it cannot be determined which of the two possible communications will succeed – it cannot be known beforehand whether SENDER will synchronise with RECEIVER$_1$ or RECEIVER$_2$. Channels, with their unique naming, cannot so naturally model such non-determinancy.

4.1 An Overview of SCCS

It is easier to understand concurrent systems if we consider them as a composition of simpler subsystems operating in unison. The design of concurrent systems devolves to the design of simpler sub-systems and their interactions. Such agents are defined by expressions consisting of operators ranging over timed sequences of actions. Agent names label a state of an object – for example $P\xrightarrow{a}Q$ denotes the transition of agent P to an agent Q by action a, where P and Q label two states of the system modelled. If only one action is needed to move P to Q, Q is called the *successor* of P.

Both actions and agent names are within the gift of the designer, who chooses action names to identify system actions and agent names to identify system states. One behaviour is linked to one name: each action name describes a unique event in a system and each agent name describes a unique state, where the state defines the behaviour of an object in terms of action sequences. It is illegal to have the same action or agent name for different behaviours. Agent and action names are either general: a, b, c ... for actions, P, Q, R ... for agents; or, when there is no ambiguity, agents can take the name of the entity they model – for example tick, request, in, ... etc. for actions and CLOCK, SCHEDULER, ... etc. for agents. External actions can support interactions with other agents; such interactions are atomic and take the name of their associated port – for example, a! is an output action over port a, a? is an input action over port a, and so on. The set of actions a particular agent can engage in is termed its sort, and the designer, by identifying and naming actions appearing in an agent's sort, makes a conscious decision as to which actions are important and which can be ignored. The designer names the external, observable actions, but all internal, unobservable actions are named in the calculus as 1 actions, sometimes referred to as ticks.

But agent names are a more general concept than simply state labels. They also label the behaviour of a system in that state. As with action names, agent names enable a designer to abstract from a system behaviour by only giving names to significant states. For example, the agent CLOCK, which ticks every ten seconds, can count minutes by naming the states separated by six tick! actions as agents ZERO, ONE, TWO, ...

ZERO $\xrightarrow{tick!}$ $\xrightarrow{tick!}$ $\xrightarrow{tick!}$ $\xrightarrow{tick!}$ $\xrightarrow{tick!}$ $\xrightarrow{tick!}$ **ONE** $\xrightarrow{tick!}$ $\xrightarrow{tick!}$ $\xrightarrow{tick!}$ $\xrightarrow{tick!}$ $\xrightarrow{tick!}$ $\xrightarrow{tick!}$ **TWO** $\xrightarrow{tick!}$ $\xrightarrow{tick!}$ $\xrightarrow{tick!}$ ...

Agent names name the future behaviour of a system in a very natural way. The above agent ZERO engages in six tick! actions before behaving as agent ONE.

Time is modelled in SCCS as particulate and advancing in integer time. Actions occur synchronously under the direction of a centralised clock, for example $P\xrightarrow{a?}\xrightarrow{1}\xrightarrow{b!}S$ describes the evolution of P into S by engaging in a sequence of atomic actions, first an observable interaction a? at time t, an internal action 1 at time t+1, followed by b! at time t+2. P is seen as the agent which engages in the sequence of actions <a?, 1, b!> before behaving as S. As agent S can be reached from agent P by engaging in one or more actions; agent S is called a *derivative* of P. More precisely, if a successor is reached by an α action it is termed an α-derivative – for example Q is an α-derivative of P in $P \xrightarrow{\alpha} Q$.

We say an agent is active if it engages in an action in every time slot. An inactive agent, with no actions to engage in, is denoted by the special agent $\mathbb{0}$. For example, the agent representing the minute counter which stops (breaks) after four tick! actions is

$$\text{START} \xrightarrow{\text{tick!}} \xrightarrow{\text{tick!}} \xrightarrow{\text{tick!}} \xrightarrow{\text{tick!}} \mathbb{0}$$

To picture an agent we use, well... a picture, called an *agent diagram*, which associates agent and port names with the interactions offered. For example, the behaviour described by agent $P \xrightarrow{a?} \xrightarrow{b!} \xrightarrow{c?} \mathbb{0}$ of sort {a?,b!,c?} can be pictured as:

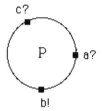

Agent diagrams abstract from time. They denote agent actions, not their order of occurrence, and as such cannot be used to denote behaviours. The set of states and transitions which plot the evolution of P into S by $P \xrightarrow{a?} \xrightarrow{b!} \xrightarrow{c?} S$ can be pictured as a timed-labelled transition system, also known as a *derivation tree*

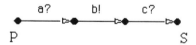

If required, we can name intermediate states of an evolution with agent names, as in

$$P \xrightarrow{a?} Q \xrightarrow{b!} R \xrightarrow{c?} S$$

While pictures are useful to describe, compose and predict the behaviours of real-time systems, we need an algebra containing a set of operators over a notation for actions and agents. Agent and action combinators of our algebra include

Over actions:
:, *prefix*, models sequentially. By prefixing existing agents with

actions a designer creates new agents. Expression Q $\stackrel{\text{def}}{=}$ a! : P defines a new agent Q which engages in action a! before behaving as existing agent P.

Over agents and actions:

×, *product*, models concurrency. The designer can take agents, P and Q, and combine them to form a new agent, P×Q, whose actions are those of agent P engaged in concurrently with those of agent Q. For example, agent ((a!:P) × (b?:Q)) has a first action a!×b? which represents actions a! and b? engaged in concurrently.

Over agents:

+, *summation*, models a choice of behaviours; a new agent, P+Q offers a choice of behaving like P or Q.

^A, *restriction*, operator supports abstraction and encapsulation. A designer can restrict an existing agent P to actions in set A denoted by P^A. It's corollaries are *pruning*, \A, which removes the actions in set A, and *synchronisation pruning*, \\A,which removes actions, both sending and receiving, in the set A.

As prefix both creates action sequences and denotes time instances, we use it to model timed sequential systems. Sequential agent P can be defined ($\stackrel{\text{def}}{=}$) in terms of the prefix operator as P $\stackrel{\text{def}}{=}$ a?:b!:c?:⓪, read as agent P engaging sequentially, at successive ticks of the global clock, in actions a?, b! and c?, before behaving as the inaction agent ⓪.

Most useful objects in the real world do not 'execute once', then die. After engaging in a sequence of actions, they're ready to engage in the same sequence again: they're recursive. For example, CLOCK, which continually offers to communicate the sound of a tick whether or not there is anyone to hear it, is described by

$$\text{CLOCK} \stackrel{\text{def}}{=} \text{tick!} : \text{CLOCK}$$

Any recursive system containing two or more states can be succinctly defined in mutually recursive terms. For example, the agent OLDCLOCK, after engaging in action tick!, behaves as MIDCLOCK which can engage in action tock!, which returns the system to the initial state OLDCLOCK.

$$\text{OLDCLOCK} \stackrel{\text{def}}{=} \text{tick!} : \text{MIDCLOCK}$$
$$\text{MIDCLOCK} \stackrel{\text{def}}{=} \text{tock!} : \text{OLDCLOCK}$$

Its behaviour can be described in terms of a transition system:

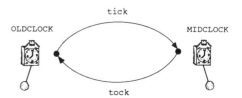

and its actions in terms of an agent diagram:

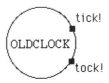

Each agent in a system has knowledge of its own identity; however, from its perspective other agents are just 'things' that collectively form an environment for it to interact with. For example, agent P in the following diagram interacts with other agents in its environment to form a complete system:

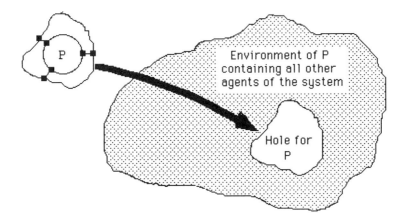

Agents interact by synchronising and, to synchronise, they must simultaneously engage in complementary input and output actions. Consider modelling a particular SENDER communicating with a particular RECEIVER, where:

the sender does something internal, sends, does something else internal, then dies;

the receiver does something internal, receives, does something else internal, then dies.

The system requires that the sender operates concurrently with the receiver:

$$\text{SENDER} \times \text{RECEIVER}$$

Time in SCCS is global; the time at which actions occur is dictated by one central clock and the first actions of all subsystems occur in the same initial time slot. To synchronise, SENDER and RECEIVER must simultaneously engage in complementary sending and receiving actions in the same time slot. Possible behaviours include: a successful synchronisation, where the sending action a! and the receiving action a? do occur in the same time slot.

$$\text{SENDER} \overset{\text{def}}{=} 1:a!:1:1:\mathbb{0}$$
$$\text{RECEIVER} \overset{\text{def}}{=} 1:a?:1:1:\mathbb{0}$$

and SENDER × RECEIVER = 1×1:a!×a?:1×1:1×1:0×0

If there are no other agents to confuse matters the sender and receiver synchronise in the second time slot, as captured in the a!×a? action.

and an unsuccessful synchronisation, where the sending action and the receiving action do not occur in the same time slot.

$$\text{SENDER} \stackrel{\text{def}}{=} 1:1:a!:1:0$$
$$\text{RECEIVER} \stackrel{\text{def}}{=} 1:a?:1:1:0$$
$$\text{and SENDER} \times \text{RECEIVER} = 1×1:1×a?:1×a!:1×1:0×0$$

We can investigate the more interesting case of successful synchronisation by considering the simple case of a sender and a receiver which continually attempt to synchronise over port a

$$\text{SENDER} \stackrel{\text{def}}{=} a!:\text{SENDER}$$
$$\text{RECEIVER} \stackrel{\text{def}}{=} a?:\text{RECEIVER}$$

and their composite is:

$$\text{SYS} \stackrel{\text{def}}{=} \text{SENDER} \times \text{RECEIVER}$$
$$= (a!:\text{SENDER}) \times (a?:\text{RECEIVER})$$
$$= a!×a?:(\text{SENDER} \times \text{RECEIVER})$$
$$= a!×a?:\text{SYS}$$

With the simultaneous, concurrent, occurrence of a! and a? represented by a?×a! it looks as if the sender will always synchronise with the receiver. In pictures:

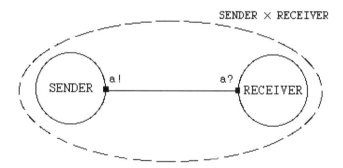

But all is not as it appears: the behaviour of SYS actually depends upon its environment. From the description of SENDER all it wishes to do is to communicate over port a; it is promiscuous, willing to synchronise with any agent executing a receive action on an a port at the same time. In other words, the sender offers to communicate with any agent in its environment, with the receiver, or with any other agent. Similarly, RECEIVER, offering to communicate with any agent in its environment, is just as indiscriminate.

We can picture SYS as:

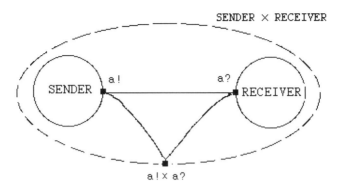

The a! and a? can synchronise sender and receiver, but equally well they can interact with any environment in which SYS finds itself. To indicated this, port a?xa! is placed on the surface of SYS.

Consider a second sender and receiver, ready to synchronise at the same time as the original pair, using the same actions. The agents could synchronise as:

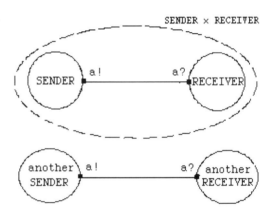

or, equally as probably, as:

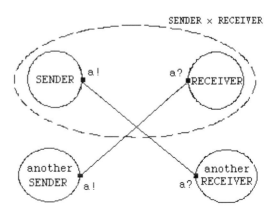

Both cases can be represented by:

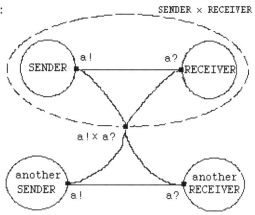

We can only ensure that the original sender and receiver synchronise with each other by making a! and a? private, preventing interaction with the environment. For this encapsulation we use the pruning operation \\A, where A is the set of interaction names to be pruned (and only on interactions – as, by definition the internal action 1 can never be a member of set A, 1∉A, pruning has no effect on the 1 action). Encapsulating SYS to SYS\\A where A={a} we get:

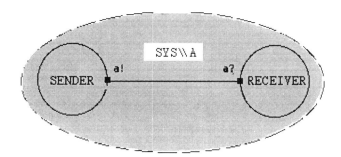

The pruning operator acts as a 'cloak of invisibility'. All actions appearing in the pruning alphabet A disappear from an expression when it is placed within the brackets of an ( )\\A operator. Actions not in A remain to interact with an environment.

Pruning does not only hide actions, it removes them, which means pruning can kill agents; for, in a synchronous universe, to show it's alive each active agent must engage in an action at each tick of the clock. Only inaction, ⓪, does nothing. So removal of actions can make an active agent inactive: for example, if Q $\stackrel{\text{def}}{=}$ d!:a?:b?:Q then Q\\{d} = ⓪, Q\\{a} = d!:⓪ and so on. Only when no actions are pruned does an agent remain intact, as in Q\\{c} = d!:a?:b?:Q\\{c}.

But it is more common to use pruning to encapsulate agents, ensuring successful synchronisation when we want it. For example, encapsulating SYS in ()\\a excludes environmental competition for synchronisation, the only behaviour remaining is for the sender's a! output action to synchronise with the receiver's a? input action:

$$\text{SYS}\backslash\backslash\text{A} \stackrel{\text{def}}{=} (\text{SENDER} \times \text{RECEIVER})\backslash\backslash\{a\}$$
$$= (a!:\text{SENDER} \times a?:\text{RECEIVER})\backslash\backslash\{a\}$$
$$= (a!\times a?:\text{SENDER} \times \text{RECEIVER})\backslash\backslash\{a\}$$

As one input action can only synchronise with one output action, the sender and receiver actions are mutually satisfied and cannot support further interactions. The inability to support interaction is noted by replacing the a?×a! with the 1 action:

$$= (1:\text{SENDER} \times \text{RECEIVER})\backslash\backslash\{a\}$$

Now, by definition an environment cannot interfere with internal actions and, as pruning is defined in terms of named observable interactions, \\{a} cannot effect the 1 action, and a tick is allowed to 'step outside' the scope of the encapsulating \\{a}

$$= 1:(\text{SYS})\backslash\backslash\{a\}$$

Thus the pruning operator, by making private certain interactions, can hide part of a design from the rest of the system:

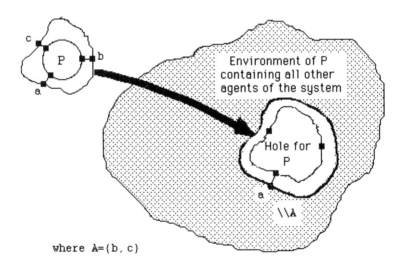

where A={b, c}

We can consider that the brackets of a ( ) \\A pruning operation form a 'hole' into which one can slot an expression. The hole prevents those actions in the expression also named in A being seen or interacted with by the outside world.

An agent which can no longer interact with its environment is a closed system. Closed systems are final systems – they don't interact with anything else. For example:

$$SYS\backslash\backslash A = 1 : SYS\backslash\backslash A$$

is closed.

We will run through an example which will illuminate the concepts of observation, interaction and pruning. The only way of observing $P \stackrel{\text{def}}{=} c? : a! : b! : \mathbb{O}$ is to experiment with it via its ports, where the observer is a further agent $Q \stackrel{\text{def}}{=} d! : a? : b? : \mathbb{O}$ operating concurrently with P:

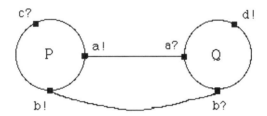

The combination $P \times Q$ represents a new machine $S \stackrel{\text{def}}{=} P \times Q$.

The concept of observation is a powerful one. It closely maps systems in which no distinction is made between who is the observer and who the observed. In our example, process P can be thought of as placed in environment Q, to be observed by Q; or, with equal validity, process Q can be placed in environment P, to be observed by P.

The new machine S, composed of P and Q, can itself be placed in a further environment. A choice can be made by the ruler of the universe containing P, Q and S as to which further observations are allowed. Such encapsulation enables a system designer to abstract a design 'in-flight'. Interactions $a!$, $a?$ and $b!$, $b?$ representing mutual observations between P and Q can be internalised (pruned) and the unsatisfied interactions ($c?$, $d!$) can remain available to cooperate with further observations.

The unrestricted Agent S_{visible} in which both potentially internally satisfied and unsatisfied observations remain visible is defined by

$$S_{\text{visible}} \stackrel{\text{def}}{=} (P \times Q) \backslash\!\backslash \{\} = c?\times d!:a!\times a?:b!\times b?:\mathbb{0}$$

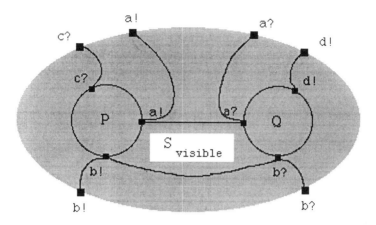

Agent S_{hide}, in which all mutual observations are internalised, pruned, is defined by

$$S_{\text{hide}} \stackrel{\text{def}}{=} (P \times Q) \backslash\!\backslash \{a,b\} = c?\times d!:1:1:\mathbb{0}$$

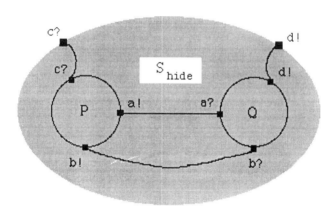

Adding extra agents, V and W, which synchronise with the c? and d! actions of S_{hide}, we get:

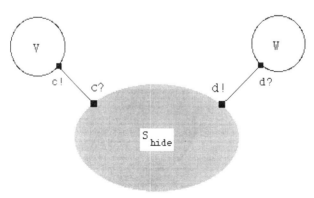

Pruning these synchronisations we get the closed system:
$$(S_{hide} \times V \times W) \backslash\backslash \{c, d\}$$
which, no longer capable of interacting with any environment, represents a final and complete system. In this example synchronisations were successful. What happens if they are not?

Agents containing actions which fail to synchronise and are pruned will result in an inactive agent $\mathbb{0}$, for example:

$$SYS \stackrel{def}{=} (1:a!:1:P \times a?:1:Q) \backslash\backslash \{a\}$$
$$= (1 \times a?:a! \times 1:1 \times 1:P \times Q) \backslash\backslash \{a\}$$
$$= (a?:a!:1:P \times Q) \backslash\backslash \{a\}$$
$$= \mathbb{0} \backslash\backslash \{a\}$$

Pruning an unsuccessful communication results in inaction. Why should this be so? All active agents are under an obligation to engage in an action in every time slot. Here the only actions the agent can engage in are $a?$ and $a!$, but the designer, by choosing to apply $\{a\}$ as a pruning set, has explicitly prevented these actions, and the agent is in a quandary. It cannot satisfy both requirements, and its only way out is to die by becoming the inaction agent $\mathbb{0}$. This it does at the first point of conflict, in the first time slot.

We will now consider what the 1 action, denoting successful synchronisation in agents like $SYS \backslash\backslash A = 1:SYS \backslash\backslash A$, actually means. The 1 action is internal to an agent. By definition it cannot be observed by any agents in its environment – for example, agent $P \stackrel{def}{=} 1:Q$ is seen to engage in nothing visible but progresses from P to Q in one time instance. The internal 1 action acts as a passage-of-time marker, indicating that the agent is actively engaged in some internal business. Any number of 1 actions, engaged in concurrently, are observed as one internal action $1 \times 1 = 1$, and any number of unobservable 1 actions can be engaged in concurrently with an observed action without changing the observation, $1 \times a? = a?$. The 1 action thus denotes either: an internally satisfied synchronisation; a private action progressing an agent without needing interaction with its environment; or an idle action where the agent is 'twiddling its thumbs', waiting for its environment to be ready to interact. As far as the environment is concerned, such actions are indistinguishable. For example, the agent $SYS \backslash\backslash A = 1:SYS \backslash\backslash A$ is continually doing something internal as far its environment is concerned : it could be idling, doing something useful, or communicating internally; the environment cannot tell the difference.

Internal actions, by allowing agents to wait, give SCCS the power to model systems with asynchronous-like behaviours. Such waiting is denoted by the delay operator δ, where $\delta P = P + 1:\delta P$. In $P \stackrel{def}{=} \delta a?:Q$ agent P can idle indefinitely, engaging in 1 actions, but, at any time it can engage in $a?$, after which it will behave as agent Q. The behaviour of P can be read as a delay for an indefinite period before engaging in $a?$, after which it will behave as agent Q.

We read the synchronous expression P $\overset{\text{def}}{=}$ a?:b!:c?:Q as: agent P will engage in a? in its first time slot, b! in its second, c? in its third, and then it will behave as agent Q. Put simply, this synchronous expression can be transformed into an asynchronous one by adding delay operators as P $\overset{\text{def}}{=}$ δa?:δb!:δc?:Q which reads: P will at some future time engage in a?, followed some time later by b!, followed some time later by c?, after which it will behave as agent Q. This P $\overset{\text{def}}{=}$ δa?:δb!:δc?:Q agent apes the behaviour of the asynchronous P $\overset{\text{def}}{=}$ a?.b!.c?.Q in CCS.

Consider adding the delay operator to our communications model by redefining the previously synchronous agents

$$\text{SENDER} \overset{\text{def}}{=} \text{a!:SENDER}$$
$$\text{RECEIVER} \overset{\text{def}}{=} \text{a?:RECEIVER}$$

as asynchronous ones:

$$\text{SENDER} \overset{\text{def}}{=} \text{δa!:SENDER}$$
$$\text{RECEIVER} \overset{\text{def}}{=} \text{δa?:RECEIVER}$$

The sender and the receiver wait to synchronise, the δ being read as a delay.

System ASYS composed of sender and receiver pruned by A={a} is redefined by:

$$\text{ASYS\\A} \overset{\text{def}}{=} (\text{δa!×δa?:SENDER×RECEIVER)\\A}$$
$$= (\text{δ1:ASYS)\\A}$$
$$= \text{δ1:ASYS\\A}$$

The sender and receiver behave asynchronously. Whichever arrives first waits until the other is ready before they synchronise. The delay before synchronisation by any number of 'ticks' is captured in the δ1 action. But is not this the definition of the blocking send protocol, a foundation of other asynchronous algebras?

As SCCS can model both asynchronous actions and the blocking send protocol, we are led to the (perhaps counter-intuitive) proposition that synchronous process algebras are more primitive than asynchronous ones. We will investigate that later on. For the present we will see how we can elevate plain-vanilla SCCS to a higher level.

To design realistic real-time systems one needs to capture interactions of a higher order than basic synchronisation. Specifically, we need to extend SCCS to model data passing – we will see, later, that such actions are generalisations of synchronisation. For the moment, however, let us consider them as objects in their own right. Action a!x outputs the contents of a data variable x over port a, and a?v inputs data over port a and binds it to local variable v. Consider agent P sending the contents of a data variable x over port a by a!x and turning into P′ by doing so; and agent Q(v), by action a?v, receiving data over port a,

---

† The subsequent behaviour of parameter passing agents depends upon the values they input, their previous behaviour generating the values they output.

binding it to its local data variable v, and turning into Q' (v) [data:=v].† We can define these agents algebraically as:

$$P \overset{\text{def}}{=} a!x:P'$$
$$Q(v) \overset{\text{def}}{=} a?v:Q'(v)$$

where Q(x) is agent Q which can communicate the value of local variable x to or from other agents. As in any parameter passing systems to operate correctly the types of data and variable must be the same.

When operating concurrently, the agents communicate, passing data item x:

$$PxQ(v) = (a!x:P')x(a?v:Q'(v))$$
$$= 1:P'xQ'(v)[v:=x]$$

Q(v)[v:=x] binds all variables named v in Q(v) to the value x. The internal action 1 indicates that the synchronisation has occurred and data passed; shown as a diagram:

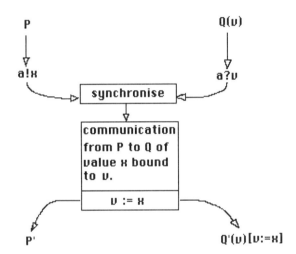

---

† As in CCS, a synchronisation is data passing without data; only the parts of the protocol dealing with synchronisation remain. For example, agent P $\overset{\text{def}}{=}$ a!:P' synchronising with Q $\overset{\text{def}}{=}$ a?:Q' is:

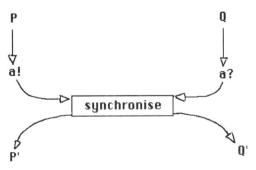

SCCS data communications[†] can be viewed as remote assignments binding data x, from the sender, to variable v, in the receiver, and we can extend this concept to model the interface parts of remote procedure calling. Consider a system in which an agent SQUARE acts as a remote procedure delivering the square of natural numbers passed to it, and an agent CALLER avails itself of this offered service. The server SQUARE, when passed a value x from the set of integers $\mathbb{N}$, x∈$\mathbb{N}$, binds it to its local variable v, returns v^2, its square, and is ready to serve another client:

$$\text{SQUARE}(v) \stackrel{\text{def}}{=} \text{in?v:out!}(v^2):\text{SQUARE}(v)$$

A client requests the squaring service by passing to it an x:

$$\text{CALLER}(x,y) \stackrel{\text{def}}{=} \text{in!x:out?y:CALLER}(x,y)$$

and their composition as:

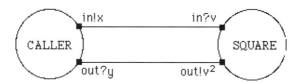

which will behave as:

```
CALLER(x,y) × SQUARE(v)
    = (in!x:out?y:CALLER(x,y) × in?v:out!(v²):SQUARE(v))
    = 1:(out?y:CALLER(x,y) × (out!(v²):SQUARE(v))[v:=x])
    = 1:(out?y:CALLER(x,y) × out!(x²):SQUARE(v)[v:=x])
    = 1:1:(CALLER(x,y)[y:=x²] × SQUARE(v)[v:=x])
```

Actually, this description CALLER(x,y) interacting with SQUARE(v) is wrong – or at any rate only partially true. We know from our previous encounter with the pruning operator that non-encapsulated agent actions can freely interact with agents in their environment, and we have not specified the environment of agent CALLER(x,y) × SQUARE(v). The only way that we can predict the behaviour of CALLER(x,y) × SQUARE(v) in any environment is to ensure that it never interacts with any environment by encapsulating its in and out actions:

$$(\text{CALLER}(x,y) \times \text{SQUARE}(v))\backslash\backslash A, \text{ where } A = \{\text{in,out}\}$$

We now obtain the predicatable client–server behaviour of CALLER(x,y) × SQUARE(v)

$$(\text{CALLER}(x,y) \times \text{SQUARE}(v))\backslash\backslash A$$
$$= 1:1:(\text{CALLER}(x,y)[y:=x^2] \times \text{SQUARE}(v)[v:=x])\backslash\backslash A$$

In this case, agents CALLER(x,y) and SQUARE(v) only have in and out actions, and pruning them closes the system.

If the caller sends a particular value of x of 2, then:

```
(CALLER(x,y)  ×  SQUARE(v))\\A
  = (in!2:out?y:CALLER(2,y)  ×  in?v:out!(v²):SQUARE(v))\\A
  = 1:(out?y:CALLER(2,y)  ×  (out!(v²):SQUARE(v))[v:=2])\\A
  = 1:(out?y:CALLER(2,y)  ×  out!(4):SQUARE(v)[v:=2])\\A
  = 1:1:(CALLER(2,y)[y:=4]  ×  SQUARE(v)[v:=2])\\A
```

A x value of 3 would have resulted in:

```
  = 1:1:(CALLER(3,y)[y:=9]  ×  SQUARE(v)[v:=3])\\A
```

We will now consider how a further operation, changing action names, can support system design. Take, for example, the design of a one-slot data buffer which can wait to accept, and hold, one data item at a time, delivering it on request:

$$\text{ONESLOT(v)} \overset{\text{def}}{=} \delta\text{bufin?v:FULLONESLOT(v)}$$
$$\text{FULLONESLOT(v)} \overset{\text{def}}{=} \delta\text{bufout!v:ONESLOT(v)}$$

To correctly connect this buffer into our existing sender–receiver system, we rename the actions of the existing SENDER $\overset{\text{def}}{=}$ δa!:SENDER and RECEIVER $\overset{\text{def}}{=}$ δa?:RECEIVER as:

$$\text{SENDER(x)} = \delta\text{bufin!x:SENDER(x)}$$
$$\text{RECEIVER(y)} = \delta\text{bufout?y:RECEIVER(y)}$$

correctly connect this buffer into our existing sender–receiver system, we rename the actions of the existing SENDER and RECEIVER, so that SENDER becomes $\overset{\text{def}}{=}$ δa!:SENDER and RECEIVER becomes $\overset{\text{def}}{=}$ δa?:RECEIVER, as:

$$\text{SENDER(x)} = \delta\text{bufin!x:SENDER(x)}$$
$$\text{RECEIVER(y)} = \delta\text{bufout?y:RECEIVER(y)}$$

to give:

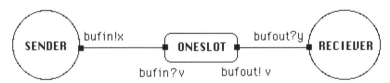

$$\text{SYS}\backslash\backslash\text{A} = (\text{SENDER(v)} \times \text{ONESLOT(v)} \times \text{RECEIVER(y)})\backslash\backslash\text{A}$$

pruning the data communications between sender, buffer and receiver by making the set of pruning actions A = {bufin,bufout}.

In SCCS, names are in the designers gift. They can be given some mnemonic connection with events modelled in the real world. The intrinsic behaviour of an agent is not captured in action names; rather it is the pattern of actions which is significant. An agent which engages in two different output actions before repeating has the same behaviour as – is indistinguishable from – any other agent which engages in two dissimilar output actions before repeating. So, changing action names does not change the behaviour of an agent but creates another agent with the same behaviour as the original. In the above example, we changed the action names of SENDER and RECEIVER and created new agents with the same behaviour as the originals but which could connect to the buffer ONESLOT.

Formally we change action names by using a *morphism function* which maps actions to others in the same set. For example, $\phi : a \rightarrow b$ represents morphism function ϕ, which, when applied to an agent, $P[\phi]$, changes all actions in P, named a to b.[†] The morphism function gives us the ability, during a design, to take copies of existing agents and connect them in a meaningful way while preserving their original behaviours. Once a system has been designed and shown to meet stated requirements, if the same behaviour is required again it can be copied by renaming and reused without further proof of correctness. As an example, we will take the previously defined single-slot buffer of:

$$\text{ONESLOT}(v) \overset{\text{def}}{=} \delta\text{bufin}?v : \delta\text{bufout}!v : \text{ONESLOT}(v)$$

and, by applying appropriate morphism functions, $\phi : \text{bufout} \rightarrow \text{common}$ and $\psi : \text{bufin} \rightarrow \text{common}$, obtain two new agents with the same behaviour, defined by:

$$\text{ONESLOT1}(x)[\phi] = \delta\text{bufin}?x : \delta\text{common}!x : \text{ONESLOT1}(x)[\phi]$$
$$\text{ONESLOT2}(y)[\psi] = \delta\text{common}?y : \delta\text{bufout}!y : \text{ONESLOT2}(y)[\psi]$$

which, when combined, models a two-slot buffer agent:

$$\text{TWOSLOT}(x,y) \overset{\text{def}}{=} (\text{ONESLOT1}(x)[\phi] \times \text{ONESLOT2}(y)[\psi]) \backslash\!\backslash\{\text{common}\}$$

behaving as:

By encapsulating, and making local the common!x and common?y communications, TWOSLOT is seen as a data buffer waiting to accept, then hold, up to two data items which it can later deliver on request.

So far, SCCS has been shown to model sequential and concurrent systems. A third, and equally important, category contains systems which offer a choice of behaviours, for example a client choosing a particular service from a server. A system offering a choice of behaviours is modelled as an agent offering several possible interactions, and, by synchronising with only one of these offered interactions, an environment can choose one behaviour while rejecting the others. For

---

† Remember that direction postfixes, ! and ?, are not formally part of the action names and cannot be changed by a morphism: a! can be changed to b! but not to a? or b?.

example, if we build a xylophone with eight bars offering the basic musical scale doh, ray, me, fah, so, la, tee, doe, and if only one xylophone bar can be struck at once, the xylophone's behaviour can be described by agent XYLO which offers the choice of striking one of eight bars before behaving as XYLO again. Using the choice operator (+), XYLO is defined as:

$$\text{XYLO} \overset{\text{def}}{=} \text{doh!:XYLO} + \text{ray!:XYLO} + \text{me!:XYLO} + \text{fah!:XYLO}$$
$$+ \text{so!:XYLO} + \text{la!:XYLO} + \text{tee!:XYLO} + \text{doe!:XYLO}$$

and, in pictures:

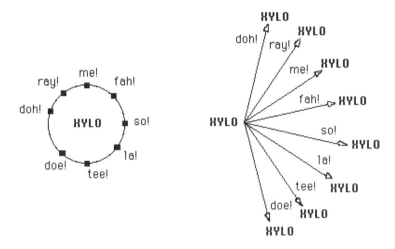

Now, consider a sequential player, capable of striking one note at a time, described by

$$\text{PLAYER} \overset{\text{def}}{=} \text{doh?:doh?:so?:so?:la?:tee?:doe?:la?:so?:PLAYER}$$

If we put the two together as XYLO × PLAYER, the actions which synchronise give:

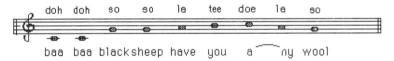

played over and over again!

By linking choice with parameter-passing we obtain predicated choice – the data communicated to an agent selects one behaviour from a set of behaviours. For example, if a data item of type Boolean received over port a of agent P by a?v as variable v can only be true or false we can use it to choose between two behaviours P' and P":

$$\text{P} \overset{\text{def}}{=} \text{a?v}: \underline{\text{if}}\ \text{v=true}\ \underline{\text{then}}\ \text{P}'\ \underline{\text{else}}\ \text{P}''$$

which can be generalised to:

$$\underline{\text{if}}\ \textit{Predicate}\ \underline{\text{then}}\ \text{P}'\ \underline{\text{else}}\ \text{P}''$$

where *Predicate* is a function returning value `true` or `false` depending upon the current values of agent variables at its point of evaluation.

Given that SCCS can model such *if...then...else* clauses, it can also model the *while...do...od*, *case...esac* clauses found in many sequential computer programs.

For an example of predicated choice we return to the client-server model. Consider a system in which a service manager offers clients two dissimilar servers, SERVER1 and SERVER2. First we defining a general server SERVER which commits the single service it controls by accepting an incoming `requestit?` from a client and responds with an outgoing `grantit!`. A server is uncommitted when it receives a `returnit?`:

$$\text{SERVER} \overset{\text{def}}{=} \delta\text{requestit?:grantit!:COMMITTED}$$
$$\text{COMMITTED} \overset{\text{def}}{=} \delta\text{returnit?:SERVER}$$

The two servers, having similar behaviours, are generated by appropriate morphisms from the general server:

$$\text{SERVER1} = \delta\text{request1?:grant1!:COMMITTED1}$$
$$\text{COMMITTED1} = \delta\text{return1?:SERVER1}$$
$$\text{SERVER2} = \delta\text{request2?:grant2!:COMMITTED2}$$
$$\text{COMMITTED2} = \delta\text{return2?:SERVER2}$$

and combined as:

$$\text{SERVERS} \overset{\text{def}}{=} \text{SERVER1} \times \text{SERVER2}$$

A manager oversees the allocation of servers to clients, committing only one server at a time. For $x \in \{1,2\}$ server x is committed to a client when the manager accepts a `req?x` and responds with a `grant?x`. For example, MAN-1(x) indicates that server 1 is committed; server x is uncommitted when the manager accepts a `ret?x`:

$$\text{MANAGER(x)} \overset{\text{def}}{=} \delta\text{req?x:}\underline{\text{if}}\ x{=}1\ \underline{\text{then}}\ \text{request1!:grant1?:grant!x:MAN-1(x)}$$
$$\underline{\text{else}}\ \text{request2!:grant2?:grant!x:MAN-2(x)}$$
$$\text{MAN-1(x)} \overset{\text{def}}{=} \delta\text{ret?1:return1!:MANAGER(x)}$$
$$\text{MAN-2(x)} \overset{\text{def}}{=} \delta\text{ret?2:return2!:MANAGER(x)}$$

The complete system is defined, pruning the internal communications between manager and servers, as:

$$\text{SYS} \overset{\text{def}}{=} (\text{MANAGER(x)} \times \text{SERVERS}) \backslash\backslash A$$
$$\text{where } A = \{\text{request1, grant1, return1}\}$$
$$\cup\ \{\text{request2, grant2, return2}\}$$

The system can be pictured as:

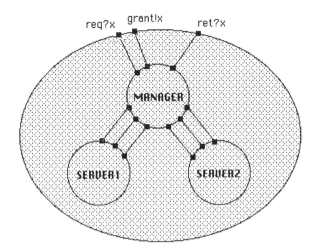

It is the clients of the environment that, via port `req?x`, determine which of the offered servers `SERVER1` or `SERVER2` is chosen. Action `request1?` gets `SERVER1`, `request2?` gets `SERVER2`. It's a *deterministic choice*, a recognisable behaviour of real-world systems.

Consider now a slight alteration, in which the services offered by `SERVER1` and `SERVER2` are identical. The two servers are still defined as:

$$
\begin{aligned}
\text{SERVER1} &= \delta \text{request1?:grant1!:COMMITTED1} \\
\text{COMMITTED1} &= \delta \text{return1?:SERVER1} \\
\text{SERVER2} &= \delta \text{request2?:grant2!: COMMITTED2} \\
\text{COMMITTED2} &= \delta \text{return2?:SERVER2}
\end{aligned}
$$

and:

$$\text{SERVERS} = \text{SERVER1} \times \text{SERVER2}$$

The manager oversees the allocation of the two servers as before, committing only one at any time; but now, as the servers offer the same service, the manager no longer needs to differentiate between them and client request parameters are redundant. But the manager still needs to inform a client which server has been assigned to it so that the client can use and return it correctly:

$$
\begin{aligned}
\text{MANAGER(x)} &\overset{\text{def}}{=} \delta \text{req?:(request1!:grant1?:grant!1:MAN-1(x)} \\
&\qquad + \text{request2!:grant2?:grant!2:MAN-2(x))} \\
\text{MAN-1(x)} &\overset{\text{def}}{=} \delta \text{ret?1:return1!:MANAGER(x)} \\
\text{MAN-2(x)} &\overset{\text{def}}{=} \delta \text{ret?2:return2!:MANAGER(x)}
\end{aligned}
$$

The system is composed as SYS $\overset{\text{def}}{=}$ (MANAGER(x) × SERVERS)\\A, and can be pictured as:

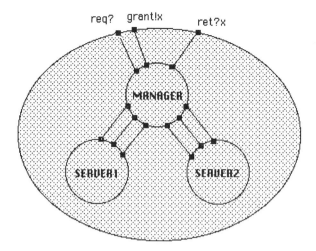

With both services available, which one is assigned is not determined by any client in the environment of SYS, but is arbitrarily determined by the manager. This is an example of *non-deterministic choice*, again a recognisable real-world situation.

We have now reached the stage where, based on the simple concept of ports and synchronous interactions, we can compose (sub-)agents into higher-order (sub-)agents using *prefix,* representing sequentiality, *product,* representing concurrency, and *summation,* representing both deterministic and non-deterministic choice. We also know how to adapt our designs 'in flight' using *pruning* to give a form of encapsulation and *morphism* to generate copies of agents. We also augmented these basic operations with data communications and predicated choice and went on to show that, using these basic tools, SCCS can address several low-complexity problems in both synchronous and asynchronous domains.

For a moment let us now pause and remember our greater goal – to design a solution to meet a given set of requirements. The logical way forward is to design and validate a set of simpler sub-solutions, and only when they are proved correct to construct a final solution from them. Using SCCS, we follow this general approach of progressing a design using simple agents (representing the basic elements of a solution) and, by combining them, construct new agents nearer and nearer to the solution, stopping only when the complete system is captured as one agent. Such a constructional approach must have a starting place. In SCCS, this starting place is the primitive SCCS agent which describes a real-world object in terms of a sequence of timed atomic actions moving the agent from one state to the next. The actions of these primitive agents are particles – truly atomic, indivisible into smaller actions or smaller units of time – that map directly to ports.

Following a constructional design strategy, we compose concurrent (sub-)agents using the product operator. However, the actions of any composed agent are no longer fully atomic: for example, the composition of P $\overset{\text{def}}{=}$ a!:b?:P' concurrently with Q $\overset{\text{def}}{=}$ c?:d!:Q' as P×Q gives:

$$P×Q = a!×c?:b?×d!:P'×Q'$$

The actions of the composite agents are themselves composite: for example, a!×c?; they are still atomic with respect to time, constrained to occur within one time slot, but, as they can be divided into smaller actions (a! and c? in this case), they are not fully atomic. As such, composites are generalisations of particles – a composite composed of one particle. We'll look closer at the implications of composite actions on SCCS later in the text. As a last stage before we do that, however, we will introduce some further notation.

While it is descriptive, the standard way of writing particles with explicit directionals, as in a! and a?, becomes a little cumbersome when used to express general behaviours. This is particularly true when presenting the laws of an algebra where all combinations of actions must be represented. For example, the synchronisation law:

$$(a!:P×a?:Q)\backslash\backslash\{a\} = (a?:P×a!:Q)\backslash\backslash\{a\} = 1:(P×Q)\backslash\backslash\{a\}$$

is a bit of a mouthful. We can use the fact that inputs are the obverse of outputs, and *vice versa*, as in $(a?)^{-1} = a!$ and $(a!)^{-1} = a?$, to simplify things, we can represent general actions by lower-case Greek characters α, β, χ ... and so on (with the exception of letters δ, ε, ϕ which have special meanings) and their obverses by α^{-1}, β^{-1}, χ^{-1} ... and so on. This enables us the write things more succinctly: for example, the above synchronisation law can now be written as:

$$(\alpha:P×\alpha^{-1}:Q)\backslash\backslash\{a\} = 1:(P×Q)\backslash\backslash\{a\}$$

That concludes this rather swift overview of SCCS. We have touched on nearly all the constructs we will meet in this chapter in an informal way, and in the sections that follow a more structured view of the basic components of SCCS precedes a more formal definition of the calculus.

4.2 Plain SCCS

4.2.1 Naming of Parts

This puts into some order, and sometimes expands upon, some of the basic concepts and terminology up to, but not including, message passing, and other, higher, concepts which we'll address later. Given its objective, there's going to be a some repetition here, and those reading the text linearly can perhaps skip over this section.

To perform a particular task the components of real-world systems must cooperate by passing information from one to another. Such co-operating (sub-)systems are modelled by SCCS using the concepts of ports, time, agents, actions, sorts and operators:[†]

- *Ports* are the observable parts of an agent which support either the sending or the receiving of information.
- *Time* is global and discrete. It advances monotonically in integer time t, t+1, t+2 ... etc.
- *Agents* are SCCS expressions which model the behaviour of objects in the real world.
- *Actions* are the atomic transitions of our models which move an agent from state to state.
- *Operators*, and the actions they act upon, define the behaviour of an agent. Operators enable us to represent sequences of actions, concurrent engagement of sequences, choices between sequences, hiding of actions from environments, and so on.

Ports

Ports are the visible interfaces by which agents interact. An agent's ports, named by the designer, are members of an infinite naming set, $\mathcal{N}$, with one unique name for each port. An agent with only port a is as pictured here. Agents can interact if they have ports with the same name, a, and one is an output, a!, the other an input, a?.

Time

Time in SCCS, as in the real world, proceeds monotonically the 'time arrow' points from the past, through 'now', to the future. Time is modelled as integer time composed of discrete and atomic *time slots* and delineated by clock ticks. Time slots are indivisible, atomic, with boundaries denoted by (:). One can imagine an SCCS expression being driven by a central clock which provides a sequence of identically sized time slots into which actions from a sequence are placed: for example, an agent engaging in the action tick! at times t, time t+1, ... and so on is represented by tick!:tick!:tick!: ...

Time is global and synchronised. Each agent in a composite system must engage in at least one action on the tick of a global clock, and the first actions of every agent occupy the same initial time slot. If at any point one (sub-)agent has no actions to perform, the system stops, and from that point on it is represented by ⓪, the inaction agent.

---

† Operator-related sections that follow contain: a formal *derivation* of the operator plus supporting *definitions*; a set of *propositions* relating to that operator, showing how it can be used algebraically, followed by an informal description of each proposition; an *interpretation* of what this abstract operator models in the real world; and finally one or more *examples* of the algebraic use of the operator. As these sections are never 'nested', their termination will be indicated by the ■ symbol.

Agents

Agents capture the important behaviours of real-world real-time systems as models in a formal algebra. An expression is a SCCS formula that relates an agent name on the left of a definition sign ($\stackrel{\mathrm{def}}{=}$) to a behaviour, a sequence of actions and (sub-)agents on the sign's right. For example, if an agent named P carries out action α its change of state into a new agent with a different behaviour is denoted by a name change to, say, Q, where P and Q are two of the possible states of the system. We say that *agent P may perform action α and in doing so becomes agent Q.* As an expression:

$$P \stackrel{\mathrm{def}}{=} \alpha:Q$$

where the class of agents is denoted by $\mathcal{P}$ and where P and Q are elements of $\mathcal{P}$

In P $\stackrel{\mathrm{def}}{=} \alpha:Q$, agent Q is called the *successor* of P, in this case an α-successor as it is reached by the single action α from P. Any expression which can be reached by any sequence of actions, including an empty one, is called a *derivative* of that first expression. In general, the set of derivatives of an expression, P, can be defined recursively as P plus the derivatives of its successors: for example, in P $\stackrel{\mathrm{def}}{=} \alpha:Q$, agents $\alpha:Q$ and Q are both derivatives of P, no action leads to $\alpha:Q$ and an α action leads to Q.

Agent constants whose behaviour relates to a particular object in the real world can be given appropriate names, such as CLOCK, CASHMACHINE, LIFT, SCHEDULER and so on. For example: CLOCK $\stackrel{\mathrm{def}}{=}$ tick!:CLOCK represents a CLOCK engages in the action tick in every time slot and acts as a real clock. Its ticks happen at set times, as against the very un-clocklike arbitrary times of a CSP or CCS version.

The capital letters P, Q, R, ... are used to denote agent variables. For example:

$$P \stackrel{\mathrm{def}}{=} \alpha:P$$

with P forever engaging in the α action. Instantiating the action name α by the particular tick! gives:

$$P \stackrel{\mathrm{def}}{=} \text{tick!}:P$$

To an observer the behaviours of P and CLOCK are indistinguishable. P represents the same behaviour as CLOCK, P = CLOCK.[†]

We have three representations of Agents. These are:

> *Agent Expressions* For example, P $\stackrel{\mathrm{def}}{=} \alpha:\beta:1:\mathbb{O}$, Q $\stackrel{\mathrm{def}}{=} \alpha:Q + \beta:P$, R $\stackrel{\mathrm{def}}{=}$
> P×Q, and so on relates user-given agent names to expressions specifying their behaviours.

[†] The definition symbol, $\stackrel{\mathrm{def}}{=}$, associates an agent name with an expression capturing how the designer thinks (rightly or wrongly) the system being modelled behaves. The symbol = is a mathematically provable relation between agent expressions. Expressions based on the latter can, in the form of laws, be applied to the former and preserve their meanings.

Derivation Trees These picture the individual actions needed to transform one agent into another. P $\stackrel{\text{def}}{=}$ α : β : 1 : ⓪ has derivation tree

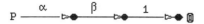

Agent diagrams These name agents and the ports by which they can can interact. Only an agent's observable actions, and not their order of execution, are described by such diagrams. P $\stackrel{\text{def}}{=}$ α : β : 1 : ⓪ has diagram

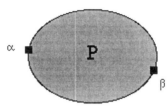

While the majority of agent names are designer-given, some behaviours are sufficiently important to have special names defined within the calculus.

definition *Inaction agent ⓪*

If at any time an agent cannot perform actions, either internal or external, it is transformed into the inaction agent ⓪. The inaction agent models the cessation of activity in a real-world artifact, either expected, in terms of correct termination, or unexpected, as in deadlock.

∎

definition *Idling agent 𝟙*

The agent that continually performs internal actions is denoted as the idling agent 𝟙. By representing an active agent which never interacts with its environment, 𝟙 represents local livelock.

∎

Actions

Ports and actions are closely related. Ports represent mechanisms by which agents can interact, their associated actions instigating such interactions. Actions model timed events moving a system between its states, and are either external and observable, supporting synchronisation, or internal, modelling the private actions of agents.

definition *Observable action names*

An agent's external actions support synchronisation; they can be observed by an environment and we name them to indicate how that agent interacts with its environment. The names themselves have no implicit meaning, they are simply labels for our convenience and they are in the gift of the designer. We tend to use single lower-case letter like a, b, c, ... to represent general activities and `tick`, `doh` etc. for actions related to real-world activities. The direction of the communications, input or output, is denoted by a special postfix, as follows:

- Output actions have a ! postfix, for example a!,
- Input actions have a ? postfix, for example a?.

Actions whose directionals are irrelevent are labelled α, β, χ, ... and so on.

■

Actions internal to an agent do not support communication, are not observable, and have no related port or user-given names. Such internal actions are private to an agent. They represent the activities of an agent which can proceed without the participation of other agents. All such internal actions are named the 1 action.

definition *The 1 action*

Internal actions are engaged in independently by an agent, and, to an observer, they simply mark the passage of time. Not supporting agent synchronisation, there is no need for them to be individually named; they are all called 1, and sometimes they are referred to as 'ticks'.

■

By informing an observer that an agent is doing something, but not what, 1 actions don't aid in the sight-reading of agent behaviours. To make things more clear we can relate specific internal actions with what those actions do. For example, instead of :
$$\text{SQUARE}(x) \stackrel{\text{def}}{=} \text{in?}x:1:\text{out?}x:\text{SQUARE}(x)$$
where the 1 represents the internal activity of actually squaring x, we could write:
$$\text{SQUARE}(x) \stackrel{\text{def}}{=} \text{in?}x:(x*x):\text{out?}x:\text{SQUARE}(x).$$

Named internal ations, like $(x*x)$, are there for our convenience, they are not formally part of the algebra in which they are treated as internal 1 actions.

It is to our advantage, when considering a general algebra over all agents, not to constrain ourselves to the actions of particular agents but, rather, to consider a larger set, *Act*, of which the actions of particular agents are a subset. Just as integer arithmetic ranges over an infinite set of integers, though when counting on our fingers we're not concerned about those over 10, similarly the set of actions of a particular agent is thought of as a subset of the actions of the system it is part of. But it also has to be a subset of the actions of systems we haven't yet thought of, which can best be accommodated by considering *Act*, the set containing all agent actions, as infinite.

definition *Act*

The infinite naming set of ports $\mathcal{N}$, with typical contents of a, b, c, ..., is used to generate a subset of action names Δ – the implication being that not all ports need associated actions, but all actions must have associated ports. From this set we create a subset of input actions $\Sigma_? = \{a? \mid a \in \Lambda\}$ with typical contents $a?$, $b?$, $c?$, and an equivalent set of output actions $\Sigma_!$ containing an output particle for every input particle, $\Sigma_! = \{a! \mid a? \in \Sigma_?\}$. The combination of these sets, $\Lambda = \Sigma_? \cup \Sigma_!$, represents the complete set. The set Act is freely generated on, and contains all products of, the particles in Λ; as such, any action in Act can be uniquely defined in terms of a finite product of particles as $\alpha = a?^{n1} \times a!^{m1} \times b?^{n2} \times \ldots$ for some integer $n1$, $m1$, $n2$ – the empty product identifying the 1 action. Elements of set Act thus include 1, $a?$, $a!\times b?$, $c?\times a?\times a?$, and so on.

■

Now that we've sorted out actions we'll look at something equally as necessary – the operators that scope over them.

Operators

The behaviour of an agent is defined by an expression containing sequences of timed actions within a framework of operators giving the relationships between these sequences. Action sequences and operators have interpretations into the real world – the sequences are sequential state machines and the operators over them represent sequences engaged in concurrently, one sequence engaged in in preference to another, and so on.

There are four fundamental operators in SCCS operating over agents and actions: *prefix*, *product*, *choice* and *restriction*. Here we represent them as both pictures and SCCS expressions.

Over actions

$:$, $prefix$ models sequentially over time:

Over agents and actions

$\times$, $product$ models concurrency:

where $P\times Q = (\alpha:P')\times(\beta:Q') = \alpha\times\beta:P'\times Q' = \alpha.\beta:P'\times Q'$
$= \alpha\beta:P'\times Q'$

Over agents

+, *summation* models a choice of behaviours:

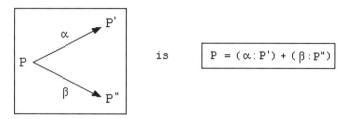

^A, *restriction* allows the designer to encapsulate agents, allowing only the actions in set A to be observed.

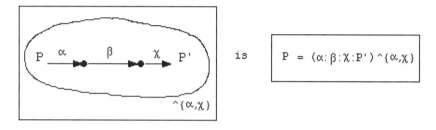

where $P^{\wedge}\{\alpha, \chi\} = (\alpha:\beta:\chi:P')^{\wedge}\{\alpha, \chi\} = \alpha:\mathbb{0}$

These operators, which form the lowest level of SCCS, mirror the most primitive actions of real-time systems and, as such, have a role akin to that of code at the assembler language level in computing systems. Once we accept that these operators truly model the real world, we can use them as axioms on which to build higher-level operators to design realistic real-world systems – but in a way which is more analogous to building macros in assembler than the dizzy heights of problem-specific high-level languages.

We need to prove that we can unambiguously use SCCS to model real-world behaviours (as we did in the overview section), and to do this we must formalise SCCS with a set of propositions over agents, actions and operators which mirror behaviours in the real world to the required level of detail. We need a complete algebra of propositions built on the simplest of foundations.

As the previous sections introduced the basic concepts of SCCS in an informal way, the next section more formally defines some of the concepts and notations to be used later on in the book.

4.2.2 Basic Operators and Propositions

4.2.2.1 Action Prefix

derivation *action prefix*
α: acts as an action prefix creating a new expression α : E by prefixing action α to an existing expression E. Expression α : E, where $\alpha \in Act$, has or admits just one action, as an axiom

$$\frac{\text{True}}{\alpha : E \xrightarrow{\alpha} E}$$

The combinator (:) in expressions such as $\alpha : \beta : \chi : E$ can be viewed as a sequential combinator delimiting the occurrence of actions. The (:) notation also divides time into individual slots. Both the time slots and the actions they contain are atomic with respect to time.

■

interpretation
Prefix models the sequential composition of synchronous events in the real world

■

definition *action prefix duplication*
(This is a shorthand for sequences composed of multiple copies of the same action.) The occurrence of a sequence of n identical actions is denoted by

$$(\alpha:)^n \text{ for } n \geq 1.$$

where $(\alpha:)^n = \alpha : \alpha : ... : \alpha$, $(\alpha:)$ repeated n times delimited internally by the action combinator. For example $(\alpha:)^3 : E$ is an expression which engages in three successive α actions before behaving as E.

$$(\alpha:)^3 : E \xrightarrow{\alpha} \xrightarrow{\alpha} \xrightarrow{\alpha} E$$

Similarly $\alpha : (\beta:)^4 : \chi : P = \alpha : \beta : \beta : \beta : \beta : \chi : P$

■

examples
a)   A bank cash machine's only action is to dispense ten-pound notes, before it breaks never to work again, and is defined by the expression:
BROKENCASHMACHINE $\stackrel{\text{def}}{=}$ £10! : ⓪

b)   A stamp machine, after accepting a coin, dispenses a stamp after a 3-second delay. Exhausted after achieving this feat, it never works again. With a clock period of 1s

$$\text{SLOW\_STAMP\_MACHINE} \stackrel{\text{def}}{=} \text{coin?}:1:1:1:\text{stamp!}:0$$
$$= \text{coin?}:(1:)^3:\text{stamp!}:0$$

c)   A revised stamp machine performs as its predecessor, slowly, but keeps on going. With a clock of 1Hz, a 1 second period

$$\text{SLOW\_STAMP\_MACHINE2} \stackrel{\text{def}}{=} \text{coin?}:(1:)^3:\text{stamp!}$$
$$:\text{SLOW\_STAMP\_MACHINE2}$$

d)   A customer offers a coin, then waits three seconds before accepting the proffered stamp

$$\text{SLOW\_CUSTOMER} \stackrel{\text{def}}{=} \text{coin!}:(1:)^3:\text{stamp?}$$
$$:\text{SLOW\_CUSTOMER}$$

e)   A tectonic plate is measured to move west at a rate equivalent to 1cm a century, causing an earthquake every 1000 years. With period of 100 years

$$\text{PLATE} \stackrel{\text{def}}{=} (\text{west\_1cm!}:)^9:\text{west\_1cm!}\times\text{quake!}:\text{PLATE}$$

f)   A dynamic memory chip is refreshed every 30 microseconds. The read and write, together making a refresh, take respectively 0.5µs and 1µs. With a period of 0.5µs

$$\text{MEMORY} \stackrel{\text{def}}{=} (1:)^{57}:\text{read?}:\text{write\_start!}$$
$$:\text{write\_end!}:\text{MEMORY}$$

g)   Given an unpopulated printed circuit board, an assembly robot populates the board with twenty memory chips, one per second, passing the board on to the next part of the process before accepting the next card. With a period of 1s

$$\text{ROBOT} \stackrel{\text{def}}{=} \text{accept\_card?}:(\text{add\_memory}:)^{20}$$
$$:\text{pass\_on\_card!}:\text{ROBOT}$$

Each internal add_memory action of the robot is operationally equivalent to a 1 action

h)   By design, the machine code instructions of most computers are atomic: once started, they cannot be interrupted by other instructions. In simpler microprocessors, these instructions take the same time, number of clock cycles, to execute. A sequence of single instructions moves the program from one state to the next. A simple example uses an accumulator to add two numbers from memory locations first and second, stores the result at location ans, then ends, uses instructions

```
lda   #first        ; load the accumulator with the contents
                    ; of location first
adda  #second       ; add to the accumulator the contents of
                    ; location second
```

```
sta    #ans              ; store the contents of the accumulator at
                         ; location ans
```

Each instruction takes a fixed time, and we can represent the above program as

PROG $\stackrel{\text{def}}{=}$ lda_#first!:adda_#second!:sta_#ans!:⓪

where the models clock period is related to the system clock speed.

i)   A traffic signal displays green for 30 seconds, red and amber for 5, and red for 20, before finally returning to green. With a clock speed of 1Hz

TRAFFIC_LIGHT $\stackrel{\text{def}}{=}$ green_on!:X
   X $\stackrel{\text{def}}{=}$ green_on!:(1:)^{29}
            :green_off!×red_on!×amber_on!:(1:)^4
            :amber_off!:(1:)^{19}:red_off!:X

j)   The assembly robot from example (g) is upgraded to insert twenty memory chips, two per second. With a clock speed of 1s

ROBOT2 $\stackrel{\text{def}}{=}$ accept_card?:(add_memory×add_memory:)^5
                        :pass_on_card!:ROBOT2

Finally, we should add some useful terminology.

Actions that prefix agent behaviours, for example α in α : P, are termed the guards of that agent.

definition *guards*
   The set of initial actions that an agent must enage in to move state, become another agent, are that agents guards. For example α is the guard of P in α : P, $\{\alpha, \beta\}$ the guards of P and Q in α : P + β : Q.

Such actions can also be used to identify agents.

definition *action derivatives*
   If an agent can engage in some action, its successor states are called its derivatives. More precisely, if an agent can engage in an α action then its successor is called an α–derivative. For example, in P $\stackrel{\text{def}}{=}$ α : Q + β : R, Q is an α–derivative, R a β–derivative. Derivatives can be defined by actions sets: for example, both Q and R are K-derivatives, where K= $\{\alpha, \beta\}$, in P $\stackrel{\text{def}}{=}$ α : Q + β : R. Derivatives can also extended to action sequences: for example, Q is an $\alpha\beta$–derivative in P $\stackrel{\text{def}}{=}$ α : β : Q. This last case also includes the special case of the empty sequence where P is the derivative of itself.

And there's a corresponding terminology for observable actions.

definition *action descendants*

> If agent P, by engaging in an α action, can be seen to become P′, ignoring
> preceding or succeeding 1 actions, then P′ is called an α–descendant of P.
> For example, Q is an α–descendant in P $\stackrel{\mathrm{def}}{=}$ $1:\alpha:1:1:Q$. By ignoring 1
> actions, ε–descendants, sequences devoid of observable actions, also can
> cause state changes, for example Q is an ε–descendant in P $\stackrel{\mathrm{def}}{=}$ $1:1:1:Q$

■

4.2.2.2 One Algebra to Rule Them All

Do we need a separate algebra over agents as well actions? For example, do agent
names have to be unique? Is prefixing an agent the same as prefixing an action?
We can circumvent such questions by arranging things so that states, and thus
agents, are written in terms of action sequences – in particular we define states
and agents in terms of system behaviours, naming states in terms of actions prefixing previous states. By doing this we link agent names directly to the algebra
over actions and remove the necessity for a further algebra over agents.

The agent which has no actions to perform is denoted $\mathbb{0}$. The state of the system
which can engage in action α before behaving as $\mathbb{0}$ is:

$$\alpha:\mathbb{0} \; \bullet \xrightarrow{\quad\alpha\quad} \mathbb{0}$$

and this previous state can be named by expression $\alpha:\mathbb{0}$ or given a label: for
example, WALTER.

$$\text{WALTER} \; \bullet \xrightarrow{\quad\alpha\quad} \mathbb{0}$$

WALTER is defined by $\alpha:\mathbb{0}$

$$\text{WALTER} \stackrel{\mathrm{def}}{=} \alpha:\mathbb{0}$$

We can continue prefixing agents with actions:

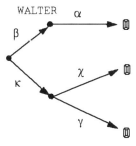

where there is a first state of $(\beta:\alpha:\mathbb{0} + \kappa:(\chi:\mathbb{0} + \gamma:\mathbb{0}))$ and two intermediary
states named by expressions $(\alpha:\mathbb{0})$ and $(\chi:\mathbb{0} + \gamma:\mathbb{0})$. These expressions

describe what actions an agent in a particular state can engage in, and we can attach our own mnemonic names to these behaviours. For example:

$$\text{FIRST} \stackrel{\text{def}}{=} (\beta:\alpha:\mathbb{0} + \kappa:(\chi:\mathbb{0} + \gamma:\mathbb{0}))$$
$$\text{WALTER} \stackrel{\text{def}}{=} \alpha:\mathbb{0}$$
$$\text{JANE} \stackrel{\text{def}}{=} (\chi:\mathbb{0} + \gamma:\mathbb{0})$$

These agent names describe possible system behaviours, and, as the associated agent names denote states, so their associated expressions also denote states.

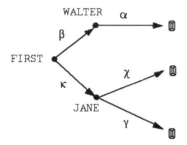

We have now captured the behaviour of a system in terms of expressions labelled with agent names. These expressions and their labels form the terms of our algebra, and, having a tractable algebra to reason about systems, derivation trees can be relegated to the role of illustrations.

We can extend this naming of states and behaviours to accommodate recursive behaviours as in:

$$\text{FIRST} \stackrel{\text{def}}{=} (\beta:\alpha:\text{FIRST} + \kappa:(\chi:\text{FIRST} + \gamma:\text{FIRST}))$$

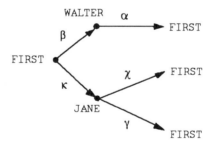

As each agent includes the behaviour of all its derivatives, we don't need to name all the states of a process, but only those of particular interest. In the above process, the expression named FIRST is sufficient to capture all subsequent behaviours.

4.2.2.3 Product

derivation *Product*

A concurrent combination of agents E and F, denoted by E×F, has the derivation rule:

$$\frac{E \xrightarrow{\alpha} E' \qquad\qquad F \xrightarrow{\beta} F' \qquad\qquad\qquad \alpha, \beta \in \mathcal{A}ct}{E{\times}F \xrightarrow{\alpha{\times}\beta} E'{\times}F'}$$

i f agent E can engage in action α in its first time slot, then behave
  like agent E'
and i f agent F can execute β in its first time slot then behave
  like F'
then the composite agent E×F can engage in α and β concurrently,
  α×β, in its first time slot before behaving as agent E'×F' .

All the actions of the agent E×F can be inferred from the independent actions of E and F.

Operators over agents, i.e. P×Q, bind less strongly than operators over actions i.e. α: P. For example α: P×Q = (α: P)×Q, α: P×β: Q = (α: P)×(β:Q)) and α: (P×Q) × (α:β:R × β:γ:Q) = (α: (P×Q)) × ((α:β:R) × (β:γ:Q))

■

examples

a)   If P $\stackrel{\text{def}}{=}$ a?:b?:c!:𝟘 and Q $\stackrel{\text{def}}{=}$ c?:b!:a?:𝟘
     Then P×Q = a?×c?:b?×b!:c!×a?:𝟘×𝟘

b)   A bank safe needs the keys held by two tellers, TELLER1 and
     TELLER2, to be operated simultaneously in order for it to be opened:
                    SAFE $\stackrel{\text{def}}{=}$ keys?:OPENSAFE
                where keys? = key1?×key2?
     Individual tellers are defined as:
                    TELLER1 $\stackrel{\text{def}}{=}$ key1!:TELLER1
                    TELLER2 $\stackrel{\text{def}}{=}$ key2!:TELLER2
     whereas both tellers operating in unison is:
                    TELLERS $\stackrel{\text{def}}{=}$ TELLER1×TELLER2
          TELLER1×TELLER2 = keys!:TELLER1×TELLER2

c)   A clock ticks every second and chimes on the hour. With a 1 second
     time slot
          CHIME $\stackrel{\text{def}}{=}$ (tick!:)^{3599}:tick!×chime!:CHIME

two copies, ticking in unison
CHIMES $\stackrel{\text{def}}{=}$ CHIME 1 × CHIME 2
= (tick1!×tick2!:)^{3599}
:tick1!×tick2!×chime1!×chime2!:CHIMES

■

As the derivation rule states that the product operator applies to both agents and actions, we need propositions over both.

Product over Agents
propositions Agents and Product ×

×1	P × Q = Q × P
×2	P × Q × R = (P × Q) × R = P × (Q × R)
×3	P × 𝟘 = 𝟘

Prop ×1 the binary product operator is commutative. The order of its parameters is not significant.

Prop ×2 the product operator is associative. The × operator can be applied to two agents in any order without disrupting equality. This is particularly powerful as it implies that propositions over product need concern only two agents, for propositions involving any greater number can be deduced from them.

Prop ×3 an agent formed by any concurrent set of subagents, of which inaction is one, is itself inaction. For a composed agent to be active, each of its subagents must contribute an action in every time interval – if even one composing subagent is inaction then the composite process cannot proceed and is itself inaction. Local inaction implies global inaction.

■

interpretation
Agent product represents the concurrent execution of process.

■

Product over Actions
In the definition of product, if we have agent E engaging in action α in its first time slot and agent F engaging in action β in its first time slot, the composite agent E×F can engage in both actions α and β concurrently, denoted α×β, in its first time slot.

definition *action dot notation*
The product operator applies to both agents and actions. To denote both by '×' overloads the notation; to relieve matters, product over agents retains the '×', but product over actions can be '.', '×', or nothing at all. For example a?×b!:P means the same as a?.b!:P and the same as a?b!:P

■

To reduce the need for brackets, we give the order of sub-expression execution in expressions by using the precedence relation '. =×> :' over actions.

For example, given P $\overset{\text{def}}{=}$ a!:b?:c!:P' and Q $\overset{\text{def}}{=}$ c?:b!:a?:Q' then

$$P×Q = (a!.c?):(b?.b!):(c!.a?):P'×Q'$$
$$= a!.c?:b?.b!:c!.a?:P'×Q'$$
$$= a!c?:b?b!:c!a?:P'×Q'$$

propositions Actions and Product ×

   ×4 $\alpha:P × \beta:Q = \alpha×\beta:(P × Q)$

   ×5 $\alpha×\beta:P = \beta×\alpha:P$

               $= \alpha.\beta:P = \beta.\alpha:P$

               $= \alpha\beta:P = \beta\alpha:P$

   ×6 $\alpha:P × 1:Q = \alpha.1:(P × Q) = \alpha:(P × Q)$

   ×7 $1:P × 1:Q = 1.1:(P × Q) = 1:(P × Q)$

Prop ×4 expresses the derivation of product as applied to actions.

Prop ×5 the operator is commutative, the order of its parameters is not significant, for actions the dot(.) notation is the same as the × notation.

Prop ×6 the visible result of an idle action engaged in concurrently with an observable action is the observable action.

Prop ×7 an idle action engaged in concurrently with other idle actions is observed as one idle action.

■

interpretation

Action product represents the concurrent execution, in the same time slot, of actions from more than one process.[†]

■

definition *Action product duplication*

The concurrent engagement of n identical actions, $n≥1$, is denoted by $(\alpha×)^n$ or $(\alpha.)^n$. Where $(\alpha.)^n = \alpha.\alpha.\;...\;.\alpha$ the sequence of the actions resulting from $(\alpha.)$ repeated n times delimited internally by the product combinator. For example $(\alpha.)^3:E$ is

$$(\alpha.)^3:E \xrightarrow{\alpha×\alpha×\alpha} E$$

Similarly $\alpha:(\beta.)^4:\chi:P = \alpha:\beta.\beta.\beta.\beta:\chi:P$

■

---

† Note the difference between concurrent operation in the synchronous algebra SCCS,

$$(a:P)×(b:Q) = a.b:P×Q$$

where the actions of concurrent processes happen concurrently, with those of the asynchronous algebra CSP

$$(a→P)||(b→Q) = (a→b→(Q||P)) \; | \; (b→a→(Q||P))$$

where there is no 'grain size' to time. As time can be infinitely subdivided to an observer, one concurrent process can always be observed to engage in an action before the other, but which one cannot be decided beforehand; here it could be either a followed by b→(Q||P) or b followed by a→(Q||P).

example

To an agent $P \stackrel{\text{def}}{=} a?:b?:1:c?:\mathbb{0}$ we'll add agent Q operating concurrently with P.

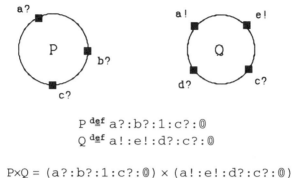

$$P \stackrel{\text{def}}{=} a?:b?:1:c?:\mathbb{0}$$
$$Q \stackrel{\text{def}}{=} a!:e!:d?:c?:\mathbb{0}$$

and

$$P{\times}Q = (a?:b?:1:c?:\mathbb{0}) \times (a!:e!:d?:c?:\mathbb{0})$$

An application of proposition ×4 gives[†]

$$= a?.a!:(b?:1:c?:\mathbb{0}) \times (e!:d?:c?:\mathbb{0})$$

proposition ×4 $= a?.a!:b?.e!:(1:c?:\mathbb{0}) \times (d?:c?:\mathbb{0})$

×6 $= a?.a!:b?.e!:d?:(c?:\mathbb{0}) \times (c?:\mathbb{0})$

×4 $= a?.a!:b?.e!:d?:c?.c?:(\mathbb{0}{\times}\mathbb{0})$

×3 $P{\times}Q = a?.a!:b?.e!:d?:(c?.)^2:\mathbb{0}$

(Note: we don't yet have a proposition for what $a!\,a?$ means.)

The final agent is represented by an agent diagram in which the ports of $P{\times}Q$ mirrors its actions.

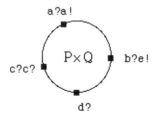

Interesting things happen when two observable actions with the same name execute simultaneously, especially if one offers to input and the other to output.

Synchronising Actions

An output action is the inverse of an input action, and we can define a function $^{-1}$ which converts one to the other, as in $(a!)^{-1}=a?$. Thus, if action α represents an offer of synchronisation (input or output), its inverse α^{-1} represents an equivalent and inverse offer of synchronisation (output or input). When operating concur-

---

† In the remainder of the text the result of the application of an SCCS proposition will be indicated by the proposition identifier to the left of the associated expression.

rently, as for example $a?\times a!$, $\alpha\times\alpha^{-1}$ represents the possibility of synchronisation. In an act of synchronisation, if each action fully satisfies its inverse, neither can support further synchronisations and, by cancelling each other out, they become an internal action. Mutually satisfied synchronisation is thus captured in $\alpha\times\alpha^{-1}=1$.

We can now complete the above example from
$$PxQ = a?.a!:b?.e!:d?:(c?.)^2:\mathbb{0}$$
as $\alpha\times\alpha^{-1}=1$
$$= 1:b?.e!:d?:(c?.)^2:\mathbb{0}$$
with agent diagram

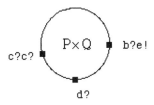

4.2.2.4 Summation

derivation

Disjunctive combination of agents modelling alternative courses of actions has the derivation rule:

$$E_i \overset{\alpha}{\rightarrow} E_i' \qquad\qquad \text{for } \alpha \in \mathcal{A}ct$$

$$\overline{}$$

$$\mathbb{E} \overset{\alpha}{\rightarrow} E_i'$$

$\mathbb{E}$ denotes a set of expressions, where $\mathbb{E} = \langle\sum E_i \mid i\in I\rangle$ is some family (possibly infinite) of expressions indexed by i. In pictures: if an agent E_i can engage in action α then behave as agent E_i':

$$E_i \xrightarrow{\quad\alpha\quad} E_i'$$

Then agent E, which contains E_i, can also engage in action α before behaving as agent E_i:

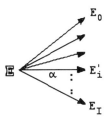

The behaviour of $\mathbb{E}$ can be derived from the sum of the initial actions of each individual E_i.

Adding this operator to our precedence relation over agents gives '×>+'; for example: $P+Q×R = P+(Q×R)$

■

interpretation *Summation*

Summation models general choice of behaviours. The agent $\mathbb{E}$ represents a system which can behave in one, and only one, of its E_i forms for $0{\leq}i{\leq}I$, and can be interpreted in the real world as a process offering several (possibly an infinite number) of behaviours. The selection can either be made by an environment or it can decide autonomously.

■

example

If we have three agents defined as:

$$E_1 \overset{def}{=} a?:E_1' \qquad E_2 \overset{def}{=} b?:E_2' \qquad E_3 \overset{def}{=} c!:E_3'$$

then *Agent Expression* $\quad \mathbb{E} \overset{def}{=} <\sum E_i \mid i \in \{1,2,3\}>$

$$= E_1 + E_2 + E_3$$
$$= a?:E_1' + b?:E_2' + c!:E_3'$$

which has the *Derivation Tree* :

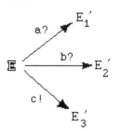

and the *Agent diagram* :

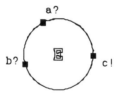

The agent diagram represents an agent capable of deterministic choice. The future behaviour of the agent depends upon which of the initial actions $a?$, $b?$ or $c!$ an environment first engaged in.

■

When the general case is given zero, one or two choices ($I= 0, 1$ and 2), the resultant behaviours are of particular interest:

When $I=0$, $\sum E_0$ has nothing to choose, there are no actions to engage in and

$I=0$ models inaction, $\Sigma E_0 = \mathbb{0}$.

When $I=1$, there is only one action to be engaged in and ΣE_1 models prefix. That is if $E_1 \stackrel{\text{def}}{=} a : E_1 '$ then $\mathbb{E} = \Sigma E_1 = \alpha : E_1 '$.

When $I=2$, ΣE_2 can be written $E_1 + E_2$, ΣE_2 can engage in one of two courses of action, a binary choice, which for general action α gives the following derivation laws:

$$\frac{E_1 \stackrel{\alpha}{\to} E_1 '}{E_1 + E_2 \stackrel{\alpha}{\to} E_1 '} \qquad\qquad \frac{E_2 \stackrel{\alpha}{\to} E_2 '}{E_1 + E_2 \stackrel{\alpha}{\to} E_2 '}$$

which, as + is associative, is the only proposition choice needs, any greater I being derived from $I=2$.

interpretation *Binary Choice*

An agent offering binary choice models the offer to engage in one of two distinct behaviours of the same system. Which is chosen, and how, we'll explore later.

■

examples

a)   An *Agent Expression* $P \stackrel{\text{def}}{=} a?:b?:\mathbb{0} + c! : (d?:\mathbb{0} + e!:\mathbb{0})$ has a *Derivation Tree*:

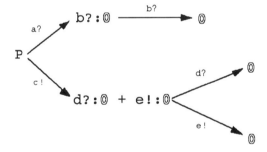

and an *Agent diagram*:

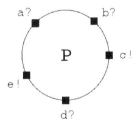

P represents an agent capable of deterministic choice, its future behaviour depending upon which of $a?$ or $c!$ its environment is engages in. Only if action c! is the initial choice can a subsequent choice between actions d? and e! be made.

b)   The stamp machine is upgraded to deliver 10p and 20p stamps for the relevant coins with a two-second delay between accepting a coin and delivering a stamp. With a clock period of 1s

10/20_SLOW_STAMP

$\overset{\text{def}}{=}$ 10pcoin?:1:10pstamp!:10/20_SLOW_STAMP

+ 20pcoin?:1:20pstamp!:10/20_SLOW_STAMP

c)   A change machine accepts a 5p coin and can deliver two possible sequences of coins in exchange. All actions take the same time.

CHANGE_MACHINE

$\overset{\text{def}}{=}$ in5p?:(out2p!:out2p!:out1p!:CHANGE_MACHINE

+ out1p!:out2p!:out2!:CHANGE_MACHINE)

d)   An adaptation of the change machine to deliver a sequence of 1p coins and at most one 2p coin. If all actions take the same time this new machine can be defined as:

$\text{CHANGE}_{0,0}$ $\overset{\text{def}}{=}$ in5p!:$\text{CHANGE}_{1,5}$

$\text{CHANGE}_{1,x}$ $\overset{\text{def}}{=}$ out2p!:$\text{CHANGE}_{0,x-2}$ + out1p:$\text{CHANGE}_{1,x-1}$, for x>2

$\text{CHANGE}_{0,x}$ $\overset{\text{def}}{=}$ out1p!:$\text{CHANGE}_{0,x-1}$, for x>0

where $\text{CHANGE}_{j,k}$ is the state of the change machine, k the change left to dispense, j=1 if 2p is not yet dispensed and j=0 when it has been.

■

propositions Sum +

+1 $P + Q = Q + P$
+2 $P + Q + R = (P + Q) + R = Q + (P + R)$
+3 $P + \mathbb{0} = P$
+4 $P + P = P$
+5 $\alpha:P + \alpha:Q \neq \alpha:(P + Q)$, unless P=Q
+6 $P \times \Sigma_i Q_i = \Sigma_i (P \times Q_i)$

Prop +1 the binary summation operator is commutative. The ordering of its parameters is not significant.

Prop +2 the + operator is associative, the order at which it is applied to two agents does not disrupt equality. Propositions regarding choice need only concern the I=2 case, as expressions involving I>2 can be deduced from them.

Prop +3 an agent formed by the summation of two agents has the choice of taking its initial action from either of them. But the inaction agent

$\mathbb{0}$ offers no actions and, in the summation of a active agent with inaction, the new agent can only choose actions from the active one and is indistinguishable from it.

Prop +4 an agent formed by the summation of two agents has a choice of performing the initial action of either; for two identical agents the individual actions are also identical, and choice between them is meaningless. The action of the summation is the same as the action of the summands.

Prop +5 we cannot 'factor out' actions in agent expressions.

Consider $P \stackrel{def}{=} \beta : P'$ and $Q \stackrel{def}{=} \mathbb{0}$

while

$def \quad \alpha : (P+Q) = \alpha : (\beta : P' + \mathbb{0})$

$+3 \qquad\qquad\qquad = \alpha : \beta : P'$

we also have

$def \quad \alpha : P + \alpha : Q = \alpha : \beta : P' + \alpha : \mathbb{0}$, which is irreducible

thus $\alpha : P + \alpha : Q \neq \alpha : (P+Q)$ as their behaviours ($\alpha : \beta : P'$) and ($\alpha : \beta : P' + \alpha : \mathbb{0}$) differ – the latter has the possibility of being inaction after its first action not present in the former. If we allowed ($\alpha : P + \alpha : Q) = \alpha : (P+Q)$ we would have the ability to *factor out* inaction from agent expressions. For example

$\alpha : P' + \alpha : \mathbb{0} = \alpha : (P' + \mathbb{0})$

$\qquad\qquad\quad = \alpha : P'$

As the major purpose of formal analysis is to detect design errors, and $\mathbb{0}$ indicates possible deadlock, we certainly don't want to factor out the very conditions we are searching for. Only when the sub-expressions P and Q are identical can we 'factor out' actions by applying prop +4 first.

Prop +6 the agents in $\sum_i Q_i$ are disjoint; only one will be chosen, thus $P \times \sum_i Q_i$ represents $P \times Q_1$ *or* $P \times Q_2$ and so on, which are also disjoint and can be written as $\sum_i (P \times Q_i)$. Summation is said to distribute over product, as in $P \times (Q+R) = (P \times Q) + (P \times R)$.

∎

(Note: infinite summation is allowed in the calculus as it infers the choice of one offered action while rejecting an infinite set of alternatives. Infinite product, though mathematically correct, infers that a single atomic event can accomplish an infinite amount of computation, which seems overly optimistic.)

4.2.2.5 Morphism

In some instances we wish to model a number of artifacts which behave identically, but for convenience we name their actions differently. For example:

DOOR $\stackrel{def}{=}$ open?:close?:DOOR

SWITCH $\stackrel{def}{=}$ on?:off?:SWITCH

FLAG $\stackrel{def}{=}$ raise?:lower?:FLAG

As external action names are in the gift of the designer we can take an existing agent and, by changing its action names, create a new agent, a 'copy', that retains the original's behaviour. The copy inherits all the validation work done on the original. Once we're happy with agents representing some generally useful behaviour, for example the above two-state system, we can reuse them in other designs by a simple renaming of actions. This changing of external action names also enables us to define and redefine interconnections between agents. For example, taking a single buffer:

we create two copies, and with new action names the copies can be connected together to form a double buffer.

Allowing a designer to change action names also allows for the possibility of inadvertently changing system behaviour. Errors are introduced if a designer renames actions using names already significant in the design. For example, such name clashes can result from changing:

$$\text{SWITCH} \overset{\text{def}}{=} \text{on?:off?:SWITCH}$$

to

$$\text{NEW\_SWITCH} \overset{\text{def}}{=} \text{on?:on?:NEW\_SWITCH}$$

But, more perniciously, problems can be introduced if we change names so that actions are pruned that, with their original names, would avoid pruning, and, vice versa, i.e. interactions that shouldn't be there are inadvertently made or wanted interactions are unmade. While errors cannot be prevented, we can make sure they are global by ensuring that name changing is carried out in a consistent manner. For this we need a formal basis for name changing: a set of propositions that tells us what to do, and when. In SCCS, the formal method of changing names is a morphism function which preserves the meaning and behaviour of agents.

derivation *Morphism*

The morphism function ϕ is a total function which, within the set of actions $\mathcal{Act}$, maps particle names (domain) to particle names (range); i.e. $\phi : \mathcal{Act} \rightarrow \mathcal{Act}$. For $\alpha, \beta, \chi \in \mathcal{Act}$ changing all αs to βs we use the function $\phi : \alpha \rightarrow \beta$ and $\psi : \beta \rightarrow \beta \times \chi$ for changing all names β to $\beta \times \chi$. Formally:

$$E \xrightarrow{\alpha} E'$$

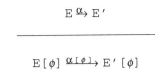

$$E[\phi] \xrightarrow{\alpha[\phi]} E'[\phi]$$

thus

if agent E can engage in action α then behave like agent E'

then agent E[φ], E with all its actions open to modification by the morphism function φ, can do action α modified by φ before behaving as agent E' with all its actions open to modification by φ.

Put more simply, E[φ] applies φ to the actions of *all* the derivatives of E.

Morphism can only change the names of visible particles. It has no effect on ticks and *always* $\phi:1\rightarrow1$

examples

a)   If P $\overset{\text{def}}{=}$ a?:b!:P and $\phi:a\rightarrow e, b\rightarrow f$ then

$$P[\phi] = e?:f!:P[\phi]$$

b)   We can convert the generalised agent

$$P \overset{\text{def}}{=} a?:b!:P$$

to a general stamp machine by use of the morphism function:

$\psi:a\rightarrow coin, b\rightarrow stamp$

$$P[\psi] = coin?:stamp!:P[\psi]$$

Defining

$$STAMP\_MACHINE \overset{\text{def}}{=} P[\psi]$$

we get

STAMP_MACHINE = coin?:stamp!:STAMP_MACHINE

The agents STAMP_MACHINE and P, as far as SCCS is concerned, have the same behaviour. By labelling actions, we put an interpretation on this behaviour

c)   This general stamp machine can in turn be converted into a particular stamp machine delivering 10p stamps for 10p coins by the morphism:

$\phi:coin\rightarrow10pcoin, stamp\rightarrow10pstamp$

$$10\_STAMP\_MACHINE \overset{\text{def}}{=} STAMP\_MACHINE[\phi]$$

Giving, with a clock period of 1s:

10_STAMP_MACHINE

$$= 10pcoin?:10pstamp!:10\_STAMP\_MACHINE$$

d)   The UK stamp machine, delivering 10p stamps for 10p coins, can be converted for export to the USA by the morphism:

$\phi:10pcoin\rightarrow10¢coin, 10pstamp\rightarrow10¢stamp$

```
        10¢_STAMP_MACHINE def 10_STAMP_MACHINE[φ]
```
Giving, with a clock period of 1s:
```
        10¢_STAMP_MACHINE
              = 10¢coin?:10¢stamp!:10¢_STAMP_MACHINE
```

e) If, due to inflation, the price of stamps rises, we can convert the 10p stamp machine to a 20p one by the morphism:
```
φ:10pcoin→20pcoin,10pstamp→20pstamp
        20_STAMP_MACHINE def 10_STAMP_MACHINE[φ]
```
Giving, with a clock period of 1s:
```
        20_STAMP_MACHINE
              = 20pcoin?:20pstamp!:20_STAMP_MACHINE
```

f) Equally the generalised agent
$$P \overset{def}{=} a?:b!:P$$
can be converted to a buffer by use of the morphism function
```
ψ:a,b→in,out
        P[ψ] = in?:out!:P[ψ]
```
Defining BUFFER def P[ψ] we get
```
        BUFFER = in?:out!:BUFFER
```
The agents P, STAMP_MACHINE, 10_STAMP_MACHINE, 10¢_STAMP_MACHINE, 20_STAMP_MACHINE and BUFFER have, as far as SCCS is concerned, the same behaviour.

g) If we represent a general NOR gate as $\gamma = \neg(\alpha \vee \beta)$, where α, β, γ $\in \{0,1\}$

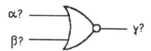

Then, applying $\phi: \alpha \rightarrow \sigma, \gamma \rightarrow \gamma \times \alpha$ and $\psi: \beta \rightarrow \rho, \gamma \rightarrow \beta \times \theta$, which results in the circuit:

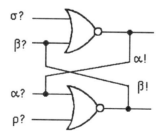

```
        FF = (NOR([φ] × NOR[ψ])
```

propositions Morphism ϕ

$\phi 1 \qquad (\alpha : P) [\phi] = \phi (\alpha) : P[\phi]$

$\phi 2 \qquad (\Sigma_i P_i) [\phi] = \Sigma_i (P_i [\phi])$

$\phi 3 \qquad (P \times Q) [\phi] = P[\phi] \times Q[\phi]$

$\phi 4a \qquad (1 : P) [\phi] = 1 : P[\phi]$

$\phi 4b \qquad 1[\phi] = 1$, corollary of $\phi 4a$

$\phi 4c \qquad (\delta P) [\phi] = \delta P[\phi]$, corollary of $\phi 4a$

$\phi 5 \qquad (P[\phi])^\wedge A = (P^\wedge \phi^{-1}(A)) [\phi]$

$\phi 6 \qquad P[\phi_1][\phi_2] = P[\phi_1 \circ \phi_2]$

$\phi 7 \qquad 0[\phi] = 0$

The first three propositions state the obvious, namely that prefix, choice and product are independent of the morphism function.

Prop $\phi 1$ is the encapsulation of the derivation of morphism

Prop $\phi 2$ morphism distributes over summation. For example: $(P+Q)[\phi]$
$= P[\phi] + Q[\phi]$. We can move a global morphism on an expression containing summation in its outermost level to operate directly on individual components of that summation. For example with $\phi : \alpha \rightarrow \gamma, \chi \rightarrow \kappa$

$$(\alpha : P + \beta : Q + \chi : R) [\phi] \qquad = (\alpha : P) [\phi]$$
$$+ (\beta : Q) [\phi] + (\chi : R) [\phi]$$
$$= \gamma : P[\phi] + \beta : Q[\phi] + \kappa : R[\phi]$$

Prop $\phi 3$ morphism distributes over product. For example: $(\alpha : P \times \beta : Q \times \chi : R) [\phi]$ can be replaced by $(\alpha : P) [\phi] \times (\beta : Q) [\phi] \times (\chi : R) [\phi]$.

The next three propositions show that morphism doesn't effect internal actions.

Prop $\phi 4a$ by *Prop $\phi 1$* $(1 : P) [\phi] = 1[\phi] : P[\phi]$ but by definition $\phi : 1 \rightarrow 1$. One cannot rename what has no name, thus $(1 : P) [\phi] = 1 : P[\phi]$

Prop $\phi 4b$ the morphism function ϕ renames actions defined in its domain. By definition 1 contains only 1 actions, and thus morphism, which can only be applied to visible actions, has no effect.

Prop $\phi 4c$ the δ operator means that an agent can delay doing something visible by engaging in any number of internal actions. Morphism has no effect on idle actions, and thus has no effect on δ, the operator.

Prop $\phi 5$ the order of application of morphism and restriction is significant; $(P[\phi])^\wedge A$ is not the same as $(P^\wedge A) [\phi]$. To change the ordering, moving the restriction 'inside' the morphism, we must neutralise the effect by first applying the inverse of the morphism function to the restriction set, as in $(P[\phi])^\wedge A = (P^\wedge \phi^{-1}(A)) [\phi]$. For example with $\phi : \alpha \rightarrow \chi, \beta \rightarrow \gamma$ and $A = \{\chi\}$

$$((\alpha : P + \beta : Q) [\phi])^\wedge A = (\chi : P[\phi] + \gamma : Q[\phi])^\wedge A$$
$$= \chi : P[\phi]^\wedge A$$

$\phi^{-1} : \chi \rightarrow \alpha, \gamma \rightarrow \beta$ and $A = \{\chi\}$ giving $\phi^{-1}A = \{\alpha\}$

$$((\alpha : P + \beta : Q) \,^\wedge \phi^{-1}A) \, [\phi] = (\alpha : P \,^\wedge \phi^{-1}A) \, [\phi]$$
$$= \chi : P \, [\phi] \,^\wedge A$$

Prop $\phi 7$ as disaster has no actions, morphism has no effect.

∎

4.2.2.6 Restriction

By limiting agent actions to a defined subset of its actions, restriction delimits the interface through which agent can interact. It allows certain paths of an agent's behaviour, tree pruning off others.

derivation

E^A behaves as expression E is only allowed to engage in the actions in set A where A is a subset of $\mathcal{A}ct$ such that $1 \in A$. The set of 'restrict to' particles, A, is a subset of possible actions of E and always implicitly includes the 1 action – one cannot influence what one cannot see.

There are three possible outcomes when restriction is applied. First the observable actions:

• If $\alpha \in A$ then

$$E \xrightarrow{\alpha} E'$$
$$\overline{\qquad\qquad}$$
$$E^\wedge A \xrightarrow{\alpha} E'^\wedge A$$

if agent E can engage in action α and become E'
and if α is contained in set A then agent E^A can engage in
    action α and then behave as E' restricted to A, E'^A.

• If $\alpha \notin A$ then

$$E \xrightarrow{\alpha} E'$$
$$\overline{\qquad\qquad}$$
$$E^\wedge A \xrightarrow{\alpha} 0$$

if agent E can engage in action α and become E'
and if α is not contained in set A, then agent E^A prevented
    from engaging in action α becomes the inaction agent 0.

Then the internal actions:

• If $\alpha = 1$, whatever A, then

$$1 : E \xrightarrow{1} E'$$
$$\overline{\qquad\qquad}$$
$$(1 : E) \,^\wedge A \xrightarrow{1} E'^\wedge A$$

Internal actions are unaffected by restriction

Adding restriction to our precedence relations over agents gives '^A>×>+'

■

examples

a) The stamp machine delivering $10p$ and $20p$ stamps for the
   relevant coins
   ```
   10/20_SLOW_STAMP
         def 10pcoin?:1:10pstamp!:10/20_SLOW_STAMP
           + 20pcoin?:1:20pstamp!:10/20_SLOW_STAMP
   ```
   has to be changed. Due to inflation, $10p$ stamps are no longer in
   use. We can model the new machine by restricting the actions to
   $20pcoin$ and $20pstamp$. For A = {1,20pcoin?,20pstamp!}
   ```
         20_SLOW_STAMP def 10/20_SLOW_STAMP^A
         20_SLOW_STAMP
                   = 20pcoin?:1:20pstamp!:20_SLOW_STAMP
   ```
   The complete $10p$ choice has been removed.

b) A $5p$ change machine delivering only $1p$ coins
   ```
         1p_CHANGE_0 def in5p!:1p_CHANGE_5
         1p_CHANGE_x def out1p!:1p_CHANGE_x-1, for x>0
   ```
   Where $CHANGE_k$ is the state of the change machine with k
   $1p$'s left to dispense can be obtained from the previous
   change machine using the restriction set A={1,5p!,1p?}
   where
   ```
         1p_CHANGE_x = CHANGE_MACHINE_x^A
   ```

■

propositions Restriction $^\wedge$, where $A \subseteq \mathcal{A}ct$, $B \subseteq \mathcal{A}ct$ and $\alpha \in \mathcal{A}ct$

$^\wedge 1$ $P^\wedge A^\wedge B = P^\wedge B^\wedge A = P^\wedge (A \cap B)$
$^\wedge 2$ $(\alpha : P)^\wedge A = \alpha : P^\wedge A$, if $\alpha \in A$
              $= \mathbb{0}$, otherwise
$^\wedge 3$ $(\sum_i P_i)^\wedge A = \sum_i (P_i^\wedge A)$
$^\wedge 4$ $(P \times Q)^\wedge A \neq (P^\wedge A) \times (Q^\wedge A)$, in general

Prop $^\wedge 1$ restrictions can be applied in any order, from the property of set
   intersection.
Prop $^\wedge 2$ is the encapsulation of the previous derivation propositions.
Prop $^\wedge 3$ restriction distributes over summation - we can move a global
   restriction on an expression containing summation to operate on
   individual components of that summation. For example
   $$(\alpha : P + \beta : Q + \chi : R)^\wedge A = (\alpha : P)^\wedge A + (\beta : Q)^\wedge A + (\chi : R)^\wedge A$$
   In particular
   $$(P + Q)^\wedge A = (P^\wedge A) + (Q^\wedge A)$$
Prop $^\wedge 4$ restriction does not generally distribute over product. For

example $(\alpha : P \times \beta : Q \times \chi : R)\,\char94 A$ cannot always be replaced by $(\alpha : P)\,\char94 A \times (\beta : Q)\,\char94 A \times (\chi : R)\,\char94 A$. We'll investigate this further, later in the book.

∎

interpretation

Restriction allows named agent actions. By keeping only certain 'restricted to' actions a designer can select parts of a process, rejecting others.

∎

To help the reader follow the application of propositions, in some examples we'll use $(\!(\,)\!)\,\char94 A$ instead of $(\,)\,\char94 A$. Naturally this notation isn't a formal part of part of the algebra.

example

A general file copy server can read in a file and, after some formatting, can copy the file to a disk or give it to a printer spooler with instructions to print it on either a fast draft-quality or a slower letter-quality printer, where:

a? = read in file	1 = format file
c! = select the disk	d! = write to disk
e! = send to printer queue	f! = write to high speed printer
g! = write to slow speed printer	

and each action takes the same time. The server can be defined by

$$\mathrm{COPY} \stackrel{\mathrm{def}}{=} a?:1:(c!:d!:\mathbb{0} + e!:(f?:\mathbb{0} + g!:\mathbb{0}))$$

which has a *Derivation Tree* of

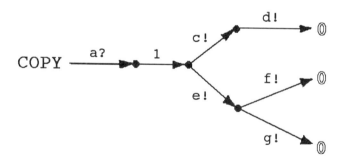

Choosing the *restrict* of $\mathrm{FAST} = \{1, a?, e!, f!, d?\}$ and applying it in $\mathrm{COPY}\char94\mathrm{FAST}$ restricts the derivation tree to

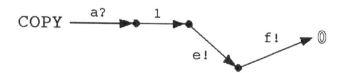

Now only one of the options offered by the COPY server, printing a file on the draft printer, is available from the COPY^FAST server. All remaining options (choices) having been disallowed by the restriction – restriction has taken a general server and turned it into one dedicated to a specialised task. The proof, for FAST = {1,a?,e!,f!,d?}:

```
COPY^FAST =  (a?:1:(c!:d!:0 + e!:(f?:0 + g!:0)))^FAST
   ^2      =  a?:(1:(c!:d!:0 + e!:(f?:0 + g!:0)))^FAST
   ^2      =  a?:1:(c!:d!:0 + e!:(f?:0 + g!:0))^FAST
   ^3      =  a?:1:((c!:d!:0)^FAST + (e!:(f?:0 + g!:0))^FAST)
   ^2      =  a?:1:(0 + e!:(f?:0 + g!:0)^FAST)
   +3      =  a?:1:e!:(f?:0 + g!:0)^FAST
   ^3      =  a?:1:e!:((f?:0)^FAST + (g!:0)^FAST)
   ^2      =  a?:1:e!:(f?:0^FAST + 0)
   +3      =  a?:1:e!:f?:0^FAST
   ^2      =  a?:1:e!:f?:0
```

which gives COPY^FAST = a?:1:e!:f?:0 as predicted by the derivation tree. Done, admittedly, very slowly, but with practice this proof will take very few lines.

Other options can be obtained by defining other '*restrict to*' sets; for example {1,a?,c!,d!} writes all files to the disk, and {1,a?,e!,f!,g!} results in a hard-copy server retaining the choice of draft or letter-quality output.

∎

Rather than moving on to consider existing operators in more depth, it's appropriate to pause a while to clear up a couple of outstanding matters and put what's been introduced so far into perspective. First, the outstanding matters. We should look at the 1 action, which, because of its central role in the algebra, has appeared in many supporting roles but hasn't found itself in the spotlight.

4.2.2.7 The Meanings of 1

In formal terms the 1 action, best known as the internal action, is the identity element in the set of observable actions, but to other agents, as well as to designers, it's simply a marker indicating that an agent is engaged in some internal activity, an agent not offering to interact with its environment, in a particular time slot. An agent may engage in such an internal action because:

- it's idling, waiting to interact;
- it's engaging in an internal synchronisation, $\alpha \times \alpha^{-1} = 1$, and cannot support other concurrent interactions;
- it's engaging in some internal activity, doing something useful to progress its own task, which is independent of any environment. Such actions naturally do not need to be observed by, or to interact with, an environment.

In all cases the environment 'sees' a 1 but is unable to distinguish the cause.

Apart from the inability to support interaction, being without an associated port, and having its given name formally specified within the algebra, the 1 action has another claim to fame: from $1 \times 1 = 1$ it is always a particle – a 1 is always operationally atomic as well as atomic in time.

While the ability of a 1 action to represent so many causes simplifies the overall algebra, its very anonymity makes designs a little obscure. To clarify things somewhat, rather than denote all internal actions by the anonymous 1 we can label internal actions with appropriate names, and without the communications directional they will be recognised as such (this was one of the reasons why the ? and ! notation was introduced). For example, internal activity progressing a task

$$\text{MULTIPLY} \stackrel{\text{def}}{=} \text{in?x:}(\text{y:=x*x}):\text{out!y:MULTIPLY}$$

and internal synchronisation

$$P \stackrel{\text{def}}{=} \text{a?:b!:0 and Q} \stackrel{\text{def}}{=} \text{a!:c?:0}$$
$$P \times Q = a_{\text{sync}}:(\text{b!:0} \times \text{c?:0})$$

are all particular synonyms for the more anonymous 1 action. Naturally these labels are transparent to the algebra and are treated as the 1 action in SCCS propositions.

Having given 1 its moment of fame, we go on to consider the remaining outstanding matter, that of whether all operators are of equal status or some are more equal than others, and can we identify an irreducible set of operators from which all others can be derived.

4.2.2.8 Derived Operators, Morphism Revisited

When we introduced morphism it was convenient to consider it as an operator of equal rank with product, summation and the like. However, not all operators have equal status; some, like pruning \\, can be derived from more basic ones, like restriction ^. Among these derived operators is morphism; for example, we can convert the α actions in $P \stackrel{\text{def}}{=} \alpha:P$ to β's, $P[\beta/\alpha]$, either by using a morphism function $\phi : \alpha \rightarrow \beta$, or by combining P with an additional agent $Q \stackrel{\text{def}}{=} \alpha^{-1}.\beta:Q$ then using the pruning operator to remove the α's.

$$P \stackrel{\text{def}}{=} \alpha:P \text{ and } Q \stackrel{\text{def}}{=} \alpha^{-1}.\beta:R$$
$$(P \times R) \backslash\backslash\alpha = (\alpha:P \times \alpha^{-1}.\beta:Q) \backslash\backslash\alpha$$
$$= \beta:(P \times Q) \backslash\backslash\alpha$$

By using delay (another derived operator which we'll look into later on) we can rename all the α actions in P (as long, that is, as P has at most one α action in each time slot) by using agent $R \stackrel{\text{def}}{=} \delta\alpha^{-1}.\beta:R$ in $(P \times R) \backslash\backslash\alpha$, R waits and synchronises with every α action in P and by doing so replaces it with a β, so that

$$P[\beta/\alpha] = P[\phi] = (P \times R) \backslash\backslash \alpha$$

It can be proved [Mil83] that any morphism can be replaced by a combination of more basic operators, giving the set of irreducible SCCS operators (the set from which all other operators can be derived) as prefix, product, summation and restriction [Pra90].

4.2.2.9 Example

We now have enough knowledge to attempt a design, in this case a simple piece of digital circuitry. An asynchronous algebra like CCS, while capturing the logical behaviour of electronic gates, would lose any sense of timing and, based on its underlying blocking send communications model, assume that gates only output when their down-stream companions are ready to accept an input. In real electronic circuits time matters, and gates change their outputs in response to changes at their inputs; no blocking send here. To keep things simple, in the following design we'll assume that gates operate with negligible delays.

To prove the design correct we must show that it behaves according to a specification. To show that an SCCS design meets its specification we write the specification as an SCCS agent and compare the emergent behaviour of our design with this specification.

Objective
Prove two behaviours, a specification and an implementation, equivalent.

Assumptions
Changes to input and output actions are atomic. Gate delays are sufficiently small that inputs and associated output changes are accommodated in the same time slot.

  a) specification
    In boolean algebra $c = \neg a \wedge b$ has as truth table

a	b	c
0	0	0
0	1	1
1	0	0
1	1	0

b) implementation

A possible implementation using AND and NOT logic gates

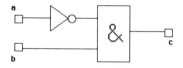

Method

Express the specification in SCCS terms, construct an implementation using SCCS, and then prove the resultant behaviours are equivalent.

Models

From the prime implicants in the truth table we can express the specification as the SCCS expression

$$\text{TRUTH} \overset{\text{def}}{=} a_0?.b_0?.c_0! : \text{TRUTH}$$
$$+ a_0?.b_1?.c_1! : \text{TRUTH}$$
$$+ a_1?.b_0?.c_0! : \text{TRUTH}$$
$$+ a_1?.b_1?.c_0! : \text{TRUTH}$$

The general forms of an AND and a NOT are

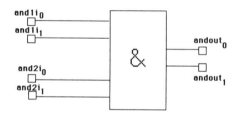

$$\text{AND} \overset{\text{def}}{=} \text{and1}i_0?.\text{and2}i_0?.\text{andout}_0! : \text{AND}$$
$$+ \text{and1}i_0?.\text{and2}i_1?.\text{andout}_0! : \text{AND}$$
$$+ \text{and1}i_1?.\text{and2}i_0?.\text{andout}_0! : \text{AND}$$
$$+ \text{and1}i_1?.\text{and2}i_1?.\text{andout}_1! : \text{AND}$$

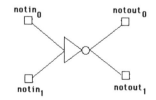

$$\text{NOT} \overset{\text{def}}{=} \text{notin}_0?.\text{notout}_1! : \text{NOT}$$
$$+ \text{notin}_1?.\text{notout}_0! : \text{NOT}$$

Knowing the behaviour of the individual components we now use SCCS to predict composite behaviour.

Composition

The agents representing general AND and NOT gates need to be connected, for which the output port of the NOT gate must have the same name as an AND gate input. This is achieved by applying appropriate morphism functions.

The function $\theta 1$: $notout_0 \rightarrow join_0$, $notout_1 \rightarrow join_1$ applied to NOT gives

$\phi 1$ $NOT[\theta 1] = notin_0?.join_1!:NOT[\theta 1]$
$+ notin_1?.join_0!:NOT[\theta 1]$

and a complementary function $\theta 2$: $and1i_0 \rightarrow join_0$, $and1i_1 \rightarrow join_1$ applied to AND gives

$\phi 1$ $AND[\theta 2] = join_0? \times and2i_0? \times andout_0!:AND[\theta 2]$
$+ join_0?.and2i_1?.andout_0!:AND[\theta 2]$
$+ join_1?.and2i_0?.andout_0!:AND[\theta 2]$
$+ join_1?.and2i_1?.andout_1!:AND[\theta 2]$

We now compose the system a step at a time restricting the observable ports to those we want to remain visible

$$SYS \stackrel{def}{=} (NOT[\theta 1] \times AND[\theta 2])\,^{\wedge}A$$
$$where\ A = \{x \in \{0,1\}, y \in \{0,1\}, z \in \{0,1\}$$
$$|\ notin_x?.and2i_y?.andout_z!\} \cup \{1\}$$

This definition of A allows combinations of binary inputs and outputs such as $notin_0?.and2i_0?.andout_0!$ and $notin_0?.and2i_1?.andout_1!$ but disallows any action which includes a $join$:

$(NOT[\theta 1] \times AND[\theta 2])\backslash\backslash A$

def $= (\!(notin_0?.join_1!:NOT[\theta 1] + notin_1?.join_0!:NOT[\theta 1])$
$\times ((join_0?.and2i_0?.andout_0!:AND[\theta 2]$
$+ join_0?.and2i_1?.andout_0!:AND[\theta 2]$
$+ join_1?.and2i_0?.andout_0!:AND[\theta 2]$
$+ join_1?.and2i_1?.andout_1!:AND[\theta 2]))$
$)\,^{\wedge}A$

+6

$= (\!(notin_0?.join_1!:NOT[\theta 1]) \times (join_0?.and2i_0?.andout_0!:AND[\theta 2])$
$+(notin_0?.join_1!:NOT[\theta 1]) \times (join_0?.and2i_1?.andout_0!:AND[\theta 2])$
$+(notin_0?.join_1!:NOT[\theta 1]) \times (join_1?.and2i_0?.andout_0!:AND[\theta 2])$
$+(notin_0?.join_1!:NOT[\theta 1]) \times (join_1?.and2i_1?.andout_1!:AND[\theta 2])$
$+(notin_1?.join_0!:NOT[\theta 1]) \times (join_0?.and2i_0?.andout_0!:AND[\theta 2])$
$+(notin_1?.join_0!:NOT[\theta 1]) \times (join_0?.and2i_1?.andout_0!:AND[\theta 2])$
$+(notin_1?.join_0!:NOT[\theta 1]) \times (join_1?.and2i_0?.andout_0!:AND[\theta 2])$

$$+(notin_1?.join_0!:NOT[\theta 1]) \times (join_1?.and2i_1?.andout_1!:AND[\theta 2])$$
$$)^{\wedge}A$$

$\wedge 3$

$$= (\!(notin_0?.join_1!:NOT[\theta 1]) \times (join_0?.and2i_0?.andout_0!:AND[\theta 2]))^{\wedge}A$$
$$+(\!(notin_0?.join_1!:NOT[\theta 1]) \times (join_0?.and2i_1?.andout_0!:AND[\theta 2]))^{\wedge}A$$
$$+(\!(notin_0?.join_1!:NOT[\theta 1]) \times (join_1?.and2i_0?.andout_0!:AND[\theta 2]))^{\wedge}A$$
$$+(\!(notin_0?.join_1!:NOT[\theta 1]) \times (join_1?.and2i_1?.andout_1!:AND[\theta 2]))^{\wedge}A$$
$$+(\!(notin_1?.join_0!:NOT[\theta 1]) \times (join_0?.and2i_0?.andout_0!:AND[\theta 2]))^{\wedge}A$$
$$+(\!(notin_1?.join_0!:NOT[\theta 1]) \times (join_0?.and2i_1?.andout_0!:AND[\theta 2]))^{\wedge}A$$
$$+(\!(notin_1?.join_0!:NOT[\theta 1]) \times (join_1?.and2i_0?.andout_0!:AND[\theta 2]))^{\wedge}A$$
$$+(\!(notin_1?.join_0!:NOT[\theta 1]) \times (join_1?.and2i_1?.andout_1!:AND[\theta 2]))^{\wedge}A$$

$\times 4$

$$= (notin_0?.join_1!.join_0?.and2i_0?.andout_0!:(NOT[\theta 1] \times AND[\theta 2]))^{\wedge}A$$
$$+(\!notin_0?.join_1!.join_0?.and2i_1?.andout_0!:(NOT[\theta 1] \times AND[\theta 2]))^{\wedge}A$$
$$+(\!notin_0?.join_1!.join_1?.and2i_0?.andout_0!:(NOT[\theta 1] \times AND[\theta 2]))^{\wedge}A$$
$$+(\!notin_0?.join_1!.join_1?.and2i_1?.andout_1!:(NOT[\theta 1] \times AND[\theta 2]))^{\wedge}A$$
$$+(\!notin_1?.join_0!.join_0?.and2i_0?.andout_0!:(NOT[\theta 1] \times AND[\theta 2]))^{\wedge}A$$
$$+(\!notin_1?.join_0!.join_0?.and2i_1?.andout_0!:(NOT[\theta 1] \times AND[\theta 2]))^{\wedge}A$$
$$+(\!notin_1?.join_0!.join_1?.and2i_0?.andout_0!:(NOT[\theta 1] \times AND[\theta 2]))^{\wedge}A$$
$$+(\!notin_1?.join_0!.join_1?.and2i_1?.andout_1!:(NOT[\theta 1] \times AND[\theta 2]))^{\wedge}A$$

and as $\alpha\alpha^{-1}=1$ then

$$= (notin_0?.join_1!.join_0?.and2i_0?.andout_0!:(NOT[\theta 1] \times AND[\theta 2]))^{\wedge}A$$
$$+(\!notin_0?.join_1!.join_0?.and2i_1?.andout_0!:(NOT[\theta 1] \times AND[\theta 2]))^{\wedge}A$$
$$+(\!notin_0?.1.and2i_0?.andout_0!:(NOT[\theta 1] \times AND[\theta 2]))^{\wedge}A$$
$$+(\!notin_0?.1.and2i_1?.andout_1!:(NOT[\theta 1] \times AND[\theta 2]))^{\wedge}A$$
$$+(\!notin_1?.1.and2i_0?.andout_0!:(NOT[\theta 1] \times AND[\theta 2]))^{\wedge}A$$
$$+(\!notin_1?.1.and2i_1?.andout_0!:(NOT[\theta 1] \times AND[\theta 2]))^{\wedge}A$$
$$+(\!notin_1?.join_0!.join_1?.and2i_0?.andout_0!:(NOT[\theta 1] \times AND[\theta 2]))^{\wedge}A$$
$$+(\!notin_1?.join_0!.join_1?.and2i_1?.andout_1!:(NOT[\theta 1] \times AND[\theta 2]))^{\wedge}A$$

$\wedge 2$

$$= \mathbb{0} + \mathbb{0} + (notin_0?.and2i_0?.andout_0!:(NOT[q1] \times AND[q2]))^{\wedge}A$$
$$+ notin_0?.and2i_1?.andout_1!:(NOT[q1] \times AND[q2])^{\wedge}A$$
$$+ notin_1?.and2i_0?.andout_0!:(NOT[q1] \times AND[q2])^{\wedge}A$$
$$+ notin_1?.and2i_1?.andout_0!:(NOT[q1] \times AND[q2])^{\wedge}A + \mathbb{0} + \mathbb{0}$$

(Phew!)

applying $+3$ gives the emergent behaviour

$$SYS = notin_0?.and2i_0?.andout_0!:SYS$$
$$+ notin_0?.and2i_1?.andout_1!:SYS$$
$$+ notin_1?.and2i_0?.andout_0!:SYS$$
$$+ notin_1?.and2i_1?.andout_0!:SYS$$

But the specification written as an SCCS theory was

$$\begin{aligned} \text{TRUTH} \;=\;& a_0?.b_0?.c_0!:\text{TRUTH} \\ &+\; a_0?.b_1?.c_1!:\text{TRUTH} \\ &+\; a_1?.b_0?.c_0!:\text{TRUTH} \\ &+\; a_1?.b_1?.c_0!:\text{TRUTH} \end{aligned}$$

Are they the same? Applying morphism

$$\theta 3:\; notin_j \rightarrow a_j,\; and2i_j \rightarrow b_j,\; andout_j \rightarrow c_j,\; \text{for } j \in \{1,2\}$$

to SYS gives

$$\phi 1 \quad \begin{aligned} \text{SYS}[\theta 3] \;=\;& a_0?.b_0?.c_0!:\text{SYS}[\theta 3] \\ &+\; a_0?.b_1?.c_1!:\text{SYS}[\theta 3] \\ &+\; a_1?.b_0?.c_0!:\text{SYS}[\theta 3] \\ &+\; a_1?.b_1?.c_0!:\text{SYS}[\theta 3] \end{aligned}$$

Now the behaviours of SYS[θ3] and TRUTH are identical, and we can write

$$\text{SYS}[\theta 3] = \text{TRUTH}$$

So now we can use SCCS and its propositions to define the behaviours, including interactions, of subagents; compose them; decide what any subsequent environment will see; and by doing so determine how the final system will behave. Then we see if it meets our requirements.

Admittedly this is all rather low-level stuff but, before we move on to higher things, there are a few items we need to sort out. In particular, we've been happily using concepts that seemed to be correct but which we've yet to prove valid. Here we'll begin to put that right, starting with recursion which we've been using without stint.

4.3 Recursion

4.3.1 Recursion in SCCS Terms

Agents which engage in some sequence of actions then stop, as with an earlier version of agent ONECOPY

$$\text{ONECOPY} \stackrel{\text{def}}{=} a?:1:(c!:d!:0 + e!:(f?:0 + y!:0))$$

where each possible behaviour is 'execute once', the agents lying broken and unusable at the end of one pass are of limited interest and more interesting objects have recursive behaviours – after engaging in a behaviour an agent is ready to offer the same behaviour again. Some examples:

- agent IDLER engages in an internal action, 1, then repeats:

$$\text{IDLER} \stackrel{\text{def}}{=} 1:\text{IDLER}$$

- a non-stopping version of ONECOPY:

  $$\text{ONECOPY} \overset{\text{def}}{=} \text{a?:1:(c!:d!:ONECOPY}$$
  $$+ \text{ e!:(f?:ONECOPY + g!:ONECOPY))}$$

- agent CLOCK continually engages in tick actions:

  $$\text{CLOCK} \overset{\text{def}}{=} \text{tick:CLOCK}$$

- DISK, a disk drive which can be read from or written to indefinitely:

  $$\text{DISK} \overset{\text{def}}{=} \text{read?:DISK + write?:DISK}$$

Recursive agents are all of the form:

$$\text{X} \overset{\text{def}}{=} \textit{...some actions... } :\text{X}$$

The behaviour of agent X is some function of X itself, an identify function:

$$\text{X} \overset{\text{def}}{=} \mathcal{F}(\text{X})$$

examples

All recursive expressions X, by returning to their initial states, have associated identity functions of the form X $\overset{\text{def}}{=}$ E where E = $\mathcal{F}(\text{X})$. Recursion can range over both simple prefixing and choice, for either complete agents or sub-expressions.

- A simple recursive agent

  $$\text{CUSTOMER} \overset{\text{def}}{=} \text{coin!:stamp?:CUSTOMER}$$

  has identity function

  $$\text{E = coin!:stamp!:X}$$

- An agent with a recursive sub-expression

  $$\text{TRAFFIC\_LIGHT} \overset{\text{def}}{=} \text{green\_on!:X}$$
  $$\text{X} \overset{\text{def}}{=} (1:)^{29}:\text{green\_off!}\times\text{red\_on!}\times\text{amber\_on!}:(1:)^4$$
  $$:\text{amber\_off!}:(1:)^{19}:\text{red\_off!}\times\text{green\_on!}:\text{X}$$

  has identity function of its recursive part E

  $$\text{TRAFFIC\_LIGHT} \overset{\text{def}}{=} \text{green\_on!:E}$$
  $$\text{E} = (1:)^{29}:\text{green\_off!}\times\text{red\_on!}\times\text{amber\_on!}:(1:)^4$$
  $$:\text{amber\_off!}:(1:)^{19}:\text{red\_off!}\times\text{green\_on!}:\text{X}$$

- A recursive agent with a choice of behaviours such as

  10/20_STAMP_MACHINE
  $$\overset{\text{def}}{=} \text{10pcoin?:10pstamp!:10/20\_STAMP\_MACHINE}$$
  $$+ \text{20pcoin?:20pstamp!:10/20\_STAMP\_MACHINE}$$

  has identity

  $$\text{E = 10pcoin?:10pstamp!:X + 20pcoin?:20pstamp!:X}$$

The solutions to identity functions of the form X $\stackrel{\text{def}}{=}$ E where E = $\mathcal{F}(X)$ are termed fixed points $\texttt{fixXE}$. A fixed point behaves identically to the expression X $\stackrel{\text{def}}{=}$ E, and, as solutions to X $\stackrel{\text{def}}{=}$ E, can replace it wherever it appears. Fixed points are just that: fixed. They represent properties that do not change in the life of a system; they represent invariants as an identity function like X $\stackrel{\text{def}}{=}$ $\mathcal{F}(X)$ says that, after engaging in activity $\mathcal{F}(\ )$, properties defined in $(\ )$ are unchanged. X is the same after application of $\mathcal{F}(X)$ as before. In the algebraic world, identity functions like $\texttt{x=f(x)}$ have fixed point solutions x, the values for which a function returns the same values as those input. Functions can have one, many or no fixed point solutions. For integer $\texttt{x>0}$:

x = square(x)	has one fixed point x=1 the left-hand side and the right-hand side have the same behaviour only when x=1 .
x = x² – x	has one fixed point x=2
x = x+1	has no fixed points
x = x	has as many fixed points as there are values of x

Fortunately, in the SCCS world each recursive expressions only has one, unique, fixed point solution.

The whole point of fixed points is that, not only do they remove recursion, but, as solutions to more complex expressions, for example the invariant x=2 as a solution to x = x² – x, they fully capture the behaviour of the more complicated expression, and such constants can replace the more complicated equivalent wherever they appear. For example, the programming fragment

```
...
if (x = x² - x) then
        print('I understand fixed points')
    else ...
...
```

can be replaced by the equivalent...

```
...
if (x = 2) then
        print('I understand fixed points')
    else ...
...
```

To prove formally that recursive equations in SCCS can be replaced by their fixed point solutions, we need to delve a little deeper. Those readers who are allergic to mathematics can avert their eyes for a page or two.

definition *fixed point*

For some I, $\mathbb{X}$ is an I indexed family of distinct agent variables, $\mathbb{X}$ = <X_i | i∈ I>, and $\mathbb{E}$ is an I indexed family of expressions containing X, $\mathbb{E}$ = <E_i | i∈ I>, $\mathbb{E}$ being a function of $\mathbb{X}$. Then $fix_i\mathbb{X}\mathbb{E}$ denotes the ith component of a solution, fixed point, of the recursive equation $\mathbb{X} \stackrel{def}{=} \mathbb{E}$. The entire family of solutions is denoted $fix_I\mathbb{X}\mathbb{E}$. For a singleton I=1, agent X $\stackrel{def}{=}$ E has a solution fixXE.

■

There is a derivation rule for $fix_i\mathbb{X}\mathbb{E}$

derivation

For some I, $\mathbb{G}$ is an I indexed family of distinct agent names, $\mathbb{G}$ = <G_i | i∈ I>, and we denote by E[$\mathbb{G}$/$\mathbb{X}$] the result of simultaneously replacing G_i for corresponding free occurrences of the variables X_i in E for each i∈ I.

Then the general rule for recursion is:

$$E_i[fix_I\mathbb{X}\mathbb{E}/\mathbb{X}] \stackrel{\alpha}{\rightarrow} E'$$

$$\overline{\qquad\qquad\qquad\qquad\qquad\qquad\qquad}$$

$$fix_i\mathbb{X}\mathbb{E} \stackrel{\alpha}{\rightarrow} E'$$

if the ith component, E_i, of a set of expressions $\mathbb{E}$, after all occurrences of the members of the family of variables $\mathbb{X}$ have been replaced by the equivalent member of the family of fixed point solutions $fix_I\mathbb{X}\mathbb{E}$, can engage in action α and then behave like agent E'
then the ith component fix_iXE of the fixed point solutions of the set of expressions $\mathbb{E}$ can also engage in action α and then behave like E'.

■

In practice, instead of having to deal with families of solutions to $\mathbb{X}$=$\mathbb{E}$, indexed by i∈ I, only the solutions to X $\stackrel{def}{=}$ E, i=1, are of real interest, where F = fixXE is the only, and thus the unique, solution to the recursive equation X $\stackrel{def}{=}$ E for E = $\mathcal{F}(X)$.

Now we can relate the behaviour of this unique fixed point solution to its parent recursive equation.

derivation

$$E[fixXE/X] \stackrel{\alpha}{\rightarrow} E'$$

$$\overline{\qquad\qquad\qquad\qquad\qquad}$$

$$fixXE \stackrel{\alpha}{\rightarrow} E'$$

if agent expression E, a function of X, E = $\mathcal{F}$(X), after all occurrences of
the variables X have been replaced by the equivalent fixed point
solution fixXE, can engage in action α and then behave like agent E'
then fixXE the fixed point solutions of expressions E can also engage in
action α before behaving like agent E'.

■

In plainer words, as the fixed point solution behaves identically to its parent, we
can replace all occurrences of variable X in a recursive equation X $\stackrel{\text{def}}{=}$ E, where
E = $\mathcal{F}$(X), by the fixed point solution fixXE. The behaviour of X $\stackrel{\text{def}}{=}$ $\mathcal{F}$(X) is
fully captured in fixXE = $\mathcal{F}$(fixXE), as it is the *only* behaviour.

Certain simple recursive expressions such as E=X, E=1:X, and so on give rise to
interesting and useful behaviours termed *derived agents*, which we will now explore

4.3.2 Derived Agents

4.3.2.1 Idler, $\mathbb{1}$

When X $\stackrel{\text{def}}{=}$ E and E = 1:X. As the fixed point F = fixXE is a solution to X $\stackrel{\text{def}}{=}$ E,
then F = fixX(1:X) is a solution to X $\stackrel{\text{def}}{=}$ 1:X. We write IDLER=fixX(1:X)
as the unique solution to X $\stackrel{\text{def}}{=}$ 1:X. But can we write IDLER $\stackrel{\text{def}}{=}$ 1:IDLER? The
derivation rule should tell us.

derivation *Idler*
    The derivation states:
$$E[fixXE/X] \stackrel{\alpha}{\rightarrow} E'$$
$$\overline{\qquad\qquad\qquad\qquad\qquad}$$
$$fixXE \stackrel{\alpha}{\rightarrow} E'$$

Substituting in the derivation rule 1:X for E, 1 for α and X for E' to obtain:
$$1:X[fixX(1:X)/X] \stackrel{1}{\rightarrow} X$$
$$\overline{\qquad\qquad\qquad\qquad\qquad}$$
$$fixX(1:X) \stackrel{1}{\rightarrow} X$$

giving
$$1:fixX(1:X) \stackrel{1}{\rightarrow} X$$
$$\overline{\qquad\qquad\qquad\qquad\qquad}$$
$$fixX(1:X) \stackrel{1}{\rightarrow} X$$

$$1 : \text{IDLER} \overset{1}{\rightarrow} X$$

$$\text{IDLER} \overset{1}{\rightarrow} X$$

Both IDLER and (1 : IDLER) can always engage in a 1 action and behave as X. Thus IDLER behaves the same as the X in X $\overset{\text{def}}{=}$ 1 : X and IDLER is a solution to the more general X $\overset{\text{def}}{=}$ 1 : X.

■

We normally write 𝟙 for IDLER. This is the formal definition of 𝟙.

propositions Idler 𝟙

Most propositions relating to idler can be derived from others by replacing the general agent names P, Q and so on by 𝟙. But note the adjective 'most': some do differ.

𝟙.1 𝟙 + 𝟙 = 𝟙
𝟙.2 𝟙 × 𝟙 = 𝟙
𝟙.3 𝟙^A = 𝟙, similarly for \A and \\A

Prop 𝟙.1 the sequence of actions offered by the two parts of the summation are identical; choice between them is vacuous, viz. prop +4.

Prop 𝟙.2 the sequence of actions offered by the two parts of the product are identical and, from prop ×7, 1×1=1, the sequence of actions of two concurrent copies of idler is indistinguishable from that of one copy.

Prop 𝟙.3 by their definitions restriction and pruning alphabets can not effect an idle action and it is impossible to change the idler by these operations.

■

interpretation 𝟙

This models a process always engaging in private internal actions and never interacting with any environment. The agent becomes incommunicado. 𝟙 models our definition of livelock

■

example

Livelocked systems do nothing useful. They are continually engaging in internal activities, never communicating with their environments. With only internal actions a livelocked agent behaves as 𝟙. Some livelocks can be easily spotted, for example:

$$P \overset{\text{def}}{=} (\text{mid}! : P)$$
$$Q \overset{\text{def}}{=} (\text{mid}? : Q)$$

where P continually outputs and Q continually inputs their combination.

$$(P \times Q) \backslash\backslash\text{mid} = ((\text{mid!}:P) \times (\text{mid?}:Q)) \backslash\backslash\text{mid}$$
$$= 1:(P \times Q) \backslash\backslash\text{mid}$$
$$= \mathbb{1}$$

P×Q continually engages in internal communication, never communicates with its environment, and by definition is not live.

In other cases the possibility of livelock is less obvious, for example:

$$\text{LIVE} \stackrel{\text{def}}{=} P \times Q$$
$$P \stackrel{\text{def}}{=} (\text{left?}:P + \text{mid!}:P)$$
$$Q \stackrel{\text{def}}{=} (\text{mid?}:Q + \text{right}:Q)$$

LIVE

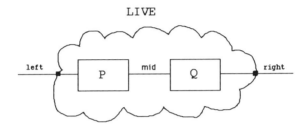

P can synchronise internally with Q over `mid`, or externally over `left`; Q can synchronise internally with P over `mid` or externally over `right`. There exists the possibility of P & Q always choosing to participate in an internal communication and always rejecting the external one – a decreasingly small possibility as the agent evolves, but nevertheless a finite one. This possible infinite internal communication is a possible livelock and is indicated in the algebra by:

$$P \times Q = (\text{left?}:P + \text{mid!}:P) \times (\text{mid?}:Q + \text{right}:Q)$$
$$= \text{mid!} \times \text{mid?}:P \times Q + \text{other possible behaviours}$$
$$= 1:P \times Q + \text{other possible behaviours}$$
$$= \mathbb{1} + \text{other possible behaviours}$$

But we needn't worry. Even the subtlest of cases will be caught by the ever-watchful eye of SCCS. In all cases, livelock will be highlighted by the appearance of a $\mathbb{1}$ in the system's emergent behaviour.

■

4.3.2.2 Inaction, ⓪

When X $\stackrel{\text{def}}{=}$ E and E=X we obtain X $\stackrel{\text{def}}{=}$ X. As the fixed point F=fixXE is a solution to X $\stackrel{\text{def}}{=}$ E, then F=fixX(X) is a solution to X $\stackrel{\text{def}}{=}$ X.

derivation *Inaction*

From the derivation rule:

$$E[fixXE/X] \xrightarrow{\alpha} E'$$

$$fixXE \xrightarrow{\alpha} E'$$

substituting X for E we obtain:

$$X[fixXX/X] \xrightarrow{\alpha} E'$$

$$fixXX \xrightarrow{\alpha} E'$$

giving:

$$fixXX \xrightarrow{\alpha} E'$$

$$fixXX \xrightarrow{\alpha} E'$$

which is a non-terminating derivation! But to be meaningful a derivation must terminate. We cannot allow X to have any actions at all. Such special agents are denoted as ⓪, the inaction agent. This is the formal derivation of agent ⓪.

■

propositions Inaction ⓪

⓪1   ⓪ + ⓪ = ⓪
⓪2   ⓪ × ⓪ = ⓪
⓪3   ⓪^A = ⓪, similarly for \A and \\A

Prop ⓪1 the action sequence offered by both parts of the summation are identically none, the choice is vacuous, viz prop +4.
Prop ⓪2 the sequence of actions offered by the two parts of the product are identically none and its behaviour is indistinguishable from one copy, viz prop ×3.
Prop ⓪3 restriction and pruning only act on visible actions. One cannot remove inaction by these operations.

■

interpretation ⓪

⓪ models a process which never performs any actions or witnesses the passage of time. As a process it never proceeds, it ceases to exist. A process can legitimately become inactive when it has finished its task, has successfully completed or unexpectedly become inactive.

■

example

Unlike livelocked systems, $\mathbb{1}$, which do nothing by being continually engaged in internal actions, deadlocked systems, $\mathbb{0}$, do nothing useful by doing nothing at all. Deadlock usually occurs when the constituent parts of composed systems cannot agree what to do next. We'll look at this later; sometimes, however, this 'do nothing' behaviour is imposed from the outside. Consider the stamp machine with the slow customer:

$$\text{STAMP\_MACHINE} \stackrel{\text{def}}{=} \text{coin?:stamp!:STAMP\_MACHINE}$$
$$\text{SLOW\_CUST} \stackrel{\text{def}}{=} \text{coin!:(1:)}^3\text{:stamp?:SLOW\_CUST}$$

pruned to allow only successful transactions:

$$(\text{STAMP\_MACHINE} \times \text{SLOW\_CUST}) \backslash\backslash\{\text{coin,stamp}\}$$
$$= (\text{coin?:stamp!:STAMP\_MACHINE}$$
$$\times \text{coin!:(1:)}^3\text{:stamp?:SLOW\_CUST})$$
$$\backslash\backslash\{\text{coin,stamp}\}$$

The first interaction is successful:

$$= 1:(\text{stamp!:STAMP\_MACHINE}$$
$$\times (1:)^3\text{:stamp?:SLOW\_CUST})$$
$$\backslash\backslash\{\text{coin,stamp}\}$$

But in the next time slot the stamp machine wants to deliver a stamp for which the customer is not ready. The ruler of the universe in which stamp machine and customer exists has decreed, by assigning the pruning, that no sole `coin` or `stamp` actions can be allowed – the only way the quandary can be satisfied is if no actions at all are allowed:

$$(\text{STAMP\_MACHINE} \times \text{SLOW\_CUST}) \backslash\backslash\{\text{coin,stamp}\} = 1:\mathbb{0}$$

and the system ceases to exist at that point.

∎

4.3.2.3 Mutual Recursion

We have seen recursion, limited to one agent expression, represented as $X \stackrel{\text{def}}{=}$ FixXE. For example, $X \stackrel{\text{def}}{=}$ FixX(read?:X + write?:X) represents a 'thing' which can be read from or written to at any time. This general agent can be written more simply as $X \stackrel{\text{def}}{=}$ read?:X ⏐ write?:X, or more specifically by replacing the variable X with constant agent names, as in DISK $\stackrel{\text{def}}{=}$ read?:DISK + write?:DISK. Can the same simplification of notation be achieved when the recursion is spread over a chain of definitions, *mutual recursion*? Consider

$$X \stackrel{\text{def}}{=} X_0$$
$$X_0 \stackrel{\text{def}}{=} \text{write!:}X_1$$
$$X_1 \stackrel{\text{def}}{=} \text{read!:}X_0$$

defining a single slot buffer which can only be read from after it has been written to. Such mutually recursive expressions can be generalised to:

$$X_0 \overset{\text{def}}{=} \alpha : X_0 + \beta : X_1$$
$$X_1 \overset{\text{def}}{=} \chi : X_0 + \gamma : X_1$$

and the unique fixed point solutions to these general equation are

$$\text{Fix}_i \langle X_0, X_1 \rangle (\alpha : X_0 + \beta : X_1, \chi : X_0 + \gamma : X_1), \text{ for } i = 0, 1$$

The derivation laws for recursion give the rules for X_0 and X_1 as:

derivation *Mutual Recursion*

$$\dfrac{\alpha : X_0 + \beta : X_1 \overset{K}{\rightarrow} X'}{X_0 \overset{K}{\rightarrow} X'} \qquad \text{and} \qquad \dfrac{\chi : X_0 + \gamma : X_1 \overset{K}{\rightarrow} X'}{X_1 \overset{K}{\rightarrow} X'}$$

There exist unique solutions for each state of a recursive expression and we can replace the agent variables in mutually recursive expressions by constant agent names.

■

From this result it is valid to replace:

$$X \overset{\text{def}}{=} X_0$$
$$X_0 \overset{\text{def}}{=} \text{write!} : X_1$$
$$X_1 \overset{\text{def}}{=} \text{read!} : X_0$$

with:

BUFFER $\overset{\text{def}}{=}$ EMPTYBUFFER
EMPTYBUFFER $\overset{\text{def}}{=}$ write! : FULLBUFFER
FULLBUFFER $\overset{\text{def}}{=}$ read! : EMPTYBUFFER

A buffer with destructive read-out.

examples
 a) A cup which can be either full or empty:
EMPTY_CUP $\overset{\text{def}}{=}$ fill! : FULL_CUP
FULL_CUP $\overset{\text{def}}{=}$ empty! : EMPTY_CUP

 b) A lift services three floors. The lift state is denoted by a suffix to the agent name: LIFT_x is the lift at floor x. For example, the lift in state LIFT_1 can go up to floor two and down to floor zero. With $x \in \{0, 1, 2\}$, and if it takes twice as long to go up between floors as it does to go down:
$\text{LIFT}_0 \overset{\text{def}}{=} \text{up} : \text{up} : \text{LIFT}_1$
$\text{LIFT}_1 \overset{\text{def}}{=} (\text{up} : \text{up} : \text{LIFT}_2) + (\text{down} : \text{LIFT}_0)$
$\text{LIFT}_2 \overset{\text{def}}{=} \text{down} : \text{LIFT}_1$

 c) A lift cabin has a simple user interface of three buttons. Action up to sends the cabin up, down down, and stop stops it. The cabin can be in one of three states: stationary, going up, or going down, each one identified by the agent names CABIN, UPCABIN and DOWNCABIN. If initially the cabin is stationary, then:

$$\text{CABIN} \stackrel{\text{def}}{=} \texttt{up?:UPCABIN + down?:DOWNCABIN}$$
$$+ \texttt{stop?:CABIN}$$
$$\text{UPCABIN} \stackrel{\text{def}}{=} \texttt{stop?:CABIN + down?:DOWNCABIN}$$
$$\text{DOWNCABIN} \stackrel{\text{def}}{=} \texttt{stop?:CABIN + up?:UPCABIN}$$

where the up and down requests are ignored if the cabin is already travelling in that direction. A set of three interlocked buttons is identified as:

$$\text{BUTTONS} \stackrel{\text{def}}{=} \texttt{up!:BUTTONS + down!:BUTTONS}$$
$$+ \texttt{stop!:BUTTONS}$$

and the complete lift:

$$\text{LIFT} \stackrel{\text{def}}{=} \texttt{(BUTTONS} \times \texttt{CABIN)} \backslash\backslash \texttt{\{stop, up, down\}}$$

So we've now shown that the calculus, at its most primitive level, is consistent and captures behaviours of real-world artifacts. And as it stands, it's all that's necessary to describe any real-time system. But, while complete, the basic algebra is not particularly usable, and we need to extend it to address higher-order, more specialised problems; for example, message passing, client server systems and so on. To be of use, these extensions must themselves be formally defined and strongly founded in the basic algebra, which we achieve by using the current algebra to derive them (and the propositions over them), which can then be used to derive operators addressing more specialised problems – and so on.

Before we can extend the algebra we have to be sure of our foundations, one of the most important being an understanding of exactly what actions are and what effects this information has on the operators and propositions over them.

4.4 Actions, Particles, Composites and All Sorts

To date we've been deliberately obscure about precisely what an action is; it was simpler to introduce the basic operators without confusing things too much, but we can't put things off forever and it's now time for a closer examination of the actions SCCS generates and how they're accommodated in its propositions.

Actions come in two interlinked flavours – particles and composites. Particles are the simplest and map directly to time slots – one particle, one time slot. Atomic time slots confer atomicity in time on particles which, as they cannot be divided into smaller actions, are also atomic operationally. But we don't always deal in agents with particulate sequences; as soon as we compose agents under product we get multiple particles per time slot and, though composite actions retain atomicity over time, they automatically lose their operational atomicity.

Particles

A particle is a special case of a composite: a composite composed of one particle.

definition *Particle*

> Particles are internal, represented by 1, or external to be observed by, and interact with, other agents. The infinite naming set $\mathcal{N}$ with typical contents of a, b, c, ..., is used to generate a subset of input particles $\Sigma_?$ with typical contents a?, b?, c? ..., and an equivalent set of co-names $\Sigma_!$ containing an output particle $a_!$ for every input particle a? in $\Sigma_?$. The combination of these sets, $\Lambda = \Sigma_? \cup \Sigma_!$, represents the complete set of particles.

■

When we combine agents we get an agent engaging concurrently in the actions of its composite parts with their individual time orders preserved – agents with n concurrent components will have at least n particles active in one time slot.

definition *Composites and* $\mathcal{A}ct$

> Composite actions can be any combination of input, output and internal particles, typical examples being 1, a!, b?, a?xb!xc!, and so on. A proviso is that, as $\alpha \times 1 = \alpha$ internal actions are subsumed within external ones, and if all the actions are internal from $1 \times 1 = 1$, they reduce to a single 1 particle.

> Every composite can be expressed in terms of powers of particulates, and the set of composites $\mathcal{A}ct$ is given by:
> $$\mathcal{A}ct = (\Sigma_? \cup \Sigma_!)^\times$$
> where $S^\times$ denotes the possibly infinite set of elements generated by product over elements from the host set S. For example if $a \in S$ then a, $a \times a$, $a \times a \times a$, ... are elements of $S^\times$

> The set $\mathcal{A}ct$ includes the internal 1 action, as a natural outcome of paired input and output actions; however, it is sometimes useful to consider the observable actions a system can engage in:
> $$\mathcal{A}ct_{-1} = \mathcal{A}ct - \{1\}$$

■

Though composite actions are more general, it is particles that provide our reference point for behaviours, and we will need a way of getting from the more general to the specific.

definition *Part*

> The set of particles present in a particular action α is denoted by $\texttt{Part}(\alpha)$; for example: $\texttt{Part}(\texttt{a!xb?}) = \{\texttt{a!}, \texttt{b?}\}$. We can extend the function $\texttt{Part}$ to operate on multiple actions as in

Part($\alpha\beta$)=Part(α)$\cup$Part(β) which can be generalised to sets of actions Part(S)=Part(S)=$\cup${Part(a)|a$\in$S}. For S={α, β}, α=a!xb? and β=a?xc! then

```
Part(S) = Part({α, β})
        = {Part(a!xb?) ∪ Part(a?xc!)} = {a!,a?,b?,c!}
```

█

As well as being able to establish the particles present in a given action, it is also useful to determine what particles a given agent can engage in. Such a set is called the sort of that agent.

definition *Sort*

Given a set of composites $L^\times$ generated on the set of particles L, $L\subseteq\Lambda$, and a particular agent P, a member of the set of agents $\mathcal{P}_L$ which range over L, then if every derivative of P can engage in an action α from $L^\times$, agent P is said to have sort L, also written P::L, and Sort(P)=L. In simpler terms, the sort of an agent is the set of particles, excluding 1, from which all the actions of that agent are formed; for example: P = a!xb?:a!xc!:P has a sort of {a!,b?,c!}.

█

We can use sorts to give us a different slant on previously defined operators:

- if P::L and $L\subseteq M$ then P::M;
- if a$\in L^\times$ and P::L then a:P::L;
- if P::L and Q::L then PxQ::L;
- if P::L and Q::L then P+Q::L;
- if P::L then P[ϕ]::Part($\phi(L)$);
- if P::L then P^A::A$\cap L$.

And, perhaps more significantly, as Sort(E) applies to each agent subexpression, we can determine, from the sorts of its constituent parts, the sort after the application of particular operators:

- Sort(α:P) = Part(α)$\cup$Sort(P);
- Sort(PxQ) = Sort(P)$\cup$Sort(Q);
- Sort(P+Q) = Sort(P)$\cup$Sort(Q);
- Sort(P[ϕ]) = Part(ϕ(Sort(P)));
- Sort(P^A) = SortP$\cap$A.

examples

- Sort($\mathbb{0}$) = {};
- Sort(1:E) = Sort(E);
- Sort(P $\overset{\text{def}}{=}$ a!xb?:c?:b!xc?:1:$\mathbb{0}$) = {a!,b?,b!,c?}

from

Sort(P) = Part(a!xb?) $\cup$ Sort(c?:b!xc?:1:$\mathbb{0}$)

$$= \{a!,b?\} \cup Part(c?) \cup Sort(b!\times c?:1:0)$$
$$= \{a!,b?\} \cup \{c?\} \cup Part(b!\times c?) \cup Sort(1:0)$$
$$= \{a!,b?,c?\} \cup \{b!,c?\} \cup Part(1) \cup Sort(0)$$
$$= \{a!,b?,b!,c?\} \cup Sort(0)$$
$$= \{a!,b?,b!,c?\}$$

- IDLECASHMACHINE has sort $\{£5!\}$;
- CLOCK has sort $\{tick!\}$;
- OLDCLOCK has sort $\{tick!, tock!\}$;
- The sort of S_{hide}, with internally satisfied communications hidden, is $\{c?,d!\}$ and sort of $S_{visible}$, when they are not hidden, is $\{a!,a?,b!,b?,c?,d!\}$;
- As $P \overset{\text{def}}{=} \alpha:\beta:\chi:1:0$ has sort $\{\alpha,\beta,\chi\}$ then $Q \overset{\text{def}}{=} \alpha:0 + \beta:P$ has sort $Sort(\alpha:0)\cup Sort(\beta:P) = \{\alpha\}\cup\{\alpha,\beta,\chi\} = \{\alpha,\beta,\chi\}$.

∎

We'll consider the effect of composite actions on propositions yet to be met as we introduce them. However, there is one problem we've already touched upon, that which occurs when a designer renames actions to names already significant in the design. We don't want to make actions dependent which were originally independent when applying a morphism. For example, α and β, originally independent, become dependent in $\alpha[\phi]$ and $\beta[\phi]$ if $\phi: \alpha\to\kappa\zeta, \beta\to\chi\zeta$ but not if $\phi: \alpha\to\kappa\zeta, \beta\to\chi$. In more formal terms, a morphism is said to be faithful on a set of action, ϕ on $\{\alpha,\beta\}$ above, if it preserves their independence. As a proposition:

$$P\backslash N[\phi] = P[\phi]\backslash Part(\phi N) \text{ if } \phi \text{ faithful on } Sort(P)\cap N$$

We now have a complete description of the kernel of SCCS, giving us the ammunition to construct specialised operators which can more directly address higher-level problems. The obvious candidates for examination are message passing systems for which we first need an understanding of agent synchronisation.

4.5 Synchronisation

4.5.1 Interaction

4.5.1.1 Agents, Actions and Synchronisation

When designing systems using SCCS our design strategy is a constructional one of repeated composition of cooperating subsystems until the solution is reached. This ties in nicely with the established client–server model of concurrent systems. In such a strategy the subsystems cooperate by passing messages, something which the operators so far introduced do not. As a first step on this road is to derive operators and propositions for agent synchronisation, before rushing in to define new operators (and their propositions), it will be to our advantage properly to introduce the inverse function and a couple of its friends.

definition $^{-1}$ *Action Inverse*

An output action is the inverse of an input action and vice versa, and we can define a function $^{-1}$ to convert one to the other; for example: $(a?)^{-1} =$ a! and $(a!)^{-1} = a?$. The inverse function is a bijection, in that a double application will get you back where you started, as in $((a?)^{-1})^{-1} = a?$. In terms of sets, the inverse function maps an element of set $\Sigma_!$ to its inverse in set $\Sigma_?$ and vice versa. The identity element of the inverse function[†] is the 1 action, $(1)^{-1} = 1$, the internal action 1. Having no associated port name, nor direction, application of the $^{-1}$ function has no effect.

◼

The $^{-1}$ function distributes over action product × in its various guises as in:
$$(a?\times b!)^{-1} = a!\times b?; \quad (a?.b!)^{-1} = a!.b?; \quad (a?b!)^{-1} = a!b?$$

Put formally, the inverse function applies to composites, it maps elements of set $\mathcal{A}ct$ $= (\Sigma_! \cup \Sigma_?)^\times$ to their inverses also in set $\mathcal{A}ct$, $^{-1}: \mathcal{A}ct{\rightarrow}\mathcal{A}ct$. For example:
$$^{-1}: a?b? \rightarrow a!b!; \quad ^{-1}: a!b! \rightarrow a?b?$$
$$\text{and } ^{-1}: (^{-1}: a?b!) \rightarrow a?b!$$

The last couple of bricks in the wall:

definition $Part^{-1}$

Given that the set of particles present in a particular action α is denoted by $Part(\alpha)$ then the set of actions that form its inverse is $Part^{-1}(\alpha) = Part(\alpha^{-1})$. We can extend the function $Part^{-1}$ to operate on multiple actions as in $Part^{-1}(\alpha\beta) = Part^{-1}(\alpha) \cup Part^{-1}(\beta)$, which itself can be generalised to action sets as in $Part^{-1}(S) = \cup\{Part^{-1}(a) \mid a \in S\}$. For example: if $S=\{\alpha, \beta\}$, $\alpha = a!\times b?$ and $\beta = a?\times c!$, then
$$Part^{-1}(S) = Part^{-1}(\{\alpha,\beta\})$$
$$= \{Part^{-1}(a!\times b?) \cup Part^{-1}(a?\times c!)\}$$
$$= \{a?, b!, a!, c?\}$$

◼

---

† The set of actions $\mathcal{A}ct$, together with the operator product (×), the inversion function $^{-1}$ and the identity element 1, form an Abelian group $(\mathcal{A}ct, \times, ^{-1})$, named after the mathematician N. H. Abel (1802-29).
- *A set with a total associative operator is called a* semigroup.
- *A semigroup with an identity element is called a* monoid.
- *A monoid in which every element has an inverse is called a* group.
- *A group whose operator is commutative is called an* Abelian group.

As actions are associative under ×, $\alpha\times\beta=\beta\times\alpha$, 1 is an identity action, for each $\alpha? \in \mathcal{A}ct$ there exists an $\alpha! \in \mathcal{A}ct$ (and vice versa) and actions are commutative under ×, $(\alpha\times\beta)\times\chi=\alpha\times(\beta\times\chi)$, then we have an Abelian group $(\mathcal{A}ct, \times, 1, ^{-1})$ which defines SCCS.

We have a similar notation for `Sort` :

definition *Sort⁻¹*

If `Sort(P)` gives the set of particles in agent `P` then `Sort⁻¹(P)` gives the set of inverse particles. For example, given `P = a!×b?:a!×c!:P` then `Sort⁻¹(P)` is `{a?,b!,c?}` .

∎

We can use this new terminology to help us formally define agent synchronisation.

Agent Synchronisation

Each observable particle is capable of supporting only one synchronisation. If at any instance an agent's guarding action is the complement of another the agents may synchronise and both actions will be satisfied. That neither particles can support further synchronisations is noted by the resultant `1` action.

Where `a!`, `a?∈Λ` this axiom over particles is captured in the derivation:

$$\frac{\texttt{true}}{\texttt{a! × a? = 1}}$$

The same concept applies to composites; for example, if $\alpha=a?\times b!$ then
$$
\begin{aligned}
\alpha\times\alpha^{-1} &= \texttt{(a?×b!)×(a!×b?)}\\
&= \texttt{(a?×a!)×(b!×b?)}\\
&= \texttt{1×1}\\
&= \texttt{1}
\end{aligned}
$$

So if one agent's α forms a complement of another's α^{-1}, when they synchronise all interactions will be satisfied. With the derivation, this time for composites $\alpha\in\mathcal{A}ct$

$$\frac{\texttt{true}}{\alpha\times\alpha^{-1} = 1}$$

and as a proposition:

proposition

↔ $\alpha \times \alpha^{-1} = 1$

`Prop` ↔ if one set of actions is the inverse of another their composition under product behaves as an internal `1` action.

∎

For two processes $\alpha : P$ and $\alpha^{-1} : Q$ where (α, α^{-1}) is a synchronisation pair:

$$\alpha : P \times \alpha^{-1} : Q$$

$$\overline{\alpha \times \alpha^{-1} : P \times Q}$$

$$\overline{1 : P \times Q}$$

the 1 denoting private synchronisations between P and Q

The pairing of an action with its inverse, because of its links to agent synchronisation, is called rather unsurprising a synchronisation pair.

definition *Synchronisation Pair*
> A pair of complementary actions by which agents can synchronise is termed a **synchronisation pair**. For example, process $\alpha : P$ and $\beta : Q$ will synchronise if $\beta = \alpha^{-1}$ as (α, α^{-1}) form a synchronisation pair.

■

interpretation
> If two processes offer, in the same time slot, to engage in sets of complementary actions, the satisfied actions synchronises their parent processes with the process executing its complement.

■

It is useful at this point to introduce the opposite of synchronisation pairs: incomplete actions – based on the premise that all actions only live to synchronise and those that contain actions yet to be paired are by definition incomplete.

definition *Incomplete Actions*
> An action α containing no internal actions in synchronisation pairs $\text{Part}(\alpha) \cap \text{Part}(\alpha^{-1}) = \emptyset$ is termed an incomplete action. Similarly, two actions (α, β) are termed externally incomplete, $\text{Part}(\alpha) \cap \text{Part}^{-1}(\beta) = \emptyset$, if their composition does not add to the synchronisation pairs in α and β when considered separately; and actions (α, β) are termed totally incomplete, $\text{Part}(\alpha\beta) \cap \text{Part}^{-1}(\alpha\beta) = \emptyset$, if their composition contains no synchronisation pairs. Some examples:
> - $a!b?c!$ is incomplete as $\{a!,b?,c!\} \cap \{a?,b!,c?\} = \emptyset$
> - $a!b?b!$ is not from $\{a!,b?,b!\} \cap \{a?,b!,b?\} \neq \emptyset$
> - $(a!b?c!, a!d?)$ are totally incomplete from
> $\{a!,b?,c!,d?\} \cap \{a?,b!,c?,d!\} = \emptyset$
> - $(a!b?c!, a!c?)$ are neither externally incomplete from
> $\{a!,b?,c!\} \cap \{a?c!\} \neq \emptyset$ nor totally incomplete from
> $\{a!,b?,c!,c?\} \cap \{a?,b!,c?,c!\} \neq \emptyset$.

- `(a!a?b?,b?c!)` are externally incomplete from
  $\{a!,a?,b?\} \cap \{b?,c?\} = \emptyset$ but not totally incomplete
  from $\{a!,a?,b?,c!\} \cap \{a?,a!,b!,c?\} \neq \emptyset$.

And over agents. Agent P is internally incomplete if none of its particles can form synchronisation pairs `Sort(P)∩Sort⁻¹(P)` $= \emptyset$. For example:

- `P=a!b?c!` : P is internally incomplete as
  $\{a!,b?,c!\} \cap \{a?,b!,c?\} = \emptyset$,
- `P=a!b?a?` : P is not as $\{a!,b?,a?\} \cap \{a?,b!,a!\} \neq \emptyset$.

Agents P and Q are externally incomplete if their combination P×Q forms no synchronisation pairs above those already present in P and Q, `Sort(P)∩Sort⁻¹(Q)` $= \emptyset$. For example:

- `P=a!b?a!` : P is not externally incomplete of `Q=a?d?` : Q, as
  $\{a!,b?\} \cap \{a!,d!\} \neq \emptyset$,
- `P=a!b?c?` : P and `Q=b?d?` : Q are, as $\{a!,b?,c?\} \cap \{b!,d!\} = \emptyset$,

■

Back to synchronisation. This is straightforward when the two agents concerned are isolated from the rest of the universe; for example: α : P placed in environment α^{-1} : Q

$$\alpha : P \times \alpha^{-1} : Q = 1 : P \times Q$$

But this is a rather simplistic view. In general, subsystems are offered synchronisation by more than one other subsystem – for example, a server with multiple clients. So what is the behaviour when α : P is placed in environment α^{-1} : Q $\times$ α^{-1} : R?

$$= \alpha : P \times \alpha^{-1} : Q \times \alpha^{-1} : R$$
$$= \alpha \times \alpha^{-1} \times \alpha^{-1} : P \times Q \times R$$
$$= 1 \times \alpha^{-1} : P \times Q \times R$$

A synchronisation has occurred, and one possible interaction remains. But has P synchronised with Q or with R?. Is it Q or R which is still offering to synchronise? The algebra doesn't tell us. In many designs we want to know beforehand – to make deterministic – which synchronisations are successful and which not. This we can do by encapsulating parts of a system, hiding them from the rest of their environment, forcing the synchronisations we want and preventing those we don't. But there is a problem: we can never tell what environment an agent may be placed in, and only by encapsulating for all possible environments can we ensure no interference and successful synchronisations – as in:

$$G \stackrel{\text{def}}{=} (E \times F) \wedge A \text{ where } \alpha, \alpha^{-1} \notin A$$
$$(E \times F) \wedge A = (\alpha : E' \times \alpha^{-1} : F') \wedge A$$
$$= (\alpha . \alpha^{-1} : E' \times F') \wedge A$$
$$= 1 : (E' \times F') \wedge A$$

The synchronisation has been encapsulated, it is internal to G, and the inability of an environment to observe or interact ensures correct synchronisation. But isn't this always the case? If an agent's actions are not in A they will be unaffected by the restriction operator and will be free to 'step outside' its scoping and remain available to interact with any environment, including each other, as in $(a!:P \times a?:Q)^\wedge\{a!a?\} = a!a?:(P \times Q)^\wedge\{a!a?\}$ and $(a!:P \times b?:Q)^\wedge\{a!b?\} = a!b?:(P \times Q)^\wedge\{a!b?\}$. If one of the guarding actions is incomplete and in the restriction set, inaction results, as in $(a!:P \times b?:Q)^\wedge\{\} = \mathbb{0}$. We can formalise these thoughts in propositions:

proposition Synchronisation $\leftrightarrow$ where $A \subseteq \mathcal{A}ct$ and $\alpha, \beta \in \mathcal{A}ct$

$\leftrightarrow$A $(\alpha:P \times \alpha^{-1}:Q)^\wedge A =$

        a) $1:(P \times Q)^\wedge A, \ \alpha\alpha^{-1} \notin A$

        b) $\alpha.\alpha^{-1}:(P \times Q)^\wedge A, \ \alpha\alpha^{-1} \in A$

$\leftrightarrow$B $(\alpha:P \times \beta:Q)^\wedge A =$

        a) $\alpha.\beta:(P \times Q)^\wedge A, \ \alpha\beta \in A$

        b) $\mathbb{0}, \ \alpha\beta \notin A$

Where guarding actions form a synchronisation pair:

Prop $\leftrightarrow$Aa) agent synchronisation is independent of any environment. When the guarding actions form a synchronisation pair within the scope of the restriction operator, synchronisation is forced, as the resultant 1 action is the only way to 'escape' the encapsulation.

Prop $\leftrightarrow$Ab) agent synchronisation is dependent upon its environment. When two agents synchronise, the 'restricted to' actions, including the synchronisation pairs, can 'step outside' the restriction and are available to interact with any environment in which the expression finds itself.

Where guarding actions do not form a synchronisation pair:

Prop $\leftrightarrow$Ba) when the agents include incomplete actions that are within the scope of an encapsulation, both actions can 'escape' the encapsulation.

Prop $\leftrightarrow$Bb) when the agents include incomplete actions not in the restriction set, inaction results.

■

interpretation

The simultaneous occurrence of input and output actions of the same port names models the synchronisation of real-world processes. We ensure that a specific synchronisation occurs by encapsulating, hiding from any environment, the relevant synchronisation pair.

■

examples

a) Consider the simple case of a server managing one unshareable resource

$$\text{FREE\_SERVER} \overset{\text{def}}{=} \alpha:\text{ASSIGNED\_SERVER}$$

placed in an environment of two clients

$$\text{CLIENT1} \overset{\text{def}}{=} \alpha^{-1}:\text{C1\&RESOURCE}$$
$$\text{CLIENT2} \overset{\text{def}}{=} \alpha^{-1}:\text{C2\&RESOURCE}$$

giving

$\text{FREE\_SERVER} \times \text{CLIENT1} \times \text{CLIENT2}$

$= \alpha:\text{ASSIGNED\_SERVER} \times \alpha^{-1}:\text{C1\&RESOURCE} \times \alpha^{-1}:\text{C2\&RESOURCE}$

$= (1:(\text{ASSIGNED\_SERVER} \times \text{C1\&RESOURCE}) \times \alpha^{-1}:\text{C2\&RESOURCE})$

$\quad + (1:(\text{ASSIGNED\_SERVER} \times \text{C2\&RESOURCE}) \times \alpha^{-1}:\text{C1\&RESOURCE})$

As the environment of FREE_SERVER contains more than one agent offering synchronisation, which client gets the resource is undetermined.

b) Reconsider our problem $\alpha:P \times \alpha^{-1}:Q \times \alpha^{-1}:R$

$\alpha:P \times \alpha^{-1}:Q \times \alpha^{-1}:R$

$\times 5 \qquad\qquad\quad = \alpha.\alpha.\alpha^{-1}:(P \times Q \times R)$

$\leftrightarrow \qquad\qquad\quad = 1.\alpha^{-1}:(P \times Q \times R)$

$\times 6 \qquad\qquad\quad = \alpha^{-1}:(P \times Q \times R)$

Which agent $\alpha:P$ has synchronised with is not determined; it is non-deterministic. To ensure $\alpha:P$ synchronises with $\alpha^{-1}:Q$ and not with $\alpha^{-1}:R$ we can use the scoping of an appropriate restriction set

$$\{\alpha, \alpha^{-1}\} \notin A:$$

$(\alpha:P \times \alpha^{-1}:Q)^\wedge A \times \alpha^{-1}:R$

$\leftrightarrow Aa \qquad\qquad = 1:(P \times Q)^\wedge A \times \alpha^{-1}:R$

c) For COPY $\overset{\text{def}}{=} \text{a}?:1:\text{c}!:\text{d}!:0$, agent COPY acts as a copy-to-disk server with agent DISK $\overset{\text{def}}{=} 1:1:\text{c}?:\text{d}?:0$. For

$(\text{c}!,\text{c}?,\text{d}!,\text{d}?) \notin A$

SYSTEM $\overset{\text{def}}{=}$ COPY $\times$ DISK

$\text{def} \quad \text{COPY} \times \text{DISK} = (\text{a}?:1:\text{c}!:\text{d}!:0 \times 1:1:\text{c}?:\text{d}?:0)^\wedge A$

$\times 6, {}^\wedge 2 \qquad\qquad\quad = \text{a}?:(1:\text{c}!:\text{d}!:0 \times 1:\text{c}?:\text{d}?:0)^\wedge A$

$\times 7, {}^\wedge 2 \qquad\qquad\quad = \text{a}?:1:(\text{c}!:\text{d}!:0 \times \text{c}?:\text{d}?:0)^\wedge A$

$\leftrightarrow Aa \qquad\qquad\quad = \text{a}?:1:1:(\text{d}!:0 \times \text{d}?:0)^\wedge A$

$\leftrightarrow Aa \qquad\qquad\quad = \text{a}?:1:1:1:(0 \times 0)^\wedge A$

$0 3 \qquad\qquad\qquad = \text{a}?:1:1:1:0$

The COPY server synchronises with the DISK and a file copied as a private interaction between them.

As obvious as single synchronisation between two agents appears to be, it's really only a special case of multiple synchronisation.

Multiple Synchronisation

Unlike interleaving algebras, the non-atomic actions of SCCS give it the capability of modelling multiple synchronisations; for example: $a!\times a!:P$ simultaneously synchronises with $a?:R$ and $a?:Q$. Put more formally:

$$\alpha\times\alpha : P \times \alpha^{-1}:Q\times\alpha^{-1}:R$$

$$\begin{array}{ll} \times 5 & = \alpha.\alpha.\alpha^{-1}.\alpha^{-1}:(P\times Q\times R) \\ \leftrightarrow & = 1.1:(P\times Q\times R) \\ \times 7 & = 1:(P\times Q\times R) \end{array}$$

Multiple synchronisation gives SCCS the capability of modelling so-called 'beacon systems' where one agent, a beacon, synchronises with a precise number of agents in its environment. For example, beacon agent $(a!:)^n:P$ can synchronise with up to n other agents whose guards contain single $a?$ actions. An obvious use for such systems is a master agent which triggers multiple slave systems.

$$(a!:)^n:MASTER \times a?:SLAVE_1 \times a?:SLAVE_2\times \ldots \times a?:SLAVE_n$$

So far we've considered successful synchronisations, but synchronisations can fail, and we need a way of handling these failures. For simplicity, we will return to the special case of single synchronisation.

Synchronisation Failure

It's all very well considering what happens when agents synchronise successfully, but what happens when they don't? Back to our customer who wants a 10p stamp:

$$10\text{CUSTOMER} \stackrel{\text{def}}{=} 10\text{pcoin}!:10\text{pstamp}?:10\text{CUSTOMER}$$

and a machine which dispenses 10p and 20p stamps:

$$10/20\_\text{STAMP\_MACHINE} \stackrel{\text{def}}{=} 10\text{pcoin}?:10\text{pstamp}!:10/20\_\text{STAMP\_MACHINE}$$
$$+ 20\text{pcoin}?:20\text{pstamp}!:10/20\_\text{STAMP\_MACHINE}$$

When we put customer and machine together we expect that their 10pcoin and 10pstamp actions would synchronise and the insertion of a 10p coin would lead to the subsequent delivery of a 10p stamp – something along the lines of the following:

$$10\text{CUSTOMER} \times 10/20\_\text{STAMP\_MACHINE}$$
$$= 1:1:10\text{CUSTOMER} \times 10/20\_\text{STAMP\_MACHINE}$$

But what do the propositions say?

```
10CUSTOMER × 10/20_STAMP_MACHINE

      = (10pcoin?:10pstamp!:10/20_STAMP_MACHINE
            + 20pcoin?:20pstamp!:10/20_STAMP_MACHINE)
          × 10pcoin!:10pstamp?:10CUSTOMER


+6    = (10pcoin?:10pstamp!:10/20_STAMP_MACHINE
            × 10pcoin!:10pstamp?:10CUSTOMER)
        + (20pcoin?:20pstamp!:10/20_STAMP_MACHINE
            × 10pcoin!:10pstamp?:10CUSTOMER)


×4    = 10pcoin?.10pcoin!
          :(10pstamp!:10/20_STAMP_MACHINE
            × 10pstamp?:10CUSTOMER)
        + (20pcoin?:20pstamp!:10/20_STAMP_MACHINE
            × 10pcoin!:10pstamp?:10CUSTOMER)


×4    = 10pcoin?.10pcoin!:10pstamp!.10pstamp?
          :10/20_STAMP_MACHINE × 10CUSTOMER
        + (20pcoin?:20pstamp!:10/20_STAMP_MACHINE
            × 10pcoin!:10pstamp?:10CUSTOMER)
```

The behaviour we wanted is there, but so are others. And these others develop to:

```
×4    = 10pcoin?.10pcoin!:10pstamp!.10pstamp?
          :10/20_STAMP_MACHINE × 10CUSTOMER
        + 20pcoin?.10pcoin!
            :(20pstamp!:10/20_STAMP_MACHINE
            × 10pstamp?:10CUSTOMER)


×4    = 10pcoin?.10pcoin!:10pstamp!.10pstamp?
          :10/20_STAMP_MACHINE × 10CUSTOMER
        + 20pcoin?.10pcoin!:20pstamp!.10pstamp?
            :10/20_STAMP_MACHINE × 10CUSTOMER
```

Both behaviours are valid. Either the $10p$ stamp transaction is successful, satisfying both agents, or the machine which offers to negotiate in $20p$ stamps and the customer in $10p$ ones are available to be satisfied by other customers and machines. We could get rid of the extra behaviours, only allowing the actions we want, by encapsulating with an appropriate 'restricted to' operation, but we can do better than that. Restriction operators tend to be too specific – one has to spell out the names of the composite actions one wishes to retain; for example: $^\wedge\{a!b?\}$ will allow only the action $a?b!$ and not $a!b?$ or even $a?$. This leads to over-complex restriction sets, such as the one given in section 4.2.2.9 where a restriction set of $A = \{x \in \{0,1\}, y \in \{0,1\}, z \in \{0,1\} \mid \text{notin}_x?.\text{and}2i_y?.\text{andout}_z!\} \cup \{1\}$

was needed. It simplifies things greatly if we address hiding, not at the the level of composite actions, but at the more basic level of particles, allowing all a! actions wherever they occur. Further, it will complement the way we progress designs if, rather than allowing actions, we remove them. Putting these things together, we arrive at the pruning operator \A which we will now investigate at more depth.

4.5.1.2 Pruning

Synchronisation between agents is pivotal in systems design, and we have seen in the previous section how encapsulation can make such synchronisations selective. But the restriction operator, E^A, which allows E to engage in specific composite actions, as a tool of encapsulation discriminates too strongly and a hiding or *pruning* operator, E\A, by coming in at a lower level – removing the particles in A from expression E – forms a more effective tool.

Action Pruning
definition *pruning operator* \

> The result of applying the pruning operator \ to agent P, as in P\A, is to remove the particles contained in set A from the agent P wherever they occur. Pruning can be defined in terms of restriction as:
>
> $$P\backslash A = P\verb|^| (\Lambda - A)^\times$$
>
> That is, pruning an agent by the set of particles in A is equivalent to restricting an agent to the complete set of actions generated by the set of particles Λ less those in A. In terms of sorts, Sort(P\A) = Sort(P) – A.
>
> (Note that, by definition, the action 1 is a member of any *'restrict to'* set, and thus is never a member of a pruning set; one cannot remove an internal action by pruning.)

Pruning removes all combinations of all the particles contained in the pruning set and hence the actions containing them.

examples
- (a?b!:c?d?:P)\{e?,e!} = a?b!:c?d?: (P)\{e?,e!}
- (a?:d?:P)\{d?} = a?:𝟘
- (a?b!:c?d?:P)\{d?} = a?b!:𝟘
- (a?b!:c?d?:P + a!b?:c?d?:P)\{a?} = a!b?:c?d?:P\{a?}
- (1:P)\A = 1: (P)\A, for all A

While the pruning operator is effective, we will only use it as a stepping-stone to an even more effective one – a hiding operator that directly addresses pruning in the context of agents communication. Cue fanfare for...

Synchronisation Pruning
definition *Synchronisation Pruning* \\

We introduce set A, a subset of the naming set $A \subseteq \mathcal{N}$, such that pruning by A performs the same function as pruning by A_1 and A_2. Subsets of the particle send and receive sets $A_1 \subseteq \Sigma_1$ and $A_2 \subseteq \Sigma_2$, such that

$$\backslash\backslash A = \backslash\{A_1 \cup A_2\}, \; 1 \notin A$$

where A_1 is the set of output particles named in A and A_2 the set of input particles named in A.

E\\A removes all input and output particles in A from E, that is $E\backslash\{a!,a?\} = E\backslash\backslash\{a\}$ and, as such, it acts directly on synchronisation pairs. In terms of sorts $\text{Sort}(P\backslash\backslash A) = \text{Sort}(P) - \{A_1 \cup A_2\}$.

■

We can provide a set of basic propositions for this new operator.

propositions Synchronisation Pruning \\ where $A \subseteq \mathcal{N}$, $B \subseteq \mathcal{N}$ and $\alpha \in \mathcal{A}ct$

\\1	$P\backslash\backslash A\backslash\backslash B = P\backslash\backslash B\backslash\backslash A = P\backslash\backslash\{A \cup B\}$
\\2	$(\alpha:P)\backslash\backslash A = \alpha:P\backslash\backslash A$, if $\text{Part}(\alpha) \cap A = \varnothing$
	$= 0$, if $\text{Part}(\alpha) \cap \text{Part}(\alpha^{-1}) \neq \varnothing$ and $\text{Part}(\alpha) \cap A \neq \varnothing$
\\3	$(\alpha \times \alpha^{-1}:P)\backslash\backslash A = 1:P\backslash\backslash A$, if $\text{Part}(\alpha) \subseteq A$
\\4	$(\Sigma_i P_i)\backslash\backslash A = \Sigma_i (P_i\backslash\backslash A)$
\\5	$(P \times Q)\backslash\backslash A \neq (P\backslash\backslash A) \times (Q\backslash\backslash A)$, in general

Prop \\1 from a property of set union synchronisation prunings can be applied in any order.

Prop \\2a if the guarding action and pruning set A have no particles in common, pruning has no effect.

Prop \\2b if the guarding action has incomplete particles also in the pruning set, inaction results.

Prop \\3 synchronising, and becoming a 1 action, is the only way a synchronisation completely contained in the pruning set can escape.

Prop \\4 synchronisation pruning distributes over summation – we can move a pruning operator, globally scoping an expression containing summation to operate on individual components of that summation. For example:

$(\alpha:P + \beta:Q + \chi:R)\backslash\backslash A = (\alpha:P)\backslash\backslash A + (\beta:Q)\backslash\backslash A + (\chi:R)\backslash\backslash A$

and in particular:

$$(P+Q) \backslash\backslash A = P\backslash\backslash A + Q\backslash\backslash A$$

Prop \\5 synchronisation pruning does not generally distribute over product. For example: $(\alpha : P \times \beta : Q \times \chi : R) \backslash\backslash A$ cannot be replaced by $(\alpha : P) \backslash\backslash A \times (\beta : Q) \backslash\backslash A \times (\chi : R) \backslash\backslash A$.

■

Knowing what $(\alpha : P) \backslash\backslash A$ is when α and A have no particles in common, while useful, is only part of the picture. We really need to know what $(\alpha : P) \backslash\backslash A$ is for all α and A. To do this we need to know more about scoping.

Pruning and Scoping

The hiding operators of restriction and pruning are used to encapsulate subdesigns by internalising certain agent actions; when applied to defined sections of expressions, these operators are said to *scope* over parts of that expression. For example: in

$$(\!(\!(\alpha!\beta!:\beta?:\chi?:P + \alpha?:1:\chi!:Q)\!)\backslash\backslash A + \alpha!\chi?:R)\!)\backslash\backslash B$$

pruning operator A scopes over the first two (sub-)agents hiding selected actions from their environment, where this environment includes the remainder of the expression, while pruning operator B scopes over the complete expression. Pruning operators control the visibility of actions in the expressions they scope over and the resultant behaviours, depending upon the contents of the pruning set. Consider the following examples, where:

- the pruning set includes some of the particles in the guarding action of the expression it scopes over. By definition, these particles, and hence the composites they are part of, will be pruned, and inaction will result. For example:

  $(a!:P)\backslash\backslash\{a\} = \mathbb{0},$
  $(a?b!:P)\backslash\backslash\{a\} = \mathbb{0},$
  $(b!a?:P)\backslash\backslash\{a\} = (b!a?:P)\backslash\backslash\{b\} = \mathbb{0}.$

- the pruning set contains none of the particles in the guarding action of the expression it scopes over. These actions 'step outside' the scope of the operator to be observed by, and be available for interaction with, agents in its environment. For example:

  $(a!:P)\backslash\backslash\{c\} = a!:P\backslash\backslash\{c\},$
  $(a?b!:P)\backslash\backslash\{c\} = a?b!:P\backslash\backslash\{c\},$
  $(a!b?:P)\backslash\backslash\{c\} = a!b?:P\backslash\backslash\{c\}.$

If only life were so simple. Things get more interesting when we scope over synchronisations; for example: how do $(a!a?b!b?:P)\backslash\backslash\{a,b\}$, $(a!a?b!b?:P)\backslash\backslash\{a\}$ or even $(a!a?b!b?:P)\backslash\backslash\{c\}$ behave? To answer such questions we need to be able to predict the outcome of pruning where some initial particles form synchronisation pairs and others do not; some particles are incomplete, some particles appear in the pruning set, and some do not (where 'none' and 'all' are included in 'some'). It's going to be simpler to cover all permutations of particulate actions if we define $(\alpha : P) \backslash A$ as $(\sigma\sigma^{-1}\gamma\gamma^{-1}\kappa\xi : P) \backslash A$ where $\sigma\sigma^{-1}$ represents synchronisation pairs not in A; $\gamma\gamma^{-1}$ synchronisation pairs in A; κ incomplete particles in A; and ξ incomplete particles not in A. Using this notion we can redefine the previous cases as:

- with no incomplete action in the pruning set, $\text{Part}(\kappa) = \varnothing$,
  $$(\alpha : P) \backslash\backslash A = 1 \times \sigma\sigma^{-1}\xi : (P \times Q) \backslash\backslash A$$
  those synchronisation pairs not in the pruning set, $\sigma\sigma^{-1}$, can escape and remain available to synchronise with other actions in the environment, as can the unpruned incomplete particles ξ; but the only way synchronisation pairs in the pruning set, $\gamma\gamma^{-1}$, can escape is to synchronise within the scoping – synchronisation pairs that are pruned over are forced to satisfy each other. For example:
  $$(a!b?a?b!c? : P) \backslash\backslash\{a\} = b?b!c? : (P) \backslash\backslash\{a\}$$
  Note that the 1 in $1 \times \sigma\xi$ is there as a reminder for the case where $\text{Part}(\xi) = \text{Part}(\sigma) = \varnothing$; for example:
  $$(a!a? : P) \backslash\backslash\{a\} = 1 : (P) \backslash\backslash\{a\}$$

- some incomplete action are in the pruning set, $\text{Part}(\kappa) \neq \varnothing$
  $$(\alpha : P) \backslash\backslash A = \mathbb{0}$$
  Inaction results, even if one particle is pruned, as in
  $$(a!b? : P) \backslash\backslash\{b\} = \mathbb{0}$$

We can use these insights to extend proposition \\2 and consider all cases of the composition of the guarding action and pruning set:

propositions Synchronisation Pruning \\6

    Where $\text{Part}(\sigma) \cap A = \varnothing$; $\text{Part}(\gamma) \subseteq A$; $\text{Part}(\kappa) \subseteq A$ and $\text{Part}(\xi) \cap A = \varnothing$

\\6   a) $(\sigma\sigma^{-1}\gamma\gamma^{-1}\xi : P) \backslash\backslash A = (\sigma\sigma^{-1}\xi : P) \backslash\backslash A = \sigma\sigma^{-1}\xi : P\backslash\backslash A$

        b) $(\sigma\sigma^{-1}\gamma\gamma^{-1}\kappa\xi : P) \backslash\backslash A = \mathbb{0}$

        c) $(\sigma\sigma^{-1} : P) \backslash\backslash A = (\sigma\sigma^{-1}\gamma\gamma^{-1} : P) \backslash\backslash A = \sigma\sigma^{-1} : P\backslash\backslash A$

        d) $(\xi : P) \backslash\backslash A = (\gamma\gamma^{-1}\xi : P) \backslash\backslash A = \xi : P\backslash\backslash A$

        e) $(\gamma\gamma^{-1} : P) \backslash\backslash A = 1 : P\backslash\backslash A$

Prop \\6

a)   incomplete actions, ξ, and synchronisation pairs, σ, not in the pruning set, $\text{Part}(\sigma) \cap A = \varnothing$ and $\text{Part}(\xi) \cap A = \varnothing$, can 'step outside' the scope of \\A and remain available for synchronisation. Synchronisation pairs in the pruning set, $\text{Part}(\gamma) \subseteq A$, can 'escape' by synchronising, becoming a 1 action to be subsumed by $\sigma\sigma^{-1}\xi$.

b) as synchronisation pairs can always escape pruning, inaction only results if the guarding action contains incomplete particles also in the pruning set, $\text{Part}(\kappa) \subseteq A$.

c) no incomplete actions. Synchronisation pairs not in the pruning set, $\text{Part}(\sigma) \cap A = \varnothing$, can escape and remain available to interact with any environment. Synchronisation pairs in the pruning set, $\text{Part}(\gamma) \subseteq A$, are forced to synchronise within the scope of the pruning, escape as a 1 action and are then subsumed within $\sigma\sigma^{-1}$.

d) no incomplete actions or synchronisation pairs in the pruning set. Incomplete actions not in the pruning set, $\text{Part}(\xi) \cap A = \varnothing$, can escape and interact with any environment. Pruned over synchronisation pairs, $\text{Part}(\gamma) \subseteq A$, are forced to synchronise within its scope to escape as a 1 action and be subsumed by ξ.

e) by themselves, pruned over synchronisation pairs, $\text{Part}(\gamma) \subseteq A$, are forced to synchronise within the scope of the pruning, escaping as a 1 action.

◼

Propositions introduced earlier are special cases:

\\2a	$(\alpha\!:\!P)\backslash\backslash A = \alpha\!:\!P\backslash\backslash A$, if $\text{Part}(\alpha) \cap A = \varnothing$ from \\6d
\\2b	$(\alpha\!:\!P)\backslash\backslash A = \mathbb{0}$, if α is an incomplete action in A from \\6b
\\3	$(\alpha\times\alpha^{-1}\!:\!P)\backslash\backslash A = 1\!:\!P\backslash\backslash A$, if $\text{Part}(\alpha) \subseteq A$ from \\6e

We can now, with more confidence, investigate emergent behaviours under pruning, starting with choice; for example: $(\alpha\!:\!P + \beta\!:\!Q)\backslash\backslash\alpha \overset{\text{def}}{=} \beta\!:\!Q\backslash\backslash\alpha$, where, given a range of behaviours, a designer can select particular ones while rejecting others.

interpretation *Pruning over Choice*
Pruning models the selection of a subset of the behaviours of a general process by removing alternative choices.

◼

As with $(\!(\,)\!)^\wedge A$, we'll sometimes use $(\!(\,)\!)\backslash\backslash A$ to highlight the application of propositions in examples; naturally this notation isn't a formal part of part of the algebra.

example
This is a reworking of the example of the restriction section. A general file copy server can read in a file and, after some formatting, can copy the file to a disk or give it to a printer spooler with instructions to print it on either a fast draft-quality printer or a slower letter-quality printer.

Where:

$a?$ = read in file 1 = format file

$c!$ = select the disk $d!$ = write to disk

$e!$ = send to printer queue $f!$ = write to high-speed printer

$g!$ = write to slow-speed printer

Each action takes 1mS. The 'restrict to' set was $\{1,a?,e!,f!,d?\}$
giving, from $\backslash\backslash A = \backslash\{A! \cup A?\}$ and $P\backslash A = P^\wedge (\Lambda - A)^\times$, the equivalent
pruning set is $\{c,g\}$

	COPY$\backslash\{c,g\}$ $= (a?:1:(c!:d!:0 + e!:(f?:0 + g!:0)))\backslash\backslash\{c,g\}$
$\backslash\backslash 6d$	$= a?:(1:(c!:d!:0 + e!:(f?:0 + g!:0)))\backslash\backslash\{c,g\}$
$\backslash\backslash 6d$	$= a?:1:(c!:d!:0 + e!:(f?:0 + g!:0))\backslash\backslash\{c,g\}$
$\backslash\backslash 4$	$= a?:1:((c!:d!:0)\backslash\backslash\{c,g\}+ (e!:(f?:0 + g!:0))\backslash\backslash\{c,g\})$
$\backslash\backslash 6b, \backslash\backslash 6d$	$= a?:1:(0 + e!:(f?:0 + g!:0)\backslash\backslash\{c,g\})$
$+3$	$= a?:1:e!:(f?:0 + g!:0)\backslash\backslash\{c,g\}$
$\backslash\backslash 4$	$= a?:1:e!:((f?:0)\backslash\backslash\{c,g\} + (g!:0)\backslash\backslash\{c,g\})$
$\backslash\backslash 6d, \backslash\backslash 6b$	$= a?:1:e!:(f?:0\backslash\backslash\{c,g\} + 0)$
$+3$	$= a?:1:e!:f?:0\backslash\backslash\{c,g\}$
03	$= a?:1:e!:f?:0$

which gives COPY$\backslash\backslash\{c,g\} = a?:1:e!:f?:0$, concurring with the
previous result. The behaviour of a general agent COPY has been reduced
to a selected subset of its original behaviour. This subset can now be used
as a system in its own right. Other restrictions of agent COPY give different
behaviours as in:

$$\text{COPY}\backslash\backslash\{c\} = a?:1:e!:(f?:0 + g!:0)$$
$$\text{COPY}\backslash\backslash\{c,f\} = a?:1:e!:g!:0$$
$$\text{COPY}\backslash\backslash\{a\} = 0$$

■

By pruning choice guards we can take a general agent, like the copy server above,
and statically convert it into a specialised agent retaining only a desired subset of
the original behaviour. More useful would be dynamic selection of behaviours,
rather as a client at run-time selects the service it wants. This we can model by
using synchronisation to select a behaviour, pruning away failed synchronisa-
tions as in $((\alpha : P + \beta : Q) \times \alpha^{-1} : R) \backslash\backslash \alpha = 1 : (P \times R) \backslash\backslash \alpha$.

interpretation

The pruning operator is a selective container of agents - it hides from
environments the particles present in the pruning set, allowing particles
not in the pruning set to freely interact.

Pruning allows us to keep necessary ports public, to receive requests and deliver results, while removing others (such encapsulations prevent outside interference in the internal workings of an agent). In effect, E\\a hides (binds) the action a to expression E.

■

All of which leads us neatly back to our customer who wants a 10p stamp:

$$\text{10CUSTOMER} \stackrel{\text{def}}{=} \text{10pcoin!:10pstamp?:10CUSTOMER}$$

and a machine which dispenses 10p and 20p stamps:

$$\text{10/20\_STAMP\_MACHINE} \stackrel{\text{def}}{=} \text{10pcoin?:10pstamp!:10/20\_STAMP\_MACHINE}$$
$$+ \text{20pcoin?:20pstamp!:10/20\_STAMP\_MACHINE}$$

When we last put the customer and the machine together we got:

$$\text{10CUSTOMER} \times \text{10/20\_STAMP\_MACHINE}$$
$$= \text{10pcoin?.10pcoin!:10pstamp!.10pstamp?}$$
$$:\text{10/20\_STAMP\_MACHINE} \times \text{10CUSTOMER}$$
$$+ \text{20pcoin?.10pcoin!:20pstamp!.10pstamp?}$$
$$:\text{10/20\_STAMP\_MACHINE} \times \text{10CUSTOMER}$$

Either the 10p stamp transaction is successful, satisfying both agents locally, or the machine offers to negotiate in 20p stamps and the customer in 10p ones and both could be satisfied by other customers and machines. We want to force a local 10p transaction and get rid of (prune away) the unsuccessful 20p actions. We want:

$$(\text{10CUSTOMER} \times \text{10/20\_STAMP\_MACHINE})\backslash\backslash\{\text{10pcoin,10pstamp,20pcoin,20pstamp}\}$$

To enable our equations to fit on the page we'll equate

$$X = \text{10CUSTOMER}$$
$$Y = \text{10/20\_STAMP\_MACHINE}$$
$$A = \{\text{10pcoin,10pstamp,20pcoin,20pstamp}\}$$

then find the emergent behaviour of GETSTAMP $\stackrel{\text{def}}{=}$ (X × Y)\\A.

Applying the propositions:

$$\text{GETSTAMP} \stackrel{\text{def}}{=} (X \times Y)\backslash\backslash A$$
$$= (\!(\text{10pcoin?:10pstamp!:X} + \text{20pcoin?:20pstamp!:X})$$
$$\times \text{10pcoin!:10pstamp?:Y})\!)\backslash\backslash A$$

+6
$$= (\!((\text{10pcoin?:10pstamp!:X} \times \text{10pcoin!:10pstamp?:Y})$$
$$+ (\text{20pcoin?:20pstamp!:X} \times \text{10pcoin!:10pstamp?:Y}))\!)\backslash\backslash A$$

\\3
$$= 1:(\!\text{10pstamp!:X} \times \text{10pstamp?:Y})\!)\backslash\backslash A$$
$$+ (\!\text{20pcoin?:20pstamp!:X} \times \text{10pcoin!:10pstamp?:Y})\!)\backslash\backslash A$$

\\3
$$= 1:1:(\!X \times Y)\!)\backslash\backslash A$$
$$+ (\!\text{20pcoin?:20pstamp!:X} \times \text{10pcoin!:10pstamp?:Y})\!)\backslash\backslash A$$

```
def     = 1:1:GETSTAMP
              + (20pcoin?:20pstamp!:X × 10pcoin!:10pstamp?:Y)\\A
```

As before, pruning has left the successful behaviour alone. But what about the other choice? The 20pcoin? part of 20pcoin?×10pcoin!, as it's in the pruning set, cannot be allowed. In detail:

```
        = 1:1:GETSTAMP
              + (20pcoin?:20pstamp!:X × 10pcoin!:10pstamp?:Y)\\A
\\6b    = 1:1:GETSTAMP + 0
+3      = 1:1:GETSTAMP
```

Almost Darwin-like, the pruning operator has killed off behaviours guarded by unsuccessful synchronisations allowing the successful one to live. Let's take another example.

example

A process P offers to output over port a, and agents Q and R both offer to input over port a. The designer wants the synchronisation between P and Q to succeed and R's synchronisation ignored. The designer defines the agents as:

$$P \overset{def}{=} a?:P', \quad Q \overset{def}{=} a!:Q', \quad R \overset{def}{=} a!:R'$$

A system design $(P \times Q \times R)$ of

$$(a?:P' \times a!:Q' \times a!:R')$$

will allow P to synchronise with Q or R. The correct design is

$$((P \times Q)\backslash\backslash A \times R) \text{ for } A = \{a\}$$

giving:

```
((P × Q)\\{a} × R)
def     = (a?:P' × a!:Q')\\{a} × a!:R'
\\3     = 1:(P'×Q')\\{a} × a!:R'
```

P has been forced to synchronise with Q and not R.

Useful as \\6 and \\2 are, they only apply to agents like $\alpha: P$. What would fit better into our design strategy would be a set of propositions that gives us the emergent behaviour of agents combined under pruning, as in $(P \times Q)\backslash\backslash A$. We already have one such proposition in \\3, but this only covers synchronisation pairs also in the pruning set; this is OK for $(a?:P \times a!:Q)\backslash\backslash\{a\}$ but not much use for $(a?:P \times b!:Q)\backslash\backslash\{a\}$. As composition, followed by scoping, is the main method of constructing systems, we need propositions which predict the emergent behaviour of agent product in general.

4.6 Constructional Design

Our SCCS design strategy is a constructional one. Starting with a set of agents representing simple and understandable components, we construct agents representing systems closer to the design objectives, stopping when our objectives are met. To control a design as it evolves we need to manage the attendant growth in information, details relevant to one stage of a design must be hidden in later stages if the model is not to get out of control. To do this we need a modelling system with the ability to simplify designs by encapsulating agents in 'black boxes' – allowing information relevant to a particular design stage to be seen but hiding the rest. The basis for such a design strategy is the combining and then pruning of two agents:

$$(\alpha:P \times \beta:Q) \backslash\backslash A$$

To use this strategy we need to understand $(\alpha:P \times \beta:Q) \backslash\backslash A$ for all permutations and combinations of action and pruning sets, and to address fully this we first need to explore scoping over agent combinations.

4.6.1 Scoping and Synchronisation

The pruning operator as a selective container of agents is exactly the tool we require for constructional design. With it we can force those behaviours we want while removing those we don't. By existing propositions we can establish that $(a!a?b!b?:P) \backslash\backslash \{a,b\} = 1:P\backslash\backslash\{a,b\}$, $(a!a!b!b?:P) \backslash\backslash\{a\} = \mathbb{0}$ and $(a!a?b!b?:P) \backslash\backslash\{c\} = a!a?b!b?:P\backslash\backslash\{c\}$ – all special cases of $(\alpha:P) \backslash\backslash A$. Scoping over prefix also encompasses scoping over product; $(\alpha:P \times \beta:Q) \backslash\backslash A$ is only $(\alpha.\beta:(P \times Q)) \backslash\backslash A$ but, as compositions are central to a design, it would be useful to have some specifically tailored laws. For example, predicting that pruning forces $a?:P$ to synchronise with $a!:Q$ in $(a?:P \times a!:Q) \backslash\backslash a = 1:(P \times Q) \backslash\backslash a$ but not in $(a?:P \times a!:Q) \backslash\backslash b = a?a!:(P \times Q) \backslash\backslash b$ would be useful. To lead up to such propositions, we will first look at a few examples to get a feel for the range of possibilities, starting with the simplest case where the initial actions of $(\alpha:P \times \beta:Q) \backslash\backslash A$ synchronise completely – the particles in the guarding actions all form synchronisation pairs, $(\alpha:P \times \alpha^{-1}:Q) \backslash\backslash A$, and:

- all particles are members of the pruning set
  $(a!b!:P \times a?b?:Q) \backslash\backslash\{a,b\} = 1:(P \times Q) \backslash\backslash\{a,b\}$;
- no particles are members of the pruning set
  $(a!b!:P \times a?b?:Q) \backslash\backslash\{c\} = a!a?b!b?:(P \times Q) \backslash\backslash\{c\}$.

followed by the equally simple case of totally incomplete actions, $(\alpha:P \times \beta:Q) \backslash\backslash A$, where $\text{Part}(\alpha\beta) \cap \text{Part}^{-1}(\alpha\beta) = \varnothing$, and:

- some particles are in the pruning set
  $(a!b!:P \times c?:Q) \backslash\backslash\{a\} = \mathbb{0}$;

- no particles are in the pruning set
  `(a!b!:P×a!c?:Q)\\{d} = a!b!a!c?:(P×Q)\\{d}`.

These are particular instances of the more general – some initial particles form synchronisation pairs and others do not; some particles are incomplete, some particles appear in the pruning set and some do not, where, again, 'none' and 'all' are included in 'some'. We can use the propositions already developed for $(\alpha:P)\backslash\backslash A$ by looking at things post -combination where $(\alpha:P \times \beta:Q)\backslash\backslash A = (\sigma\sigma^{-1}\gamma\gamma^{-1}\kappa\xi:P \times Q)\backslash\backslash A$ and $\sigma\sigma^{-1}$ represents synchronisation pairs not in A; $\gamma\gamma^{-1}$ synchronisation pairs in A; κ incomplete particles in A and ξ incomplete particles not in A. This gives us the particular cases of:

- some incomplete actions are in the pruning set, $\text{Part}(\kappa) \neq \varnothing$
  $$(\alpha:P \times \beta:Q)\backslash\backslash A = \mathbb{0}.$$
  Inaction results even if one such particle is pruned, as in
  $$(a!b?:P×a?b!c?:Q)\backslash\backslash\{c\} = \mathbb{0};$$

- no incomplete actions are in the pruning set, $\text{Part}(\kappa) = \varnothing$, but some of the synchronisation pairs are, $\text{Part}(\sigma) \neq \varnothing$,
  $$(\alpha:P \times \beta:Q)\backslash\backslash A = 1×\sigma\sigma^{-1}\xi:(P \times Q)\backslash\backslash A.$$

Those synchronisation pairs not in the pruning set, $\sigma\sigma^{-1}$, can escape and remain available to synchronise with other actions in the environment, as can the unpruned incomplete particles ξ; but the only way those synchronisation pairs in the pruning set, $\gamma\gamma^{-1}$, can escape is to synchronise within the scoping and convert to an internal 1 action – synchronisation pairs in the pruning set are forced to synchronise with each other. For example: `(a!b?:P×a?b!c?:Q)\\{a} = b?b!c?:(P×Q)\\{a}`. Note that the 1 is there as a reminder to cover the case where $\text{Part}(\xi) = \text{Part}(\sigma) = \varnothing$, for example in
$$(a!:P×a?:Q)\backslash\backslash\{a\} = 1:(P \times Q)\backslash\backslash\{a\}.$$

To use these concepts we need the strength of propositions round us. The product operator is associative $\text{Prop} \times 2$ and, as above, we only need to consider combinations of two agents. As its useful to have laws over successful and unsuccessful synchronisation, we will propose the following propositions based on the earlier \\6 propositions.

propositions Synchronisation Pruning $\leftrightarrow$
  Where $\alpha\alpha^{-1}$ contains only complete synchronisation pairs,
  $\text{Part}(\alpha) \cap \text{Part}^{-1}(\alpha) \neq \varnothing$
  $\leftrightarrow 1 \quad (\alpha:P \times \alpha^{-1}:Q)\backslash\backslash A =$
  $\qquad\qquad$ a) $1:(P \times Q)\backslash\backslash A$, if $\text{Part}(\alpha) \subseteq A$
  $\qquad\qquad$ b) $\alpha\alpha^{-1}:(P \times Q)\backslash\backslash A$, if $\text{Part}(\alpha) \cap A = \varnothing$

Where $\alpha\beta$ contains no synchronisation pairs,

$\texttt{Part}(\alpha\beta)\cap\texttt{Part}^{-1}(\alpha\beta)=\varnothing$

$\leftrightarrow 5 \quad (\alpha:\texttt{P}\times\beta:\texttt{Q})\backslash\backslash\texttt{A} =$
  a) $\alpha\beta:(\texttt{P}\times\texttt{Q})\backslash\backslash\texttt{A}$, if $\texttt{Part}(\alpha\beta)\cap\texttt{A}=\varnothing$
  b) $\mathbb{0}$, if $\texttt{Part}(\alpha\beta)\cap\texttt{A}\neq\varnothing$

$\texttt{Prop}\leftrightarrow\texttt{1a}$ based on $\backslash\backslash\texttt{6e}$, all particles form synchronisation pairs which are also part of the pruning set, all particles synchronise, metamorphose to an internal action and escape pruning.

$\texttt{Prop}\leftrightarrow\texttt{1b}$ based on $\backslash\backslash\texttt{6c}$, all particles form synchronisation pairs, none of which are in the pruning set, no particles are pruned, all escape ready to synchronise with any suitable action in their environment.

$\texttt{Prop}\leftrightarrow\texttt{5a}$ based on $\backslash\backslash\texttt{6d}$, no synchronisation pairs, no incomplete particles in the pruning set, no particles synchronise or are pruned.

$\texttt{Prop}\leftrightarrow\texttt{5b}$ based on $\backslash\backslash\texttt{6b}$, no synchronisation pairs, some incomplete particles are in the pruning set, and inaction results.

■

While such propositions are necessary, luckily they're not always required, and a sight reading is all that is needed. In most cases we use $(\texttt{P}\times\texttt{Q})\backslash\backslash\texttt{A}$, as it holds on to particles in set $\texttt{A}$, to force the guarding action of $\texttt{P}$ and $\texttt{Q}$ in $\texttt{A}$ to synchronise, where, if all synchronisations succeed, the system survives, but if even one fails, the system dies, and in practice the other propositions are only used to arbitrate over disputes and sort out the more obscure cases.

Synchronous pruning removes unsatisfied ends of possible synchronisations while allowing satisfied ones, which means an environment can be used to determine the behaviour of an agent. To demonstrate, we need another example:

example

GETSTAMP, where we want to force a local $10\texttt{p}$ transaction and to get rid of, prune away, the unsuccessful $20\texttt{p}$ actions, is simplified to

$$(10\texttt{CUSTOMER}\times10/20\_\texttt{STAMP\_MACHINE})\backslash\backslash\texttt{A}$$

where

$$\texttt{A} = \{10\texttt{pcoin},10\texttt{pstamp},20\texttt{pcoin},20\texttt{pstamp}\}$$
$$\texttt{X} = 10\texttt{CUSTOMER}$$
$$\texttt{Y} = 10/20\_\texttt{STAMP\_MACHINE}$$

$\texttt{GETSTAMP} \stackrel{\text{def}}{=} (\texttt{X}\times\texttt{Y})\backslash\backslash\texttt{A}$

$\quad = (\!(10\texttt{pcoin?}:10\texttt{pstamp!}:\texttt{X} + 20\texttt{pcoin?}:20\texttt{pstamp!}:\texttt{X})$
$\qquad \times\ 10\texttt{pcoin!}:10\texttt{pstamp?}:\texttt{Y})\!)\backslash\backslash\texttt{A}$

$+6 \quad = (\!(10\texttt{pcoin?}:10\texttt{pstamp!}:\texttt{X}\times10\texttt{pcoin!}:10\texttt{pstamp?}:\texttt{Y})$
$\qquad + (20\texttt{pcoin?}:20\texttt{pstamp!}:\texttt{X}\times10\texttt{pcoin!}:10\texttt{pstamp?}:\texttt{Y})\!)\backslash\backslash\texttt{A}$

$\backslash\backslash\texttt{4},\leftrightarrow\texttt{1a},\leftrightarrow\texttt{5b} \quad = 1:(\!10\texttt{pstamp!}:\texttt{X}\times10\texttt{pstamp?}:\texttt{Y})\!)\backslash\backslash\texttt{A} + \mathbb{0}$

```
+3,↔1a        = 1:1:(X × Y)\\A
def           = 1:1:GETSTAMP
```

■

And over choice:

example

Consider P $\stackrel{\text{def}}{=}$ a?:b?:0 + c!:(d?:0 + e!:0) which has the following derivation tree:

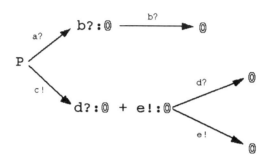

P is placed in an environment Q $\stackrel{\text{def}}{=}$ a!:1:0. Then pruning over the interaction a

```
     (P×Q)\\a
                = ((a?:b?:0 + c!:(d?:0 + e!:0)) × a!:1:0)\\a
+6              = ((a?:b?:0 × a!:1:0) + (c!:(d?:0 + e!:0) × a!:1:0))\\a
\\4             = (a?:b?:0 × a!:1:0)\\a + (c!:(d?:0 + e!:0) × a!:1:0)\\a
↔1a,↔5b         = 1:(b?:0 × 1:0)\\a + 0
+3              = 1:(b?:0 × 1:0)\\a
↔5a             = 1:b?.1:(0 × 0)\\a
×6,×3           = 1:b?:0\\a
03              = 1:b?:0
```

■

In the above example Q selects whichever behaviour of P it wants. Pruning allowing successful synchronisations – representing wanted behaviours – to persist, while removing unsuccessful synchronisations – representing unwanted behaviours. We now have enough ammunition to return to the problem we left hanging in the last section.

example

A general file copy server can read in a file and, after some formatting, can copy the file to a disk or give it to a printer spooler with instructions to print it on either a fast draft-quality printer or a slower letter-quality printer.

Where:

a? = read in file	1 = format file
c! = select the disk	d! = write to disk
e! = send to printer queue	f! = write to high-speed printer
g! = write to slow-speed printer	

For COPY $\overset{\text{def}}{=}$ a?:1:(c!:d!:$\mathbb{0}$ + e!:(f?:$\mathbb{0}$ + g!:$\mathbb{0}$))

and DISK $\overset{\text{def}}{=}$ 1:1:c?:d?:$\mathbb{0}$

SYSTEM\\{c,d} $\overset{\text{def}}{=}$ (COPY × DISK)\\{c,d}

def	= ((a?:1:(c!:d!:$\mathbf{0}$+ e!:(f?:$\mathbf{0}$+ g!:$\mathbf{0}$))) × (1:1:c?:d?:$\mathbf{0}$))\\{c,d}
↔5a	= a?:((1:(c!:d!:$\mathbf{0}$ + e!:(f?:$\mathbf{0}$ + g!:$\mathbf{0}$)) × (1:c?:d?:$\mathbf{0}$))\\{c,d}
↔5a	= a?:1:((c!:d!:$\mathbf{0}$ + e!:(f?:$\mathbf{0}$ + g!:$\mathbf{0}$)) × (c?:d?:$\mathbf{0}$))\\{c,d}
+6,\\4	= a?:1:(((c!:d!:$\mathbf{0}$) × (c?:d?:$\mathbf{0}$))\\{c,d}
	+ (e!:(f?:$\mathbf{0}$ + g!:$\mathbf{0}$)× (c?:d?:$\mathbf{0}$))\\{c,d})
↔1a,↔5b	= a?:1:(1:((d!:$\mathbf{0}$) × (d?:$\mathbf{0}$))\\{c,d} + $\mathbf{0}$)
+3	= a?:1:1:((d!:$\mathbf{0}$) × (d?:$\mathbf{0}$))\\{c,d}
↔1a	= a?:1:1:1:$\mathbf{0}$

The general copy server has synchronised with the disk and has specified that the file be written to disk.

Only the a?:1:c!:d!:$\mathbb{0}$ behaviour of COPY satisfied by the 1:1:c?:d?:$\mathbb{0}$ behaviour of DISK remains post-composition with all other behaviours of the general COPY agent removed.

◼

Note that what is being modelled here is a dynamic deterministic selection of behaviours at 'run-time'. This directly maps into the concept of client–servers in which a client, by communicating its desires to a server, selects the service it wants when it wants it. Here the choice of server behaviours is dynamic in comparison with the restriction operator in a previous example which changed the agent statically, before it met its environment.

It gives us confidence in the abstract SCCS calculus when we find that it can accurately and easily model the results of process synchronisation, an essential building block in any multi-process design. But though synchronisation can dynamically select certain behaviours and discard others, we need to be aware of the limitations a designer has over such selections.

4.6.2 Choice of Choices

In the real world, choices come in two flavours: deterministic – when the outcome can be predicted; and non-deterministic – when the outcome appears to be randomly chosen. When we select an item from a menu and we get the dish we ordered, that is determinism; non-determinism is where we ask for the dish of the day. Agents behave deterministically if it is the environment which selects the behaviour; agents behave non-deterministically if they autonomously decide their own future. For deterministic systems, given information about how the agents interact, a designer can predict behaviour and only those outcomes need checking against a specification. However, with non-deterministic systems, all outcomes have the same probability and all possible behaviours have to be verified.

4.6.2.1 Deterministic Choice

The summation operator models deterministic choice – the choice of behaviour can be influenced by the environment.

example

Consider agent $E \overset{\text{def}}{=} a?:b!:0 + c!:d?:0$ placed in environment $F \overset{\text{def}}{=} a!:c?:0$

E represents an agent capable of choice – its behaviour depends upon which of the actions $a?$ or $c?$ is first engaged in. As these interactions are observable they can be used by an environment to influence the choice.

$$
\begin{aligned}
(E \times F) &= (a?:b!:0 + c!:d?:0) \times a!:c?:0 \\
+6 \quad &= (a?:b!:0 \times a!:c?:0) \\
&\quad + (c!:d?:0 \times a!:c?:0)
\end{aligned}
$$

The future behaviour is that of F concurrently with one of E's. The resultant behaviour is still open to environmental influence. To make the choice deterministic we need an encapsulation so, not only does F determine the outcome, but F is the only influence on E; we exclude all other environments.

$$
\begin{aligned}
(E \times F) \backslash\backslash a \quad &= (\!(a?:b!:0 \times a!:c?:0) \\
&\quad\quad + (c!:d?:0 \times a!:c?:0)\!) \backslash\backslash a \\
\backslash\backslash 4 \quad\quad &= (\!(a?:b!:0 \times a!:c?:0)\!) \backslash\backslash a \\
&\quad\quad + (\!(c!:d?:0 \times a!:c?:0)\!) \backslash\backslash a \\
\leftrightarrow 1a, \leftrightarrow 5b \quad &= 1:(\!(b!:0 \times c?:0)\!) \backslash\backslash a + 0 \\
+3 \quad\quad &= 1:(\!(b!:0 \times c?:0)\!) \backslash\backslash a
\end{aligned}
$$

F has selected one behaviour, rejecting the other.

■

4.6.2.2 Non-Deterministic Choice

If an agent is capable of engaging in more than one possible behaviour, the selection of which cannot be influenced by its environment, the choice is non-deterministic. There are two types of non-determinism, external and internal.

> *External* non-determinism: the environment is involved at the point of choice but has limited control over any outcome. For example, agent a!:P + a!:Q in environment a?:R; the choice of subsequently behaving as P×R or Q×R is not influenced by the environment – the environment interacts with the agent but doesn't affect the outcome.
>
> *Internal* non-determinism: the environment is not involved at the point of choice, for example agent 1:P + 1:Q in any environment; at the point of choice the agent is executing internal events, unobserved by and not offering interaction to any environment.

example
Consider agent E ᵈᵉᶠ a?:b!:0 + a?:d?:0 placed in environment F ᵈᵉᶠ a!:c?:0

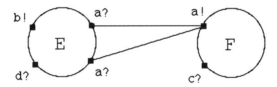

Here, E is capable of choice. But with identical choice guards the environment cannot use them to influence E's future behaviour. To keep things clean we encapsulate E and F.

(E×F)\\a = ((a?:b!:0 + a?:d?:0) × a!:c?:0)\\a

F is involved at the point of choice but cannot influence it, the joint behaviour becomes:

(E×F)\\a = 1:b!.c?:0 + 1:d?.c?:0

which neatly turns into internal choice, as no further environment can select a behaviour of (E×F)\\a. Why? Because not only are its choice guards identical but they're internal and cannot support any interactions. The composition of agent E, which exhibits *external non-determinism*, with agent F has created an agent (E×F)\\a exhibiting *internal non-determinism*.

■

SCCS, using the familiar summation, communication and pruning operations, has modelled both deterministic and non-deterministic choice without 'breaking its stride'. We will conclude this section on constructional design with a relevant example.

4.6.3 Example: Software Interrupts

It is notoriously difficult to predict how systems containing software interrupts behave. The use of testing is particularly fraught, and more than a few designs are implemented with fingers crossed. But perhaps SCCS, being a real-time algebra, will illuminate what is happening in such cases. The design process follows the normal route of interpreting the separate parts of the real-world problem into SCCS expressions, using the calculus to predict the behaviour of the composite system, and, finally, interpreting these predictions back into the real world. The component parts of a this real-time system are:

- an *interrupting process* which provides a periodic interrupt;
- the *main process* to be interrupted;
- an *interrupt service routine* called to service the interrupt.

The main process and the interrupting process operate concurrently. Generation of an interrupt causes the main process to cease execution and an interrupt service routine to be activated. On termination of the interrupt service routine, the main process resumes from the point it was interrupted. With a system clock of 1MHz, period $1\mu s$, their SCCS interpretations are:

Interrupting process R
> Idles for $4\mu s$, four time slots, generating an interrupt request every fifth slot over port int, then repeats.
> $$R \stackrel{def}{=} 1:1:1:1:int!:R = (1:)^4:int!:R$$

Interrupt Service Routine $B_{i,N}$
> Carries out action d three times, which takes $1\mu s$ each, then returns control back to the main process.
> $$B_{i,N} \stackrel{def}{=} d:d:d:Q_{i,N} = (d:)^3:Q_{i,N}$$

Main Process $Q_{n,N}$
> Engages in a series of a and b actions, each taking $1\mu s$, executes continually and is always ready to receive an interrupt request. With interrupts enabled, this main process is defined by:
> $$Q_{n,N} \stackrel{def}{=} int?:B_{n,N} + a:Q_{n-1,N} \quad for \ 0<n{\le}N.$$
> $$Q_{0,N} \stackrel{def}{=} int?:B_{0,N} + b:Q_{N,N}$$
> where constant N gives the number of a actions engaged in by Q prior to its

sole b action; and where the n in $Q_{n,N}$ defines the current state of Q, how many a's remain in the current cycle. All subscript arithmetic is modulo N-1. For example, $Q_{4,2}$ has two a's to complete in a four a cycle. Without interrupts, we have:

$$Q_{n,N} \stackrel{\text{def}}{=} (a:)^N : b : Q_{n,N}$$

For N=2:

$$Q_{2,2} = \text{int?}:B_{2,2} + a:(\text{int?}:B_{1,2} + a:(\text{int?}:B_{0,2} + b:Q_{2,2}))$$

giving, in the absence of interrupts:

$$Q_{2,2} = a:a:b:Q_{2,2}$$

To aid comprehension, internal actions a, b and d are specifically named. Naturally these actions are transparent to SCCS and treated as the 1 action in propositions.

Now, as we are a little more familiar with compositional design, we relax the strict application of propositions, particularly the effect of the pruning of unsuccessful synchronisations, and determine the emergent behaviour as we would a sight reading. The composite systems is:

```
     S  def  [R × Q₂,₂]\\int
sub   = ((1:1:1:1:int!:R) × (int?:B₂,₂ + a:Q₁,₂))\\int
↔5a   = a:((1:1:1:int!:R) × (Q₁,₂))\\int
sub   = a:((1:1:1:int!:R) × (int?:B₁,₂ + a:Q₀,₂))\\int
↔5a   = a:a:((1:1:int!:R) × (Q₀,₂))\\int
sub   = a:a:((1:1:int!:R) × (int?:B₀,₂ + b:Q₂,₂))\\int
↔5a   = a:a:b:((1:int!:R) × (Q₂,₂))\\int ──────────────────── (*)
sub   = a:a:b:((1:int!:R) × (int?:B₂,₂ + a:Q₁,₂))\\int
↔5a   = a:a:b:a:((int!:R) × (Q₁,₂))\\int
sub   = a:a:b:a:((int!:R) × (int?:B₁,₂ + a:Q₀,₂))\\int
↔1a   = a:a:b:a:1:((R) × (B₁,₂))\\int
sub   = a:a:b:a:1:((1:1:1:1:int!:R) × (d:d:d:Q₁,₂))\\int
↔5a   = a:a:b:a:1:d:d:d:((1:int!:R) × (Q₁,₂))\\int
sub   = a:a:b:a:1:d:d:d:((1:int!:R) × (int?:B₁,₂ + a:Q₀,₂))\\int
↔5a   = a:a:b:a:1:d:d:d:a:((int!:R) × (Q₀,₂))\\int
sub   = a:a:b:a:1:d:d:d:a:((int!:R) × (int?:B₀,₂ + b:Q₂,₂))\\int
↔1a   = a:a:b:a:1:d:d:d:a:1:((R) × (B₀,₂))\\int
sub   = a:a:b:a:1:d:d:d:a:1:((1:1:1:1:int!:R) × (d:d:d:Q₀,₂))\\int
↔5a   = a:a:b:a:1:d:d:d:a:1:d:d:d:((1:int!:R) × (Q₀,₂))\\int
↔5a   = a:a:b:a:1:d:d:d:a:1:d:d:d:b:((int!:R) × (Q₂,₂))\\int
sub   = a:a:b:a:1:(d:)³:a:1:(d:)³:b:((int!:R) × (int?:B₂,₂ + a:Q₁,₂))\\int
↔1a   = a:a:b:a:1:d:d:d:a:1:d:d:d:b:1:((R) × (B₂,₂))\\int
↔5a   = a:a:b:a:1:d:d:d:a:1:d:d:d:b:1:d:d:d:((1:int!:R) × (Q₂,₂))\\int
```

which recurses with the expression at stage (*) to give:

$$S \overset{\text{def}}{=} a:a:b:X$$
$$X \overset{\text{def}}{=} a:1:d:d:d:a:1:d:d:d:d:b:1:d:d:d:X$$

We can interpret this derived SCCS expression as:

a sequential process consisting of repetitions of the internal actions of the main process $a:a:b$ indispersed with those of the interrupt service routine $d:d:d$, interactions which cause the changeover denoted by a 1 action. With no interrupts, the behaviour is as for the main process.

4.6.4 Distributing Pruning over Product

In a large design, each stage may require the composition/abstraction of many agents and, calling on the associativity of the product operator, we've already produced some relevant propositions about combining two agents at a time. But if we can establish that pruning always distributes over product $(P \times Q) \backslash\backslash A = (P\backslash\backslash A) \times (Q\backslash\backslash A)$ we won't need exotic propositions over $(P \times Q) \backslash\backslash A$ but will get away with working out what $(P\backslash\backslash A)$ and $(Q\backslash\backslash A)$ do individually. But we strike a snag here, as:

$$^4 \qquad (P \times Q)^{\wedge}A \neq (P^{\wedge}A) \times (Q^{\wedge}A), \text{ in general}$$
$$\backslash\backslash 5 \qquad (P \times Q) \backslash\backslash A \neq (P\backslash\backslash A) \times (Q\backslash\backslash A), \text{ in general}$$

It's not always the case that encapsulation distributes through product. Applying a pruning operator to sub-expressions before they are combined is not necessarily the same as pruning them afterwards.

If true, this means that for each different order to which we apply the same pruning we may get different final systems. Consider two agents pruned by A, $(\alpha:P \times \beta:Q) \backslash\backslash A$, when is it equivalent to $(P\backslash\backslash A) \times (Q\backslash\backslash A)$ and when not? Let's look at some examples.

examples

Starting with the case of different guarding actions, none of whose particles appear in the pruning set and $\text{Part}(\alpha\beta) \cap A = \emptyset$, then:

$$(a!:0 \times b?:0) \backslash\backslash c$$
$$\leftrightarrow 5a \qquad = a!b?:(0 \times 0) \backslash\backslash c$$
$$\times 3, 03 \qquad = a!b?:0$$

and:

$$(a!:0) \backslash\backslash c \times (b?:0) \backslash\backslash c$$
$$\backslash\backslash 2 \qquad = a!:(0) \backslash\backslash c \times b?(0) \backslash\backslash c$$
$$\times 4 \qquad = a!b?:(0) \backslash\backslash c \times (0) \backslash\backslash c$$
$$03, \times 3 \qquad = a!b?:0$$

Pruning distributes over product.

Now, consider the case where the guarding actions are complete

synchronisation pairs and these actions are included in the pruning set,
$\alpha=\beta^{-1}$ and `Part(α)⊆A`. Then:

    (a!:P×a?:Q)\\a
    ↔1a   = 1:(P×Q)\\a

and the right hand side as:

    (a!:P)\\a × (a?:Q)\\a
    \\2   = 0 × 0
    ×3   = 0

Pruning does not distribute over product.

In the first case, P and Q synchronise before pruning, whereas in the second the possible synchronisation is pruned before it can succeed.

■

Whether or not pruning distributes over product in $(\alpha:P\times\beta:Q)\backslash\backslash A$ depends on whether α and β form an external synchronisation pair, that is their product has synchronisation possibilities not present in either of them individually, and these external synchronisations are in the pruning set. In $(\alpha:P\times\beta:Q)\backslash\backslash A$ such synchronisation pairs can successfully come together, become a 1, and escape the pruning. However, in $(\alpha:P)\backslash\backslash A\times(\beta:Q)\backslash\backslash A$ the actions never come together and are picked off by the pruning operator, playing havoc with the rules of distribution. More formally, only by removing these synchronisations, as in \\6 for `Part(γ)=∅`, is distribution ensured:

$$(\alpha:P\times\beta:Q)\backslash\backslash A = \alpha\beta:(P\times Q)\backslash\backslash A \text{ if Part}(\gamma)=\emptyset$$

This is consistent with the intuition that pruning does not distribute over the product when the scoped-over agents interact through the pruning operator [Mil83], or, put the other way round, 'synchronisation pruning distributes over product if the scoped-over agents do not interact through actions in the pruning set'. More formally:

$$(P\times Q)\backslash\backslash A = P\backslash\backslash A\times Q\backslash\backslash A$$

if P and Q are externally incomplete for all actions in A

As A contains both input and output actions, we can write this as:

proposition Synchronisation Pruning \\5

    \\5   (α:P×β:Q)\\A = (α:P)\\A × (β:Q)\\A, if
           Sort(P)∩Sort(Q)∩A=∅

    Prop \\5 synchronisation pruning distributes over product if the agents
           are externally incomplete for all actions in the pruning set.

■

Similar conclusions and propositions hold for restriction.

interpretation

Application of pruning at different stages of a design may result in different final behaviours. One can prune interactions which may have synchronised successfully in the future. But isn't this what we designers want? As with the scoping of variables in block -structured programming languages, some variable may be defined as local, internal, to a procedure, and hidden from the rest of the program. In a similar way, SCCS supports the scoping of actions in a concurrent system and it is the responsibility of the designer to decide at what stage to enforce scoping to achieve the desired level of abstraction. Don't hide too early, as this may remove possible synchronisations with future subagents; but don't hide too late if the design requires that certain actions of certain agents need to be hidden to limit interference by an environment.

■

example

Due to the symmetry of the product operator we can compose systems by adding one new agent at a time, and, as each agent is added, the designer can use scoping to control the level of abstraction. Consider the case of a Boolean circuit with two observable inputs a and b, and an observable output c, where c = f (a, b). All the internal details are hidden.

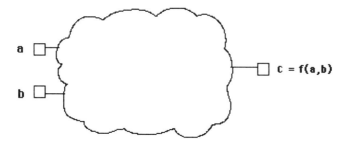

For an f (a, b) = ¬a ∧ ¬b, the output is the AND of its inverted inputs. We can suggest that an extension of our previous NOT and AND circuit will do the job.

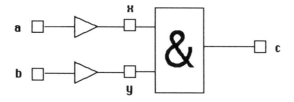

Using appropriate morphisms on the basic NOT and AND gates we obtain the subagents:

$$\text{NOT1} \stackrel{\text{def}}{=} a_0?.x_1!:\text{NOT1} + a_1?.x_0!:\text{NOT1}$$
$$\text{NOT2} \stackrel{\text{def}}{=} b_0?.y_1!:\text{NOT2} + b_1?.y_0!:\text{NOT2}$$
$$\text{AND} \stackrel{\text{def}}{=} x_0?.y_0?.c_0!:\text{AND} + x_0?.y_1?.c_0!:\text{AND}$$
$$+ x_1?.y_0?.c_0!:\text{AND} + x_1?.y_1?.c_1!:\text{AND}$$

and the complete system is:

$$\text{SYS} \stackrel{\text{def}}{=} (\text{NOT1} \times \text{NOT2} \times \text{AND}) \backslash\backslash\{x,y\}$$
$$= (\text{NOT1} \times \text{NOT2} \times \text{AND}) \backslash\backslash x \backslash\backslash y$$

AND and NOT1 interact via x but NOT2 doesn't

$\backslash\backslash 5$ $\text{SYS} = ((\text{NOT1} \times \text{AND}) \backslash\backslash x \times \text{NOT2}\backslash\backslash x) \backslash\backslash y$

and NOT2 has no x actions

$\leftrightarrow 5a$ $\text{SYS} = ((\text{NOT1} \times \text{AND}) \backslash\backslash x \times \text{NOT2}) \backslash\backslash y$

We have our desired template for two-at-a-time composition abstracting at each stage.

$\text{NOT1AND} \stackrel{\text{def}}{=} (\text{NOT1} \times \text{AND}) \backslash\backslash x$

$\text{def} \qquad = ((a_0?.x_1!:\text{NOT1} + a_1?.x_0!:\text{NOT1})$
$\qquad\qquad \times (x_0?.y_0?.c_0!:\text{AND} + x_0?.y_1?.c_0!:\text{AND}$
$\qquad\qquad\quad + x_1?.y_0?.c_0!:\text{AND} + x_1?.y_1?.c_1!:\text{AND})) \backslash\backslash x$

Rather than plod on regardless we can be clever and reuse the previous NOT AND result:

$\text{TRUTH} \stackrel{\text{def}}{=} a_0?.b_0?.c_0!:\text{TRUTH} + a_0?.b_1?.c_1!:\text{TRUTH}$
$\qquad\qquad + a_1?.b_0?.c_0!:\text{TRUTH} + a_1?.b_1?.c_0!:\text{TRUTH}$

Applying suitable morphisms $a, b, c \rightarrow a, y, c$ gives:

$\text{NOT1AND} \stackrel{\text{def}}{=} a_0?.y_0?.c_0!:\text{NOT1AND} + a_0?.y_1?.c_1!:\text{NOT1AND}$
$\qquad\qquad + a_1?.y_0?.c_0!:\text{NOT1AND} + a_1?.y_1?.c_0!:\text{NOT1AND}$

Now add in the other agent NOT2 :

$\text{SYS} \stackrel{\text{def}}{=} (\text{NOT1AND} \times \text{NOT2}) \backslash\backslash y$

$\text{def} \qquad = ((a_0?.y_0?.c_0!:\text{NOT1AND} + a_0?.y_1?.c_1!:\text{NOT1AND}$
$\qquad\qquad + a_1?.y_0?.c_0!:\text{NOT1AND} + a_1?.y_1?.c_0!:\text{NOT1AND})$
$\qquad\qquad\quad \times (b_0?.y_1!:\text{NOT2} + b_1?.y_0!:\text{NOT2})$
$\qquad\qquad) \backslash\backslash y$

$+6, \backslash\backslash 4 \qquad = (a_0?.y_0?.c_0!:\text{NOT1AND} \times b_0?.y_1!:\text{NOT2}) \backslash\backslash y$
$\qquad\qquad + (a_0?.y_0?.c_0!:\text{NOT1AND} \times b_1?.y_0!:\text{NOT2}) \backslash\backslash y$
$\qquad\qquad + (a_0?.y_1?.c_1!:\text{NOT1AND} \times b_0?.y_1!:\text{NOT2}) \backslash\backslash y$
$\qquad\qquad + (a_0?.y_1?.c_1!:\text{NOT1AND} \times b_1?.y_0!:\text{NOT2}) \backslash\backslash y$
$\qquad\qquad + (a_1?.y_0?.c_0!:\text{NOT1AND} \times b_0?.y_1!:\text{NOT2}) \backslash\backslash y$
$\qquad\qquad + (a_1?.y_0?.c_0!:\text{NOT1AND} \times b_1?.y_0!:\text{NOT2}) \backslash\backslash y$
$\qquad\qquad + (a_1?.y_1?.c_0!:\text{NOT1AND} \times b_0?.y_1!:\text{NOT2}) \backslash\backslash y$
$\qquad\qquad + (a_1?.y_1?.c_0!:\text{NOT1AND} \times b_1?.y_0!:\text{NOT2}) \backslash\backslash y$

$$\leftrightarrow 1a, \leftrightarrow 5b, +3 \quad = \; a_0?.c_0!.b_1?: (\text{NOT1AND} \;\times\; \text{NOT2}) \backslash\backslash y$$
$$+ \; a_0?.c_1!.b_0?: (\text{NOT1AND} \;\times\; \text{NOT2}) \backslash\backslash y$$
$$+ \; a_1?.c_0!.b_1?: (\text{NOT1AND} \;\times\; \text{NOT2}) \backslash\backslash y$$
$$+ \; a_1?.c_0!.b_0?: (\text{NOT1AND} \;\times\; \text{NOT2}) \backslash\backslash y$$

$$\text{def} \qquad \text{SYS} = a_0?.b_0?.c_1!:\text{SYS} + a_1?.b_0?.c_0!:\text{SYS}$$
$$+ \; a_0?.b_1?.c_0!:\text{SYS} + a_1?.b_1?.c_0!:\text{SYS}$$

Which is the behaviour we require, $c = \neg a \wedge \neg b$, with ports a, b and c available for further synchronisations – check it with truth tables if you're not convinced!

■

4.7 Message Passing

To date we've formally modelled interactions between real-world systems only in terms of synchronisations. We've yet to see the message passing we need to model things like: procedure calling; interprocess communication; client–server systems, and so on. As the usefulness of a calculus which does not address such concepts will be limited, we will now introduce some SCCS notation especially built for the job. Our approach will be to state the sort of data passing constructs we'd expect – the simpler and more comprehensible the better – and then prove them strongly founded in the existing SCCS.

4.7.1 Parameter Passing

If we had a data passing mechanism we would intuitively expect that **a!x** would send a data item x via a particulate a! action and **a?v** would receive the data via a particulate a? action, binding the data received to local variable v. The definitions of two agents P and Q using these communication actions would be:

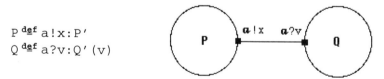

$$P \overset{\text{def}}{=} a!x:P'$$
$$Q \overset{\text{def}}{=} a?v:Q'(v)$$

and the behaviour captured in:

$$(P \times Q) \backslash\backslash a = 1: (P' \times Q'(v)[v:=x]) \backslash\backslash a$$

an internal communication after which all occurrences of local (bound) variable v in Q' are bound to the communicated value x from P denoted by $[v:=x]$. This is also sometimes written as $(P \times Q) \backslash\backslash a = 1: (P' \times Q'[v/x]) \backslash\backslash a$. We will use either form as appropriate.

In detail, of the two agents, one, P, has the ability to send all values of some type (all members of a set) $\mathcal{D}$ but chooses to communicate a particular value, $x \in \mathcal{D}$. Agent, Q, receptive to all values from set $\mathcal{D}$, receives the x value sent by P and assigns it to its local variable v where $v \in \mathcal{D}$. In computer terms a parameter of type $\mathcal{D}$ is passed from P to Q where it is bound to the latter's formal parameter v.

This description infers that parameter passing is akin to choice. If we map the set of values to be communicated to a set of ports indexed by $x \in \mathcal{D}$, for example $\mathcal{D}$ = {yes, no}, we get a sending and a receiving port for each value. As a picture:

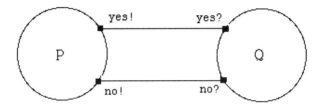

We can express the behaviour of P, the transmitter, and Q, the receiver, as:

P $\overset{\text{def}}{=}$ yes!:P(yes) + no!:P(no) and Q $\overset{\text{def}}{=}$ yes?:Q(yes) + no?:Q(no)

Agent P after sending a yes behaves as P(yes) and as P(no) after sending a no. Similarly agent Q after receiving a yes behaves as Q(yes), and Q(no) after a no.

If agent P chooses to engage in action yes

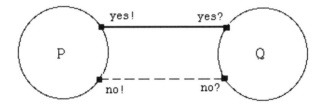

while Q is still ready to engage in either yes or no

P $\overset{\text{def}}{=}$ yes!:P(yes) and Q $\overset{\text{def}}{=}$ yes?:Q(yes) + no?:Q(no)

Putting them together and hiding all interactions:

(P×Q)\\{yes,no} = ((yes!:P(yes)) × (yes?:Q(yes) + no?:Q(no)))\\{yes,no}

Turning the handle on the SCCS propositions:

$$
\begin{aligned}
&= ((\text{yes!:P(yes)}) \times (\text{yes?:Q(yes)} + \text{no?:Q(no)}))\backslash\backslash\{\text{yes,no}\}\\
+6, \backslash\backslash 4 \quad &= (\text{yes!:P(yes)} \times \text{yes?:Q(yes)})\backslash\backslash\{\text{yes,no}\}\\
&\quad + (\text{yes!:P(yes)} \times \text{no?:Q(no)})\backslash\backslash\{\text{yes,no}\}\\
\leftrightarrow 1a, \leftrightarrow 5b \quad &= 1:(\text{P(yes)}\times\text{Q(yes)})\backslash\backslash\{\text{yes,no}\} + \mathbb{0}\\
+3 \quad &= 1:(\text{P(yes)}\times\text{Q(yes)})\backslash\backslash\{\text{yes,no}\}
\end{aligned}
$$

After the agents synchronise by yes, P reacts as if it has sent a yes and Q as if it has received one – they behave as if the message yes really had been passed. If agent P had decided to send a no rather than a yes the resultant behaviour would have been $(P \times Q) \setminus\setminus \{yes, no\} = 1 : (P(no) \times Q(no)) \setminus\setminus \{yes, no\}$ as if a no had actually been passed.

So synchronisation, by a suitable combination of choice and concurrency, simulates data passing. We can make bare synchronisation more like message passing by parametrising actions, one parametrised action per element of data set $\mathcal{D}$.

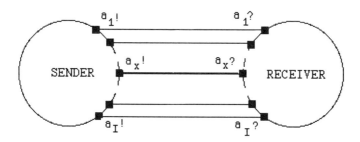

After sending over port a_x the sender's future behaviour, P_x, is parametrised by this port's identifier x. After receiving over port a_v the receiver's future behaviour, Q_v, is parametrised by v the identifier of the receiving port.

The case of the sender choosing to activate one (of a set of) sending action and the receiver ready to receive any action from the same set is expressed algebraically as:

$$P \stackrel{\text{def}}{=} \Sigma_{x \in \mathcal{D}} a_x! : P_x \text{ and } Q \stackrel{\text{def}}{=} \Sigma_{v \in \mathcal{D}} a_v? : Q_v$$

composing $P \times Q$

$$P \times Q = (\Sigma_{x \in \mathcal{D}} a_x! : P_x) \times (\Sigma_{v \in \mathcal{D}} a_v? : Q_v)$$

for $\mathcal{D} = \{0, 1\}$ and a particular x, $x = 1$

	$P \times Q$	$= a_1! : P_1 \times \Sigma_{v \in (0,1)} a_v? : Q_v$
def		$= a_1! : P_1 \times (a_0! : Q_0 + a_1? : Q_1)$
+6		$= (a_1! : P_1 \times a_0? : Q_0) + (a_1! : P_1 \times a_1? : Q_1)$

pruning over all the links $(a_x \mid x \in \mathcal{D})$

\\4		$= (a_1! : P_1 \times a_0? : Q_0) \setminus\setminus (a_x \mid x \in \mathcal{D})$
		$+ (a_1! : P_1 \times a_1? : Q_1) \setminus\setminus (a_x \mid x \in \mathcal{D})$
↔1a, ↔5b		$= 0 + 1 : (P_1 \times Q_1) \setminus\setminus (a_x \mid x \in \mathcal{D})$
+3		$= 1 : (P_1 \times Q_1) \setminus\setminus (a_x \mid x \in \mathcal{D})$

After communication, the behaviour of both sender and receiver is parametrised by $v = x = 1$, the value communicated.

The particular form of passing binary values can be extended to any data set by defining a general sender and receiver pair:

$$P \stackrel{\text{def}}{=} \sum_i a_i : P_i \text{ and } Q \stackrel{\text{def}}{=} \sum_i b_i : Q_i \text{ where } 0 \le i \le I$$

the sender has a set of I output ports a_i, the receiver a set of I input ports b_i

Choice has proved to model the parameter passing we want, and it only requires a small change to give us the simpler, more evocative, parameter passing notation of:

$$P \stackrel{\text{def}}{=} a!x:P_x$$
$$Q \stackrel{\text{def}}{=} a?v:Q_v$$
$$(P \times Q) \backslash\backslash a = 1 : (P_x \times Q_v[v:=x]) \backslash\backslash a, \text{ for } x, v \in \mathcal{D}$$

and from now on we will use $a!x$ and $b?v$ as shorthands of $a_x!$ and $\sum_{v \in \mathcal{D}} b_v?$.

As a picture:

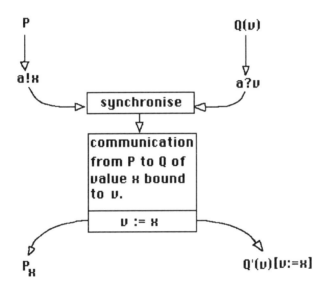

definition *remote assignment*
> The passing of parameter x from P to Q and its subsequent binding to variable v in Q interprets as assigning x to v, $v:=x$, a remote assignment between the two processes.

■

definition *Particulate communications pair*
> Synchronisation, and hence parameter passing, will only occur between actions $a!(x)$ and $b?(v)$ if $b=a^{-1}$ over the data set of which x and v are both members is termed a *particulate communication pair*.

■

In terms of propositions[†] (based on previous synchronisation propositions, so they should look familiar), a particulate communication is forced if the communication pair is scoped over

$$(a!x:P \times a?v:Q) \backslash\backslash A = 1: (P \times Q[v:=x]) \backslash\backslash A, \text{ if } a \in A$$

but if the guarding actions do not form a communication pair and neither are scoped over, then both can escape the pruning, and, if they are, inaction results.

$$(a!x:P \times b?v:Q) \backslash\backslash A = a!x.b?v: (P \times Q) \backslash\backslash A, \text{ if } a \notin A \text{ and } b \notin A$$
$$= \mathbb{0}, \text{ if } a \in A \text{ or } b \in A$$

We can now write the successful parameter passing construct as a derivation.

derivation *parameter passing*

Where x and v have the same data type, $x, v \in \mathcal{D}$

$$P \xrightarrow{a!x} P' \text{ and } Q \xrightarrow{a?v} Q'(v) \text{ and } (P \times Q) \backslash\backslash a$$

$$1: (P' \times Q'(v)[v:=x]) \backslash\backslash a$$

■

This is not an additional concept in SCCS but a syntactic 'shorthand' for a portmanteau of concurrency, choice and pruning, so previously defined propositions apply where appropriate.

We are not, of course, restricted to particulate communications; just as the general form of actions are composite so are those involved in parameter passing. Each action can simultaneously support multiple data passing, input and output, and, while the algebra has no problem with such concepts, we humans have to apply some constraints to keep things understandable. To this end we limit ourselves to bidirectional communication between two agents, as in $a_1!x.a_2!y.a_3?u:P \times a_1?v.a_2?w.a_3!z:Q$ based on multiple unidirectional communication, as in $a_1!x.a_2!y:P \times a_1?v.a_2?w:Q$, which is itself based on single unidirectional communication, as in $a!x:P \times a?v:Q$. All this without a loss of generality but a gain in comprehensibility. Time for some notation.

At the lowest level we have particles interchanging single data items, as in $a!x:P \times a?v:Q$; this can be extended to multiple actions each conveying one item of data, as in $a_1!x.a_2!y:P \times a_1?v.a_2?w:Q$, which could also be written more generally, in composite form, as $\alpha(!x.!y):P \times \alpha^{-1}(?v.?w):Q$. An extension to bidirectional data passing, as in $\alpha(!x.?w):P \times \alpha^{-1}(?v.!y):Q$ is quite natural – all this with the proviso that data types are respected, as in

---

[†] In SCCS there's no inherent directionality in data passing. It's irrelevant which process selects the value to pass as long as they're both of the same mind. Anthropomorphically, we tend to think it's the sender that selects the data to be sent, and our propositions tend to reflect this.

α (! x::$\mathcal{D}_1$. ?w::$\mathcal{D}_2$) : P $\times$ α^{-1} (?v::$\mathcal{D}_1$. ! y::$\mathcal{D}_2$) : Q. So, step-by-step we've moved away from the realms of strict parameter passing – one data item at a time – to the realisation that the same SCCS concepts support data passing of any complexity and we've blurred the traditional distinction between parameter passing and message passing.

4.7.2 Message Passing

Conditioned by programming, we tend to think of parameters as single, simply typed, variables passed between procedures, and messages as a longer, possibly multi-typed, communication between processes, extrapolated in distributed systems to client requests and server replies. From the Collins Dictionary we get the definition of 'message' as '*a communication, usually brief, from one person or group, to another*'.

SCCS sides with Collins. The algebra does not differentiate between parameters and messages, since they are both conveyors of information and both are interpretations of agent synchronisation. As a simple nod towards the door can pass the message 'let's get out of here', the a! of process P synchronising with the a! of process Q could mean '3::$\mathcal{INT}$', or, '3::$\mathcal{INT}$, 78.6::$\mathcal{REAL}$, true::$\mathcal{BOOL}$', or '[1,27,18,3]::$\mathcal{LISTOFINT}$', or, 'a-long-message::$\mathcal{LISTOFCHAR}$', or the complete text of Shakespeare's *Romeo and Juliet*, or whatever the processes agree that's what the synchronisations means. As long as we obey the rules of data typing we can be as exotic as we like. Some examples:

examples

a)   Concurrent data passing can be constructed by combining single element communications under the $\times$ operator; such data passing can be written as ((a::$\mathcal{D}_1$)$\times$(b::$\mathcal{D}_2$)$\times$(a::$\mathcal{D}_3$)) and so on. For example:

$$P \stackrel{\text{def}}{=} a! \ (1::\mathcal{INT}) \ \times a! \ (2::\mathcal{INT}) \ \times a! \ (3::\mathcal{INT}) : P'$$
$$Q \stackrel{\text{def}}{=} a? \ (x::\mathcal{INT}) \ \times a? \ (y::\mathcal{INT}) \ \times a? \ (z::\mathcal{INT}) : Q'$$
$$(P \times Q) \backslash\backslash a = 1 : (P' \times Q' \ [(x:=1),(y:=2),(z:=3)]) \backslash\backslash a$$

The same effect can be obtained by replacing the three particulates with one composite.

$$P \stackrel{\text{def}}{=} a! \ ((1 \times 2 \times 3)::\mathcal{INT}) : P'$$
$$Q \stackrel{\text{def}}{=} a? \ ((x \times y \times z)::\mathcal{INT}) : Q'$$
$$(P \times Q) \backslash\backslash a = 1 : (P' \times Q' \ [(x:=1),(y:=2),(z:=3)]) \backslash\backslash a$$

b)   Sequential data passing can be constructed by concatenating smaller sequential messages. For example, the passing of a list of three items (1,2,3) of type $\mathcal{INT}$ from agent P to agent Q over port a may be represented as several 'one slot' sub-messages and expressed as items composed under the action prefix ':'. For example: $((a:b:c)::\mathcal{D})$ or: $((a::\mathcal{D}_1):(b::\mathcal{D}_2):(c::\mathcal{D}_3))$.

The passing of a list of three items $(1,2,3)$ of type $\mathcal{INT}$ from agent P to agent Q over ports a as separate actions

$$P \stackrel{\text{def}}{=} (a!1:a!2:a!3)::\mathcal{INT}):P'$$
$$Q \stackrel{\text{def}}{=} (a?x:a?y:a?z)::\mathcal{INT}):Q'$$
$$(P \times Q) \backslash\backslash a = 1:1:1:(P' \times Q'[(x:=1),(y:=2),(z:=3)])\backslash\backslash a$$

Using an equivalent notation

$$P \stackrel{\text{def}}{=} a!((1:2:3)::\mathcal{INT}):P'$$
$$Q \stackrel{\text{def}}{=} a?((x:y:z)::\mathcal{INT}):Q'$$
$$(P \times Q) \backslash\backslash a \stackrel{\text{def}}{=} 1:1:1:(P' \times Q'[(x:=1),(y:=2),(z:=3)])\backslash\backslash a$$

c) Data passing items containing both sequential and concurrent elements can be represented by combining elements under the ':' and 'x' operators. For example, communication of an instance of the composite data type $\mathcal{RECORD}$ containing instances of data types $\mathcal{INT}$, $\mathcal{REAL}$ and $\mathcal{BOOL}$.

Communicated serially:

$$P \stackrel{\text{def}}{=} a!(1::\mathcal{INT}):a!(3.171::\mathcal{REAL}):a!(true::\mathcal{BOOL}):P'$$
$$Q \stackrel{\text{def}}{=} a?(x::\mathcal{INT}):a?(y::\mathcal{REAL}):a?(z::\mathcal{BOOL}):Q'$$
$$(P \times Q) \backslash\backslash a = 1:1:1:(P' \times Q'[(x:=1),(y:=3.171),(z:=true)])\backslash\backslash a$$

Communicated concurrently:

$$P \stackrel{\text{def}}{=} a!((1 \times 3.171 \times true)::\mathcal{RECORD}):P'$$
$$Q \stackrel{\text{def}}{=} a?((x \times y \times z)::\mathcal{RECORD}):Q'$$
$$(P \times Q) \backslash\backslash a = 1:(P' \times Q'[(x:=1),(y:=3.171),(z:=true)])\backslash\backslash a$$

∎

We can now formalise the notation before looking at some propositions.

definition *Communications pair*
Synchronisation and hence parameter passing will only occur between actions $\alpha(!x.?w:)^n$ and $\beta(!y.?v:)^n$ if $\beta=\alpha^{-1}$; $x, v \in \mathcal{D}_1$ and $y, w \in \mathcal{D}_2$, where $\beta=\alpha^{-1}$ is called a communications pair.

∎

We repackage our propositions of interaction as propositions over data passing, starting with bidirectional data passing.

propositions *general data passing*
For $(x, v::\mathcal{D}_1)$ and $(y, w::\mathcal{D}_2)$

Where $\alpha\alpha^{-1}$ contains only complete synchronisation pairs

$\leftrightarrow$10 $\qquad$ $(\alpha(!x.?w):P \times \alpha^{-1}(!y.?v):Q) \backslash\backslash A =$

a) $1:(P[w:=y] \times Q[v:=x]) \backslash\backslash A$, if $\text{Part}(\alpha) \subseteq A$

b) $\alpha(!x.?w).\alpha^{-1}(!y.?v):(P \times Q) \backslash\backslash A$, if $\text{Part}(\alpha) \cap A \neq \varnothing$

Where $\alpha\beta$ contains no synchronisation pairs, $\text{Part}(\alpha\beta) \cap \text{Part}^{-1}(\alpha\beta) = \varnothing$

$\leftrightarrow$14 $\qquad$ $(\alpha(!x.?w):P \times \beta(!y.?v):Q) \backslash\backslash A =$

a) $\alpha(!x.?w).\beta(!y.?v):(P \times Q) \backslash\backslash A$, if $\text{Part}(\alpha\beta) \cap A = \varnothing$

b) $\mathbb{0}$, if $\text{Part}(\alpha\beta) \cap A \neq \varnothing$

> Where $\alpha(!x.?w)$ indicates port α sending data item x simultaneously as it receives data item w. Items x and v can, of course, themselves be composed of several concurrently communicated data items.

Prop $\leftrightarrow$10a based on $\backslash\backslash$6e, two agents whose actions form an encapsulated communications pair successfully synchronise and pass data.

Prop $\leftrightarrow$10b based on $\backslash\backslash$6c, two agents whose actions do not form encapsulated particulate communications pairs escape pruning and remain available to communicate with an environment, including each other.

Prop $\leftrightarrow$14a based on $\backslash\backslash$6d, no encapsulated particulate communications, all escape and remain available for communication with an environment.

Prop $\leftrightarrow$14b based on $\backslash\backslash$6b, if any of the independent particulate communications are encapsulated, inaction results.

∎

And the simpler case of unidirectional data passing.

proposition *unidirectional data passing*

For $(x, v::\mathcal{D})$

Where $\alpha\alpha^{-1}$ contains only complete synchronisation pairs

$\leftrightarrow$I $\qquad$ $(\alpha(!x):P \times \alpha^{-1}(?v):Q) \backslash\backslash A =$

a) $1:(P \times Q[v:=x]) \backslash\backslash A$, if $\text{Part}(\alpha) \subseteq A$

b) $\alpha(!x).\alpha^{-1}(?v):(P \times Q) \backslash\backslash A$, if $\text{Part}(\alpha) \cap A \neq \varnothing$

Where $\alpha\beta$ contains no synchronisation pairs, $\text{Part}(\alpha\beta) \cap \text{Part}^{-1}(\alpha\beta) = \varnothing$

$\leftrightarrow$II $\qquad$ $(\alpha(!x):P \times \beta(?v):Q) \backslash\backslash A =$

a) $\alpha(!x).\beta(?v):(P \times Q) \backslash\backslash A$, if $\text{Part}(\alpha\beta) \cap A = \varnothing$

b) $\mathbb{0}$, if $\text{Part}(\alpha\beta) \cap A \neq \varnothing$

Prop ↔Ia two agents, whose initial actions form a communications pair, encapsulated with respect to a successful synchronisation, can successfully pass a message.

Prop ↔Ib if the communications pair is not encapsulated, either a message will be passed between the agents, or they remain available to interact with an environment.

Prop ↔IIa if the initial actions of the two agents do not form a communications pair and are not pruned, communication will fail, but the actions remain to interact with an environment

Prop ↔IIb if any of the particulate communications are encapsulated inaction results.

■

examples

a) two buffers connected together

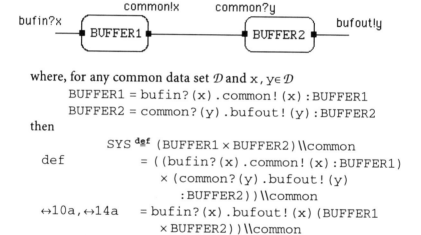

where, for any common data set $\mathcal{D}$ and x, y∈ $\mathcal{D}$

    BUFFER1 = bufin?(x).common!(x):BUFFER1
    BUFFER2 = common?(y).bufout!(y):BUFFER2

then

          SYS ≝ (BUFFER1 × BUFFER2)\\common
def   = ((bufin?(x).common!(x):BUFFER1)
          × (common?(y).bufout!(y)
          :BUFFER2))\\common
↔10a,↔14a = bufin?(x).bufout!(x)(BUFFER1
          × BUFFER2))\\common
def   = bufin?(x).bufout!(x):SYS

b) A revisit to our circuit composed of AND and NOT logic gates

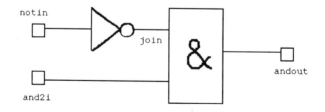

where the general AND is defined by:
    AND = join?(v) × and2i?(y) × andout!(z:=v∧y):AND

and the NOT as:

```
NOT = notin?(x).join(¬x)!:NOT
```

which, when connected, becomes:

SYS $\stackrel{\text{def}}{=}$ (NOT × AND)\\join

```
def          = ((join?(v).and2i?(y)
                                .andout!(z:=v∧y):AND)
              × (notin?(x).join(¬x)!:NOT))\\join
```

↔10a,↔14a   = notin?(x).and2i?(y)
```
                                .andout!(z:=¬x∧y):SYS
```

■

Message passing, while a useful tool in its own right, has another trick up its sleeve: the data passed can be used to influence the behaviour of the receiving agent.

4.7.3 Predicated Choice

From a?v, which binds data communicated to variable v in the receiving agent, it only takes a small sleight of hand to produce a construct for predicated choice where the future behaviour of the receiving agents depends on the value of v received. The simplest choice is between two such behaviours, and we use a predicate, based on the current values of an agent's bound variables, to choose between them. In computer languages such predicated choices are written as:

IF *predicate* THEN *choice1* ELSE *choice2*.

which also form the basis of iterative DO loops, WHILE loops, multiple choice CASE statements and so on. The simplest SCCS expression for predicated choice is:

P $\stackrel{\text{def}}{=}$ α?x: *if* x=*const* *then* P' *else* P''

where x and *const* have the same data type and the evaluation of the predicate is an internal action of the system.

We could develop a predicated choice construct from parameter passing, but it is more satisfying to go back to first principles – to the case where the sender can choose to activate one (of a set of) sending action and the receiver receive any one of this set, expressed algebraically as:

$$P \stackrel{\text{def}}{=} \sum_{x \in \mathcal{D}} a_x! : P_x \text{ and } Q \stackrel{\text{def}}{=} \sum_{v \in \mathcal{D}} a_v? : Q_v$$

For binary choice we need a $\mathcal{D}=\{\text{true}, \text{false}\}$, then, composing P×Q and restricting over the ports, we get:

$$P \times Q = ((\sum_{x \in \mathcal{D}} a_x! : P_x) \times (\sum_{v \in \mathcal{D}} a_v? : Q_v)) \setminus\!\setminus (a_x | x \in \mathcal{D})$$

For x=true

$$P \times Q = (a_{\text{true}}! : P_{\text{true}} \times \sum_{v \in (\text{false}, \text{true})} a_v? : Q_v) \setminus\!\setminus \{a_{\text{true}}, a_{\text{false}}\}$$

$+6$

$$= ((a_{true}!:P_{true} \times a_{false}?:Q_{false})$$
$$+ (a_{true}!:P_{true} \times a_{true}?:Q_{true}))\backslash\backslash\{a_{true}, a_{false}\}$$

$\leftrightarrow 1a, \leftrightarrow 5b, +3$

$$= 1:(P_{true} \times Q_{true})\backslash\backslash\{a_{true}, a_{false}\}$$

For x=false

$$P \times Q = (a_{false}!:P_{false} \times \Sigma_{v\in(false,true)} a_v?:Q_v)\backslash\backslash\{a_{true}, a_{false}\}$$

$+6$

$$= ((a_{false}!:P_{false} \times a_{false}?:Q_{false})$$
$$+ (a_{false}!:P_{false} \times a_{true}?:Q_{true}))\backslash\backslash\{a_{true}, a_{false}\}$$

$\leftrightarrow 1a, \leftrightarrow 5b, +3$

$$= 1:(P_{false} \times Q_{false})\backslash\backslash\{a_{true}, a_{false}\}$$

After communication, the behaviours of sender and receiver are determined by the value of x communicated. We can replace these rather messy SCCS expressions using our parameter passing notation of

$$P \stackrel{\text{def}}{=} \alpha!x:P_x$$
$$Q \stackrel{\text{def}}{=} \alpha?x:\underline{if}\ x=true\ \underline{then}\ Q_{true}\ \underline{else}\ Q_{false}$$

for x∈{true, false}. Again, this is *not* an additional concept in SCCS but a syntactic 'shorthand' for a combination of concurrency, choice and pruning. Using this notation, the NOT gate of the previous section could be rewritten as:

$$\text{NOT} \stackrel{\text{def}}{=} \text{notin}?x:\underline{if}\ x=0\ \underline{then}\ \text{notout}!1:\text{NOT}$$
$$\underline{else}\ \text{notout}!0:\text{NOT}$$

Naturally the predicate is not restricted to one variable but can be as complex as required, as long as it evaluates to the binary true or false. For example, we could have:

$$P \stackrel{\text{def}}{=} \alpha?x:\alpha?y:\underline{if}\ x=y\ \underline{then}\ P'\ \underline{else}\ P''$$

We represent all such cases of predicated choice by the expression:

$$\underline{if}\ Pred\ \underline{then}\ P\ \underline{else}\ Q$$

which we can formalise in terms of a derivation.

derivation *predicated binary choice*

$$P \stackrel{\alpha}{\rightarrow} P'\ \text{and}\ Pred = true$$

$$(\underline{if}\ Pred\ \underline{then}\ P\ \underline{else}\ Q) \stackrel{\alpha}{\rightarrow} P'$$

and:

$$Q \stackrel{\alpha}{\rightarrow} Q'\ \text{and}\ Pred = false$$

$$(\underline{if}\ Pred\ \underline{then}\ P\ \underline{else}\ Q) \stackrel{\alpha}{\rightarrow} Q'$$

where *Pred* is an expression which evaluates to true or false and contains variables bound by input actions up to the time it is evaluated. Each predicate uses the current state of the agent to select one of many possible behaviours, where the current state includes the values of all variables previously input.

■

examples

a) Agent EXOR inputs over a? and b? and outputs their exclusive OR over c!. where $a, b, c \in \{0, 1\}$
EXOR $\stackrel{\text{def}}{=}$ a?x:b?y:<u>if</u> x=y <u>then</u> c!0:EXOR
<u>else</u> c!1:EXOR

b) If asked, an agent will deliver the compete text of the Bible, otherwise it will deliver the complete text of the Koran.
TEXT $\stackrel{\text{def}}{=}$ a?x:<u>if</u> x=bible <u>then</u> b!Bible:TEXT
<u>else</u> b!Koran:TEXT

■

proposition *predicated choice*

*Pred*1   (<u>if</u> *Pred* <u>then</u> P <u>else</u> Q) = P, if *Pred* = true,
                                        = Q otherwise

■

We can generalise binary predicated choice[†] over behaviour sets
$$\underline{if} \; Pred \; \underline{then} \; \Sigma_i P \; \underline{else} \; \Sigma_j Q, \text{ for some i and some j}$$
and formalise this in terms of a derivation.

derivation *predicated choice*

A generalisation formed by the combination of the derivations of predicated binary choice and that of choice itself:

$$\frac{P_i \stackrel{\alpha}{\rightarrow} P' \text{ and } Pred = \text{true}}{(\underline{if} \; Pred \; \underline{then} \; \mathbb{P} \; \underline{else} \; \mathbb{Q}) \stackrel{\alpha}{\rightarrow} P'}$$

and:

$$\frac{Q_j \stackrel{\alpha}{\rightarrow} Q' \text{ and } Pred = \text{false}}{(\underline{if} \; Pred \; \underline{then} \; \mathbb{P} \; \underline{else} \; \mathbb{Q}) \stackrel{\alpha}{\rightarrow} Q'}$$

Where *Pred* is an expression evaluating to true or false containing

---

† Note: the predicate has to be evaluated and this must be reflected in the calculus. Predicate evaluation is modelled as the requisite number of internal 1 actions of the agent concerned.

elements of the set of bound variables available at the point when $Pred$ is evaluated.

$\mathbb{P} = \langle \Sigma P_i \mid i \in I \rangle$ is a possibly infinite family of expressions indexed by i.

$\mathbb{Q} = \langle \Sigma Q_j \mid j \in I \rangle$ is a possibly infinite family of expressions indexed by j.

The predicated choice selects a subset of possible behaviours based on the current state of the agent.

■

proposition *predicated general choice*

$Pred2$ $(\underline{if}\ Pred\ \underline{then}\ \mathbb{P}\ \underline{else}\ \mathbb{Q}) = \mathbb{P}$, if $Pred = \texttt{true}$
$\qquad\qquad\qquad\qquad\qquad\qquad = \mathbb{Q}$, if $Pred = \texttt{false}$

Where further distinctions can be made over a chosen set by descending the predicate branches until a binary choice over the leaves is attained.

■

As SCCS predicated choice can model the IF...THEN...ELSE clause which forms the basis of WHILE...DO...OD, CASE...ESAC and other sequential programming control constructs, and as we have previously shown that it can model both data typing and procedure calling, it looks like SCCS can be used to model and reason about sequential computer programs. But before we do that we need formally to introduce the last major concept – that of giving agents the ability to delay their observable behaviours.

4.8 Agents Lurking

Rather than have the one chance to synchronise, if, by engaging in internal actions, one agent could wait until the other was ready, we would greatly increase the probability of successful synchronisation.

4.8.1 Delay, δ

Agent δE behaves as agent E, except that it can delay indefinitely before engaging in its first observable action. Formally δE has a derivation tree:

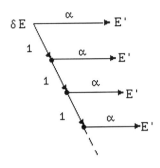

Agent δE can engage in action α and then behave as E', or it can engage in a 1 action before engaging in α and then behave as E', or it can engage in a 1 action before, ..., and so on. δE can engage in any number (including zero) of 1s before engaging in α.

This can represented by the simpler:

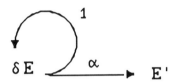

The unary delay operator δ, the solution to δE $\stackrel{\text{def}}{=}$ 1 : δE + E, can be defined by the fixed point

$$δE = fixX(1:X + E)$$

the solution to

$$X \stackrel{\text{def}}{=} 1 : X + X$$

derivation *Delay*

$$δE \stackrel{1}{\rightarrow} δE \qquad\qquad and \qquad\qquad E \stackrel{α}{\rightarrow} E'$$

$$\overline{δE \stackrel{α}{\rightarrow} E'}$$

δE may idle indefinitely before behaving like E

In terms of precedence over agents, δ binds stronger than summation or product, δP+δQ = (δP) + (δQ) and δP×δQ = (δP) × (δQ), but less than restriction and prunings, δP^A = δ(P^A), δP\A = δ(P\A), δP\\A = δ(P\\A), giving '^A=\A=\\A>δ>×>+'. In terms of actions, prefix and product bind more strongly than δ, δα:P = δ(α:P) and δα.β:P = δ(α.β:P), giving '.=×>:>δ'.

■

examples

a) A stamp machine sits and waits for a customer to insert a coin. After a delay of one second, for internal machinations, it delivers the stamp.

$$S\_MACH \stackrel{\text{def}}{=} δcoin?:1:stamp!:S\_MACH$$

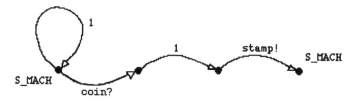

b) A customer, after inserting a coin, is prepared to wait for a stamp to be delivered.

$$S\_CUST \stackrel{\text{def}}{=} coin!:\delta stamp?:S\_CUST$$

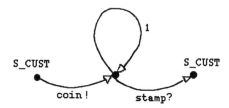

c) When the above stamp machine and customer get together the coin action can only be successful in the first time slot. The customer then waits for the machine to deliver a stamp. As the machine does its internal things in the second time slot, synchronisation of the stamp action can only occur in the third. Something like:

```
S_MACH × S_CUST = X
        X def  coin?xcoin!:1:stamp!xstamp?:X
```

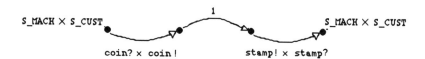

d) An electronic clock, E_CLOCK, displays time to the nearest minute. To do this it relies upon another system, MINS, which counts seconds and tells the clock, via action update, when a minute has passed, whereupon the clock increments its local ticks counter, converts it to hours and minutes and displays the result by action display_time. With a clock period of 1Hz and a period of 1sec.

```
E_CLOCK def  ticks:=0:X
        X def  δupdate?:ticks:=ticks+1:display_time:X
    MINS def  1:Y;
        Y def  (1) 59 :update!:MINS
```

e) A program occasionally calls a security function and awaits its return. The function waits to be called, and returns after taking ten seconds to check things out. With a clock speed of 1Hz and time slots of 1sec.

PROG ^{def} ... :sub!:δreturn?: ...

SEC_SUB ^{def} δsub!:(check things)[10]: return?:SEC_SUB

f)   An initially undefined Boolean variable, UNDEFINED, can be written
to via port WTrue and take the value TRUE, or be written to via port
WFalse and take the value FALSE

UNDEFINED ^{def} δ(WFalse?:FALSE + WTrue?:TRUE)

When in state TRUE the variable can either be read from, via port
RTrue, and maintain the value TRUE, be written to, via port WTrue,
and maintain the value TRUE, or be written to, via port WFalse, and
take the value FALSE

TRUE ^{def} δ(RTrue?:TRUE + WTrue?:TRUE + WFalse?:FALSE)

When in state FALSE the variable can either be read from, via port
RFalse, and maintain the value FALSE, be written to, via port WFalse,
and maintain the value FALSE, or be written to, via port WTrue, and
take the value TRUE

FALSE ^{def} δ(RFalse?:FALSE + WFalse?:FALSE + WTrue?:TRUE)

propositions Delay δ

δ1a	$\delta P = P + 1:\delta P$
δ1b	$= P + \delta P$
δ2	$1:\delta P = \delta(1:P)$
δ3	$\delta\delta P = \delta P$
δ4	$(\delta P)\,^\wedge A = \delta(P\,^\wedge A)$, also for \A and \\A
δ5	$\delta P \times \delta Q = \delta((P \times \delta Q) + (\delta P \times Q))$
δ6	$\delta P + \delta Q \neq \delta(P + Q)$
δ7	$\delta \mathbb{1} = \mathbb{1}$
δ8	$\delta \mathbb{0} = \delta \mathbb{0}$

Prop δ1a by definition then δ1b by

δ1a $P + \delta P = P + P + 1:\delta P$

+4,δ1a $= P + 1:\delta P = \delta P$

Prop δ2 a process delaying one time slot before delaying an indefinite
time, is the same as one delaying an indefinite time before delaying
one time slot. Both are delayed by at least one time slot.

Prop δ3 delaying an indefinite time twice is the same as delaying an
indefinite time once.

Prop δ4 restriction and pruning by definition never affect an idle action;
delay, consisting of sequences of 1 actions, is unaffected by these
operations and can be moved outside their scope.

Prop δ5 $\delta P \times \delta Q \neq \delta(P \times Q)$ as in $\delta(P \times Q)$ the first actions of P and Q

happen simultaneously after a common delay, while in
$\delta P \times \delta Q$ the delays of P and Q are independent.

Prop δ6   take the counter example of P $\stackrel{\text{def}}{=}$ a?:$\mathbb{0}$ and Q $\stackrel{\text{def}}{=}$ b?:$\mathbb{0}$.

Agent $(\delta P + \delta Q)$ persistently offers a choice between 1, a? and b?. It can autonomously engage in a 1 action and select P or Q, rejecting other behaviours $(\delta P + \delta Q)$ $\stackrel{1}{\gt}$ Q is an uncontrollable rejection of P. For example, in:

$$(\delta P + \delta Q) = \delta(a?:\mathbb{0}) + \delta(b?:\mathbb{0})$$

either $\delta(a?:\mathbb{0})$ or $\delta(b?:\mathbb{0})$ can engage in an internal action, silently rejecting the other behaviour – the outcome is non-deterministic, not under the control of any environment. But in:

$$\delta(P + Q) = \delta(a?:\mathbb{0} + b?:\mathbb{0})$$

after a common delay a deterministic choice of a? or b? is always exhibited.

Prop δ7   delaying an indefinite time, δ, before delaying for ever, $\mathbb{1}$, is indistinguishable from just delaying forever.

Prop δ8   delaying an indefinite time, δ, before inaction is irreducible. Inaction will occur, though it might be delayed.

■

δE behaves like E but is willing to wait any number of time slots before actually proceeding to its next observable action. Using the δ operator, an agent can 'wait' for a synchronisation.

interpretation

The delay operator models the non-real-time parts of processes. A process can 'twiddle its thumbs' while waiting to synchronise with another process.

■

The understanding is that δE waits until its environment is ready to participate in a synchronisation. By weakening the relationship between actions and the time, the δ operator enables SCCS to model non-real-time systems; for example: the SCCS expression

$$P \stackrel{\text{def}}{=} \delta a : \delta b : \delta c : \delta d : \dots$$

denotes a temporal asynchronous ordering of actions where *'at some time in the future'* event a will happen followed *'some time later'* by event b followed *'some time later'* by event c, and so on. This is rather like the behaviour captured in the CCS expression:

$$P \stackrel{\text{def}}{=} a.b.c.d. \dots$$

Does this mean that a synchronous algebra like SCCS can model asynchronous systems in the same way as asynchronous algebras like CCS, CSP and so on? Well, to an extent. SCCS cannot escape the bonds of the central clock which dictates all actions, it cannot directly model continuous time, which infers an infinite divisibility, it can only model granulated time. For example, when SCCS models a delay it does so as a number of time slots. This isn't really so much of a problem, for theoretically granulated time can approach continuous time, sufficient for all practical purposes, by simply speeding up the clock, and most real-world systems operate in granulated time anyway.

But a note of caution here. The designer should be aware that, though delay adds to the power of the algebra, gains are rarely made without concomitant losses, and using δs as prefixes has its pitfalls, for δP may never get around to doing anything – a sort of self-imposed livelock. But, even more pernicious, $\delta P + \delta Q$, a generalisation of $(1:P) + (1:Q)$, can not only delay for ever; it is non-deterministic, for when it does act it can autonomously decide to reject Q and behave as P.

example

We can now use the introduced propositions to determine the joint behaviour of the customer:

$$\texttt{S\_CUST} \overset{\text{def}}{=} \texttt{coin!:}\delta\texttt{stamp?:S\_CUST}$$

and the stamp machine:

$$\texttt{S\_MACH} \overset{\text{def}}{=} \delta\texttt{coin?:1:stamp!:S\_MACH}$$

Starting from

```
S_MACH × S_CUST
        = (coin!:δstamp?:S_CUST) × (δcoin?:1:stamp!:S_MACH)

δ1a     = (coin!:δstamp?:S_CUST)
            × (coin?:1:stamp!:S_MACH + 1:δcoin?:1:stamp!:S_MACH)

+6      = (coin!:δstamp?:S_CUST × coin?:1:stamp!:S_MACH)
          + (coin!:δstamp?:S_CUST × 1:δcoin?:1:stamp!:S_MACH)
```

The first part of the expression is heading for the behaviour we expected, but the alternative, in which the customer inserts a coin while the machine idles, is a valid behaviour which we had not considered. The only way to get the behaviour we want is to remove the unsuccessful synchronisations by pruning. Instead of $(\texttt{S\_MACH} \times \texttt{S\_CUST})$ the system we need is $(\texttt{S\_MACH} \times \texttt{S\_CUST}) \backslash\backslash A$ where $A = \{\texttt{coin}, \texttt{stamp}\}$

```
(S_MACH × S_CUST)\\{coin,stamp}
    \\4       = (coin!:δstamp?:S_CUST × coin?:1:stamp!:S_MACH)\\A
                 + (coin!:δstamp?:S_CUST
                      × 1:δcoin?:1:stamp!:S_MACH)\\A

↔1a,↔5b = 1:(δstamp?:S_CUST × 1:stamp!:S_MACH)\\A + ⓪

    +3        = 1:(δstamp?:S_CUST × 1:stamp!:S_MACH)\\A
```

That gives the first synchronisation between the `coin` of customer and machine, the synchronisation representing a coin insertion as expected. Now for the rest:

δ1a   = 1:((stamp?:S_CUST + 1:δstamp?:S_CUST)
                        × 1:stamp!:S_MACH))\\A

+6   = 1:((stamp?:S_CUST × 1:stamp!:S_MACH)
                        + (1:δstamp?:S_CUST × 1:stamp!:S_MACH))\\A

\\4   = 1:((stamp?:S_CUST × 1:stamp!:S_MACH)\\A
                        + (1:δstamp?:S_CUST × 1:stamp!:S_MACH)\\A)

↔5b,×7,\\2 = 1:(0 + 1:(δstamp?:S_CUST × stamp!:S_MACH)\\A)

+3   = 1:1:(δstamp?:S_CUST × stamp!:S_MACH)\\A

In the second time slot the customer idles, waiting for the machine to do its internal action. Now we're looking for delivery of the stamp.

δ1a   = 1:1:((stamp?:S_CUST + 1:δstamp?:S_CUST)
                        × stamp!:S_MACH))\\A

+6   = 1:1:((stamp?:S_CUST × stamp!:S_MACH)
                        + (1:δstamp?:S_CUST × stamp!:S_MACH))\\A)

\\4   = 1:1:((stamp?:S_CUST × stamp!:S_MACH)\\A
                        + (1:δstamp?:S_CUST × stamp!:S_MACH)\\A)

↔1a,↔5b   = 1:1:(1:(S_CUST × S_MACH)\\A + 0)

+3   = 1:1:1:(S_CUST × S_MACH)\\A

In the third time slot the customer and the machine synchronise, `stamp` representing the delivery of a stamp. The complete action is:

(S_MACH × S_CUST)\\{coin,stamp}
            = 1:1:1:(S_CUST × S_MACH)\\{coin,stamp}

The successful transaction we expected – the stamp machine waiting for a coin and the customer waiting for the delivery of a stamp – is now fully modelled as an SCCS expression.

■

The proof is rather long winded. Why? Because we're limited to existing propositions. As the encapsulation of communicating agents with action delay is going to be a common occurrence, some simpler propositions targeted at this requirement would be more useful. Now we have seen the need, we will introduce the propositions.

In the above example, one agent can wait until another is ready, and only when both are ready can the communication occur. Does this ring any bells? This is the blocking-send protocol. The addition of the delay operator has given SCCS, based on a synchronising protocol, the power to model behaviour of the blocking-send communications protocol. The underpinnings of SCCS, modelling synchronous actions, can model the primitives used in algebras which model asynchronous ones, giving rise to the (possibly counter-intuitive) hypothesis that synchronous calculi are more primitive than, and can model, asynchronous ones.

A situation in which one process waits for another to be ready is central to many real-world systems; for example, client–server systems where the server waits for a client to come along, the client waits for the server to perform, and so on. As with synchronisation itself, it would be useful to have some higher level propositions for the common cases of synchronisation plus delay. We need propositions for different types of waiting: for when one or both participants are delayed, and for both successful and unsuccessful synchronisation. To keep things simple, first we will derive the propositions, then we will look at some examples.

As before, we will base our investigations on $(\alpha : P \times \beta : Q) \backslash\backslash A$ for all values of α and β, whether or not they are members of A; whether or not some of their particles form synchronisation pairs; and with the added ability of either, or both, agents to wait.

4.8.2 One Agent Waits

Synchronisation between agents in SCCS is symmetrical; it doesn't really matter which is the 'sender' and which the 'receiver', the difference is purely syntactic. Similarly, whether it is the sender or the receiver which waits to synchronise is irrelevant to the algebra, and we need only consider the case of one agent delayed with respect to the other; however, having one set of propositions for waiting senders and another for waiting receivers makes things easier when it come to applying them. As sender and receiver are interchangeable, we will introduce the case for delayed sender, and, using the symmetry of SCCS synchronisations, determine the propositions of delayed receiver.

The general expression of a sending agent waiting to synchronise, and a receiving agent ready to receive in the next time slot with pruning, is $((\delta\alpha : P) \times (\beta : Q)) \backslash\backslash A$, for, as the product operator is associative, from this basis we can derive all other cases.

$$((\delta\alpha:P) \times (\beta:Q))\backslash\backslash A$$

$\delta 1a \qquad = ((\alpha:P + 1:\delta\alpha:P) \times (\beta:Q))\backslash\backslash A$

$+6 \qquad = ((\alpha:P \times \beta:Q) + (1:\delta\alpha:P \times \beta:Q))\backslash\backslash A$

$\backslash\backslash 4 \qquad = (\alpha:P \times \beta:Q)\backslash\backslash A + (1:\delta\alpha:P \times \beta:Q)\backslash\backslash A$

which is a combination of $(\alpha:P \times \beta:Q)\backslash\backslash A$, the undelayed case, and the instance where $\delta\alpha$ engages in a tick. We've already developed propositions, special cases of $\backslash\backslash 6$, that cover both, and we could leave things at that. However, it would be useful to have propositions that help us with the more common cases, leaving the designer to go 'back to basics' only for the exceptional ones. The cases of interest are those where the initial actions synchronise completely – the particles in the guarding actions all form synchronisation pairs, $(\delta\alpha:P \times \alpha^{-1}:Q)\backslash\backslash A$, and:

- all particles are members of the pruning set
  $(\delta a!b!:P \times a?b?:Q)\backslash\backslash\{a,b\} = 1:(P \times Q)\backslash\backslash\{a,b\}$
- or no particles are members of the pruning set
  $(\delta a!b!:P \times a?b?:Q)\backslash\backslash\{c\} = a!a?b!b?:(P \times Q)\backslash\backslash\{c\}$
  $+ a?b?:(\delta a!b!P \times Q)\backslash\backslash\{c\}$

and the equally straightforward case of completely incomplete actions, $(\delta\alpha:P \times \beta:Q)\backslash\backslash A$, where $\text{Part}(\alpha\beta)\cap\text{Part}^{-1}(\alpha\beta)=\varnothing$, and:

- some particles are in the pruning set
  $(\delta a!b!:P \times c?:Q)\backslash\backslash\{c\} = \mathbb{0};$
- or no particles in the pruning set
  $(\delta a!b!:P \times a!c?:Q)\backslash\backslash\{d\} = a!b!a!c?:(P \times Q)\backslash\backslash\{d\}$
  $+ a?c?:(\delta a!b!P \times Q)\backslash\backslash\{d\}$

examples

a) $(a?:P \times \delta a!:Q)\backslash\backslash a = (\delta a?:P \times a!:Q)\backslash\backslash a = 1:(P \times Q)\backslash\backslash a$

b) $(\delta a?:P \times a!:Q)\backslash\backslash b = a?a!:(P \times Q)\backslash\backslash b + a!:(\delta a?:P \times Q)\backslash\backslash a$

c) $(\delta a?:P \times b!:Q)\backslash\backslash b = \mathbb{0}$

d) $(a?:P \times \delta b!c?:Q)\backslash\backslash d = a?b!c?:(P \times Q)\backslash\backslash c$
  $+ a?:(P \times \delta b!c?:Q)\backslash\backslash c$

■

At this point we will develop the case of complete synchronisation pairs, $\alpha\alpha^{-1}$, where $\text{Part}(\alpha)\cap\text{Part}^{-1}(\alpha)\neq\varnothing$

First where the all particles are pruned, $\text{Part}(\alpha)\subseteq A$

$((\delta\alpha:P) \times (\alpha^{-1}:Q))\backslash\backslash A$

$\qquad = (\alpha:P \times \alpha^{-1}:Q)\backslash\backslash A + (1:\delta\alpha:P \times \alpha^{-1}:Q)\backslash\backslash A$

$\leftrightarrow 1a, \leftrightarrow 5b \qquad = 1:(P \times Q)\backslash\backslash A + \mathbb{0}$

$+3 \qquad = 1:(P \times Q)\backslash\backslash A, \text{ if } \text{Part}(\alpha)\subseteq A$

And then when they aren't, $\text{Part}(\alpha)\cap A=\varnothing$

$((\delta\alpha:P) \times (\alpha^{-1}:Q))\backslash\backslash A$

$$= (\alpha : P \times \alpha^{-1} : Q) \backslash\backslash A + (1 : \delta\alpha : P \times \alpha^{-1} : Q) \backslash\backslash A$$

$\leftrightarrow 1b, \leftrightarrow 5a$ $\quad = \alpha\alpha^{-1} : (P \times Q) \backslash\backslash A + \alpha^{-1} : (\delta\alpha : P \times : Q) \backslash\backslash A,$
$$\text{if } \mathtt{Part}\,(\alpha) \cap A = \varnothing$$

Then, where $\alpha\beta$ contains no synchronisation pairs, $\mathtt{Part}\,(\alpha\beta) \cap \mathtt{Part}^{-1}\,(\alpha\beta) = \varnothing$
First for some α particles pruned, $\mathtt{Part}\,(\alpha) \cap A \neq \varnothing$

$((\delta\alpha : P) \times (\beta : Q)) \backslash\backslash A$

$$= (\alpha : P \times \beta : Q) \backslash\backslash A + (1 : \delta\alpha : P \times \beta : Q) \backslash\backslash A$$

$\leftrightarrow 5b, \leftrightarrow 5a$ $\quad = 0 + \beta : (\delta\alpha : P \times Q) \backslash\backslash A$

$+3$ $\qquad\quad = \beta : (\delta\alpha : P \times Q) \backslash\backslash A, \text{ if } \mathtt{Part}\,(\alpha) \cap A \neq \varnothing$

then some β particles pruned, $\mathtt{Part}\,(\beta) \cap A \neq \varnothing$

$((\delta\alpha : P) \times (\beta : Q)) \backslash\backslash A$

$$= (\alpha : P \times \beta : Q) \backslash\backslash A + (1 : \delta\alpha : P \times \beta : Q) \backslash\backslash A$$

$\leftrightarrow 5b, \leftrightarrow 5b$ $\quad = 0 + 0$

$+3$ $\qquad\quad = 0, \text{ if } \mathtt{Part}\,(\beta) \cap A \neq \varnothing$

finally where no particles are pruned, $\mathtt{Part}\,(\alpha\beta) \cap A = \varnothing$

$((\delta\alpha : P) \times (\beta : Q)) \backslash\backslash A$

$$= (\alpha : P \times \beta : Q) \backslash\backslash A + (1 : \delta\alpha : P \times \beta : Q) \backslash\backslash A$$

$\leftrightarrow 5a, \leftrightarrow 5a$ $\quad = \alpha\beta\,(P \times Q) \backslash\backslash A + \beta : (\delta\alpha : P \times Q) \backslash\backslash A,$
$$\text{if } \mathtt{Part}\,(\alpha\beta) \cap A = \varnothing$$

By corollary, we can define a set of propositions for a delayed receiver to give a set of general propositions.

Propositions *One agent delayed*

Where $\alpha\alpha^{-1}$ contains complete synchronisation pairs,
$\mathtt{Part}\,(\alpha) \cap \mathtt{Part}^{-1}\,(\alpha) \neq \varnothing$

$\leftrightarrow 2$ $\qquad ((\delta\alpha : P) \times (\alpha^{-1} : Q)) \backslash\backslash A =$
    a) $1 : (P \times Q) \backslash\backslash A, \text{ if } \mathtt{Part}\,(\alpha) \subseteq A$
    b) $\alpha\alpha^{-1} : (P \times Q) \backslash\backslash A + \alpha^{-1} : (\delta\alpha : P \times Q) \backslash\backslash A, \text{ if } \mathtt{Part}\,(\alpha) \cap A = \varnothing$

$\leftrightarrow 3$ $\qquad ((\alpha : P) \times (\delta\alpha^{-1} : Q)) \backslash\backslash A =$
    a) $1 : (P \times Q) \backslash\backslash A, \text{ if } \mathtt{Part}\,(\alpha) \subseteq A$
    b) $\alpha\alpha^{-1} : (P \times Q) \backslash\backslash A + \alpha : (P \times \delta\alpha^{-1} : Q) \backslash\backslash A, \text{ if } \mathtt{Part}\,(\alpha) \cap A = \varnothing$

Where $\alpha\beta$ contains no synchronisation pairs,
$\mathtt{Part}\,(\alpha\beta) \cap \mathtt{Part}^{-1}\,(\alpha\beta) = \varnothing$

$\leftrightarrow 6$ $\qquad ((\delta\alpha : P) \times (\beta : Q)) \backslash\backslash A =$
    a) $\beta : (\delta\alpha : P \times Q) \backslash\backslash A, \text{ if } \mathtt{Part}\,(\alpha) \cap A \neq \varnothing$
    b) $0, \text{ if } \mathtt{Part}\,(\beta) \cap A \neq \varnothing$
    c) $\alpha\beta\,(P \times Q) \backslash\backslash A + \beta : (\delta\alpha : P \times Q) \backslash\backslash A, \text{ if } \mathtt{Part}\,(\alpha\beta) \cap A = \varnothing$

↔7 $((\alpha : P) \times (\delta\beta : Q)) \backslash\backslash A =$
a) $\alpha : (P \times \delta\beta : Q) \backslash\backslash A$, if $\text{Part}(\beta) \cap A \neq \emptyset$
b) $\mathbb{0}$, if $\text{Part}(\alpha) \cap A \neq \emptyset$
c) $\alpha\beta (P \times Q) \backslash\backslash A + \alpha : (P \times \delta\beta : Q) \backslash\backslash A$, if $\text{Part}(\alpha\beta) \cap A = \emptyset$

Prop ↔2a, ↔3a all particles form synchronisation pairs which are also
part of the pruning set. Only if all particles synchronise,
metamorphose to an internal action, can they escape pruning.

Prop ↔2b, ↔3b all particles form synchronisation pairs, none of which
are scoped over, no particles are pruned, a non-deterministic choice
exists between either escaping together or the delayed agent
contributing a tick. In both cases, escaped actions remain ready to
synchronise with an environment.

Prop ↔6a, ↔7a there are no synchronisation pairs. The incomplete
particles in the delayed agent are in the pruning set and can only
escape by contributing a tick and waiting for later synchronisations.
Particles in the non-delayed action cannot wait, but, as they are not in
the pruning set, they can escape, ready to interact with an
environment.

Prop ↔6b, ↔7b there are no synchronisation pairs. The incomplete
particles in the non-delayed agent cannot wait, are pruned, and
inaction results.

Prop ↔6c, ↔7c there are no synchronisation pairs, and no particles in
the pruning set. Either the actions escape together, or the delayed
agent contributes a tick and waits for later synchronisations. Escaped
actions remain ready to synchronise with their environment.

■

interpretation

If we expect two processes to synchronise, their guard actions forming a
synchronisation pair one of which can wait, and we set the environment to
prevent outside interference, either we force immediate synchronisation,
or, if the non-delayed agents' guarding actions are not in the pruning set,
they can be rolled off until synchronisation. In effect, the \\a over
$(P \times \delta a : Q) \backslash\backslash a$ holds the a action back until it can escape by synchronising
with an action from P. If synchronisation fails and one of the failures
includes particles from the pruning set, inaction, $\mathbb{0}$, results. In essence, the
delay enables a process to wait for successful synchronisations, removing
unsuccessful ones – a sort of Darwinistic selection of the fittest.

■

example *Delayed Sender*

This is that well known phenomenon, the broken lift. In this case, the only working control button is the one which stops the lift.

The cabin keeps looking for a button action

CABIN $\overset{\text{def}}{=}$ up?:UPCABIN + down?:DOWNCABIN + stop?:CABIN

UPCABIN $\overset{\text{def}}{=}$ stop?:CABIN + down?:DOWNCABIN

DOWNCABIN $\overset{\text{def}}{=}$ stop?:CABIN + up?:UPCABIN

The stop button can be pushed at any time

BUTTONS $\overset{\text{def}}{=}$ δstop!:BUTTONS

The complete lift is described as:

	LIFT $\overset{\text{def}}{=}$ (BUTTONS × CABIN)\\{stop,up,down}	
def	=	(δstop!:BUTTONS × (up?:UPCABIN + down?:DOWNCABIN
		+ stop?:CABIN))\\{stop,up,down}
+6,\\4	=	(δstop!:BUTTONS × up?:UPCABIN)\\{stop,up,down}
		+ (δstop!:BUTTONS × down?:DOWNCABIN)\\ {stop,up,down}
		+ (δstop!:BUTTONS × stop?:CABIN)\\ {stop,up,down})
↔6b,↔2a	=	0 + 0 + 1:(BUTTONS × CABIN)\\{stop,up,down}
+3	=	1:(BUTTONS × CABIN)\\{stop,up,down}
def	=	1:LIFT

The lift remains stationary.

■

example *Delayed Receiver*

The signal and wait actions on semaphore s are used to control access to an associated resource. With an initial value of s=1, a system composed of this semaphore and client processes A and B should exhibit mutual exclusion. Rather than denote internal actions of the processes by the 1 action, we will denote the critical section of process x by CS_x.

A must synchronise with the semaphore via a! before it can enter its critical section, and informs the semaphore it has exited its critical section via b!. Similarly, B uses q! and c!.

A $\overset{\text{def}}{=}$ δa!:CS_A:b!:A, B $\overset{\text{def}}{=}$ δg!:CS_B:c!:B

To keep things simple, we will use a semaphore with a pair of ports for each client.

SEM $\overset{\text{def}}{=}$ SEM_A + SEM_B = a?:δb?:SEM + g?:δc?:SEM

The complete system:

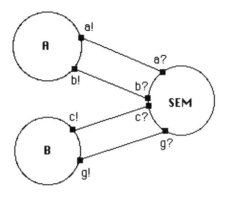

$$\text{SYS} \stackrel{\text{def}}{=} (A \times B \times SEM) \backslash\backslash \{a, b, c, g\}$$

For mutual exclusion derivations of SYS must not include A and B in their critical sections in the same time slot, that is $(CS_A . CS_B)$ must not be an action of SYS.

$$\begin{aligned}
\text{SYS} \stackrel{\text{def}}{=}\ & (A \times B \times SEM) \backslash\backslash\{a,b,c,g\} \\
\text{def} \quad =\ & (A \times B \times (SEM_A + SEM_B)) \backslash\backslash\{a,b,c,g\}
\end{aligned}$$

As SEM_A and A interact through actions a, b and SEM_B and B interact through actions g, c, then

$$\backslash 5 \quad = ((A \times SEM_A) \backslash\backslash\{a,b\} \times B) \backslash\backslash\{c,g\} + ((B \times SEM_B) \backslash\backslash\{c,g\} \times A) \backslash\backslash\{a,b\}$$

Starting with $(A \times SEM_A) \backslash\backslash\{a,b\}$

$$\begin{aligned}
\text{def} \quad =\ & (\!(\delta a! : CS_A : b! : A \times a? : \delta b? : SEM)\!) \backslash\backslash\{a,b\} \\
\leftrightarrow 2a \quad =\ & 1 : (\!(CS_A : b! : A \times \delta b? : SEM)\!) \backslash\backslash\{a,b\} \\
\leftrightarrow 7a \quad =\ & 1 : CS_A : (\!(b! : A \times \delta b? : SEM)\!) \backslash\backslash\{a,b\} \\
\leftrightarrow 3a \quad =\ & 1 : CS_A : 1 : (A \times SEM) \backslash\backslash\{a,b\}
\end{aligned}$$

Adding B, $((A \times SEM_A) \backslash\backslash\{a,b\} \times B) \backslash\backslash\{c,g\}$

$$\begin{aligned}
\text{def} \quad =\ & (\!(1 : CS_A : 1 : (A \times SEM) \backslash\backslash\{a,b\} \times (\delta g! : CS_B : c! : B)\!)) \backslash\backslash\{c,g\} \\
\leftrightarrow 7a \quad =\ & 1 : CS_A : 1 : (\!(A \times SEM) \backslash\backslash\{a,b\} \times (\delta g! : CS_B : c! : B)\!)) \backslash\backslash\{c,g\} \\
\text{def} \quad =\ & 1 : CS_A : 1 : (\!(A \times SEM) \backslash\backslash\{a,b\} \times B)\!) \backslash\backslash\{c,g\} \\
\text{def} \quad =\ & 1 : CS_A : 1 : SYS_A
\end{aligned}$$

Starting with $(B \times SEM_B) \backslash\backslash\{c,g\}$

$$\begin{aligned}
\text{def} \quad =\ & (\!(\delta g! : CS_B : c! : B \times g? : \delta c? : SEM)\!) \backslash\backslash\{c,g\} \\
\leftrightarrow 2a \quad =\ & 1 : (\!(CS_B : c! : B \times \delta c? : SEM)\!) \backslash\backslash\{c,g\} \\
\leftrightarrow 7a \quad =\ & 1 : CS_B : (\!(c! : B \times \delta c? : SEM)\!) \backslash\backslash\{c,g\} \\
\leftrightarrow 3a \quad =\ & 1 : CS_B : 1 : (B \times SEM) \backslash\backslash\{c,g\}
\end{aligned}$$

Adding A, $((B \times SEM_B) \backslash\backslash\{c,g\} \times A) \backslash\{a,b\}$

$$
\begin{array}{rl}
\text{def} & = (\!(1\!:\!CS_B\!:\!1\!:\!(B\ \times\ SEM)\!)\backslash\!\backslash\{c,g\}\ \times\ (\delta a!\!:\!CS_A\!:\!b!\!:\!A)\,)\!)\backslash\!\backslash\{a,b\} \\
\leftrightarrow7a & = 1\!:\!CS_B\!:\!1\!:\!(\!(B\ \times\ SEM)\!)\backslash\!\backslash\{c,g\}\ \times\ (\delta a!\!:\!CS_A\!:\!b!\!:\!A)\,)\!)\backslash\!\backslash\{a,b\} \\
\text{def} & = 1\!:\!CS_B\!:\!1\!:\!(\!(B\ \times\ SEM)\!)\backslash\!\backslash\{c,g\}\ \times\ A)\!)\backslash\!\backslash\{a,b\} \\
\text{def} & = 1\!:\!CS_B\!:\!1\!:\!SYS_B
\end{array}
$$

Putting it all together

$$
\begin{array}{rl}
\text{def} & = 1\!:\!CS_A\!:\!1\!:\!SYS_A\ +\ 1\!:\!CS_B\!:\!1\!:\!SYS_B
\end{array}
$$

giving

$$
SYS\ =\ 1\!:\!CS_A\!:\!1\!:\!SYS_A\ +\ 1\!:\!CS_B\!:\!1\!:\!SYS_B
$$

the equivalent of

$$
+4 \qquad\qquad SYS\ =\ 1\!:\!1\!:\!1\!:\!SYS
$$

This meets the required specification that A and B are never simultaneously in their critical sections. The semaphore, by serialising access to the resource, preserves mutual exclusion.

∎

example *Sender and Receiver Delayed (at different times)*
In an earlier section we explored the behaviour of a stamp machine which sits and waits for a customer to insert a coin, then, after a delay of one second for internal machinations, it delivers a stamp.

$$
S\_MACH\ \overset{\text{def}}{=}\ \delta coin?\!:\!1\!:\!stamp!\!:\!S\_MACH
$$

and that of a customer who, after inserting a coin, is prepared to wait for a stamp to be delivered

$$
S\_CUST\ \overset{\text{def}}{=}\ coin!\!:\!\delta stamp?\!:\!S\_CUST
$$

We hypothesised that, when the above stamp machine and customer get together, the coin action is successful in the first time slot. As the machine therefore does its internal things in the second time slot, synchronisation of the stamp action can only occur in the third. Will our new SCCS propositions bear this out?

Composing and encapsulating the system with respect to the coin and stamp actions

$$
(S\_MACH\ \times\ S\_CUST)\backslash\!\backslash\{coin, stamp\}
$$

$$
\begin{array}{rl}
\text{def} & = (\delta coin?\!:\!1\!:\!stamp!\!:\!S\_MACH \\
& \qquad\qquad \times\ coin!\!:\!\delta stamp?\!:\!S\_CUST)\backslash\!\backslash\{coin, stamp\} \\
\leftrightarrow2a & = 1\!:\!(1\!:\!stamp!\!:\!S\_MACH\ \times\ \delta stamp?\!:\!S\_CUST)\backslash\!\backslash\{coin, stamp\} \\
\leftrightarrow7a & = 1\!:\!1\!:\!(stamp!\!:\!S\_MACH\ \times\ \delta stamp?\!:\!S\_CUST)\backslash\!\backslash\{coin, stamp\} \\
\leftrightarrow3a & = 1\!:\!1\!:\!1\!:\!(S\_MACH\ \times\ S\_CUST)\backslash\!\backslash\{coin, stamp\}
\end{array}
$$

Which gives the expected

$$
(S\_MACH\ \times\ S\_CUST)\backslash\!\backslash\{coin, stamp\}
$$

$$= 1:1:1:(\text{S\_MACH} \times \text{S\_CUST})\backslash\backslash\{\text{coin},\text{stamp}\}$$
– no problem.

We can, of course, label the rather anonymous internal actions in any way we choose. To highlight the synchronisations, we could rename them as:
$(\text{S\_MACH} \times \text{S\_CUST})\backslash\backslash\{\text{coin},\text{stamp}\}$
$$= \text{coin}_{\text{sync}}:\text{idle}:\text{stamp}_{\text{sync}}:(\text{S\_MACH} \times \text{S\_CUST})\backslash\backslash\{\text{coin},\text{stamp}\}$$

∎

The obvious next step is to look at the concurrent execution of two waiting agents.

4.8.3 Both Agents Wait

A situation in which both the sending and the receiving agents are waiting to synchronise can be expressed in the general
$$((\delta\alpha:P) \times (\delta\beta:Q))\backslash\backslash A$$

$\delta 5 \qquad = (\!(\delta((\delta\alpha:P \times \beta:Q) + (\alpha:P \times \delta\beta:Q))\!))\backslash\backslash A$

$\delta 4 \qquad = \delta(\!((\delta\alpha:P \times \beta:Q) + (\alpha:P \times \delta\beta:Q))\!)\backslash\backslash A$

$\backslash\backslash 4 \qquad = \delta(\!(\delta\alpha:P \times \beta:Q)\!)\backslash\backslash A + (\!(\alpha:P \times \delta\beta:Q)\!)\backslash\backslash A)$

which is a delayed choice over the behaviours we examined in the previous section. As before, we will consider some common cases as candidates for elevation to propositions – which will, after all, give us a chance to try out the propositions introduced in the previous section.

First, where $\beta=\alpha^{-1}$ and $\alpha\alpha^{-1}$ contain only complete synchronisation pairs, $\text{Part}(\alpha)\cap\text{Part}^{-1}(\alpha)\neq\varnothing$, behaviour differs depending upon whether the pruning set A includes particles in α or not.

Where all particles are pruned, $\text{Part}(\alpha)\subseteq A$
$((\delta\alpha:P) \times (\delta\alpha^{-1}:Q))\backslash\backslash A$
$$= \delta((\delta\alpha:P \times \alpha^{-1}:Q)\backslash\backslash A + (\alpha:P \times \delta\alpha^{-1}:Q)\backslash\backslash A)$$
$\leftrightarrow 2a, \leftrightarrow 3a \qquad = \delta(1:(P \times Q)\backslash\backslash A + 1:(P \times Q)\backslash\backslash A)$
$+4 \qquad = \delta 1:(P \times Q)\backslash\backslash A, \text{ if } \text{Part}(\alpha)\subseteq A$

the behaviour is context-independent, the two agents always eventually synchronise.

Where they aren't, $\text{Part}(\alpha)\cap A=\varnothing$
$((\delta\alpha:P) \times (\delta\alpha^{-1}:Q))\backslash\backslash A$
$$= \delta((\delta\alpha:P \times \alpha^{-1}:Q)\backslash\backslash A + (\alpha:P \times \delta\alpha^{-1}:Q)\backslash\backslash A)$$
$\leftrightarrow 2b, \leftrightarrow 3b \qquad = \delta(\alpha\alpha^{-1}:(P \times Q)\backslash\backslash A + \alpha^{-1}:(\delta\alpha:P \times Q)\backslash\backslash A$
$$+ \alpha\alpha^{-1}:(P \times Q)\backslash\backslash A + \alpha:(P \times \delta\alpha^{-1}:Q)\backslash\backslash A)$$
$+4 \qquad = \delta(\alpha\alpha^{-1}:(P \times Q)\backslash\backslash A + \alpha^{-1}:(\delta\alpha:P \times Q)\backslash\backslash A$
$$+ \alpha:(P \times \delta\alpha^{-1}:Q)\backslash\backslash A), \text{ if } \text{Part}(\alpha)\cap A=\varnothing$$

the behaviour is context-dependent, the choice between internal and external synchronisation is dependent upon the environment in which the agent finds itself, and, since we do not know the environment, we leave all options open.

Second, where $\alpha\beta$ contains no synchronisation pairs, $\texttt{Part}(\alpha\beta) \cap \texttt{Part}^{-1}(\alpha\beta) = \varnothing$, behaviour depends on A allowing the agents it scopes over to interact with an environment.

Where some α and some β particles are pruned, $\texttt{Part}(\alpha) \cap A \neq \varnothing$ and $\texttt{Part}(\beta) \cap A \neq \varnothing$

```
((δα:P) × (δ β:Q))\\A
                = δ((δα:P × β:Q)\\A + (α:P × δβ:Q)\\A)
↔6b             = δ(0 + (α:P × δβ:Q)\\A), if Part(β)∩A≠∅
↔7b             = δ(0 + 0), if Part(β)∩A≠∅ and Part(α)∩A≠∅
01              = δ0, if Part(β)∩A≠∅ and Part(α)∩A≠∅
```

Where some α particles are pruned, $\texttt{Part}(\alpha) \cap A \neq \varnothing$

```
((δα:P) × (δ β:Q))\\A
                = δ((δα:P × β:Q)\\A + (α:P × δβ:Q)\\A)
↔6a,↔7b         = δ(β:(δα:P × Q)\\A + 0)
+3              = δβ:(δα:P × Q)\\A, if Part(α)∩A≠∅
```

Where some β particles are pruned, $\texttt{Part}(\beta) \cap A \neq \varnothing$

```
((δα:P) × (δβ:Q))\\A
                = δ((δα:P × β:Q)\\A + (α:P × δβ:Q)\\A)
↔6b,↔7a         = δ(0 + α:(P × δβ:Q)\\A)
+3              = δα:(P × δβ:Q)\\A, if Part(β)∩A≠∅
```

Where no particles are pruned, $\texttt{Part}(\alpha\beta) \cap A = \varnothing$

```
((δα:P) × (δβ:Q))\\A
                = δ((δα:P × β:Q)\\A + (α:P × δβ:Q)\\A)
↔6c,↔7c         = δ(αβ(P × Q)\\A + β:(δα:P × Q)\\A
                    + αβ(P × Q)\\A + α:(P × δβ:Q)\\A)
+4              = δ(αβ(P × Q)\\A + β:(δα:P × Q)\\A
                    + α:(P × δβ:Q)\\A), if Part(αβ)∩A=∅
```

All of the above we can express as propositions.

propositions

Where $\alpha\alpha^{-1}$ contains complete synchronisation pairs, $\texttt{Part}(\alpha) \cap \texttt{Part}^{-1}(\alpha) \neq \varnothing$

```
↔4  ((δα:P) × (δα⁻¹:Q))\\A =
    a) δ1:(P×Q)\\A, if Part(α)⊆A
```

$\quad$ b) $\delta(\alpha\alpha^{-1}: (P \times Q) \backslash\backslash A + \alpha^{-1}: (\delta\alpha: P \times Q) \backslash\backslash A$
$$+ \alpha: (P \times \delta\alpha^{-1}: Q) \backslash\backslash A), \text{ if } \mathtt{Part}(\alpha) \cap A = \varnothing$$

Where $\alpha\beta$ contains no synchronisation pairs, $\mathtt{Part}(\alpha\beta) \cap \mathtt{Part}^{-1}(\alpha\beta) = \varnothing$

$\leftrightarrow 8 \quad ((\delta\alpha: P) \times (\delta\beta: Q)) \backslash\backslash A =$

$\quad$ a) $\delta 0$, if $\mathtt{Part}(\beta) \cap A \neq \varnothing$ and $\mathtt{Part}(\alpha) \cap A \neq \varnothing$

$\quad$ b) $\delta\beta: (\delta\alpha: P \times Q) \backslash\backslash A$, if $\mathtt{Part}(\alpha) \cap A \neq \varnothing$

$\quad$ c) $\delta\alpha: (P \times \delta\beta: Q) \backslash\backslash A$, if $\mathtt{Part}(\beta) \cap A \neq \varnothing$

$\quad$ d) $\delta(\alpha\beta: (P \times Q) \backslash\backslash A + \beta: (\delta\alpha: P \times Q) \backslash\backslash A$
$$+ \alpha: (P \times \delta\beta: Q) \backslash\backslash A), \text{ if } \mathtt{Part}(\alpha\beta) \cap A = \varnothing$$

Prop $\leftrightarrow 4a$ all particles form synchronisation pairs, and these are in the pruning set. Only complete internal synchronisation is possible, either immediately or at some time in the future, as denoted by $\delta 1$.

Prop $\leftrightarrow 4b$ all particles form synchronisation pairs, none of which are in the pruning set, no particles are pruned, and a non-deterministic choice exists: either the actions escape together, or the delayed agent contributes a tick. Escaped actions remain ready to synchronise with their environment.

Prop $\leftrightarrow 8a$ there are no synchronisation pairs, some of the initial particles of both actions appear in the pruning set, no actions except tick can escape, and inaction results after the simultaneous ticks run out.

Prop $\leftrightarrow 8b, \leftrightarrow 8c$ there are no synchronisation pairs, the incomplete particles in the scoped over agent can only put off pruning by contribute a tick and waiting for later synchronisations, incomplete particles that are not scoped over can either wait, contributing a tick to the proceedings, or escape ready to interact with an environment.

Prop $\leftrightarrow 8d$ there are no synchronisation pairs, and no particles in the pruning set. Either the actions escape together, or each delayed agent contributes a tick and waits for later synchronisations. Escaped actions remain ready to synchronise with their environment.

interpretation

If we have two processes waiting to synchronise and we set the environment such that the act will be encapsulated, they will synchronise either immediately or at some time in the future. If the guards do not synchronise, while one or both guards are not scoped over they can be rolled out of the pruning; if one of the guards is in the pruning set the encapsulation holds it back while the other agent's actions are rolled out until its guard is scoped over and held. If the two held guards synchronise, they can escape to start the process over again; but if they cannot, inaction will eventually ensue.

It does a great deal to our confidence in SCCS as a design tool that this abstract mathematical calculus models exactly the synchronisation of asynchronous systems that we observe in the real world.

example *Both Agents Delayed*

In the earlier 'Agents, Actions and Synchronisation' section we had an example, SYSTEM $\stackrel{\text{def}}{=}$ COPY × DISK, where we needed to pad the head of the disk definition with idle actions so that the COPY↔DISK communications synchronise correctly. We promised to return to it when we had the modelling tools to make this unnatural activity unnecessary. We do that here. Defining the processes as:

COPY $\stackrel{\text{def}}{=}$ δa?:format:δc!:δd!:COPY

DISK $\stackrel{\text{def}}{=}$ δc?:δd?:DISK

where:

a? = read in file	format = format file
c! = select the disk	d! = write to disk

Both processes are now recursive and, more importantly, both wait for interactions with each other. Composing the system and encapsulating over these interactions

SYSTEM $\stackrel{\text{def}}{=}$ (COPY × DISK)\\{c,d}

def	= (δa?:format:δc!:δd!:COPY × δc?:δd?:DISK)\\{c,d}
↔8c	= δa?:(format:δc!:δd!:COPY × δc?:δd?:DISK)\\{c,d}
↔7a	= δa?:format:(δc!:δd!:COPY × δc?:δd?:DISK)\\{c,d}
↔4a	= δa?:format:δ1:(δd!:COPY × δd?:DISK)\\A
↔4a	= δa?:format:δ1:δ1:(COPY × DISK)\\A
def	= δa?:format:δ1:δ1:SYS

After reading and formatting the data into a file, the COPY server, when both processes are ready, synchronises with DISK to select a disk and writes the file.

■

example *Both Agents Delayed plus Choice*

In the section introducing communications and concurrency we proved that agent P $\stackrel{\text{def}}{=}$ a?:b?:P + c!:(d?:P + e!:P) placed in an environment Q $\stackrel{\text{def}}{=}$ a!:1:Q and pruned over by a had behaviour

(P×Q)\\a = 1:b?:(P×Q)\\a

This, like the previous example, was a rather contrived solution relying upon correct padding by 1 actions to ensure the two agents synchronised successfully. We can now rectify this by allowing P to wait to synchronise, as in

P $\stackrel{\text{def}}{=}$ δa?:b?:P + c!:(d?:P + e!:P)

Q $\stackrel{\text{def}}{=}$ a!:δQ

Now

$$\text{SYS} \stackrel{\text{def}}{=} (P \times Q) \backslash\backslash a$$

```
def              = (((δa?:b?:P + c!:(d?:P + e!:P))) × a!:δQ))\\a
+6               = (((δa?:b?:P × a!:δQ)
                     + (c!:(d?:P + e!:P)) × a!:δQ))\\a
\\4              = ((δa?:b?:P × a!:δQ))\\a
                     + ((c!:(d?:P + e!:P) × a!:δQ))\\a
↔2a,↔5b          = 1:((b?:P × δQ))\\a + ⓞ
+3,↔7a           = 1:b?:((P × Q))\\a
def              = 1:b?:SYS
```

If we define the environment slightly differently, this time both P and Q wait to synchronise,

$$P \stackrel{\text{def}}{=} \delta a?:b?:P + c!:(d?:P + e!:P)$$
$$Q \stackrel{\text{def}}{=} \delta a!:Q$$

We get a different behaviour

$$\text{SYS} \stackrel{\text{def}}{=} (P \times Q) \backslash\backslash a$$

```
def              = (((δa?:b?:P + c!:(d?:P + e!:P)) × δa!:Q))\\a
+6               = (((δa?:b?:P × δa!:Q)
                     + (c!:(d?:P + e!:P)) × δa!:Q))\\a
\\4              = ((δa?:b?:P × δa!:Q))\\a
                     + ((c!:(d?:P + e!:P) × δa!:Q))\\a
↔4a,↔7a          = δ1:((b?:P × Q))\\a
                     + c!:(d?:P + e!:P) × δa!:Q))\\a
def,+6           = δ1:((b?:P × δa!:Q))\\a
                     + c!:(((d?:P × δa!:Q) + (e!:P × δa!:Q)))\\a
↔7a,\\4          = δ1:b?:((P × Q))\\a
                     + c!:(((d?:P × δa!:Q))\\a + (e!:P × δa!:Q))\\a)
↔5a              = δ1:b?:((P × Q))\\a
                     + c!:(d?:((P × δa!:Q))\\a + e!:((P × δa!:Q))\\a)
def              = δ1:b?:SYS + c!:(d?:SYS + e!:SYS)
```

The possibility of the two agents successfully synchronising remains, but, while Q waits to synchronise, P can go off and engage in its non-encapsulated actions.

Previous examples have shown the recommended route of constructing a design, composing agents two at a time and encapsulating as we go. But what if we cannot approach a design using this method? We can still reach a correct result, but with less finesse.

Consider the case of two agents, $\delta\alpha : P$ and $\delta\alpha : Q$, with the same guarding actions, placed in an environment, $\delta\alpha^{-1}:R$, which satisfies that guard. Encapsulating the resultant system with respect to α we get:

$$(\delta\alpha:P \times \delta\alpha:Q \times \delta\alpha^{-1}:R)\backslash\backslash\alpha$$

which interprets into 'some time in the future, either $\delta\alpha^{-1}:R$ synchronises with $\delta\alpha:P$ or with $\delta\alpha:Q$' – the partner 'rejected' by R waits for future cooperation possibilities. All other behaviours are pruned by the $\backslash\backslash\alpha$ encapsulation. This rather useful result we will elevate to the status of a proposition:

proposition

$\leftrightarrow9$ $(\delta\alpha:P \times \delta\alpha:Q \times \delta\alpha^{-1}:R)\backslash\backslash\alpha$

$\quad = \delta1:(\delta\alpha:P \times Q \times R)\backslash\backslash\alpha + \delta1:(P \times \delta\alpha:Q \times R)\backslash\backslash\alpha$

Prop $\leftrightarrow9$ Some time in the future, R will synchronise with either Q or P

example *Realistic Semaphores*

The previous attempt at modelling a binary semaphore was rather contrived; the semaphore needed a pair of interactions for each client. A more realistic general semaphore could serve any number of clients using only two interactions, one representing *signal* and the other *wait*. A system composed of this semaphore agent and two clients A and B is:

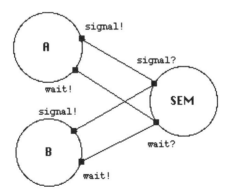

The system preserves mutual exclusion by controlling entry to critical sections. The semaphore waits for requests from clients, and clients wait for subsequent semaphore permission to enter their critical sections. Each client process talks to the semaphore via a `wait!`, asking to enter its critical section, and, later informs the semaphore via a `signal!` that it has exited its critical section

$$A \stackrel{\text{def}}{=} \delta\text{wait!}:CS_{AH}:CS_{AT}:\delta\text{signal!}:A$$
$$B \stackrel{\text{def}}{=} \delta\text{wait!}:CS_{BH}:CS_{BT}:\delta\text{signal!}:B$$

What is the significance of $CS_{AH}:CS_{AT}$? While we have shown that SCCS can detect failure in mutual exclusion for atomic critical sections, let us instead consider the more general, non-atomic critical sections. To do this, we make the critical section divisible by giving them head and tail parts:

$\quad CS_{xH}$ head part of the critical section of process x

$\quad CS_{xT}$ tail part of the critical section of process x

In the semaphore S_n, n represents a count of the number of currently available unshareable resources. For example, the semaphore S_2 is associated with two remaining resources. S_n is always initialised to the maximum number of resources.

$\quad SEM \stackrel{\text{def}}{=} S_{max}$

$\quad S_{max} \stackrel{\text{def}}{=} \delta\texttt{wait?}:S_{max-1}$

$\quad S_n \stackrel{\text{def}}{=} \delta\texttt{wait!}:S_{n-1} + \delta\texttt{signal!}:S_{n+1}$ for 0<n<max

$\quad S_0 \stackrel{\text{def}}{=} \delta\texttt{signal!}:S_1$

For a single unshareable resource we use a binary semaphore, a special case of the general semaphore, for which max=1, giving:

$\quad SEM \stackrel{\text{def}}{=} S_1$

$\quad S_1 \stackrel{\text{def}}{=} \delta\texttt{wait?}:S_0$

$\quad S_0 \stackrel{\text{def}}{=} \delta\texttt{signal!}:S_1$

The complete system is:

$\quad\quad SYS \stackrel{\text{def}}{=}$ (A×B×SEM)\\{wait,signal}

To show that the complete system exhibits mutual exclusion, we must prove that no more than one critical section action executes at the same time, and, after a head action, no other critical section action can occur before a related tail action.

Writing wait and signal as s and w

SYS $\stackrel{\text{def}}{=}$ (A×B×SEM)\\{w,s}

def $\quad$ = (δw!:CS_{AH}:CS_{AT}:δs!:A

$\quad\quad\quad$ × δw!:CS_{BH}:CS_{BT}:δs!:B × δw?:δs?:SEM)\\{w,s}

Using the result of our last example now encapsulated in proposition ↔9

↔9 $\quad$ = δ1:(CS_{AH}:CS_{AT}:δs!:A × δw!:CS_{BH}:CS_{BT}:δs!:B × δs?:SEM)\\{w,s}

$\quad\quad$ + δ1:(δw!:CS_{AH}:CS_{AT}:δs!:A × CS_{BH}:CS_{BT}:δs!:B × δs?:SEM)\\{w,s}

↔7a $\quad$ = δ1:CS_{AH}:CS_{AT}:(δs!:A × δw!:CS_{BH}:CS_{BT}:δs!:B × δs?:SEM)\\{w,s}

$\quad\quad$ + δ1:CS_{BH}:CS_{BT}:(δw!:CS_{AH}:CS_{AT}:δs!:A × δs!:B × δs?:SEM)\\{w,s}

$$\leftrightarrow 4a \quad = \delta 1 : CS_{AH} : CS_{AT} : \delta 1 : (A \times \delta w! : CS_{BH} : CS_{BT} : \delta s! : B \times SEM) \backslash\backslash \{w, s\}$$

$$+ \ \delta 1 : CS_{AH} : CS_{AT} : \delta 1 : (\delta w! : CS_{BH} : CS_{BT} : \delta s! : A \times B \times SEM) \backslash\backslash \{w, s\}$$

$$\mathtt{def} \quad = \delta 1 : CS_{AH} : CS_{AT} : \delta 1 : (A \times B \times SEM) \backslash\backslash \{w, s\}$$

$$+ \ \delta 1 : CS_{BH} : CS_{BT} : \delta 1 : (A \times B \times SEM) \backslash\backslash \{w, s\}$$

$$\mathtt{def} \quad = \delta 1 : CS_{AH} : CS_{AT} : \delta 1 : SYS \ + \ \delta 1 : CS_{BH} : CS_{BT} : \delta 1 : SYS$$

giving

$$SYS \ \overset{\mathtt{def}}{=} \ \delta 1 : CS_{AH} : CS_{AT} : \delta 1 : SYS \ + \ \delta 1 : CS_{BH} : CS_{BT} : \delta 1 : SYS$$

This meets the required specification – the semaphore has serialised access to the resource.

■

4.8.4 Examples

We now have tools to model synchronous systems, asynchronous systems, and mixtures of both. We will put these abilities to use and explore concepts introduced in earlier chapters, in particular proving whether certain scheduler algorithms are correct.

Non-pre-emptive Scheduler

Consider the simple case of a single processor, multi-process computer system composed of a scheduler S orchestrating the granting of access to a processor to two processes A and B; to be active, a process has to be in possession of the processor resource. If the process, rather than the scheduler, decides when deactivation occurs, it is termed non-pre-emptive scheduling. Without loss of generality, we simplify things by allowing process A to engage in two internal actions and process B to engage in one.

Requirements

The scheduler S interacts with processes A and B to activate and deactivate them.

S first starts A by communicating with it via port α. A runs to completion; its last act is to inform the scheduler, via port β, that it has completed.

S then starts B by communicating with it via port γ. B runs to completion; its last act is to communicate with the scheduler, via port χ.

S then starts A ... and so on.

Pictorial view

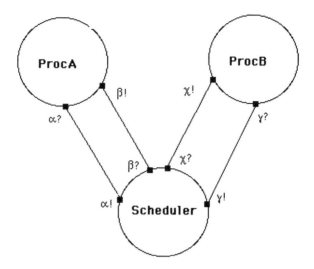

Specification

Viewed externally, the system is seen to engage in the actions of process A, followed by the actions of process B, repeated indefinitely. Hidden from the outside observer are the internal actions synchronising processes to the scheduler. Denoting A's two internal actions as a : a, and B's as b, the required system behaviour is:

$$SAB \stackrel{def}{=} (S \times A \times B) \backslash\backslash \{\alpha,\beta,\gamma,\chi\} = 1:a:a:1:1:b:1:SAB$$

where the internal 1 action indicates synchronisations activating and deactivating processes A and B.

Possible implementations

We move the problem to the SCCS domain, capturing the semantics of the problem.

Pictures and expressions

Process A

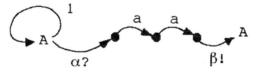

$$A \stackrel{def}{=} \delta\alpha?:a:a:\beta!:A$$

Process B

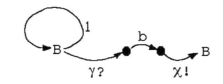

$$B \stackrel{\text{def}}{=} \delta\gamma?:b:\chi!:B$$

Scheduler S

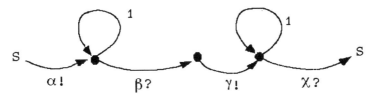

$$S \stackrel{\text{def}}{=} \alpha!:\delta S_1$$
$$S_1 \stackrel{\text{def}}{=} \beta?:\gamma!:\delta S_2$$
$$S_2 \stackrel{\text{def}}{=} \chi?:S$$

Composition

$$SAB \stackrel{\text{def}}{=} (S \times A \times B) \backslash\backslash \{\alpha,\beta,\gamma,\chi\}$$

We will ease the task by taking things in stages, composing two agents at a time, commencing with A composed with S up to recursion.

SA $\stackrel{\text{def}}{=}$	$(S \times A) \backslash\backslash \{\alpha,\beta\}$	
sub	$= ((\alpha!:\delta S_1) \times (\delta\alpha?:a:a:\beta!:A)) \backslash\backslash \{\alpha,\beta\}$	
$\leftrightarrow$3a	$= 1:(\delta S_1 \times (a:a:\beta!:A)) \backslash\backslash \{\alpha,\beta\}$	
sub	$= 1:((\delta\beta?:\gamma!:\delta S_2) \times (a:a:\beta!:A)) \backslash\backslash \{\alpha,\beta\}$	
$\leftrightarrow$6a	$= 1:a:a:((\delta\beta?:\gamma!:\delta S_2) \times (\beta!:A)) \backslash\backslash \{\alpha,\beta\}$	
$\leftrightarrow$2a	$= 1:a:a:1:((\gamma!:\delta S_2) \times A) \backslash\backslash \{\alpha,\beta\}$	
sub	$= 1:a:a:1:((\gamma!:\delta\chi?:S) \times (\delta\alpha?:a:a:\beta!:A)) \backslash\backslash \{\alpha,\beta\}$	
$\leftrightarrow$7a	$= 1:a:a:1:\gamma!:((\delta\chi?:S) \times (\delta\alpha?:a:a:\beta!:A)) \backslash\backslash \{\alpha,\beta\}$	
$\leftrightarrow$8c	$= 1:a:a:1:\gamma!:\delta\chi?:(S \times (\delta\alpha?:a:a:\beta!:A)) \backslash\backslash \{\alpha,\beta\}$	
def	$= 1:a:a:1:\gamma!:\delta\chi?:(S \times A) \backslash\backslash \{\alpha,\beta\}$	
dcf	SA $-$ $1:a \cdot a \cdot 1:\gamma!:\delta\chi?:SA$	

Now, add process B

SAB $\stackrel{\text{def}}{=}$	$(SA \times B) \backslash\backslash \{\gamma,\chi\}$	
sub	$= ((1:a:a:1:\gamma!:\delta\chi?:SA) \times (\delta\gamma?:b:\chi!:B)) \backslash\backslash \{\gamma,\chi\}$	
$\leftrightarrow$7a	$= 1:a:a:1:((\gamma!:\delta\chi?:SA) \times (\delta\gamma?:b:\chi!:B)) \backslash\backslash \{\gamma,\chi\}$	
$\leftrightarrow$3a	$= 1:a:a:1:1:((\delta\chi?:SA) \times (b:\chi!:B)) \backslash\backslash \{\gamma,\chi\}$	
$\leftrightarrow$6a	$= 1:a:a:1:1:b:((\delta\chi?:SA) \times (\chi!:B)) \backslash\backslash \{\gamma,\chi\}$	
$\leftrightarrow$2a	$= 1:a:a:1:1:b:1:(SA \times B) \backslash\backslash \{\gamma,\chi\}$	
def	SAB $= 1:a:a:1:1:b:1:SAB$	

The asynchronous agents have combined to form a synchronous system. Our required specification was

$$SAB = 1:a:a:1:1:b:1:SAB$$

The implementation has met our specification.

The definitions of the implementations A, B and S are correct, and they can be implemented or further refined.

Instead of evaluating the complete system in one go as:

$$SAB \stackrel{def}{=} (\!(S \times A \times B)\!) \backslash\backslash \{\alpha,\beta,\gamma,\chi\}$$

we opted for the route of composing two agents at a time:

$$(\!((\!(S \times A)\!) \backslash\backslash \{\alpha,\beta\} \times B)\!) \backslash\backslash \{\gamma,\chi\}$$

as this seemed the natural thing to do to keep our task simple. But is it a valid route?

$$(\!(S \times A \times B)\!) \backslash\backslash \{\alpha,\beta,\gamma,\chi\}$$
$$\backslash\backslash 1 \qquad\qquad \stackrel{def}{=} (\!(S \times A \times B)\!) \backslash\backslash \{\alpha,\beta\} \backslash\backslash \{\gamma,\chi\}$$

Now S and A interact through $\{\alpha,\beta\}$ but B does not, so by:

$$\backslash\backslash 5 \qquad\qquad = (\!((\!(S \times A)\!) \backslash\backslash \{\alpha,\beta\} \times B\backslash\backslash\{\alpha,\beta\})\!) \backslash\backslash \{\gamma,\chi\}$$

But B contains no actions $\{\alpha,\beta\}$, $Sort\,(B) \cup \{\alpha,\beta\} = \varnothing$

$$\backslash\backslash 2 \qquad\qquad = (\!((\!(S \times A)\!) \backslash\backslash \{\alpha,\beta\} \times B)\!) \backslash\backslash \{\gamma,\chi\}$$

which is as far as we can go, as agents $(S \times A)$ and B interact through $\{\gamma,\chi\}$.

The design strategy was to model the component parts of the proposed system as individual SCCS agents, the SCCS definitions forming the formal design; then, using the propositions of the algebra, to establish the emergent behaviour of the total system; finally comparing the emergent behaviour with that desired. If we're successful we can proceed to translate the design to an implementation; if not, for example if it deadlocks, livelocks, isn't safe, or just does not do what is required, SCCS should help us identify the errors so we can modify things and resubmit the new design to the SCCS test.

All this hinges on having the requirements and the design defined in comparable SCCS forms; this is all rather primitive compared with the CSP method of checking the behaviour of components in terms of traces and, from that, predicting if the design will satisfy a specification or not. We will have to leave the development of comparable methods in SCCS until a later chapter. However, in the meantime, using the imperfect tools we have at our disposal, we can still carry out some validations. Let us move on to the next example.

Time Sliced Round Robin Scheduler

Consider again the case of a single processor, multi-process computer system with a scheduler S orchestrating the activation of processes A and B, but this time the scheduler decides when processes are to be deactivated. Processes run pre-emptively, the scheduler giving the processor to a process for a set period of time, a time slice. Without losing generality, we allow process A to engage in three internal actions and process B four.

Requirements

The scheduler S communicates with processes A and B to activate and deactivate them.

S first starts A by communicating with it via port α, idles for two time periods, then deactivates A via its β port.

S then starts B by communicating with it via port γ, idles for two time periods, then deactivates B via its χ port.

The scheduler then starts A ... and so on.

Process A, initially idle, waits for a start synchronisation from the scheduler via α. When A starts processing it remains ready to receive a stop signal from the scheduler over β.

Process B, initially idle, waits for a start synchronisation from the scheduler via γ. When B starts processing it remains ready to receive a stop signal from the scheduler over χ.

Pictorial view

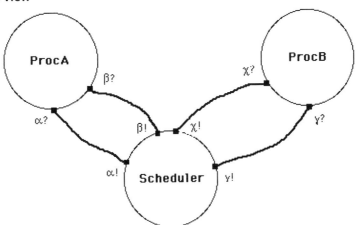

Specification

Viewed externally the system will be seen to engage in actions of process A, followed by actions of process B, and repeated indefinitely. Interaction between scheduler and processes is hidden from the observer. Denoting A's three internal actions as a_x for $x=1,2,3$ and B's four internal action as b_x for $x=1,2,3,4$, the required system behaviour is

$$SAB \overset{def}{=} (S \times A \times B) \setminus\!\setminus\{\alpha,\beta,\gamma,\chi\}$$
$$= 1\!:\!a_1\!:\!a_2\!:\!1\!:\!1\!:\!b_1\!:\!b_2\!:\!1\!:\!1\!:\!a_3\!:\!1\!:\!1\!:\!1\!:\!b_3\!:\!b_4\!:\!SAB$$

In the case of $a_3:1$ the 1 indicates an idle action of process A when, having been granted two time slots, it only needs one to complete. Other instances of 1 indicate the synchronisations activating and deactivating A and B.

Possible implementation

To keep the design general, the agents should not be over-specified, and the process agents should not be defined with foreknowledge of possible environments but specified to interact correctly with any environment granting arbitrarily long time slots. The only certainties are that an agent's actions occur in their predetermined sequences. A general model of processes A and B allows them to be deactivated at any time, including immediately, after activation.

Process A, has three a actions:

$$A \overset{def}{=} \delta A_1$$
$$A_1 \overset{def}{=} \alpha?\!:\!(a_1\!:\!(a_2\!:\!(a_3\!:\!\delta A_4 + \beta?\!:\!\delta A_3) + \beta?\!:\!\delta A_2) + \beta?\!:\!A)$$
$$A_2 \overset{def}{=} \alpha?\!:\!(a_2\!:\!(a_3\!:\!\delta A_4 + \beta?\!:\!\delta A_3) + \beta?\!:\!\delta A_2)$$
$$A_3 \overset{def}{=} \alpha?\!:\!(a_3\!:\!\delta A_4 + \beta?\!:\!\delta A_3)$$
$$A_4 \overset{def}{=} \beta?\!:\!A$$

Process B, has four b actions:

$$B \overset{def}{=} \delta B_1$$
$$B_1 \overset{def}{=} \gamma?\!:\!(b_1\!:\!(b_2\!:\!(b_3\!:\!(b_4\!:\!\delta B_5 + \chi?\!:\!\delta B_4) + \chi?\!:\!\delta B_3) + \chi?\!:\!\delta B_2) + \chi?\!:\!B)$$
$$B_2 \overset{def}{=} \gamma?\!:\!(b_2\!:\!(b_3\!:\!(b_4\!:\!\delta B_5 + \chi?\!:\!\delta B_4) + \chi?\!:\!\delta B_3) + \chi?\!:\!\delta B_2)$$
$$B_3 \overset{def}{=} \gamma?\!:\!(b_3\!:\!(b_4\!:\!\delta B_5 + \chi?\!:\!\delta B_4) + \chi?\!:\!\delta B_3)$$
$$B_4 \overset{def}{=} \gamma?\!:\!(b_4\!:\!\delta B_5 + \chi?\!:\!\delta B_4)$$
$$B_5 \overset{def}{=} \chi?\!:\!B$$

The scheduler, S, initiates all communications, idling for two time slots after process activation

$$S = \alpha!\!:\!1\!:\!1\!:\!\beta!\!:\!\gamma!\!:\!1\!:\!1\!:\!\chi!\!:\!S$$

Composition

Composition is as in the previous example. We will evaluate the complete system two agents at a time.

$$(\!(S \times A \times B)\!) \setminus\!\setminus\{\alpha,\beta,\gamma,\chi\}$$
$$\setminus\!\setminus 1 \qquad = (\!(S \times A \times B)\!) \setminus\!\setminus\{\alpha,\beta\} \setminus\!\setminus\{\gamma,\chi\}$$

Only S and A interact through $\{\alpha,\beta\}$ so

$$\backslash\backslash 5 \qquad = (\!(\,(\!(S \times A)\,) \backslash\backslash\{\alpha,\beta\} \times B\backslash\backslash\{\alpha,\beta\}\,)\!) \backslash\backslash\{\gamma,\chi\}$$

But $\text{Sort}(B) \cup \{\alpha,\beta\} = \varnothing$

$$\backslash\backslash 2 \qquad = (\!(\,(\!(S \times A)\,) \backslash\backslash\{\alpha,\beta\} \times B\,)\!) \backslash\backslash\{\gamma,\chi\}$$

Commencing with A composed with S up to recursion.

$$\text{SA} \overset{\text{def}}{=} (S \times A) \backslash\backslash\{\alpha,\beta\}$$

sub $= (\,(\alpha!:1:1:\beta!:\gamma!:1:1:\chi!:S)$
$\qquad\qquad \times \delta\alpha?:(a_1:(a_2:(a_3:\delta A_4 + \beta?:\delta A_3) + \beta?:\delta A_2) + \beta?:A)$
$\qquad\qquad)\backslash\backslash\{\alpha,\beta\})$

$\leftrightarrow$3a $= 1:(\,(1:1:\beta!:\gamma!:1:1:\chi!:S)$
$\qquad\qquad \times (a_1:(a_2:(a_3:\delta A_4 + \beta?:\delta A_3) + \beta?:\delta A_2))\backslash\backslash\{\alpha,\beta\}$

$\leftrightarrow$5a $= 1:a_1:(\,(1:\beta!:\gamma!:1:1:\chi!:S)$
$\qquad\qquad \times a_2:(a_3:\delta A_4 + \beta?:\delta A_3))\backslash\backslash\{\alpha,\beta\}$

$\leftrightarrow$5a $= 1:a_1:a_2:(\,(\beta!:\gamma!:1:1:\chi!:S)$
$\qquad\qquad \times (a_3:\delta A_4 + \beta?:\delta A_3))\backslash\backslash\{\alpha,\beta\}$

$\leftrightarrow$1a $= 1:a_1:a_2:1:(\,(\gamma!:1:1:\chi!:S) \times \delta A_3)\backslash\backslash\{\alpha,\beta\}$

sub $= 1:a_1:a_2:1:(\,(\gamma!:1:1:\chi!:S)$
$\qquad\qquad \times \delta\alpha?:(a_3:\delta A_4 + \beta?:\delta A_3))\backslash\backslash\{\alpha,\beta\}$

$\leftrightarrow$7a $= 1:a_1:a_2:1:\gamma!:1:1:\chi!:(S \times \delta\alpha?:(a_3:\delta A_4 + \beta?:\delta A_3))\backslash\backslash\{\alpha,\beta\}$

sub $= 1:a_1:a_2:1:\gamma!:1:1:\chi!:(\,(\alpha!:1:1:\beta!:\gamma!:1:1:\chi!:S)$
$\qquad\qquad \times \delta\alpha?:(a_3:\delta A_4 + \beta?:\delta A_3))\backslash\backslash\{\alpha,\beta\}$

$\leftrightarrow$3a $= 1:a_1:a_2:1:\gamma!:1:1:\chi!:1:(\,(1:1:\beta!:\gamma!:1:1:\chi!:S)$
$\qquad\qquad \times (a_3:\delta A_4 + \beta?:\delta A_3))\backslash\backslash\{\alpha,\beta\}$

$\leftrightarrow$5a,sub $= 1:a_1:a_2:1:\gamma!:1:1:\chi!:1:a_3:(\,(1:\beta!:\gamma!:1:1:\chi!:S)$
$\qquad\qquad \times (\delta\beta?:A))\backslash\backslash\{\alpha,\beta\}$

$\leftrightarrow$7a $= 1:a_1:a_2:1:\gamma!:1:1:\chi!:1:a_3:1:(\,(\beta!:\gamma!:1:1:\chi!:S)$
$\qquad\qquad \times (\delta\beta?:A))\backslash\backslash\{\alpha,\beta\}$

$\leftrightarrow$3a $= 1:a_1:a_2:1:\gamma!:1:1:\chi!:1:a_3:1:1:(\,(\gamma!:1:1:\chi!:S) \times A)\backslash\backslash\{\alpha,\beta\}$

sub $= 1:a_1:a_2:1:\gamma!:1:1:\chi!:1:a_3:1:1:(\,(\gamma!:1:1:\chi!:S)$
$\qquad\qquad \times (\delta\alpha?:a_1:(a_2:(a_3:\delta A_4 + \beta?:\delta A_3) + \beta?:\delta A_2)))\backslash\backslash\{\alpha,\beta\}$

$\leftrightarrow$7a,sub $= 1:a_1:a_2:1:\gamma!:1:1:\chi!:1:a_3:1:1:\gamma!:1:1:\chi!:(S \times A)\backslash\backslash\{\alpha,\beta\}$

def SA $= 1:a_1:a_2:1:\gamma!:1:1:\chi!:1:a_3:1:1:\gamma!:1:1:\chi!:\text{SA}$

Now add process B

$$\text{SAB} = (\text{SA} \times B)\backslash\backslash\{\gamma,\chi\}$$

sub $= (\,(1:a_1:a_2:1:\gamma!:1:1:\chi!:1:a_3:1:1:\gamma!:1:1:\chi!:\text{SA})$
$\qquad\qquad \times \delta\gamma?:(b_1:(b_2:(b_3:(b_4:\delta B_5 + \chi?:\delta B_4)+\chi?:\delta B_3)+\chi?:\delta B_2)+\chi?:B$
$\qquad\qquad)\backslash\backslash\{\gamma,\chi\}$

$\leftrightarrow$7a $= 1:a_1:a_2:1:(\,(\gamma!:1:1:\chi!:1:a_3:1:1:\gamma!:1:1:\chi!:\text{SA})$
$\qquad\qquad \times \delta\gamma?:(b_1:(b_2:(b_3:(b4:\delta B_5 + \chi?:\delta B_4)+\chi?:\delta B_3)+\chi?:\delta B_2)+\chi?:B$
$\qquad\qquad)\backslash\backslash\{\gamma,\chi\}$

$\leftrightarrow$3a $= 1:a_1:a_2:1:1:(\,(1:1:\chi!:1:a_3:1:1:\gamma!:1:1:\chi!:\text{SA})$

$$\times \ (b_1 : (b_2 : (b_3 : (b_4 : \delta B_5 \ + \ \chi? : \delta B_4) \ + \ \chi? : \delta B_3) \ + \ \chi? : \delta B_2) \ + \ \chi? : B)$$
$$) \backslash\backslash \{\gamma, \chi\}$$

$\leftrightarrow 5a$
$$= \ 1 : a_1 : a_2 : 1 : 1 : b_1 : b_2 : (\ (\chi! : 1 : a_3 : 1 : 1 : \gamma! : 1 : 1 : \chi! : SA)$$
$$\times \ (b_3 : (b_4 : \delta B_5 \ + \ \chi? : \delta B_4) \ + \ \chi? : \delta B_3)$$
$$) \backslash\backslash \{\gamma, \chi\}$$

$\leftrightarrow 1a$
$$= \ 1 : a_1 : a_2 : 1 : 1 : b_1 : b_2 : 1 : (\ (1 : a_3 : 1 : 1 : \gamma! : 1 : 1 : \chi! : SA) \ \times \ (\delta B_3) \ ) \backslash\backslash \{\gamma, \chi\}$$

sub
$$= \ 1 : a_1 : a_2 : 1 : 1 : b_1 : b_2 : 1 : (\ (1 : a_3 : 1 : 1 : \gamma! : 1 : 1 : \chi! : SA)$$
$$\times \ (\delta \gamma? : (b_3 : (b_4 : \delta B_5 \ + \ \chi? : \delta B_4) \ + \ \chi? : \delta B_3))$$
$$) \backslash\backslash \{\gamma, \chi\}$$

$\leftrightarrow 7a$
$$= \ 1 : a_1 : a_2 : 1 : 1 : b_1 : b_2 : 1 : 1 : a_3 : 1 : 1 : (\ (\gamma! : 1 : 1 : \chi! : SA)$$
$$\times \ (\delta \gamma? : (b_3 : (b_4 : \delta B_5 \ + \ \chi? : \delta B_4) \ + \ \chi? : \delta B_3))$$
$$) \backslash\backslash \{\gamma, \chi\}$$

$\leftrightarrow 3a$
$$= \ 1 : a_1 : a_2 : 1 : 1 : b_1 : b_2 : 1 : 1 : a_3 : 1 : 1 : 1 : (\ (1 : 1 : \chi! : SA)$$
$$\times \ (b_3 : (b_4 : \delta B_5 \ + \ \chi? : \delta B_4) \ + \ \chi? : \delta B_3) \ ) \backslash\backslash \{\gamma, \chi\}$$

$\leftrightarrow 5a$
$$= \ 1 : a_1 : a_2 : 1 : 1 : b_1 : b_2 : 1 : 1 : a_3 : 1 : 1 : 1 : b_3 : b_4 : (\ (\chi! : SA) \times (\delta B_5) \ ) \ \backslash\backslash \{\gamma, \chi\}$$

sub
$$= \ 1 : a_1 : a_2 : 1 : 1 : b_1 : b_2 : 1 : 1 : a_3 : 1 : 1 : 1 : b_3 : b_4 : (\ (\chi! : SA)$$
$$\times \ (\delta \chi? : B) \ ) \backslash\backslash \{\gamma, \chi\}$$

$\leftrightarrow 3a$
$$= \ 1 : a_1 : a_2 : 1 : 1 : b_1 : b_2 : 1 : 1 : a_3 : 1 : 1 : 1 : b_3 : b_4 : 1 : (SA \times B) \ ) \backslash\backslash \{\gamma, \chi\}$$

def SAB
$$= \ 1 : a_1 : a_2 : 1 : 1 : b_1 : b_2 : 1 : 1 : a_3 : 1 : 1 : 1 : b_3 : b_4 : 1 : SAB$$

Our required specification was
$$SAB = 1 : a_1 : a_2 : 1 : 1 : b_1 : b_2 : 1 : 1 : a_3 : 1 : 1 : 1 : b_3 : b_4 : SAB$$

The expressions for the specification and the implementation differ by a 1 action just prior to the SAB state. The implementation has not met the specification; does this imply that the implementation is wrong? Possibly, but remember we say that an implementation has met (satisfied) a specification if there is a transformation route from the specification to the implementation, or vice versa. All we can imply from the failure of an implementation to meet a specification is that the specification and implementation differ – no distinction of which of them is 'right' can be made, and the possibilities exist that the specification is correct but the implementation is wrong or the implementation is correct and the specification is wrong.

We decide which, if any, is correct by mapping the semantics of the expressions back into the problem domain.

In this instance it is the specification that is at fault. For, after B's b_4 action, it must be deactivated. This is described by the implementation but not the specification. The correct specification of the system is:
$$SAB = 1 : a_1 : a_2 : 1 : 1 : b_1 : b_2 : 1 : 1 : a_3 : 1 : 1 : 1 : b_3 : b_4 : 1 : SAB$$
and our implementation satisfies this (modified) specification.

We could, of course, have made the distinction between synchronisation and internal action stronger by denoting specific synchronisations as in:

$$\text{SAB} = \alpha_{sync} : a_1 : a_2 : \beta_{sync} : \gamma_{sync} : b_1 : b_2 : \chi_{sync} : \alpha_{sync} : a_3 : a\_idle : \beta_{sync}$$
$$: \gamma_{sync} : b_3 : b_4 : \chi_{sync} : \text{SAB}$$

4.8.5 Message Passing and Waiting

4.8.5.1 Introduction

Earlier we took the basic synchronisation model and from it derived a set of propositions for asynchronous like behaviours. In this section we extend synchronous data passing to their asynchronous equivalent. For simplicity we consider the most commonly used cases, but even this results in a rather involved section, which, though informative and useful, is still involved.

We only need to consider two cases of data passing: when one agent waits; and when both wait.

4.8.5.2 Parameter Passing

One Agent Waits to Pass Data

The general case of data passing between two agents where data can be sent and received simultaneously is $\alpha(!x.?w):P \times \alpha^{-1}(!y.?v):Q$ and, as sender and receiver are interchangeable, we only need to explore the case of one agent waiting, using symmetry to define the alternative case. Our aim is therefore to explore $(\delta\alpha(!x.?w):P \times \beta(!y.?v):Q)\backslash\backslash A$

δ1a	=	$((\alpha(!x.?w):P + 1:\delta\alpha(!x.?w):P) \times (\beta(!y.?v):Q))\backslash\backslash A$
+6	=	$((\alpha(!x.?w):P \times \beta(!y.?v):Q)$
		$+ (1:\delta\alpha(!x.?w):P \times \beta(!y.?v):Q))\backslash\backslash A$
\\4	=	$(\alpha(!x.?w):P \times \beta(!y.?v):Q)\backslash\backslash A$
		$+ (1:\delta\alpha(!x.?w):P \times \beta(!y.?v):Q)\backslash\backslash A$

This has resonances with the derivation of delayed synchronisation – not too surprising, as parameter passing is only a repackaging of synchronisation. Following the lead of the previous section, we will consider only the most useful cases for elevation to propositions; the reader will have to make recourse to the basic propositions for other cases.

First we consider $\alpha=\beta^{-1}$, where the guards form complete communication pairs, $\text{Part}(\alpha)\cap\text{Part}^{-1}(\alpha)\neq\emptyset$, whose subsequent behaviour depends upon whether the pruning includes particles from α or not.

Where all the particles are pruned, $\text{Part}(\alpha)\subseteq A$

$$(\delta\alpha(!x?w):P \times \alpha^{-1}(!y?v):Q)\backslash\backslash A$$
$$= (\alpha(!x?w):P \times \alpha^{-1}(!y?v):Q)\backslash\backslash A$$
$$+ (1:\delta\alpha(!x?w):P \times \alpha^{-1}(!y?v):Q)\backslash\backslash A$$

$\leftrightarrow$10a, $\leftrightarrow$5b $= 1:(P[w:=y] \times Q[v:=x])\backslash\backslash A + 0$

+3 $= 1:(P[w:=y] \times Q[v:=x])\backslash\backslash A$

the behaviour is context independent, the two agents always successfully synchronise and pass their data

When they aren't, $\text{Part}(\alpha) \cap A = \varnothing$

$$(\delta\alpha(!x?w):P \times \alpha^{-1}(!y?v):Q)\backslash\backslash A$$
$$= (\alpha(!x?w):P \times \alpha^{-1}(!y?v):Q)\backslash\backslash A$$
$$+ (1:\delta\alpha(!x?w):P \times \alpha^{-1}(!y?v):Q)\backslash\backslash A$$

$\leftrightarrow$10b, $\leftrightarrow$5a $= \alpha(!x.?w)\alpha^{-1}(!y.?v):(P \times Q)\backslash\backslash A$
$$+ \alpha^{-1}(!y?v):(\delta\alpha(!x?w):P \times Q)\backslash\backslash A$$

the behaviour is context-dependent, the choice between internal and external synchronisation depends upon the environment in which the agent subsequently finds itself, and, not knowing what that environment is, we leave all options open.

Second, where $\alpha\beta$ contains no synchronisation pairs, $\text{Part}(\alpha\beta) \cap \text{Part}^{-1}(\alpha\beta) = \varnothing$.

Where some α particles are pruned, $\text{Part}(\alpha) \cap A \neq \varnothing$

$$(\delta\alpha(!x?w):P \times \beta(!y?v):Q)\backslash\backslash A$$
$$= (\alpha(!x?w):P \times \beta(!y?v):Q)\backslash\backslash A$$
$$+ (1:\delta\alpha(!x?w):P \times \beta(!y?v):Q)\backslash\backslash A$$

$\leftrightarrow$14b, $\leftrightarrow$5a $= 0 + \beta(!y?v):(\delta\alpha(!x?w):P \times Q)\backslash\backslash A$

+3 $= \beta(!y?v):(\delta\alpha(!x?w):P \times Q)\backslash\backslash A$

Where some β particles are pruned, $\text{Part}(\beta) \cap A \neq \varnothing$

$$(\delta\alpha(!x?w):P \times \beta(!y?v):Q)\backslash\backslash A$$
$$= (\alpha(!x?w):P \times \beta(!y?v):Q)\backslash\backslash A$$
$$+ (1:\delta\alpha(!x?w):P \times \beta(!y?v):Q)\backslash\backslash A$$

$\leftrightarrow$14b, $\leftrightarrow$5b $= 0 + 0$

+3 $= 0$

Where no particles are pruned, $\text{Part}(\alpha\beta) \cap A = \varnothing$

$$(\delta\alpha(!x?w):P \times \beta(!y?v):Q)\backslash\backslash A$$
$$= (\alpha(!x?w):P \times \beta(!y?v):Q)\backslash\backslash A$$
$$+ (1:\delta\alpha(!x?w):P \times \beta(!y?v):Q)\backslash\backslash A$$

$\leftrightarrow$14a, $\leftrightarrow$5a $= \alpha(!x.?w)\beta(!y.?v):(P\times Q)\backslash\backslash A$
$$+ \beta(!y?v):(\delta\alpha(!x?w):P \times Q)\backslash\backslash A$$

By corollary we can define a set of propositions where only the second agent is delayed, combining both into a complete set of propositions.

propositions *Data passing with one agent delayed*

Where $\alpha\alpha^{-1}$ contains only complete synchronisation pairs and the variables, (x,v) and (y,w), if they are there, are of comparable data types: $x, v \in \mathcal{D}_1$ and $y, w \in \mathcal{D}_2$

$\leftrightarrow$11 $(\delta\alpha(!x?w):P \times \alpha^{-1}(!y?v):Q)\backslash\backslash A =$

    a) 1: $(P[w:=y] \times Q[v:=x])\backslash\backslash A$, if Part$(\alpha)\subseteq A$

    b) $\alpha(!x?w)\alpha^{-1}(!y?v):(P \times Q)\backslash\backslash A$

         $+ \alpha^{-1}(!y?v):(\delta\alpha(!x?w):P \times Q)\backslash\backslash A$, if Part$(\alpha)\cap A=\varnothing$

$\leftrightarrow$12 $(\alpha(!x?w):P \times \delta\alpha^{-1}(!y?v):Q)\backslash\backslash A =$

    a) 1: $(P[w:=y] \times Q[v:=x])\backslash\backslash A$, if Part$(\alpha)\subseteq A$

    b) $\alpha(!x?w)\alpha^{-1}(!y?v):(P \times Q)\backslash\backslash A$

         $+ \alpha(!x?w):(P \times \delta\alpha^{-1}(!y?v):Q)\backslash\backslash A$, if Part$(\alpha)\cap A=\varnothing$

Where $\alpha\beta$ contains no communication pairs, Part$(\alpha\beta) \cap$ Part$^{-1}(\alpha\beta) =\varnothing$

$\leftrightarrow$15 $(\delta\alpha(!x?w):P \times \beta(!y?v):Q)\backslash\backslash A =$

    a) $\beta(!y?v):(\delta\alpha(!x?w):P \times Q)\backslash\backslash A$, if Part$(\alpha)\cap A\neq\varnothing$

    b) 0, if Part$(\beta)\cap A\neq\varnothing$

    c) $\alpha(!x.?w)\beta(!y.?v)):(P \times Q)\backslash\backslash A$

         $+ \beta(!y?v):(\delta\alpha(!x?w):P \times Q)\backslash\backslash A$, if Part$(\alpha\beta)\cap A=\varnothing$

$\leftrightarrow$16 $(\alpha(!x?w):P \times \delta\beta(!y?v):Q)\backslash\backslash A =$

    a) $\alpha(!x?w):(P \times \delta\beta(!y?v):Q)\backslash\backslash A$, if Part$(\beta)\cap A\neq\varnothing$

    b) 0, if Part$(\alpha)\cap A\neq\varnothing$

    c) $\alpha(!x.?w)\beta(!y.?v):(P \times Q)\backslash\backslash A$

         $+ \alpha(!x?w):(P \times \delta\beta(!y?v):Q)\backslash\backslash A$, if Part$(\alpha\beta)\cap A=\varnothing$

Prop $\leftrightarrow$11a,$\leftrightarrow$12a all particles form communication pairs which are also part of the pruning set. All particles are forced to synchronise, data is passed successfully and privately. The resulting internal tick escapes pruning.

Prop $\leftrightarrow$11b,$\leftrightarrow$12b all particles form commnication pairs, none of which are in the pruning set. A choice exists: either all communication pairs escape to communicate with each other, or with any environment; or the delayed agent contributes a tick and only the non-delayed action escapes.

Prop $\leftrightarrow$15a,$\leftrightarrow$16a there are no communication pairs, and no data passing. The incomplete particles in the delayed agent can only escape pruning by contributing a tick and waiting for later communications; particles in the non-delayed action cannot wait and, not being pruned, escape, ready to interact with an environment.

Prop $\leftrightarrow$15b,$\leftrightarrow$16b there are no communication pairs, and no data passing. The incomplete particles in the non-delayed agent cannot wait, are pruned, and inaction results.

Prop $\leftrightarrow$15c,$\leftrightarrow$16c there are no communication pairs, and no data passing, nothing is pruned. Either the actions escape together or the delayed agent contributes a tick and waits for later synchronisations. Escaped actions remain ready to communicate with an environment.

■

And we move seamlessly on to…

Both Agents Wait to Pass Data

propositions

Where $\alpha\alpha^{-1}$ contains only complete synchronisation pairs and the variables, (x, v) and (y, w), if they are there, are of comparable data types: $x, v \in \mathcal{D}_1$ and $y, w \in \mathcal{D}_2$

$\leftrightarrow$13 $(\delta\alpha(!x?w):P \times \delta\alpha^{-1}(!y?v):Q)\backslash\backslash A =$

   a) $\delta1:(P[w:=y] \times Q[v:=x])\backslash\backslash A$, if Part$(\alpha)\subseteq A$

   b) $\delta(\alpha(!x?w)\alpha^{-1}(!y?v):(P \times Q)\backslash\backslash A$

      $+ \alpha^{-1}(!y?v):(\delta\alpha(!x?w):P \times Q)\backslash\backslash A$

      $+ \alpha(!x?w):(P \times \delta\alpha^{-1}(!y?v):Q)\backslash\backslash A)$, if Part$(\alpha)\cap A=\varnothing$

Where $\alpha\beta$ contains no synchronisation pairs, Part$(\alpha\beta)\cap$ Part$^{-1}(\alpha\beta)=\varnothing$

$\leftrightarrow$17 $(\delta\alpha(!x?w):P \times \delta\beta(!y?v):Q)\backslash\backslash A =$

   a) $\delta\mathbf{0}$, if Part$(\beta)\cap A\neq\varnothing$ and Part$(\alpha)\cap A\neq\varnothing$

   b) $\delta\beta(!y?v):(\delta\alpha(!x?w):P \times Q)\backslash\backslash A$, if Part$(\alpha)\cap A\neq\varnothing$

   c) $\delta\alpha(!x?w):(P \times \delta\beta(!y?v):Q)\backslash\backslash A$, if Part$(\beta)\cap A\neq\varnothing$

   d) $\delta(\alpha(!x.?w)\beta(!y.?v):(P \times Q)\backslash\backslash A$

      $+ \beta(!y?v):(\delta\alpha(!x?w):P \times Q)\backslash\backslash A$

      $+ \alpha(!x?w):(P \times \delta\beta(!y?v):Q)\backslash\backslash A)$, if Part$(\alpha\beta)\cap A=\varnothing$

Prop $\leftrightarrow$13a) all particles form communication pairs which are also in the pruning set. Only complete internal communication is possible, either immediately or at some time in the future, as denoted by the $\delta1$.

Prop $\leftrightarrow$13b all particles form communication pairs, none of which are in the pruning set, and no communication is pruned. There is a non-deterministic choice: all communications escape together, or the delayed agent contributes a tick. Escaped communications remain, ready to synchronise with an environment.

Prop $\leftrightarrow$17a there are no communication pairs, some of the particles in the agent guards appear in the pruning set. No actions, except tick, can escape, and inaction results after the simultaneous ticks run out.

Prop $\leftrightarrow$17b,$\leftrightarrow$17c there are no communication pairs, the incomplete particles in the scoped over agent can only put off pruning by

contributing a tick and waiting for later communications. Incomplete
particles that are not scoped over can either wait, contributing a tick
to the proceedings, or escape ready to communicate with an
environment.

Prop ↔17d there are no communication pairs, and no particles in the
pruning set. Either all communications escape together, or each
delayed agent contributes a tick and waits for later communications.
Escaped communications remain, ready to synchronise with an
environment.

■

Next, some examples.

4.8.5.3 Examples

example 1

Agent DOUBLE waits for integers to be input over channel in and outputs
double their value over channel out.

DOUBLE(x,y) = δin?x:(y:=2x):out!y:DOUBLE(x,y)

For clarity, the internal action is denoted by (y:=2x) instead of the
normal 1.

Adding an asynchronous generator of integers,

INTGEN ^{def} δin!int:INTGEN

we get an agent that generates even integers over port out.

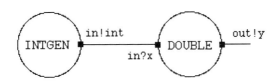

SYS ^{def} (INTGEN × DOUBLE(x,y))\\in

def   = ((δin!int:INTGEN) × (δin?x:(y:=2x):out!y:DOUBLE(x,y)))\\in

↔13a   = δ1:(INTGEN × ((y:=2int):out!2int:DOUBLE(x,y)))\\in

After double application of ↔15a followed by application of the pruning
operator all actions of INTGEN, except its idle actions, are pruned, giving

= δ1:(y:=2int):out!2int:(INTGEN × (DOUBLE(x,y)))\\in

SYS = δ1:(y:=2int):out!2int:SYS

■

example 2

Given two buffers, `ONESLOT1` and `ONESLOT2`, defined as

$$\texttt{ONESLOT1} \overset{\text{def}}{=} \delta\texttt{bufin?x:}\delta\texttt{mid!x:ONESLOT1}$$
$$\texttt{ONESLOT2} \overset{\text{def}}{=} \delta\texttt{mid?x:}\delta\texttt{bufout!x:ONESLOT2}$$

how does their combination,

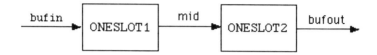

$$\texttt{TWOSLOT} \overset{\text{def}}{=} \texttt{(ONESLOT1} \times \texttt{ONESLOT2)}\backslash\backslash\texttt{mid}$$

with their common communication internalised, behave?

Rewriting the component parts in normal form[†]

$$\texttt{ONESLOT1} \overset{\text{def}}{=} \delta\texttt{bufin?x:FULLSLOT2(x)}$$
$$\texttt{FULLSLOT1(x)} \overset{\text{def}}{=} \delta\texttt{mid!x:ONESLOT1}$$
$$\texttt{ONESLOT2} \overset{\text{def}}{=} \delta\texttt{mid?x:FULLSLOT2(x)}$$
$$\texttt{FULLSLOT2(x)} \overset{\text{def}}{=} \delta\texttt{bufout!x:ONESLOT2}$$

`TWOSLOT` $\overset{\text{def}}{=}$	`(ONESLOT1 × ONESLOT2)\\mid`
def	`= (δbufin?x:FULLSLOT1(x) × δmid?x:FULLSLOT1(x))\\mid`
↔17c	`= δbufin?x:(FULLSLOT1(x) × δmid?x:FULLSLOT1(x))\\mid`
def	`= δbufin?x:(δmid!x:ONESLOT1 × δmid?x:FULLSLOT1(x))\\mid`
↔13a	`= δbufin?x:δ1:(ONESLOT1 × FULLSLOT1(x))\\mid`
def	`= δbufin?x:δ1:`
	`(δbufin?x:FULLSLOT1(x) × δbufout!x:ONESLOT2)\\mid`
↔17d	`= δbufin?x:δ1:`
	`δ(bufout!x:(δbufin?x:FULLSLOT1(x) × ONESLOT2)\\mid`
	`+ bufin?x:(FULLSLOT1(x) × δbufout!x:ONESLOT2)\\mid`
	`+ bufin?x.bufout!x:(FULLSLOT1(x) × ONESLOT2)\\mid)`

which is

def	`= δbufin?x:δ1:`
	`δ(bufout!x:(ONESLOT1 × ONESLOT2)\\mid`
	`+ bufin?x:(FULLSLOT1(x) × FULLSLOT2(x))\\mid`
	`+ bufin?x.bufout!x:(FULLSLOT1(x) × ONESLOT2)\\mid)`

`TWOSLOT` waits to accept and deliver data, after it inputs a value it's ready to output that last input, input a new one, or both.

■

[†]   Normal form redrafts a behaviour into single guards prefixing states; for example: P=α:Q and Q=β:R in place of P=α:β:R.

example 3

Let us look again at the asynchronous circuit:

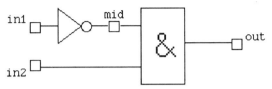

In the synchronous domain we can model each constituent gate using parameter passing. From the general form of the NOT gate which waits for input and delivers its output within the same time slot of

$$\text{NOT} \stackrel{\text{def}}{=} \delta notin_0?.notout_1!:\text{NOT}$$
$$+ \delta notin_1?.notout_0!:\text{NOT}$$

we get the parameter passing form

$$\text{NOT} \stackrel{\text{def}}{=} \delta notin?x.notout!\neg x:\text{NOT}, \text{ for } x \in \{0,1\}$$

from which with appropriate morphisms we obtain the necessary NOT gate

$$\text{NOT} = \delta in1?x.mid!\neg x:\text{NOT}, \text{ for } x \in \{0,1\}$$

An AND gate, waiting for input, delivering output in the same time slot is

$$\text{AND} \stackrel{\text{def}}{=} \delta and1i_0?.and2i_0?.andout_0!:\text{AND}$$
$$+ \delta and1i_0?.and2i_1?.andout_0!:\text{AND}$$
$$+ \delta and1i_1?.and2i_0?.andout_0!:\text{AND}$$
$$+ \delta and1i_1?.and2i_1?.andout_1!:\text{AND}$$

from which we get, for $y, z \in \{0,1\}$

$$\text{AND} \stackrel{\text{def}}{=} \delta and1i?z.and2i?y.andout!(z \wedge y):\text{AND}$$

which, with appropriate morphisms, leads us to the AND gate used in the circuit, for $y, z \in \{0,1\}$

$$\text{AND} \stackrel{\text{def}}{=} \delta mid?z.in2?y.out!(z \wedge y):\text{AND}$$

The model, consisting of gates connected by wires, each of which carry signals representing logical 0 and 1, is now closer to the real world and, being asynchronous, the circuit has different behaviours dependent upon the relative speeds of its constituent gates. An idealised circuit with no gate delays between inputs and output gives the timing diagram:

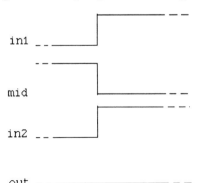

The output out keeps its 0 value even though in1 and in2 change from
0 to 1. But this is only true if we assume that inputs can change
simultaneously and gates have zero delays.

But no physical gate operates in zero time. A system in which the NOT gate
does have a delay would look like:

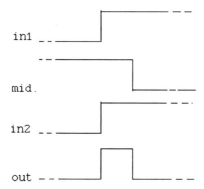

The 'blip' in 'out' is caused by the delay in communicating the change of
in1 to the AND gate, via the NOT gate, relative to that of in2.

Modelling the circuit as the set of interconnected agents

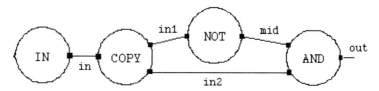

We include the necessary relative delay by giving the NOT component a delay:

IN $\stackrel{\text{def}}{=}$ in!0:IN1
IN1 $\stackrel{\text{def}}{=}$ in!1:IN1
COPY $\stackrel{\text{def}}{=}$ δ(in?x.in1!x.in2!x):COPY
NOT $\stackrel{\text{def}}{=}$ δ(in1?x_t.mid!¬x_{t-1}):NOT
AND $\stackrel{\text{def}}{=}$ δ(mid?z.in2?y.out!(z∧y)):AND

where t−1 represents the value in the time slot preceding t.

First we need to do some renaming, to fit things onto a page:

IN $\stackrel{\text{def}}{=}$ I
  I $\stackrel{\text{def}}{=}$ in!0:I1
  I1 $\stackrel{\text{def}}{=}$ in!1:I1
COPY $\stackrel{\text{def}}{=}$ C
  C $\stackrel{\text{def}}{=}$ δin?x.in1!x.in2!x:C

NOT $\stackrel{\text{def}}{=}$ N
  N $\stackrel{\text{def}}{=}$ δin1?x_t.mid!$\neg x_{t-1}$:N, where x_{t-1} is the previous input
AND $\stackrel{\text{def}}{=}$ A
  A $\stackrel{\text{def}}{=}$ δ(mid?z.in2?y.out!(z$\wedge$y)):A

SYS $\stackrel{\text{def}}{=}$ (I$\times$C$\times$N$\times$A)\\{in,mid,in1,in2}

For convenience, assume the current output of the NOT gate $\neg x_{t-1}$ is 1

def   = (in!0:I1 $\times$ δin?x.in1!x.in2!x:C $\times$ δin1?x_t.mid!1:N
              $\times$ δ(mid?z.in2?y.out!(z$\wedge$y)):A)\\{in,mid,in1,in2}

       = out!(1$\wedge$0):(in!1:I1 $\times$ C $\times$ N $\times$ A)\\{in,mid,in1,in2}

       = out!(0):(in!1:I1 $\times$ δin?x.in1!x.in2!x:C
                       $\times$ δin1?x_t.mid!1:N $\times$ δmid?z.in2?y.out!(z$\wedge$y):A
)\\{in,mid,in1,in2}

       = out!(0):out!(1$\wedge$1):
              (in!1:I1 $\times$ C $\times$ N $\times$ A)\\{in,mid,in1,in2}

       = out!(0):out!(1):
              (in!1:I1 $\times$ δin?x.in1!x.in2!x:C $\times$ δin1?x_t.mid!0:N
               $\times$ δmid?z.in2?y.out!(z$\wedge$y):A)\\{in,mid,in1,in2}

SYS = out!(0):out!(1):out!(0):(in!1:I1 $\times$ C$\times$N$\times$A)\\{in,mid,in1,in2}

Is this the expected output? In this case our synchronous SCCS model has sampled the asynchronous system at times t_0, t_1 and t_2.

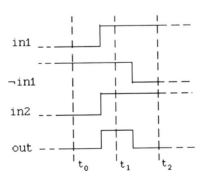

4.9 Specifications and Proof

Introduction

In SCCS we have the facility to model real-time and asynchronous systems, to manipulate these models, and to predict the behaviour of their composites – we can design concurrent and real-time systems. Such designs form hypotheses expressing how we expect a particular system to behave, but, as yet, we have no formal framework to prove these hypotheses are correct. There is one great difficulty with a good hypothesis: when it is completed – the corners smoothed, the contents cohesive and coherent – it is likely to become a thing in itself, a work of art, like a finished painting or a sonnet, and one hates to disturb it. But we must eschew the inevitable feeling of ownership, and disinterestedly subject our creation to the rigours of a proving ground before releasing it to the public.

To prove a design, we check that it performs the function required, that it meets its specification, that at all times it is deadlock free, that live, safe, unshareable resources are used under mutual exclusion, and so on. It must be bulletproof. But how do we prove it so? We need a way of expressing these requirements within a formal framework, but while we have a formal algebra to construct our design, we have no formal equivalent for writing specifications or comparing designs and specifications. So, while we have an obligation to prove our designs sound, we don't as yet have a mechanism to fulfil it. The foundation of such proof systems is that 'two objects are considered equal if, by observation alone, we cannot tell them apart'. To equate two such behaviours, they must be defined in terms which can be equated, in the same or equivalent algebras. Here we equate designs and specifications by returning to the basic premise, as we capture system behaviours in terms of labelled transition systems; two systems are equivalent if their derivation trees are equivalent, i.e. if their SCCS expressions capture the same behaviours.

By expressing the behaviours of both systems in term of SCCS we can equate them, and SCCS expression denote the same behaviours if we can transform one into the other. For example, the expresions

$$P \stackrel{\text{def}}{=} a!:b?:P \text{ and } Q \stackrel{\text{def}}{=} x!:y?:Q$$

are equivalent, as one can be transformed into the other using an appropriate morphism: behaviours are transparent to morphisms. So, to prove a design meets a specification, we can express both in SCCS terms and determine if one can be converted into the other. This should not come as a surprise, as we have used this same approach in previous chapters. The formal development of such approaches and a investigation ino the benefits and drawbacks we will leave to later chapters.

Having proved that a design meets a specification, the designer cannot breathe a sigh of relief and make tracks to the local hostelry until his design can be proved to be deadlock free, live, and so on. This we will start to explore in the coming chapter.

4.9.1 Mutual Exclusion

In an earlier section we introduced several algorithms and attempted to prove whether or not they provided processes with mutual exclusive access to unshareable resources. A program was deemed incorrect if we found even one counter-example in which the algorithm didn't meet our stated requirements, and considered correct if we could not find any such counter-examples. It was concluded at the time that, even for fairly simple programs, the operational proof method was inadequate since, while we could ask questions of an algorithm (e.g. does it have properties such as liveness, lack of deadlock, does it meet its specification, etc.?) the answers could not be relied upon, because the algorithms were expressed in an informal computer language with no semantics.

We now have a more formal framework in which to reason about concurrent systems. Surely this can do a better job than operational 'proof' techniques? By translating systems into SCCS, with an atomic action for each atomic system event, we can 'bolt on' the semantics of SCCS, propositions and all. But we do not always have the luxury of mapping atomic actions in our model to atomic events in the real system, in some cases because it would give too large a search space to check for errors, and in others because the system events aren't atomic and we know nothing about their lower implementation levels. However, validating a high-level design is useful as long as we are aware of the approximations made. Although we know that formalising our algorithms into SCCS is not entirely valid, we also know that if the algorithms fail at the program instruction level, they will, by definition, also fail at lower atomic levels. As examples we will use SCCS formally to check some of the mutual exclusion algorithms proposed earlier, starting with proposed solution three which we concluded probably did not deliver mutual exclusion.

```
program mutual V3;
var inprocone, inproctwo : integer;

    procedure processone;
        begin
            while TRUE do
                first part of processone;
                while inproctwo do
                    nothing;
                endwhile
                inprocone := TRUE;
```

```
                    critical section one;
                    inprocone := FALSE;
                    rest of processone;
               endwhile
        end (*processone*)


    procedure processtwo;
        begin
            while TRUE do
                first part of processtwo;
                while inprocone do
                    nothing;
                endwhile
                inproctwo := TRUE
                critical section two;
                inproctwo := FALSE;
                rest of processtwo;
            endwhile
        end (*processtwo*)


begin
    inprocone := FALSE;
    inproctwo := FALSE;
    parbegin
        processone;
        processtwo;
    parend
end. (*mutual V3*)
```

For an SCCS model we use the notation

> inprocx   flag set if process x is in its critical section
> CSx   the critical section of process x
> NCSx   non-critical section of process x.

Processes one and two can now be defined in the more formal and tractable SCCS domain as

$$P1 \stackrel{def}{=} \delta if(inproc2) \ then \ P1$$
$$\qquad\qquad else \ \delta(inproc1:=true):\delta CS1:\delta(inproc1:=false):\delta NCS1:P1$$
$$P2 \stackrel{def}{=} \delta if(inproc1) \ then \ P2$$
$$\qquad\qquad else \ \delta(inproc2:=true):\delta CS2:\delta(inproc2:=false):\delta NCS2:P2$$

and the complete system as

$$V3 \stackrel{def}{=} \delta inproc1:=false:\delta inproc2:=false:P1 \times P2$$

An expansion of this expression will test all the states of the V3 algorithm. V3 must provide mutual exclusion for all possible interleavings of P1 and P2, but, as the number of states is large, this straightforward approach is best left to theorem provers. We can be more selective by considering probable error 'hot spots' in this case, where P1 and P2 simultaneously attempt to enter their critical sections. If this fails to meet the specification, the algorithm has failed, and we need search no further for failure conditions.

The specification to be met is that the action (CS1.CS2) must not appear in the design.

```
V3 def inproc1:=false:inproc2:=false:P1×P2
P1 def if(inproc2) then P1
            else (inproc1:=true):CS1:(inproc1:=false):NCS1:P1
P2 def if(inproc1) then P2
            else (inproc2:=true):CS2:(inproc2:=false):NCS2:P2


     V3 def inproc1:=false:inproc2:=false:P1×P2
def     = inproc1:=false:inproc2:=false:
                  (inproc1:=true):CS1:(inproc1:=false):NCS1:P1
                x (inproc2:=true):CS2:(inproc2:=false):NCS2:P2
×7      = inproc1:=false:inproc2:=false:inproc1:=true.inproc2:=true:
            CS1:(inproc1:=false):NCS1:P1
                x CS2:(inproc2:=false):NCS2:P2
×7      = inproc1:=false:inproc2:=false:inproc1:=true.inproc2:=true:
            CS1.CS2:(inproc1:=false):NCS1:P1
                  x (inproc2:=false):NCS2:P2
```

P1 and P2 are both in their critical sections at the same time. Mutual exclusion is not preserved, so the SCCS design does not satisfy the specification.

Encouraged by this success we will try another of our tendered solutions to mutual exclusion. This time we will check solution four.

```
program mutual V4;
var p1wants, p2wants : boolean;

    procedure processone;
        begin
            while TRUE do
                first part of processone;
                p1wants := TRUE;
                while p2wants do
                    nothing;
                endwhile;
```

```
                    critical section one;
                    p1wants := FALSE;
                    rest of processone;
                endwhile
          end (*processone*)


      procedure processtwo;
          begin
              while TRUE do
                    first part of processtwo;
                    p2wants := TRUE
                    while p1wants do
                          nothing;
                    endwhile;
                    critical section two;
                    p2wants := FALSE;
                    rest of processtwo;
                endwhile
          end (*processtwo*)


  begin
      p1wants := FALSE;
      p2wants := FALSE;
      parbegin
          processone;
          processtwo;
      parend
  end (*mutual V4*)
```

For this SCCS model we use the notation

pxw	process x's want flag
CSx	the critical section of process x
NCSx	non-critical section of process x.

Processes one and two can now be defined for the synchronous case as

P1 $\stackrel{\text{def}}{=}$ p1w:=true:X

P2 $\stackrel{\text{def}}{=}$ p2w:=true:Y

where

X $\stackrel{\text{def}}{=}$ if(p2w) then X
            else CS1:p1w:=false:NCS1:P1

Y $\stackrel{\text{def}}{=}$ if(p1w) then Y
            else CS2:p2w:=false:NCS2:P2

and the complete system is

$$V4 \overset{\text{def}}{=} \text{p1w:=false:p2w:=false:P1×P2}$$
$$×7 \qquad = \text{p1w:=false:p2w:=false:p1w:=true.p2w:=true:X×Y}$$

The last two traces of V4 do nothing, for ever.[†]

SCCS has again highlighted a design failure – deadlock was not a desired behaviour of the envisaged system, and it is up to the designer to remodel the solution and resubmit it until a viable solution, one which satisfies the specification, is found.

While looking at mutual exclusion, we've stumbled upon deadlock detection. Within SCCS we have two agents, inaction 𝟘 and idler 𝟙, which characterise deadlock and livelock, both of which are common causes of failure in concurrent systems; and we have seen how, if a composition under SCCS exhibits one of these unwanted 'pathological' behaviours, the expression indicates its presence. We will return to deadlock after considering an example of livelock

4.9.2 Livelock – Software Scheduler

Let's consider our Round Robin example again, keeping the same requirements but choosing different agents of implementation. For example, what would be the behaviour of the composite if we kept the definitions of the processes as

Process A, has three a actions:

$$A \overset{\text{def}}{=} \delta A_1$$
$$A_1 \overset{\text{def}}{=} \alpha?: (a_1: (a_2: (a_3:\delta A_4 + \beta?:\delta A_3) + \beta?:\delta A_2) + \beta?:A)$$
$$A_2 \overset{\text{def}}{=} \alpha?: (a_2: (a_3:\delta A_4 + \beta?:\delta A_3) + \beta?:\delta A_2)$$
$$A_3 \overset{\text{def}}{=} \alpha?: (a_3:\delta A_4 + \beta?:\delta A_3)$$
$$A_4 \overset{\text{def}}{=} \beta?:A$$

Process B, has four b actions:

$$B \overset{\text{def}}{=} \delta B_1$$
$$B_1 \overset{\text{def}}{=} \gamma?: (b_1: (b_2: (b_3: (b_4:\delta B_5 + \chi?:\delta B_4) + \chi?:\delta B_3) + \chi?:\delta B_2) + \chi?:B)$$
$$B_2 \overset{\text{def}}{=} \gamma?: (b_2: (b_3: (b_4:\delta B_5 + \chi?:\delta B_4) + \chi?:\delta B_3) + \chi?:\delta B_2)$$
$$B_3 \overset{\text{def}}{=} \gamma?: (b_3: (b_4:\delta B_5 + \chi?:\delta B_4) + \chi?:\delta B_3)$$
$$B_4 \overset{\text{def}}{=} \gamma?: (b_4:\delta B_5 + \chi?:\delta B_4)$$
$$B_5 \overset{\text{def}}{=} \chi?:B$$

But redefined the scheduler S as

$$S \overset{\text{def}}{=} \alpha!:\beta!:\gamma!:\chi!:S$$

[†] If the predicate 'if(x) then ...' were modelled as an internal action V4 would degenerate to a 𝟙.

Composition

As in the last example We'll evaluate the complete system two agents at a time.

$$(S \times A \times B) \backslash\backslash \{\alpha, \beta, \gamma, \chi\}$$
$$\backslash\backslash 5 \quad = ((S \times A) \backslash\backslash \{\alpha, \beta\} \times B) \backslash\backslash \{\gamma, \chi\}$$

Commencing with the evaluation of A composed with S.

$$
\begin{aligned}
\text{SA} \ \overset{\text{def}}{=} \ & (S \times A) \backslash\backslash \{\alpha, \beta\} \\
\text{sub} \quad = \ & ((\alpha!:\beta!:\gamma!:\chi!:S) \\
& \times (\delta\alpha?:(a_1:(a_2:(a_3:\delta A_4 \ + \ \beta?:\delta A_3) + \ \beta?:\delta A_2) + \ \beta?:A)))\backslash\backslash \{\alpha, \beta\} \\
\leftrightarrow 3a \quad = \ & 1:((\beta!:\gamma!:\chi!:S) \\
& \times (a_1:(a_2:(a_3:\delta A_4 \ + \ \beta?:\delta A_3) + \ \beta?:\delta A_2) + \ \beta?:A))\backslash\backslash \{\alpha, \beta\} \\
\leftrightarrow 1a \quad = \ & 1:1:((\gamma!:\chi!:S) \ \times \ \delta A_1)\backslash\backslash \{\alpha, \beta\} \\
\leftrightarrow 7a \quad = \ & 1:1:\gamma!:\chi!:(S \times A)\backslash\backslash \{\alpha, \beta\} \\
\text{def SA} = \ & 1:1:\gamma!:\chi!:\text{SA}
\end{aligned}
$$

Now add process B

$$
\begin{aligned}
\text{SAB} \ \overset{\text{def}}{=} \ & (\text{SA} \times B) \backslash\backslash \{\gamma, \chi\} \\
\text{sub} \quad = \ & ((1:1:\gamma!:\chi!:\text{SA}) \\
& \times \delta(\gamma?:(b_1:(b_2:(b_3:(b_4:\delta B_5 + \ \chi?:\delta B_4) + \ \chi?:\delta B_3) + \ \chi?:\delta B_2) + \ \chi?:B)) \\
&)\backslash\backslash \{\gamma, \chi\} \\
\leftrightarrow 7a \quad = \ & 1:1:((\gamma!:\chi!:\text{SA}) \\
& \times \delta(\gamma?:(b_1:(b_2:(b_3:(b_4:\delta B_5 + \ \chi?:\delta B_4) + \ \chi?:\delta B_3) + \ \chi?:\delta B_2) + \ \chi?:B)) \\
&)\backslash\backslash \{\gamma, \chi\} \\
\leftrightarrow 3a \quad = \ & 1:1:1:((\chi!:\text{SA}) \\
& \times (b_1:(b_2:(b_3:(b_4:\delta B_5 \ + \ \chi?:\delta B_4) + \ \chi?:\delta B_3) + \ \chi?:\delta B_2) + \ \chi?:B) \\
&)\backslash\backslash \{\gamma, \chi\} \\
\leftrightarrow 1a \quad = \ & 1:1:1:1:(\text{SA} \times B)\backslash\backslash \{\gamma, \chi\} \\
\text{def} \quad = \ & 1:1:1:1:\text{SAB} \\
\text{def SAB} = \ & \mathbb{1}
\end{aligned}
$$

The implementation has not met our specification. It exhibits livelock, denoted by idler $\mathbb{1}$. A few seconds of thought would show that this behaviour should have been expected; as the system spends all its time communicating, the two processes never do any useful work. It is reassuring that SCCS has illuminated the fact so well.

4.9.3 Deadlock – Software Scheduler

Consider a less obvious case. The system (in which the previous design plays a part) has been modified by a later review involving a change to the system specification – not an infrequent occurrence in the real world. To test the system code it is though necessary to log each communication occurrence; this extra code added to each process takes three internal actions to execute, and it seems reasonable to allow this extra code to execute after each activation or deactivation communication, and to do so atomically. What happens now?

Process A :

$$A \overset{def}{=} \delta A_1$$
$$A_1 \overset{def}{=} \alpha?:1^3:(a_1:(a_2:(a_3:\delta A_4 + \beta?:1^3:\delta A_3) + \beta?:1^3:\delta A_2) + \beta?:1^3:A)$$
$$A_2 \overset{def}{=} \alpha?:1^3:(a_2:(a_3:\delta A_4 + \beta?:1^3:\delta A_3) + \beta?:1^3:\delta A_2)$$
$$A_3 \overset{def}{=} \alpha?:1^3:(a_3:\delta A_4 + \beta?:1^3:\delta A_3)$$
$$A_4 \overset{def}{=} \beta?:1^3:A$$

Process B :

$$B \overset{def}{=} \delta B_1$$
$$B_1 \overset{def}{=} \gamma?:1^3:(b_1:(b_2:(b_3:(b4:\delta B_5 + \chi?:1^3:\delta B_4) + \chi?:1^3:\delta B_3) + \chi?:1^3:\delta B_2)$$
$$+ \chi?:1^3:B)$$
$$B_2 \overset{def}{=} \gamma?:1^3:(b_2:(b_3:(b4:\delta B_5 + \chi?:1^3:\delta B_4) + \chi?:1^3:\delta B_3) + \chi?:1^3:\delta B_2)$$
$$B_3 \overset{def}{=} \gamma?:1^3:(b_3:(b4:\delta B_5 + \chi?:1^3:\delta B_4) + \chi?:1^3:\delta B_3)$$
$$B_4 \overset{def}{=} \gamma?:1^3:(b_4:\delta B_5 + \chi?:1^3:\delta B_4)$$
$$B_5 \overset{def}{=} \chi?:1^3:B$$

The scheduler S :

$$S \overset{def}{=} \alpha!:1:1:\beta!:\gamma!:1:1:\chi!:S$$

Composition

$$(S \times A \times B)\backslash\backslash\{\alpha,\beta,\gamma,\chi\}$$
$$\backslash\backslash 5 \qquad = ((S \times A)\backslash\backslash\{\alpha,\beta\} \times B)\backslash\backslash\{\gamma,\chi\}$$

We commence with the evaluation of A composed with S:

$$SA \overset{def}{=} (S \times A)\backslash\backslash\{\alpha,\beta\}$$

$$\begin{aligned}
\text{sub} \quad &= ((\alpha!:1:1:\beta!:\gamma!:1:1:\chi!:S) \\
&\qquad \times (\delta\alpha?:1^3:(a_1:(a_2:(a_3:\delta A_4 + \beta?:1^3:\delta A_3)\beta?:1^3:\delta A_2) \\
&\qquad + \beta?:1^3:A)))\backslash\backslash\{\alpha,\beta\})
\end{aligned}$$

$$\begin{aligned}
\leftrightarrow 3a \quad &= 1:((1:1:\beta!:\gamma!:1:1:\chi!:S) \\
&\qquad \times (1^3:(a_1:(a_2:(a_3:\delta A_4 + \beta?:1^3:\delta A_3) + \beta?:1^3:\delta A_2) \\
&\qquad + \beta?:1^3:A)))\backslash\backslash\{\alpha,\beta\}
\end{aligned}$$

$$\begin{aligned}
\leftrightarrow 5a \quad &= 1:1:1:((\beta!:\gamma!:1:1:\chi!:S) \\
&\qquad \times (1:(a_1:(a_2:(a_3:\delta A_4 + \beta?:1^3:\delta A_3) + \beta?:1^3:\delta A_2) \\
&\qquad + \beta?:1^3:A)))\backslash\backslash\{\alpha,\beta\}
\end{aligned}$$

$$\leftrightarrow 5b \quad = 1:1:1:\mathbb{0}$$
$$\text{def } SA = 1:1:1:\mathbb{0}$$

Now add process B:

$$SAB \overset{def}{=} (SA \times B)\backslash\backslash\{\gamma,\chi\}$$

$$\begin{aligned}
\text{sub} \quad &= ((1:1:1:\mathbb{0}) \times \\
&\qquad \delta(\gamma?:(b_1:(b_2:(b_3:(b_4:\delta B_5+ \chi?:\delta B_4)+ \chi?:\delta B_3)+ \chi?:\delta B_2)+ \chi?:B)))
\end{aligned}$$

$$)\backslash\backslash\{\gamma,\chi\}$$

$\leftrightarrow 7a \quad = 1:1:1:(0 \times$

$\delta(\gamma?:(b_1:(b_2:(b_3:(b_4:\delta B_5+ \chi?:\delta B_4)+ \chi?:\delta B_3)+ \chi?:\delta B_2)+ \chi?:B)))$

$)\backslash\backslash\{\gamma,\chi\}$

$\times 3,03 \quad = 1:1:1:0$

$\text{def SAB} = 1:1:1:0$

The composite system exhibits three internal actions before it dies. So what has happened? Process A is started by the scheduler. It then uses two of the slots granted to it by the scheduler for two communication logging actions. At this point Process A still needs one more slot, without interruption, to complete the logging task, but the scheduler wants to stop A in the next time slot, which results in an unresolvable conflict.

4.9.4 Comments

The previous sections make SCCS look quite healthy. We can translate designs of real-world, real-time, behaviours into expressions in an algebra, then use the algebra to determine the emergent behaviour of the designs. We can then check if the design satisfies its specification by comparing this behaviour against the required one. The first stage of mapping a behaviour into the formal SCCS framework and derivation of a composite behaviour is sound. It is proving the behaviour meets the required specification that gives pause for thought.

So far, to prove a design is equivalent to a specification, we have expressed them both in the calculus and checked if all possible actions in all equivalent states are the same. This is fine if we quickly find a counter example but, if the counter example is obscure, we have a tedious job in front of us. Worse still, if the design is error-free we have to check all actions in all possible system states, and we're back to exhaustive testing. Well almost; this time our exhaustive testing has a formal basis which means we can write provable specifications, designs can be checked against specifications using proved propositions and, last but not least, we can build automated tools to do the checking for us.

The different types of equivalence, the writing of more subtle specifications, the automation of proofs and the consideration of non-trivial examples are dealt with in the next chapter.

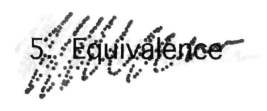

5. Equivalence

5.0 The Need For Equivalence

A design is only completed when we have proved it meets its specification, and to do this we need to prove an equivalence between specification and design. In more specific terms, we must prove, before implementation, that our designs meet their requirements (satisfy their specifications) and only those requirements (no over-specification).

We don't just need equivalence to check a completed design against its specification but, as designs are progressed by combining together (sub)systems, we need an equality to equate (sub)designs and (sub)specifications; and if we can equate (sub)designs with (sub)designs we can replace one design by an equivalent if it's simpler, or cheaper, or whatever. Equivalence is also needed to construct the algebra we use to progress a design. We need to know if the order of evaluation matters, if the behaviour of $(\mathcal{E}xpr_1 + \mathcal{E}xpr_2) + \mathcal{E}xpr_3$ is the same as $\mathcal{E}xpr_2 + (\mathcal{E}xpr_1 + \mathcal{E}xpr_3)$, if we can replace one sub-expression $(\alpha:\mathcal{E}xpr + \text{NIL})$ with another $\alpha:\mathcal{E}xpr$, and so on.

While it is convenient to talk about equivalences between objects like agents P and Q, it must not be forgotten that what we're actually talking about here are equivalences between expressions describing behaviours, of which agents, sub-agents and specifications are all special cases. In various parts of what follows in proving that certain expressions are isomorphic, $\mathcal{E}xpr_1 \equiv \mathcal{E}xpr_2$, we prove that $\mathcal{E}xpr_1$ and $\mathcal{E}xpr_2$ represent equivalent behaviours; this is the general case of equating agents $P \equiv Q$ and comparing agents representing a design and a specification $\mathcal{E}xpr_{\text{design}} \equiv \mathcal{E}xpr_{\text{spec}}$, also written $\mathcal{D}esign \equiv \mathcal{S}pecification$.

This leads us to the question of when two expressions are equivalent and describe the 'same' system, and of what is meant by same.

- 0, $(a?:0)\backslash\backslash a$, 0×0 and $0 + 0$ all describe systems which do nothing.
- $a!:0$, $(b!:0)[a/b]$, $a!:0 + 0$, $a!:0 + a!:0$ and $a!:(0 \times 0)$ all

describe systems which can do a! and then nothing.

- a?:0 + b?:0, b?:0 + a?:0, (b?:0 + c?:0) [a/c] all describe systems which can do either a? or b? and then nothing.
- 0, 1:0, 0 + 1:0, (b?:0 × b!:0) \\b all describe systems which do nothing visible.
- a?:0, a?:1:0, 0 + 1:a?:0, (b?:a?:0 × b!:1:0) \\b all describe systems whose only visible behaviour is a single a?.

Intuitively, two systems are said to be *equivalent* when no observation can distinguish them. Two (sub)systems are said to be *congruent* if the result of placing them in the same system context yields two equivalent systems. We can state that P is congruent to Q if P is equivalent to Q, and for every suitable context, $\mathcal{C}[\![\ ]\!]$ the systems formed are also equivalent, $\mathcal{C}[\![P]\!] = \mathcal{C}[\![Q]\!]$; unfortunately, systems which are equivalent in isolation are not necessarily congruent and we will take time out to consider what we mean by congruence before we proceed.

Congruence

Two agent expressions $\mathit{Expr_1}$ and $\mathit{Expr_2}$ are congruent if, when placed in the same context $\mathcal{C}[\![\ ]\!]$, an expression with zero or more 'holes' which can be filled by expressions, the resulting behaviours are equivalent. Consider an analogy with arithmetic. If we accept that a=b then, for particular expressions $\mathit{Expr_1}$=a and $\mathit{Expr_2}$=b in context $\mathcal{C}[\![\ ]\!] = [\![\ ]\!] +3$ we are equating

$$a+3 = b+3$$

and for a $\mathcal{C}[\![\ ]\!] = (x + (2 \times [\![\ ]\!] - 1)/3)$

$$x + (2 \times a - 1)/3 = x + (2 \times b - 1)/3$$

and so on.

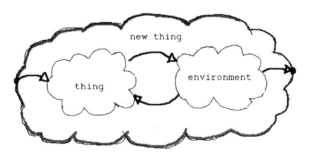

The idea of congruences underpins our constructional design strategy. Once we have a description of a thing and we place this in an environment with which it can interact, we have created a more complex thing.

We can now model systems of any complexity as
individual objects, each viewing the others as an
environment to interact with. Now, proving each
subdesign meets its specification verifies that it
can perform as required, and if we can show that
two designs are congruent, one can replace the
other without changing the behaviour of the
overall system.

To construct a design, and determine emergent
behaviours when we combine expressions, we
need an algebra over expressions and the algebra needs propositions that tell us
which expression can replace which, whatever the environment; for example:

$$P1 + P2 = P2 + P1$$
$$P \times 0 = 0$$

That is, if such propositions are congruences they can be used to simplify other
expression; for example, after proving

$$a : P \times 1 : Q = a : (P \times Q)$$

is context independent wherever $(a : P \times 1 : Q)$ appears, we can replace it with
$(a : (P \times Q))$. For example, in context $c[\![]\!] = c : R \times ([\![]\!]) \backslash b$

$$c : R \times (a : P \times 1 : Q) \backslash b = c : R \times (a : (P \times Q)) \backslash b$$

We can also use congruences to prove the basic propositions of an algebra which,
in turn, can be used to derive other, higher-level, propositions. For example,
developing $\alpha : P$ slotted into environment $([\![]\!] \times \alpha^{-1} : Q) \backslash\backslash A$ into

$$(\alpha : P \times \alpha^{-1} : Q) \backslash\backslash A = 1 : (P \times Q) \backslash\backslash A, \quad \text{Part}(\alpha) \subseteq A$$

from

$$(\alpha : P \times \alpha^{-1} : Q) \backslash\backslash A$$
$$\times 4 \qquad\qquad = (\alpha . \alpha^{-1} : (P \times Q)) \backslash\backslash A$$
$$\backslash\backslash 3 \qquad\qquad = 1 : (P \times Q) \backslash\backslash A, \text{if } \text{Part}(\alpha) \subseteq A$$

And we use equality between expressions to build our algebras, after validating a minimum set of expressions which form the kernel of SCCS; for example: $P + Q = Q + P$,
$(\alpha : P) \wedge \beta = 0$, ... etc. We can use these propositions to derive further propositions
until an algebra of the relevant level of abstraction for a particular problem is reached.

While we've made the case for needing equivalence and congruence, we have yet
to say how we get them. Both require us to compare behaviours, and to compare
behaviours we observe them, which means we need a formal notion over observations upon which we can compare behaviours. The simplest of such notions of
observation consist of traces which simply list the sequences of actions an object
is observed to engage in; and this is our starting-point.

5.1 Traces

Traces are lists of actions seen by an observer as an agent moves from state to state.

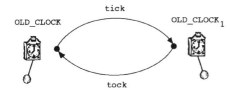

OLD_CLOCK would be observed to repeat forever the sequence tick, tock

definition *traces*

The trace of an agent is a finite sequence recording the actions of an agent from a particular state. Individual traces are written as lists of actions enclosed in <brackets>; for example:

$<\alpha, \beta>$	a two-action trace, α followed by β.
$<\alpha>$	a one-action trace.
$<>$	an empty trace, recording no actions.

The empty trace describes the behaviour of an agent before it engages in its first action.

■

The future behaviour of any agent is described by a set of traces. The future traces of P are <>, before it engages in any actions, $<\alpha>$, after it engages in its first action, $<\alpha, \alpha>$, after it engages in its second action, and so on up to $<\alpha>^n$, for some integer n, giving the set of traces

$$\{<>, <\alpha>, <\alpha, \alpha>, \ldots, <\alpha>^n\}$$

It is convenient to define $A*$ as the set of all finite traces, including <>, which can be formed from symbols in the set A. $A*$ describes all possible behaviours of an agent with alphabet A. In our example

$$A = \{\alpha\} \text{ so } A* = \{<>, <\alpha>, <\alpha, \alpha>, \ldots, <\alpha>^n\}$$

To predict the behaviour of agent P we use the function Traces(P) which returns the set of all traces of agent P. For example, the above agent has Traces(P) = $\{\alpha\}*$. More complex examples include are given below.

example

OLD_CLOCK represents an agent which ticks before it tocks.

$$OLD\_CLOCK \stackrel{\text{def}}{=} tick: OLD\_CLOCK_1$$
$$OLD\_CLOCK_1 \stackrel{\text{def}}{=} tock: OLD\_CLOCK$$

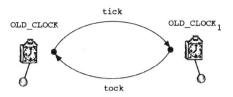

and

Traces(OLD_CLOCK) =

    {<>,<tick>,<tick,tock>,<tick,tock,tick>, ...etc.}

Traces(OLD_CLOCK$_1$) =

    {<>,<tock>,<tock,tick>,<tock,tick,tock>, ...etc.}

example

STAMP_MACHINE represents an agent which usually accepts a coin and delivers a stamp in a pull-out drawer. Occasionally the machine needs a kick before the drawer can be pulled out, and even then it sometimes fails to deliver a stamp, evoking a curse from the coin-giver.

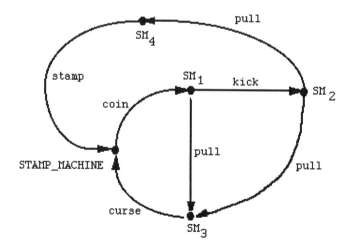

STAMP_MACHINE $\overset{\text{def}}{=}$ SM

        SM $\overset{\text{def}}{=}$ coin:(kick:(pull:stamp:SM

               + pull:curse:SM) + (pull:curse:SM))

and

    Traces(SM) =

      {<>,<coin>,<coin,kick>,<coin,pull>,<coin,pull,curse>, ... etc.}

    Traces(SM$_1$) =

      {<>,<kick>,<pull>,<kick,pull>,<pull,curse>, ... etc.}

The complete behaviour of any system P is described by `Traces(P)`, the set of all possible sequences of actions of P from its initial state. For example `Traces(SM)` generates all the traces of STAMP_MACHINE from its initial state and fully describes STAMP_MACHINE, just as `Traces(P)` = `{α}*` fully describes P $\stackrel{\text{def}}{=}$ α : P.

So far, so good. Traces appear to capture agent behaviour with an effortless simplicity. But, to see if traces can support tests of equality in SCCS, we need to delve a bit deeper.

5.2 From Traces to Bisimulations

We prove that two agents P and Q describe the same systems by proving that P and Q are isomorphic, P ≅ Q. But how do we prove systems isomorphic?

We need to observe the actions of systems to compare them. Two systems are the same if they are observed to engage in the same sequences of actions. We know that traces contain the lists of actions a system can engage in, so perhaps we can use traces as a proxy and compare two systems by comparing their traces. We could propose that:
(P) is equivalent to (Q) if and only if `Traces(P)` is the same as `Traces(Q)` written as:
$$((P) \cong (Q)) \Leftrightarrow (\text{Traces}(P) = \text{Traces}(Q))$$

The proposition will be `false` if we can find a counter-example; and here is such a counter-example: consider the two systems P $\stackrel{\text{def}}{=}$ α : P and Q $\stackrel{\text{def}}{=}$ α : Q + α : Q₁, pictured as:

We can see that the two systems differ. P, at any moment in its infinite life is capable of engaging in action α and returning to state P; while Q, which can also engage in any number of α actions to return to state Q, can also at any time engage in an α action, move to state Q_1 and stop. In terms of their future actions, the systems behave the same; both can engage in any number of α actions. More formally, their sets of traces include the elements <>, <α>, <α,α>, <α,α,α>, …, <$α^n$> for some integer n, written as <α>*, and `Traces(P)` = `Traces(Q)` = <α>*.

Thus, while the traces of P and Q are the same, the systems P and Q are not. Perhaps rather than using traces, which predicted behaviours, we can use actual behaviours to distinguish systems. Unfortunately not, as while the actions of processes seen by an observer happen in sequence, *when* they occur is not specified and, for P and Q, an observer, after seeing both systems perform α, can never be sure if Q is in its initial state, ready to engage in another α, or in state Q_1, never to engage in an α again. Hence traces alone cannot be used to differentiate between systems.[†] To be safe, we need to compare systems by comparing all possible actions in all possible states, up to and including their final states; and to compare systems we have to compare the traces from every state of both systems. Thankfully this is simpler than it sounds – after all, a system's behaviour is the sum of its behaviours in its individual states and, with the exception of the initial state, each state of a system's derivation tree is reached by a single action from a previous state. We can describe the behaviour of any system in terms of actions and successor states. This recursive definition should enable us to produce an algorithm by which we can compare agent actions in all reachable states. Comparing agents in this way is termed *bisimulation*, of which there are many flavours, each with different and sometimes useful equivalence properties.

5.3 Bisimulation

Two agents are considered the same if they behave the same. Two agents, in particular states, have the same behaviour if they engage in the same actions, and this we can check.

By this test the following agents are the same when in states P, Q and P_1, Q_1:

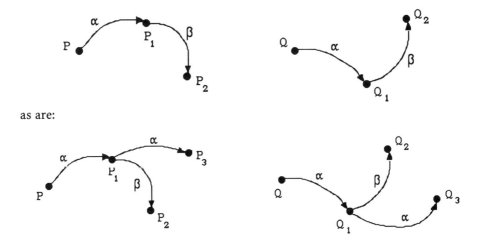

as are:

---

† CSP gets round the problem by considering not only what a system can do, its traces, but also what a system cannot do, its refusals [Hoa85]. In the above example, it is the fact that P cannot refuse to engage in an a action whilst Q as Q_1 can, that distinguishes the two systems.

We relate equivalent states if their subsequent actions are the same; more formally, we define a binary relationship, **R**, between two agents in their initial states, for
example P**R**Q, if the agents can engage in the same next actions. To compare the
complete behaviours of two agents we need to extend this relationship over all
agent states, as only if two agents behave the same as they evolve through their
derivation trees can we consider them equivalent. What we want is an easily
automated algorithm that will test agents for such equivalence:

> To compare two agents we need to compare the actions that move the agents
> from initial states to successor states, the actions that move them from these suc-
> cessor states to further states, the actions that move them from these further
> states, ... and so on.

But for our algorithm to work it is not sufficient to show that one agent simulates,
behaves the same as, the other. We need to show that each simulates the other.

Consider two agents, P and Q. We can say that agent P behaves like, simulates,
agent Q if P engages in the same initial actions as Q, P's successor states have the
same actions as Q in its successor states, and so on. By proving that P simulates Q
we've proved that P performs at least the actions of Q; it may do more. To check
that one agent doesn't simply contain the other, and to prove agents P and Q are
the exactly the same, we need to check not only that P simulates Q but *also* that Q
simulates P.

We need to prove a bisimulation between P and Q by proving that each simulates
the other. More formally, if $\mathbf{R}_i$ is a bisimulation between comparable states of two
agents, then we denote $\cup_{i \in I} \mathbf{R}_i$, for all I comparisons, as the bisimulation relation $\mathbf{\hat{B}}$. Comparing agents by bisimulation was first reported in [Park81].

example
Where P and Q can be pictured as

While Q can simulate P, as P cannot simulate Q we do not have a
bisimulation.

■

Two agents are in bisimulation only if there exists a bisimulation relationship containing all their states. What we now need is an algorithm which, given two

agents, works this out for us. Our first algorithm is for the strong bisimulation, which checks all agent actions.

5.3.1 Strong Bisimulation

Strong bisimulation checks to see if two agents are equivalent for all their actions, both internal and external. We check external actions because they tells us how an agent behaves at its interface, but, without including internal actions denoting the passage of time, the time response of such systems will be lost. Thus, to compare real-time systems, we need to account for all actions, in other words actions in set *Act*.

strong bisimulation

P is bisimilar to Q, Q$\mathcal{B}$P, if and only if for each α action, $\alpha\in$ *Act*

a) if P$\xrightarrow{\alpha}$P', then there exists a Q' such that Q$\xrightarrow{\alpha}$Q' and P' is bisimilar to Q', P'$\mathcal{B}$Q', and it can be said that Q simulates P.

And the corollary is:

b) if Q$\xrightarrow{\alpha}$Q', then there exists a P' such that P$\xrightarrow{\alpha}$P' and P' is bisimilar to Q', Q'$\mathcal{B}$P', and it can be said that P simulates Q.

In the above algorithm α is a place marker, not for just one, but for any number of actions. Consider agents FRED and GEORGE:

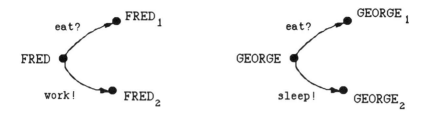

To use the algorithm we first make P=FRED and Q=GEORGE, then in part (a) we consider both α=eat? and α=work! as actions of P that Q must match, and in part (b) both α=eat? and α=sleep! as possible actions of Q that P must match. In this case, FRED and GEORGE aren't bisimilar as, in their initial states, they engage in different actions.

Unfortunately, the algorithm for strong bisimulation has a weakness. It is based on a circular argument: 'is bisimilar to' appears on both sides of the 'if and only if' statement. To prove P and Q bisimilar it is necessary to prove P' and Q' bisimilar, and so on. But an algorithm is only an algorithm if it knows when to stop. This one stops when either the bisimulation is complete or it has failed. To prove a bisimulation has failed it is only necessary to find a pair of non-bisimilar states that should be bisimilar – either initial states or ones upon which previous bisimilarities rely. To prove a bisimulation complete, on the other hand, it has to be shown that all agent states have been checked by appearing (at least once) in the bisimulation relation. How we prove a bisimulation fails is straightforward, but to prove it complete needs more investigation.

We will content ourselves with an informal argument. If an agent is closed, it is completely defined and the actions associated with each state are known; such agents are either fully recursive, contain paths returning to initial states, are internally recursive, or have paths ending in a $\mathbb{0}$ or a $\mathbb{1}$.

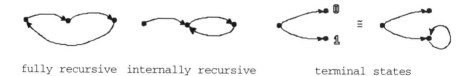

fully recursive internally recursive   terminal states

If the agent is recursive the algorithm will revisit previously checked states; for terminal states, $\mathbb{0}$ or $\mathbb{1}$, the agents have known future behaviour, and in all cases the sequence of actions leading to each state completely defines the behaviour up to and including that state. That only leaves agents which aren't closed, whose behaviour in certain agent states is unknown:

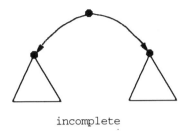

incomplete

The two agent will only be bisimilar if their future, but undefined, behaviours are bisimilar.

A successful bisimulation of agents P and Q must compare all the states of both. Our bisimulation algorithm should start by comparing behaviours of the agents in their initial states and follow those behaviours until all states, of both derivation trees, have been compared. For agents with initial states P and Q it is thus only necessary to check that the resultant bisimulation is complete and contains P$\mathcal{B}$Q.

Now we can prove if agents are bisimilar, but can we say that, because two agents are bisimilar, they are equivalent? Unfortunately, not just yet; because bisimulation looks like an equivalence relation doesn't mean that it *is* one - it has to be proved to be one.

5.3.2 From Strong Bisimulation to an Equivalence

To prove that bisimilar agents are also equivalent, we must prove that the bisimulation relation over expressions is also an equivalence relation[†] over expressions. To do this we have to prove that there is a relation which satisfies its definition, that it is the largest, and that it is an equivalence. The proof would require a detour through the land of backward Es and upside down As, so we will take the mathematicians on trust and accept that $\mathcal{B}$ does meet these criteria. For those who really must have the proof, see [Mil83].

If designers had any say in the equivalence relation which is used to compare *Specifications* with *Designs* they would pick the one that is most easily satisfied, as,

---

† Any relation is an equivalence if it can be shown to be reflexive, symmetrical and transitive. For example the relation = is an equivalence for integers. Given x and y are integers as
$$x=x, \text{ reflexive}$$
$$(x=y) \Rightarrow (y=x), \text{ symmetric}$$
$$(x=y) \wedge (y=z) \Rightarrow (x=z), \text{ transitive}$$
To prove the bisimulation relation over expressions is also an equivalence we must prove that $\mathcal{B}$ is:
- Reflexive, P $\mathcal{B}$ P
- Symmetrical, P $\mathcal{B}$ Q $\Rightarrow$ Q $\mathcal{B}$ P
- Transitive, P $\mathcal{B}$ Q $\wedge$ Q $\mathcal{B}$ R $\Rightarrow$ P $\mathcal{B}$ R.

by picking the weakest, most generous, relation they would have the one that the maximum number of expressions would satisfy, thus making the task of designing, and later implementing, solutions all the simpler. Again the mathematicians come to the rescue: in [Mil89] we are told we can weaken the bisimulation by replacing the 'iff' with the weaker 'implies'.

We can now rewrite the definition of strong bisimulation[†] as an equivalence relation, noting its promotion by replacing $\mathcal{B}$ with the more evocative $\sim$.

strong bisimulation $\sim$

$P \sim Q$ implies that, for each α action, $\alpha \in \mathcal{A}ct$

    a) if $P \xrightarrow{\alpha} P'$, then for some Q', $Q \xrightarrow{\alpha} Q'$ and $P' \sim Q'$

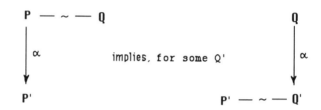

and conversely,

    b) if $Q \xrightarrow{\alpha} Q'$, then for some P', $P \xrightarrow{\alpha} P'$ and $P' \sim Q'$

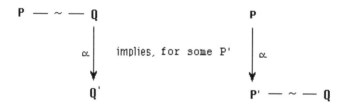

■

(Note: as $\sim$ is reflexive we've replaced the $Q' \sim P'$ in (b) by $P' \sim Q'$)

To prove agent equivalence using bisimulation we have to compare the actions of the agents in all comparable states. To make things clearer we will follow the algorithm in small steps, a task made easier by labelling each state and by writing each agent expression in normal form, in terms of guards and successor states. In normal form $P \stackrel{\text{def}}{=} \alpha : \beta : P + \chi : 1 : P$ is rewritten as $P \stackrel{\text{def}}{=} \alpha : P_1 + \chi : P_2$, $P_1 \stackrel{\text{def}}{=} \beta : P, P_2 \stackrel{\text{def}}{=} 1 : P$.

---

† An alternative proof which considers strong bisimulation as a fixed point can be found in [Mil89].

Now, some examples of testing for strong equivalence using normal form:

example
Where $P \stackrel{def}{=} \alpha : P$ and $Q \stackrel{def}{=} \alpha : Q_1, Q_1 \stackrel{def}{=} \alpha : Q$ can be pictured as

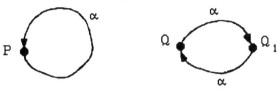

P and Q look to be equivalent, but can we prove it?
P and Q are equivalent if the bisimulation relation contains all states, including $P \sim Q$. This we test by constructing the bisimulation relation from initial state through all successor states.

In the initial state, $P \sim Q$

$$\text{if } P \xrightarrow{\alpha} P \Rightarrow Q \xrightarrow{\alpha} Q_1 \text{ and } P \sim Q_1$$
$$\text{if } Q \xrightarrow{\alpha} Q_1 \Rightarrow P \xrightarrow{\alpha} P \text{ and } P \sim Q_1$$

which can be rewritten as:

$$\text{Given } P \xrightarrow{\alpha} P \Rightarrow Q \xrightarrow{\alpha} Q_1$$
$$\text{and } Q \xrightarrow{\alpha} Q_1 \Rightarrow P \xrightarrow{\alpha} P$$

then $P \sim Q$ if $P \sim Q_1$, which can be expressed as $(P,Q) \subseteq \sim$ if $P \sim Q_1$.

Checking (P, Q_1)

$$P \xrightarrow{\alpha} P \Rightarrow Q_1 \xrightarrow{\alpha} Q$$
$$\text{and } Q_1 \xrightarrow{\alpha} Q \Rightarrow P \xrightarrow{\alpha} P$$

$\{(P,Q), (P,Q_1)\} \subseteq \sim$ if $P \sim Q$.

But (P,Q) is already in $\sim$. We've examined all agents' states and for each state the agents simulate each other, giving the strong bisimulation relation

$$\sim = \{(P,Q), (P_1,Q)\}$$

which is complete and contains (P,Q) proving

$$P \sim Q$$

■

Back to the example that started this search for an equivalence

example
Where $P \stackrel{def}{=} \alpha : P$ and $Q \stackrel{def}{=} \alpha : Q + \alpha : Q_1$ can be pictured as:

To prove P and Q equivalent we prove P~Q to be a member of a complete bisimulation relation.

Q can engage in an α and return to state Q; this is matched by P engaging in an α action and then returning to state P, and vice versa. In its initial state Q can engage in an α action and move to state Q_1, which again can be matched by P, and vice versa.

Checking (P,Q)

$$P\xrightarrow{\alpha}P \Rightarrow Q\xrightarrow{\alpha}Q$$
$$\text{and } Q\xrightarrow{\alpha}Q \Rightarrow P\xrightarrow{\alpha}P$$

$$Q\xrightarrow{\alpha}Q_1 \Rightarrow P\xrightarrow{\alpha}P$$
$$\text{and } P\xrightarrow{\alpha}P \Rightarrow Q\xrightarrow{\alpha}Q_1$$

$(P,Q)\subseteq\sim$ if $(P{\sim}Q)$ and $(P{\sim}Q_1)$.

(P,Q) is already in the bisimulation and the two agents are only equal if (P,Q_1) is also there. But Q_1 has no further actions, $Q_1=0$, while P has, and
$$P\xrightarrow{\alpha}P \Rightarrow 0\xrightarrow{\alpha}0 \text{ is false.}$$
Thus $(P,Q_1)\notin\sim$, the bisimulation relation is incomplete and
$$\neg\,(P{\sim}Q)$$

■

Dissimilar agents, which could not be distinguished by traces from initial states, have their non-equivalence confirmed by bisimulation.

To complete things, we will consider a few more cases; for example, agents with undefined states:

example
Are $P \overset{\text{def}}{=} \alpha: (1:P' + \beta:P'')$ and $Q \overset{\text{def}}{=} \alpha: (1:Q' + \beta:Q'')$ strongly bisimilar by our algorithm?

Where
$$P \stackrel{\text{def}}{=} \alpha : P_1$$
$$P_1 \stackrel{\text{def}}{=} 1 : P' + \beta : P''$$

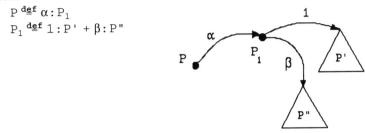

and

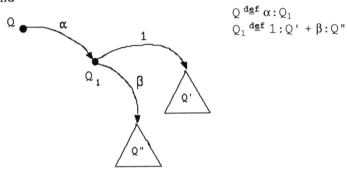

$$Q \stackrel{\text{def}}{=} \alpha : Q_1$$
$$Q_1 \stackrel{\text{def}}{=} 1 : Q' + \beta : Q''$$

In their initial states P and Q both engage α and will be in bisimulation if their successor states, P_1 and Q_1, are also in bisimulation, $(P_1 \sim Q_1)$. P_1 and Q_1 can engage 1 or β actions and will be in bisimulation if $(P' \sim Q')$ and $(P'' \sim Q'')$.

All known states have been visited, and only if the undefined states are in the relation as $(P' \sim Q')$ and $(P'' \sim Q'')$ will
$$Q \sim P$$

Now consider agents with inaction; for example: the previous agent with $P' = P'' = Q' = Q'' = \mathbb{0}$.

example
Checking $(P \sim Q)$, where

$$P \stackrel{\text{def}}{=} \alpha : P_1 \qquad\qquad Q \stackrel{\text{def}}{=} \alpha : Q_1$$
$$P_1 \stackrel{\text{def}}{=} 1 : \mathbb{0} + \beta : \mathbb{0} \qquad\qquad Q_1 \stackrel{\text{def}}{=} 1 : \mathbb{0} + \beta : \mathbb{0}$$

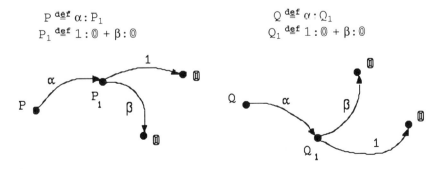

In their initial states P and Q engage in the same α action, but will only be in bisimulation, $(P{\sim}Q)$, if their successor states P_1 and Q_1 are in bisimulation, $(P_1{\sim}Q_1)$. In states P_1 and Q_1 they can engage in the same 1 and β actions and are in bisimulation as $\mathbb{0}{\sim}\mathbb{0}$. Working backwards, the full bisimulation relation is:

$$\sim = \{\,(P,Q)\,,\,(P_1,Q_1)\,,\,(\mathbb{0},\mathbb{0})\,\}$$

As this complete bisimulation relation contains (P,Q) we can declare
$$Q{\sim}P$$

Alternatively we could have included the previous example, where the previously unknown future behaviours are now known, $P'=P''=Q'=Q''=\mathbb{0}$, which gives $(P'{\sim}Q')$ and $(P''{\sim}Q'')$ leading to $Q{\sim}P$.

∎

Note the last example would have the same result if we'd used any bisimilar agents for P',Q' and P'',Q'' including $P'=P''=Q'=Q''=\mathbb{1}$.

example
   Where
$$P \stackrel{\text{def}}{=} \alpha:P_1$$
$$P_1 \stackrel{\text{def}}{=} \chi:P + \beta:P_2$$
$$P_2 \stackrel{\text{def}}{=} 1:\mathbb{0}$$

   and
$$Q \stackrel{\text{def}}{=} \alpha:Q_1$$
$$Q_1 \stackrel{\text{def}}{=} \chi:Q_3 + \beta:Q_2$$
$$Q_2 \stackrel{\text{def}}{=} 1:\mathbb{0}$$
$$Q_3 \stackrel{\text{def}}{=} \alpha:Q_4$$
$$Q_4 \stackrel{\text{def}}{=} \chi:Q_5 + \beta:Q_6$$
$$Q_5 \stackrel{\text{def}}{=} \alpha:Q_4$$
$$Q_6 \stackrel{\text{def}}{=} 1:\mathbb{0}$$

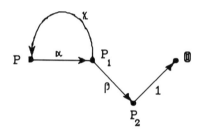

To prove $P{\sim}Q$ we must prove they simulate each other. Starting from their initial states we 'walk through' their actions.

Checking (P, Q)

$$P \xrightarrow{\alpha} P_1 \Rightarrow Q \xrightarrow{\alpha} Q_1$$
$$\text{and } Q \xrightarrow{\alpha} Q_1 \Rightarrow P \xrightarrow{\alpha} P_1$$

giving $\{(P, Q)\} \subseteq \sim$ if $P_1 \sim Q_1$

Checking (P_1, Q_1)

$$P_1 \xrightarrow{\chi} P \Rightarrow Q_1 \xrightarrow{\chi} Q_3$$
$$\text{and } Q_1 \xrightarrow{\chi} Q_3 \Rightarrow P_1 \xrightarrow{\chi} P$$

$$P_1 \xrightarrow{\beta} P_2 \Rightarrow Q_1 \xrightarrow{\beta} Q_2$$
$$\text{and } Q_1 \xrightarrow{\beta} Q_2 \Rightarrow P_1 \xrightarrow{\beta} P_2$$

$\{(P, Q), (P_1, Q_1)\} \subseteq \sim$ if $P \sim Q_3$ and $P_2 \sim Q_2$

Checking (P, Q_3)

$$P \xrightarrow{\alpha} P_1 \Rightarrow Q_3 \xrightarrow{\alpha} Q_4$$
$$\text{and } Q_3 \xrightarrow{\alpha} Q_4 \Rightarrow P \xrightarrow{\alpha} P_1$$

and (P_2, Q_2)

$$P_2 \xrightarrow{1} \mathbb{0} \Rightarrow Q_2 \xrightarrow{1} \mathbb{0}$$
$$\text{and } Q_2 \xrightarrow{1} \mathbb{0} \Rightarrow P_2 \xrightarrow{1} \mathbb{0}$$

$\{(P, Q), (P_1, Q_1), (P, Q_3), (P_2, Q_2), (\mathbb{0}, \mathbb{0})\} \subseteq \sim$ if $P_1 \sim Q_4$

Checking (P_1, Q_4)

$$P_1 \xrightarrow{\beta} P_2 \Rightarrow Q_4 \xrightarrow{\beta} Q_6$$
$$\text{and } Q_4 \xrightarrow{\beta} Q_6 \Rightarrow P_1 \xrightarrow{\beta} P_2$$

$$P_1 \xrightarrow{\chi} P \Rightarrow Q_4 \xrightarrow{\chi} Q_5$$
$$\text{and } Q_4 \xrightarrow{\chi} Q_5 \Rightarrow P_1 \xrightarrow{\chi} P$$

$\{(P, Q), (P_1, Q_1), (P, Q_3), (P_2, Q_2), (P_1, Q_4), (\mathbb{0}, \mathbb{0})\} \subseteq \sim$ if $P_2 \sim Q_6$ and $P \sim Q_5$

Checking (P_2, Q_6)

$$P_2 \xrightarrow{1} \mathbb{0} \Rightarrow Q_6 \xrightarrow{1} \mathbb{0}$$
$$\text{and } Q_6 \xrightarrow{1} \mathbb{0} \Rightarrow P_2 \xrightarrow{1} \mathbb{0}$$

and (P, Q_5)

$$\text{if } P \xrightarrow{\alpha} P_1 \Rightarrow Q_5 \xrightarrow{\alpha} Q_4$$
$$\text{if } Q_5 \xrightarrow{\alpha} Q_4 \Rightarrow P \xrightarrow{\alpha} P_1$$

$\{(P, Q), (P_1, Q_1), (P, Q_3), (P_2, Q_2), (P_1, Q_4), (P_2, Q_6), (P, Q_5), (\mathbb{0}, \mathbb{0})\} \subseteq \sim$ if $P_1 \sim Q_4$.

But, as (P_1, Q_4) is already in the bisimulation, we've finished, giving the complete bisimulation relation:

$$\{(P, Q), (P_1, Q_1), (P, Q_3), (P_2, Q_2), (P_1, Q_4), (P_2, Q_6), (P, Q_5), (\mathbb{0}, \mathbb{0})\}$$

Each action in each state of each agent can be simulated by an action of the other in an associated state, and, as the relation contains (P, Q) we have:

$$P \sim Q$$

The states of the two systems which are in bisimulation
$$(P \sim Q \sim Q_3 \sim Q_5) , \quad (P_1 \sim Q_1 \sim Q_4) \text{ and } (P_2 \sim Q_2 \sim Q_6)$$
are said to be in the same bisimulation class.

■

As one can see, checking if agents are bisimilar isn't difficult, the only real problem is keeping track of those states you've visited and what states to check next. One could employ a stricter regime to ensure one didn't miss things out, as in [Koo91], but it would be much easier to leave the simple and repetitive tasks of an equivalence check to automation, as we will see in the next chapter.

But all is not yet over. Though we may have proved strong bisimulation is an equivalence, we have yet to prove it can be used to equate expressions. To prove two agents equal we have to prove they have the same behaviour in all circumstances, whatever environment they find themselves in, and to do this we have to prove they are not just equivalent but congruent, which leads to the following question.

Is ~ a Congruence?

To prove ~ is a congruence we have to show that expressions declared bisimilar when placed in the same context result in equivalent systems; that is, if $Expr_1 \sim Expr_2$ then in all relevant contexts $C[\![ ]\!]$ we need to prove that
$$(Expr_1 \sim Expr_2) \Rightarrow (C[\![Expr_1]\!] \sim C[\![Expr_2]\!])$$

In our case the appropriate contexts are those formed by the SCCS operators themselves. For example, it has to be proved that, given $(Expr_1 \sim Expr_2)$, $(Expr_1) \backslash \alpha \sim (Expr_2) \backslash \alpha$, and this has to be shown for all combinations of the relevant operators, the relevant operators being the irreducible set from which all other operators can be defined. Prasad, in [Pra90],[†] defined this minimum set to be prefix, product, summation and restriction, and Milner showed ~ to be a congruence over them, and in particular that

1) $E \sim F$ implies $a : E \sim a : F$, $E \times G \sim F \times G$, $E \hat{~} A \sim F \hat{~} A$,
2) $\mathbb{E} \sim \mathbb{F}$ implies $\Sigma \mathbb{E} \sim \Sigma \mathbb{F}$, $fix_i \mathbb{X} \mathbb{E} \sim fix_i \mathbb{X} \mathbb{F}$.

Having defined ~ as a congruence over agents, the quotient $\mathcal{P}/\sim$, where $\mathcal{P}$ is the class of agents, helps define the SCCS as a pair of Abelian[††] monoids and laws over choice and product.

---

† Prasad in [Pra90] established the irreducible set of independent SCCS operators by finding out which of them cannot be derived from others.

†† (Aside) The class of $\mathcal{P}$ of agents, together with the operator product ($\times$) and the identity element $\mathbb{1}$, form an Abelian monoid $(\mathcal{P}/\sim, \times, \mathbb{1})$, named after the mathematician N. H. Abel (1802-29).

(continued)

1) $(\mathcal{P}/\sim, \times, \mathbb{1})$
2) $(\mathcal{P}/\sim, +, \mathbb{0})$
3) $P \times \mathbb{0} \sim \mathbb{0}$ and $P \times (Q + R) \sim P \times Q + P \times R$.
4) $P + P \sim P$.

Once each basic SCCS operator is shown to maintain its equality in the context of others, we are able to raise certain equivalences between SCCS expressions to propositions. These propositions, by placing existing congruent expressions in congruent environments, can be used to define new propositions over new operators.

Strong bisimulation, $\sim$, is a formal equivalence between SCCS expressions, and we should replace the = we've previously used in propositions with the more correct $\sim$. For example proposition $\times 1$, $P \times Q = Q \times P$, should read $P \times Q \sim Q \times P$. But as = has a longer history of meaning 'the same as', we will continue in its use, remembering that = is a particular form of congruence based on strong bisimulation, not to be confused with other equalities based on different ways of observing systems – one of which we are about to consider.

5.3.3 Observational Equivalence

We differentiate between objects only if they are observed to have different behaviours. In the world of process algebras, if a third agent, the observer, cannot detect any difference between two agents, we declare them equal. But different observers can detect different things. For strong congruence to check timings, the observer 'sees' all actions, both internal 1 and external a!, a?, ..., etc. ones.[†] Such an observer is synchronous; by acknowledging internal actions, the observer has the same concept of time as the agents it observes and would be able to differentiate between $1 : a : \mathbb{0}$ and $a : \mathbb{0}$ in particular and $1 : P$ and P in general. By ignoring 1 actions, destroying timing information, such an observer views agents as black boxes; it can distinguish the order external actions come in, but not when they occur or what is going on 'inside the box'.

But is comparing systems by external behaviour alone of any benefit? If we

(continues)
(Another aside)
- A set with a total associative operator is called a *semigroup*.
- A semigroup with an identity element is called a *monoid*.
- A monoid whose operator is commutative is called an *Abelian monoid*.

As agents are associative under $\times$, $P \times Q = Q \times P$, $\mathbb{1}$ is the identity agent under $\times$, $\mathbb{1} \times \mathbb{1} = \mathbb{1}$, and agents are commutative under $\times$, $(P \times Q) \times R = P \times (Q \times R)$, then we have the Abelian monoid $(\mathcal{P}/\sim, \times, \mathbb{1})$. The same holds for $(\mathcal{P}/\sim, +, \mathbb{0})$.

[†] Note: to avoid clutter in the rest of this section, where convenient we'll dispense with the input/output qualifiers and simply write a for external actions a? and a!.

express a system specification, *Specification*, in terms of a required input–output behaviour, then implementation, *Imp*, could be said to satisfy *Specification* if it has the same external behaviour as an ordering of external events. For some systems we're not interested in when things happen, and we only need assurance that they will, or will not, happen. For example, for a system to be live we want that resource to be granted at some time in the future. For other systems we are only interested in their 'black box' behaviour – we need to know that certain outputs result from certain inputs, rather than what goes on inside to make this happen. A unit which satisfactorily multiplies two integer numbers by a successive addition, and another which uses a look-up table, are the same in terms of what they input and output. Any asynchronous procedure using them would be none the wiser, and we should not distinguish between them.

If we are not concerned with the internal activities of an object, only that certain outputs result from certain inputs, more solutions will be acceptable than if we demand, for example, that so much time must pass between inputs and associated outputs. The specification required by an asynchronous observer will be weaker than that of a synchronous one, and, being weaker, it will be easier to satisfy.

If two agents differ only in the amount of delay between external actions, strong bisimulation is too distinctive. As such asynchronous agents are not strongly congruent, and, to compare them we use a different type of equivalence, we need an observational equivalence, $\approx$, only concerned with observable behaviours, and we write P$\approx$Q if P and Q are observationally equivalent. Just as strong bisimulation was used as the basis for our strong equivalence, we will look for an analogous bisimulation to develop observational equivalence. The most obvious step is simply to ignore all 1 actions by replacing the *Act* in strong bisimulation with Act_{-1} to give bisimulation **O**.

bisimulation O

P **O** Q implies that, for each observable α action, $\alpha \in Act_{-1}$

a)   if P$\xrightarrow{\alpha}$P ', then for some Q ', Q$\xrightarrow{\alpha}$Q ' and P '**O** Q ',
and conversely,

b)   if Q$\xrightarrow{\alpha}$Q ', then for some P ', P$\xrightarrow{\alpha}$P ' and P '**O** Q '

■

Such a bisimulation would accept $1 : a : \mathbb{O}$ and $a : \mathbb{O}$ as equivalent. Just what we want. Unfortunately, this simple approach falls down when it encounters unstable agents; that is, agents which, by internal actions, can autonomously change states. For example, by ignoring internal actions, this bisimulation would not differentiate

$1 : a : \mathbb{0} + b : \mathbb{0}$ and $a : \mathbb{0} + b : \mathbb{0}$

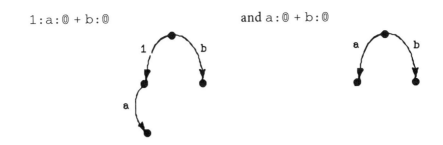

But in real life these agents behave differently. The second can engage in an a or a b action, but the first, if it first performs an internal action, may never engage in b. As in real life, the most obvious solution isn't always the best. We need to rethink.

Perhaps we can equate observable behaviours, not by ignoring what we consider unimportant, but by concentrating on what is important and matching actions with the same visible content. More formally:

> $P \approx Q$ if, for every action of P, visible or invisible, $P \xrightarrow{\alpha} P'$, Q can engage in an α action (surrounded by any number, possibly zero, of internal actions), and move to state Q' such that $P' \approx Q'$. And the same holds if P and Q are interchanged.

To clarify things we introduce a notation $\xRightarrow{\alpha}$, a transition composed of an α action surrounded by any number, possibly zero, of internal actions.

definition $\xRightarrow{\alpha}$

> $Q \xRightarrow{\alpha} Q'$ is equivalent to $Q \xrightarrow{1^*} \xrightarrow{\alpha} \xrightarrow{1^*} Q'$ where 1^* represents zero or more 1 actions.

■

When considering observers which could 'see' all actions we found it useful to refer to next states in terms of derivatives of previous states, for example Q, in $P \xrightarrow{\alpha} Q$, is an α–derivative of P. As this will not translate directly to observers blind to internal actions, we use the term descendants to identify states reached by observable actions alone; for example, in $P \xRightarrow{a} Q$, Q is termed an α-descendant of P.

example

> Where $Q \stackrel{\text{def}}{=} 1 : \alpha : 1 : Q'$
> then the following all hold true
> $$Q \xRightarrow{1} \alpha : 1 : Q'$$
> $$Q \xRightarrow{\alpha} 1 : Q'$$
> $$Q \xRightarrow{\alpha} Q'$$

■

Agents can change state by engaging in external actions or internal actions, or no actions, so, when comparing agents, we have three cases to match:

- we can match a visible action, $P \xrightarrow{a} P'$, $\alpha = <a>$ by action sequence $Q \xrightarrow{<a>} Q'$, the same external action bracketed by any number, including zero, of internal actions, $Q \xrightarrow{1^*} \xrightarrow{a} \xrightarrow{1^*} Q'$;
- we can match $P \rightarrow P'$, $\alpha = <>$, the empty sequence, by action sequence $Q \xrightarrow{<>} Q'$, zero or more internal actions, $Q \xrightarrow{1^*} \xrightarrow{<>} \xrightarrow{1^*} Q'$; (Note: We usually write $P \Rightarrow P'$ for $P \xrightarrow{<>} P'$.)
- we can match an internal action, $P \xrightarrow{1} P'$, $\alpha = 1$ by the action sequence $Q \xrightarrow{1} Q'$, the occurrence of at least one internal action, $Q \xrightarrow{1^*} \xrightarrow{1} \xrightarrow{1^*} Q'$.

We can now formally propose an algorithm for checking an observational bisimulation.

observational bisimulation relation $\mathcal{R}$

P is observationally bisimilar to Q, $Q \mathcal{R} P$, if and only if, for each α action, $\alpha \in \mathcal{A}ct$

a)   if $P \xrightarrow{\alpha} P'$, then for some Q', $Q \xrightarrow{\alpha} Q'$ and $P' \mathcal{R} Q'$,

and conversely

b)   if $Q \xrightarrow{\alpha} Q'$, then for some P', $P \xrightarrow{\alpha} P'$ and $Q' \mathcal{R} P'$.

■

Each single action, internal or external, of P can be matched by a descendant of Q with the same visible content. But is this what we want? This implies that every tick of one agent would have to be matched by a sequence of at least one tick of the other. Under this bisimulation, while we would differentiate $a:P + b:Q$ from $1:a:P + b:Q$, whether it differentiated $1:P$ from P would depend upon the P – it would say $1:a:\mathbb{0}$ and $1:1:a:\mathbb{0}$ were the same but $1:\mathbb{0}$ and $\mathbb{0}$ were different. This is not what we want – but it *is* coming closer.

To get nearer our goal, we modify the previous bisimulation to sort out those 1 actions once and for all.

weak (or observational) bisimulation $\mathcal{W}$

P is weakly bisimilar to Q, $P \mathcal{W} Q$, if and only if, for each α action, $\alpha \in \mathcal{A}ct$

a) if $P \xrightarrow{\alpha} P'$, then either

1) $\alpha = 1$ and $P' \mathcal{W} Q$, or

2) for some Q', $Q \xrightarrow{\alpha} Q'$ and $P' \mathcal{W} Q'$

and conversely,

b) if $Q \xrightarrow{\alpha} Q'$, then either

1) $\alpha = 1$ and $P \mathcal{W} Q'$, or

2) for some P', $P \xrightarrow{\alpha} P'$ and $Q' \mathcal{W} P'$

■

The definition for visible action remains the same, but now each 1 action of P doesn't have to be matched by one or more 1 actions of Q, as long as Q is equivalent to P after P's 1 action; and similarly with P and Q interchanged. Now, under this modification, $\mathcal{W}$ will not distinguish $1:P$ from P but will distinguish $a:P+b:Q$ from $1:a:P+b:Q$.

As in the case of our strong bisimulation, $\mathcal{W}$ cannot be promoted to an equivalence until it has been proved that there is a relation which satisfies its definition, it is the largest, and it is an equivalence. Once again we accept that $\mathcal{W}$ does meet these criteria. We rename $\mathcal{W}$ observational equivalence ≈ and define P≈Q in the following way:

observational equivalence ≈

P≈Q, if and only if, for each α action, $\alpha \in \mathcal{A}ct$

    a) if $P \xrightarrow{\alpha} P'$, then either

        1) $\alpha=1$ and $P' \approx Q$, or

        2) for some Q', $Q \xRightarrow{\alpha} Q'$ and $P' \approx Q'$

  and conversely,

    b) if $Q \xrightarrow{\alpha} Q'$, then either

        1) $\alpha=1$ and $P \approx Q'$, or

        2) for some P', $P \xRightarrow{\alpha} P'$ and $P' \approx Q'$.

■

We can use this newly acquired equivalence to test various theories. For example, is $P \approx 1:P$? Where P can be any agent, we have to consider the case when an agent's initial actions are external, $P=a:Q$; and that when they are internal, $P=1:Q$.

    Checking $(P \approx 1:P)$ in two parts

        Checking $(a:Q, 1:a:Q)$

            $a:Q \xrightarrow{a} Q \Rightarrow 1:a:Q \xRightarrow{a} Q$ and $Q \approx Q$

          $1:a:Q \xrightarrow{1} a:Q$ as $\alpha=1$ we need $a:Q \approx a:Q$

        Checking $(1:Q, 1:1:Q)$

            $1:Q \xrightarrow{1} Q \Rightarrow 1:1:Q' \Rightarrow Q$ and $Q \approx Q$

          $1:1:Q \xrightarrow{1} 1:Q$ as $\alpha=1$ we need $1:Q \approx 1:Q$

    Accepting $Q \approx Q$, $a:Q \approx a:Q$ and $1:Q \approx 1:Q$ we've proved $(P \approx 1:P)$

example

    Where

        $P \xlongequal{\text{def}} 1:P_1$

        $P_1 \xlongequal{\text{def}} a:P_2$

        $P_2 \xlongequal{\text{def}} 1:P_3$

        $P_3 \xlongequal{\text{def}} b:\mathbb{0}$

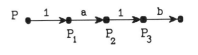

and
$$Q \stackrel{\text{def}}{=} a : Q_1$$
$$Q_1 \stackrel{\text{def}}{=} b : \emptyset$$

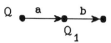

Checking (P, Q)

$$P \stackrel{1}{\longrightarrow} P_1 \text{ as } \alpha=1 \text{ we need } P_1 \approx Q$$
$$\text{and } Q \stackrel{a}{\longrightarrow} Q_1 \Rightarrow P \stackrel{a}{\longrightarrow} P_3 \text{ and } P_3 \approx Q_1$$
giving $\{ (P, Q) \} \subseteq \approx$ if $P_1 \approx Q$ and $P_3 \approx Q_1$

Checking (P_1, Q)

$$P_1 \stackrel{a}{\longrightarrow} P_2 \Rightarrow Q \stackrel{a}{\longrightarrow} Q_1 \text{ and } P_2 \approx Q_1$$
$$Q \stackrel{a}{\longrightarrow} Q_1 \Rightarrow P_1 \stackrel{a}{\longrightarrow} P_3 \text{ and } P_3 \approx Q_1$$
giving $\{ (P, Q), (P_1, Q) \} \subseteq \approx$ if $P_2 \approx Q_1$ and $P_3 \approx Q_1$

Checking (P_2, Q_1)

$$P_2 \stackrel{1}{\longrightarrow} P_3 \text{ as } \alpha=1 \text{ we need } P_3 \approx Q_1$$
$$\text{and } Q_1 \stackrel{b}{\longrightarrow} \emptyset \Rightarrow P_2 \stackrel{b}{\longrightarrow} \emptyset \text{ and } \emptyset \approx \emptyset$$
giving $\{ (P, Q), (P_1, Q), (P_2, Q_1), (\emptyset, \emptyset) \} \subseteq \approx$ if $P_3 \approx Q_1$

Checking (P_3, Q_1)

$$P_3 \stackrel{b}{\longrightarrow} \emptyset \Rightarrow Q_1 \stackrel{b}{\longrightarrow} \emptyset \text{ and } \emptyset \approx \emptyset$$
$$Q_1 \stackrel{b}{\longrightarrow} \emptyset \Rightarrow P_3 \stackrel{b}{\longrightarrow} \emptyset \text{ and } \emptyset \approx \emptyset$$

We've ended up with the complete bisimulation relation
$$\{ (P, Q), (P_1, Q), (P_2, Q_1), (P_3, Q_1), (\emptyset, \emptyset) \}$$

Each action in each state of each agent can be simulated by an action of the other in an associated state, and, as the relation contains (P, Q) we have:
$$P \approx Q$$

The states of the two systems which are in bisimulation, in the same bisimulation class, are
$$(P \approx P_1 \approx Q), (P_2 \approx P_3 \approx Q_1) \text{ and } (\emptyset \approx \emptyset)$$

■

example

Where
$$P \stackrel{\text{def}}{=} a : \emptyset + b : \emptyset$$

and

$$Q \stackrel{\text{def}}{=} 1 : Q_1 + b : 0$$
$$Q_1 \stackrel{\text{def}}{=} a : 0$$

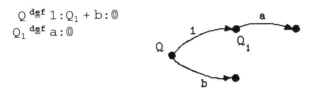

Checking (P, Q)

$P \stackrel{b}{\longrightarrow} 0 \Rightarrow Q \stackrel{b}{\Longrightarrow} 0$ and $0 \approx 0$
and $Q \stackrel{b}{\longrightarrow} 0 \Rightarrow P \stackrel{b}{\Longrightarrow} 0$ and $0 \approx 0$
$P \stackrel{a}{\longrightarrow} 0 \Rightarrow Q \stackrel{a}{\Longrightarrow} 0$ and $0 \approx 0$
and from $Q \stackrel{1}{\longrightarrow} Q_1$ as $\alpha = 1$ we need $P \approx Q_1$

giving $\{ (P, Q), (0, 0) \} \subseteq \approx$ if $P \approx Q_1$

Checking (P, Q_1)

$P \stackrel{a}{\longrightarrow} 0 \Rightarrow Q_1 \stackrel{a}{\Longrightarrow} 0$ and $0 \approx 0$
$Q_1 \stackrel{a}{\longrightarrow} 0 \Rightarrow P \stackrel{a}{\Longrightarrow} 0$ and $0 \approx 0$
$P \stackrel{b}{\longrightarrow} 0 \Rightarrow Q_1 \stackrel{b}{\Longrightarrow} ?$

While P can always engage in an a or a b, Q_1 cannot. The bisimulation is incomplete and

$$\neg (P \approx Q)$$

∎

example

Where

$$P \stackrel{\text{def}}{=} a : P_1 + a : P_2$$
$$P_1 \stackrel{\text{def}}{=} b : P_1$$
$$P_2 \stackrel{\text{def}}{=} 1 : P_3$$
$$P_3 \stackrel{\text{def}}{=} b : P_3$$

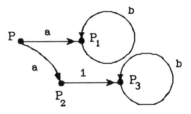

and

$$Q \stackrel{\text{def}}{=} a : Q_1$$
$$Q_1 \stackrel{\text{def}}{=} 1 : Q_2$$
$$Q_2 \stackrel{\text{def}}{=} 1 : Q_3$$
$$Q_3 \stackrel{\text{def}}{=} b : Q_3$$

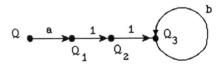

To prove agent P and Q behaviourally equivalent we must prove that they weakly simulate each other. Starting from their initial states we 'walk through' their actions.

Checking (P,Q)

$$P\xrightarrow{a}P_1 \Rightarrow Q\xRightarrow{a}Q_3 \text{ and } P_1\approx Q_3$$
$$\text{and } Q\xrightarrow{a}Q_1 \Rightarrow P\xRightarrow{a}P_1 \text{ and } P_1\approx Q_1$$
$$P\xrightarrow{a}P_2 \Rightarrow Q\xRightarrow{a}Q_3 \text{ and } P_2\approx Q_3$$
$$\text{and } Q\xrightarrow{a}Q_1 \Rightarrow P\xRightarrow{a}P_3 \text{ and } P_3\approx Q_1$$

giving $\{(P,Q)\}\subseteq\approx$ if $P_1\approx Q_1$, $P_1\approx Q_3$, $P_2\approx Q_3$ and $P_3\approx Q_1$

Checking (P_1,Q_1)

$$P_1\xrightarrow{b}P_1 \Rightarrow Q_1\xRightarrow{b}Q_3 \text{ and } P_1\approx Q_3$$
$$\text{and from } Q_1\xrightarrow{1}Q_2 \text{ as } \alpha=1 \text{ we need } P_1\approx Q_2$$

$\{(P,Q),(P_1,Q_1)\}\subseteq\approx$ if $P_1\approx Q_2$, $P_1\approx Q_3$, $P_2\approx Q_3$ and $P_3\approx Q_1$

Checking (P_1,Q_2)

$$P_1\xrightarrow{b}P_1 \Rightarrow Q_2\xRightarrow{b}Q_3 \text{ and } P_1\approx Q_3$$
$$\text{and from } Q_2\xrightarrow{1}Q_3 \text{ as } \alpha=1 \text{ we need } P_1\approx Q_3$$

$\{(P,Q),(P_1,Q_1),(P_1,Q_2)\}\subseteq\approx$ if $P_1\approx Q_3$, $P_2\approx Q_3$ and $P_3\approx Q_1$

Checking (P_1,Q_3)

$$P_1\xrightarrow{b}P_1 \Rightarrow Q_3\xRightarrow{b}Q_3 \text{ and } P_1\approx Q_3$$
$$\text{and } Q_3\xrightarrow{b}Q_3 \Rightarrow P_1\xRightarrow{b}P_1 \text{ and } P_1\approx Q_3$$

$\{(P,Q),(P_1,Q_1),(P_1,Q_2),(P_1,Q_3)\}\subseteq\approx$ if $P_2\approx Q_3$ and $P_3\approx Q_1$

Checking (P_2,Q_3)

$$P_2\xrightarrow{1}P_3 \text{ as } \alpha=1 \text{ we need } P_3\approx Q_3$$
$$\text{and } Q_3\xrightarrow{b}Q_3 \Rightarrow P_2\xRightarrow{b}P_3 \text{ and } P_3\approx Q_3$$

$\{(P,Q),(P_1,Q_1),(P_1,Q_2),(P_1,Q_3),(P_2,Q_3)\}\subseteq\approx$
if $P_3\approx Q_1$ and $P_3\approx Q_3$

Checking (P_3,Q_1)

$$P_3\xrightarrow{b}P_3 \Rightarrow Q_1\xRightarrow{b}Q_3 \text{ and } P_3\approx Q_3$$
$$\text{and from } Q_1\xrightarrow{1}Q_2 \text{ as } \alpha=1 \text{ we need } P_3\approx Q_2$$

$\{(P,Q),(P_1,Q_1),(P_1,Q_2),(P_1,Q_3),(P_2,Q_3),(P_3,Q_1)\}\subseteq\approx$
if $P_3\approx Q_2$ and $P_3\approx Q_3$

Checking (P_3,Q_2)

$$P_3\xrightarrow{b}P_3 \Rightarrow Q_2\xRightarrow{b}Q_3 \text{ and } P_3\approx Q_3$$
$$\text{and from } Q_2\xrightarrow{1}Q_3 \text{ as } \alpha=1 \text{ we need } P_3\approx Q_3$$

$\{ (P,Q), (P_1,Q_1), (P_1,Q_2), (P_1,Q_3), (P_2,Q_3), (P_3,Q_1), (P_3,Q_2) \} \subseteq \approx$
if $P_3 \approx Q_3$

Checking (P_3, Q_3)

$$P_3 \xrightarrow{\text{b}} P_3 \Rightarrow Q_3 \xRightarrow{\text{b}} Q_3 \text{ and } P_3 \approx Q_3$$
$$\text{and } Q_3 \xrightarrow{\text{b}} Q_3 \Rightarrow P_3 \xRightarrow{\text{b}} P_3 \text{ and } P_3 \approx Q_3$$

We've finished with the bisimulation relation

$$\{ (P,Q), (P_1,Q_1), (P_1,Q_2), (P_1,Q_3), (P_2,Q_3),$$
$$(P_3,Q_1), (P_3,Q_2), (P_3,Q_3) \}$$

Each action in each state of each agent can be simulated by an action of the other in an associated state, and, as the relation contains (P,Q) we have

$$P \approx Q$$

with bisimulation classes

$$(P \approx Q) \text{ and } (P_1 \approx P_2 \approx P_3 \approx Q_1 \approx Q_2 \approx Q_3)$$

∎

Now we have two forms of equivalence, strong ~, based on strong bisimulation, and observational $\approx$, based on weak bisimulation.

- Strong bisimulation is a relationship comparing both internal and external behaviours, and can be used to compare real-time expressions. This view is inherited by strong congruence ~ which it fathers.
- Weak bisimulation is a relation which compares only the external behaviours of agents. This view is inherited by observational equivalence $\approx$ which it fathers.

Observational equivalence contains less information that strong equivalence and, as such, is a weaker form of equivalence; if we prove two systems strongly equivalent they are also weakly equivalent, but the same does not always hold the other way round. More formally, strong equivalence implies observational equivalence.

proposition

$$(\mathit{Expr}_1 \sim \mathit{Expr}_2) \Rightarrow (\mathit{Expr}_1 \approx \mathit{Expr}_2)$$

∎

The set of systems found equivalent under strong bisimulation contains, as a subset, systems equivalent under weak bisimulation, $\approx \subseteq \sim$.

Having shown we can use observational equivalence to compare systems, we now need to see if it can be extended to a congruence.

Is ≈ a congruence?

To shown an equivalence is also a congruence for a particular set of behaviours, we need to account for the equivalence in all possible contexts $C[\![\ ]\!]$ formed by those behaviours. The SCCS contexts we need to examine are that for prefix, $a:[\![\ ]\!]$, summation $[\![\ ]\!]+R$, product $[\![\ ]\!]\times R$, and restriction $[\![\ ]\!]\wedge A$. For each context we have to prove that

$$(\mathit{Expr}_1 \approx \mathit{Expr}_2) \Rightarrow (C[\![\mathit{Expr}_1]\!] \approx C[\![\mathit{Expr}_2]\!])$$

For example, if $(\mathit{Expr}_1 \approx \mathit{Expr}_2)$ then $(a:\mathit{Expr}_1 \approx a:\mathit{Expr}_2)$, $(\mathit{Expr} + \mathit{Expr}_1 \approx \mathit{Expr} + \mathit{Expr}_2)$, and so on. Unfortunately an equivalence is not automatically a congruence, and so it proves with ≈. While $(\mathit{Expr}_1 \approx \mathit{Expr}_2)$, it does not always follow that $(\mathit{Expr} + \mathit{Expr}_1 \approx \mathit{Expr} + \mathit{Expr}_2)$. Consider agents $a:\mathbb{0}$ and $1:a:\mathbb{0}$ in context $C[\![\ ]\!] = [\![\ ]\!] + b:\mathbb{0}$; while $a:\mathbb{0} \approx 1:a:\mathbb{0}$ agent $(a:\mathbb{0} + b:\mathbb{0})$ can engage in a or b but $(1:a.\mathbb{0} + b:\mathbb{0})$, by engaging in the hidden 1 action, can autonomously reject the b action. So

$$\neg ((\mathit{Expr}_1 \approx \mathit{Expr}_2) \Rightarrow (\mathit{Expr} + \mathit{Expr}_1 \approx \mathit{Expr} + \mathit{Expr}_2))$$

More subtly, $a:\mathbb{0}$ and $1:a:\mathbb{0}$ in context $C[\![\ ]\!] = [\![\ ]\!] \times b:\mathbb{0}$, though $a:\mathbb{0} \approx 1:a:\mathbb{0}$ the agent $(a:\mathbb{0} \times b:\mathbb{0})$ can engage axb but $(1:a:\mathbb{0} \times b:\mathbb{0})$ cannot. So

$$\neg ((\mathit{Expr}_1 \approx \mathit{Expr}_2) \Rightarrow (\mathit{Expr} \times \mathit{Expr}_1 \approx \mathit{Expr} \times \mathit{Expr}_2))$$

While rejecting ≈ as a congruence, $\approx^c$, it was almost there. Only when combining unstable agents under summation or product does it break down. The difference between ≈ and a congruence is thus only a matter of the initial actions of agents – if the agents combined are stable, ≈ is a congruence.

proposition
   If P and Q are stable and P ≈ Q then P $\approx^c$ Q

■

We can thus promote ≈ to a congruence if we insist that only expressions guarded by external actions are considered. This is sufficient for most purposes and is the limit to which we can push things within SCCS. We can, however, strengthen our observational equality, and turn it into a congruence, if we step outside of strict SCCS and relax its timing constraints to create an asynchronous algebra, ASCCS.

5.3.4 Observational Congruence

Just as the ~ equivalence, based on a synchronous observer, was used to define the synchronous algebra SCCS, an equivalence based on an asynchronous observer can define an asynchronous version ASCCS. But how do we introduce asynchronicity into SCCS? An obvious step would be to prefix each action with the delay operator and ignore internal actions when we compare expressions. This would change expressions like $a:b:0$, in which b immediately follows a, into $\delta a:\delta b:\delta 0$, which can delay indefinitely before a and b. But, again, the obvious way isn't always the best. There's a problem. If we add the delay operator to all actions when we combine agents by summation we will *always* get an unstable result. For example, combining $P = \delta a:\delta P$ and $Q = \delta b:\delta Q$ the resultant $(\delta a:\delta P + \delta b:\delta Q)$ can perform an internal action

$$(\delta a:\delta P + \delta b:\delta Q) \bullet \xrightarrow{\quad 1 \quad} \bullet (\delta a:\delta P)$$

The unseen action autonomously rejects one of the behaviours. Just as an unstable agent is one which can ignore its environment, autonomously choosing its future behaviour, a stable agent can be controlled by its environment. To be stable, subject to environmental influence, the guards at the point of choice must be observable. We can prevent the introduction of instabilities into ASCCS by ensuring that, during conversion, SCCS agents like $a:P$ are converted into $a:\delta P$ and not $\delta a:\delta P$.

While this definition does preserve strong congruence, it doesn't preserve all SCCS operators: in particular, prefix, and we have to revise our old prefix $a:$ into $a.$ where $a.E$ behaves identically to $a:\delta E$ – which does conform to the definition and the congruence.

We can now define the basic syntax of this asynchronous algebra, called ASCCS, by:
$$E ::= X \mid a.E \mid \delta E \mid \Sigma E \mid E{\times}E \mid E{\char`^}A \mid \text{fix}_i XE$$

> Plus a new operator over agents such that ΔP behaves like P except that it can delay between any of its actions. ΔP has derivation rule

$$\frac{E \xrightarrow{a} E'}{\Delta E \xrightarrow{a} \delta \Delta E'}$$

ΔP prefixes all but the initial action of P with δ. For example $P \overset{\text{def}}{=} a:b:0$ in SCCS becomes $\Delta P \overset{\text{def}}{=} a.b.0$ in ASCCS.

Now, if two asynchronous agents differ only in the amount of delay between actions, they cannot be told apart by an observer who cannot distinguish between hidden action sequence lengths. If $P \overset{\text{def}}{=} a:\delta b:\delta 0$ and $Q \overset{\text{def}}{=} a:\delta 1:\delta b:\delta 0$ both can delay indefinitely between their a and b actions, but, while in P that delay can be of length zero, in Q it must be of length at least one. However, an asynchronous observer, blind to how long delays are, will not differentiate P from Q. As such, asynchronous processes like P and Q are no longer strongly congruent, and, to compare them, we require a different type of congruence. We need an observational congruence $\approx^c$, mainly concerned with the external or so-called observable behaviour of agents, where $P\approx^c Q$ if P and Q are observationally congruent.

observational congruence $\approx^c$

P $\approx^c$ Q, if, for each α action, $\alpha \in \mathcal{A}ct$

a) if P$\xrightarrow{\alpha}$P' then, for some Q', Q$\xrightarrow{\alpha}\Longrightarrow$Q' and P'$\approx$Q'

and conversely,

b) if Q$\xrightarrow{\alpha}$Q' then, for some P', P$\xrightarrow{\alpha}\Longrightarrow$P' and P'$\approx$Q'

■

This definition of $\approx^c$ imposes a stronger condition than $\approx$. Whilst the initial actions of P and Q still have to be exactly matched, it is only necessary to prove P'$\approx$Q' for subsequent actions. But, as this definition allows us to ignore internal actions, it is a weaker relation than strong bisimulation, $\sim$. Giving the hierarchy of equivalence relations:

proposition

$$(\mathcal{E}xpr_1 \sim \mathcal{E}xpr_2) \Rightarrow (\mathcal{E}xpr_1 \approx^c \mathcal{E}xpr_2) \Rightarrow (\mathcal{E}xpr_1 \approx \mathcal{E}xpr_2)$$

■

The congruence relation, $\approx^c$, lies somewhere between $\approx$ and $\sim$. such that $\approx \subseteq \approx^c \subseteq \sim$. However, the only contexts for which $\approx^c$ is valid are asynchronous ones; in other words, $\approx^c$ is only valid within the context of ASCCS. In [Mil83] Milner declared $\approx^c$ to be both an equivalence and a congruence, albeit one restricted to the asynchronous expressions of ASCCS.

Endnote

By relaxing the need to observe certain internal actions, we have weakened the strong equivalence of SCCS in which all actions are compared, in the direction of observational equivalence where only eternal behaviours are compared. Though, by weakening our equivalence, only comparing external, mainly input/output, behaviours, we have lost the ability to equate timings, having two forms of equivalence gives us the best of both worlds. We can check if designs meet real-time criteria by using strong equivalence, and test their atemporal properties using the simpler observational equivalence.

Equating agents by observed behaviours alone gives us a congruence effective within the asynchronous algebra ASCCS. Of additional interest is that, by imposing further constraints on ASCCS and considering only non-overlapping actions, ASCCS becomes isomorphic to Milner's asynchronous algebra CCS, the family resemblance being reinforced in [Mil89] where, after an in-depth presentation of CCS, the author then refines CCS in the direction of synchronous algebras – the same path as we have taken, although in the opposite direction.

In all cases, agents have been compared by some form of bisimulation. The concept of bisimulation, with its simple and repetitive parts, is ideal for mechanisation. Researchers at Edinburgh University were among the first to explore this in their Concurrency Workbench, initially aimed at CCS but later expanded to encompass TSCCS, Meije and SCCS. Its usefulness as a design tool is explored in the next chapter.

6. Automating SCCS

The process of manually checking SCCS formula is time-consuming, repetitive and error prone; one slip at the beginning and the whole thing is wrong. What we need is an automated tool to take out both tedium and errors, and the sort of automated tool we would wish for would be interactive, and intuitive; would help novices to learn about SCCS; would help designers explore the behaviour of SCCS agents; would check the emergent behaviours of combinations of agents; would help us compare both-real time and observational behaviours of agents; and ultimately would check if designs meet their specifications. A tool which goes a long way to meet these objectives is the Concurrency Work Bench (CWB) produced by those nice people at the Laboratory for the Foundation of Computer Science (LFCS), at the University of Edinburgh, and most of this chapter is devoted to its use.

6.0 Concurrency Work Bench: an Introduction

The Concurrency Work Bench is a tool to support the automatic verification of finite-state processes. It supports the analysis of processes written in TCCS, Temporal CCS – a super set of CCS – as well as in CCS and SCCS.[†] Copies of the workbench are available over the Internet: the current web page, to be found at `http://www.dcs.ed.ac.uk`, gives instructions upon how to get a copy of CWB, the user manual [Mol94] and the relevant papers. How the workbench does what it does is not explored in this chapter; if you are interested, you should refer to [ClPaSt94]. Our main interest here is to see how we can use the workbench to investigate, compare and verify SCCS agents.

We want to use the concurrency work bench for several things.

- As an interactive tool to assist users to explore the behaviour of an agent: to find its sort; its state space; its initial actions; to unroll (action by action) its transition graph; to see if it is stable, free of deadlocks; to see if it diverges; and so on.

---

† For the extension of CWB to cover SCCS we have to thank Faron Moller, who was then with Edinburgh University's LFCS.

- To determine the result of agent composition, the emergent behaviour of a system, so that we can check our 'pencil and paper' predictions.
- To compare agent behaviours using bisimulation – strong bisimulation to compare real-time behaviours and weak bisimulation for observable behaviours. With such comparisons we will also be able to check the special bisimulations on which we can base higher-order laws.
- To compare agents with modal logic specifications, using strong forms to check if an agent has specific properties at specific times, and weaker forms to check less temporal concerns.

We will explore these uses of CWB in the next three sections, but first we will describe the dialect of SCCS used by CWB.

SCCS syntax according to CWB

Although the workbench supports a cut-down version of SCCS, the basic elements of SCCS remain the same. CWB's SCCS is still about synchronous agents which engage in a mixture of external and internal particles, but CWB has its own interpretation of SCCS syntax, complementary to the other algebras it supports and rather different both from Milners original and that used in this text.

The CWB syntax of SCCS particles, actions and agents is as follows:

Agent Names can be any collection of printable characters, each name to start with an uppercase letter. Certain characters which cannot be used in names are: ':', ',', '=', '@', '$', '(', ')', '[', ']', '{', '}', '/', '\', '+', '|', '#', '*', a space, a tab, or a carriage return.

Particulate Action Names can be any sequence of printable characters whose first character is not an uppercase letter. Inverse particles are prefixed by a single quotation mark. (In our version we've used a?=a and a!=`a.)

```
PARTICLE p ::= name        : cannot start with
                           : uppercase letter
             | `name       : coname
```

Actions are either empty observations eps, an internal action 1, particles, non-negative powers of a particle, or products of particles and/or actions.

```
ACT a ::= eps     : empty observation (for weak
                  : modalities)
        | 1       : tick (for strong modalities)
        | p       : particle
        | p^n     : exponentiation, n a positive
                  : integer
        | a#a     : product
```

SCCS process constructors are:

Nil the constant 0 represents the SCCS agent with no further actions
(our version ⓪);

Bottom the constant @ is the SCCS agent ⊥, divergence. It represents
'infinite internal computation' or 'undefinedness';

Action Prefix the agent a : A represents the agent A prefixed by action a;

Summation if $A_1, A_2, ..., A_n$ are agents then $A_1 + A_2 + ... + A_n$ is also an
agent;

Delay the agent $A represents an agent which can delay indefinitely before
behaving as agent A, $A = A + 1 : $A (our version δA);

Product if $A_1, A_2, ..., A_n$ are agents, then their parallel combination $A_1 \mid A_2$
$\mid ... \mid A_n$ is also an agent (our version $A_1 \times A_2$);

Restriction if A is an agent and $p, p_1, ..., p_n$ are particles and S is a set of
particles, then A\p is an agent whose behaviour is restricted to
external action p; A\ $\{p_1, p_1, ..., p_n\}$ to external actions $\{p_1, p_1, ...,$
$p_n\}$ and A\ S to the external actions in set S (our version
A^{p!,p?}; there is no direct equivalent to \\a);

Morphism if A is an agent, $a_1, ..., a_n$ and $b_1, ..., b_n$ particles and/or
actions, then A[b/a] is agent A with all particles and/or actions
named a (including `a) replaced by b (including `b) actions, similarly
for A[$a_1/b_1, ..., a_n/b_n$], (we also use A[ψ] where ψ : a→b).

An agent previously represented as P $\stackrel{def}{=}$ a? : (b! . c? : ⓪ + c! : P×Q))
^{a!,a?} would be submitted to CWB as P = a : (`b#c : 0 + `c : P|Q)\{a}.
Unfortunately there is no direct way of representing *Pruning* or *Parameter Passing*.

With regard to precedence,[†] summation binds weakest, then product, prefixing,
restriction and morphism; all of which can be changed by appropriate bracketing.

example

A machine which can deliver two types of stamp

    STAMP $\stackrel{def}{=}$ δ(xcoin? : xstamp! : STAMP + ycoin? : ystamp! : STAMP)

can be instantiated into the example in Chapter 5 which dispensed 10p and

---

[†] The binding of the delay operator in CWB is rather different from our usage. In CWB, $
binds weaker than other operators, such that: $a:$P=$(a:$P)); δP+Q=$(P+Q);
δP×Q=$(P×Q).

20p stamps by

```
10/20_STAMP def STAMP[xstamp/10pstamp,xcoin/10pcoin,
                         ystamp/20pstamp,ycoin/20pcoin]
        = δ(10pcoin?:10pstamp!:10/20_STAMP
                         + 20pcoin?:20pstamp!:10/20_STAMP)
```

A customer wanting a 10p stamp is

```
10CUSTOMER def 10pcoin!:δ10pstamp?:10CUSTOMER
```

In (10/20_STAMP × 10CUSTOMER) the customer will synchronise with the 10p actions of the machine paying for and getting a 10p stamp. To prune unsuccessful actions we'd define the total system as

```
SYS def (10/20_STAMP × 10CUSTOMER)\\A
A = {10pcoin,10pstamp,20pcoin,20pstamp}
```

For CWB we need to translate the above to

```
STAMP def $(xcoin:'xstamp:STAMP + ycoin:'ystamp:STAMP)
```
and
```
STAMPS def STAMP[xstamp/10pstamp, xcoin/10pcoin,
                   ystamp/20pstamp, ycoin/20pcoin]
CUST def '10pcoin:$10pstamp:CUST
```

As there is no direct equivalent to pruning in CWB we have to use the equivalent in terms of a 'restriction to' set of allowed actions; in this case pruning all external actions is equivalent to allowing none:

```
SYS def (STAMPS|CUST)\{}
```

■

CWB does not, as yet, handle parametrised actions, a?x or a!v. Instead we have to go back to basics and 'spell out' such transactions with a set of separate actions, a pair for each for each parameter.

example

A memory element, capable of acting as a binary variable, can be written, overwritten and read any time after initialisation, is defined as

```
VARINIT def δin?x:VAR
VAR def δ(in?x:VAR + out!x:VAR)
```
where x∈{true,false}.

The CWB equivalent requires two agents, one for each binary variable:

```
VARINT def $('var_write_true:VART + 'var_write_false:VARF)
VART def $(var_read_true:VART + 'var_write_true:VART
                   + 'var_write_false:VARF)
```

$$VARF \stackrel{\text{def}}{=} \$(var\_read\_false:VARF + `var\_write\_false:VARF$$
$$+ `var\_write\_true:VART)$$

A successful `var_write_true is equivalent to writing the value true to the variable and a successful var_read_true is equivalent to reading the value true. Similarly, actions var_write_false and `var_read_false emulate the reading and writing of false.

■

The lack of such shorthands makes CWB rather ungainly as a design tool; however, its relative ease of use, its low cost, and its interactive facilities – which make SCCS come alive – far outweigh this slight disadvantage.

6.1 CWB and Agent Behaviours

The syntax of SCCS relates to the real world. In this section we use CWB to help us understand SCCS and how to use it to model real-world behaviours correctly, as only when once we're sure of our ground can we proceed and combine our subsystems.

Interfacing to CWB
To start the workbench in SCCS mode we use the command:

```
Command: cwb sccs
```

Once activated, the workbench prompts for input with a 'Command:'. To signal that user input is ready for evaluation, user responses are terminated by a ';'.

Once CWB is running, a most useful command is:

```
Command: help;
```

then just follow the directions for specific assistance. The next most useful command for graceful, or even hurried, retreats from the system is:

```
Command: quit;
```

which exits CWB, returning the user to the Unix command level.

CWB has a suite of commands which allows the user to define a working environment for a session. These include commands to create agents and action sets, combine agents, analyse agent behaviour and review the state of the environment at any time. What follows is a selection of these commands used in this text; for more detail go to the source of your own CWB or the documents produced by the LFCS, at Edinburgh University.

Agent Environment Commands

`agent;`   binds a given identifier to a given agent. Without the definition part it prints what's currently bound to the identifier.

    `Command: agent A = a:0;`
    `Command: agent A;`
        `** Agents **`
    `agent A = a.0`

`set;`   binds a given identifier to a given set of actions. Without the definition part it prints what's currently bound to the identifier.

    `Command: set S = {a,b,c};`
    `Command: set S;`
        `** Agents **`
    `set S = {a,b,c}`

`print;`   prints all bindings of all working environments.

`clear;`   removes all current bindings from all environments.

Bindings are dynamic. For example, binding a behaviour to an agent name already in use will overwrite the old binding and have a 'knock-on' effect, in that the behaviour of all other agents defined in terms of the changed agent will also be changed. The `clear` command clears the decks by removing all bindings.

All CWB actions are particles, atomic operationally and over time. Composites are constructed using the binary infix # operator. For example, the composite a#b represents the simultaneous execution of the a and b particles.

Actions in CWB responses come in two flavours, observable external actions, denoted $==$ a $\Longrightarrow$, and the occurrence of both internal and external actions, shown as $—$ a $\rightarrow$.

Once we have defined (and manipulated) our environment, we can ask questions about its current state using derivative and analysis commands.

Derivative Commands

transitions(A); lists the (one-step) transitions of agent A.

derivatives(a,A); lists the agents reachable from A via action a.

closure(a,A); lists the agents reachable from A via action a, where a can be any action including eps.

closure(a,b,…,A); lists the agents reachable from A via the observation a, b, …, where the sequence a, b, … can only be observable actions.

init A; lists the observable action that A can perform next.

obs(n,A); lists all action sequences of length n from A and the final state of each. Only works if agent state space finite.

vs(n,A); lists all visible action sequences of length n from A, if agent state space finite.

Analysis Commands

`stable A;` returns `true` if A is stable (A can initially perform only observable external actions), `false` otherwise.

`diverges A;` returns `true` if A contains an unguarded (by an observable action) of bottom.

`freevars A;` lists the free variables of an agent.

`sort A;` prints the sort of an agent.

`size A;` prints the number of states of an agent, if finite.

`states A;` lists the state space, the reachable states, of an agent, if finite.

`statesexp A;` lists the state space of a given agent, if finite, and for each such state a sequence of actions to get there from the initial state is printed.

`statesobs A;` lists the state space of an agent, if finite, and for each such state a sequence of observable actions to get there from the initial state.

`findinit (a,b,…,A);` lists the states of given agent which have actions a, b, … as initial observable actions. Only works if agent state space finite.

`deadlocks A;` prints any deadlock states of an agent. For each deadlocked state the sequence of actions from the initial state is printed.

`deadlocksobs A;` as "`deadlocks A`" but with observable action sequences.

Interfacing the workbench with the Unix file system gives the user the capability of saving working environments for later recall as well as session outputs for printing, and so on.

File Handling Commands

save "filename"; writes into named file the current workbench
environments in a form suitable for the workbench to read back
using the input command. Files can be nested within files.

input "filename"; read file previously created by the save
command and use the definitions it contains to update current
environments.

output "filename"; redirects the output of all subsequent
commands from stdout to "filename". Without a file name,
output returns to stdout.

Let us put some of this to practice by using it to investigate the behaviour of particular agents.

Exploring Agents with SCCS

We'll introduce the SCCS operators by considering various agents, starting with the simple prefix.

```
****************************************************
* Create a simple sequential agent
****************************************************
  Command: agent P = `a:b:P;

  Command: size P;              * it has two states
  P has 2 states.

  Command: states P;
  1:  b:P
  2:  P

  Command: sort P;              * and these actions.
  {a,b}

  Command: transitions P;       * its first action is
  — `a ⟶ b:P

  Command: obs(2,P);            * its first two observable
  = `a b ⟹ P                    * actions are `a then b
```

```
Command: statesexp P;        * and its state space
—  `a ⟶ b:P
—    ⟶ P


Command: closure(a,P);       * One state b:P
1: b:P                       * reached by action a


Command: closure(`a,b,P);    * the state reached
1:  P                        * after `a then b
```

Add an agent with a choice of behaviours.

```
*****************************************************
* Create an agent with guarded choice
*****************************************************
Command: agent Q = c:`d:Q + e:`f:Q;


Command: size Q;             * has three states
Q has 3 states.


Command: states Q;           * namely
1:  `f:Q
2:  `d:Q
3:  Q


Command: sort Q;             * Four actions
{c,d,e,f}


Command: transitions Q;      * these initial actions and
—  c ⟶ `d:Q
—  e ⟶ `f:Q


Command: obs(2,Q);           * these two observable sequences
=  c `d ⟹ Q
=  e `f ⟹ Q


Command: statesexp Q;        * Its state space is
—  e ⟶ `f:Q
—  c ⟶ `d:Q
—    ⟶ Q


Command: closure(e,Q);       * The state reached by e
1:  `f:Q
```

```
     Command: closure(e,`f,Q);    * and after e then `f
     1: Q
```

Then add morphism.

```
     **************************************************
     * Create new agent STAMP, based on Q,
     * representing a particular stamp machine -
     * one which accepts 10p and 20p coins
     * and delivers a stamp of the same value
     **************************************************
     Command: agent STAMPS = Q[10pcoin/c,10pstamp/d,
                                    20pcoin/e,20pstamp/f];

     Command: sort STAMPS;
     {10pcoin,10pstamp,20pcoin,20pstamp}

     Command: statesexp STAMPS;
     — 10pcoin `10pstamp ⟶ Q[10pcoin/c,10pstamp/d,20pcoin/e,20pstamp/f]
     — 20pcoin ⟶ (`f:Q)[10pcoin/c,10pstamp/d,20pcoin/e,20pstamp/f]
     — 10pcoin ⟶ (`d:Q)[10pcoin/c,10pstamp/d,20pcoin/e,20pstamp/f]
     — ⟶ STAMPS
```

Finally, add restriction.

```
     **************************************************
     * which when restricted to 10p actions becomes
     **************************************************
     Command: statesexp STAMPS\{10pcoin, 10pstamp};
     — 10pcoin `10pstamp ⟶ Q[10pcoin/c,10pstamp/d,20pcoin/e,
                                    20pstamp/f]\{10pcoin,10pstamp}
     — 10pcoin ⟶ (`d:Q)[10pcoin/c,10pstamp/d,20pcoin/e,
                                    20pstamp/f]\{10pcoin,10pstamp}
     — ⟶ STAMPS\{10pcoin,10pstamp}


     **************************************************
     * Before quitting we can save the
     * agent environments for later use
     **************************************************
     Command: save Stamp.eg;
     Command: quit;
```

We've now seen all CWB representations of operators except delay. However, given the differing precedences of CWB $ to SCCS δ, to make things simple we'll use the more universal form of delay based on the definition of $\delta P = P + 1 : \delta P$ when considering binary variable VAR.

```
***************************************************
* Create an agent representing a binary variable
* which, after initialisation, can be written to,
* overwritten and read from
***************************************************
  Command: agent VARINT = `var_write_true:VART
                          + `var_write_false:VARF + 1:VARINT;
  Command: agent VARF = var_read_false:VARF
                          + `var_write_false:VARF
                          + `var_write_true:VART + 1:VARF;
  Command: agent VART = var_read_true:VART
                          + `var_write_true:VART
                          + `var_write_false:VARF + 1:VART;

  Command: size VARINT;        * has three states
  VARINT has 3 states.

  Command: states VARINT;      * namely
  1: VART
  2: VARF
  3: VARINT

  Command: sort VARINT;        * and can take these actions
  {var_read_false,var_read_true,var_write_false,var_write_true}

  Command: statesexp VARINT;  * this its state space with
  — `var_write_true —> VART   * one path to each state
  — `var_write_false —> VARF
  — —> VARINT

  Command: statesobs VARINT;  * for the complete picture
  = `var_write_true => VART
  = `var_write_false => VARF
  = => VARINT

  Command: statesexp VART;    * here's the
  — `var_write_false —> VARF
  — —> VART

  Command: statesobs VART;    * state spaces with
  = `var_write_false => VARF
```

```
        = ⇒ VART


     Command: statesexp VARF;      * one path to each
     — `var_write_true ⟶ VART
     — ⟶ VARF


     Command: statesobs VARF;      * for the rest of the system
     = `var_write_true ⟹ VART
     = ⟹ VARF


     Command: quit;
```

Agents are more interesting when we operate them concurrently with communication between the bits.

Agent Composition

We'll start with the simplest combination, the two agents $P \stackrel{def}{=} a:P$ and $Q \stackrel{def}{=} b:Q$

```
********************************************************
* First declare the agents
********************************************************
  Command: agent P = a:P;
  Command: agent Q = b:Q;


********************************************************
* when combined without no actions hidden...
********************************************************
  Command: statesexp SYSviz;
  — a#b ⟶ P | Q
  — ⟶ SYSviz


********************************************************
* ...the combination of their initial actions
* remains available to communicate with
* other agents.
* But if we hide all action, by allowing none...
********************************************************
  Command: agent Shid = (P|Q)\{};
  Command: statesexp Shid;
  — ⟶ SYShid
```

```
******************************************************
* ...the composite action is pruned and, as its
* only action is prohibited, inaction results.
******************************************************
   Command: transitions(Shid);
   No transitions
```

Things get more interesting If we combine two agents that can communicate; for example, P $\stackrel{\text{def}}{=}$ a : P and Q $\stackrel{\text{def}}{=}$ `a : Q

```
******************************************************
* First declare the agents.
******************************************************
   Command: agent P = a:P;
   Command: agent Q = `a:Q;


******************************************************
* When combined, we would expect to
* behave as
*      (a:P | `a:Q) = a#`a:(P | Q)
******************************************************
   Command: agent SYSviz = (P | Q);
   Command: statesexp SYSviz;
   — 1 ⟶ P | Q
   —   ⟶ SYSviz
```

Not what we had expected. What's wrong? Well, nothing really; it's all a matter of perspective. Our version (a : P | `a : Q) = a#`a : (P | Q) thinks of (P|Q) as a possible component of a larger system and, as such, its behaviour depends upon the environment in which it eventually finds itself; synchronisation between P and Q, 1 : (P | Q) is just one possible behaviour. The workbench assumes that, as we haven't specified any environment, there is no environment. The agent is a complete system and the only valid behaviour is for P to synchronise with Q. But don't worry, when we consider complete systems, both views give the same result. For example, harmony returns when we turn the agent combination into a complete system by hiding the synchronisation pair from all possible environments.

```
******************************************************
* Hide the joint action, forcing the synchronisation.
* \{} does not permit unresolved external actions,
* restricts nothing, and is the same as
* pruning all external actions.
******************************************************
   Command: agent SYShid = (P | Q)\{};
```

```
   Command: statesexp SYShid;
   — 1 —→ (P | Q)\{}
   —   —→ SYShid


****************************************************
* This also works if the agents are delayed
****************************************************
   Command: agent Pd = $a:Pd;
   Command: agent Qd = $'a:Qd;

   Command: agent SYSdviz = Pd|Qd;
   Command: statesexp SYSdviz;
   — 1 —→ Pd | Qd
   — a —→ Pd | $'a:Qd
   — 'a —→ $a:Pd | Qd
   — 1 —→ $a:Pd | $'a:Qd
   —   —→ SYSdviz


   Command: agent SYSdhid = (Pd|Qd)\{};
   Command: statesexp SYSdhid;
   — 1 —→ (Pd | Qd)\{}
   — 1 —→ ($a:Pd | $'a:Qd)\{}
   —   —→ SYSdhid


*********************************************************************
* And if there's a choice of synchronisation
*********************************************************************
   Command: agent Pd = $a:Pd;
   Command: agent Qd = $`a:Qd;
   Command: agent Rd = $`a:Rd;

   Command: agent SYSdRviz = (Pd | Qd | Rd);
   Command: statesexp SYSdRviz;
   — `a —→ Pd | Qd | Rd
   — 1 —→ Pd | Qd | $`a:Rd
   — 1 —→ Pd | $`a:Qd | Rd
   — a —→ Pd | $`a:Qd | $`a:Rd
   — `a^2 —→ $a:Pd | Qd | Rd
   — `a —→ $a:Pd | Qd | $`a:Rd
   — `a —→ $a:Pd | $`a:Qd | Rd
   — 1 —→ $a:Pd | $`a:Qd | $`a:Rd
   —   —→ SYSdRviz


   Command: agent SYSdRhid = (Pd | Qd | Rd)\{};
```

```
Command: statesexp SYSdRhid;
— 1 ⟶ (Pd | Qd | $`a:Rd)\{}
— 1 ⟶ (Pd | $`a:Qd | Rd)\{}
— 1 ⟶ ($a:Pd | $`a:Qd | $`a:Rd)\{}
—   ⟶ SYSdRhid
```

Now let's go back to our example of a stamp machine, but, this time, to make
things more interesting, have it serving a customer.

```
*****************************************************
* The agents we intend to combine are
* already 'saved' in Stamp.eg
*****************************************************
  Command: input Stamp.eg;     * input previously saved
                               * agent environments

  Command: print;              * check they're what we want
   ** Agents **
  agent Q = c:`d:Q + e:`f:Q
  agent STAMPS = Q[10pcoin/c,10pstamp/d,20pcoin/e,20pstamp/f]

  Command: statesexp STAMPS;;
  — 10pcoin `10pstamp ⟶ Q[10pcoin/c,10pstamp/d,20pcoin/e,20pstamp/f]
  — 20pcoin ⟶ (`f:Q)[10pcoin/c,10pstamp/d,20pcoin/e,20pstamp/f]
  — 10pcoin ⟶ (`d:Q)[10pcoin/c,10pstamp/d,20pcoin/e,20pstamp/f]
  —   ⟶ STAMPS


*****************************************************
* We convert P to an agent representing a customer who can
* negotiate with the stamp machine for a 10p stamp
*****************************************************
  Command: agent P = `a:b:P;
  Command: agent CUST = P[10pcoin/a,10pstamp/b];

  Command: statesexp CUST;
  — `10pcoin 10pstamp ⟶ P[10pcoin/a,10pstamp/b]
  — `10pcoin ⟶ (b:P)[10pcoin/a,10pstamp/b]
  —   ⟶ CUST


*****************************************************
* Define their combination and examine the behaviour
* when we only allow successful synchronisations to proceed
*****************************************************
  Command: agent SYS = (STAMPS|CUST)\{};
```

```
Command: states SYS;
1: (Q[10pcoin/c,10pstamp/d,20pcoin/e,20pstamp/f]
                        | P[10pcoin/a,10pstamp/b])\{}
2: ((`d:Q)[10pcoin/c,10pstamp/d,20pcoin/e,20pstamp/f]
                        | (b:P)[10pcoin/a,10pstamp/b])\{}
3: SYS


Command: statesexp SYS;
— 1 1 —→ (Q[10pcoin/c,10pstamp/d,20pcoin/e,20pstamp/f]
                        | P[10pcoin/a,10pstamp/b])\{}
— 1 —→ ((`d:Q)[10pcoin/c,10pstamp/d,20pcoin/e,20pstamp/f]
                        | (b:P)[10pcoin/a,10pstamp/b])\{}
— —→ SYS
```

A successful `10pcoin` transaction, followed by a `10pstamp` transaction.

Now we can start to tackle larger, more realistic, systems, starting with the hardware design of an AND/NOT gate combination.

```
*****************************************************
* Define a two-input AND gate as
*****************************************************
  Command: agent AND = and1i0#and2i0#`andout0:AND
                     + and1i1#and2i0#`andout0:AND
                     + and1i0#and2i1#`andout0:AND
                     + and1i0#and2i1#`andout1:AND;


*****************************************************
* Define a one-input NOT gate as
*****************************************************
  Command: agent NOT = notin0#`notout1:NOT
                     + notin1#`notout0:NOT;


*****************************************************
* By changing suitable port names...
*****************************************************
  Command: agent ANDR = (AND)[join0/and1i0,join1/and1i1];
  Command: agent NOTR = (NOT)[join0/notout0,join1/notout1];


*****************************************************
* ...connect them together, hiding the
* connection join...
*****************************************************
```

```
Command: set A = {notin0,notin1,and2i0,and2i1,andout0,andout1};
Command: agent SYS = (NOTR|ANDR)\A;
```

```
*****************************************************
* ...which gives the following visible behaviour
*****************************************************
Command: vs(1,SYS);
  == and2i0#`andout0#notin0 ⟹
  == and2i0#`andout0#notin1 ⟹
  == and2i1#`andout0#notin1 ⟹
  == and2i1#`andout1#notin0 ⟹
```

Now we'll revisit two earlier examples of software scheduler algorithms starting
with the non-pre-emptive scheduler.

```
*****************************************************
* Non-pre-emptive scheduler
*
* The scheduler S interacts with processes A and B to
* activate and deactivate them.
* The processes wait to be activated. When active, A engages
* in two internal actions, a1 and a2, and B in one, b1.
*****************************************************
Command: agent A = $astart:a1:a2:astop:A;
Command: agent B = $bstart:b1:bstop:B;
```

```
*****************************************************
* S first starts A by communicating with it via port astart.
* A runs to completion; its last act is to inform the
* scheduler, via port astop, that it has completed.
* S then starts B by communicating with it via port bstart.
* B runs to completion; its last act is to communicate with
* the scheduler via port bstop.
* S then starts A ... and so on.
*****************************************************
Command: agent S = `astart:$`astop:`bstart:$`bstop:S;
```

```
*****************************************************
* The complete system, hiding scheduler/process interactions
*****************************************************
Command: agent SAB = (A|B|S)\{a1,a2,b1};
```

```
*****************************************************
* This behaves as
*****************************************************
```

```
Command: statesexp SAB;
 — 1 a1 a2 1 1 b1 1 ⟶ ($astart:a1:a2:astop:A | B | S)\{a1,a2,b1}
 — 1 a1 a2 1 1 b1 ⟶ ($astart:a1:a2:astop:A | bstop:B
                                  | $`bstop:S)\{a1,a2,b1}
 — 1 a1 a2 1 1 ⟶ ($astart:a1:a2:astop:A | b1:bstop:B
                                  | $`bstop:S)\{a1,a2,b1}
 — 1 a1 a2 1 ⟶ (A | $bstart:b1:bstop:B | `bstart:$`bstop:S)\{a1,a2,b1}
 — 1 a1 a2 ⟶ (astop:A | $bstart:b1:bstop:B
                                  | $`astop:`bstart:$`bstop:S)\{a1,a2,b1}
 — 1 a1 ⟶ (a2:astop:A | $bstart:b1:bstop:B
                                  | $`astop:`bstart:$`bstop:S)\{a1,a2,b1}
 — 1 ⟶ (a1:a2:astop:A | $bstart:b1:bstop:B
                                  | $`astop:`bstart:$`bstop:S)\{a1,a2,b1}
 — ⟶ SAB
```

Now we follow on with the Round Robin scheduler.

```
**************************************************
* Round Robin scheduler
*
* The scheduler S interacts with processes A and B to activate
* and deactivate them. Processes wait to be activated and can
* be deactivated at any time.
* When active, A engages in three internal actions, B in four.
**************************************************
  Command: agent A = $A0;
  Command: agent A0 = astart:A1 + astop:A;
  Command: agent A1 = a1:A2 + astop:$astart:A1;
  Command: agent A2 = a2:A3 + astop:$astart:A2;
  Command: agent A3 = a3:A + astop:$astart:A3;

  Command: agent B = $B0;
  Command: agent B0 = bstart:B1 + bstop:B;
  Command: agent B1 = b1:B2 + bstop:$bstart:B1;
  Command: agent B2 = b2:B3 + bstop:$bstart:B2;
  Command: agent B3 = b3:B4 + bstop:$bstart:B3;
  Command: agent B4 = b4:B + bstop:$bstart:B4;


**************************************************
* S first starts A by communicating with it via port astart,
* idles for two ticks, then deactivates A via port astop.
* S then starts B by communicating with it via port bstart,
* idles for two ticks, then deactivates B via port bstop.
* S then starts A … and so on.
**************************************************
```

```
  Command: agent S = `astart:1:1:`astop:`bstart:1:1:`bstop:S;


**************************************************
* The complete system, hiding scheduler/process interactions
**************************************************
  Command: agent SAB = (A | B | S)\{a1,a2,a3,b1,b2,b3,b4};


**************************************************
* The complete system behaviour
**************************************************
  Command: statesexp SAB;
  — 1 a1 a2 1 1 b1 b2 1 1 a3 1 1 1 b3 b4 1 —→ ($A0 | B |S)
                                                   \{a1,a2,a3,b1,b2,b3,b4}
  — 1 a1 a2 1 1 b1 b2 1 1 a3 1 1 1 b3 b4 —→ ($A0 | B | `bstop:S)
                                                   \{a1,a2,a3,b1,b2,b3,b4}
  — 1 a1 a2 1 1 b1 b2 1 1 a3 1 1 1 b3 —→ ($A0 | B4 | 1:`bstop:S)
                                                   \{a1,a2,a3,b1,b2,b3,b4}
  — 1 a1 a2 1 1 b1 b2 1 1 a3 1 1 1 —→ ($A0 | B3 | 1:1:`bstop:S)
                                                   \{a1,a2,a3,b1,b2,b3,b4}
  — 1 a1 a2 1 1 b1 b2 1 1 a3 1 1 —→ (A | $bstart:B3 | `bstart:1:1:`bstop:S)
                                                   \{a1,a2,a3,b1,b2,b3,b4}
  — 1 a1 a2 1 1 b1 b2 1 1 a3 1 —→ ($A0 | $bstart:B3
                                   | `astop:`bstart:1:1:`bstop:S)
                                                   \{a1,a2,a3,b1,b2,b3,b4}
  — 1 a1 a2 1 1 b1 b2 1 1 a3 —→ (A | $bstart:B3
                                   | 1:`astop:`bstart:1:1:`bstop:S)
                                                   \{a1,a2,a3,b1,b2,b3,b4}
  — 1 a1 a2 1 1 b1 b2 1 1 —→ (A3 | $bstart:B3
                                   | 1:1:`astop:`bstart:1:1:`bstop:S)
                                                   \{a1,a2,a3,b1,b2,b3,b4}
  — 1 a1 a2 1 1 b1 b2 1 —→ ($astart:A3 | $bstart:B3 | S)
                                                   \{a1,a2,a3,b1,b2,b3,b4}
  — 1 a1 a2 1 1 b1 b2 —→ ($astart:A3 | B3 | `bstop:S)
                                                   \{a1,a2,a3,b1,b2,b3,b4}
  — 1 a1 a2 1 1 b1 —→ ($astart:A3 | B2 | 1:`bstop:S)\{a1,a2,a3,b1,b2,b3,b4}
  — 1 a1 a2 1 1 —→ ($astart:A3 | B1 | 1:1:`bstop:S)\{a1,a2,a3,b1,b2,b3,b4}
  — 1 a1 a2 1 —→ ($astart:A3 | $B0 | `bstart:1:1:`bstop:S)
                                                   \{a1,a2,a3,b1,b2,b3,b4}
  — 1 a1 a2 —→ (A3 | $B0 | `astop:`bstart:1:1:`bstop:S)
                                                   \{a1,a2,a3,b1,b2,b3,b4}
  — 1 a1 —→ (A2 | $B0 | 1:`astop:`bstart:1:1:`bstop:S)
                                                   \{a1,a2,a3,b1,b2,b3,b4}
  — 1 —→ (A1 | $B0 | 1:1:`astop:`bstart:1:1:`bstop:S)
                                                   \{a1,a2,a3,b1,b2,b3,b4}
  — —→ SAB
```

Both these examples verified our earlier 'pencil and paper' predictions of emergent behaviours, and we will finish off with a rewrite of the interrupt example.

```
*****************************************************
* Interrupts
*
* From the general case we take the particular case of:
* Main Process Q
* which repeatedly engages in two a actions followed by one
* b action, each taking one time slot.
* The process is always ready to receive an interrupt request.
* With interrupts enabled, the main process is defined by:
*              Q def int?:B + a:Q1
*              Q1 def int?:B1 + a:Q2
*              Q2 def int?:B2 + b:Q
*
* giving, in the absence of interrupts:
*              Q = a:a:b:Q
*****************************************************
  Command: agent Q = int:B + a:Q1;
  Command: agent Q1 = int:B1 + a:Q2;
  Command: agent Q2 = int:B2 + b:Q;


*****************************************************
* Interrupting process R
* idles for four ticks, generating an interrupt request
* every fifth tick over port int, then repeats.
*              R def 1:1:1:1:int!:R
*****************************************************
  Command: agent R = 1:1:1:1:`int:R;


*****************************************************
* Interrupt Service Routine B
* carries out three d actions, taking one time slot each, then
* returns control to the main process at the point of interrupt.
*              B def d:d:d:Q
*              B1 def d:d:d:Q1
*              B2 def d:d:d:Q2
*****************************************************
  Command: agent B = d:d:d:Q;
  Command: agent B1 = d:d:d:Q1;
  Command: agent B2 = d:d:d:Q2;
```

```
*****************************************************
* The composite systems is S def [R × Q]\\int...
*****************************************************
  Command: agent SYS = (R | Q)\{a,b,d};


*****************************************************
* ...with state space...
*****************************************************
  Command: statesexp SYS;
  — a a b a 1 d d d a 1 d d d b 1 d d  ⟶ (1:1:`int:R | d:Q)\{a,b,d}
  — a a b a 1 d d d a 1 d d d b 1 d  ⟶ (1:1:1:`int:R | d:d:Q)\{a,b,d}
  — a a b a 1 d d d a 1 d d d b 1  ⟶ (R | B)\{a,b,d}
  — a a b a 1 d d d a 1 d d d b  ⟶ (`int:R | Q)\{a,b,d}
  — a a b a 1 d d d a 1 d d d  ⟶ (1:`int:R | Q2)\{a,b,d}
  — a a b a 1 d d d a 1 d d  ⟶ (1:1:`int:R | d:Q2)\{a,b,d}
  — a a b a 1 d d d a 1 d  ⟶ (1:1:1:`int:R | d:d:Q2)\{a,b,d}
  — a a b a 1 d d d a 1  ⟶ (R | B2)\{a,b,d}
  — a a b a 1 d d d a  ⟶ (`int:R | Q2)\{a,b,d}
  — a a b a 1 d d d  ⟶ (1:`int:R | Q1)\{a,b,d}
  — a a b a 1 d d  ⟶ (1:1:`int:R | d:Q1)\{a,b,d}
  — a a b a 1 d  ⟶ (1:1:1:`int:R | d:d:Q1)\{a,b,d}
  — a a b a 1  ⟶ (R | B1)\{a,b,d}
  — a a b a  ⟶ (`int:R | Q1)\{a,b,d}
  — a a b  ⟶ (1:`int:R | Q)\{a,b,d}
  — a a  ⟶ (1:1:`int:R | Q2)\{a,b,d}
  — a  ⟶ (1:1:1:`int:R | Q1)\{a,b,d}
  — ⟶ SYS


*****************************************************
* ...and observable actions
*****************************************************
  Command: obs(15,SYS);
  === a a b a d d d a d d d b d d d ===> (1:`int:R | Q)\{a,b,d}

  Command: vs(15,SYS);
  === a a b a d d d a d d d b d d d ===>
```

Again, this is good enough to agree with our previous prediction of emergent behaviours.

However, just checking that a system behaves itself by visual inspection of its emergent behaviour seems perverse when we have bisimulation checkers and other tools to do it properly.

6.2 Agents, Bisimulation and CWB

To compare, and check, agent behaviours CWB comes equipped with the following relational commands

---

Relational Commands

All the relational commands (except `min`) take two agents names as parameters, return `true` if the relation holds and `false` if it doesn't. None will work if either agent's state space is infinite.

`eq(A,B);` observational equivalence.

`cong(A,B);` observational congruence.

`strongeq(A,B);` strong bisimulation.

`diveq(A,B);` observational equivalence which respects divergence.

`min(X,A);` minimises the state space of A with respect to weak equivalence, binding the result to X.

`pb(A,B);` prints the largest bisimulation over the state space of the two agents divided into bisimulation classes. Equivalent agents appear in the same bisimulation class.

The way we set about comparing expressions, to see if they have the same behaviour, depends upon the observer; of the two main types, strong bisimulation, equating all actions, compares real-time behaviours; weak bisimulation, equating only observable actions, compares external behaviours. CWB supports strong bisimulation, which is both an equivalence and a congruence, and weak bisimulation which, though an observational equivalence, is not implicitly a congruence. By supporting such comparison techniques, CWB gives us an automated tool to take the tedium out of proving agents are equal/congruent. Checking previous 'manual' predictions should increase our confidence in the workbench. We will start with the example that showed that traces alone were an unsafe base for comparing agents. We will then follow the progression from strong bisimulation to observational equivalence and congruences. In the final examples we will rework some more realistic problems from SCCS

So, first let us look again at where deadlock fooled simple traces into declaring two disparate systems equal.

example

$P \stackrel{\text{def}}{=} \alpha : P$ and $Q \stackrel{\text{def}}{=} \alpha : Q + \alpha : Q_1$ can be pictured as

P differs from Q as P can always engage in an α while Q, which can also indefinitely engage in α actions, has the possibility of moving to state Q_1 and stopping. While they have different behaviours, as their possible future actions are the same they have the same traces:
Traces (P) = Traces (Q) = <α>*.

Turning to the concurrency workbench,[†]

```
************************************************
* We declare the two agents
************************************************
  Command: agent P = a:P;
  Command: agent Q = a:0 + a:Q;


************************************************
* and compare their traces
************************************************
  Command: dftrace(P,Q);        * they have the same traces
  true


************************************************
* To prove if P are Q equivalent we look at their bisimulation
************************************************
  Command: pb(P,Q);
  The largest bisimulation on these agents:       this is the first
  ---------------------------------------            bisimulation class
  1: Q
  ---------------------------------------
  1: 0                                           this the second
  ---------------------------------------
  1: P
                                                 and this the third
```

[†] Note: actual workbench session printouts have been condensed here, as they tend to be rather free with white space. What you see in these pages is *almost* what you get.

```
*********************************************************
* P and Q are not in the same bisimulation class and
* are therefore not bisimilar. In fact, each of the
* three classes has only one occupant and none of the
* agent states are bisimilar.
******
* If we are only interested in establishing if two systems are
* equivalent, and not the details, there are appropriate
* commands for each type of comparison.
* In this case we check their strong bisimulation.
*********************************************************
```
```
Command: strongeq(P,Q);       * they are not strongly bisimilar
false
```

Thus we establish that $\mathtt{Traces(P)} = \mathtt{Traces(Q)}$ while $\neg(P \sim Q)$.

■

Two agents, which could not be distinguished by traces alone, have their non-equivalence confirmed by bisimulation, which agrees with our previous finding. Now let's look at a straightforward case of using strong bisimulation to compare agents. One such comparison, previously tackled the long way round, is demonstrated in the next example.

example
Where
$$P \stackrel{\text{def}}{=} \alpha : P_1$$
$$P_1 \stackrel{\text{def}}{=} \chi : P + \beta : P_2$$
$$P_2 \stackrel{\text{def}}{=} 1 : \mathbb{0}$$

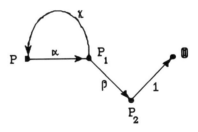

and
$$Q \stackrel{\text{def}}{=} \alpha : Q_1$$
$$Q_1 \stackrel{\text{def}}{=} \chi : Q_3 + \beta : Q_2$$
$$Q_2 \stackrel{\text{def}}{=} 1 : \mathbb{0}$$
$$Q_3 \stackrel{\text{def}}{=} \alpha : Q_4$$
$$Q_4 \stackrel{\text{def}}{=} \chi : Q_5 + \beta : Q_6$$
$$Q_5 \stackrel{\text{def}}{=} \alpha : Q_4$$
$$Q_6 \stackrel{\text{def}}{=} 1 : \mathbb{0}$$

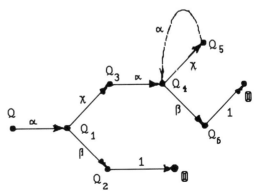

To prove agent P and Q equivalent we must prove they simulate each other, are in the same bisimulation class. The bisimulation classes we obtained previously were:

$$(P \sim Q \sim Q_3 \sim Q_5) , \ (P_1 \sim Q_1 \sim Q_4) \text{ and } (P_2 \sim Q_2 \sim Q_6)$$

```
**************************************************
* We rewrite the two agents in CWB-speak
**************************************************
  Command: agent P = a:P1;
  Command: agent P1 = c:P + b:P2;
  Command: agent P2 = 1:0;

  Command: agent Q = a:Q1;
  Command: agent Q1 = c:Q3 + b:Q2;
  Command: agent Q2 = 1:0;
  Command: agent Q3 = a:Q4;
  Command: agent Q4 = c:Q5 + b:Q6;
  Command: agent Q5 = a:Q4;
  Command: agent Q6 = 1:0;


**************************************************
* To prove P and Q equivalent we must
* prove that P~Q is a member of a
* complete bisimulation relation.
* In this case the largest weak
* bisimulation over P and Q is…
**************************************************
  Command: pb(P,Q);
  The largest bisimulation on these agents:
  ---------------------
  1: P2
  2: 0
  3: Q2
  4: Q6
  ---------------------
  1: P1
  2: Q1
  3: Q4
  ---------------------
  1: P
  2: Q
  3: Q3
  4: Q5
```

```
*****************************************************
* Which all agrees with our pencil and paper proof.
* As the last bisimulation class includes P and Q the
* two systems are equivalent under strong bisimulation
*****************************************************
   Command: strongeq(P,Q);     * they are strongly bisimilar
   true

   Command: eq(P,Q);           * hence they are also equivalent
   true                        * observationally
```

■

So much for strong bisimulation. For some agents, a weaker form of equivalence, observational equivalence based on an observational bisimulation that matches only external actions, may be more appropriate.

example
Where

$$P \stackrel{\text{def}}{=} 1 : P_1$$
$$P_1 \stackrel{\text{def}}{=} a : P_2$$
$$P_2 \stackrel{\text{def}}{=} 1 : P_3$$
$$P_3 \stackrel{\text{def}}{=} b : \mathbb{0}$$

and

$$Q \stackrel{\text{def}}{=} a : Q_1$$
$$Q_1 \stackrel{\text{def}}{=} b : \mathbb{0}$$

```
*****************************************************
* We rewrite the two agents as
*****************************************************
   Command: agent P = 1:a:1:b:0;
   Command: agent Q = a:b:0;


*****************************************************
* Their complete state spaces differ from
* their observable state spaces.
*****************************************************
   Command: statesobs(P);
   == a b ⟹ 0
   == a ⟹ b:0
   == a ⟹ 1:b:0
   == ⟹ a:1:b:0
   == ⟹ P


   Command: statesexp(P);
```

```
  — 1 a 1 b —→ 0
  — 1 a 1 —→ b:0
  — 1 a —→ 1:b:0
  — 1 —→ a:1:b:0
  — —→ P


Command: statesexp(Q);
  — a b —→ 0
  — a —→ b:0
  — —→ Q


Command: statesobs(Q);
  == a b ==> 0
  == a ==> b:0
  == ==> Q
```

```
*********************************************************
* which is reflected in their having identical traces
* of observable actions, equivalence under observational
* equivalence but not strong bisimulation.
*********************************************************
  Command: dftrace(P,Q);
  true

  Command: eq(P,Q);
  true

  Command: strongeq(P,Q);
  false
```

Thus $P \approx Q$ but $\neg (P \sim Q)$.

■

But the crunch comes when comparing observable behaviours. We do not want to equate agents which can engage in the same external action sequences if one silently rejects particular behaviours by unseen 1 actions.

example
Where
$$P \stackrel{\text{def}}{=} a:0 + b:0$$

and

$$Q \stackrel{\text{def}}{=} 1 : Q_1 + b : \mathbb{0}$$
$$Q_1 \stackrel{\text{def}}{=} a : \mathbb{0}$$

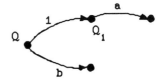

```
****************************************************
* We rewrite the two agents as
****************************************************
  Command: agent P = a:0 + b:0;
  Command: agent Q = 1:Q1 + b:0;
  Command: agent Q1 = a:0;


****************************************************
* P's complete state space is the same as its observable
* state space, but Q's is different
****************************************************
  Command: statesexp P;
  — a —→ 0
  — —→ P


  Command: statesobs P;
  = a ⟹ 0
  = ⟹ P


  Command: statesexp Q;
  — b —→ 0
  — 1 —→ Q1
  — —→ Q


  Command: statesobs Q;
  = b ⟹ 0
  = ⟹ Q1
  = ⟹ Q


****************************************************
* While they have identical traces, they are equivalent under
* neither observational equivalence nor strong bisimulation.
****************************************************
  Command: dftrace(P,Q);
  true


  Command: eq(P,Q);
```

```
false

Command: strongeq(P,Q);

false
```

While P can always engage in a or b, Q_1 can autonomously reject the b, hence $\neg(P \approx Q)$.

The next example has a positive result.

example

Where

$$P \stackrel{\text{def}}{=} a : P_1 + a : P_2$$
$$P_1 \stackrel{\text{def}}{=} b : P_1$$
$$P_2 \stackrel{\text{def}}{=} 1 : P_3$$
$$P_3 \stackrel{\text{def}}{=} b : P_3$$

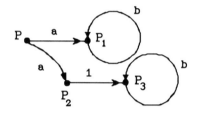

and

$$Q \stackrel{\text{def}}{=} a : Q_1$$
$$Q_1 \stackrel{\text{def}}{=} 1 : Q_2$$
$$Q_2 \stackrel{\text{def}}{=} 1 : Q_3$$
$$Q_3 \stackrel{\text{def}}{=} b : Q_3$$

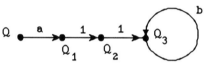

```
*******************************************************
* We rewrite the two agents as
*******************************************************
  Command: agent P = a:P1 + a:P2;
  Command: agent P1 = b:P1;
  Command: agent P2 = 1:P3;
  Command: agent P3 = b:P3;


  Command: agent Q = a:Q1;
  Command: agent Q1 = 1:Q2;
  Command: agent Q2 = 1:Q3;
  Command: agent Q3 = b:Q3;


*******************************************************
* giving their state spaces
*******************************************************
  Command: statesexp P;
  — a 1 ⟶ P3
  — a ⟶ P2
```

```
— a —→ P1
— —→ P

Command: statesobs P;
= a ⟹ P3
= a ⟹ P2
= a ⟹ P1
= ⟹ P

Command: statesexp Q;
— a 1 1 —→ Q3
— a 1 —→ Q2
— a —→ Q1
— —→ Q

Command: statesobs Q;
= a ⟹ Q3
= a ⟹ Q2
= a ⟹ Q1
= ⟹ Q


*************************************************
* While their full action sequences are different,
* their observable action sequences are the same.
* Thus they have the same traces;
* i.e. they are equivalent under observational
* equivalence but not under strong bisimulation
*************************************************
Command: dftrace(P,Q);
true

Command: eq(P,Q);
true

Command: strongeq(P,Q);
false


*************************************************
* 'For fun', here are the bisimulation classes
*************************************************
Command: pb(P,Q);
The largest bisimulation on these agents:
--------------------
1: P1
```

```
2:  P2
3:  P3
4:  Q1
5:  Q2
6:  Q3
--------------------
1:  P
2:  Q
```

Which is the same as the hand-crafted result, $P \approx Q$.

■

Sometimes proving agents equivalent isn't sufficient and we also need to prove them congruent. Strong bisimulation is a congruence, and agents proved strongly bisimilar are also congruent. Unfortunately, this isn't true for observational equivalence. To raise observational equivalence to a congruence we'd have to show that placing observationally equivalent expressions in the same contexts $C[\![\,]\!]$ results in observational equivalent expressions. For contexts $[\![\,]\!]+R$ and $[\![\,]\!]\times R$, observational equivalence is not a congruence.

First summation, $\mathit{Expr}_1 = a:\mathbb{0}$ and $\mathit{Expr}_2 = 1:a:\mathbb{0}$ in context $C[\![\,]\!] = [\![\,]\!] + \mathit{Expr}$, where $\mathit{Expr} = b:\mathbb{0}$. Whilst $a:\mathbb{0} \approx 1:a:\mathbb{0}$ agent $(a:\mathbb{0} + b:\mathbb{0})$ can engage in a or b but $(1:a:\mathbb{0} + b:\mathbb{0})$ by engaging in the hidden 1 action can autonomously reject the b action. So

$$\neg\left((\mathit{Expr}_1 \approx \mathit{Expr}_2) \Rightarrow (\mathit{Expr} + \mathit{Expr}_1 \approx \mathit{Expr} + \mathit{Expr}_2) \right)$$

For product we have the counter-example $a.\mathbb{0}$ and $1.a.\mathbb{0}$ in context $C[\![\,]\!] = [\![\,]\!] \times \mathit{Expr}$, where $\mathit{Expr} = b:\mathbb{0}$, though $a:\mathbb{0} \approx 1:a:\mathbb{0}$ agent $(a:\mathbb{0} \times b:\mathbb{0})$ can engage axb but $(1:a:\mathbb{0} \times b:\mathbb{0})$ cannot. So

$$\neg\left((\mathit{Expr}_1 \approx \mathit{Expr}_2) \Rightarrow (\mathit{Expr} \times \mathit{Expr}_1 \approx \mathit{Expr} \times \mathit{Expr}_2) \right)$$

Does the workbench concur?

```
***************************************************
* We rewrite the three agents as
***************************************************
  Command: agent P = a:0;
  Command: agent Q = 1:a:0;
  Command: agent R = b:0;


***************************************************
* Agents P and Q are bisimilar
***************************************************
  Command: eq(P,Q);
  true
```

```
****************************************************
* as they are in a prefix context
****************************************************
   Command: eq(a:P,a:Q);
   true


****************************************************
* but not in summation or product contexts
****************************************************
   Command: eq(P+R,Q+R);
   false


   Command: eq(P|R,Q|R);
   false


****************************************************
* All of this is covered by
****************************************************
   Command: cong(P,Q);
   false
```

Once we have some confidence in CWB – after all, its predictions do compute with our pencil and paper attempts – we can check laws we've derived from the basic SCCS; for example, law $\leftrightarrow 1$, that

$(\alpha:P \times \alpha^{-1}:Q) \backslash\backslash A = 1 : (P \times Q) \backslash\backslash A, \; \mathrm{Part}(\alpha) \subseteq A.$

```
   Command: agent P = a:P;
   Command: agent Q = `a:Q;


****************************************************
* First we look at their individual
* behaviours. Remember: \{} prunes all
* external actions.
****************************************************
   Command: statesexp (a:P|`a:Q)\{};
   — 1 ⟶ (P | Q)\{}
   — ⟶ (a:P | `a:Q)\{}


   Command: statesexp 1:(P|Q)\{};
   — 1 ⟶ (P | Q)\{}
   — ⟶ 1:(P | Q)\{}


****************************************************
* And as strong equivalence is a congruence
****************************************************
```

```
Command: strongeq (((a:P)|(`a:Q))\{}, 1:(P|Q)\{});
true
```

While CWB has proved useful to check the occasional law, we are more likely to use it to check a design. This we do by comparing an agent, representing an implementation, with another, representing a specification, and for this we need to use CWB equivalences and congruences in all their forms, which we will illustrate by revisiting previous examples.

Agent Validation

The design of the NOT/AND gate combination:

```
Command: agent AND = and1i0#and2i0#`andout0:AND
                   + and1i0#and2i1#`andout0:AND
                   + and1i1#and2i0#`andout0:AND
                   + and1i1#and2i1#`andout1:AND;
Command: agent NOT = notin0#`notout1:NOT
                   + notin1#`notout0:NOT;
```

when suitably converted and restricted the combined agents become design NEWSYS

```
Command: agent ANDR = (AND)[join0/and1i0,join1/and1i1];
Command: agent NOTR = (NOT)[join0/notout0,join1/notout1];
Command: agent SYS = (NOTR|ANDR)\A;
Command: set A = {notin0,notin1,and2i0,and2i1,andout0,andout1};
Command: agent NEWSYS = (SYS)[a0/notin0,a1/notin1,b0/and2i0,
                         b1/and2i1,c0/andout0,c1/andout1];
```

so it can be compared with the expected behaviour

```
Command: agent TRUTH = a0#b0#`c0:TRUTH + a0#b1#`c1:TRUTH
                     + a1#b0#`c0:TRUTH + a1#b1#`c0:TRUTH;
```

They seem to have the same actions

```
Command: init NEWSYS;
{a0#b0#`c0,a0#b1#`c1,a1#b0#`c0,a1#b1#`c0}
```

```
Command: init TRUTH;
{a0#b0#`c0,a0#b1#`c1,a1#b0#`c0,a1#b1#`c0}
```

However, to be acceptable with respect to the timing, the two agents must be strongly bisimilar

```
Command: strongeq(NEWSYS,TRUTH);
true
```

which they are, QED. In the last example, time was of the essence and we had to prove strong equivalence. However, other designs may only require observational equivalence to a specification. Next we revisit a slightly revised non-pre-emptive scheduler

```
******************************************************
* Non-preemptive scheduler (see section 4.8.4)
***
* The scheduler S activates and deactivates processes A and B.
* The processes wait to be activated. When active, A engages
* in two internal actions, a1 and a2, and B in one, b1.
******************************************************
   Command: agent A = $astart:a1:a2:astop:A;
   Command: agent B = $bstart:b1:bstop:B;


******************************************************
* S first starts A by communicating with it via port astart.
* A runs to completion; its last act is to inform the
* scheduler, via port astop, that it has completed.
* S then starts B by communicating with it via port bstart.
* B runs to completion; its last act is to communicate with
* the scheduler via port bstop.
* S then starts A ... and so on.
******************************************************
   Command: agent S = `astart:$`astop:`bstart:$`bstop:S;


******************************************************
* The complete design, hiding scheduler/process interaction
******************************************************
   Command: agent SAB = (A|B|S)\{a1,a2,b1};


******************************************************
* Expected behaviour
******************************************************
   Command: agent Spec = 1:a1:a2:1:1:b1:1:Spec;


******************************************************
* The state spaces of design and specification
******************************************************
   Command: statesexp Spec;
   — 1 a1 a2 1 1 b1 —→ 1:Spec
   — 1 a1 a2 1 1 —→ b1:1:Spec
   — 1 a1 a2 1 —→ 1:b1:1:Spec
   — 1 a1 a2 —→ 1:1:b1:1:Spec
   — 1 a1 —→ a2:1:1:b1:1:Spec
   — 1 —→ a1:a2:1:1:b1:1:Spec
```

```
—  —→  :Spec

Command: statesexp SAB;
— 1 a1 a2 1 1 b1 1 —→ ($astart:a1:a2:astop:A | B | S)\{a1,a2,b1}
— 1 a1 a2 1 1 b1 —→ ($astart:a1:a2:astop:A | bstop:B
                                  | $`bstop:S)\{a1,a2,b1}
— 1 a1 a2 1 1 —→ ($astart:a1:a2:astop:A | b1:bstop:B
                                  | $`bstop:S)\{a1,a2,b1}
— 1 a1 a2 1 —→ (A | $bstart:b1:bstop:B | `bstart:$`bstop:S)\{a1,a2,b1}
— 1 a1 a2 —→ (astop:A | $bstart:b1:bstop:B
                                  | $`astop:`bstart:$`bstop:S)\{a1,a2,b1}
— 1 a1 —→ (a2:astop:A | $bstart:b1:bstop:B
                                  | $`astop:`bstart:$`bstop:S)\{a1,a2,b1}
— 1 —→ (a1:a2:astop:A | $bstart:b1:bstop:B
                                  | $`astop:`bstart:$`bstop:S)\{a1,a2,b1}
—  —→ SAB


*****************************************************
* If we want to check that actions and timing are correct
* the design and specification must be strongly bisimilar
*****************************************************
Command: strongeq(SAB,Spec);
true


*****************************************************
* Here we are only interested in the observable behaviours
* and weak bisimulation is sufficient
*****************************************************
Command: eq(SAB,Spec);
true
```

With a revised Round Robin scheduler, observational equivalence is also sufficient.

```
*****************************************************
* Round Robin scheduler (see section 4.8.4)
***
* The scheduler S activates and deactivates processes A and B.
* The processes wait to be activated and can be deactivated
* at any time; when active, A engages in three internal
* actions, and B in four.
*****************************************************
Command: agent A = $A0;
Command: agent A0 = astart:A1 + astop:A;
```

```
Command: agent A1 = a1:A2 + astop:$astart:A1;
Command: agent A2 = a2:A3 + astop:$astart:A2;
Command: agent A3 = a3:A + astop:$astart:A3;


Command: agent B = $B0;
Command: agent B0 = bstart:B1 + bstop:B;
Command: agent B1 = b1:B2 + bstop:$bstart:B1;
Command: agent B2 = b2:B3 + bstop:$bstart:B2;
Command: agent B3 = b3:B4 + bstop:$bstart:B3;
Command: agent B4 = b4:B + bstop:$bstart:B4;


**************************************************
* S first starts A over port astart, idles for two ticks,
* then deactivates A via port astop.
* S then starts B over port bstart, idles for two ticks,
* then deactivates B via port bstop.
* S then starts A … and so on.
**************************************************
  Command: agent S = `astart:1:1:`astop:`bstart:1:1:`bstop:S;


**************************************************
* The complete system, hiding scheduler/ process interactions
**************************************************
  Command: agent SAB = (A | B | S)\{a1,a2,a3,b1,b2,b3,b4};


**************************************************
* The expected emergent behaviour
**************************************************
  Command: agent Emerge
             = 1:a1:a2:1:1:b1:b2:1:1:a3:1:1:1:b3:b4:1:Emerge;


**************************************************
* Comparing design and specification by strong bisimulation
**************************************************
  Command: strongeq(SAB,Emerge);
  true


**************************************************
* Here we are only interested in process actions,
* not the scheduling, and observational equivalence
* is sufficient.
**************************************************
  Command: eq(SAB,Emerge);
  true
```

Any system which is in strong bisimulation with a specification is automatically also observationally equivalent with that specification, but not vice versa. Now we go back to systems where time is part of the requirement with that specification; for example, in systems with interrupts, to prove the system correct only strong bisimulation will do.

```
*****************************************************
* Interrupts (see section 4.6.3)
***
* Main Process Q
* Repeatedly engages in two a actions followed by one b action,
* each taking one time slot.
* The process is always ready to receive an interrupt request.
* With interrupts enabled, the main process is defined by:
*               Q def int?:B + a:Q1
*               Q1 def int?:B1 + a:Q2
*               Q2 def int?:B2 + b:Q
* giving, in the absence of interrupts:
*               Q def a:a:b:Q
*****************************************************
   Command: agent Q = int:B + a:Q1;
   Command: agent Q1 = int:B1 + a:Q2;
   Command: agent Q2 = int:B2 + b:Q;


*****************************************************
* Interrupting process R
* Idles for four ticks, generating an interrupt request
* every fifth tick over port int, then repeats.
*               R def 1:1:1:1:int!:R
*****************************************************
   Command: agent R = 1:1:1:1:`int:R;


*****************************************************
* Interrupt Service Routine B
* Carries out three d actions, taking one time slot each, then
* returns control to the main process at the point of interrupt
*               B def d:d:d:Q
*               B1 def d:d:d:Q1
*               B2 def d:d:d:Q2
*****************************************************
   Command: agent B = d:d:d:Q;
   Command: agent B1 = d:d:d:Q1;
   Command: agent B2 = d:d:d:Q2;
```

```
****************************************************
* The composite systems is
*               S def (R × Q)\\int
****************************************************
  Command: agent SYS = (R | Q)\{a,b,d};


****************************************************
* Expected behaviour
****************************************************
  Command: agent S = a:a:b:X;
  Command: agent X = a:1:d:d:d:a:1:d:d:d:b:1:d:d:d:X;

  Command: statesexp SYS;
  — a a b a 1 d d d a 1 d d d b 1 d d —→ (1:1:`int:R | d:Q)\{a,b,d}
  — a a b a 1 d d d a 1 d d d b 1 d —→ (1:1:1:`int:R | d:d:Q)\{a,b,d}
  — a a b a 1 d d d a 1 d d d b 1 —→ (R | B)\{a,b,d}
  — a a b a 1 d d d a 1 d d d b —→ (`int:R | Q)\{a,b,d}
  — a a b a 1 d d d a 1 d d d —→ (1:`int:R | Q2)\{a,b,d}
  — a a b a 1 d d d a 1 d d —→ (1:1:`int:R | d:Q2)\{a,b,d}
  — a a b a 1 d d d a 1 d —→ (1:1:1:`int:R | d:d:Q2)\{a,b,d}
  — a a b a 1 d d d a 1 —→ (R | B2)\{a,b,d}
  — a a b a 1 d d d a —→ (`int:R | Q2)\{a,b,d}
  — a a b a 1 d d d —→ (1:`int:R | Q1)\{a,b,d}
  — a a b a 1 d d —→ (1:1:`int:R | d:Q1)\{a,b,d}
  — a a b a 1 d —→ (1:1:1:`int:R | d:d:Q1)\{a,b,d}
  — a a b a 1 —→ (R | B1)\{a,b,d}
  — a a b a —→ (`int:R | Q1)\{a,b,d}
  — a a b —→ (1:`int:R | Q)\{a,b,d}
  — a a —→ (1:1:`int:R | Q2)\{a,b,d}
  — a —→ (1:1:1:`int:R | Q1)\{a,b,d}
  — —→ SYS

  Command: vs(15,S);
  === a a b a d d d a d d d b d d d ===>
  Command: vs(15,SYS);
  === a a b a d d d a d d d b d d d ===>

  Command: strongeq(S,SYS);
  true
```

Now we have the ability to check a design against a specification, as long as both are written as SCCS expressions. If we capture desired properties as an SCCS specification we can check to see if a design has these properties or not. As an example of this, we'll check a set of SCCS algorithms against a specification for

mutual exclusion. Two clients access a shared resource which, to maintain its
integrity, is accessed under mutual exclusion. Each client tries to grab the
resource when it wants it, paying no heed to the state of the resource or other
clients. Can these anarchists succeed?

```
****************************************************
* Mutual Exclusion by anarchy
***
* Two customers...
****************************************************
   Command: agent CUST1 = $enter:cs1:$exit:CUST1;
   Command: agent CUST2 = $enter:cs2:$exit:CUST2;


****************************************************
* ...accessing the same resource by entering and exiting
* their critical sections whenever they like
****************************************************
   Command: agent USERS = CUST1 |CUST2;


****************************************************
* Can such anarchy meet the specification?
****************************************************
   Command: agent ObsSPEC = (Obs1SPEC + Obs2SPEC);
   Command: agent Obs1SPEC = $enter:cs1:$exit:ObsSPEC;
   Command: agent Obs2SPEC = $enter:cs2:$exit:ObsSPEC;


****************************************************
* As we are only interested in observable actions
****************************************************
   Command: statesobs ObsSPEC;
   == enter cs1 ⟹ $exit:ObsSPEC
   == enter ⟹ cs2:$exit:ObsSPEC
   == enter ⟹ cs1:$exit:ObsSPEC
   == ⟹ $enter:cs2:$exit:ObsSPEC
   == ⟹ $enter:cs1:$exit:ObsSPEC
   == ⟹ ObsSPEC


   Command: statesobs USERS;
   == enter^2 cs1#cs2 exit^2 ⟹ CUST1 | CUST2
   == enter cs1#enter cs2#exit ⟹ CUST1 | $exit:CUST2
   == enter cs1 enter#exit ⟹ CUST1 | cs2:$exit:CUST2
   == enter cs1 exit ⟹ CUST1 | $enter:cs2:$exit:CUST2
   == enter cs2#enter cs1#exit ⟹ $exit:CUST1 | CUST2
   == enter cs2 enter#exit ⟹ cs1:$exit:CUST1 | CUST2
```

```
= enter cs2 exit ⟹ $enter:cs1:$exit:CUST1 | CUST2
= enter^2 cs1#cs2 ⟹ $exit:CUST1 | $exit:CUST2
= enter cs1#enter ⟹ $exit:CUST1 | cs2:$exit:CUST2
= enter cs1 ⟹ $exit:CUST1 | $enter:cs2:$exit:CUST2
= enter cs2#enter ⟹ cs1:$exit:CUST1 | $exit:CUST2
= enter cs2 ⟹ $enter:cs1:$exit:CUST1 | $exit:CUST2
= enter^2 ⟹ cs1:$exit:CUST1 | cs2:$exit:CUST2
= enter ⟹ cs1:$exit:CUST1 | $enter:cs2:$exit:CUST2
= enter ⟹ $enter:cs1:$exit:CUST1 | cs2:$exit:CUST2
= ⟹ $enter:cs1:$exit:CUST1 | $enter:cs2:$exit:CUST2
= ⟹ USERS
```

```
*****************************************************
* Failure is confirmed by a lack of observational equivalence
*****************************************************
  Command: eq(USERS,ObsSPEC);
  false
```

Mutual exclusion is violated in many different ways – which is not surprising, given the lack restraint of the users. This is a design to forget. We'd expect better of a semaphore-based design

```
*****************************************************
* Semaphores (see section 4.8.3)
***
* Define two agents which, in their critical
* section, use the same resource where
*            csah = head of process A's critical section
*            csat = tail of process A's critical section
*****************************************************
  Command: agent A = $`wait:csah:csat:$`signal:A;
  Command: agent B = $`wait:csbh:csbt:$`signal:B;
```

```
*****************************************************
* To preserve mutual exclusion they signal
* and wait on a common binary semaphore
*****************************************************
  Command: agent SEM = S1;
  Command: agent S1 = $wait:S0;
  Command: agent S0 = $signal:S1;
```

```
*****************************************************
* The compete system
*****************************************************
  Command: agent SYS = (A | B | SEM)\{csah,csat,csbh,csbt};
```

```
***************************************************
* We want to compare with this the behaviour we require,
* namely, that mutual exclusion is not violated,
* that is, that csa and csb are executed serially.
***************************************************
  Command: agent ObsASPEC = $csah:$csat:ObsSPEC;
  Command: agent ObsBSPEC = $csbh:$csbt:ObsSPEC;
  Command: agent ObsSPEC = ObsASPEC + ObsBSPEC;


***************************************************
* We want to equate the observable behaviours
* of SYS and ObsSPEC.
***
* Their observable state spaces are
***************************************************
  Command: statesobs ObsSPEC;
  == csbh ==> $csbt:ObSPEC
  == csah ==> $csat:ObSPEC
  == ==> $csbh:$csbt:ObSPEC
  == ==> $csah:$csat:ObSPEC
  == ==> ObSPEC


  Command: statesobs SYS;
  == csah csat ==> (A | $`wait:csbh:csbt:$`signal:B | S1)
                                    \{csah,csat,csbh,csbt}
  == csbh csbt ==> ($`wait:csah:csat:$`signal:A | B | S1)
                                    \{csah,csat,csbh,csbt}
  == csah csat ==> ($`signal:A | $`wait:csbh:csbt:$`signal:B | $signal:S1)
                                    \{csah,csat,csbh,csbt}
  == csbh csbt ==> ($`wait:csah:csat:$`signal:A | $`signal:B | $signal:S1)
                                    \{csah,csat,csbh,csbt}
  == csah ==> (csat:$`signal:A | $`wait:csbh:csbt:$`signal:B | $signal:S1)
                                    \{csah,csat,csbh,csbt}
  == csbh ==> ($`wait:csah:csat:$`signal:A | csbt:$`signal:B | $signal:S1)
                                    \{csah,csat,csbh,csbt}
  == ==> (csah:csat:$`signal:A | $`wait:csbh:csbt:$`signal:B | S0)
                                    \{csah,csat,csbh,csbt}
  == ==> ($`wait:csah:csat:$`signal:A | csbh:csbt:$`signal:B | S0)
                                    \{csah,csat,csbh,csbt}
  == ==> ($`wait:csah:csat:$`signal:A | $`wait:csbh:csbt:$`signal:B
                                  | $wait:S0)
                                    \{csah,csat,csbh,csbt}
  == ==> SYShid
```

```
*****************************************************
* Their observational equivalence is
*****************************************************
  Command: eq(ObsSPEC,SYS);
  true
```

The semaphore allows the two users to access the shared resource with mutual exclusion.

That CWB tells us if an algorithm is wrong is agreeable, but it would be better if it could also tell us in what way it's wrong, and why. As an example, we'll use an algorithm suggested earlier to provide mutual exclusion.

```
*****************************************************
* Mutual Exclusion (see section 4.9.1)
***
* Two processes, defined by
*               P1 def p1w:= true:X
*               P2 def p2w:= true:Y
*                   where
*               X def if(p2w) then X
*                           else cs1:p1w:=false:NCS1:P1
*               Y def if(p1w) then Y
*                           else cs2:p2w:=false:NCS2:P2
* use want flags in an attempt to ensure that only
* one is in its critical section, cs, at any one
* time. When not in their critical sections,
* NCS, they proceed concurrently. Where
*       p1wfr = read p1wants when false
*       p1wfw = write p1wants making it false
*       p1wtr = read p1wants when true
*       p1wtw = write p1wants making it true
*****************************************************
  Command: agent P1 = p1wtw:X;
  Command: agent X = p2wfr:X + p2wfr:enter1:p1wfw:exit1:P1;

  Command: agent P2 = p2wtw:Y;
  Command: agent Y = p1wtr:Y + p1wfr:enter2:p2wfw:exit2:P2;


*****************************************************
* The two processes want flags
*               P1WT = p1wants true
*               P1WF = p1wants false
*               P2W has similar forms
*****************************************************
```

```
Command: agent P1WT = `p1wtr:P1WT + `p1wtw:P1WT
                         + `p1wfw:P1WF + 1:P1WT;
Command: agent P1WF = `p1wfr:P1WF + `p1wfw:P1WF
                         + `p1wtw:P1WT + 1:P1WF;
Command: agent P2WT = `p2wtr:P2WT + `p2wtw:P2WT
                         + `p2wfw:P2WF + 1:P2WT;
Command: agent P2WF = `p2wfr:P2WF + `p2wfw:P2WF
                         + `p2wtw:P2WT + 1:P2WF;


*****************************************************
* The complete system
*****************************************************
  Command: agent V4 = (P1|P2|P1WF|P2WF)\B;
  Command: set B = {enter1, exit1, enter2, exit2};


*****************************************************
* All meet the specification
*****************************************************
  Command: agent ObsSPEC = $(Obs1SPEC + Obs2SPEC);
  Command: agent Obs1SPEC = enter1:$exit1:ObsSPEC;
  Command: agent Obs2SPEC = enter2:$exit2:ObsSPEC;


*****************************************************
* Are the design and specification bisimilar?
*****************************************************
  Command: eq(ObsSPEC,V4);
  false


*****************************************************
* Why not? Let us look at their behaviours
*****************************************************
  Command: statesexp ObsSPEC;
  — enter2 —→ $exit2:ObsSPEC
  — enter1 —→ $exit1:ObsSPEC
  — 1 —→ $Obs1SPEC + Obs2SPEC
  — —→ ObsSPEC

  Command: statesexp V4;
  — 1 —→ (X | Y | P1WT | P2WT)\B
  — —→ V4
```

```
*********************************************************
* Rather then search through derivation trees, we have
* commands which get to the root of certain problems
* and tell us how they arose.
* For example, deadlock:
*********************************************************
  Command: deadlocks V4;
  — —→ V4
  — 1 —→ (X | Y | P1WT | P2WT)\B
```

With a lot less fuss than the pencil and paper method, CWB tells us the algorithm ends in deadlock.

Just to show that things would work out when there is no conflict, consider the case when only one process attempts to use the resource.

```
*********************************************************
* Mutual Exclusion – only one process
*               P1 def p1w:= true:X
*                   where
*              X def if(p2w) then X
*                         else cs1:p1w:=false:NCS1:P1
* which uses the same want flags to ensure
* mutual exclusion is maintained
*********************************************************
  Command: agent P1 = p1wtw:X;
  Command: agent X = p2wtr:X + p2wfr:enter1:p1wfw:exit1:P1;


*********************************************************
* The want flags remain
*********************************************************
  Command: agent P1WT = `p1wtr:P1WT + `p1wtw:P1WT
                         + `p1wfw:P1WF + 1:P1WT;
  Command: agent P1WF = `p1wfr:P1WF + `p1wfw:P1WF
                         + `p1wtw:P1WT + 1:P1WF;
  Command: agent P2WT = `p2wtr:P2WT + `p2wtw:P2WT
                         + `p2wfw:P2WF + 1:P2WT;
  Command: agent P2WF = `p2wfr:P2WF + `p2wfw:P2WF
                         + `p2wtw:P2WT + 1:P2WF;
```

```
*****************************************************
* The complete system
*****************************************************
   Command: agent V4 = (P1|P1WF|P2WF)\B;
   Command: set B = {enter1,exit1};


*****************************************************
* All meet the specification
*****************************************************
   Command: agent Obs1SPEC = $enter1:$exit1:Obs1SPEC;


*****************************************************
* Their observational behaviours...
*****************************************************
   Command: statesexp Obs1SPEC;
   ── enter1 ──→ $exit1:Obs1SPEC
   ── 1 ──→ $enter1:$exit1:Obs1SPEC
   ── ──→ Obs1SPEC


   Command: statesexp V4;
   ── 1 1 enter1 1 exit1 ──→ (P1 | P1WF | P2WF)\B
   ── 1 1 enter1 1 ──→ (exit1:P1 | P1WF | P2WF)\B
   ── 1 1 enter1 ──→ (p1wfw:exit1:P1 | P1WT | P2WF)\B
   ── 1 1 ──→ (enter1:p1wfw:exit1:P1 | P1WT | P2WF)\B
   ── 1 ──→ (X | P1WT | P2WF)\B
   ── ──→ V4


*****************************************************
* ...are the same, which is supported by
*****************************************************
   Command: eq(Obs1SPEC,V4);
   true
```

6.3 Comments

The workbench has automated the checking equalities between expressions: strong bisimulation for real-time systems; observational equivalence and congruence for asynchronous systems; and by doing so CWB has automated the design validation process. Well, almost. Using SCCS expressions as specifications has limitations; in many cases, being constrained to compare a design with a specification by comparing them action for action is too strong, and the next section introduces a more flexible way of writing specifications.

7. Proving Things Correct

Introduction

So far we've checked to see if a design is correct by taking two SCCS agents, one representing the specification and the other the proposed design, and compared their behaviours action by action using bisimulations – strong bisimulation for complete system behaviour and weaker observational bisimulation for external behaviours. While this method scores on simplicity, in lots of cases action by action comparison is too distinctive; rather than proving two agents identical, we're more likely to want to prove that they either have or do not have certain properties. Following an approached used in [Fen96], consider agents:

$$P \stackrel{\text{def}}{=} \mathbb{0}$$
$$Pa \stackrel{\text{def}}{=} a:\mathbb{0}$$
$$P1 \stackrel{\text{def}}{=} 1:a:b:\mathbb{0}$$
$$Q \stackrel{\text{def}}{=} a:Q$$
$$R \stackrel{\text{def}}{=} a:(b:\mathbb{0} + c:\mathbb{0})$$
$$S \stackrel{\text{def}}{=} a:b:\mathbb{0} + c:\mathbb{0}$$
$$T \stackrel{\text{def}}{=} a:b:\mathbb{0} + c:\mathbb{0} + d:\mathbb{0}$$
$$U \stackrel{\text{def}}{=} 1:b:(b:\mathbb{0} + c:\mathbb{0})$$

None of these is equal under bisimulation, but they do have behaviours in common; for example, agents R, S, T and U all have 'b' as possible second actions; all agents except Q terminate; P1 and U both engage in an internal action before their first observable action; and so on. While this selection of properties allows us to controllably weaken specifications to the limit of what is appropriate (the weaker the specification, the greater the number of acceptable solutions and the easier will be to find the simplest of them) its main attraction is that it gives us a different way of specifying, and ultimately of verifying, longer-term behaviours such as liveness and safety, which proved difficult with process algebras alone. But more of that later; first we need to explore just how to write such specifications.

The simplest way of expressing behaviours is in terms of immediate properties – what the next actions are. For example, P has no first action; the first actions of

Pa, Q and R are all 'a'; the first actions of P1 and U internal; we can then go on to define what properties we want from second actions, and so on. Now, if we had a logic over combinations of these simple properties, we could selectively check the behaviour of an agent for its complete life. The types of properties we could look for could include: whether an agent is live, i.e. something good eventually happens – for example, if action b is itself good, or guards a good state, then agents P1 and U are live; whether an agent is safe, i.e. nothing bad ever happens – for example, if action c is bad, or guards a bad state, then agents P, Pa, P1, Q and T are safe; and so on.

To decide which agents meet a specification, we need to show which agents have the properties cited in a specification as they evolve – in their initial states they pass the first test, their successors pass the second test, and so on. For example, agent P $\stackrel{\text{def}}{=}$ request:δget:0 has property 'first action request' and 'subsequent action get', and will meet the specification 'after a request agent will eventually get' whereas Q $\stackrel{\text{def}}{=}$ request:0 won't. To validate designs using agent properties we need a basic and sufficient framework that not only can describe simple behaviours but also may be used as a foundation for higher-order formulas capable of specifying system behaviours of any complexity. This is where Modal Logics, and in particular Hennessy-Milner Logic (HML), step in. Rather as traces are to CSP, HML is distinct from, but isomorphic to, transition-system-based process algebras like CSP and SCCS – their isomorphism gives us the ability to directly compare SCCS designs with HML specifications.

7.1 Modal Logics

7.1.1 Hennessy–Milner Logic

Modal logics think of systems in terms of their properties in given states, using as underlying models labelled transition systems ($\mathcal{P}$, { $\stackrel{\alpha}{\longrightarrow}$ | $\alpha \in \mathcal{A}ct$ }), where $\mathcal{P}$ is a non-empty set of states, $\mathcal{A}ct$ is an action set, and α a transition from $\mathcal{A}ct$, $\alpha \in \mathcal{A}ct$, where systems move between states by engaging in actions from $\mathcal{A}ct$. We, on the other hand, are more interested in process algebra models where states and agents are interchangeable concepts and, without loss of generality, we can apply modal logic to the transition system underlying SCCS where $\mathcal{P}$ is a non-empty set of agents, $\mathcal{A}ct$ is an action set, and α a transition from $\mathcal{A}ct$ by which agents transforms themselves into other agents. To distinguish between actions we use lower-case Greek letters α, β, χ, ξ, ... to label general actions (except for ϵ, δ, ϕ and φ, which are reserved); 1 for internal actions; for particular external actions whose directions are unimportant, we use lower-case letters a, b, c, ...; if directionals are important we use a?, b?, c?, ... for input actions and a!, b!, c!, ... for output actions; and for actions linked to real-world events we use labels like tick, croak, ... and so on.

The modal logic of particular interest to us is Hennessy–Milner logic (HML), which complements process algebras by describing agent behaviours in terms of formulas over agent properties. The simplest logic formulas (see [HenMil80] and [HenMil85]) are:

$$\phi ::= \mathtt{tt} \mid \neg\phi \mid \phi_1 \wedge \phi_2 \mid [K]\phi$$

A formula, ϕ, is either the constant formula true $\mathtt{tt}$; the negation of a formula $\neg\phi$; the conjunction of two formulas $\phi_1 \wedge \phi_2$; or $[K]\phi$ a modalised formula. $[K]\phi$ which is true if, after *every* action in K, property ϕ holds, where K is a subset of the action set $\mathcal{Act}$, $K\subseteq\mathcal{Act}$. To keep things simple, when a specific action set is used for K it is usual to write $[\alpha_1, \alpha_2, \ldots, \alpha_n]$ instead of $[\{\alpha_1, \alpha_2, \ldots, \alpha_n\}]$.

To give a semantics to the logic we use a satisfaction relation; where $P \models \phi$ means agent P has property ϕ, and $P \not\models \phi$ means that it hasn't, we can write:

$$P \models \mathtt{tt}, \mathtt{tt} \text{ satisfies all agents}$$
$$P \models \neg\phi, \text{ iff } P \not\models \phi$$
$$P \models \phi_1 \wedge \phi_2, \text{ iff } P \models \phi_1 \text{ and } P \models \phi_2$$
$$P \models [K]\phi, \text{ iff } \forall P' \in \mathcal{P}. \ \forall\alpha\in K. \ (P\xrightarrow{\alpha}P' \Rightarrow P' \models \phi)$$

If we put that into words: by the act of existing, every agent has property $\mathtt{tt}$, where every agent includes $\mathbb{0}$; an agent has property $\neg\phi$ if it does not have property ϕ; an agent has property $\phi_1 \wedge \phi_2$ if it has both properties ϕ_1 and ϕ_2; and P satisfies $[K]\phi$, P $\models [K]\phi$, if for all $\alpha\in K$, whenever $P\xrightarrow{\alpha}P'$ then P' satisfies ϕ, $[K]\phi = \bigwedge_{\alpha\in K}[\alpha]\phi$. Informally, agent P has property $[K]\phi$ if, after every K action, all the resulting agents have the property ϕ. A special case, $[K]\mathtt{tt}$, looks on first sight to be capable of discriminating between agents that can perform K actions and those that cannot. However, things aren't always what they seem; with an implication in its definition, $\forall P' \in \mathcal{P}. \ (P\xrightarrow{K}P' \Rightarrow P'\models\mathtt{tt})$, as $(P\xrightarrow{K}P'\Rightarrow\mathtt{true})=\mathtt{true}$[†] whatever the K, $[K]\mathtt{tt}$ holds for all agents including $\mathbb{0}$. But all is not lost; a small change from $[K]\mathtt{tt}$ to $[K]\mathtt{ff}$ gives us the formula we seek. First the change. Using formula $\phi := \neg\phi$ and constant formula true, $\mathtt{tt}$, we can define the constant formula false, $\mathtt{ff}$:

$$\mathtt{ff} = \neg\mathtt{tt}$$

Now, just as $\mathtt{tt}$ is a property of all agents, $\mathtt{ff}$ is a property of none. By replacing the $\mathtt{tt}$ in $[K]\mathtt{tt}$ with $\mathtt{ff}$ we get $[K]\mathtt{ff}$, which represents an inability to perform *any* action in K. Specifically, $P \models [K]\mathtt{ff}$ holds if P has no K-derivatives and $P \models [\alpha]\mathtt{ff}$ holds if P has no α-derivatives.

---

† Truth tables for IMPLIES $\Rightarrow$, AND $\wedge$ and OR $\vee$

x	y	x$\Rightarrow$y	x$\wedge$y	x$\vee$y
false	false	true	false	false
false	true	true	false	true
true	false	false	false	true
true	true	true	true	true

proof

For $P \stackrel{\text{def}}{=} \alpha : P'$

α is a valid initial action of P and, as no agents satisfy ff, $P' \models \text{ff}$ is false, from $(\text{true} \Rightarrow \text{false}) = \text{false}$ we see that formula $[\alpha]\text{ff}$ does not satisfy P.

$P \models [\alpha]\text{ff}$ is false from

$$P' \in \mathcal{P}. \ \alpha \in K. \ (P \stackrel{\alpha}{\longrightarrow} P' \Rightarrow P' \models \text{ff})$$
$$(\text{true} \Rightarrow \text{false})$$
$$\text{false}$$

Written as $(\alpha : P') \not\models [\alpha]\text{ff}$

■

examples

(a) Given FROG $\stackrel{\text{def}}{=}$ croak:$\mathbb{0}$

FROG has a croak-derivative, [croak]ff cannot satisfy FROG and it's not true that FROG cannot croak.

FROG $\not\models$ [croak]ff

As FROG has no quack-derivatives [quack]ff satisfies FROG. FROG cannot quack.

FROG $\models$ [quack]ff

Similarly, as FROG has neither quack- nor moo-derivatives, FROG cannot quack or moo.

FROG $\models$ [quack,moo]ff

Finally, though FROG has a croak-derivative it has no quack-derivative, so it's not true that FROG cannot croak or quack.

FROG $\not\models$ [croak,quack]ff

(b) Given DUCK $\stackrel{\text{def}}{=}$ fly:$\mathbb{0}$ + quack:$\mathbb{0}$

DUCK has no moo-derivative so DUCK cannot moo.

DUCK $\models$ [moo]ff

As DUCK has both quack- and fly-derivatives it isn't true that DUCK cannot croak or fly.

DUCK $\not\models$ [quack,fly]ff

Whilst DUCK has no moo-derivatives it has a quack-derivative, so it's not true that DUCK cannot moo or quack.

DUCK $\not\models$ [quack,moo]ff

As DUCK has neither croak- nor moo-derivatives, it cannot croak or moo.

DUCK $\models$ [croak,moo]ff

■

As well as double negatives, for example $\phi = \neg(\neg\phi)$, we also have duals:

$$\phi_1 \vee \phi_2 = \neg(\neg\phi_1 \wedge \neg\phi_2)$$

a disjunction of properties, which holds if either ϕ_1 or ϕ_2 holds; and:

$$\langle K \rangle \phi = \neg [K] \neg \phi$$

a direct reading of which is $\langle K \rangle \phi$ holds if ϕ doesn't hold after not all actions in K; which is more conventionally expressed as '$\langle K \rangle \phi$ holds if there exists at least one K action after whose performance ϕ holds'.[†] Their associated satisfaction relations are:

$$P \not\models \text{ff}$$
$$P \models \phi_1 \vee \phi_2, \text{ iff } P \models \phi_1 \text{ or } P \models \phi_2$$

and as $\neg(a \Rightarrow (\neg b)) = a \wedge b$, the definition of $\langle K \rangle \phi$ derived from that of $[K]\phi$ is:

$$P \models \langle K \rangle \phi, \text{ iff } \exists P' \in \mathcal{P}. \ \exists a \in K. \ (P \xrightarrow{\alpha} P' \wedge P' \models \phi)$$

where P satisfies $\langle K \rangle \phi$ if there are some $a \in K$ such that $P \xrightarrow{\alpha} P'$ *and* P' satisfies ϕ, $\langle K \rangle \phi = \bigvee_{\alpha \in K} \langle \alpha \rangle \phi$. That is, $P \models \langle K \rangle \phi$ holds if P *has at least one* K-derivative for which ϕ holds. Special cases of $P \models \langle K \rangle \phi$ include $P \models \langle K \rangle \text{tt}$, P has at least one K-derivative, and $P \models \langle \alpha \rangle \text{tt}$, P has at least one α-derivative.

proof

For $P \stackrel{\text{def}}{=} \alpha : P'$

α is a valid initial action of P, it has an α–derivative, which satisfies tt and as $(\text{true} \wedge \text{true}) = \text{true}$ then $\langle a \rangle \text{tt}$ satisfies P, $P \models \langle \alpha \rangle \text{tt}$.

From

$$P \models \langle \alpha \rangle \text{tt is true from}$$
$$P' \in \mathcal{P}. \ a \in K. \ (P \xrightarrow{\alpha} P' \wedge P' \models \text{tt})$$
$$(\text{true} \wedge \text{true})$$
$$\text{true}$$

∎

examples

(a) Given FROG $\stackrel{\text{def}}{=}$ croak : ⓪

FROG has a croak-derivative, FROG can croak.

     FROG $\models$ ⟨croak⟩tt

While FROG has a no quack-derivative, it has a croak-derivative. FROG can either croak or quack.

     FROG $\models$ ⟨croak, quack⟩tt

FROG has neither moo- nor quack-derivative, it can neither moo nor quack.

     FROG $\not\models$ ⟨moo, quack⟩tt

(b) Given DUCK $\stackrel{\text{def}}{=}$ fly : ⓪ + quack : ⓪:

DUCK $\models$ ⟨fly⟩tt	DUCK can fly,
DUCK $\models$ ⟨fly, quack⟩tt	can either fly or quack,
DUCK $\models$ ⟨fly, croak⟩tt	can either fly or croak,
DUCK $\not\models$ ⟨moo, croak⟩tt	but can neither moo nor croak.

∎

---

† Warning: As the English language is not a precise vehicle, these textual 'interpretations' of modal logic formulas may mislead and it is advisable, especially for the more complicated expressions, to return to the modal world for unambiguous definitions.

As well as deciding if a particular agent satisfies a given formula we could also look upon each ϕ property as defining that subset of processes $\|\phi\| \subseteq \mathcal{P}$ which have property ϕ, where the function $\| \ \|$ takes a formula as an argument and delivers a set of agents as a result. We can now consider a specification as an expression over properties that denote a set of validated agents, an agent satisfying a specification if it is a member of that set. This gives

$$\|tt\| = \mathcal{P}$$
$$\|\neg\phi\| = \mathcal{P} - \|\phi\|$$
$$\|\phi_1 \wedge \phi_2\| = \|\phi_1\| \cap \|\phi_2\|$$
$$\|[K]\phi\| = [\overline{K}] \ \|\phi\|$$

As the formula tt holds for any agent it, defines the set of all agents $\mathcal{P}$, the formula $\|\neg\phi\|$ describes agents which do not have the property ϕ and hence is the set of all agents $\mathcal{P}$ less those which do satisfy ϕ; the formula $\phi_1 \wedge \phi_2$ defines agents which satisfy both ϕ_1 and ϕ_2, the intersection of sets $\|\phi_1\|$ and $\|\phi_2\|$. The last formula $\|[K]\phi\| = [\overline{K}] \ \|\phi\|$ uses the function $[\overline{K}]$ which takes the complete set of agents $\mathcal{P}$ and delivers the subset $\mathcal{P}'$, $\mathcal{P}' \subseteq \mathcal{P}$, which have the following properties:

$$[\overline{K}]\mathcal{P}' = \{ P \in \mathcal{P} \mid \forall P' \in \mathcal{P}. \forall \alpha \in K. \ \text{if } P \xrightarrow{\alpha} P' \text{ then } P' \in \mathcal{P}' \}$$

$\|\phi\| \subseteq \mathcal{P}$ defines the agents that have property ϕ, $[\overline{K}] \ \|\phi\|$ defines the set of agents from $\mathcal{P}$ whose every K–derivative has property ϕ; and this is just what we want.

We can extend these definitions into their duals in

$$\|ff\| = \|\neg tt\| = \mathcal{P} - \mathcal{P} = \{ \}$$
$$\|\phi_1 \vee \phi_2\| = \|\phi_1\| \cup \|\phi_2\|$$

The formula ff holds for no agents and $\|ff\|$ defines the empty set $\{ \}$. The formula $\phi_1 \vee \phi_2$ defines agents which satisfy ϕ_1 or ϕ_2 and is the union of sets $\|\phi_1\|$ and $\|\phi_2\|$. For any $\mathcal{P}' \subseteq \mathcal{P}$ the function $\langle \overline{K} \rangle$ in $\|\langle K \rangle \phi\| = \langle \overline{K} \rangle \ \|\phi\|$ is defined by:

$$\langle \overline{K} \rangle \mathcal{P}' = \{ P \in \mathcal{P} \mid \exists P' \in \mathcal{P}'. \exists \alpha \in K. \ P \xrightarrow{\alpha} P' \}$$

giving $\|\langle K \rangle \phi\|$ as the set of agents each with at least one K–derivative.

Fine; we now have a logic of agent properties that, when considered as specifications, can separate agents into those that have certain properties, satisfy a specification, and those that do not. But to write clear and understandable specifications our existing logic is too verbose – what we want is terse forms which precisely capture agent behaviours, the simpler the better. After the constants tt and ff, which define all agents and no agents; the simplest, most appropriate formulas are the modal terms $[\alpha]tt$, $[\alpha]ff$, $\langle\alpha\rangle tt$, $\langle\alpha\rangle ff$; but are these the most appropriate? If they are, which of them would form the best foundations for a specification language? To make such decisions, first we have to assure ourselves as to what these term mean. $\langle\alpha\rangle ff$ holds for no agents, $[\alpha]tt$ for all agents, $\langle\alpha\rangle tt$ for those agents which can perform an α action and $[\alpha]ff$ for those which cannot. The proofs follow.

proof

- $[\alpha]$tt holds for all agents.

  The set $\|[\alpha]\text{tt}\|$ is defined by $\{P \in \mathcal{P} \mid \forall P' \in \mathcal{P}.\ P\overset{\alpha}{\longrightarrow}P' \Rightarrow P' \vDash \text{tt}\}$. As all agents satisfy tt, $P' \vDash$ tt is always true, which gives $P\overset{\alpha}{\longrightarrow}P' \Rightarrow$ true. From the definition of $\Rightarrow$, $P\overset{\alpha}{\longrightarrow}P' \Rightarrow$ true is always true, therefore all agents $P \in \mathcal{P}$ have property $[\alpha]$tt and
  $$\|[\alpha]\text{tt}\| = \mathcal{P}$$

- $[\alpha]$ff holds for agents which have no α-derivatives.

  The set $\|[\alpha]\text{ff}\|$ is defined by $\{P \in \mathcal{P} \mid \forall P' \in \mathcal{P}.\ P\overset{\alpha}{\longrightarrow}P' \Rightarrow P' \vDash \text{ff}\}$. As no agents satisfy ff, $P' \vDash$ ff is always false, giving $P\overset{\alpha}{\longrightarrow}P' \Rightarrow$ false. $P\overset{\alpha}{\longrightarrow}P' \Rightarrow$ false is only true if $P\overset{\alpha}{\longrightarrow}P'$ is false, $\|[\alpha]\text{ff}\|$ holds for agents with no α-derivatives
  $$\|[\alpha]\text{ff}\| = \{\text{agents with no } \alpha\text{-derivatives}\}$$

- $\langle\alpha\rangle$tt holds for agents which have α-derivatives.

  The set $\|\langle\alpha\rangle\text{tt}\|$ is defined by $\{P \in \mathcal{P} \mid \exists P' \in \mathcal{P}.\ P\overset{\alpha}{\longrightarrow}P' \wedge P' \vDash \text{tt}\}$. As all agents satisfy tt, $P' \vDash$ tt is always true, giving $P\overset{\alpha}{\longrightarrow}P' \wedge$ true. $P\overset{\alpha}{\longrightarrow}P' \wedge$ true is true if $P\overset{\alpha}{\longrightarrow}P'$ is true, $\|\langle\alpha\rangle\text{tt}\|$ holds for agents with α-derivatives
  $$\|\langle\alpha\rangle\text{tt}\| = \{\text{agents with } \alpha\text{-derivatives}\}$$

- $\langle\alpha\rangle$ff holds for no agents.

  The set $\|\langle\alpha\rangle\text{ff}\|$ is defined by $\{P \in \mathcal{P} \mid \exists P' \in \mathcal{P}.\ P\overset{\alpha}{\longrightarrow}P' \wedge P' \vDash \text{ff}\}$. As no agents satisfy ff, $P' \vDash$ ff is always false, giving $P\overset{\alpha}{\longrightarrow}P' \wedge$ false. As $P\overset{\alpha}{\longrightarrow}P' \wedge$ false is always false, $\|\langle\alpha\rangle\text{ff}\|$ holds for no agents
  $$\|\langle\alpha\rangle\text{ff}\| = \{\ \}$$

■

So two of the formulas
$$\|[\alpha]\text{tt}\| = \|\text{tt}\| = \mathcal{P}$$
$$\|\langle\alpha\rangle\text{ff}\| = \|\text{ff}\| = \{\ \}$$
add nothing to the logic, covered as they are by existing constants, but the other two,
$$\|[\alpha]\text{ff}\| = \{\text{agents with no } \alpha\text{-derivatives}\}$$
$$\|\langle\alpha\rangle\text{tt}\| = \{\text{agents with } \alpha\text{-derivatives}\}$$
more than make up for this lapse. To compare agents, we check their actions as they evolve; agents are equivalent if they can always perform the same actions, different if they cannot – which is precisely what $\langle\alpha\rangle$tt and $[\alpha]$ff gives us.

example

Consider agents
$$P \overset{\text{def}}{=} \textcircled{0}$$
$$Pa \overset{\text{def}}{=} a : \textcircled{0}$$
$$P1 \overset{\text{def}}{=} 1 : a : b : \textcircled{0}$$
$$Q \overset{\text{def}}{=} a : Q$$

$$R \overset{\text{def}}{=} a:(b:\mathbb{0} + c:\mathbb{0})$$
$$S \overset{\text{def}}{=} a:b:\mathbb{0} + c:\mathbb{0}$$
$$T \overset{\text{def}}{=} a:b:\mathbb{0} + c:\mathbb{0} + d:\mathbb{0}$$
$$U \overset{\text{def}}{=} 1:b:(b:\mathbb{0} + c:\mathbb{0})$$

the specification $\|[a]tt\|$ is met by all the processes, including $\mathbb{0}$

$$\|[a]tt\| = \{P, Pa, P1, Q, R, S, T, U\}$$

$\|[a]ff\|$ by agents which cannot engage in a, have no a-derivatives.

$$\|[a]ff\| = \{P, P1, U\}$$

$\|\langle a\rangle tt\|$ by agents which can engage in a, have a-derivatives.

$$\|\langle a\rangle tt\| = \{Pa, Q, R, S, T\}$$

$\|\langle a\rangle ff\|$ by none.

$$\|\langle a\rangle ff\| = \{\ \}$$

In particular

$\|\langle 1\rangle tt\|$ is met by agents which can idle

$$\|\langle 1\rangle tt\| = \{P1, U\}$$

$\|[1]ff\|$ by agents which cannot

$$\|[1]ff\| = \{P, Pa, Q, R, S, T\}$$

■

We can now write modal logic specifications in terms of these two formulas:

$P \vDash \langle\alpha\rangle tt$ holds if P has an α–derivative;

$P \vDash [\alpha]ff$ holds if P has no α–derivatives and this includes $\mathbb{0}$;

and use them to prove if an agent does, or does not, meet a given specification by simply checking to see if it does, or does not, have the necessary derivatives which satisfy the required properties. We can humanise the sight reading of agent behaviours by expressing these formula in terms of capabilities: what agents are capable or not capable of; or conversely, refusals: what agents can or cannot refuse to do:

$P \vDash \langle\alpha\rangle tt$ – P cannot refuse α, it expresses the capability of performing α,

$P \vDash [\alpha]ff$ – P refuses α, it expresses the inability to perform α.

using whichever term best fits the circumstances.

examples

a) $P \overset{\text{def}}{=} 1:a:P'$ and $Q \overset{\text{def}}{=} a:Q'$ have different first actions.
$\langle 1\rangle tt$ is true for P, P has a 1–derivative and cannot refuse a 1; and
$\langle a\rangle tt$ is true for Q, Q has an a–derivative and cannot refuse an a.
P satisfies $\langle 1\rangle tt$ but Q does not, Q satisfies $\langle a\rangle tt$ but P does not.

b) $P \overset{\text{def}}{=} a:P' + b:P''$ and $Q \overset{\text{def}}{=} a:Q'$ have different choices of initial
actions. $\langle a\rangle tt$ is true for both P and Q – neither P or Q can refuse an
a. But $\langle b\rangle tt$ is true for P only – P cannot refuse an b but Q can. P
satisfies $\langle b\rangle tt$ but Q does not.

c)   When checking an agent against a formula, their properties, in the terms of actions, have to match precisely. In SCCS terms, action particles must match, and, while a! : P satisfies ⟨a!⟩tt, it needs a!xb? : P to satisfy ⟨a!xb?⟩tt.

■

As modal formulas return boolean values, we can use boolean connectives to compose grander formulas. For example, ⟨tick⟩tt ∧ [tock]ff defines agents which can tick and not tock. Further, as single occurrences of [ ] and ⟨ ⟩ check an agent's immediate actions, by combining them into strings we can check evolving agents. For example, with ⟨α⟩⟨β, χ⟩⟨ξ⟩ ... the first bit, ⟨α⟩, checks the first action, ⟨β, χ⟩ the second action, ⟨ξ⟩ its derivatives, and so on.

Strings of ⟨ ⟩s are natural parallels of traces; if P can perform trace $\alpha_1, \alpha_2, \ldots, \alpha_n$, then P has the property ⟨α_1⟩⟨α_2⟩ ... ⟨α_n⟩tt. For example, P $\stackrel{\text{def}}{=}$ α:β:χ:P′ has the property ⟨α⟩⟨β⟩⟨χ⟩tt. In more detail, P, written in normal form P $\stackrel{\text{def}}{=}$ α:P′, P′ $\stackrel{\text{def}}{=}$ β:P″ and P″ $\stackrel{\text{def}}{=}$ χ:P‴, will satisfy ⟨α⟩⟨β⟩⟨χ⟩tt from

$(P \stackrel{\alpha}{\to} P' \wedge P' \models ⟨\beta⟩⟨\chi⟩tt)$, if P has an α–derivative and P′ ⊨ ⟨β⟩⟨χ⟩tt

and following the nesting, P′ ⊨ ⟨β⟩⟨χ⟩tt if

$(P' \stackrel{\beta}{\to} P'' \wedge P'' \models ⟨\chi⟩tt)$, P′ has a β–derivative and P″ ⊨ ⟨χ⟩tt

and again, P′ ⊨ ⟨χ⟩tt if

$(P'' \stackrel{\chi}{\to} P''' \wedge P''' \models tt)$, P″ has a χ–derivative

We can, of course, mix modalities, as with P which will satisfy [α]⟨β⟩tt if $(P \stackrel{\alpha}{\to} P' \Rightarrow P' \models ⟨\beta⟩tt)$, P has no α–derivatives, or if all P's α–derivatives have a β–derivative.

We can thus use strings to check agent behaviours by effectively 'unrolling' a specification against an agent, 'action by action', until we get to the terminating tt or ff; where P ⊨ [α]ff can refuse an α and P ⊨ ⟨α⟩tt cannot refuse an α. For example, as α:β:0 has an α–derivative that satisfies [α]ff it satisfies [α][α]ff which α:α:0 fails to do; alternatively, as α:α:0 has an α–derivative that satisfies ⟨α⟩tt it satisfies [α]⟨α⟩tt which α:β:0 does not. In sight reading terms, α:β:0, after accepting an initial α, can refuse another, whereas α:α:0, after an initial α, cannot.

As composite formulas will fail if one of their propositions fails, it is not always necessary to evaluate the complete string but only to go as far as the point where the outcome is determined. For example, ⟨α⟩⟨β⟩⟨χ⟩tt cannot hold for agents with no α–derivatives, those with no αβ–derivatives, or those with no αβχ–derivatives. In particular, we only need go as far as the second action in P $\stackrel{\text{def}}{=}$ α:α:χ:P′ to show P⊭⟨α⟩⟨β⟩⟨χ⟩tt.

examples

a) P $\stackrel{\text{def}}{=}$ a:b:P′ and Q $\stackrel{\text{def}}{=}$ a:0 + a:b:Q′ differ in their second actions
     [a]tt holds for both P and Q,

[a]⟨b⟩tt for P but not for Q.

After performing a P has to engage in b but Q may have chosen not to. P satisfies [a]⟨b⟩tt but Q does not.

Or we can appeal to the more formal:
   P has no a–derivatives that don't satisfy tt, P⊨[a]tt
   Q has no a–derivatives that don't satisfy tt, Q⊨[a]tt
and
   P has no a–derivatives that don't have β–derivatives, P⊨[a]⟨b⟩tt
   Q has a–derivatives that don't have β–derivatives, Q⊭[a]⟨b⟩tt

b)   P $\stackrel{def}{=}$ a:b:0 and Q $\stackrel{def}{=}$ a:(b:0 + 1:b:0) differ in their choice of second actions

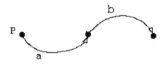 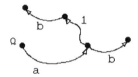

⟨a⟩tt holds for both P and Q
⟨a⟩[1]ff holds for P but not for Q.
P, after performing a, can refuse a 1 but Q cannot. P satisfies ⟨a⟩[1]ff but Q does not.

c)   Remember P $\stackrel{def}{=}$ a:P and Q $\stackrel{def}{=}$ a:Q + a:0

 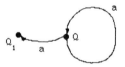

While both ⟨a⟩tt and ⟨a⟩⟨a⟩tt hold for P and Q we can differentiate them by ⟨a⟩[a]ff which holds for Q but not P.

d)   And the similar P $\stackrel{def}{=}$ a:P and Q $\stackrel{def}{=}$ a:Q + 1:a:0

 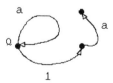

in which Q can engage in an internal 1 whereas P cannot. P satisfies [1]ff but Q does not.

e) STAMP $\stackrel{\text{def}}{=}$ 10pcoin?:10pstamp!:STAMP + 20pcoin?:20pstamp!:STAMP

STAMP $\models$ ⟨10pcoin?⟩tt   can accept a 10p coin,

STAMP $\models$ ⟨10pcoin?⟩tt ∧ ⟨20pcoin?⟩tt   accepts both 10p and 20p coins,

STAMP $\models$ [10pstamp!,20pstamp!]ff   but won't deliver stamps as a
                                             first action

nor accept two coins in a row.

STAMP $\models$ [10pcoin?,20pcoin?][10pcoin?,20pcoin?]ff

■

To make things simpler, rather than enumerating each action in a specification, for both [ ] and ⟨ ⟩ we can call upon some shorthand forms. Where $\mathcal{A}ct$ is the universal set of actions and { } none

'−' is an abbreviation of '−{ }' representing all actions as in $[-]\phi = [\mathcal{A}ct]\phi$
'−$\mathcal{K}$' means all actions except those in $\mathcal{K}$, as in $\langle-\mathcal{K}\rangle\phi = \langle\mathcal{A}ct - \mathcal{K}\rangle\phi$

P satisfies $[-]\phi$, P $\models$ $[-]\phi$, if it satisfies $[\alpha]\phi$ for *all* $\alpha \in \mathcal{A}ct$, and P satisfies $\langle-\rangle\phi$, P $\models$ $\langle-\rangle\phi$, if it satisfies $\langle\alpha\rangle\phi$ for *some* $\alpha \in \mathcal{A}ct$. Specifically,

$$\text{P} \models [-]\text{tt if P} \models [\alpha]\text{tt for all } \alpha \in \mathcal{A}ct$$
$$\text{and P} \models \langle-\rangle\text{tt if P} \models \langle\alpha\rangle\text{tt for some } \alpha \in \mathcal{A}ct.$$

These shorthands give us neat ways of capturing some interesting properties:

- $[-]$ff defines agents which reject all actions. $[-]$ff agents have terminated, and if this is unexpected, such inactive agents may be deadlocked; for example, P $\models$ $[-]$ff is true for P $\stackrel{\text{def}}{=}$ 0 but false for P $\stackrel{\text{def}}{=}$ 1:P′ + 0.
- $\langle-\rangle$tt, the obverse of $[-]$ff, defines agents that cannot refuse any actions and represent agents that have not terminated, aren't deadlocked. For example, P $\models$ $\langle-\rangle$tt is true for P $\stackrel{\text{def}}{=}$ 1:P′ + 0 but false for P $\stackrel{\text{def}}{=}$ 0.

Each '−' simply means some undefined action; in particular $[-]$tt is true for all agents, and, in general, the previous modal logic forms apply with '−' plugged-in in place of named actions. For example, $[-]\langle\alpha\rangle$tt holds for initially inactive agents, or, if active, all those whose derivatives have at least one α−derivative, i.e. agents that are capable of α as a second action. For example, for

$$\text{P0} \stackrel{\text{def}}{=} 0$$
$$\text{Pa} \stackrel{\text{def}}{=} \alpha:\text{Pa}$$
$$\text{Pb} \stackrel{\text{def}}{=} \beta:\text{Pb}$$
$$\text{Pba} \stackrel{\text{def}}{=} \beta:\alpha:\text{Pba}$$
$$\text{we get } \|[-]\langle\alpha\rangle\text{tt}\| = \{\text{P0},\text{Pa},\text{Pba}\}$$

Following their definitions, while $[-]$ prefixes must hold for all (or no) paths, $\langle-\rangle$s need only hold for some. In particular, in a string of ⟨ ⟩s, used to represent action traces, all non-terminal $\langle-\rangle$s represent some action, it doesn't matter what, and only the identity of the last action is of interest; for example, $\langle-\rangle\langle\alpha\rangle$tt holds for agents that may be capable of α as a second action.

'$-\mathcal{K}$', by defining what actions are not being considered in a proposition, helps us write some tight definitions. Take as an example our previous $\langle a \rangle$tt which does not mean 'only action α is possible' but rather 'α is one among perhaps many possible actions', and if we really want 'only action α is possible' we then have to spell out what is impossible, for example in P $\stackrel{\text{def}}{=}$ $\alpha : P'$ we would have to say that α is possible $\langle \alpha \rangle$tt, as well as what other actions, β, χ, etc. are not, giving a proposition along the lines of $(\langle \alpha \rangle$tt $\wedge [\beta]$ff $\wedge [\chi]$ff $\wedge \dots)$. Now, using the $-\mathcal{K}$ abbreviation, we can rewrite this more succinctly as $[-\alpha]$ff which, being satisfied by agents whose next action can be nothing but α, is true only of agents whose initial actions are α or by agents with no actions, $\mathbb{0}$. Because $[-\alpha]$ff is satisfied by $\mathbb{0}$ we need $\langle - \rangle$tt[†] to ride shotgun and see off such agents, giving $(\langle - \rangle$tt $\wedge [-\alpha]$ff$)$ is satisfied by agents with only α–derivatives; for example, P $\stackrel{\text{def}}{=}$ $\alpha : P$ but not P $\stackrel{\text{def}}{=}$ $\beta : P$ or P $\stackrel{\text{def}}{=}$ $\alpha : P + \beta : P$.

'$-\mathcal{K}$' also helps to define agents with a choice of behaviours where, again, not only do we have to specify what initial choices are acceptable but also we must enumerate those that are not. For example, in P $\stackrel{\text{def}}{=}$ $\alpha : P' + \beta : P''$ we would need the conjunction of the formulas allowing actions α and β disjuncted with formulas specifying which actions are to be refused. To contain the explosion of detail we can include within a specification the term $[-\mathcal{K}]$ff which is true for agents which only have an initial choice of actions from $\mathcal{K}$; for example, $[-\alpha, \beta]$ff is satisfied by agents with zero, α or β–derivatives and as such allows $\mathbb{0}$, $\alpha : \mathbb{0}, \beta : \mathbb{0}$ and $\alpha : \mathbb{0} + \beta : \mathbb{0}$ but not $\chi : \mathbb{0}$, $\alpha : \mathbb{0} + \chi : \mathbb{0}$ or $\alpha : \mathbb{0} + \beta : \mathbb{0} + \chi : \mathbb{0}$ – which is nearly what we want. We can then use $\neg[-\alpha]$ff$)$ to exclude agents with only α–derivatives, and $\neg[-\beta]$ff$)$ for those with only β–derivatives, giving $([-\alpha, \beta]$ff $\wedge \neg[-\alpha]$ff $\wedge \neg[-\beta]$ff$)$ which accepts $\alpha : \mathbb{0} + \beta : \mathbb{0}$ and rejects $\mathbb{0}$, $\alpha : \mathbb{0}, \beta : \mathbb{0}$ and $\alpha : \mathbb{0} + \beta : \mathbb{0} + \chi : \mathbb{0}$.

So, while this new notation is no more than that, a notation, it adds greatly to the expressive power of the logic, and hence our ability to write specifications. For example:

- $[-]$ff describes an agent incapable of performing any action, has terminated.
- $\langle - \rangle$tt describes an agent capable of performing any action, has not terminated.
- $(\langle - \rangle$tt $\wedge [-\alpha]$ff$)$ describes an agent capable only of performing α.

---

† As $\langle - \rangle$tt is true for agents which cannot refuse to engage in any action, so it is false for agents that have terminated For this reason we'll see $\langle - \rangle$tt appear in many formulas where we do not want terminated agents as solutions and where such solutions may be allowed by the other components of the formula. For example, all [ ] modalities hold for terminated agents and we need a $\langle - \rangle$tt to insure some action is performed; for example, with $[\alpha]$ff we add the $\langle - \rangle$tt to ensure terminated agents are not considered as solutions. In general the $\langle - \rangle$tt ensures that some action occurs, what those action are being determined the rest of the formula.

- [-α, β]ff describes an agent with an initial choice between α and β.
- ([-α, β]ff ∧ ¬[-α]ff ∧ ¬[-β]ff) describes an agent with an initial choice between only α and β, rejecting those with initially only α or only β.

examples

a) If P0 $\stackrel{\text{def}}{=}$ 0, Pa $\stackrel{\text{def}}{=}$ a:0 and Pab $\stackrel{\text{def}}{=}$ a:0 + b:0

P0 ⊨ [-]ff	P0 ⊨ [a][-]ff	P0 ⊨ [b][-]ff
Pa ⊭ [-]ff	Pa ⊨ [a][-]ff	Pa ⊨ [b][-]ff
Pab ⊭ [-]ff	Pab ⊨ [a][-]ff	Pab ⊨ [b][-]ff

b) If STAMP $\stackrel{\text{def}}{=}$ 10pcoin?:10pstamp!:0 + 20pcoin?:20pstamp!:0

After a 10pcoin only a 10pstamp and not a 20p one can be collected
$$\text{STAMP} ⊨ [10\text{pcoin}?](\langle 10\text{pstamp}!\rangle\text{tt} ∧ [20\text{pstamp}!]\text{ff})$$

As ⟨-⟩tt checks that some action happens and [-a]ff checks that such actions can only be a, the above can be rewritten as:
$$\text{STAMP} ⊨ [10\text{pcoin}?](\langle-\rangle\text{tt} ∧ [-10\text{pstamp}!]\text{ff})$$

c) After a tick, all OLD_CLOCK $\stackrel{\text{def}}{=}$ tick:tock:OLD_CLOCK can do is tock
$$\text{OLD\_CLOCK} ⊨ [\text{tick}](\langle-\rangle\text{tt} ∧ [-\text{tock}]\text{ff})$$

It cannot tick
$$\text{OLD\_CLOCK} ⊭ [\text{tick}](\langle-\rangle\text{tt} ∧ [-\text{tick}]\text{ff})$$

If we want the second action of OLD_CLOCK to be tock, and we don't care about the first action, OLD_CLOCK must satisfy
$$\langle-\rangle\text{tt} ∧ [-] (\langle-\rangle\text{tt} ∧ [-\text{tock}]\text{ff})$$

d) P $\stackrel{\text{def}}{=}$ a:c:P + b:d:P would satisfy [-a, b]ff. Initially either actions a or b are possible, but this can be strengthened to exclude inaction as a solution ([-a,b]ff ∧ ⟨-⟩tt) and further strengthened to (([-a,b]ff) ∧ [-]([-c,d]ff ∧ ⟨-⟩tt) ∧ ⟨-⟩tt) – after an initial choice of a and b, all actions except c and d are impossible. However, impressive as this formula looks, and it does hold for P $\stackrel{\text{def}}{=}$ a:c:P + b:d:P, it also holds for P $\stackrel{\text{def}}{=}$ a:c:P + b:c:P. Now, rather than press on and generate even more complex forms to check for P $\stackrel{\text{def}}{=}$ a:c:P + b:d:P, it is sometimes better to rethink along more modest lines. In this case, thinking of expressions as trace generators to check P $\stackrel{\text{def}}{=}$ a:c:P + b:d:P, we can use (⟨a⟩⟨c⟩tt ∧ ⟨b⟩⟨d⟩tt).

■

With modal logic we have the ability to define system requirements in terms of enumerated sequences of actions to which our solution must conform. Such formulas divide possible solution sets into those agents which satisfy the requirement and those which do not, and, by considering both internal and external actions, as we've done here, we can decide if the behaviour of an agent meets its timing requirements. Sometimes, however, we're only interested in an agent's observational behaviour, and, just as we can have strong and weak equivalences, so we have two sorts of modal logic. The observational variety of modal logic is the topic of the next section.

Observational Properties

We can use SCCS to represent the behaviour of the same object in two forms, depending upon whether or not the observer employed 'sees' internal, 1, actions or not. The resulting algebras have different transition relations, $\rightarrow$ and $\Rightarrow$; different sets of actions; and different equivalences, strong $\sim$ and weak $\approx$, and transition systems defined by $(\mathcal{P}, \{\stackrel{\alpha}{\rightarrow} \mid \alpha \in \mathcal{A}ct\})$ and $(\mathcal{P}, \{\stackrel{\alpha}{\Rightarrow} \mid \alpha \in \mathcal{A}ct'\})$, $\mathcal{A}ct' = (\mathcal{A}ct-\{1\}) \cup \{\varepsilon\}$. Remember, there is no $\stackrel{1}{\Rightarrow}$ relation, only a $\stackrel{\varepsilon}{\Rightarrow}$ which represents zero or more 1 transitions. For each transition system we have logics that differ only in their modalities, $K \subseteq \mathcal{A}ct$ for [K] , modified by $K \subseteq \mathcal{A}ct'$ to [[K]], and we exchange derivatives, which take account of all actions in $\mathcal{A}ct$, for descendants, which acknowledge only the observational subset $\mathcal{A}ct'$. Where

$$P \models [[K]]\phi, \text{ iff } \forall P' \in \mathcal{P}. \ \forall \alpha \in K. \ (P\stackrel{\alpha}{\Rightarrow}P' \Rightarrow P' \models \phi)$$

P satisfies [[K]]ϕ, if *every* K–descendant has property ϕ.

$\langle\langle K \rangle\rangle$, the dual of [[K]], is defined by

$$P \models \langle\langle K \rangle\rangle\phi, \text{ iff } \exists P' \in \mathcal{P}. \ \exists \alpha \in K. \ (P\stackrel{\alpha}{\Rightarrow}P' \wedge P' \models \phi)$$

P satisfies $\langle\langle K \rangle\rangle\phi$, if *at least one* K–descendant has property ϕ.

Rather as observable actions $\Rightarrow$ were defined in terms of all actions $\rightarrow$, the modalities [[K]]ϕ and $\langle\langle K \rangle\rangle\phi$ can be defined in terms of [K] ϕ and $\langle K \rangle\phi$

$$[[K]]\phi = [[\ ]][K][[\ ]]\phi \text{ and } \langle\langle K \rangle\rangle\phi = \langle\langle \ \rangle\rangle\langle K\rangle\langle\langle \ \rangle\rangle\phi$$

where internal sequences are covered by

$$P \models [[\ ]]\phi, \text{ iff } \forall Q \in \{P' : (P\stackrel{\varepsilon}{\Rightarrow}P'\}. \ Q \models \phi)$$
$$P \models \langle\langle \ \rangle\rangle\phi, \text{ iff } \exists Q \in \{P' : (P\stackrel{\varepsilon}{\Rightarrow}P'\}. \ Q \models \phi)$$

We also have $\langle\langle\alpha\rangle\rangle$tt and [[$\alpha$]]ff, analogous to $\langle\alpha\rangle$tt and [α]ff.

$\|\langle\langle\alpha\rangle\rangle$tt$\|$ is the set of agents capable of performing observable action α.

$\|[[\alpha]]$ff$\|$ is the set of agents incapable of performing observable action α.

For example, the property $\langle\langle$croak$\rangle\rangle$tt describes a system capable of observable action croak after any number of internal actions and [[moo]]ff describes a system refusing observable action moo no matter how many internal actions it does first.

Observable modalities also have analogies with the special cases and abbreviations of strong modalities, but, rather than go through the list, we'll illustrate them by examples.

examples

a) FROG $\overset{\text{def}}{=}$ croak:FROG and ILL_FROG $\overset{\text{def}}{=}$ croak:ILL_FROG + 1:0. Both satisfy $\langle\langle$croak$\rangle\rangle$tt, but ILL_FROG, after performing a croak, can silently expire – it has the property $\langle\langle$croak$\rangle\rangle$[[croak]]ff which FROG, locked into croaking forever, does not.

b) P $\overset{\text{def}}{=}$ 1:a:P' and Q $\overset{\text{def}}{=}$ a:Q' have different first actions, but one is internal, and, while under strong modality only P satisfies $\langle 1\rangle$tt when ignoring 1 actions, observationally we cannot tell them apart
$\langle\langle$a$\rangle\rangle$tt is true for both P and Q

c) P $\overset{\text{def}}{=}$ a:P and Q $\overset{\text{def}}{=}$ a:Q + 1:a:Q are indistinguishable observationally.

■

Like observational equivalence, observable modal logic is blind to how many internal actions occur, but by use of ε it retains the capability of distinguishing between $\alpha:0 + \beta:0$, whose environment can control choice, and $\alpha:0 + 1:\beta:0$, which can autonomously withdraw its α action. The second can engage in an internal action, $\langle\langle\varepsilon\rangle\rangle$tt, before refusing an α, [[α]]ff, the first cannot, and we differentiate them by:

$$\alpha:0 + 1:\beta:0 \models \langle\langle\varepsilon\rangle\rangle[[\alpha]]ff$$
$$\alpha:0 + \beta:0 \not\models \langle\langle\varepsilon\rangle\rangle[[\alpha]]ff$$

Similarly, we can differentiate FROG $\overset{\text{def}}{=}$ δcroak:FROG and ILL_FROG $\overset{\text{def}}{=}$ croak:ILL_FROG + 1:0. FROG always croaks after any number (including zero) of internal actions and will satisfy [[ε]]$\langle\langle$croak$\rangle\rangle$tt which ILL_FROG cannot.

While it is useful to consider external behaviours, and for real-time systems formulas with 1's still intact, there's a major problem with both these forms: they only define what is happening at the point of inspection – [α], $\langle\alpha\rangle$, [[α]] and $\langle\langle\alpha\rangle\rangle$ only refer to current states, [α]tt holds for $\alpha:P'$ whatever the P'; and, though such formulas can be used to answer questions about the immediate properties of agents (such as 'can FROG, in its current state, croak?') we cannot use them to address long-term liveness and safety issues (such as whether or not FROG will always croak, or CLOCK will eventually tick). To investigate these longer-term properties, we need to extend the current logic to longer agent runs where a run is a finite (including zero) or an infinite sequence of agent transitions of the form $P_0 \overset{\alpha_1}{\to} P_1 \overset{\alpha_2}{\to} P_2 \overset{\alpha_3}{\to} \ldots$. As such, one can think of a run as the act of traversing a path through an agent's derivation tree. An agent's complete behaviour can now be described in terms of all runs involving maximal sequences of actions where a finite run is simply a maximal run whose final state is incapable of further transitions.

The longer-term questions we wish to ask of agents can now be couched in terms of runs – agents can be considered safe if no runs contain an unsafe property (unwanted properties never hold), and can be considered live if all runs contain good properties (wanted properties eventually hold). We can change these strong temporal properties that hold for all runs to weak safety and weak liveness which need only hold for some runs. But weak or strong, such long-term temporal properties are in reference to an agent's total behaviour, and can only be checked if we consider the agent's properties for all runs – which, for recursive systems, will be infinite. For example, to check if a single state system like CLOCK $\overset{\text{def}}{=}$ tick:CLOCK always ticks, we would have to show that CLOCK satisfies the infinite set of formulas $\langle$tick$\rangle$tt, [tick]$\langle$tick$\rangle$tt, [tick][tick]$\langle$tick$\rangle$tt, and so on. Checking for infinite behaviours needs infinitely long formulas – not a very satisfactory basis for a specification. Fortunately the recursive modal formulas that represent infinite behaviours in modal logic are identity functions like X = $\langle$tick$\rangle$X; and we know all about them. It's time to reach for the fixed points.

7.1.2 Propositional Modal Mu-Calculus – Modal Logic *plus* Fixed Points

The logic used here is termed the mu-calculus, formed by the addition of fixed point operators to modal logic and, though this was first proposed by Kozens in [Koz83], most of what follows is based on the papers of Stirling [Stir91] and [Stir96].

In SCCS, to describe the agent that can, at any time in an infinite life, engage in an α action, we don't use an infinite SCCS expression like P $\overset{\text{def}}{=}$ $\alpha:\alpha:\alpha:\alpha: \ldots$, but the simpler recursive form P $\overset{\text{def}}{=}$ $\alpha:$P. Similarly, rather than describe this behaviour as an infinite set of modal formulas, $\langle\alpha\rangle$tt and [α]$\langle\alpha\rangle$tt and [α][α]$\langle\alpha\rangle$tt and ..., the obvious thing to do is use a recursive formula like

$$X = \langle\alpha\rangle\text{tt} \wedge [\alpha]X$$

where the property of P is described as a property of X. This looks right, as unrolling X gives the desired $\{\langle\alpha\rangle\text{tt}, [\alpha]\langle\alpha\rangle\text{tt}, [\alpha][\alpha]\langle\alpha\rangle\text{tt}, \ldots\}$ and P is a termed a maximal solution of X = $\langle\alpha\rangle$tt $\wedge$ [α]X. But are we allowed to expand modal logic to include recursion? As with SCCS, we have to show that such recursions are well founded, which is made more difficult as they have more than one solution. For example, X $\overset{\text{def}}{=}$ ff, representing the inactive agent P $\overset{\text{def}}{=}$ $\mathbb{0}$, is also a valid minimal solution to X = $\langle\alpha\rangle$tt $\wedge$ [α]X. We need to delve deeper, particularly into what these minimal and maximal solutions are.

The simple formula X $\overset{\text{def}}{=}$ $\langle$tick$\rangle$X, in the context of agent CLOCK $\overset{\text{def}}{=}$

tick:CLOCK, has one maximal solution, the set {CLOCK}, and one minimal solution, the set {}, ordered as {}⊆{CLOCK}. If we change the context of X, the agents we associate with X, we can get different solutions, again bracketed by maximal and minimal extremes. The formal proof that recursive modal logic equations have such unique minimal, a least fixed point, and maximal, a greatest fixed point, solutions is based on a general theory due to Knaster-Tarski [Tar55]:

Where S is any set, 2^S is the set of all subsets of S, and the function $f: 2^S{\to}2^S$ is monotonic in the sets it ranges over, where f is monotonic if $f(\mathcal{E}) \subseteq f(\mathcal{F})$ for any $\mathcal{E}, \mathcal{F} \subseteq S$ and $\mathcal{E} \subseteq \mathcal{F}$, then f

a) has a least fixed point given by $\bigcap\{\mathcal{E} \subseteq S \mid f(\mathcal{E}) \subseteq \mathcal{E}\}$

b) has a greatest fixed point given by $\bigcup\{\mathcal{E} \subseteq S \mid \mathcal{E} \subseteq f(\mathcal{E})\}$

As all the operators of the modal mu-calculus can be shown to induce semantically monotonic functions [Stir96], the above result applies to any modal equation $Z \stackrel{\text{def}}{=} \phi$ where ϕ contains modal operators, boolean connectives, constants and Z. The property given by the least solution to $Z \stackrel{\text{def}}{=} \phi$ is donated by $\mu Z . \phi$, and $\nu Z . \phi$ denotes the property given by its largest solution.

To add fixed points to our existing modal logic, as well as more notation, we need to include them in the world of properties, formulas and satisfaction relations. Starting with the maximal fixed point operator νZ, our existing modal logic is extended to:

$$\phi ::= Z \mid \neg\phi \mid \phi_1 \wedge \phi_2 \mid [K]\phi \mid \nu Z . \phi$$

where formulas ϕ are built from a set Var of variables X, Y, Z, ... , a set $\mathcal{A}ct$ of labels $\alpha, \beta, \chi, ...$ and K as a subset of $\mathcal{A}ct$. The previous extensions $\langle\,\rangle, \langle\langle\,\rangle\rangle, [[\,]]$, etc. are preserved.

$\nu Z . \phi$ represents the greatest fixed point, the maximal solution of the formula $Z \stackrel{\text{def}}{=} \phi$, where νZ binds free occurrences of Z in ϕ. The constant tt is defined by $\nu Z . Z$, the maximal solution to Z=Z, and ff by $\neg$tt.

Operationally, $\nu Z . \phi$ can be replaced by its unfolding, $\phi[\nu Z . \phi/Z]$, replacing Z by $\nu Z . \phi$ as we go, ϕ holding along any path of the unfolding. For example, we can generalise the previous X = $\langle\alpha\rangle$tt $\wedge$ [α]X into greatest fixed point form, replacing the $\langle u\rangle$tt by general property φ giving

$$\begin{aligned}
\nu Z . \varphi{\wedge}[\alpha]Z &= \varphi{\wedge}[\alpha]\,(\nu Z . \varphi{\wedge}[\alpha]Z\,) \\
&= \varphi{\wedge}[\alpha]\,(\varphi{\wedge}[\alpha]\,(\nu Z . \varphi{\wedge}[\alpha]Z\,)\,) \\
&= \varphi{\wedge}[\alpha]\,(\varphi{\wedge}[\alpha]\,(\varphi{\wedge}[\alpha]\,(\nu Z . \varphi{\wedge}[\alpha]Z\,)\,)\,) \\
&= \varphi{\wedge}[\alpha]\,(\varphi{\wedge}[\alpha]\,(\varphi{\wedge}[\alpha]\,(\varphi{\wedge}[\alpha]\, ...\,)\,)\,)
\end{aligned}$$

which interprets as φ holds initially, after the first α action, after the second, and after all subsequent α actions. That is, φ holds along all execution paths of α actions; as such, maximal fixed points, by checking the invariance of φ, can be used to test the safety properties of agents.

example

P ⊨ νZ.⟨a⟩tt∧[−]Z defines agents always ready to engage in a; at every point along every path from P, checked by [−]Z, an a can be performed, checked by ⟨a⟩tt, and this is true for P ^{def} a : P but not for P ^{def} 0 or for P ^{def} a : b : P.

∎

We can move this safeness test to a more general P ⊨ νZ.φ∧[K]Z, which defines agents where φ holds along all paths composed of actions from K; then to the even more general P ⊨ νZ.φ∧[−]Z, which defines agents with property φ holding along all paths whatever the actions accepted along the way.

But we don't always want to know if all the states of a system have or have not certain properties; sometimes we only need to know if these properties may eventually hold. For this, we need to look to minimal fixed points, $\mu Z.\phi$, the dual of $\nu Z.\phi$, with ⟨ ⟩ for [ ] and ∨ for ∧, these represent minimal forms, an infinite disjunction of properties

$$\mu Z.\phi \overset{def}{=} \neg \nu Z.\neg\phi[\neg Z/Z]$$

where $\phi[\psi/Z]$ is the property obtained by substituting ψ for free occurrences of Z in ϕ.

$\mu Z.\varphi\vee\langle\alpha\rangle Z$ holds for an agent that can evolve into another, satisfying φ after a finite number (including zero) of occurrences of α, and as such defines agents weakly live with respect to φ. We can move this to the more general $\mu Z.\varphi\vee\langle K\rangle Z$ which defines agents where φ holds initially or after some runs composed of K actions – φ holds on some K–paths, and then to the more general $\mu Z.\varphi\vee\langle-\rangle Z$ which defines agents where φ holds on some runs.

example

P ⊨ μZ.⟨a⟩tt∨⟨−⟩Z holds if along some path from P consisting of any actions, checked by ⟨−⟩Z, at some point a can be performed, checked by ⟨a⟩tt – there exists at least one path where eventually a is possible. This is true for P ^{def} a : P, P ^{def} b : a : P, P ^{def} c : b : a : P and P ^{def} b : a : P + c : 0 but not P ^{def} 0, P ^{def} b : P or P ^{def} c : P. By replacing the ⟨−⟩Z with a specific action P ⊨ μZ.⟨a⟩tt∨⟨b⟩Z holds if along paths from P consisting solely of b actions, checked by ⟨b⟩Z, at some point a is possible, checked by ⟨a⟩tt. This is true for P ^{def} a : P, P ^{def} b : a : P and P ^{def} : b : a : P + c : 0 but not P ^{def} 0, P ^{def} b : P, P ^{def} c : P or P ^{def} c : b : a : P.

∎

For the moment we will just accept that maximal fixed points model infinite behaviours and minimal fixed points are satisfied with finite ones. We will look at the formal basis for this in a moment; in the meantime we will illustrate the difference by considering invariance Always(φ): where φ holds in all states of all runs; as against Eventually(φ): where φ holds at least once in all runs. As formulae:

$$\text{Eventually}(\phi) \overset{\text{def}}{=} \mu Z . \phi \vee ([-]Z \wedge \langle - \rangle tt)$$
$$\text{Always}(\phi) \overset{\text{def}}{=} \nu Z . \phi \wedge [-]Z$$

The unfolding of `Eventually`(ϕ) gives 'either ϕ holds now, or for all successors, and there is at least one, either ϕ holds now or...'; the unfolding of `Always`(ϕ) gives 'ϕ holds now, and for all successors ϕ holds now and for all successors...'.

Eventually(ϕ), using μZ as least fixed points, formed by the disjunction of properties as agents evolve, is concerned with finite behaviours: ϕ holds eventually in some (unbounded but) finite time; whereas Always(ϕ) using the maximal fixed points, formed by the conjunction of an agent's properties, ' "anding" together' tests as an agent evolves, is concerned with infinite behaviours: ϕ always holds, even along infinite paths. In both the above examples, the engine for recursion is the $[-]Z$ which ensures that any associated property, like the ϕ in $\phi \wedge [-]Z$, is checked along all paths, as against $\langle - \rangle Z$ which is satisfied with some paths. As well as the standard $[-]Z$ term there are others, such as $[\alpha]Z$, which checks for α–derivatives, and $[K]Z$, which checks for K–derivatives. These non-standard versions are just as useful, and we will see some examples later. First some particular cases:

- `Always`(ϕ) with $\phi = \langle - \rangle tt$ is special. As agents with the property $\langle - \rangle tt$ can engage in any action, and as the maximal fixed point checks every state in a behaviour tree, agents that satisfy $\nu Z . \langle - \rangle tt \wedge [-]Z$ can always engage in some action, they never terminate. For example , $\nu Z . \langle - \rangle tt \wedge [-]Z$ holds for P $\overset{\text{def}}{=}$ a : P but not a : 0 or $(a? : 0 \times b! : 0) \backslash \backslash \{a, b\}$.

- `Always`(ϕ) with $\phi = \langle 1 \rangle tt$, as agents with the property $\langle 1 \rangle tt$, can accept a 1, and as the maximal fixed point checks every state in a behaviour tree, agents that satisfy $\nu Z . \langle 1 \rangle t \wedge [-]Z$ can engage in any action as long as in every active state a 1 is possible and, as such, it holds for P $\overset{\text{def}}{=}$ 1 : P and $(\delta a : 0 \times \delta b : 0) \backslash \backslash \{a, b\}$ but not for 1 : 1 : a : 0 or P $\overset{\text{def}}{=}$ 1 : P + 1 : 1 : a : 0.

As with modal logic, when using the mu-calculus for specifications it would be convenient if we had some way of establishing which agents satisfy which formulas. An obvious solution would be to use the function $\| \; \|$, which takes a formula ϕ as an argument and delivers $\mathcal{P}$, the set of agents which satisfy ϕ, $\|\phi\| \subseteq \mathcal{P}$; but to accommodate fixed points, or rather the propositional variables introduced by fixed points, we introduce the concept of valuations, $\mathcal{V}$. Valuations map propositional variables to sets of processes, $\mathcal{V} : \text{Var} \to 2^{\mathcal{P}}$, and we use $\mathcal{V}$ to assign to each variable Z a subset of processes $\mathcal{V}(\mathcal{P})$ from $\mathcal{P}$. Now, rewriting the previous rules in terms of agents with property ϕ under valuation $\mathcal{V}$

$$\|Z\|_{\mathcal{V}} = \mathcal{V}(Z)$$
$$\|\neg\phi\|_{\mathcal{V}} = \mathcal{P} - \|\phi\|_{\mathcal{V}}$$
$$\|\phi_1 \wedge \phi_2\|_{\mathcal{V}} = \|\phi_1\|_{\mathcal{V}} \cap \|\phi_2\|_{\mathcal{V}}$$
$$\|\phi_1 \vee \phi_2\|_{\mathcal{V}} = \|\phi_1\|_{\mathcal{V}} \cup \|\phi_2\|_{\mathcal{V}}$$

$$\|[K]\phi\|_{\mathcal{V}} = \|[\overline{K}]\| \, \|\phi\|_{\mathcal{V}}$$
$$\|\langle K\rangle\phi\|_{\mathcal{V}} = \|\langle\overline{K}\rangle\| \, \|\phi\|_{\mathcal{V}}$$

where the set of agents with the property Z is a subset of $\mathcal{P}$ as determined by their valuations $\mathcal{V}$. Additionally, where $\mathcal{E}$ is a subset of processes $\mathcal{P}$ and $\mathcal{V}[\mathcal{E}/Z]$ is the valuation $\mathcal{V}'$ which agrees with $\mathcal{V}$ save $\mathcal{V}'(Z) = \mathcal{E}$. Using Tarski's result, Stirling [Stir96] defines the set of agents with property $vZ.\phi$ as

$$\|vZ.\phi\|_{\mathcal{V}} = \bigcup\{\mathcal{E} \subseteq \mathcal{P} \mid \mathcal{E} \subseteq \|\phi\|_{\mathcal{V}[\mathcal{E}/Z]}\}$$

and for $\mu Z.\phi$

$$\|\mu Z.\phi\|_{\mathcal{V}} = \bigcap\{\mathcal{E} \subseteq \mathcal{P} \mid \|\phi\|_{\mathcal{V}[\mathcal{E}/Z]} \subseteq \mathcal{E}\}$$

Here the fixed points are the set of processes $\mathcal{E}$ that satisfy the condition $\mathcal{E} = \|\phi\|_{\mathcal{V}[\mathcal{E}/Z]}$, and these fall into two categories: those solutions, prefixed points, for which $\|\phi\|_{\mathcal{V}[\mathcal{E}/Z]} \subseteq \mathcal{E}$; and those, postfixed points, for which $\mathcal{E} \subseteq \|\phi\|_{\mathcal{V}[\mathcal{E}/Z]}$. The interpretation is that if one thinks of the solution sets as being on a continuum, from ff representing the set of no processes through $\mathcal{E}$ to tt representing the set of all processes; and given that a greatest fixed point is the union of all postfixed points from $\mathcal{E}$ to infinity, a greatest fixed point defines a property that will always be true in an infinite behaviour; and as a least fixed point is the intersection of a finite number of prefixed points, from none to $\mathcal{E}$, a least fixed point is one which sometimes will be true in a finite behaviour. For example:

- $vZ.\langle K\rangle Z$ represents the capability of performing K actions forever, and has special cases:
  - $vZ.\langle\alpha\rangle Z$ the capability of infinitely performing α;
  - $vZ.\langle 1\rangle Z$ the capability of engaging in infinite internal activity;
  - $vZ.\langle -\rangle Z$ defines agents with undefined and infinite behaviours - agents which can engage in an infinite number of actions internal or external.

And in complement:

- $\mu Z.[K]Z$ represents the capability of performing a finite number (including none) of K actions, and the has special cases:
  - $\mu Z.[\alpha]Z$ an incapability of continually performing α actions;
  - $\mu Z.[1]Z$ represents convergence - the agent can engage in a non-infinite number (including none) of internal actions;
  - $\mu Z.[-]Z$ defines agents which eventually terminate.

examples

a) To check that CLOCK can only tick, and will do for ever, we need the recursion from $[-]Z$ to check each action, $[-tick]ff$ to check if each action is a tick and only a tick, and $\langle-\rangle tt$ to reject termination

$$vZ.(([-tick]ff \wedge \langle-\rangle tt) \wedge [-]Z)$$

which is false for OLD_CLOCK. Conversely,

$$vZ.[-]([-tock]ff \wedge [-]Z),$$

each even action is a tock, holds for OLD_CLOCK but not CLOCK.

b) Back to our running example. We can distinguish P $\overset{\text{def}}{=}$ a : P and Q $\overset{\text{def}}{=}$ a : Q + a : $\mathbb{0}$

As Q can terminate and P cannot, only P has property
$$vZ . \langle - \rangle tt \wedge [-]Z$$

But this is rather weak. More precisely: Q, as Q_1, can refuse to engage in everything, including a, while P can never refuse an a. Hence only P has property
$$vZ . \langle a \rangle tt \wedge [-]Z$$

c) We can distinguish P $\overset{\text{def}}{=}$ a : P + 1 : P from Q $\overset{\text{def}}{=}$ a : Q

For Q, observable action a must happen, and the possibility of infinite internal actions does not exist. As P can forever engage in internal actions, we can use $vZ . \langle 1 \rangle Z$ to distinguish the two. Alternatively, as Q will always engage in a actions and P need not, we can use the stronger $vZ . [-a] ff \wedge \langle - \rangle tt \wedge [-]Z$ to distinguish between them.

d) A system is safe if nothing bad happens. We can make a system, one that would get into an unwanted state by engaging in K actions, safe by ensuring that it never does engage in K actions, [K]ff, and this property must hold for all paths – it must be an invariant, we need to prove the system satisfies the maximal fixed point $vZ . ([K]ff \wedge [-]Z)$.

Take a particular instance:
Two processes use critical sections to access to an unshareable resource, and the unsafe state we want to avoid is one in which both agents simultaneously use the resource, indicated by simultaneously active critical sections. For two SCCS clients we need to ensure that no state is ever reached where action cs1×cs2 (cs1 is the first client in its critical section and cs2 the second client, in its) can be performed. That is, it should always be true that clients cannot get into states where action cs1×cs2 is possible. We have mutual

exclusion if:
$$\nu Z.\,([cs1 \times cs2]ff \wedge [-]Z) = true$$

e)   A system will be live if something good eventually happens –
     eventually a certain property holds along all execution paths. If good
     things are from set K, to be live with respect to K the agents must
     eventually execute an action from K and the desired state is reached
     after a finite number of actions, $\mu Z.\,\langle K\rangle tt \vee (\langle -\rangle tt \wedge [-]Z)$.

In particular, a stamp can eventually be collected in

$$STAMP \stackrel{\mathrm{def}}{=} in1p?:1pstamp?:collect!:STAMP$$
$$+ in2p?:2pstamp?:collect!:STAMP$$

and

$$STAMP \models \mu Z.\,\langle collect\rangle tt \vee (\langle -\rangle tt \wedge [-]Z)$$

f)   Different formulas can capture quite subtle behaviours. For example,
     slightly different formulas put different spins on what is meant by
     'eventually'. Consider a rogue chocolate machine that sometimes
     delivers a chocolate after accepting a coin, sometimes accepts any
     number of coins without delivering a chocolate, or sometimes – after
     accepting two or more coins – goes bang and expires. In normal form:

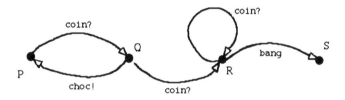

```
COINCHOC def P
P def coin?:Q
Q def choc!:P + coin?:R
R def coin?:R + bang:S
S def 0
```

First we have 'coin? happens eventually' – along all paths
$$\mu Z.\,\langle -\rangle tt \wedge [-coin?]Z$$
Following the unfolding of the minimal fixed point: as we pass
through Z a finite number of times there can be no infinite -coin?
runs and $\langle -\rangle tt$ ensures we cannot terminate before a coin?.

Then we have 'eventually coin? must happen'
$$\mu Z.\,([-coin?]ff \vee [-]Z) \wedge \langle -\rangle tt$$
A point is reached where coin? is the only possible action.

Finally, 'eventually coin? may happen'

$$\mu Z.\langle coin?\rangle tt \lor ([-]Z \land \langle -\rangle tt)$$

A point is always reached where coin? is possible.

Which, applied to the chocolate machine, gives:

$$\|\mu Z.\langle -\rangle tt \land [-coin?]Z\|_\mathcal{V} = \{P,Q\}$$

for R can bang instead, and S does nothing;

$$\|\mu Z.([-coin?]ff \lor [-]Z) \land \langle -\rangle tt\|_\mathcal{V} = \{P\}$$

As Q can engage in a coin or a choc, R in a coin or a bang and S does nothing, so only P must engage in a coin;

$$\|\mu Z.\langle coin?\rangle tt \lor ([-]Z) \land \langle -\rangle tt)\|_\mathcal{V} = \{P,Q,R\}$$

as only S has no coin in any of its futures.

■

At the simplest level, with no fixed points, mu-calculus is our original modal logic. By adding single fixed points we increased the expressive power of the calculus which we exploited by using single fixed points to check invariance properties, something always (or never) happens, to check system safety: a system never deadlocks; critical sections are never subject to multiple occupancy; and so on. But, to capture the subtleties of longer-term liveness (that requests made are eventually granted; users eventually exit previously entered critical sections; hardware units output some function of previous inputs; etc.; generalised to a check for 'if a given action occurs then a given action invariably follows') we are sometimes going to need something more expressive. In this case multiple fixed points – one fixed point to check for the second action embedded in other which checks for the first. Consider a liveness specification for a client–server system used to check that users are eventually given resources they've requested here, as we're only interested in the request and grant actions, not any preceding, intervening or subsequent actions, we will need a specification along the lines of 'whenever a user makes a request, eventually it's granted' or, more generally, ignoring all other actions, 'whenever action α action β follows'. To check for 'whenever action α action β follows', also written as '$\alpha...\beta$' (where '...' is an arbitrary action sequence) in all possible systems, we're going to need not one but several formulas. Checking if '$\alpha...\beta$' holds for every run;[†] is different from checking if '$\alpha...\beta$' holds for some runs; and so on. Such formulas may contain no, one, or several fixed points, and we will go about their construction in a systematic way, working up to multiple fixed points via single fixed points but starting with no fixed points.

Without fixed points we can only check if α and β occur at specific times, for example, $[\alpha]\langle\beta\rangle tt$, also written $[\alpha]Happens\_\beta$, checks if β immediately follows an initial α.

$[\alpha]Happens\_\beta$

'If α is an initial action then an immediate β is possible.'

---

† Note: As runs include the empty sequence as possible transitions they include the behaviour of an agent in its initial state, before it engages in its first action.

We can strengthen this formula to include a check for 'α and only α is the initial action' by adding $[-\alpha]\text{ff}$, to reject agents that satisfy 'whenever initial action is not α', and $\langle-\rangle\text{tt}$, to reject initial inaction, giving

$$Only\_happens\_\alpha = ([-\alpha]\text{ff} \wedge \langle-\rangle\text{tt})$$

and

$$Only\_happens\_\alpha \wedge [\alpha]Happens\_\beta$$

'If α, and only α, is an initial action then an immediate β is possible.'

This can be further strengthened to check if the second action is 'β and only β' by replacing the $Happens\_\beta$ with an $Only\_happens\_\beta$ of $([-\beta]\text{ff} \wedge \langle-\rangle\text{tt})$, giving

a) 'α: β...',

'β immediately follows an initial α'

$$Only\_happens\_\alpha \wedge [\alpha]Only\_happens\_\beta$$

'If α, and only α, is an initial action then inevitably β, and only β, immediately follows.'

By employing a single fixed point we can relax the constraint that β must immediately follow an α to 'β eventually happens' of

$$Event\_happens\_\beta = \mu X . (\langle-\rangle\text{tt} \wedge [-\beta]X)$$

b) 'α...β...',

'β eventually happens in every run from an initial α'

$$[\alpha]Event\_happens\_\beta$$

'after an initial α eventually β happens.'

To check for 'α: (...β... + ...)', where '...α...β...' only holds on some paths, our current $Event\_happens\_\beta$ of $\mu X . (\langle-\rangle\text{tt} \wedge [-\beta]X)$ is too strong. But, by replacing the $[-\beta]X$, which checks all paths, in $Event\_happens\_\beta$, with $\langle-\beta\rangle X$, that is satisfied with some, we get $\mu X . (\langle-\rangle\text{tt} \vee \langle-\beta\rangle X)$, 'β happens on some paths', also called $Some\_happens\_\beta$. Now, by using $Some\_happens\_\beta = \mu X . (\langle-\rangle\text{tt} \vee \langle-\beta\rangle X)$ to check that β occurs on some runs, we get:

$$[\alpha]Some\_happens\_\beta$$

'after an initial α then β sometimes happens.'

Well, we would, except that this formula also accepts agents like 'α: ...' which perform no β actions. For our purposes the stronger

$$Some\_may\_\beta = \mu X . (\langle\beta\rangle\text{tt} \vee \langle-\rangle X)$$

that rejects such cases is more suitable, giving:

c) 'α... (...β... + ...)',

'β is a possible next action in at least one run from an initial α'

$$[\alpha]Some\_may\_\beta$$

'after an initial α then sometimes β is possible.'

Where necessary we can strengthen the above formulas to check that 'α and only α is the initial action' by adding $Only\_happens\_\alpha$, as in

> *Only_happens_α* ∧ *[α]Event_happens_β*
> 'after an initial α, and only α, then β eventually happens.'

and

> *Only_happens_α* ∧ *[α]Some_may_β*
> 'after an initial α, and only α, then sometimes β is possible.'

Formulas a) through c) rely upon α being the initial action – not always what we want. To check for '...α...β...' we use two fixed points, one to check for the eventual occurrence of β, *Event_happens_β*, embedded in another which checks that the preceding α is always present, *Always([α]Event_happens_β)*, of $\nu Z. ([\alpha]\mu X. (\langle - \rangle tt \wedge [-\beta]X)) \wedge [-]Z)$, with an additional fixed point to ensure that α does eventually occur all paths, giving:

d) '...α...β...',
   'α is an action in every run from the initial state and β is an action in every run from α'
   Event_happens_α ∧ *Always([α]Event_happens_β)*
   'eventually α happens and if α ever happens then eventually β happens.'

To check for '...α...(...β... + ...)', where '...α...β...' only holds on some paths, we again need a *Some_may* in place of the *Event_happens* above, giving:

e) '...α...(...β... + ...)',
   'α is an action in every run from the initial state and β is a possible next action in at least one run from α'
   Event_happens_α ∧ *Always([α]Some_may_β)*
   'eventually α happens and if α ever happens then sometimes β is possible.'

f) '...(...α...β...) + ...',
   'α is a possible next action in at least one run from the initial state and β is an action in every run from α'
   Some_may_α ∧ *Always([α]Event_happens_β)*
   'sometimes α is possible and if α ever happens then eventually β happens.'

g) '(...α. (...β... + ...)) + ...',
   'α is a possible next action in at least one run from the initial state and β is a possible next action in at least one run from α'
   Some_may_α ∧ *Always([α]Some_may_β)*
   'sometimes α is possible and if α ever happens then sometimes β is possible.'

Though fairly obvious, it is probably worth reinforcing our understanding that 'formulas a) through f)' form a hierarchy of weaker and weaker tests – the *Some* clauses accepting at least those agents accepted by associated *Event* clauses. For example, as all previous formulas are included in '$(\ldots\alpha\ldots(\ldots\beta\ldots+\ldots))+\ldots$' then 'formula g)' will accept all agents that satisfy 'formulas a) through f)' plus those that meet '$(\ldots\alpha\ldots(\ldots\beta\ldots+\ldots))+\ldots$'. It is all dependent upon the interpretation of '...': for example, if all but one '...' in '$(\ldots\alpha\ldots(\ldots\beta\ldots+\ldots))+\ldots$' is an empty sequence we get '$\alpha:\beta\ldots$' and so on.

Sometimes, instead of satisfying ourselves that a particular action inevitably happens, we only need to check if such an action eventually may happen. This we can achieve by replacing the *Event_happens* in the above formula with

$$Event\_may\_\chi = \mu X.\,(\langle\chi\rangle tt \vee (\langle-\rangle tt \wedge [-]X))$$

'χ is possible next action in every run'. We can, for example, modify the above d) to:
  'α is a possible next action in every run from the initial state and β is a possible next action in every run from α'

$$Event\_may\_\alpha \wedge Always([\alpha]Event\_may\_\beta)$$

  'eventually α may happen and if α ever happens then eventually β may happen'. Which not only checks for '$\ldots\alpha\ldots\beta\ldots$' but also '$(\alpha\ldots\beta\ldots)+\ldots$'

Not only can we 'mix and match' any of the above components to achieve the result we desire, we can, of course, extend any such formula to check systems with a choice of behaviours by replacing the singular α and β actions by sets containing the actions that guard each choice. For example

$$\mu X.\,(\langle K\rangle tt \vee (\langle-\rangle tt \wedge [-]X))$$
$$\wedge\, \nu Z.\,([K]\mu X.\,(\langle M\rangle tt \vee \langle-\rangle X))\wedge\langle-\rangle Z)$$

read as 'eventually an action from K is possible and, if such an action occurs, then sometimes an action from M is possible.'

examples

The design department of the Innovative Vending Machine Company is given the task of designing a machine to launch the company's first foray into stamp vending with a design constraint of 'goods paid for can eventually be delivered'.

Their first successful attempt

       Proto1 $\stackrel{\text{def}}{=}$ in1p?:collect1p!:Proto1

is checked by specification

   *Only_happens_*in1p? $\wedge$ [in1p?]*Only_happens_*collect1p!

of

       [-in1p?]ff $\wedge$ $\langle-\rangle$tt $\wedge$ [in1p?]([-collect1p!]ff $\wedge$ $\langle-\rangle$tt)

'an initial in1p? followed immediately by a collect1p!'.

Prior to extending the machine to handle more than one denomination of stamp a button was added to select the stamp required

       Proto2 $\stackrel{\text{def}}{=}$ in1p?:1pstamp?:collect1p!:Proto2

which met specification
  *Only_happens_*in1p? ∧ [in1p?]*Event_happens_*collect1p!
of
      [−in1p?]ff ∧ ⟨−⟩tt ∧ [in1p?]μX. (⟨−⟩tt ∧ [−collect1p!]X)
'after an initial in1p then eventually collect1p! happens', which gives
the confidence to introduce a machine delivering two types of stamp. But
the fault in
     Proto3 ^{def} in1p?:1pstamp?:collect1p!:Proto3
               + in2p:2pstamp?:collect1p!:Proto3
is not picked up by
       *Only_happens_*{in1p?,in2p?}
             ∧ [in1p?,in2p?]*Event_happens_*collect1p!
of

     [−in1p?,in2p?]ff ∧ ⟨−⟩tt
          ∧ [in1p?,in2p?]μX. (⟨−⟩tt ∧ [−collect1p!]X)
'after an initial in1p? or in2p? then eventually collect1p! happens',
as this accepts possible 'in2p?...collect1p!' sequences. To detect the
failure we need something like
    *Event_may_*in1p?
      ∧ *Always*([in1p?]*Event_happens_*collect1p!)
    ∧
    *Event_may_*in2p?
      ∧ *Always*([in2p?]*Event_happens_*collect2p!)
of
    (μX. (⟨in1p?⟩tt ∨ (⟨−⟩tt ∧ [−]X))
       ∧ νZ. ([in1p?]μX. (⟨−⟩tt ∧ [−collect1p!]X) ∧ [−]Z))
   ∧ (μX. (⟨in2p?⟩tt ∨ (⟨−⟩tt ∧ [−]X))
       ∧ νZ. ([in2p?]μX. (⟨−⟩tt ∧ [−collect2p!]X) ∧ [−]Z))
which checks for 'eventually in1p? may happen and if in1p? ever
happens then eventually collect1p! happens' = true, and, 'eventually
in2p? may happen and if in2p? ever happens then eventually
collect2p! happens' = false.

This fault was corrected in a new machine:
      Proto4 ^{def} in1p?:1pstamp?:collect1p!:Proto4
            + in2p?:2pstamp?:collect2p!:Proto4
            + bang:0
which unfortunately could die after an internal explosion. When checking
1pstamp transactions, this is missed in:
    *Event_may_*in1p?
      ∧ *Always*([in1p?]*Event_happens_*collect1p!)
of
    μX. (⟨in1p?⟩tt ∨ (⟨−⟩tt ∧ [−]X))
      ∧ νZ. ([in1p?]μX. (⟨−⟩tt ∧ [−collect1p!]X) ∧ [−]Z)

To detect the inaction we can use an 'always' wrapper of:

> *Always* (
>   *Event_may_*in1p?
>   ∧ *Always* ([in1p?]*Event_happens_*collect1p!)
>)

of:

> vY. (µX. (⟨in1p?⟩tt ∨ (⟨-⟩tt ∧ [-]X))
>   ∧ vZ. ([in1p?]µX. (⟨-⟩tt ∧ [-collect1p!]X) ∧ [-]Z)
>) ∧ [-]Y

to check 'it is always true that if in1p? may happen then collect1p! eventually happens'. While Proto4 fails the test, it is met by the machine eventually released:

> STAMPS ᵈᵉᶠ in1p?:1pstamp?:collect1p!:STAMPS
>   + in2p?:2pstamp?:collect2p!:STAMPS

A prototype 'eco-friendly' machine, which switches itself off when not in use, needs wakening before use

> Proto5 ᵈᵉᶠ wake?:(in1p?:1pstamp?:collect1p!:Proto5
>   + in2p?:2pstamp?:collect2p!:Proto5)

and meets

*Some_may_*in1p? ∧ *Always* ([in1p?]*Event_happens_*collect1p!)

of

> µX. (⟨in1p?⟩tt ∨ ⟨-⟩X)
>   ∧ vZ. ([in1p?]µX. (⟨-⟩tt ∧ [-collect1p!]X) ∧ [-]Z)

'sometimes in1p? is possible and if in1p? ever happens then eventually collect1p! happens'.

Another prototype, a development of the 'eco-machine', but designed for the niche market of football stadiums, usually displays the current match score but, after a kick, will negotiate the delivery of a stamp or chewing gum

> Proto6 ᵈᵉᶠ kick?:in1p?:(1pstamp?:collect1p!:Proto6
>   + gum?:collectgum!:Proto6)
>   + score!:Proto6

was checked against

*Some_may_*in1p? ∧ *Always* ([in1p?]*Some_may_*collect1p!)

of

> µX. (⟨in1p?⟩tt ∨ ⟨-⟩X)
>   ∧ vZ. ([in1p?]µX. (⟨collect1p?⟩tt ∨ ⟨-⟩X) ∧ [-]Z)

'sometimes in1p? is possible and if in1p? ever happens then sometimes collect1p! is possible'.

∎

By using multiple fixed points we have selectively checked actions of real interest whilst ignoring all others. This selectivity will be particularly useful when we need to check something inherently simple, like clients eventually getting previously requested resources, in complex environments, like multiprocess client–server systems, where action interleavings can be many and varied.

Mu-calculus and SCCS

In mu-calculus, actions like $\alpha,\beta,\chi,...$ from set $\mathcal{A}ct$ are used in formulas such as $\langle\alpha\rangle tt$ and $[\alpha]ff$ to check if an agent can or cannot engage in α, and while it is usual to think of these actions as atomic particles by definition $\alpha,\beta,\chi,...$ also represent combinations of particles into non-atomic composites – as, for example, the $[cs1\times cs2]ff$ met when checking for mutual exclusion; similarly the SCCS action $\delta\alpha$, which can delay engaging in α by engaging in none, one, two or up to an infinite number of internal 1 actions, can also be modelled by mu-calculus as 1 is always a member of $\mathcal{A}ct$. But whilst non-atomic and delayed actions are both modelled in mu-calculus, how we interpret these concepts needs a little thought. For example, to check that P $\stackrel{\text{def}}{=}$ a?:P can always engage in an a? action we can use formula $\nu X. (\langle a?\rangle tt \wedge [-]X)$ but when combined with Q $\stackrel{\text{def}}{=}$ x!:Q, as P×Q = a?×x!:P×Q, we need formula $\nu X. (\langle a?\times x!\rangle tt \wedge [-]X)$ as it is necessary not only to identify the action of concern but the composites of which it forms a part. Consider two agent P $\stackrel{\text{def}}{=}$ a?:b?:c?:P and Q $\stackrel{\text{def}}{=}$ x!:y!:Q in P×Q; every action of one agent will eventually be combined with every action of the other, and to check if action c? eventually occurs we have to check for the composites it is part of by using $\mu Z. (\langle c?\times x!, c?\times y!\rangle tt \vee ([-]Z \wedge \langle-\rangle tt))$. Similar care has to be taken in the presence of the delay operator; consider P $\stackrel{\text{def}}{=}$ δa?:P combined with Q $\stackrel{\text{def}}{=}$ δx!:Q, the resulting P×Q has possible initial actions 1, a?, x! or a?×x!.

To show how all this affects the way we go about proving SCCS agents correct, we will consider how we prove a particular system live and safe, where a system is live if eventually something good happens and safe if nothing bad ever happens. In a multi-client single-server system a particular 'something good' is that each client eventually gets the resource it requests; a particular 'nothing bad' is that never more than one client uses an unshareable resource at the same time. First we look at a single client in isolation.

Pc1 $\stackrel{\text{def}}{=}$ req1:enter!:cs1:exit?:Pc1

cs1 is the client's critical section during which it has access to the resource; enter! and exit? are the entry and exit guards of the critical section, to be used later for negotiating with the arbiter that allocates the resource; and req1 is simply there to help us 'see' when a particular client makes a resource request.

To check if, after making a request, a client gains entry to a critical section we need a specification along the lines of 'whenever a client requests entry to its critical section, eventually the request is granted'. From a client's perspective this is another instance of checking for '$\alpha...\beta$' and, in this case, we can use a modified form of the previous 'formula b)' of:

b)   'α: β....' or '$\alpha...\beta$...',
      'β eventually happens in every run from an initial, and only an initial, α'
      $Only\_happens\_\alpha \wedge [\alpha]Event\_happens\_\beta$
      'after an initial α, and only α, then β eventually happens'.

Instantiated for client Pc1
$$[-req1]ff \wedge \langle-\rangle tt \wedge [req1]\mu X. (\langle-\rangle tt \wedge [-cs1]X)$$
'after an initial req1, and only req1, then eventually cs1 happens'.

Things get more complex when we introduce competition in the form of another client
$$Pc1 \stackrel{\text{def}}{=} req1:enter!:cs1:exit?:Pc1$$
$$Pc2 \stackrel{\text{def}}{=} req2:enter!:cs2:exit?:Pc2$$

In combination the clients operate in 'lock step'
$$Pc1 \times Pc2 = req1 \times req2:enter! \times enter!:cs1 \times cs2:$$
$$exit? \times exit?:CLIENT1 \times CLIENT2$$

Here we can use $\nu Z. ([cs1 \times cs2]ff \wedge [-]Z)$ to check if mutual exclusion is preserved (it isn't) and $\nu Z. (\langle-\rangle tt \wedge [-]Z)$ to check that the system does not terminate unexpectedly (it doesn't). But to check the system is live, 'req1 eventually leads to cs1', we can no longer use
$$Only\_happens\_req1 \wedge [req1]Event\_happens\_cs1$$
as actions req1 and cs1 no longer exist in isolation. Instead we need to modify the formula and check for composites that include req1 and cs1. In this case
$$Only\_happens\_req1 \times req2 \wedge [req1 \times req2]Event\_happens\_cs1 \times cs2$$
of
$$[-req1 \times req2]ff \wedge \langle-\rangle tt \wedge [req1 \times req2]\mu X. (\langle-\rangle tt \wedge [-cs1 \times cs2]X)$$

Less frenetic clients, who can wait to enter and exit their critical sections, take a more 'laid-back' attitude to acquiring the resource
$$CLIENT1 \stackrel{\text{def}}{=} req1:\delta enter!:cs1:\delta exit?:CLIENT1$$
$$CLIENT2 \stackrel{\text{def}}{=} req2:\delta enter!:cs2:\delta exit?:CLIENT2$$

Now, when we form CLIENT1×CLIENT2, to check for liveness we have to check that req1, in any its combinations, leads eventually to cs1, in any of its forms. This would be as straightforward as that if it wasn't for the delays. Delays confuse things. Consider the case of $\delta\alpha:P$, where $\delta\alpha:P$ can engage in any number (including zero) of internal action before behaving as $\alpha:P$. As such, $\delta\alpha:P$ forms the root of an infinite derivation tree with zero to an infinite number of internal (silent) 1's preceding the α:

$$\delta\alpha : P = \alpha : P + 1 : \delta\alpha : P$$

As α is eventually possible for all runs of δα : P then agents commencing with 'δα...' are satisfied by *Event_may _α*, as is '...δα...'. However, if the action of concern is 'behind' another delayed action, as in '...δχ...α...', some runs may never get past δχ to the α action, and such sequences will only meet the weaker *Some_may_α*. Based on the above we can extend our previous formulas to check for 'α...β' in the presence of delays to:

h)   For '...α...δβ...' and '...δα...β...' and '...δα...δβ...'; delay before β, before α and before both,
     Event_may_α ∧ Always([α]*Event_may_β*)
     'eventually α may happen and if α ever happens then eventually β may happen'.

i)   '...α...δγ...β...', β follows another delay,
     Event_may_α ∧ Always([α]*Some_may_β*)
     'eventually α may happen and if α ever happens then sometimes β is possible'.

j)   '...δχ...α...β...', α follows another delay,
     Some_may_α ∧ Always([α]*Event_may_β*)
     'sometimes α is possible and if α ever happens then eventually β may happen'.

k)   '...δχ...α...δγ...β...', both α and β follow delays,
     Some_may_α ∧ Always([α]*Some_may_β*)
     'sometimes α is possible and if α ever happens then sometimes β is possible'.

examples

A client, after issuing a request, immediately enters its critical section
         Pab = req1 : enter! : cs1 : exit? : Pab
and another, that can wait to exit its critical section
         Padb = req1 : enter! : cs1 : δexit? : Padb
As req1 is an initial action of both, and occurs before any delays, when checking for 'req1...cs1' both satisfy
     Only_happens_req1 ∧ [req1]Event_hap_cs1
of
     [-req1]ff ∧ ⟨-⟩tt ∧ [req1]μX. (⟨-⟩tt ∧ [-cs1]X)
'after an initial req1, and only req1, then eventually cs1 is possible'.

A client that can wait to enter but not exit its critical section

$$\text{Pdab} = \text{req1}:\delta\text{enter}!:\text{cs1}:\text{exit}?:\text{Pdab}$$

and another, that waits both to enter and exit its critical section

$$\text{Pdadb} = \text{req1}:\delta\text{enter}!:\text{cs1}:\delta\text{exit}?:\text{Pdadb}$$

When checking for 'req1...cs1' both meet specification

$$Only\_happens\_\text{req1} \wedge [\text{req1}]Some\_may\_\text{cs1}$$

of

$$[-\text{req1}]\text{ff} \wedge \langle-\rangle\text{tt} \wedge [\text{req1}]\mu X.\,(\langle\text{cs1}\rangle\text{tt} \vee \langle-\rangle X)$$

'after an initial req1, and only a req1, then sometimes cs1 is possible'.

Finally, when checking for 'enter!...exit?' all four, amongst other things, satisfy an

$$Event\_may\_\text{enter}! \wedge Always([\text{enter}!]Event\_may\_\text{exit}?)$$

of

$$\mu X.\,(\langle\text{enter}!\rangle\text{tt} \vee (\langle-\rangle\text{tt} \wedge [-]X))$$
$$\wedge \nu Z.\,([\text{enter}!]\mu X.\,(\langle\text{exit}?\rangle\text{tt} \vee (\langle-\rangle\text{tt} \wedge [-]X)) \wedge [-]Z)$$

'eventually enter! may happen and if enter! ever happens then eventually exit? may happen'.

■

But be careful. As $Some\_\alpha$ means 'α is possible on some runs', it also means α is not a certainty – agents that meet $Some\_\alpha$ can have runs in which no α occurs. For example, $Some\_may\_\text{cs1}$ actually interprets as 'on a particular run a client may, or may not, get the resource'. This is not a fault in the mu-calculus but rather a true reflection of the lack of liveness implicit in the SCCS delay operator.

To round things off, consider a pair of clients that start together but wait for a semaphore to give them permission to enter and exit their critical sections:

$$\text{Cs1} \stackrel{\text{def}}{=} \text{req1}:\delta\text{enter}!:\text{cs1}:\delta\text{exit}?:\text{Cs1}$$
$$\text{Cs2} \stackrel{\text{def}}{=} \text{req2}:\delta\text{enter}!:\text{cs2}:\delta\text{exit}:\text{Cs2}$$

The binary semaphore that guards the critical sections is

$$\text{Sem} \stackrel{\text{def}}{=} \delta\text{enter}?:\delta\text{exit}!:\text{Sem}$$

and the complete system

$$\text{SYS} = (\text{Cs1} \times \text{Cs2} \times \text{Sem}) \backslash\backslash \{\text{enter}, \text{exit}\}$$

When analysing SYS we can use $\nu Z.\,([\text{cs1}\times\text{cs2}]\text{ff} \wedge [-]Z)$ to check if mutual exclusion is preserved, and $\nu Z.\,(\langle-\rangle\text{tt} \wedge [-]Z)$ to check for unexpected termination. But to check that if client cs1 issues a request it may eventually enter its critical section we need to account for all composites containing req1 and cs1. Here, as SYS is defined with {enter, exit} pruned, and we separately check that cs1×cs2 is not an action of SYS, we need only consider the request action, req1×req2, and critical section cs1. Now in deference to the possibility of infinite delays we use as a specification

of
$$Only\_happens\_req1 \times req2 \wedge [req1 \times req2] Some\_may\_cs1$$

$$[-req1 \times req2] ff \wedge \langle - \rangle tt \wedge [req1 \times req2] \mu X. (\langle cs1 \rangle tt \vee \langle - \rangle X)$$

'after an initial req1, and only a req1, in any of its combinations, then sometimes cs1, in any of its combinations, is possible'.

Interesting though all this detail is, mu-calculus is only of use if it helps us decide whether particular designs are correct; and, whilst the raw calculus is flexible and can produce specifications of incredible subtlety, these same formulas can get very complex and counter-intuitive very quickly, and its sometimes easier to package useful formulas, as we've already begun to do with *Always*, *Event* and *Some*, into parametrisable macros. These can humanise formulas so they can be read at a glance, or, at worst, with a hard look.

Macros

Luckily we tend to ask the same types of questions in a specification, and, instead of building complex formulas from scratch, it is more convenient to package them into higher, more user-friendly, forms that capture in an intuitive way these basic behaviours. Most authors choose to emulate temporal logic operators (for a starting point on such logics you could do worse than [Bar86]) – a sensible move, as, by emulating temporal logics, we can hitch a ride on their past successes in specifying concurrent systems. All we need to do is identify these convenient forms and construct parameterised compositional formulas to fit them. We have already met Always and Event_happens, and by using these we can check if the double buffer can never engage in infinite internal activity using

$$\text{TWOBUFF} \not\models \text{Always} (\text{Event\_happens\_in?}$$
$$\vee \text{Event\_happens\_out!}$$
$$\vee \text{Event\_happens\_in?} \times \text{out!})$$

interpreted as the buffer is live if it can always eventually engage in either in?, out!, or in?×out! actions. Useful macros over agent properties that map onto the basic questions we wish to ask of our designs include:

- Always (ϕ), $\nu Z . \phi \wedge [-]Z$, also called strong invariance, holds when ϕ always holds along all execution paths, Always $([-\alpha]ff)$ holds for P $\stackrel{\text{def}}{=} \alpha: P$ but not P $\stackrel{\text{def}}{=} \alpha: P + \beta: P$ and the special case of NeverDies $\stackrel{\text{def}}{=}$ Always $(\langle - \rangle tt)$ checks that an agent can always engage in a further action, does not deadlock, and holds for P $\stackrel{\text{def}}{=} \alpha: P$ but not P $\stackrel{\text{def}}{=} \alpha: P + \alpha: \mathbb{0}$.

- Sometimes (ϕ), $\mu Z . \phi \vee \langle - \rangle Z$, the inverse of Always (ϕ), holds for agents where ϕ holds initially or which can evolve into at least one agent where ϕ holds. For example, Sometimes $(\langle \chi \rangle tt)$ holds for P $\stackrel{\text{def}}{=} \chi: P$ and P $\stackrel{\text{def}}{=} \alpha: \chi: \mathbb{0} + \beta: P$ but not P $\stackrel{\text{def}}{=} \alpha: P + \beta: P$.

- Delay(ϕ),$\mu Z.\phi \vee \langle 1 \rangle Z$), a special case of Sometimes (ϕ), holds for agents where ϕ holds initially or along some 1 paths. For example, Delay($\langle \alpha \rangle$tt) holds for P $\stackrel{\text{def}}{=}$ α:P and P $\stackrel{\text{def}}{=}$ $\delta \alpha$:P but not P $\stackrel{\text{def}}{=}$ δb:P or P $\stackrel{\text{def}}{=}$ $\delta 1$:P. As such, Delay(ϕ) defines $\langle\!\langle \ \rangle\!\rangle \phi$ and, in a similar way, $\nu Z.\phi \wedge [1]Z$ defines $[\![\ ]\!]\phi$.

- Eventually(ϕ),$\mu Z.\phi \vee (\langle - \rangle$tt $\wedge [-]Z$), a strengthened form of Sometimes (ϕ), holds for agents for which ϕ initially holds, or the agents have derivatives and Eventually(ϕ) holds for all. For example, Eventually($\langle \chi \rangle$tt) holds for P $\stackrel{\text{def}}{=}$ χ:P and P $\stackrel{\text{def}}{=}$ α:χ:P + β:χ:P but not P $\stackrel{\text{def}}{=}$ α:χ:$\mathbb{0}$ + β:P or P $\stackrel{\text{def}}{=}$ α:P + β:P.

- WeakUntil(ϕ,ψ),$\nu Z.\psi \vee (\phi \wedge [-]Z$), holds for agents where, along each execution path, ϕ holds until ψ does or ψ never does hold. For example, WeakUntil($\langle \alpha \rangle$tt,$\langle \gamma \rangle$tt) holds for P $\stackrel{\text{def}}{=}$ α:γ:P, P $\stackrel{\text{def}}{=}$ α:P and P $\stackrel{\text{def}}{=}$ α:P + β:γ:P but not P $\stackrel{\text{def}}{=}$ α:1:γ:P.

- StrongUntil(ϕ,ψ),$\mu Z.\psi \vee (\phi \wedge \langle - \rangle$tt $\wedge [-]Z$), a strengthened WeakUntil(ϕ,ψ), holds for agents where, along each execution path, ϕ holds until ψ does and ϕ is guaranteed to hold eventually. For example, StrongUntil($\langle \alpha \rangle$tt,$\langle \gamma \rangle$tt) holds for P $\stackrel{\text{def}}{=}$ α:γ:P but not P $\stackrel{\text{def}}{=}$ α:P or P $\stackrel{\text{def}}{=}$ α:P + β:γ:P.

In each case, single action properties can be generalised; for example, from Always ($\langle \alpha \rangle$tt) to Always ($\langle K \rangle$tt), which holds for all continuous performance of actions from K, as in Always ($\langle \alpha, \beta \rangle$tt) holds for P $\stackrel{\text{def}}{=}$ α:P and P $\stackrel{\text{def}}{=}$ α:P + β:P but not P $\stackrel{\text{def}}{=}$ α:P + β:γ:P; WeakUntil($\langle \alpha, \beta \rangle$tt,$\langle \gamma \rangle$tt) which holds for P $\stackrel{\text{def}}{=}$ α:P, P $\stackrel{\text{def}}{=}$ α:γ:P and P $\stackrel{\text{def}}{=}$ α:P + β:γ:P; StrongUntil($\langle \alpha, \beta \rangle$tt,$\langle \gamma \rangle$tt) which holds for P $\stackrel{\text{def}}{=}$ α:γ:P but not P $\stackrel{\text{def}}{=}$ α:P or P $\stackrel{\text{def}}{=}$ α:P + β:γ:P; and so on. The other shorthands of '$-$' and '$-K$' apply, as you would expect.

We can now use these more user-friendly forms to decide important questions about our designs and see that, while these packaged formulas don't have the expressive power of the raw calculus, they certainly do make things easier.

- Agents where a required property ϕ is an invariant – always true in all its derivatives, Always (ϕ) =true – are safe with respect to that property. For example, agents always prepared to engage in some action, Always ($\langle - \rangle$tt) =true, do not terminate. Its complement – an unwanted property ϕ never holds in any derivatives – is said to be safe from that property. For example, an agent which never allows two agents to be in their critical sections at the same time - one which always refuses cs1#cs2, Always ([cs1#cs2]ff) =true – is safe with respect to mutual exclusion.

- Agents, some of whose derivatives have property ϕ, Sometimes(ϕ)=true, are possibly live with respect to ϕ; while the property cannot be guaranteed to hold for all futures, neither can it be guaranteed not to hold. An offered service may be used, philosophers may eat, and so on. This can be strengthened to: agents, all of whose derivatives have property ϕ, Eventually(ϕ)=true, are live with respect to ϕ; offered services are always used, philosophers always eat, and so on. In particular, Sometimes($\langle\alpha\rangle$tt) holds for P $\stackrel{\text{def}}{=}$ 1:α:0 + 1:β:0 but Eventually($\langle\alpha\rangle$tt) does not.

- To check if one property may follow a previous continuous property, we can use WeakUntil(ϕ, ψ), ϕ holds until ψ holds but ψ may never hold at any time; for example, WeakUntil($\langle K\rangle$tt, ψ) which holds if, after the continuous possibility of K actions, ψ holds, or the agent can engage in K actions forever, without ψ ever becoming true. WeakUntil can be strengthened to StrongUntil(ϕ, ψ) where ϕ holds until ψ holds and ψ is guaranteed to hold at some point. For example, StrongUntil($\langle K\rangle$tt, ψ) holds if, after the continuous possibility of K actions, ψ holds. In particular, both WeakUntil($\langle\alpha\rangle$tt, $\langle\beta\rangle$tt) and StrongUntil($\langle\alpha\rangle$tt, $\langle\beta\rangle$tt) hold for P $\stackrel{\text{def}}{=}$ α:β:P but only WeakUntil($\langle\alpha\rangle$tt, $\langle\beta\rangle$tt) holds for P $\stackrel{\text{def}}{=}$ α:β:P + γ:P.

The above 'standard' property-related macros can be modified into the already introduced, but here properly parametrised, set of action related macros, of:

- Only_hap(-act),[-act]ff $\wedge$ $\langle-\rangle$tt, holds for agents whose next action is act, and only act, and are not immediately inactive.

- Event_may(act),μZ.$\langle$act$\rangle$tt $\vee$ ($\langle-\rangle$tt $\wedge$ [-]Z), true if action act eventually may happen on all runs.

- Event_hap(-act),μZ.$\langle-\rangle$tt $\wedge$ [-act]Z, true if action act eventually happens on all runs

- Some_may(act),μZ.$\langle$act$\rangle$tt $\vee$ $\langle-\rangle$Z, true if action act is possible on some runs.

We can also increase the readability of formulas by using macros to name constants, such as the previously introduced NeverDies $\stackrel{\text{def}}{=}$ Always($\langle-\rangle$tt), which is true for non-terminating agents.

These prepackaged formula can also be used in combination with each other, as in Always[α](Event_may(β)) – after the occurrence of an α eventually β may happen; or we can combine them with raw mu-calculus; for example: $\langle\langle\alpha\rangle\rangle$Always([-$\beta$]ff $\wedge$ $\langle-\rangle$tt), that defines agents which, after an initial observable α, always engage in β.

examples

a) CLOCK does always `tick`, `CLOCK ⊨ Always([-tick]ff ∧ ⟨-⟩tt)`,
but `OLD_CLOCK`

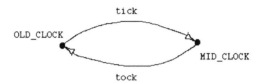

cannot, `OLD_CLOCK ⊭ Always([-tick]ff ∧ ⟨-⟩tt)`. However, as
`OLD_CLOCK` alternates ticks with tocks, `OLD_CLOCK ⊨`
`Always([tick]⟨tock⟩tt)`, and only the older clock can evolve into
an agent which can `tock`, `OLD_CLOCK ⊨ Event_hap(-tock)`.

b) We can detect the termination present in Q $\stackrel{\text{def}}{=}$ a : Q + a : ◎ missing
from P $\stackrel{\text{def}}{=}$ a : P

as only P satisfies
$$\text{Always}(\langle-\rangle\text{tt})$$
or, more strongly, every agent that P evolves into can engage in an a
but Q can evolve into Q_1 which cannot engage in an a; only P has
property
$$\text{Always}(\langle a\rangle\text{tt})$$
and can never refuse an a
$$\text{Always}(\text{Only\_hap}(-a))$$

c) We can distinguish P $\stackrel{\text{def}}{=}$ a : P + 1 : P from Q $\stackrel{\text{def}}{=}$ a : Q

Neither terminate
$$\text{Always}(\langle-\rangle\text{tt})$$
but only Q is always ready to engage in observable action a, and only
a, without the possibility of infinite internal actions
$$\text{Always}(\text{Only\_hap}(-a))$$
Alternatively, only P may perform an internal action

Some_may(1)

or, more accurately, only P will eventually perform an internal action

Event_hap(-1)

which can be further strengthened to 'only P can always perform an internal action'

Always(⟨1⟩tt)

Only Q can perform an internal action after an a

StrongUntil(⟨a⟩tt,⟨1⟩tt)

d) If a system only gets into an unwanted state by engaging in K actions, we can make it safe by ensuring the system never engages in K actions, [K]ff. For the system to be safe throughout its life, this property must always hold; it must be an invariant

Always([K]ff)

For two SCCS clients that use critical sections to access an unshareable resource, to ensure mutual exclusion we need to prove that

Always([cs1×cs2]ff) = true

e) That a stamp can always be collected in

STAMP $\stackrel{\text{def}}{=}$ in1p?:1pstamp?:collect!:STAMP

+ in2p?:2pstamp?:collect!:STAMP

is checked by

STAMP ⊨ Event_hap(-collect!)

f) We saw earlier how different formulas can capture quite subtle behaviours by looking at

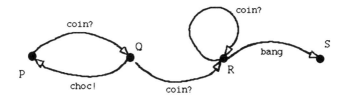

COINCHOC $\stackrel{\text{def}}{=}$ P

P $\stackrel{\text{def}}{=}$ coin?:Q

Q $\stackrel{\text{def}}{=}$ choc!:P + coin?:R

R $\stackrel{\text{def}}{=}$ coin?:R + bang:S

S $\stackrel{\text{def}}{=}$ 0

to give us three different flavours of eventually:

'eventually coin? happens' – along all paths $\mu Z.\langle-\rangle tt \wedge [-coin?]Z$

'eventually coin? must happen' $\mu Z.([-coin?]ff \vee [-]Z) \wedge \langle-\rangle tt$

'eventually coin? may happen' $\mu Z.\langle coin?\rangle tt \vee ([-]Z \wedge \langle-\rangle tt)$

We can also express these in prepackaged form:

First 'coin? happens eventually' – along all paths
$$\texttt{Event\_hap(-coin?)}$$
where $\texttt{Event\_hap(-act)} \stackrel{\text{def}}{=} \texttt{min(Z.} \langle\texttt{-}\rangle\texttt{tt} \wedge \texttt{[-act]Z)}$
Then, 'eventually coin? must happen'
$$\texttt{Event\_must(-coin?)}$$
where $\texttt{Event\_must(-act)}$
$$\stackrel{\text{def}}{=} \texttt{min(Z.([-act]ff} \vee \texttt{[-]Z)} \wedge \langle\texttt{-}\rangle\texttt{tt)}$$
Finally, 'eventually coin? may happen'
$$\texttt{Event\_may(coin?)}$$
where $\texttt{Event\_may(act)}$
$$\stackrel{\text{def}}{=} \texttt{min(Z.}\langle\texttt{act}\rangle\texttt{tt} \vee \texttt{([-]Z} \wedge \langle\texttt{-}\rangle\texttt{tt))}$$

All resulting in
$$\|\texttt{Event\_hap(-coin?)}\|_{\mathcal{V}} = \{\texttt{P,Q}\}$$
$$\|\texttt{Event\_must(-coin?)}\|_{\mathcal{V}} = \{\texttt{P}\}$$
$$\|\texttt{Event\_may(coin?)}\|_{\mathcal{V}} = \{\texttt{P,Q,R}\}$$

g) To check a system is live with respect to certain behaviours, we need to show that, for every execution path where property ϕ holds, property ψ eventually holds. For example, in
$$\texttt{STAMP} \stackrel{\text{def}}{=} \texttt{in1p?:1pstamp?:collect!:STAMP}$$
$$\texttt{+ in2p?:2pstamp?:collect!:STAMP}$$
while clients would be happy if stamps can be collected (paid for or not), and the vendor would be happy just to get money, to be fair to both we need to check that stamps paid for can be subsequently collected.
$$\texttt{Only\_hap(-\{in1p?,in2p?\})}$$
$$\wedge \texttt{[in1p?,in2p?]Event\_hap(-collect!)}$$

In a more selective stamp machine
$$\texttt{STAMPS} \stackrel{\text{def}}{=} \texttt{in1p?:1pstamp?:collect1p!:STAMPS}$$
$$\texttt{+ in2p?:2pstamp?:collect2p!:STAMPS}$$
we need to prove that the user can only collect the type of stamp paid for
$$\texttt{Event\_may(in1p?)}$$
$$\wedge \texttt{Always([in1p?]Event\_hap(-collect1p!))}$$

h) Two clients requesting access to critical sections accessing the same resource:
$$\texttt{CLIENT1} \stackrel{\text{def}}{=} \texttt{req1:}\delta\texttt{enter!:cs1:}\delta\texttt{exit?:CLIENT1}$$
$$\texttt{CLIENT2} \stackrel{\text{def}}{=} \texttt{req2:}\delta\texttt{enter!:cs2:}\delta\texttt{exit?:CLIENT2}$$
with critical sections guarded by binary semaphore
$$\texttt{SEM} \stackrel{\text{def}}{=} \delta\texttt{enter?:}\delta\texttt{exit!:SEM}$$

in SYS = (CLIENT1 × CLIENT2 × SEM) \\{enter,exit}
We can use Always([cs1×cs2]ff) to check if mutual exclusion is
preserved, and Always(⟨-⟩tt) to check the system never terminates
unexpectedly, but to check that every time a client issues a request it may
get to enter its critical section, allowing for all possible combinations of
actions containing req1 and cs1, we need to check that:
    'on those paths commencing with req1, in any of its
    combinations, req1×req2, then sometimes cs1 is possible'
Only_hap(-req1×req2) ∧ [req1×req2]Some_may(cs1)

i)   A buffer BUFF ^{def} in?:BUFF + out!:BUFF can always either input
or output Always(⟨in?⟩tt ∨ ⟨out!⟩tt), but if two copies of a
buffer are connected by mid actions
    BUFF1 = (in?:BUFF1 + mid!:BUFF1)
    BUFF2 = (mid?:BUFF2 + out!:BUFF2)
    SYS = (BUFF1 × BUFF2)\\mid
there is a possibility of always choosing the internal communication,
rejecting the external ones. We can test for this by checking if
any/none of the possible combinations of observable actions always
eventually occurs
    Always(Event_hap(-in?) ∨ Event_hap(-out!)
            ∨ Event_hap(-in?×out!))

j)   A non-pre-emptive scheduler
    S ^{def} astart!:δastop?:bstart!:δbstop?:S;
first starts process A via astart. A runs to completion, its last act
being to inform the scheduler via astop that it has completed. The
scheduler then starts B with bstart which, when completed,
communicates with the scheduler with bstop. The scheduler then
starts A, … and so on.
    Process A engages in two a actions and B in a b
        ProcA ^{def} δastart?:a:a:astop!:ProcA
        ProcB ^{def} δbstart?:b:bstop!:ProcB
The complete design, hiding scheduler/process interactions, is
    SAB = (ProcA×ProcB×S)\\{astart,astop,bstart,bstop}
If the system is working correctly, it must not unexpectedly
terminate, and, ignoring internal actions, after continuous a actions
a b action occurs
    NeverDies ∧ StrongUntil(⟨⟨a⟩⟩tt,⟨⟨b⟩⟩tt)

End Note

This text was conceived as as adjunct to an undergraduate course, and what we've covered here only skirts the lower slopes of mu-calculus. However, even in the foothills there are pitfalls. Take the example of multi-client systems: our formulas, pretty as they look, don't actually check if client requests and resource accesses are matched – one client request gives one resource access, `req:grant`; but they will allow things like multiple requests resulting in only one access, `req:req:grant`. To show causality, we will have to extend our specification and uniquely label each request and grant pairs so that the `i`th request, req_i, leads inevitably to an `i`th grant, $grant_i$. More generally, in our quick rattle through modal logic, we've constrained ourselves to the non-alternating version of embedded fixed points, where one formula lies snug and complete inside another, and we've avoided the turbulent world of alternating fixed points needed to explore even subtler specifications. Also, the text does little to advance the ongoing question of how one can prove large systems live and safe. For those readers wishing to scale these higher peaks, and in the need of maps and reliable mountain guides, I suggest they first look in [Stir96] and [Bra92]; in the meantime, we will travel a different road and consider mechanising what we've done so far.

7.2 Modal Logic, CWB and Satisfaction

With a modal logic, having the ability to write succinct specifications is one thing, but it's another thing to prove that a design meets such specifications. To help us in these tasks we have CWB, which, unfortunately, employs a notation which, constrained by the lowest common denominator of character-oriented interfaces, is rather idiosyncratic.

CWB Modal Logic Notation

The workbench includes a model checker to compare agent behaviour against modal propositions. The CWB syntax of modal logic, starting with proposition identifiers, is:

Identifiers can be any collection of printable characters, starting with an upper
case letter. Certain characters which cannot be used as identifiers are: '.',
'`,`', '-', '~', '&', '(', ')', '[', ']', '<', '>', '{', '}', '|', '*', a space, a tab, or a
carriage return;

Propositional Logic if P and Q are propositional formulas then so are T(true),
F(false), ~P(negation), P&Q(conjunction), P|Q(disjunction), and
P⇒Q(implication). Unary operators bind stronger than binary ones, ⇒
having lower precedence than & and |, which have equal precedence. All
of which can be changed by appropriate bracketing.

Modal Operators if P is a proposition, $a_1, ... , a_n$ are actions and L an action
set then the following are propositions:
- $[a_1, ..., a_n]$P and [L]P   strong necessity
- $[-a_1, ..., a_n]$P and [-L]P   strong complement necessity
- $[[a_1, ..., a_n]]$P and [[L]]P   weak necessity
- $[[-a_1, ..., a_n]]$P and [[-L]]P   weak complement necessity
- $<a_1, ..., a_n>$P and <L>P   strong possibility
- $<-a_1, ..., a_n>$P and <-L>P   strong complement possibility
- $<<a_1, ..., a_n>>$P and <<L>P   weak possibility
- $<<-a_1, ..., a_n>>$P and <<-L>>P   weak complement possibility

As well as complements, we can specify 'wild card' actions [-], <->, and
so on.

Fixed Point Operators if X is an identifier and P is a proposition in which free
occurrences of X appear within an even number of negations (including
zero of course) then max(X,P) and min(X,P) are propositions representing maximal and minimal fixed points.

The work bench command used to build a working propositional environment is:
prop which binds an identifier to a proposition. Without the definition part it
prints what is currently bound to the identifier.

Command: prop Prop = [a]<->T;

Command: prop Prop;

** Propositions **

prop Prop = [a]<->T

The prop command can also be used to build parameterised propositions in the
form: *Name(param(s)) = definition*, as in

Command: prop Always(P) = max(Z. P & [-]Z);

Once we have a proposition, the workbench contains a set of commands to help us check agent behaviours against it.

---

cp(A,prop); checkprop returns true if agent A satisfies proposition prop, false otherwise, where proposition prop may be parametrised. Only works if agent state space is finite.

dfstrong(A,B); if A and B differ under strong bisimulation the command returns a strong modal formula which is true for A and false for B. If the two agents cannot be distinguished the return is "The two agents are indistinguishable".

dfweak(A,B); if A and B differ under observational equivalence the command returns a weak modal formula which is true for A and false for B. If the two agents cannot be distinguished the return is "The two agents are indistinguishable".

dftrace(A,B); if agents not trace equivalent returns the action sequence generated by one agent but not the other. If they are trace equivalent returns true.

Macros

The work bench comes with some pre-written macros which can be used to check agent properties, namely:

---

diverges A; returns true if there is an unguarded occurrence of bottom – representing a divergent or undefined process .

deadlocks A; prints the deadlocked states of an agent, if it has any, and an action sequence from the initial state to each such deadlocked state. Only works if agent state space is finite.

deadlocksobs A; prints the deadlocked states of an agent, if it has any, and an observable action sequence from the initial state to each such deadlocked state. Only works if agent state space is finite.

stable A; returns true if an agents stable – it cannot initially perform an unobservable action, false otherwise.

To these 'build-in' macros we can add some of our own. First, some dealing in general properties.

```
**************************************************
* Always(P)
*    true if P always holds
**************************************************
   prop Always(P) = max(Z. P & [-]Z);


**************************************************
* Sometimes(P)
*    true if P holds on some runs
**************************************************
   prop Sometimes(P) = min(Z. P | <->Z);


**************************************************
* Eventually(P)
*    true if P eventually holds on all runs
**************************************************
   prop Eventually(P) = min(Z. P | ([-]Z & <->T));


**************************************************
* StrongUntil(P,Q)
*    true if on all runs P holds until Q
*    holds and Q holds at some point
**************************************************
   prop StrongUntil(P,Q) = min(Z. Q | (P & [-]Z & <->T));


**************************************************
* WeakUntil(P,Q)
*    true if on all runs P holds until Q
*    holds but Q need never hold
**************************************************
   prop WeakUntil(P,Q) = max(Z. Q | (P & [-]Z));


**************************************************
* Delay(P)
*    true if P holds on all runs of zero
*    or more internal actions
**************************************************
   prop Delay(P) = min(Z. P | <1>Z);
```

Then, some dealing in particular actions:

```
****************************************************
*  Only_hap(-act)
*     true of processes whose next action is act, and
*     only act, and do not immediately terminate.
****************************************************
   prop Only_hap(-act) = [-act]F & <->T;


****************************************************
*  Event_may(act)
*     true of processes for which action act
*     is eventually possible on all runs
****************************************************
   prop Event_may(act) = min(Z. <act>T | ([-]Z & <->T));


****************************************************
*  Event_hap(-act)
*     true of processes for which action act
*     eventually happens on all runs
****************************************************
   prop Event_hap(-act) = min(Z. <->T & [-act]Z);


****************************************************
*  Some_may(act)
*     true of processes for which action act
*     is possible on some runs
****************************************************
   prop Some_may(act) = min(Z. <act>T | <->Z);


****************************************************
*  NeverDies
*     true of processes that always have a next
*     action to engage in.
*     True for agents that do not terminate
****************************************************
   prop NeverDies = min(Z. <->T & [-]Z);
```

Design Validation

We have modal logic as a flexible way of writing specifications, and CWB to do all the menial work for us. All we now need is some assurance that things work as we expect. To do this we will revisit some earlier examples.

```
*************************************************
* Our old friends CLOCK and OLD_CLOCK.
*************************************************
  Command: agent CLOCK = tick:CLOCK;
  Command: agent OLD_CLOCK = tick:tock:OLD_CLOCK;


*************************************************
* A specification which requires that an agent
* only ticks and...
*************************************************
  Command: prop Tick = max(Z.([-tick]F & <->T) & [-]Z);

  Command: cp(CLOCK,Tick);              * is met by CLOCK
  true
  Command: cp(OLD_Tick,Tick);           * but not by OLD_CLOCK
  false


*************************************************
* ...a specification which requires that an agent's
* even actions are tock.
*************************************************
  Command: prop EvenTock = max(Z.[-]([-tock]F & [-]Z));

  Command: cp(CLOCK,EvenTock);          * is not met by CLOCK
  false
  Command: cp(OLD_CLOCK,EvenTock);      * but is by OLD_CLOCK
  true
```

We can more also express some of these checks using the Always macro.

```
*************************************************
* Checking against a specification that
* requires an agent always to tick.
*************************************************
  Command: prop AllTick = Always(Only_hap(-tick));

  Command: cp(CLOCK,AllTick);           * is met by CLOCK
  true
  Command: cp(OLD_CLOCK,AllTick);       * but not OLD_CLOCK
  false
```

While use of the Always macro is fairly self-evident, that of Sometimes and Eventually is less obvious. Sometimes(φ) holds if φ can hold on some runs whereas Eventually(φ) only holds if φ can hold on all runs.

```
*****************************************************
* Both Sometimes(φ) and Eventually(φ)
* hold if φ holds on all runs...
*****************************************************
  Command: cp(1:a:0, Sometimes(<a>T));
  true
  Command: cp(1:a:0, Eventually(<a>T));
  true


*****************************************************
* ...and fail where φ holds on none
*****************************************************
  Command: cp(b:0, Sometimes(<a>T));
  false
  Command: cp(b:0, Eventually(<a>T));
  false


*****************************************************
* However Sometimes(φ) holds if φ holds on at
* least one run, and Eventually(φ) fails
* if φ fails on at least one run.
*****************************************************
  Command: cp(1:b:0 + 1:a:0, Sometimes(<a>T));
  true
  Command: cp(1:b:0 + 1:a:0, Eventually(<a>T));
  false
```

We can apply this to our interrupt algorithm.

```
*****************************************************
* Main Process Q
* Repeatedly engages in two a actions followed by one
* b action, each taking one time slot.
* The process is always ready to receive an interrupt request.
*****************************************************
  Command: agent Q = int:B + a:Q1;
  Command: agent Q1 = int:B1 + a:Q2;
  Command: agent Q2 = int:B2 + b:Q;


*****************************************************
* Interrupting Process R
* Idles for four ticks, generating an interrupt request
* every fifth tick over port int, then repeats.
* We add action ireq to act as an interrupt request marker.
*****************************************************
```

```
Command: agent R = 1:1:1:1:`int#ireq:R;


*******************************************************
* Interrupt Service Routine B
* Carries out three d actions, taking one time
* slot each, then returns control to the
* main process at the point of interrupt.
*******************************************************
  Command: agent B = d:d:d:Q;
  Command: agent B1 = d:d:d:Q1;
  Command: agent B2 = d:d:d:Q2;


*******************************************************
* The composite system is
*******************************************************
  Command: agent SYS = (R | Q)\{ireq,a,b,d};

  Command: statesexp SYS;
  — a a b a ireq d d d a ireq d d d b ireq d d ⟶ (1:1:`int#ireq:R
                                                    | d:Q)\{a,b,d,ireq}
  — a a b a ireq d d d a ireq d d d b ireq d ⟶ (1:1:1:`int#ireq:R
                                                  | d:d:Q)\{a,b,d,ireq}
  — a a b a ireq d d d a ireq d d d b ireq ⟶ (R | B)\{a,b,d,ireq}
  — a a b a ireq d d d a ireq d d d b ⟶ (`int#ireq:R | Q)\{a,b,d,ireq}
  — a a b a ireq d d d a ireq d d d ⟶ (1:`int#ireq:R | Q2)\{a,b,d,ireq}
  — a a b a ireq d d d a ireq d d ⟶ (1:1:`int#ireq:R | d:Q2)\{a,b,d,ireq}
  — a a b a ireq d d d a ireq d ⟶ (1:1:1:`int#ireq:R | d:d:Q2)\{a,b,d,ireq}
  — a a b a ireq d d d a ireq ⟶ (R | B2)\{a,b,d,ireq}
  — a a b a ireq d d d a ⟶ (`int#ireq:R | Q2)\{a,b,d,ireq}
  — a a b a ireq d d d ⟶ (1:`int#ireq:R | Q1)\{a,b,d,ireq}
  — a a b a ireq d d ⟶ (1:1:`int#ireq:R | d:Q1)\{a,b,d,ireq}
  — a a b a ireq d ⟶ (1:1:1:`int#ireq:R | d:d:Q1)\{a,b,d,ireq}
  — a a b a ireq ⟶ (R | B1)\{a,b,d,ireq}
  — a a b a ⟶ (`int#ireq:R | Q1)\{a,b,d,ireq}
  — a a b ⟶ (1:`int#ireq:R | Q)\{a,b,d,ireq}
  — a a ⟶ (1:1·`int#ireq:R | Q2)\{a,b,d,ireq}
  — a ⟶ (1:1:1:`int#ireq:R | Q1)\{a,b,d,ireq}
  —   ⟶ SYS


*******************************************************
* The expected behaviour of...
*******************************************************
  Command: agent S = a:a:b:X;
  Command: agent X = a:ireq:d:d:d:a:ireq:d:d:d:b:ireq:d:d:d:X;
```

```
**************************************************
* ...is met by the design.
**************************************************
   Command: strongeq(S,SYS);
   true


**************************************************
* Also interrupts come immediately they're requested.
**************************************************
   Command: cp(SYS, Event_hap(-ireq)
                       & Always([ireq]Only_hap(-d)));
   true
```

We can check if an agent is not live by showing it can always engage in internal actions.

```
**************************************************
* If two agents continually synchronise with each other
* and that's all they do something bad has happened.
* By not engaging in any external actions of
* communication the system is no longer live.
**************************************************
   Command: agent P = a:P;
   Command: agent Q = 'a:Q;

   Command: transitions (P|Q)\{};
   — 1 —→ (P | Q)\{}

   Command: cp((P|Q)\{}, max(Z.<1>Z));
   true
```

But can we pick up a deadlock? We can if we associate deadlock with unexpected termination.

First we detect termination.

```
**************************************************
* Termination
***
* We distinguish P ᵈᵉᶠ a:P which does not terminate
* from Q ᵈᵉᶠ a:Q + a:① which does...
**************************************************
   Command: agent P = a:P;
   Command: agent Q = a:Q + a:0;
```

```
****************************************************
* ...by seeing if either unexpectedly terminates.
****************************************************
  Command: cp(P, NeverDies);            * P does not
  true
  Command: cp(Q, NeverDies);            * but Q does
  false


****************************************************
* Now if two agents fail to synchronise and the
* unsatisfied actions are pruned by the
* environment, deadlock ensues
****************************************************
  Command: agent P = a:P;
  Command: agent Q = `b:P;

  Command: transitions (P|Q)\{};
  No transitions.

  Command: cp(P, max(Z.<->T & [-]Z));
  true
  Command: cp((P|Q)\{}, max(Z.<->T & [-]Z));
  false


****************************************************
* In macro form
****************************************************
  Command: cp(P, NeverDies);                * P never dies
  true
  Command: cp((P|Q)\{}, NeverDies);      * but (P|Q)\{} does
  false
```

A slightly more complex task is to check if one event eventually follows another, an agent is live with respect to these events.

```
****************************************
* Stamp machine
****************************************
  Command: agent STAMP = in1p:1pstamp:collect:STAMP
                       + in2p:2pstamp:collect:STAMP;


****************************************
* initially either a 1p or a 2p can be input
* and stamps paid for are eventually collected.
****************************************
```

```
Command: prop Ev_collect = min(Y.<->T & [-collect]Y);
Command: prop Pay'n'collect
             = [-in1p,in2p]F & <->T & [in1p,in2p]Ev_collect;


*****************************************************
* Checked by:
*****************************************************
Command: cp(STAMP, Pay'n'collect);
true


*****************************************************
* In macro form, checking that we collect paid-
* for stamps and the machine never terminates.
*****************************************************
Command: prop Spec = Only_hap(-{in1p,in2p})
                           & [in1p,in2p]Event_hap(-collect);
Command: cp(STAMP, Spec & NeverDies);
true
```

In the case of a less naive stamp machine:

```
*****************************************************
* Stamp machine defined by
*****************************************************
Command: agent STAMPS = in1p:1pstamp:collect1p:STAMPS
                      + in2p:2pstamp:collect2p:STAMPS;


*****************************************************
* Whenever a 1p coin is deposited only a 1p stamp
* can eventually be collected
*****************************************************
cp(STAMPS, Event_may(in1p)
              & Always([in1p]Event_hap(-collect1p)));
true
```

Now we have the ability to check designs against a modal logic specification, checking if a design has certain properties such as deadlock, we can also use it to check other properties of interest, like mutual exclusion (for CCS, CWB and mutual exclusion, see [Wal89]). Here a shared resource which, to maintain its integrity, has to be accessed under mutual exclusion, is accessed by two clients. First the anarchists.

```
****************************************************
* Mutual Exclusion
***
* Two clients:
* accessing the same resource by entering and exiting
* their critical sections whenever they like...
****************************************************
  Command: agent CLIENT1 = req1:$enter1:cs1:$exit1:CLIENT1;
  Command: agent CLIENT2 = req2:$enter2:cs2:$exit2:CLIENT2;
  Command: agent USERS = CLIENT1|CLIENT2;


****************************************************
* ...with a behaviour of
****************************************************
  Command: statesobs USERS;
  == req1#req2 enter1#enter2 cs1#cs2 exit1#exit2 ⟹ CLIENT1 | CLIENT2
  == req1#req2 enter1 cs1#enter2 cs2#exit1 ⟹ CLIENT1 | $exit2:CLIENT2
  == req1#req2 enter1 cs1 enter2#exit1 ⟹ CLIENT1 | cs2:$exit2:CLIENT2
  == req1#req2 enter1 cs1 exit1 ⟹ CLIENT1 | $enter2:cs2:$exit2:CLIENT2
  == req1#req2 enter2 cs2#enter1 cs1#exit2 ⟹ $exit1:CLIENT1 | CLIENT2
  == req1#req2 enter2 cs2 enter1#exit2 ⟹ cs1:$exit1:CLIENT1 | CLIENT2
  == req1#req2 enter2 cs2 exit2 ⟹ $enter1:cs1:$exit1:CLIENT1 | CLIENT2
  == req1#req2 enter1#enter2 cs1#cs2 ⟹ $exit1:CLIENT1 | $exit2:CLIENT2
  == req1#req2 enter1 cs1#enter2 ⟹ $exit1:CLIENT1 | cs2:$exit2:CLIENT2
  == req1#req2 enter1 cs1 ⟹ $exit1:CLIENT1 | $enter2:cs2:$exit2:CLIENT2
  == req1#req2 enter2 cs2#enter1 ⟹ cs1:$exit1:CLIENT1 | $exit2:CLIENT2
  == req1#req2 enter2 cs2 ⟹ $enter1:cs1:$exit1:CLIENT1 | $exit2:CLIENT2
  == req1#req2 enter1#enter2 ⟹ cs1:$exit1:CLIENT1 | cs2:$exit2:CLIENT2
  == req1#req2 enter1 ⟹ cs1:$exit1:CLIENT1 | $enter2:cs2:$exit2:CLIENT2
  == req1#req2 enter2 ⟹ $enter1:cs1:$exit1:CLIENT1 | cs2:$exit2:CLIENT2
  == req1#req2 ⟹ $enter1:cs1:$exit1:CLIENT1 | $enter2:cs2:$exit2:CLIENT2
  == ⟹ USERS


****************************************************
* We wouldn't expect it to meet the specification...
****************************************************
  Command: prop Spec2 = max(Z.([cs1#cs2]F) & [-]Z);


****************************************************
* ...and it doesn't
****************************************************
  Command: cp(USERS, Spec2);
  false
```

We can see in the response to 'statesobs' that the specification is frequently violated – not surprising given the lack restraint of the users. We would expect better of a semaphore-based design.

```
*******************************************************
* Semaphores
***
* Define two agents and a binary semaphore.
*******************************************************
   Command: agent CLIENT1 = req1:$enter:cs1:$`exit:CLIENT1;
   Command: agent CLIENT2 = req2:$enter:cs2:$`exit:CLIENT2;

   Command: agent SEM = S1;
   Command: agent S1 = $`enter:S0;
   Command: agent S0 = $exit:S1;


*******************************************************
* put together as...
*******************************************************
   Command: set A = {req1,req2,cs1,cs2};
   Command: agent SYS = (CLIENT1|CLIENT2|SEM)\A;


*******************************************************
* ...behaves as
*******************************************************
   Command: statesobs SYS;
   = req1#req2 cs1 ⟹ ($`exit:CLIENT1 | $enter:cs2:$`exit:CLIENT2
                                    | $exit:S1)\A
   = req1#req2 cs2 ⟹ ($enter:cs1:$`exit:CLIENT1 | $`exit:CLIENT2
                                    | $exit:S1)\A
   = req1#req2 ⟹ (cs1:$`exit:CLIENT1 | $enter:cs2:$`exit:CLIENT2
                                    | S0)\A
   = req1#req2 ⟹ ($enter:cs1:$`exit:CLIENT1 | cs2:$`exit:CLIENT2
                                    | S0)\A
   = req1#req2 ⟹ ($enter:cs1:$`exit:CLIENT1
                                    | $enter:cs2:$`exit:CLIENT2
                                    | $`enter:S0)\A
   = ⟹ SYS


*******************************************************
* which we'd expect to meet the mutual exclusion
* specification
*******************************************************
   Command: prop Spec = max(Z.[cs1#cs2]F & [-]Z);
```

```
Command: cp(SYS, Spec);
true
```

```
*****************************************************
* and never deadlock.
*****************************************************
   Command: cp(SYS, NeverDies & Always([cs1#cs2]F));
   true
```

This says what SYS doesn't do. But processes which never attempt to enter a critical section will also satisfy the above. What we really want is something stronger, something along the lines of 'does a resource request, reqx, lead to a resource access, csx?'.

```
*****************************************************
* We check the liveness specification
*****************************************************
   Command: cp(SYS, Only_hap(-req1#req2) &
                          [req1#req2]Some_may(cs1));
   true
```

The semaphore allows the two clients to access the shared resource with mutual exclusion. It never unexpectedly terminates, and when client one requests the resource eventually it gets it.

End Note
Unfortunately, CWB doesn't as yet handle agent or action indexing, nor the mathematics on such indexing. Which means no parametrised actions, no a?x or a?v, and, as a result, systems succinctly expressed in SCCS can get rather verbose when rewritten for CWB. Whilst these deficiencies do restrict CWB as a design tool, with its relative ease of use, its interactive facilities, its ability to equate agents, handle modal logic and compare modal specifications with proposed designs, etc. – all in the public domain – something about gift horses springs to mind.

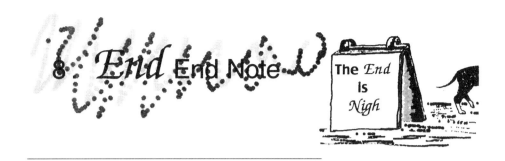

8 End End Note

I hope this record of the journey of an electrical engineer, whose only truck with discrete maths was using boolean algebra to design simple digital electronics and who thought sets were something best left to tennis players, into the intricacies of congruence in SCCS and multiple fixed points in mu-calculus, will be of some use to those who have shared part, if not all, of my voyage. My thanks go to Professor Milner, the progenitor of CCS, SCCS and HML; to Professor Stirling, whose facility of making difficult concepts understandable has given me what insight I have into modal logics; to the Electrical Engineering Department of the University of Surrey, which, though not sure why I wanted to write a book on the subject, let me make my post part-time when the project got out of hand (you should have seen the length of the manuscript before the cleaver was applied); and, finally, to those readers who stuck it out to the end – well done, and I hope your future investigations into the formal world bring you as much pleasure as have mine.

Appendix 1

Some of the More Useful SCCS Propositions

The Operators

SCCS has three basic combinational operators

Prefix(:)	occurrence of a single indivisible event, sequentially
Product(×)	concurrent combinator of agents, concurrency
Summation(+)	disjunctive combination of agents, choice

one hiding operator

Restriction(^)	delimits interfaces through which agents can interact, abstraction

and one action renaming operator

Morphism(φ)	creates new agents

These have been extended to give

Pruning(\)	the obverse of restriction
Synchronisation pruning(\\)	encapsulates interacting agents

As one would expect, operators acting on actions within agents, '. =×> : >δ', bind more strongly than those over agents '\A=\\A=^A>δ>×>+'.

1. Product ×

$\times 1$ $P \times Q = Q \times P$

$\times 2$ $P \times Q \times R = (P \times Q) \times R = P \times (Q \times R)$

$\times 3$ $P \times 0 = 0$

$\times 4$ $\alpha{:}P \times \beta{:}Q - \alpha{\times}\beta \cdot (P \times Q)$

$\times 5$ $\alpha{\times}\beta{:}P = \beta{\times}\alpha{:}P$
                 $= \alpha.\beta{:}P = \beta.\alpha{:}P$
                 $= \alpha\beta{:}P = \beta\alpha{:}P$

$\times 6$ $\alpha{:}P \times 1{:}Q = \alpha.1{:}(P \times Q) = \alpha{:}(P \times Q)$

$\times 7$ $1{:}P \times 1{:}Q = 1.1{:}(P \times Q) = 1{:}(P \times Q)$

2. Sum +

+1 $P + Q = Q + P$

+2 $P + Q + R = (P + Q) + R = Q + (P + R)$

+3 $P + \mathbb{0} = P$

+4 $P + P = P$

+5 $\alpha{:}P + \alpha{:}Q \neq \alpha{:}(P + Q)$, unless $P{=}Q$

+6 $P \times \Sigma_i Q_i = \Sigma_i (P \times Q_i)$

3. Morphism ϕ

$\phi 1$ $(\alpha{:}P)[\phi] = \phi(\alpha){:}P[\phi]$

$\phi 2$ $(\Sigma_i P_i)[\phi] = \Sigma_i (P_i[\phi])$

$\phi 3$ $(P \times Q)[\phi] = P[\phi] \times Q[\phi]$

$\phi 4a$ $(1{:}P)[\phi] = 1{:}P[\phi]$

$\phi 4b$ $\mathbb{1}[\phi] = \mathbb{1}$

$\phi 4c$ $(\delta P)[\phi] = \delta P[\phi]$

$\phi 5$ $(P[\phi])^{\wedge}A = (P^{\wedge}\phi^{-1}(A))[\phi]$

$\phi 6$ $P[\phi_1][\phi_2] = P[\phi_1 \circ \phi_2]$

$\phi 7$ $\mathbb{0}[\phi] = \mathbb{0}$

4. Restriction $^{\wedge}$ where $A \subseteq \mathcal{Act}$, $B \subseteq \mathcal{Act}$ and $\alpha \in \mathcal{Act}$

$^{\wedge}1$ $P^{\wedge}A^{\wedge}B = P^{\wedge}B^{\wedge}A = P^{\wedge}(A \cap B)$

$^{\wedge}2$ $(\alpha{:}P)^{\wedge}A = \alpha{:}P^{\wedge}A$, if $\alpha \in A$

            $= \mathbb{0}$, otherwise

$^{\wedge}3$ $(\Sigma_i P_i)^{\wedge}A = \Sigma_i (P_i{}^{\wedge}A)$

$^{\wedge}4$ $(P \times Q)^{\wedge}A \neq (P^{\wedge}A) \times (Q^{\wedge}A)$, in general

5. Idler $\mathbb{1}$

$\mathbb{1}1$ $\mathbb{1} + \mathbb{1} = \mathbb{1}$

$\mathbb{1}2$ $\mathbb{1} \times \mathbb{1} = \mathbb{1}$

$\mathbb{1}3$ $\mathbb{1}^{\wedge}A = \mathbb{1}$, similarly for $\backslash A$ and $\backslash\backslash A$

6. Inaction $\mathbb{0}$

$\mathbb{0}1$ $\mathbb{0} + \mathbb{0} = \mathbb{0}$

$\mathbb{0}2$ $\mathbb{0} \times \mathbb{0} = \mathbb{0}$

$\mathbb{0}3$ $\mathbb{0}^{\wedge}A = \mathbb{0}$, similarly for $\backslash A$ and $\backslash\backslash A$

7. Delay δ

$\delta 1a$ $\delta P = P + 1{:}\delta P$

$\delta 1b$ $= P + \delta P$

$\delta 2$ $1{:}\delta P = \delta(1{:}P)$

$\delta 3$ $\delta\delta P = \delta P$

$\delta 4$ $(\delta P)^{\wedge}A = \delta(P^{\wedge}A)$, also for $\backslash A$ and $\backslash\backslash A$

$\delta 5$ $\delta P \times \delta Q = \delta((P \times \delta Q) + (\delta P \times Q))$

$\delta 6$ $\delta P + \delta Q \neq \delta(P + Q)$

$\delta 7$ $\delta 1 = 1$

$\delta 8$ $\delta 0 = \delta 0$

8. Synchronisation Pruning $\backslash\backslash$ where $A \subseteq \mathcal{N}$, $B \subseteq \mathcal{N}$ and $\alpha \in \mathcal{A}ct$

$\backslash\backslash 1$ $P\backslash\backslash A\backslash\backslash B = P\backslash\backslash B\backslash\backslash A = P\backslash\backslash\{A \cup B\}$

$\backslash\backslash 2$ $(\alpha:P)\backslash\backslash A = \alpha:P\backslash\backslash A$, if $Part(\alpha) \cap A = \emptyset$

               $= 0$, if $Part(\alpha) \cap Part(\alpha^{-1}) \neq \emptyset$ and $Part(\alpha) \cap A \neq \emptyset$

$\backslash\backslash 3$ $(\alpha \times \alpha^{-1}:P)\backslash\backslash A = 1:P\backslash\backslash A$, if $Part(\alpha) \subseteq A$

$\backslash\backslash 4$ $(\sum_i P_i)\backslash\backslash A = \sum_i (P_i\backslash\backslash A)$

$\backslash\backslash 5$ $(P \times Q)\backslash\backslash A = P\backslash\backslash A \times Q\backslash\backslash A$, if $Sort(P) \cap Sort(Q) \cap A = \emptyset$

$\backslash\backslash 6$ Where $Part(\sigma) \cap A = \emptyset$; $Part(\gamma) \subseteq A$; $Part(\kappa) \subseteq A$ and $Part(\xi) \cap A = \emptyset$

     a) $(\sigma\sigma^{-1}\gamma\gamma^{-1}\xi:P)\backslash\backslash A = (\sigma\sigma^{-1}\xi:P)\backslash\backslash A = \sigma\sigma^{-1}\xi:P\backslash\backslash A$

     b) $(\sigma\sigma^{-1}\gamma\gamma^{-1}\kappa\xi:P)\backslash\backslash A = (\kappa:P)\backslash\backslash A = 0$

     c) $(\sigma\sigma^{-1}:P)\backslash\backslash A = (\sigma\sigma^{-1}\gamma\gamma^{-1}:P)\backslash\backslash A = \sigma\sigma^{-1}:P\backslash\backslash A$

     d) $(\xi:P)\backslash\backslash A = (\gamma\gamma^{-1}\xi:P)\backslash\backslash A = \xi:P\backslash\backslash A$

     e) $(\gamma\gamma^{-1}:P)\backslash\backslash A = 1:P\backslash\backslash A$

9. Pruning and Synchronisation

Where $\alpha\alpha^{-1}$ contains only complete synchronisation pairs

$\leftrightarrow 1$ $(\alpha:P \times \alpha^{-1}:Q)\backslash\backslash A =$

     a) $1:(P \times Q)\backslash\backslash A$, if $Part(\alpha) \subseteq A$

     b) $\alpha\alpha^{-1}:(P \times Q)\backslash\backslash A$, if $Part(\alpha) \cap A = \emptyset$

$\leftrightarrow 2$ $((\delta\alpha:P) \times (\alpha^{-1}:Q))\backslash\backslash A =$

     a) $1:(P \times Q)\backslash\backslash A$, if $Part(\alpha) \subseteq A$

     b) $\alpha\alpha^{-1}:(P \times Q)\backslash\backslash A + \alpha^{-1}:(\delta\alpha:P \times Q)\backslash\backslash A$, if $Part(\alpha) \cap A = \emptyset$

$\leftrightarrow 3$ $((\alpha:P) \times (\delta\alpha^{-1}:Q))\backslash\backslash A =$

     a) $1:(P \times Q)\backslash\backslash A$, if $Part(\alpha) \subseteq A$

     b) $\alpha\alpha^{-1}:(P \times Q)\backslash\backslash A + \alpha:(P \times \delta\alpha^{-1}:Q)\backslash\backslash A$, if $Part(\alpha) \cap A = \emptyset$

$\leftrightarrow 4$ $((\delta\alpha:P) \times (\delta\alpha^{-1}:Q))\backslash\backslash A =$

     a) $\delta 1:(P \times Q)\backslash\backslash A$, if $Part(\alpha) \subseteq A$

     b) $\delta(\alpha\alpha^{-1}:(P \times Q)\backslash\backslash A + \alpha^{-1}:(\delta\alpha:P \times Q)\backslash\backslash A$

          $+ \alpha:(P \times \delta\alpha^{-1}:Q)\backslash\backslash A)$, if $Part(\alpha) \cap A = \emptyset$

Where $\alpha\beta$ contains no synchronisation pairs.

$\leftrightarrow 5$ $(\alpha:P \times \beta:Q)\backslash\backslash A =$

     a) $\alpha\beta:(\Gamma \times Q)\backslash\backslash A$, if $Part(\alpha\beta) \cap A = \emptyset$

     b) 0, if $Part(\alpha\beta) \cap A \neq \emptyset$

$\leftrightarrow 6$ $((\delta\alpha:P) \times (\beta:Q))\backslash\backslash A =$

     a) $\beta:(\delta\alpha:P \times Q)\backslash\backslash A$, if $Part(\alpha) \cap A \neq \emptyset$

     b) 0, if $Part(\beta) \cap A \neq \emptyset$

     c) $\alpha\beta(P \times Q)\backslash\backslash A + \beta:(\delta\alpha:P \times Q)\backslash\backslash A$, if $Part(\alpha\beta) \cap A = \emptyset$

$\leftrightarrow 7$ $((\alpha:P) \times (\delta\beta:Q))\backslash\backslash A =$

     a) $\alpha:(P \times \delta\beta:Q)\backslash\backslash A$, if $Part(\beta) \cap A \neq \emptyset$

     b) 0, if $Part(\alpha) \cap A \neq \emptyset$

       c) $\alpha\beta(P \times Q)\backslash\backslash A + \alpha:(P \times \delta\beta:Q)\backslash\backslash A$, if $Part(\alpha\beta)\cap A=\varnothing$

$\leftrightarrow 8$ $((\delta\alpha:P) \times (\delta\beta:Q))\backslash\backslash A =$

       a) $\delta 0$, if $Part(\beta)\cap A\neq\varnothing$ and $Part(\alpha)\cap A\neq\varnothing$

       b) $\delta\beta:(\delta\alpha:P \times Q)\backslash\backslash A$, if $Part(\alpha)\cap A\neq\varnothing$

       c) $\delta\alpha:(P \times \delta\beta:Q)\backslash\backslash A$, if $Part(\beta)\cap A\neq\varnothing$

       d) $\delta(\alpha\beta:(P \times Q)\backslash\backslash A + \beta:(\delta\alpha:P \times Q)\backslash\backslash A$

          $+ \alpha:(P \times \delta\beta:Q)\backslash\backslash A)$, if $Part(\alpha\beta)\cap A=\varnothing$

$\leftrightarrow 9$ $((\delta\alpha:P) \times (\delta\alpha:Q) \times (\delta\alpha^{-1}:R))\backslash\backslash A$

       $= \delta 1:(\delta\alpha:P \times Q \times R)\backslash\backslash A$

          $+ \delta 1:(P \times \delta\alpha:Q \times R)\backslash\backslash A$, $Part(\alpha)\subseteq A$

10. Data Passing

Where $\alpha\alpha^{-1}$ contains only complete synchronisation pairs and the variables, (x,v) and (y,w), if there, are of comparable data types, $x, v\in \mathcal{D}_1$ and $y, w\in \mathcal{D}_2$

$\leftrightarrow 10$ $(\alpha(!x.?w):P \times \alpha^{-1}(!y.?v):Q)\backslash\backslash A =$

       a) $1:(P[w:=y] \times Q[v:=x])\backslash\backslash A$, if $Part(\alpha)\subseteq A$

       b) $\alpha(!x.?w)\alpha^{-1}(!y.?v):(P \times Q)\backslash\backslash A$, if $Part(\alpha)\cap A\neq\varnothing$

$\leftrightarrow 11$ $(\delta\alpha(!x?w):P \times \alpha^{-1}(!y?v):Q)\backslash\backslash A =$

       a) $1:(P[w:=y] \times Q[v:=x])\backslash\backslash A$, if $Part(\alpha)\subseteq A$

       b) $\alpha(!x?w)\alpha^{-1}(!y?v):(P \times Q)\backslash\backslash A$

          $+ \alpha^{-1}(!y?v):(\delta\alpha(!x?w):P \times Q)\backslash\backslash A$, if $Part(\alpha)\cap A=\varnothing$

$\leftrightarrow 12$ $(\alpha(!x?w):P \times \delta\alpha^{-1}(!y?v):Q)\backslash\backslash A =$

       a) $1:(P[w:=y] \times Q[v:=x])\backslash\backslash A$, if $Part(\alpha)\subseteq A$

       b) $\alpha(!x.?w)\alpha^{-1}(!y.?v):(P \times Q)\backslash\backslash A$

          $+ \alpha(!x?w):(P \times \delta\alpha^{-1}(!y?v):Q)\backslash\backslash A$, if $Part(\alpha)\cap A=\varnothing$

$\leftrightarrow 13$ $(\delta\alpha(!x?w):P \times \delta\alpha^{-1}(!y?v):Q)\backslash\backslash A =$

       a) $\delta 1:(P[w:=y] \times Q[v:=x])\backslash\backslash A$, if $Part(\alpha)\subseteq A$

       b) $\delta(\alpha(!x?w)\alpha^{-1}(!y?v):(P \times Q)\backslash\backslash A$

          $+ \alpha^{-1}(!y?v):(\delta\alpha(!x?w):P \times Q)\backslash\backslash A$

          $+ \alpha(!x?w):(P \times \delta\alpha^{-1}(!y?v):Q)\backslash\backslash A)$, if $Part(\alpha)\cap A=\varnothing$

Where $\alpha\beta$ contains no synchronisation pairs

$\leftrightarrow 14$ $(\alpha(!x.?w):P \times \beta(!y.?v):Q)\backslash\backslash A =$

       a) $\alpha(!x.?w)\beta(!y.?v):(P \times Q)\backslash\backslash A$, if $Part(\alpha\beta)\cap A=\varnothing$

       b) 0, if $Part(\alpha\beta)\cap A\neq\varnothing$

$\leftrightarrow 15$ $(\delta\alpha(!x?w):P \times \beta(!y?v):Q)\backslash\backslash A =$

       a) $\beta(!y?v):(\delta\alpha(!x?w):P \times Q)\backslash\backslash A$, if $Part(\alpha)\cap A\neq\varnothing$

       b) 0, if $Part(\beta)\cap A\neq\varnothing$

       c) $\alpha(!x.?w)\beta(!y.?v):(P \times Q)\backslash\backslash A$

          $+ \beta(!y?v):(\delta\alpha(!x?w):P \times Q)\backslash\backslash A$, if $Part(\alpha\beta)\cap A=\varnothing$

$\leftrightarrow 16$ $(\alpha(!x?w):P \times \delta\beta(!y?v):Q)\backslash\backslash A =$

       a) $\alpha(!x?w):(P \times \delta\beta(!y?v):Q)\backslash\backslash A$, if $Part(\beta)\cap A\neq\varnothing$

       b) 0, if $Part(\alpha)\cap A\neq\varnothing$

       c) $\alpha(!x.?w)\beta(!y.?v):(P \times Q)\backslash\backslash A$

$$+ \;\alpha(!x?w):(P \times \delta\beta(!y?v):Q)\backslash\backslash A, \text{ if Part}(\alpha\beta)\cap A=\emptyset$$

↔17 $(\delta\alpha(!x?w):P \times \delta\beta(!y?v):Q)\backslash\backslash A =$

a) $\delta 0$, if Part$(\beta)\cap A\neq\emptyset$ and Part$(\alpha)\cap A\neq\emptyset$

b) $\delta\beta(!y?v):(\delta\alpha(!x?w):P \times Q)\backslash\backslash A$, if Part$(\alpha)\cap A\neq\emptyset$

c) $\delta\alpha(!x?w):(P \times \delta\beta(!y?v):Q)\backslash\backslash A$, if Part$(\beta)\cap A\neq\emptyset$

d) $\delta(\alpha(!x.?w)\beta(!y.?v):(P \times Q)\backslash\backslash A$

$$+ \;\beta(!y?v):(\delta\alpha(!x?w):P \times Q)\backslash\backslash A$$

$$+ \;\alpha(!x?w):(P \times \delta\beta(!y?v):Q)\backslash\backslash A), \text{ if Part}(\alpha\beta)\cap A=\emptyset$$

Appendix 2

Notation Used Throughout the Book

Logic

p,q	propositions
¬ p	not p, the negation of proposition p: ¬p true if p false
p ∧ q	p and q, the conjunction of p,q: p∧q true if both p and q true
p ∨ q	p or q, the disjunction of p,q: p∨q true if either p or q true
p ⇒ q	p implies q: if p then q
p ⇔ q	equivalence of p and q: p if and only if q
iff	if and only if
∀x	for *all* x (the universal quantifier)
	∀x.p(x) for all x, p holds
∃x	for *some* x (the existential quantifier)
	∃x.p(x) there exists an x such that p holds

Set Theory

{x,y,z}	the set of elements x, y and z
{x | p(x)}	the set of all elements x for which p holds
x∈A	element x is a member of set A
x∉A	element x is not a member of set A
A⊆B, B⊇A	A is a subset of B
A⊈B	A is a not a subset of B
A⊂B, B⊃A	A is a proper subset of B
A⊄B	A is a not a proper subset of B
Ø = {}	the empty, or null, set
A∩B	the intersection of sets A, B: {x | x∈A and x∈B}
A∪B	the union of sets A, B: {x | x∈A or x∈B}
A − B	the relative complement of set B in set A: {x | x∈A and x∉B}

$\bigcup_{i \in I} A_i$	$\{x \mid x \in A_i,$ for at least one $i \in I\}$, where I is an index set
$\bigcap_{i \in I} A_i$	$\{x \mid x \in A_i,$ for every $i \in I\}$, where I is an index set

Special Sets

$\mathbb{Z}$	the set of integers: $\{0,1,-1,2,-2,3,...\}$
$\mathbb{N}$	the set of non negative integers (natural numbers): $\{0,1,2,3,...\}$
$\mathbb{Z}^+$	the set of positive integers: $\{1,2,3,...\}$
$\mathbb{B}$	the Boolean set: $\{\text{true},\text{false}\}$

Relations

$A \times B$	the cross, or Cartesian, product of sets A, B
$\mathbf{R} \subseteq A \times B$	$\mathbf{R}$ is a relation from A to B
$a\,\mathbf{R}\,b;\ (a,b) \in \mathbf{R}$	a is related to b
reflexive	$\mathbf{R}$ is *reflexive* if $\forall x \in A\,.\,x\mathbf{R}x$
symmetric	$\mathbf{R}$ is *symmetric* if $\forall x, y \in A\,.\,x\mathbf{R}y \Rightarrow y\mathbf{R}x$
antisymmetric	$\mathbf{R}$ is *antisymmetric* if $\forall x, y \in A\,.\,x\mathbf{R}y \wedge y\mathbf{R}x \Rightarrow x=y$
transitive	$\mathbf{R}$ is *transitive* if $\forall x, y, z \in A\,.\,x\mathbf{R}y \wedge y\mathbf{R}z \Rightarrow x\mathbf{R}z$
equivalence	$\mathbf{R}$ is an equivalence relation if it is reflexive, transitive and symmetric
partial order	a relation that's reflexive, antisymmetric and transitive

Functions

$f: A \rightarrow B$	f is a function, a mapping from elements in set A to unique elements in set B. For each a in A function f defines an element b in B
domain	of $f: A \rightarrow B$, that subset of A for which f gives a value in B
range	of $f: A \rightarrow B$, that subset of B to which f maps a value
f^{-1}	the inverse of function f
$g \circ f$	for $f: A \rightarrow B$ and $g: B \rightarrow C$ the composite function $g \circ f: A \rightarrow C,\ (g \circ f)(a) = g(f(a))$
$f(a) = a$	f is an identity function for all a
monotonic	a function that respects partial order

Operators

idempotent	a binary operator O such that $x\,O\,x = x$
identity	an element I such that $I\,O\,x = x\,O\,I = x$

commutative	a binary operator O such that $x \, O \, y = y \, O \, x$
associative	a binary operator O such that $x \, O \, (y \, O \, z)$ $= (x \, O \, y) \, O \, z$
distributive	operator O_1 distributes through O_2 if $x \, O_1 \, (y \, O_2 \, z) = (x \, O_1 \, y) \, O_2 \, (x \, O_1 \, z)$

Traces

ε, $<>$	empty trace
$<a,b>$	action a followed by action b
Traces(P)	returns the possible traces of agent P
NextActions(P)	returns the set of next actions of agent P
Final(P,seq)	returns the set of states reached by P engaging in action sequence seq

CCS

$\alpha,\beta,...$	observable actions
$\alpha?$	input action
$\alpha!$	output action
τ	silent action
E,F,G,...	agent expressions
$\alpha.E$	prefix
$\alpha?(x).E$	input of values
$\alpha!(x).E$	output of values
E + F	summation
E | F	composition
E\L	restriction
E[f]	relabelling
0	inaction

SCCS

Basics

a,b,c,...	port names
$\mathcal{N}$	naming set
1	idle, internal, particle
a?,b?,c?,...	input particles, input synchronisation offer on ports a,b,c,...
a!,b!,c!,...	output particles, output synchronisation offer on ports a,b,c,...
$()^{-1}$	inversion, $(a?)^{-1}=a!$
$\Sigma_!$	input particle set
$\Sigma_?$	output particle set

Λ	particle set, $\Lambda = \Sigma_? \cup \Sigma_!$
L, $L \subseteq \Lambda$	a particle subset
L^x	set of composites generated by x acting on a set of L particles
$L(E)$	the sort of E, the set of particles that E can engage in
Sort(E)	returns the sort of expression E

Actions

$\alpha, \beta, \chi, \ldots$	general actions
$\alpha^{-1}, \beta^{-1}, \chi^{-1}, \ldots$	inverse general actions
$\alpha \times \beta$	composite action
$\mathcal{A}ct$	$\mathcal{A}ct = (\Sigma_? \cup \Sigma_!)^x$ composite action naming set
$\mathcal{A}ct_{-1}$	observable action set, $\mathcal{A}ct - \{1\}$
$\alpha \times \alpha^{-1}$	synchronisation pair $\alpha \times \alpha^{-1} = 1$
$\alpha!w$	outputs, over port α, the value w
$\alpha?v$	assigns, to variable v, data input over port α
$\mathcal{D}$	data type set
Part(α)	returns the set of particles present in action α

Agents

E,F,G,...	agent expressions
X,Y,...	agent variables
P,Q,R,...	agents
$\mathcal{P}$	a class of agents
$\mathbb{0}$	Inaction agent, does not engage in any actions
$\mathbb{1}$	idler agent, continually engages in 1 actions

Operations

$\alpha : E$	action prefix, sequentiality, engages in α before behaving as E
guard	action α is said to guard E in $\alpha : E$
E + F	binary summation, choice of behaving as E or F
$\Sigma_{i \in I}(E_i)$	general summation, choice of behaving as a particular E_i from an indexed family of agents $<E_i \mid i \in I>$
E × F	binary composition, E and F operating concurrently
$\Pi_{i \in I}(E_i)$	general product, the set of $<E_i \mid i \in I>$ agents operating concurrently
E^L	restriction, only actions in L allowed
E\L	pruning, actions in L disallowed
E\\L	synchronisation pruning, disallows both input and output versions of actions named in L
$E[f]$, $f : a \to b$	relabelling, change action names in E
δE	delay, can delay indefinitely before behaving as E
fixXE	fixed point solution of X $\overset{\text{def}}{=}$ E, where E $= \mathcal{F}(X)$

Equivalence

d<u>e</u>f	is defined by
≅	behavioural equivalence
~	strong equivalence
≈	observational equivalence
≈^{c}	observational congruence

Modal Logic and Mu-calculus

Basics

$\mathcal{A}ct$ '	observable action set, $\mathcal{A}ct$ ' = ($\mathcal{A}ct$ − {1}) ∪ {ε}
K−derivatives	an agent has a K−derivative if it can engage an action from K, K⊆$\mathcal{A}ct$
K−descendants	as K−derivatives with only observable actions considered, K⊆$\mathcal{A}ct$ '
P ⊨ φ	agent P has property φ
P ⊭ φ	agent P doesn't have property φ
‖φ‖	defines the set of agents which have property φ

Formulas over properties

tt	the constant formula true
ff	the constant formula false
[K]φ	holds if every K−derivative has property φ
[[K]]φ	holds if every K−descendant has property φ
⟨K⟩φ	holds if at least one K−derivative has property φ
⟨⟨K⟩⟩φ	holds if at least one K−descendant has property φ
μZ.φ	minimal fixpoint
νZ.φ	maximal fixpoint

Macros

Always(φ)	true if φ always holds on all runs
Sometimes(φ)	true if φ holds on some runs
Eventually(φ)	true if φ eventually holds on all runs
WeakUntil(φ,ψ)	true if on all runs φ holds until ψ holds but ψ need never hold
StrongUntil(φ,ψ)	true if on all runs φ holds until ψ holds and ψ holds at some point
Delay(φ)	true if φ holds on all runs of zero or more

	internal actions
`Only_hap(-act)`	`true` for agents whose next action is `act`, and only `act`, and are not immediately inactive
`Event_may(act)`	`true` if action `act` eventually may happen on all runs
`Event_hap(-act)`	`true` if action `act` eventually happens on all runs
`Some_may(act)`	`true` if action `act` is possible on some runs

Concurrency Work Bench
SCCS
Basics

Agents	any collection of printable characters, starting with an upper case letter, except: ‘:’, ‘,’,‘=’, ‘@’, ‘$’, ‘(’, ‘)’, ‘[’, ‘]’, ‘{’, ‘}’, ‘/’, ‘\’, ‘+’, ‘|’, ‘#’, ‘*’, a space, a tab, or a carriage return
Particulates	can be any sequence of printable characters whose first character is not an upper case letter, a, - inverse particles are prefixed by a single quotation mark, `'a`
Actions	an empty observation, `eps`, an internal action `1`, a particle, a nonnegative power of a particle, or a product of particles and/or actions
Inaction	`0`
Bottom	the constant `@` is the SCCS agent $\perp$, divergence. It represents 'infinite internal computation' or 'undefinedness'
Action Prefix	`a:A`
Summation	`A + B + C`
Delay	`$A` can delay indefinitely before behaving as A
Product	`A	B	C`
Restriction	`A\S` where S is a particle set
Morphism	`A[b/a]` is agent A with all particles and/or actions named a (including `'a`) replaced by b (including `'b`) actions

Agent Environment Commands

`agent`	binds a given identifier to a given agent. Without the definition part it prints what's

	currently bound to the identifier
`set`	binds a given identifier to a given set of actions. Without the definition part it prints what's currently bound to the identifier
`print`	prints all bindings of all working environments
`clear`	removes all current bindings from all environments

Derivative Commands

`transitions(A)`	lists the one step transitions of agent A
`derivatives(a,A)`	lists the agents reachable from A via action a
`closure(a,A)`	lists the agents reachable from A via action a. Where a can be any action including `eps`
`closure(a,b,...,A)`	lists the agents reachable from A via the observation 'a,b,...'. Where the sequence 'a,b,...' can only be observable actions
`init A`	lists the observable action that A can perform next
`obs(n,A)`	lists all action sequences of length n from A and the final state of each. Only works if agent state space finite
`vs(n,A)`	lists all visible action sequences of length n from A, if agent state space finite

Analysis Commands

`stable A`	returns `true` if A is stable (A's can initially perform only observable external actions), `false` otherwise
`diverges A`	returns `true` if A contains an unguarded (by an observable action) occurrence of bottom
`freevars A`	lists the free variables of an agent
`sort A`	prints the sort of an agent
`size A`	prints the number of states of an agent, if finite
`states A`	lists the state space, the reachable states, of an agent, if finite
`statesexp A`	lists the state space of given agent, if finite, and for each such state a sequence of actions to get there from the initial state is printed
`statesobs A`	lists the state space of an agent, if finite, and for each such state a sequence of observable

	actions to get there from the initial state
findinit(a,b,...,A)	lists the states of given agent which have 'a,b,...' as initial observable actions. Only works if agent state space finite
deadlocks A	prints any deadlock states of an agent. For each deadlocked state the sequence of actions from the initial state is printed
deadlocksobs A	as 'deadlocks A' but with observable action sequences

File Handling Commands

save 'filename'	writes into file filename the current workbench environments in a form suitable for the workbench to read back using the input command. Files can be nested within files
input 'filename'	read file filename previously created by the save command and use the definitions it contains to update current environments
output 'filename'	redirects the output of all subsequent commands from Unix stdout to filename. Without a file name output returns to stdout

Relational Commands

eq(A,B)	observational equivalence
cong(A,B)	observational congruence
strongeq(A,B)	strong bisimulation
diveq(A,B)	observational equivalence which respects divergence
min(X,A)	minimises the state space of A with respect to weak equivalence, binding the result to X
pb(A,B)	prints the largest bisimulation over the state space of agents A and B as a set of bisimulation classes. Equivalent agents appear in the same bisimulation class

Modal Logic
Notation

Identifiers	can be any collection of printable characters, starting with an upper case letter. Certain characters which cannot be used as identifiers are: '.', ',', '-', '~', '&', '(', ')', '[', ']', '<', '>', '{', '}', '|', '*', a

Propositional Logic

space, a tab, or a carriage return
if P and Q are propositional formulas then
so are T(true), F(false),
~P(negation), P&Q(conjunction),
P|Q(disjunction), and
P⇒Q(implication). Unary operators
bind stronger than binary ones, ⇒ having
lower precedence than & and |, which have
equal precedence. All of which can be
changed by appropriate bracketing

Modal Operators

if P is a proposition, $a_1, ..., a_n$ are actions
and L an action set then the following are
propositions:

● [a_1, ..., a_n] P and [L] P strong
necessity

● [-a_1, ..., a_n] P and [-L] P strong
complement necessity

● [[a_1, ..., a_n]] P and [[L]] P weak
necessity

● [[-a_1, ..., a_n]] P and [[-L]] P weak
complement necessity

● <a_1, ..., a_n>P and <L>P strong
possibility

● <-a_1, ..., a_n>P and <-L>P strong
complement possibility

● <<a_1, ..., a_n>>P and <<L>>P weak
possibility

● <<-a_1, ..., a_n>>P and <<-L>>P weak
complement possibility

As well as complements we can specify 'wild
card' actions [-], <->, and so on

Fixed Point Operators

if X is an identifier and P is a proposition in
which free occurrences of X appear within
an even number of negations (including
zero of course) then max(X, P) and
min(X, P) are propositions representing
maximal and minimal fixed points

Propositions

cp(A,prop)

returns true if agent A satisfies
proposition prop, false otherwise. Only
works if agent state space is finite

dfstrong(A,B)

if A and B differ under strong bisimulation
the command returns a strong modal

	formula which is `true` for A and `false` for B. If the two agents cannot be distinguished the return is "The two agents are indistinguishable"
`dfweak(A,B)`	if A and B differ under observational equivalence the command returns a weak modal formula which is `true` for A and `false` for B. If the two agents cannot be distinguished the return is "The two agents are indistinguishable"
`dftrace(A,B)`	if agents not trace equivalent returns the action sequence generated by one agent but not the other. If they are trace equivalent returns `true`

Built-in Macros

`diverges A`	returns `true` if there is an unguarded occurrence of bottom – representing a divergent or undefined process
`deadlocks A`	prints the deadlocked states of agent A, if it has any, and an action sequence from A to each such deadlocked state. Only works if agent state space is finite
`deadlocksobs A`	prints the deadlocked states of agent A, if it has any, and an observable action sequence from A to each such deadlocked state. Only works if agent state space is finite
`stable A`	returns `true` if an agent is stable – it cannot initially perform an unobservable action, `false` otherwise

References

Bar86   Barringer H., *Program Logics – a short survey*, Technical Report UMCS-86-11-1, Department of Computer Science, University of Manchester, 1986.

Ben82   Ben-Ari M., *Principles of Concurrent Programming*, Prentice Hall, 1982, ISBN 0-13-701078-8.

Ben90   Ben-Ari M., *Principles of Concurrent and Distributed Programming*, Prentice Hall, 1990, ISBN 0-13-7711821-X.

Bra92   Bradfield J. C., *Verifying Temporal Properties of Systems*, Progress in Theoretical Computer Science Series, Birkhäuser, 1992, ISBN 0-8176-3625-0.

Bri75   Brinch Hansen P., 'The Programming Language Concurrent Pascal', *IEEE Transactions on Software Engineering*, SE1, 2, June 1975.

Bri77   Brinch Hansen P., *The Architecture of Concurrent Programs*, Prentice Hall, 1977.

Bur88   Burns A., *Programming in OCCAM 2*, Addison-Wesley, 1988, ISBN 0-201-17371-9.

BuWe90   Burns A. and Wellings A., *Real-Time Systems and their Programming Languages*, Addison-Wesley, 1990, ISBN 0-201-17529-0.

ClPaSt94   Cleaveland R., Parrow J. and Steffen B., *The Concurrency Workbench: A Semantics Based Verification Tool for the Verification of Concurrent Systems,* Proc Workshop on Automated Verification Methods for Finite-state Systems, Lecture Notes in Computer Science 407, Springer-Verlag, 1989.

Dei84   Deitel H. M., *An Introduction to Operating Systems*, Addison-Wesley, 1984, ISBN 0-201-14502-2.

Dijk65   Dijkstra E. W., 'Solution of a Problem in Concurrent Programming Control', *Communications of the ACM*, 8(5), 1966.

Dijk68   Dijkstra E. W., *Co-operating Sequential Processes: Programming Languages*, (ed. F. Genvys), Academic Press, 1968.

Dow88   Dowsing R. D., *Introduction to Concurrency using OCCAM*, Van Nostrand Reinhold, 1988, ISBN 0-278-00059-2.

Fen96   Fencott C., *Formal Methods for Concurrency*, Thomson Computer Press, 1996, ISBN 1-85032-173-6.

Gal90   Galletly J., *OCCAM2*, Pitman, 1990, ISBN 0-273-03067-1.

GeGe88   Gehani N. and McGettrick A. D., (eds): *Concurrent Programming*; Addison-Wesley, 1988, ISBN 0-273-03067-1

HenMil80   Hennessy M. and Milner R., *On Observing Nondeterminism and Concurrency*, Lecture Notes in Computer Science 85, Springer-Verlag, 1980.

HenMil85   Hennessy M. and Milner R., 'Algebraic Laws for Nondeterminism and Concurrency', *J. Assoc. Comput. Mach.* 32, 137–61, 1985.

Hoa74   Hoare C. A. R., 'Monitors: an Operating System Structuring Concept', *Communications of the ACM*, 21(8), August 1974, 549–57.

Hoa85   Hoare C. A. R., *Communicating Sequential Processes*, Prentice Hall, 1985, ISBN 0-13-153289-8.

Hym66   Hymann H., 'Proving Monitors', *Communications of the ACM*, 19(5), 1976.

Inm84   Inmos Ltd, *OCCAM Programming Language*, Prentice Hall, 1984, ISBN 0-13-629296-8.

Knu66   Knuth D. E., 'Additional Comments on a Problem in Concurrent Programming Control', *Communications of the ACM*, 9(5), 1966

Koo91   Koomen C. J., *The Design of Communicating Systems*, Kluwer, 1991, ISBN 0-7923-9203-5.

Koz83
Kozens D., 'Results on the Propositional Mu-Calculus', *Theoretical Computer Science*, 27, 333–45, 1983.

Lam74
Lamport L., 'A New Solution to Dijkstra's Concurrent Programming Problem', *Communications of the ACM*, 17, 453–5, 1974.

Mil82a
Milner R., *Calculi for Synchrony and Asynchrony*, University of Edinburgh, Internal report CSR-104-82, Feb 1982.

Mil82b
Milner R., *A Finite Delay Operator in Synchronous CCS*, University of Edinburgh, Internal report CSR-116-82, May 1982.

Mil83
Milner R., 'Calculi for Synchrony and Asynchrony', *Theoret. Comp. Sci.* 25, 267–310, 1983.

Mil89
Milner R., *Communication and Concurrency*, Prentice Hall, 1989, ISBN 0-13-115007-3.

Moll94
Moller F., *The Edinburgh Concurrency Workbench (version 7)*, Manual available from Department of Computer Science, University of Edinburgh, 1994.

Park81
Park D., *Concurrency and Automata on Infinite Sequences*, Proc. 5th Gl. Conf., Lecture Notes in Comp. Sci., Springer, 104, 167–83, 1981.

Pet85
Peterson J. L. and Silberschatz A., *Operating System Concepts*, 2nd edition, Addison-Wesley, 1985.

Pra90
Prasad K. V. S., *On the Non-derivability of Operators in CCS*, Report 55, Programming Methodology Group, University of Göteborg, 1990.

Stir91
Stirling C., *An Introduction to Modal and Temporal Logics for CCS*, Proc 1989 Joint UK/Japan Workshop on Concurrency, Lecture Notes in Computer Science 491, 2–20, Springer-Verlag, 1991. Paper also available via Edinburgh University's Internet site at http://www.dcs.ed.ac.uk/home/cwb/refs.html.

Stir96
Stirling C., 'Modal and Temporal Logics for Processes', in *Logics for Concurrency: Structure versus Automata*, ed Moller and Birtwhistle, Springer, 1996, ISBN 3-540-60915-6. Paper also available via Edinburgh University's Internet site at http://www.dcs.ed.ac.uk/ home/cwb/refs.html.

Tar55
Tarski A., 'A Lattice-Theoretical Fixpoint Theorem and its Applications', *Pacific Journal of Mathematics*, 5, 1955.

Wal89   Walker D. J., 'Automated Analysis of Mutual Exclusion Algorithms using CCS', *Formal Aspects of Computing*, Vol. 1 No. 3, 273–92, Springer International, 1989.

Wir77   Wirth N., 'Modula, a Language for Modular Multiprogramming', *Software Practice and Experience*, 7(1), 1977.

Index